Lecture Notes in Artificial Intelligence 1747

Subseries of Lecture Notes in Computer Science
Edited by J. G. Carbonell and J. Siekmann

Lecture Notes in Computer $

Edited by G. Goos, J. Hartmanis and

Springer

Berlin
Heidelberg
New York
Barcelona
Hong Kong
London
Milan
Paris
Singapore
Tokyo

Norman Foo (Ed.)

Advanced Topics in Artificial Intelligence

12th Australian Joint Conference
on Artificial Intelligence, AI'99
Sydney, Australia, December 6-10, 1999
Proceedings

Springer

Series Editors

Jaime G. Carbonell, Carnegie Mellon University, Pittsburgh, PA, USA
Jörg Siekmann, University of Saarland, Saarbrücken, Germany

Volume Editor

Norman Foo
University of New South Wales
School of Computer Science and Engineering
Sydney, NSW 2052, Australia
E-mail: norman@cse.unsw.edu.au

Cataloging-in-Publication data applied for

Die Deutsche Bibliothek - CIP-Einheitsaufnahme

Advanced topics in artificial intelligence : proceedings / 12th Australian Joint
Conference on Artificial Intelligence, AI '99, Sydney, Australia, December 6 -
10, 1999 / Norman Foo (ed.). - Berlin ; Heidelberg ; New York ; Barcelona ;
Hong Kong ; London ; Milan ; Paris ; Singapore ; Tokyo : Springer, 1999
(Lecture notes in computer science ; Vol. 1747 : Lectures notes in artificial
intelligence)
ISBN 3-540-66822-5

CR Subject Classification (1998): I.2

ISBN 3-540-66822-5 Springer-Verlag Berlin Heidelberg New York

Typesetting: Camera-ready by author
SPIN 10750039   06/3142 – 5 4 3 2 1 0   Printed on acid-free paper

Preface

The 12th Australian Joint Conference on Artificial Intelligence (AI'99) held in Sydney, Australia, 6-10 December 1999, is the latest in a series of annual regional meetings at which advances in artificial intelligence are reported. This series now attracts many international papers, and indeed the constitution of the program committee reflects this geographical diversity. Besides the usual tutorials and workshops, this year the conference included a companion symposium at which papers on industrial applications were presented. The symposium papers have been published in a separate volume edited by Eric Tsui. AI'99 is organized by the University of New South Wales, and sponsored by the Australian Computer Society, the Commonwealth Scientific and Industrial Research Organisation (CSIRO), Computer Sciences Corporation, the KRRU group at Griffith University, the Australian Artificial Intelligence Institute, and Neuron-Works Ltd.

AI'99 received over 120 conference paper submissions, of which about one-third were from outside Australia. From these, 39 were accepted for regular presentation, and a further 15 for poster display. These proceedings contain the full regular papers and extended summaries of the poster papers. All papers were refereed, mostly by two or three reviewers selected by members of the program committee, and a list of these reviewers appears later.

The technical program comprised two days of workshops and tutorials, followed by three days of conference and symposium plenary and paper sessions. Distinguished plenary speakers were invited to share their experience and expertise in AI with our delegates. Some workshops (Knowledge Acquisition, Commonsense Reasoning, AI Applications to Plant and Animal Production) also had their own invited speakers.

The plenary speakers were: Paul Beinat (NeuronWorks), Ussama Fayed (Microsoft Research), Michael Georgeff (Australian Artificial Intelligence Institute), Hiroshi Motoda (Osaka University), and Eugene C. Freuder (University of New Hampshire). The workshop speakers were: Takahira Yamaguchi (Shizuoka University) in Knowledge Acquisition, John McCarthy (Stanford University) and Michael Thielscher (Dresden University) in Commonsense Reasoning, and M.H. Rasmy (University of Cairo) in AI Applications in Plant and Animal Production. We thank our sponsors and the workshop organizers for supporting their visit.

The smooth running of AI'99 was largely due to its program committee, the administrative staff, the reviewers, the conference organizers CIM Pty Ltd, and the managers of the venue Coogee Holiday Inn.

We thank Springer-Verlag and its representative Alfred Hofmann for efficient assistance in producing these proceedings of AI'99 as a volume in Lecture Notes in Artificial Intelligence series.

October 1999

Norman Foo
the Conference Chair

AI'99 gratefully acknowledges financial support from the following sponsors:

The Artificial Intelligence and Expert Systems Committee of the Australian Computer Society
Commonwealth Scientific and Industrial Research Organisation (CSIRO)
Computer Sciences Corporation (CSC)
Knowledge Representation and Reasoning Unit (KKRU), Griffith University
The Australian Artificial Intelligence Institute
NeuronWorks Ltd

Organizing Committee

General Chair:
John Debenham   University of Technology, Sydney

Conference Chair:
Norman Foo   The University of New South Wales

Symposium Chair:
Eric Tsui   Computer Sciences Corporation

Local Arrangements Chairs:
Graham Mann   The University of New South Wales
Paul Compton   The University of New South Wales

Workshop Chair:
Chengqi Zhang   Deakin University

Tutorial Chair:
Mehmet Orgun   Macquarie University

Conference Organizer:
CIM Conference and Incentive Management

Program Committee

Leila Alem	CSIRO Sydney
Michael Brooks	University of Adelaide
Robert Dale	Macquarie University
Patrick Doherty	University of Linköping
Phan Minh Dung	Asian Institute of Technology
Peter Eklund	Griffith University
John Gero	University of Sydney
Greg Gibbon	University of Newcastle
Jane Hsu	National Taiwan University
William Havens	Simon Fraser University
Joxan Jaffar	National University of Singapore
Ray Jarvis	Monash University
Dayou Liu	Jilin University
Cara MacNish	University of Western Australia
Kim Marriott	Monash University
Tim Menzies	NASA/WVU Software Research
Toshiro Minami	Fujitsu Japan
Erica Mellis	University of Saarland and DFKI
Maurice Pagnucco	Macquarie University

Jeff Pelletier	University of Alberta
S. Ramesh	Indian Institute of Technology, Bombay
John Slaney	Australian National University
Liz Sonenberg	University of Melbourne
Geoff Sutcliffe	James Cook University
Geoff Webb	Deakin University
Mary-Anne Williams	University of Newcastle
Vilas Wuwongse	Asian Institute of Technology
Wai Kiang Yeap	University of Otago
Xinghuo Yu	Central Queensland University
Soe-Tsyr Yuan	Fu-Jen Catholic University
Nevin Zhang	Hong Kong University of Science & Technology

Administrators/Programmers

Dirk Freykamp	The University of New South Wales
Jane Brennan	The University of New South Wales

Workshop Organizers

Debbie Richards	Macquarie University
Abdul Sattar	Griffith University
Hussein Aly Abbass	Queensland University of Technology
Mary-Anne Williams	University of Newcastle
Ryszard Kowalczyk	CSIRO

Tutorial Presenters

Abdul Sattar	Griffith University
Ann Nicholson	Monash University
David Dowe	Monash University

AI'99 Reviewers

AI'99 is indebted to the following reviewers:

David Albrecht	Leila Alem	Jose Alferes
Grigoris Antoniou	Chutiporn Anutariya	Takayuki Baba
Chitta Baral	Ghassan Beydoun	Pushpak Bhattacharya
Bob Bogner	Damien Brain	Derek Bridge
Marianne Brown	Stefanie Bruninghaus	Mike Cameron-Jones
Mike Carbonaro	Lawrence Cavedon	Scott Chase
Bruce Cheek	Jie Cheng	Shing-Chi Cheung
Richard Cole	Stephen Cranefield	Ingo Dahn
Honghua Dai	Robert Dale	Phan Minh Dung
Peter Eklund	Yakov Frayman	Alan M. Frisch
Daya Gaur	Hector Geffner	John Gero
Aditya Ghose	Greg Gibbon	H. Gotanda
Stephen Green	Russ Greiner	Bernd Groh
Joakim Gustafsson	Michael Harries	Patrik Haslum
Bill Havens	Clint Heinze	Tim Hendtlass
Anton van den Hengel	Achim Hoffmann	Michael C. Horsch
Shinya Hosogi	Zhiyi Huang	M. Irgens
Rosemary Irrgang	Joxan Jaffar	R. A. Jarvis
Margaret E. Jefferies	Jun Jo	A. C. Kakas
Mike Kalish	Joarder Kamruzzaman	Manfred Kerberk
David Kinny	Supanat Kitcharoensakul	Alistair Knott
Kevin Korb	Victor Korotkich	Krishna Kottathra
Rex Kwok	Henry Kyburg	Willem Labuschagne
Wai Lam	Evelina Lamma	Jimmy Lee
Ho-fung Leung	Jean Lieber	Dekang Lin
Fangzhen Lin	Bruce Litow	Wei Liu
Phil Long	David R Lovell	Witold Lukaszewicz
Xudong Luo	Sofian Maabout	Cara MacNish
Anna Maclachlan	N. Mani	Heiko Mantel
Xiyun Mao	Kim Marriott	Ryusuke Masuoka
Gord McCalla	Eric McCreath	Ian McDonald
Erica Mellis	Tim Menzies	Nicolas Meuleau
Josef Meyer	Michela Milano	David Morley
Fazel Naghdy	Ekawit Nantareewarawat	Abhaya Nayak
Eric Neufeld	Douglas Newlands	Ann Nicholson
Koichi Niijima	Toshihiko Ono	Tom Osborn
Robyn Owens	Maurice Pagnucco	Andrew P. Paplinski
Cecile Paris	Noel Patson	Lawrence Peh
Pavlos Peppas	Y. Permpoontanalarp	Mark Peters
Tuan Pham	Richard Price	Daniel Pun
Maryam Purvis	Cateen Quayle	Monzur Rahman
Sid Ray	Wayne Read	Ingrid Rewitzky

Debbie Richards
Joseph Ryan
Erik Sandewall
Helen Shen
Hiroshi Shiratsuchi
John Slaney
Zbigniew Stachniak
D. Suter
Thanaruk
   Theeramunkong
Kai Ming Ting
Thilo Trapp
Olivier de Vel
Margaret Wasko
Geoff Webb
Peter Wigham
Graham Wrightson
Wai Kiang Yeap
Soe-Tsyr Yuan
Lynn Zelmer

Mike Rosenman
Chiaki Sakama
Ken Satoh
Uday V. Shenoy
Simeon Simoff
Liz Sonenberg
Nigel Stanger
Andrzej Szalas
Sylvie Thiebaux
Boon Toh Low
Andre Trudel
Matt Vernooy
Nobuo Watanabe
Virginia Wheway
Mary-Anne Williams
Baolin Wu
Jia-Huai You
Nobuhiro Yugami
DongMei Zhang
Zijian Zheng

Hans Rott
M. Abdus Salam
A. Sattar
Sin Shimozono
G. Sivakumar
Bruce Spencer
Geoff Sutcliffe
Choh Man Teng
John Thornton
Francesca Toni
C. P. Tsang
Steven Versteeg
Sam Waugh
Lyndon While
Andreas Wolf
Vilas Wuwongse
Xinghuo Yu
Alex Zelinsky
Weihong Zhang
Jackson Zhu

Table of Contents

Belief Revision

Adaptive Algorithms

Automated Reasoning

Neural Learning

Knowledge Representation II

Heuristics

Knowledge Representation III

Machine Learning II

Applications

Poster Papers (Extended Summary)

Generating Rule Sets from Model Trees

Geoffrey Holmes, Mark Hall, and Eibe Frank

Department of Computer Science
University of Waikato, New Zealand
Phone +64 7 838-4405
{geoff,mhall,eibe}@cs.waikato.ac.nz

Abstract. Model trees—decision trees with linear models at the leaf nodes—have recently emerged as an accurate method for numeric prediction that produces understandable models. However, it is known that decision lists—ordered sets of If-Then rules—have the potential to be more compact and therefore more understandable than their tree counterparts.

We present an algorithm for inducing simple, accurate decision lists from model trees. Model trees are built repeatedly and the best rule is selected at each iteration. This method produces rule sets that are as accurate but smaller than the model tree constructed from the entire dataset. Experimental results for various heuristics which attempt to find a compromise between rule accuracy and rule coverage are reported. We show that our method produces comparably accurate and smaller rule sets than the commercial state-of-the-art rule learning system Cubist.

1 Introduction

Recent work in knowledge discovery on time series data [3], indicates that the scope of application of machine learning algorithms has gone beyond the relatively "straightforward" classification of nominal attributes in data. These applications are important to business, medicine, engineering and the social sciences, particularly in areas concerned with understanding data from sensors [8].

Of equal importance, particularly for business applications is the prediction, and consequent interpretation, of numeric values. For example, the 1998 KDD-Cup concentrated on predicting whether or not someone would donate to a charity. It is arguable that the charity would like to know both the amount someone is likely to donate and the factors which determine this donation from historical data so that they can produce a more effective marketing campaign.

Predicting numeric values usually involves complicated regression formulae. However, in machine learning it is important to present results that can be easily interpreted. Decision lists presented in the If-Then rule format are one of the most popular description languages used in machine learning. They have the potential to be more compact and more predictive than their tree counterparts [16]. In any application, the desired outcome is a small descriptive model

N. Foo (Ed.): AI'99, LNAI 1747, pp. 1–12, 1999.

which has strong predictive capability. It has to be small to be interpretable and understandable, and it has to be accurate so that generalization capabilities can be attributed to the model.

In this paper we present a procedure for generating rules from model trees [10], based on the basic strategy of the PART algorithm [4], that produces accurate and compact rule sets. Section 2 discusses the motivation for PART and alternative approaches to continuous class prediction. Section 3 describes the adaptation of PART to model trees. Section 4 presents an experimental evaluation on standard datasets. We compare the accuracy and size of the rule sets of our procedure with model trees and the rule-based regression learner Cubist[1], the commercial successor of M5 [10]. Section 5 concludes with a discussion of the results and areas for further research on this problem.

2   Related Work

Rule learning for classification systems normally operates in two-stages. Rules are induced initially and then refined at a later stage using a complex global optimization procedure. This is usually accomplished in one of two ways; either by generating a decision tree, mapping the tree to a rule set and then refining the rule set based on boundary considerations of the coverage achieved by each rule, or by employing the separate-and-conquer paradigm. As with decision trees this strategy usually employs a rule optimization stage.

Frank and Witten (1998) combined these two approaches in an algorithm called PART (for partial decision trees) in order to circumvent problems that can arise with both these techniques. Rules induced from decision trees are computationally expensive and this expense can grow alarmingly in the presence of noise [2], while separate-and-conquer methods suffer from a form of overpruning called "hasty generalization" [4].

PART works by building a rule and removing its cover, as in the separate-and-conquer technique, repeatedly until all the instances are covered. The rule construction stage differs from standard separate-and-conquer methods because a partial pruned decision tree is built for a set of instances, the leaf with the largest coverage is made into a rule, and the tree is discarded. The pruned decision tree helps to avoid the overpruning problem of methods that immediately prune an individual rule after construction. Also, the expensive rule optimization stages associated with decision tree rule learning are not performed. Results on standard data sets show smaller rule sizes with no loss in accuracy when compared with the decision tree learner C4.5 [11] and greater accuracy when compared with the separate-and-conquer rule learner RIPPER [2]. In this paper we adapt the basic procedure of PART to continuous class prediction to examine whether similar results can be obtained, namely smaller rule sets with no loss in accuracy.

Although the literature is light in the area of rule-based continuous class prediction, a taxonomy can be found. A first split can be made on whether a

---

[1] A test version of Cubist is available from http://www.rulequest.com

technique generates interpretable results. Those that do not include neural networks, and various statistical approaches at dealing with non-linear regression, such as MARS [5] and projection pursuit [6]. Those that do produce readable output are further split on whether or not they are based on the two major paradigms for rule generation—rule sets represented as regression or model trees, and the separate-and-conquer rule-learning approach. Examples from the regression tree family include: CART [1], RETIS [7] and M5 [10]. Separate-and-conquer methods include a system that maps a regression problem into a classification problem [16], and a propositional learning system [14].

3   Generating Rules From Model Trees

Model trees [10] are a technique for dealing with continuous class problems that provide a structural representation of the data and a piecewise linear fit of the class. They have a conventional decision tree structure but use linear functions at the leaves instead of discrete class labels. The first implementation of model trees, M5, was rather abstractly defined in [10] and the idea was reconstructed and improved in a system called M5' [15]. Like conventional decision tree learners, M5' builds a tree by splitting the data based on the values of predictive attributes. Instead of selecting attributes by an information theoretic metric, M5' chooses attributes that minimise intra-subset variation in the class values of instances that go down each branch.

After constructing a tree, M5' computes a linear model for each node; the tree is then pruned back from the leaves, so long as the expected estimated error decreases. The expected error for each node is calculated by averaging the absolute difference between the predicted value and the actual class value of each training example that reaches the node. To compensate for an optimistic expected error from the training data, this average is multiplied by a factor that takes into account the number of training examples that reach the node and the number of parameters in the model that represent the class value at that node.

This process of tree construction can lead to sharp discontinuities occurring between adjacent linear models at the leaves of the pruned tree. A procedure called smoothing is used to compensate for these differences. The smoothing procedure computes a prediction using the leaf model, and then passes that value along the path back to the root, smoothing it at each node by combining it with the value predicted by the linear model for that node.

3.1   Rule Generation

The method for generating rules from model trees, which we call M5'Rules, is straightforward and works as follows: a tree learner (in this case model trees) is applied to the full training dataset and a pruned tree is learned. Next, the best leaf (according to some heuristic) is made into a rule and the tree is discarded. All instances covered by the rule are removed from the dataset. The process is applied recursively to the remaining instances and terminates when all instances are covered by one or more rules. This is the basic separate-and-conquer strategy for learning rules; however, instead of building a single rule, as it is done usually, we build a full model tree at each stage, and make its "best" leaf into a rule. This avoids potential for over-pruning called hasty generalization [4]. In contrast to PART, which employs the same strategy for categorical prediction, M5'Rules builds full trees instead of partially explored trees. Building partial trees leads to greater computational efficiency, and does not affect the size and accuracy of the resulting rules.

This paper concentrates on generating rules using unsmoothed linear models. Because the tree from which a rule is generated is discarded at each stage, smoothing for rules would have to be done as a post processing stage after the full set of rules has been produced. This process is more complicated than smoothing model trees—it would involve determining the boundaries between rules and then installing linear models to smooth over them.

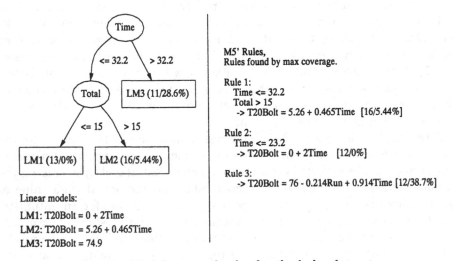

Fig. 1. Model tree and rules for the bolts dataset.

3.2   Rule Selection Heuristics

So far we have described a general approach to extracting rules from trees, applicable to either classification or regression. It remains to determine, at each stage, which leaf in the tree is the best candidate for addition to the rule set. The most obvious approach [4] is to choose the leaf which covers the most examples. Figure 1 shows a tree produced by M5' and the rules generated by M5'Rules using the coverage heuristic for the dataset *bolts* [13]. The values at the leaves of the tree and on the consequent of the rules are the coverage and percent root mean squared error respectively for instances that reach those leaves (satisfy those rules).

Note that the first rule will always map directly to one branch of the tree, however, subsequent rules often do not. In Figure 1, Rule 1 and LM2 are identical as are Rule 2 and LM1, however, Rule 3 and LM3 are very different.

We have experimented with three other heuristics, designed to identify accurate rules and to trade off accuracy against coverage. These measures are similar to those used in the separate-and-conquer procedure when evaluating the specialization of one rule from another [14].

The first of these calculates the percent root mean squared error as shown in Equation 1:

$$\% \text{ RMS} = \frac{\sqrt{\sum_{i=1}^{N_r}(Y_i - y_i)^2/N_r}}{\sqrt{\sum_{i=1}^{N}(Y_i - \overline{Y})^2/N}}, \tag{1}$$

where Y_i is the actual class value for example i, y_i is the class value predicted by the linear model at a leaf, N_r is the number of examples covered by leaf, $\overline{Y}$ is the mean of the class values, and N is the total number of examples. In this case, small values of % RMS (less than 1) indicate that the model at a leaf is doing better than simply predicting the mean of the class values.

One potential problem with percent root mean squared error is that it may favour accuracy at the expense of coverage. Equations 2 and 3 show two heuristic measures designed to trade off accuracy against coverage. The first, simply normalises the mean absolute error at a leaf using the number of examples it covers; the second, multiplies the correlation between the predicted and actual class values for instances at a leaf by the number of instances that reach the leaf.

$$\text{MAE / Cover} = \frac{\sum_{i=1}^{N_r}|Y_i - y_i|}{2N_r}, \tag{2}$$

$$\text{CC} \times \text{Cover} = \frac{\sum_{i=1}^{N_r} Y_i y_i}{N_r \sigma_Y \sigma_y} \times N_r. \tag{3}$$

In Equation 3, Y_i and y_i are the actual value and predicted value for instance i expressed as deviations from their respective means.

4   Experimental Results

In order to evaluate the performance of M5′Rules on a diverse set of machine learning problems, experiments were performed using thirty continuous class datasets. The datasets and their properties are listed in Table 1, and can be obtained from the authors upon request. Nineteen of these datasets were used by Kilpatrick and Cameron-Jones [9], six are from the StatLib repository [13], and the remaining five were collected by Simonoff [12].

As well as M5′Rules using each of the rule-selection heuristics described above, M5′ (with unsmoothed linear models) and the commercial regression

Table 1. Continuous class datasets used in the experiments

Dataset values (%)	Instances attributes	Missing attributes	Numeric	Nominal
auto93	93	0.7	16	6
autoHorse	205	1.1	17	8
autoMpg	398	0.2	4	3
autoPrice	159	0.0	15	0
baskball	96	0.0	4	0
bodyfat	252	0.0	14	0
breastTumor	286	0.3	1	8
cholesterol	303	0.1	6	7
cleveland	303	0.1	6	7
cloud	108	0.0	4	2
cpu	209	0.0	6	1
echoMonths	131	7.5	6	3
elusage	55	0.0	1	1
fishcatch	158	6.9	5	2
housing	506	0.0	12	1
hungarian	294	19.0	6	7
lowbwt	189	0.0	2	7
mbagrade	61	0.0	1	1
meta	528	4.3	19	2
pbc	418	15.6	10	8
pharynx	195	0.1	1	10
pollution	60	0.0	15	0
pwLinear	200	0.0	10	0
quake	2178	0.0	3	0
sensory	576	0.0	0	11
servo	167	0.0	0	4
sleep	62	2.4	7	0
strike	625	0.0	5	1
veteran	137	0.0	3	4
vineyard	52	0.0	3	0

rule learning system Cubist were run on all the datasets. Default parameter settings were used for all algorithms. The mean absolute error, averaged over ten ten-fold cross-validation runs and the standard deviations of these ten error estimates were calculated for each algorithm-dataset combination. The same folds were used for each algorithm.

Table 2 compares the results for M5'Rules with those for M5' unsmoothed. Results for M5'Rules are marked with a ∘ if they show a significant improvement over the corresponding results for M5', and with a • if they show a significant degradation. Results marked with a √ show where M5'Rules has produced significantly fewer rules than M5'; those marked with a × show where M5'Rules has produced significantly more rules than M5'. Results are considered "significant" if the difference is statistically significant at the 1% level according to a paired two-sided t-test, each pair of data points consisting of the estimates obtained in one ten-fold cross-validation run for the two learning algorithms being compared.

Table 2. Experimental results: comparing M5'Rules with M5'. The values are mean absolute error averaged over ten ten-fold cross-validation runs. Results are marked with a o if they show a significant improvement over M5' unsmoothed, and with a • if they show a significant degradation. Results marked with a √ show where M5' Rules has produced significantly fewer rules than M5'; those marked with a × show where M5' Rules has produced significantly more rules than M5'.

Dataset	M5' Unsmoothed	M5'R % RMS		M5'R MAE/Cover		M5'R CC×Cover		M5'R Cover	
auto93	3.66±0.2	3.66±0.2		3.66±0.2		3.66±0.2		3.66±0.2	
autoHorse	8.97±0.5	9.44±0.5	√	9.36±0.5	√	9.40±0.5	•√	9.32±0.5	√
autoMpg	2.08±0.0	2.10±0.1	√	2.08±0.1	√	2.08±0.0	√	2.08±0.0	√
autoPrice	1522.96±53.2	1636.90±96.6	•√	1655.50±109.9	•√	1650.81±129.0	√	1637.44±124.7	•√
baskball	0.07±0.0	0.07±0.0		0.07±0.0		0.07±0.0		0.07±0.0	
bodyfat	0.37±0.1	0.40±0.0	×	0.38±0.1	×	0.37±0.1		0.36±0.1	
breastTumor	8.06±0.1	8.06±0.1		8.06±0.1		8.06±0.1		8.06±0.1	
cholesterol	40.98±1.4	40.91±1.4		40.99±1.4		40.77±1.4		40.98±1.4	
cleveland	0.66±0.0	0.65±0.0		0.66±0.0		0.66±0.0		0.66±0.0	
cloud	0.29±0.0	0.28±0.0		0.28±0.0		0.29±0.0		0.29±0.0	
cpu	13.40±1.2	13.31±1.3		13.33±1.3		13.18±1.5		13.27±1.4	
echoMonths	8.90±0.1	8.90±0.1		8.90±0.1		8.90±0.1		8.90±0.1	
elusage	9.57±0.6	9.57±0.6		9.57±0.6		9.57±0.6		9.57±0.6	
fishcatch	38.70±1.6	39.47±1.5	√	41.55±1.5	•√	38.53±1.9	√	38.61±1.8	√
housing	2.75±0.2	2.64±0.1	√	2.71±0.2	√	2.71±0.1	√	2.77±0.1	√
hungarian	0.28±0.0	0.28±0.0	√	0.28±0.0	√	0.28±0.0		0.28±0.0	
lowbwt	370.93±6.7	370.93±6.7		370.93±6.7		370.93±6.7		370.57±6.4	
mbagrade	0.23±0.0	0.23±0.0		0.23±0.0		0.23±0.0		0.23±0.0	
meta	115.73±13.3	123.82±24.5	√	135.33±22.8	√	131.29±12.8	√	127.72±25.1	√
pbc	716.13±12.8	715.67±12.2		716.13±12.8		716.13±12.8		716.13±12.8	
pharynx	352.85±5.8	352.66±6.1		351.82±7.5		352.76±7.9		353.24±5.9	
pollution	35.15±2.0	35.15±2.0		35.03±2.1		34.99±2.1		35.03±2.1	
pwLinear	1.15±0.0	1.15±0.0		1.15±0.0		1.15±0.0		1.15±0.0	
quake	0.15±0.0	0.15±0.0	√	0.15±0.0		0.15±0.0	•√	0.15±0.0	
sensory	0.58±0.0	0.58±0.0	√	0.58±0.0	√	0.59±0.0	√	0.58±0.0	√
servo	0.31±0.0	0.32±0.0	√	0.32±0.0	√	0.32±0.0	√	0.32±0.0	√
sleep	2.56±0.1	2.56±0.1		2.56±0.1		2.56±0.1		2.56±0.1	
strike	215.87±7.1	231.12±9.7	•√	220.14±4.9	√	222.95±6.4	√	214.91±7.4	√
veteran	92.06±4.3	90.48±4.8		90.49±4.8		90.91±4.5		91.52±4.7	
vineyard	2.48±0.1	2.51±0.2	√	2.51±0.1	√	2.43±0.1	√	2.51±0.1	√

o,•(√,×) statistically significant improvement or degradation

From Table 2 it can be seen that all four heuristic methods for choosing rules give results that are rarely significantly worse than M5'. In fact, choosing rules simply by coverage gives an excellent result—accuracy on only one dataset is significantly degraded. Each of the remaining three heuristics degrade accuracy on two datasets.

As well as accuracy, the size of the rule set is important because it has a strong influence on comprehensibility. Correlation times coverage and plain coverage never result in a larger rule set than M5'. These two heuristics reduce the size of the rule set on eleven, and ten datasets respectively. Both percent root mean squared error and mean absolute error over cover increase the size of the rule set on one dataset, while decreasing size on twelve and eleven datasets respectively.

Table 3. Experimental results: comparing accuracy of M5′Rules with Cubist. The values are mean absolute error averaged over ten ten-fold cross-validation runs. Results are marked with a o if they show a significant improvement over Cubist, and with a • if they show a significant degradation (the precision of the results shown in the table is such that some appear identical but in fact are significantly different, e.g. baskball).

Dataset	Cubist	M5′R % RMS		M5′R MAE/Cover		M5′R CC×Cover		M5′R Cover	
auto93	4.07±0.2	3.66±0.2	o	3.66±0.2	o	3.66±0.2	o	3.66±0.2	o
autoHorse	9.27±0.5	9.44±0.5		9.36±0.5		9.40±0.5		9.32±0.5	
autoMpg	2.24±0.1	2.10±0.1	o	2.08±0.1	o	2.08±0.0	o	2.08±0.0	o
autoPrice	1639.12±63.8	1636.90±96.6		1655.50±109.9		1650.81±129.0		1637.4±124.74	
baskball	0.07±0.0	0.07±0.0	o	0.07±0.0	o	0.07±0.0	o	0.07±0.0	o
bodyfat	0.33±0.0	0.40±0.0	•	0.38±0.1		0.37±0.1		0.36±0.1	
breastTumor	8.97±0.1	8.06±0.1	o	8.06±0.1	o	8.06±0.1	o	8.06±0.1	o
cholesterol	43.02±1.5	40.91±1.4	o	40.99±1.4		40.77±1.4	o	40.98±1.4	
cleveland	0.65±0.0	0.65±0.0		0.66±0.0		0.66±0.0		0.66±0.0	
cloud	0.26±0.0	0.28±0.0	•	0.28±0.0	•	0.29±0.0	•	0.29±0.0	•
cpu	10.96±1.1	13.31±1.3	•	13.33±1.3	•	13.18±1.5	•	13.27±1.4	•
echoMonths	9.41±0.2	8.90±0.1	o	8.90±0.1	o	8.90±0.1	o	8.90±0.1	o
elusage	7.59±0.2	9.57±0.6	•	9.57±0.6	•	9.57±0.6	•	9.57±0.6	•
fishcatch	41.66±0.8	39.47±1.5	o	41.55±1.5		38.53±1.9	o	38.61±1.8	o
housing	2.37±0.1	2.64±0.1	•	2.71±0.2	•	2.71±0.1	•	2.77±0.1	•
hungarian	0.23±0.0	0.28±0.0	•	0.28±0.0	•	0.28±0.0	•	0.28±0.0	•
lowbwt	340.29±7.2	370.93±6.7	•	370.93±6.7	•	370.93±6.7	•	370.57±6.4	•
mbagrade	0.23±0.0	0.23±0.0		0.23±0.0		0.23±0.0		0.23±0.0	
meta	107.26±9.8	123.82±24.5		135.33±22.8	•	131.29±12.8	•	127.72±25.1	•
pbc	774.76±16.3	715.67±12.2	o	716.13±12.8	o	716.13±12.8	o	716.13±12.8	o
pharynx	448.93±2.7	352.66±6.1	o	351.82±7.5	o	352.76±7.9	o	353.24±5.9	o
pollution	34.68±2.4	35.15±2.0		35.03±2.1		34.99±2.1		35.03±2.1	
pwLinear	1.14±0.0	1.15±0.0		1.15±0.0		1.15±0.0		1.15±0.0	
quake	0.15±0.0	0.15±0.0		0.15±0.0		0.15±0.0		0.15±0.0	
sensory	0.61±0.0	0.58±0.0	o	0.58±0.0	o	0.59±0.0	o	0.58±0.0	o
servo	0.38±0.0	0.32±0.0	o	0.32±0.0	o	0.32±0.0	o	0.32±0.0	o
sleep	2.84±0.2	2.56±0.1	o	2.56±0.1	o	2.56±0.1	o	2.56±0.1	o
strike	201.31±5.0	231.12±9.7	•	220.14±4.9	•	222.95±6.4	•	214.91±7.4	•
veteran	88.76±5.5	90.48±4.8		90.49±4.8		90.91±4.5		91.52±4.7	
vineyard	2.28±0.1	2.51±0.2	•	2.51±0.1	•	2.43±0.1	•	2.51±0.1	•

o,• statistically significant improvement or degradation

Table 3 compares accuracy for M5′Rules with those for Cubist. Table 4 and Table 5 compare the average number of rules produced and average number of conditions per rule set respectively. The results for both accuracy and number of rules—as well as Table 2—are summarised for quick comparison in Table 6. Each entry in Table 6 has two values: the first indicates the number of datasets for which the method associated with its column is significantly more accurate than the method associated with its row; the second (in braces) indicates the number of datasets for which the method associated with its column produces significantly smaller rule sets than the method associated with its row.

From the first row and the first column of Table 6 it can be noted that all four versions of M5′Rules—as well as (perhaps surprisingly) M5′—outperform Cubist on more datasets than they are outperformed by Cubist. % RMS and CC × Cover are more accurate than Cubist on twelve datasets, Cover on eleven datasets and MAE / Cover on ten datasets. By comparison, Cubist does better than all four

Table 4. Experimental results: number of rules produced by M5′Rules compared with number of rules produced by Cubist

Dataset	Cubist	M5′R % RMS	M5′R MAE/Cover	M5′R CC×Cover	M5′R Cover
auto93	2.92±0.2	1.08±0.1 ∘	1.08±0.1 ∘	1.08±0.1 ∘	1.08±0.1 ∘
autoHorse	5.31±0.3	2.12±0.6 ∘	2.20±0.6 ∘	2.83±0.7 ∘	2.79±0.5 ∘
autoMpg	6.21±0.5	3.41±0.4 ∘	3.87±0.4 ∘	3.94±0.4 ∘	3.91±0.4 ∘
autoPrice	3.28±0.2	4.88±0.5 •	4.70±0.4 •	4.75±0.5 •	4.24±0.4 •
baskball	5.17±0.2	1.00±0.0 ∘	1.00±0.0 ∘	1.00±0.0 ∘	1.00±0.0 ∘
bodyfat	1.38±0.2	3.97±0.6 •	3.73±0.4 •	3.58±0.4 •	3.51±0.4 •
breastTumor	22.19±0.6	1.06±0.1 ∘	1.06±0.1 ∘	1.06±0.1 ∘	1.06±0.1 ∘
cholesterol	18.63±0.8	2.33±0.4 ∘	2.45±0.5 ∘	2.08±0.4 ∘	2.46±0.5 ∘
cleveland	8.27±0.8	1.07±0.1 ∘	1.06±0.1 ∘	1.16±0.3 ∘	1.18±0.3 ∘
cloud	1.09±0.1	2.62±0.5 •	2.55±0.4 •	2.60±0.4 •	2.63±0.4 •
cpu	2.00±0.0	2.74±0.2 •	2.72±0.2 •	2.70±0.2 •	2.71±0.2 •
echoMonths	6.24±0.4	1.00±0.0 ∘	1.00±0.0 ∘	1.00±0.0 ∘	1.00±0.0 ∘
elusage	2.00±0.0	1.62±0.2 ∘	1.62±0.2 ∘	1.62±0.2 ∘	1.62±0.2 ∘
fishcatch	2.00±0.0	3.47±0.3 •	2.87±0.4 •	3.63±0.3 •	3.63±0.3 •
housing	6.90±0.4	9.61±1.6 •	8.44±0.8 •	8.32±0.8 •	8.57±0.7 •
hungarian	9.15±0.5	1.56±0.2 ∘	1.56±0.2 ∘	1.65±0.2 ∘	1.69±0.3 ∘
lowbwt	6.45±0.2	1.05±0.1 ∘	1.05±0.1 ∘	1.05±0.1 ∘	1.04±0.1 ∘
mbagrade	3.57±0.1	1.00±0.0 ∘	1.00±0.0 ∘	1.00±0.0 ∘	1.00±0.0 ∘
meta	12.90±0.3	5.40±0.4 ∘	5.00±0.4 ∘	5.40±0.6 ∘	4.66±0.5 ∘
pbc	21.63±0.9	1.63±0.1 ∘	1.64±0.1 ∘	1.65±0.1 ∘	1.64±0.1 ∘
pharynx	7.96±0.1	2.07±0.5 ∘	2.20±0.5 ∘	2.16±0.4 ∘	2.18±0.4 ∘
pollution	1.53±0.2	1.22±0.1 ∘	1.19±0.1 ∘	1.20±0.1 ∘	1.21±0.1 ∘
pwLinear	2.00±0.0	2.00±0.0	2.00±0.0	2.00±0.0	2.00±0.0
quake	4.53±0.9	2.45±0.3 ∘	3.61±0.4	1.98±0.2 ∘	3.66±0.4
sensory	45.31±1.1	4.19±0.5 ∘	4.04±0.4 ∘	3.97±0.3 ∘	4.13±0.5 ∘
servo	5.77±0.1	5.05±0.3 ∘	5.20±0.4 ∘	4.18±0.3 ∘	4.09±0.3 ∘
sleep	2.17±0.2	1.00±0.0 ∘	1.00±0.0 ∘	1.00±0.0 ∘	1.00±0.0 ∘
strike	16.65±1.5	4.68±0.9 ∘	4.78±0.9 ∘	4.95±1.0 ∘	4.86±1.1 ∘
veteran	6.48±0.6	1.26±0.3 ∘	1.27±0.3 ∘	1.29±0.2 ∘	1.36±0.3 ∘
vineyard	2.77±0.1	2.27±0.2 ∘	2.07±0.2 ∘	2.18±0.2 ∘	2.07±0.2 ∘

∘,• statistically significant improvement or degradation

M5′Rules variants on nine datasets, eight of which are the same for all variants. When rule set sizes are compared, it can be seen that M5′Rules produces smaller rule sets than Cubist more often than not. % RMS and CC × Cover produce smaller rule sets than Cubist on twenty-three datasets, and MAE / Cover and Cover produce smaller ones on twenty-two datasets. Cubist, on the other hand, produces smaller rule sets than all variants of M5′Rules on only six datasets. From Table 4, it can be seen that in many cases M5′Rules produces far fewer rules than Cubist. For example, on the sensory dataset Cubist produces just over forty-five rules, while M5′Rules is more accurate with approximately four rules. Furthermore, from Table 5 it can be seen that M5′Rules generates fewer conditions per rule set than Cubist—it is significantly better on twenty-four and worse on at most five. For some datasets (sensory, pbc, breastTumor, cholesterol) the differences are dramatic.

5 Conclusion

We have presented an algorithm for generating rules for numeric prediction by applying the separate-and-conquer technique to generate a sequence of model

Table 5. Experimental results: average number of conditions per rule set produced by M5'Rules compared with average number of conditions per rule set produced by Cubist

Dataset	Cubist	M5'R % RMS	M5'R MAE/Cover	M5'R CC×Cover	M5'R Cover
auto93	4.37±0.6	0.08±0.1 o	0.08±0.1 o	0.09±0.1 o	0.09±0.1 o
autoHorse	11.60±1.1	4.47±2.2 o	3.89±1.5 o	3.96±2.2 o	3.63±1.3 o
autoMpg	14.13±1.6	5.17±1.1 o	3.50±0.4 o	3.53±0.5 o	3.49±0.5 o
autoPrice	5.63±0.6	8.61±1.7 •	7.64±1.4 •	7.19±1.0 •	5.98±0.7
baskball	11.75±0.7	0.00±0.0 o	0.00±0.0 o	0.00±0.0 o	0.00±0.0 o
bodyfat	0.76±0.5	6.86±1.7 •	4.07±0.8 •	3.00±0.6 •	3.08±0.6 •
breastTumor	81.32±3.9	0.06±0.1 o	0.06±0.1 o	0.06±0.1 o	0.06±0.1 o
cholesterol	81.86±4.7	1.78±0.8 o	1.48±0.6 o	1.58±0.6 o	1.47±0.5 o
cleveland	27.37±4.3	0.19±0.3 o	0.15±0.3 o	0.24±0.4 o	0.21±0.4 o
cloud	0.18±0.1	2.23±0.7 •	1.59±0.4 •	1.79±0.6 •	1.76±0.6 •
cpu	2.00±0.0	1.91±0.2	1.86±0.3	1.82±0.2	1.82±0.2
echoMonths	16.53±1.7	0.00±0.0 o	0.00±0.0 o	0.00±0.0 o	0.00±0.0 o
elusage	2.00±0.0	0.64±0.2 o	0.63±0.2 o	0.62±0.2 o	0.62±0.2 o
fishcatch	2.00±0.0	4.43±1.1 •	3.66±0.9 •	3.40±0.6 •	3.40±0.6 •
housing	18.28±1.6	30.44±6.9 •	18.28±2.7	16.30±2.6	15.73±2.1
hungarian	33.04±3.3	0.88±0.3 o	0.79±0.3 o	0.81±0.3 o	0.84±0.4 o
lowbwt	21.19±0.9	0.06±0.1 o	0.05±0.1 o	0.06±0.1 o	0.06±0.1 o
mbagrade	6.61±0.4	0.00±0.0 o	0.00±0.0 o	0.00±0.0 o	0.00±0.0 o
meta	25.87±0.6	8.81±1.0 o	7.34±0.7 o	10.53±1.8 o	6.49±0.9 o
pbc	100.86±5.6	0.65±0.1 o	0.65±0.1 o	0.65±0.1 o	0.65±0.1 o
pharynx	7.96±0.1	2.70±1.5 o	1.86±0.9 o	1.60±0.6 o	1.79±0.7 o
pollution	1.18±0.5	0.28±0.2 o	0.25±0.1 o	0.25±0.1 o	0.25±0.1 o
pwLinear	2.00±0.0	1.00±0.0 o	1.00±0.0 o	1.00±0.0 o	1.00±0.0 o
quake	9.64±3.0	3.04±0.5 o	2.66±0.4 o	3.62±0.9 o	2.69±0.5 o
sensory	218.80±6.8	8.88±1.6 o	5.43±1.1 o	5.70±0.9 o	5.40±1.2 o
servo	13.33±0.2	7.42±0.9 o	7.15±0.9 o	5.19±0.6 o	5.05±0.5 o
sleep	2.38±0.8	0.00±0.0 o	0.00±0.0 o	0.00±0.0 o	0.00±0.0 o
strike	46.55±5.2	9.27±2.9 o	4.98±1.2 o	7.40±2.1 o	5.25±1.6 o
veteran	19.63±2.5	0.50±0.5 o	0.42±0.3 o	0.41±0.3 o	0.41±0.4 o
vineyard	4.13±0.4	1.90±0.2 o	1.56±0.2 o	1.53±0.2 o	1.56±0.2 o

o,• statistically significant improvement or degradation

trees, reading one rule off each of the trees. The algorithm is straightforward to implement and relatively insensitive to the heuristic used to select competing rules from the tree at each iteration. M5'Rules using the coverage heuristic is significantly worse, in terms of accuracy, on only one (autoPrice) of the thirty bench mark datasets when compared with M5'. In terms of compactness, M5'Rules never produces larger rule sets and produces smaller sets on ten datasets. When compared to the commercial system Cubist, M5'Rules outperforms it on size and is comparable on accuracy. When based on the number of leaves it is more than three times more likely to produce significantly fewer rules. When the number of conditions per rule are used to estimate rule size M5'Rules is eight times more likely to produce rules with fewer conditions than Cubist.

Published results with smoothed trees [15] indicate that the smoothing procedure substantially increases the accuracy of predictions. Smoothing cannot be applied to rules in the same way as for trees because the tree containing the relevant adjacent models is discarded at each iteration of the rule generation process. It seems more likely that improvements to M5'Rules will have to be made as a post-processing optimization stage. This is unfortunate because gen-

Table 6. Results of paired t-tests ($p = 0.01$): number indicates how often method in column significantly outperforms method in row; number in braces indicates how often method in column produces significantly fewer rules than method in row.

	Cubist	M5′	% RMS	MAE / Cover	CC × Cover	Cover
Cubist	-	12 {20}	12 {23}	10 {22}	12 {23}	11 {22}
M5′	8 {6}	-	0 {12}	0 {11}	0 {11}	0 {10}
% RMS	9 {6}	2 {1}	-	1 {2}	0 {4}	1 {5}
MAE / Cover	9 {6}	2 {1}	1 {2}	-	1 {4}	1 {2}
CC × Cover	9 {6}	2 {0}	1 {2}	1 {1}	-	1 {2}
Cover	9 {6}	1 {0}	0 {3}	0 {1}	0 {2}	-

eration of accurate rule sets without global optimization is a compelling aspect of the basic PART procedure, on which M5′Rules is based. However, smoothing usually increases the complexity of the linear models at the leaf nodes, making the resulting predictor more difficult to analyze.

Acknowledgements

We would like to thank Gordon Paynter for suggesting the problem and Yong Wang for helpful discussions on model trees.

References

1. L. Breiman, J. Olshen, and C. Stone. *Classification and Regression Trees.* Wadsworth, Monterrey, Ca, 1984.
2. W. W. Cohen. Fast effective rule induction. In *Proc. of the Twelfth International Conference on Machine Learning*, pages 115–123. Morgan Kaufmann, 1995.
3. G. Das, K. I. Lin, G. Renganathan, and P. Smyth. Rule discovery from time series. In *Proc. of the Fourth International Conference on Knowledge Discovery and Data Mining*, pages 16–22. AAAI Press, 1998.
4. E. Frank and I. H. Witten. Generating accurate rule sets without global optimization. In *Proc. of the Fifteenth International Conference on Machine Learning*, pages 144–151. Morgan Kaufmann, 1998.
5. J. Freidman. Multivariate adaptive regression splines. *Annals of Statistics*, 19(1):1–141, 1991.
6. J. Freidman and W. Stuetzle. Projection pursuit regression. *J. American Statistics Association*, 76:817–823, 1981.
7. A. Karalic. Employing linear regression in regression tree leaves. In *Proc. of the Tenth European Conference on Artificial Intelligence*, Vienna, Austria, 1992.
8. E. J. Keogh and M. J. Pazzani. An enhanced representation of time series which allows fast and accurate classification, clustering and relevance feedback. In *Proc. of the Fourth International Conference on Knowledge Discovery and Data Mining*, pages 239–243. AAAI Press, 1998.

9. D. Kilpatrick and M. Cameron-Jones. Numeric prediction using instance-based learning with encoding length selection. In Nikola Kasabov, Robert Kozma, Kitty Ko, Robert O'Shea, George Coghill, and Tom Gedeon, editors, *Progress in Connectionist-Based Information Systems*, volume 2, pages 984–987. Springer-Verlag, 1998.

10. J. R. Quinlan. Learning with continuous classes. In *Proc. of the Fifth Australian Joint Conference on Artificial Intelligence*, pages 343–348, World Scientific, Singapore, 1992.

11. J. R. Quinlan. *C4.5: Programs for Machine Learning*. Morgan Kaufmann, San Mateo, CA., 1993.

12. J. Simonoff. *Smoothing Methods in Statistics*. Springer-Verlag, New York, 1996.

13. StatLib. Department of Statistics, Carnegie Mellon University, 1999. http://lib.stat.cmu.edu.

14. L. Torgo. Data fitting with rule-based regression. In J. Zizka and P. Brazdil, editors, *Proc. of the Workshop on Artificial Intelligence Techniques (AIT'95)*, Brno, Czech Republic, 1995.

15. Y. Wang and I. H. Witten. Induction of model trees for predicting continuous classes. In *Proc. of the poster papers of the European Conference on Machine Learning*, pages 128–137, Prague, Czech Republic, 1997.

16. S. Weiss and N. Indurkhya. Rule-based machine learning methods for functional prediction. *Journal of Artificial Intelligence Research*, 3:383–403, 1995.

Classifying and Learning Cricket Shots Using Camera Motion

Mihai Lazarescu, Svetha Venkatesh, and Geoff West

Curtin University of Technology,
GPO Box U1987, Perth 6001, WA
{lazarescu,svetha,geoff}@computing.edu.au

Abstract. This paper presents a method to classify and learn cricket shots. The procedure begins by extracting the camera motion parameters from the shots. Then the camera parameter values are converted to symbolic form and combined to generate a symbolic description that defines the trajectory of the cricket ball. The description generated is used to classify the cricket shot and to dynamically expand or update the system's knowledge of shots. The first novel aspect of this approach is that by using the camera motion parameters, a complex and difficult process of low level image segmenting of either the batsman or the cricket ball from video images is avoided. Also the method does not require high resolution images. Another novel aspect of this work is the use of a new incremental learning algorithm that enables the system to improve and update its knowledge base. Unlike previously developed algorithms which store training instances and have simple method to prune their concept hierarchies, the incremental learning algorithm used in this work generates compact concept hierarchies and uses evidence based forgetting. The results show that the system performs well in the task of classifying four types of cricket shots.

1 Introduction

In this paper we present a system which uses camera motion to recognise and learn cricket shots. The work is part of a multimedia project which aims to use transcripts of commentary and image clues to recognise, learn and produce a natural language description of action/s taking place in the video segment. The domain of our work is sports and we have previously developed a system that is able to recognise and learn American Football plays based on the transcript of the commentary and video clues [7], [6], [8]. Essentially the transcript clues are used to constrain the search for a match for the play in the video segment while the video clues are used to refine the solution. The system develops detailed spatio-temporal models of the American Football plays which can be easily converted into detailed text descriptions of them. This offers the advantage that the system can generate descriptions for the plays which are far more detailed than that present in normal commentary.

In the current work we explore the possibility of applying the work done in American Football to other sports, in this case, cricket. The reason for choosing

N. Foo (Ed.): AI'99, LNAI 1747, pp. 13–23, 1999.

cricket is that though cricket is a lot simpler than American Football, it still involves well defined actions — *cricket shots* — for which accurate representations can be built. We define a cricket shot as the way in which the batsman hits the ball he is facing and propose a classification scheme based on the direction in which the ball is hit and the distance covered by the ball.

The objective of our research is to combine camera motion estimation with incremental machine learning to classify and learn types of cricket shots. The video processing is fast, does not require high resolution images and avoids complex low level segmentation. An important aspect of this work is the use of a new incremental learning algorithm. The incremental learning involves updating existing symbolic descriptions of the cricket shots in order to keep them consistent with incoming data.

The paper is organised as follows. Section two presents some background information on camera motion estimation and incremental machine learning. Section three covers the way in which we extract the data from video and process it. Section four presents the results and section five contains the conclusions.

2   Previous Work

The problem of estimating motion parameters has been researched extensively in the past since it provides a simple, fast and accurate way to search multimedia databases for specific shots (for example a shot of a landscape is likely to involve a significant amount of pan, whilst a shot of an aerobatic sequence is likely to contain roll).

Bergen's *et al.* [4] method is based on two models: a global model that constrains the overall motion estimated and a local model that is used in the estimation process. Affine flow, planar flow, rigid body motion and general optic flow are the four specific models chosen. The same objective function is used in all models and the minimisation is performed with respect to different parameters.

Akutsu *et al.* [1] have proposed a method based on analysing the distribution of motion vectors in Hough space. Seven categories of camera motion are estimated: pan, tilt, zoom, pan and tilt, pan and zoom, tilt and zoom, and pan, tilt and zoom. Each category has a different signature curve in the Hough space. Estimation of the motion parameters is based on Hough-transformed optic-flow vectors measured from the image sequence and determining which of the signatures best matches the data in a least squares sense.

Park *et al.* [11] describe a method of estimating camera parameters that establishes feature based correspondence between frames. The camera parameters representing zoom, focal length and 3D rotation are estimated by fitting the correspondence data to a transformation model based on perspective projection.

Tse and Baker [13] present an algorithm to compensate for camera zoom and pan. The global motion in each frame is modelled by just two parameters: a zoom factor and a pan and tilt factor based on local displacement vectors found by conventional means.

Wu and Kittler [14] present a technique to extract rotation, change of scale, and translation from an image sequence without establishing correspondence. A multi-resolution iterative algorithm that uses a Taylor series approximation of the spatial and temporal gradient of the image is used.

To extract the camera motion parameters from a sequence of images we use a method developed by Srinivasan *et al* [10]. The method can qualitatively estimate camera pan, tilt, zoom, roll, and horizontal and vertical tracking. Unlike most other comparable techniques, this method can distinguish pan from horizontal tracking, and tilt from vertical tracking.

Several methods of learning have been developed but the one that is best suited for real world situations is *incremental learning*. Human beings *learn incrementally* because facts are generally received in the form of a sequential flow of information. Typically the information received comes in steps and human beings have to learn how to deal with a situation long before all the facts are available. Further, humans have limited memory and processing power [12].

There are several important issues in incremental learning which have been identified: bias, concept drift, memory size and forgetting. Several systems have been designed (ILF [7], [5], GEM [12], COBWEB [3], [2] and UNIMEM [9]) to address some of the issues mentioned above.

We use the incremental learning algorithm ILF [7,5]. The concepts developed by our algorithm are stored in a hierarchy in which all descriptions share all the features observed in the training instances. The descriptions in our structure do not store the individual instances of the cricket shots and any feature's range of values is defined with the help of a set which covers all the values encountered in the training instances which were used in the generalisation process. There are several reasons for choosing this type of representation. The reason for not storing the instances is that it allows the system to detect any drift in the target concept and also by using all observed features to build the concepts, the system is able to handle cases of missing or noisy data. Furthermore this representation substantially reduces the size of the concept and as a result the amount of memory required to store the hierarchy.

3 Extracting and Converting the Camera Motion Parameters

There are two ways in which a cricket shot can be determined. One method involves segmenting out either the batsman or the ball. Unlike American Football where it is possible to track *some* of the players in the play, in cricket it is much more difficult to track the batsman because of two reasons: the high speed of the shot (few frames, too much blur as shown in Figure 1) and the batsman is often occluded by the wicket keeper. Furthermore, even if the batsman could be consistently segmented out from the image, it is still difficult to distinguish the action of the batsman (the bat cannot be identified consistently so its pattern of movement cannot be accurately classified). It is similarly difficult to segment out the cricket ball in video especially since the cricket ball is *small* and difficult to distinguish from the background (generally there is no *significant* difference between the ball and backgound). An alternative method is to use the camera motion parameters to determine the path of the ball. Throughout the cricket game the camera generally focuses on the ball trajectory and hence it is possible to generate a hypothesis on the type of cricket shot based on the camera motion parameters which in turn define the direction of the ball. There are three stages

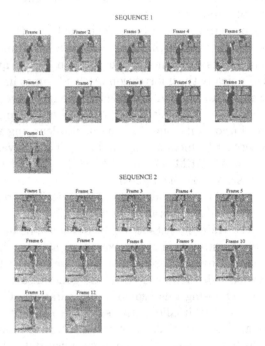

Fig. 1. Two typical sequences of a batsman attempting a shot. Images provided with the courtesy of Wide World of Sports - Channel 9 Australia.

in the processing of the camera motion parameters.

In the first stage the system attempts to determine the size of the window that contains the cricket shot, that is the start and end of the shot sequence containing the shot (the camera position is assumed to be behind one the two bowling ends of the cricket ground to capture the bowling action). The cricket action consists of two parts: the bowler action and the batsman action. The bowler's action is defined by a sequence of frames in which there is a substantial amount of zoom and tilt but little pan. This is because the camera is tracking and zooming on the bowler and the cricket ball. Both the bowler and the ball move fairly straight and hence there is no substantial panning. The batsman action is defined by a sudden change in the direction of the ball which involves a significant amount of pan. The cricket shot ends with a cut when the camera focuses on the crowd, the ground or a field player who has fielded the cricket ball. The *cricket shot window* therefore starts at the frame where the system has detected a sudden change in the camera parameters and ends at the frame where the system detects a cut.

The second stage involves determining the *dominant motion* of the camera in the cricket shot. The reason for checking for a *dominant motion* is that the movement of the camera during a shot is not always smooth and contains varying amounts of zoom and tilt as it all depends on how good the camera man is at tracking the ball: the more experienced, the smoother the action. Hence it is quite likely that a drive on the left side will contain some small movement to the right which occurs while the camera man attempted to track the ball. Such movement is essentially noisy and must be eliminated to be able to determine the real camera movement. The system analyses the entire sequence and determines the *dominant movement* of the camera (for example whether the overall movement was to the left or to the right) by computing the frequency of the *negative* and *positive* values for the camera parameters. The *most frequent sign determines the dominant motion* for that category of camera parameters. For example if the values for the pan parameter are mostly positive then the dominant motion is to the right otherwise the movement is to the left. The symbolic values classifying the dominant motion for all camera parameters are shown in Table 1 (the actual pan/tilt/roll value is not considered at this stage when converting it to symbolic form — just the sign).

Table 1. Symbolic values classifying the dominant camera motion.

Camera Parameter	Symbolic Value	Value Sign
Pan	Right	Positive
Pan	Left	Negative
Tilt	Up	Positive
Tilt	Down	Negative
Roll	Clockwise	Positive
Roll	Anticlockwise	Negative
Zoom	Zoom-In	Positive
Zoom	Zoom-Out	Negative

The third stage involves a more refined classification of the camera motion. Once the *dominant motion* has been identified much of the noise is removed. Then for each camera parameter in turn, the system collects all the values from the sequence and computes an average. This average value indicates how far and how fast the camera moved during the cricket shot. The average value is also converted into a symbolic value (the threshold values defining the boundaries of the types of camera motion were obtained using a simple clustering technique — generally the values fall into three intervals, for example for the Gabba Cricket

Table 2. Symbolic values for the average camera motion parameter value.

Camera Parameter	Symbolic Value	Average Value
Pan	Right	High Positive Values
Pan	Left	High Negative Values
Pan	Middle	Close To Zero
Tilt	Up	High Positive Values
Tilt	Down	High Negative Values
Tilt	Centered	Close To Zero
Roll	Clockwise	High Positive Values
Roll	Anticlockwise	High Negative Values
Roll	Static	Close To Zero
Zoom	Zoom-In	High Positive Values
Zoom	Zoom-Out	High Negative Values
Zoom	Steady	Close To Zero

ground the intervals were [-30...-1],[-0.1..0.1], [1..30]). Table 2 shows the symbolic values used to describe the average camera parameter values.

Once symbolic values for both the dominant motion and the average camera motion have been obtained for each of the four camera parameters, the system can identify the type of the cricket shot. Each shot can, therefore, be expressed as a sequence of symbolic values. Figure 2 shows types of cricket shot which the system is attempting to indentify. Besides the eight symbolic values representing the camera parameters, the system also generates a ninth symbolic value which defines the length of the shot. The length of the shot is simply derived from the duration of the video shot sequence (the number of frames in a shot). For example consider the shot *long straight drive* (on the left side). One possible set of symbolic values for the camera parameters is shown in Table 3.

Table 3. Symbolic values classifying the dominant camera motion and average motion for a long straight drive (on the left side).

Camera Parameter	Dominant Motion	Average Value
Pan	Left	Close To Zero
Tilt	Down	High Negative Value
Roll	Clockwise	High Negative Value
Zoom	Zoom-Out	High Negative Value

Extracting camera parameters for the frames that make up a window containing the cricket shot provides information about the ball trajectory. To determine its type, we classify the shot based on the three parameters: dominant motion,

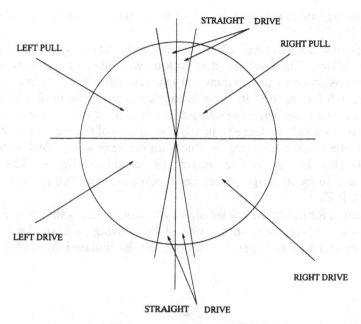

Fig. 2. The six cricket shots the system attempts to identify: the drive shot (left ,right or straight), the pull shot (left or right) and the hook shot.

average camera motion value and length. However the values of two of the parameters along which a shot is classified namely, dominant motion and average camera motion value, vary from game to game. This is due to the following factors:

- Camera position varies on different cricket grounds mainly in the angle at which the shot is captured (right behind wicket or at a slight angle) and the perspective from which the shot is taken (low down or high up in the stands).
- Ground shape and size also varies on different cricket grounds (for example the Brisbane Gabba Cricket Ground is smaller than the Melbourne Cricket Ground and a shot such as a drive involves slightly different camera motion — different pan and zoom).

The goal of our work has been to build general cricket shot descriptions to enable the system to classify shots from different cricket grounds and therefore any ground specific information needs to removed. To deal with variations in the parameters we use incremental learning. We build representations of the shots using symbolic data and update these representations when necessary.

4   Classifying and Learning Cricket Shots

Training data is extracted from a video sequence, such that several shots are extracted and their description are derived in terms of symbolic movement data, symbolic average value and shot length. We use the incremental learning algorithm ILF [7], [5].

The way in which the system learns from the incoming cricket shot descriptions is as follows. The symbolic descriptions generated by the data analysis module are passed on to the incremental learning module which first attempts to find a match for the shot in the existing hierarchy of shots. Each new shot description is compared with the current description in the hierarchy to determine if there is enough evidence to justify the update of the current description. Each description in the hierarchy produces an evidence score which determines whether the shot does or does not match the current description. The score is computed as a function of age, where age records the duration in time the shot is known to ILF.

The general format of the cricket shot type description is shown in Figure 3. This shows that there are n shots, with shot 3 having m examples in its description. In this way multiple descriptions can be updated (provided enough

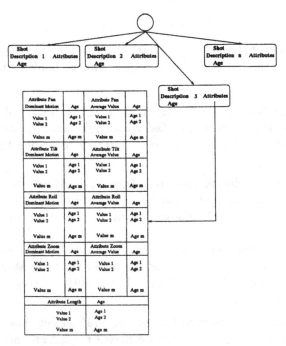

Fig. 3. A typical description hierarchy used by the incremental learning algorithm. Each shot description has an age and 9 attributes and each one of the attributes has a set of data values+age values associated with it.

evidence was found) by the same shot. While this procedure results in the system updating descriptions which should not be updated when one considers the overall set of shots, results show that over time the unnecessary modifications are "aged out" of the descriptions. That is unless a particular shot description gets reinforced by other similar ones, it forgotten. The main reason for choosing to update multiple descriptions is that it is a simple way of representing a fuzzy match between the existing description and the input cricket shot which is more appropriate than an absolute match (as we mentioned above, the camera parameters vary from game to game). The update process is based on data ageing. The algorithm uses ageing at two levels: the *data level* and the *description level*. Therefore, when a new cricket shot is processed there are three possible outcomes. The first is that the system finds a match for it in the existing hierarchy of shot descriptions. The description that matches the input cricket shot is updated to be consistent with the new data. The second outcome is that the system does not find a match for the new cricket shot so a new description is added to the hierarchy while updating the existing shot descriptions. The third outcome from processing a new cricket shot is that one (or possibly more) description in the hierarchy get removed since the data is "aged out".

5 Results

We have trained the system on 63 cricket shots and tested it on 80 shots. The video segments used in our work had a length varying from 24 to 190 frames. The shots have been collected from 5 cricket games and cover five types of shots. Two of the shots occur rarely (most players tend to avoid them since they are high risk shots) and as a result very few instances were present in either the training or the test sets. The training data is shown in Table 4 and the test data is shown in Table 5. The results of the classification are shown in Table 6. The system performed very well when classifying four types of shots: the pull shot (left and right) and drive shot (left and right). The overall success rate averaged at 77% (slightly higher on right hand side — this was due to the fact that more data were available to train the system on the right hand side). The results also show that the system was not able to build an accurate description for the straight drive shot and hence it was unable to accurately classify the shot. In the case of the straight drive shot the system has simply been unable to identify any significant differences between the camera parameters for a straight drive and a drive on each side of the ground (the pan values do not vary as much as expected).

Table 4. The training data.

Number of Shots	Side	Shot Type
25	Right	Drive
15	Left	Drive
18	Right	Pull
14	Left	Pull

Table 5. The test data.

Number of Shots	Side	Shot Type
24	Right	Drive
20	Left	Drive
20	Right	Pull
18	Left	Pull

Table 6. The results of the tests.

Side	Shot Type	Correct	Incorrect
Right	Drive	19	5
Left	Drive	18	2
Right	Pull	15	5
Left	Pull	12	6

6   Conclusions

We have developed a system which classifies and learns cricket shots. The system uses the camera motion parameters to estimate the direction of the ball in a cricket shot. The procedure to extract the camera parameters is fast, robust and avoids complex and costly low level image segmentation. The camera motion parameters are converted into a symbolic description of the camera movement which defines the trajectory of the ball. The symbolic description is then used to classify and learn cricket shots. The learning process uses forgetting and allows the system to keep existing cricket shot descriptions consistent with incoming data. The results show that the system performs well in the task of classifying four types of cricket shot with an average success rate at 77%.

References

1. H. Hashimoto A. Akutsu, Y. Tonomura and Y. Ohba. Video indexing using motion vectors. In *Conference Proceedings of SPIE Visual Communication and Image Processing 1992*, pages 1522–1530, 1992.
2. Douglas H. Fisher. Knowledge aquisition via incremental conceptual clustering. In Jude W. Shavlik and Thomas G. Diettrich, editors, *Readings in Machine Learning*, pages 267–284. Morgan Kauffman, 1990.
3. John H. Gennari, Pat Langley, and Doug Fisher. Models of incremental concept formation. *Artificial Intelligence*, 40:11–61, 1989.
4. K. Hanna J. R. Bergen, P. Anandan and J. Hingorani. Hierarchical model based estimation. In *Proceedings of ECCV92*, pages 232–252, 1992.
5. Mihai Lazarescu, Svetha Venkatesh, and Geoff West. Incremental learning with forgetting (i.l.f.). In *Proceedings of ICML-99 Workshop on Machine Learning in Computer Vision*, June 1999.

6. Mihai Lazarescu, Svetha Venkatesh, Geoff West, and Terry Caelli. Combining nl processing and video data to query american football. In *Proceedings of IAPR'98*, pages 1238–1241, August 1998.
7. Mihai Lazarescu, Svetha Venkatesh, Geoff West, and Terry Caelli. Using natural language and video data to query and learn american football plays. In *Proceedings of ICAPR'98*, pages 63–73, nov 1998.
8. Mihai Lazarescu, Svetha Venkatesh, Geoff West, and Terry Caelli. On the automated interpretation and indexing of american football. In *Proceedings of ICMCS'99*, pages 802–807, June 1999.
9. M. Lebowitz. Experiments with incremental concept formation : Unimem. *Machine Learning*, 2(2):103–138, 1987.
10. Srinivasan M., S. Venkatesh, and R. Hosie. Qualitative estimation of camera motion parameters from video sequences. *Pattern Recognition*, 30:593–606, 1997.
11. J. Park, N. Yagi, K. Enami, and E. Kiyoharu. Estimation of camera parameters from image sequence for model video based coding. *IEEE Transactions on Circutis Systems and Video Technology*, 3(4):288–296, 1994.
12. R. E. Reinke and R. S. Michalski. Incremental learning of concept descriptions : A method and experimental results. In J. E. Hayes, D. Mitchie, and J. Richards, editors, *Machine Intelligence*, volume 11, pages 263–289. 1988.
13. Y.T. Tse and R.L. Baker. Global zoompan estimation and compensation for video compression. In *ICASSP'91*, pages 2725–2728, 1991.
14. S.F. Wu and J. Kittler. A differential method for simultaneous estimation of motion change of scale and translation. *Signal Process. Image Comm.*, 2:69–80, 1990.

Unsupervised Learning in Metagame

Graham E. Farr and David R. Powell

School of Computer Science and Software Engineering,
Monash University (Clayton Campus)
Clayton, Vic. 3168 Australia
{gfarr,powell}@csse.monash.edu.au

Abstract. The Metagame approach to computer game playing, introduced by Pell, involves writing programs that can play many games from
some large class, rather than programs specialised to play just a single
game such as chess. Metagame programs take the rules of a randomly
generated game as input, then do some analysis of that game, and then
play the game against an opponent. Success in Metagame competitions
is evidence of a more general kind of ability than that possessed by (for
example) a chess program or a draughts program. In this paper, we take
up one of Pell's challenges by building a Metagame player that can learn.
The learning techniques used are a refinement of the regression methods
of Christensen and Korf, and they are applied to unsupervised learning, from self-play, of the weights of the components (or *advisors*) of the
evaluation function. The method used leads to significant improvement
in playing strength for many (but not all) games in the class. We also
shed light on some curious behaviour of some advisor weights. In order
to conduct this research, a new and more efficient Metagame player was
written.

1 Introduction

Metagame is a relatively new field of Artificial Intelligence research originated by
Pell [8,9,10,11,12]. The basic idea is to develop and compare programs which can
analyse and play any game from some general class, rather than just a single
game. A Metagame program takes the rules (suitably encoded) to some new
game (possibly randomly generated), performs some analysis of the game, then
plays that game against other players. The performance of such programs can
be compared quantitatively using the results of games and tournaments. The
hope is that success (by a program) at Metagame is indicative of a more general
kind of problem solving ability than that possessed by a program which plays a
single game such as Chess. Analysis of particular games in the class is intended
to be done by the program rather than a human. Metagame is thus intended as
a testbed for AI ideas, and in many respects may be a better one than Chess.

Pell introduced the class SCL of Symmetric Chess-Like games as a domain for
Metagame play. This class consists of games between two players on a rectangular
board, with pieces, moves, captures, promotion, goals and other ingredients. For
full details of the SCL class, see [11]; we give a little more detail in §3.

N. Foo (Ed.): AI'99, LNAI 1747, pp. 24–35, 1999.

Pell developed a Metagame player (in Prolog) called METAGAMER for the SCL class, and ran some tournaments with several Metagame-playing algorithms as participants (playing several randomly generated games from the class). The tournament participants themselves were fairly elementary (being just bit-players in Pell's work) but the work did serve to demonstrate the feasibility of the Metagame paradigm. Pell pointed to many useful avenues for further research, including the use of Metagame as a testbed for learning.

The purpose of this paper is to take up that challenge, in particular to apply some unsupervised learning techniques to Metagame. It is natural for the learning to be unsupervised because of the lack of prior human expertise on the SCL class as a whole. We construct what may well be the world's best Metagame player (albeit for a slight restriction of the SCL class). It is able to learn well enough to significantly improve play over much of the class considered. We find, though, that learning well enough to improve play at every single game in (even our restriction of) the whole SCL class is beyond our methods. We will discuss some of the problems faced and the lessons learned.

The game playing algorithms considered here are of a very standard type: fixed depth α-β search, with the positions at the leaves of this search tree being valued according to an evaluation function. The evaluation function is a linear combination of *advisors*, where an advisor is a function of the position which returns something helpful like material balance or mobility. Advisors in Metagame capture concepts which apply across (at least a large portion of) the SCL class. Advisors are symmetric in the sense that interchanging colours in a position will simply negate an advisor's value. Further information on the actual advisors used is given in the next Section. The coefficients of the advisors are the *weights*. If the choice of advisors and search depth are given, then playing strategy is entirely determined by these weights. In this paper we study a method of learning the weights.

The learning techniques used are a refinement of the regression methods of Christensen and Korf [2]. Their method involved starting with some initial estimates of the weights in the static evaluation function and solving a series of linear regression problems to obtain a series of successively improved sets of weights. A variety of initial estimates may be tried in order to increase the chance of finding a good local optimum. They apply their method to learning weights of pieces in Chess, obtaining interesting results which they discuss. Here the technique is adapted to learn weights of evaluation function components in Metagame. This is apparently more difficult and we describe the refinements we found it necessary to introduce. We also shed light on correlations between advisors, the effect this has on the advisor weights learned, and the import of negative weights (which turn out not to be a problem after all).

The experiments conducted required extensive computations. Pell's Metagame player (in Prolog), while having many nice features, was too slow for this purpose. One of us (Powell) wrote a new Metagame player, for most of the SCL class, in C, which was fast enough.

We briefly describe some other relevant work. Epstein [4] constructed a program, Hoyle, which also plays games from some class, but does no analysis of the rules of the game. It does some supervised learning: for each game, it requires a game-specific program written by a human expert from which to learn. More recently, Epstein, Gelfand and Lesniak [5] have added a pattern-based learning capability to Hoyle. The program MorphII, due to Levinson [6,7], can play a very general class of games defined in predicate logic, and a couple of learning methods have been implemented. Samuel [13] did pioneering work on the unsupervised learning of evaluation function weights (applied to Draughts), although he used an iterative updating method different to the regression technique employed here and in [2]. Abramson [1] applied regression to learning evaluation functions that estimate the expected outcome (under random play) of a game. The technique is widely applicable, and he tried it out on Othello and Chess with interesting results. Pell [11,12] has suggested applying the Temporal Difference (TD) methods of Sutton [15], and applied with notable success to Backgammon by Tesauro [16,17], to Metagame. One practical difficulty for us, if such methods were to be applied to Metagame, is the much greater number of games required.

   In the remainder of this paper we describe the learning methods we use, report the experimental results obtained, discuss them, draw some conclusions and offer some suggestions for future work.

2   Methods

As usual (e.g. [14]), an evaluation function v_0 is a linear combination of components a_j, $j = 1, \ldots, n$ (which, in the context of Metagame, Pell [11] calls *advisors*). Both v_0 and its advisors are functions of the position P. The coefficients (or *weights*) of the advisors are denoted by λ_j, $j = 1, \ldots, n$ and are independent of position. It is often convenient to speak of the *weight vector* $\lambda = (\lambda_j)_{j=1}^{n}$. Thus:

$$v_0(\lambda, P) = \sum_{j=1}^{n} \lambda_j a_j(P).$$

This is assumed to be some sort of estimate of the value of the position P. It is assumed that a better estimate of the "true" value of P can be obtained by searching to depth d and backing up the static evaluations given by v_0 at the leaves of this search tree; denote this depth-d evaluation of P by $v_d(\lambda, P)$. These assumptions are standard, although not rigorously justified (see [1]).

   As in [13], then, one way to improve a set of weights is to adjust them so that the resulting evaluation function more nearly approximates the backed up value obtained from using the current weights at the leaves. As in [2], we do this adjustment by starting with some initial weight vector $\lambda^{(0)}$ and then, for each iteration $k = 1, 2, \ldots$, assembling equations

$$v_0(\lambda^{(k)}, P) = v_d(\lambda^{(k-1)}, P)$$

for a suitably large number of positions P and finding the least squares solution of this over-constrained system for $\lambda^{(k)}$. This process may converge on a new weight vector λ.

We thus need a large number of positions P. We generate these positions by getting our program to play the current game (i.e., the particular SCL game which the program is trying to learn) many times, and introducing some randomness into its play in order to ensure that we get a reasonably wide variety of positions. Such self-play allows us to sample positions from a game in a way that is natural for each game, as well as showing (from the results of the games) how well a particular learning method is doing (see below). The resulting weights are average weights over all stages of the game, as in [2].

Of course, as noted in [2], the weight vector λ found by the above process might not be globally optimum (with respect to playing strength). In fact just doing the above procedure may result in a weight vector that is worse than the initial one (since some least squares solutions of the system

$$\forall P \quad v_0(\lambda) = v_d(\lambda, P)$$

are bad, i.e. may cause poorer play if used as weights), so care needs to be taken to prevent such degeneration. As well as picking a reasonable initial vector (typically, having all components equal to 1; such "uniform" vectors were used by Pell [11]), we find it helpful to periodically check on the game-playing performance of our weight vectors and take steps to ensure that what we do does actually improve things.

We now summarise our learning procedure.

Fix:

$$d = \text{depth of search (typically, 3)};$$

$$N = \text{number of equations per learning iteration}$$

$$\text{(typically, 1000; see below)}.$$

1. Input: rules of new SCL game G.
   Aim: to learn a good weight vector λ for G.
2. Initialisation:
   $$\lambda^{(0)} := \mathbf{1} \quad \text{(i.e., vector of } n \text{ ones)}$$
3. Games to be played between two computer players, each using α-β search to depth d:
   – one player uses fixed weights $\lambda^{(0)}$ (and does not learn);
   – the other uses the current weights $\lambda^{(k)}$ (the "Learning Player").
4. $k := 1$
5. k-th Learning Iteration:
   Repeat the following until a predetermined number of games have been played.
   1. Play enough games between these two players to collect N linear equations in λ, one for each position P and each equation having the form
   $$v_0(\lambda, P) = v_d(\lambda^{(k-1)}, P).$$

Also keep a record of the Learning Player's score over these games (where, for each game, win $= 1$, draw $= 1/2$, loss $= 0$). Let this score, as a fraction of games played during this Learning Iteration, be p_{k-1}. (Thus, for each k, p_k is an indication of how successful the weight vector $\lambda^{(k)}$ was.)

2. Use linear regression to find the least squares solution to this system of equations for λ. (We used LAPACK version 2.0.)

3. Update weight vector according to how much of an improvement it is over the previous weight vector:

$$\lambda^{(k)} := (1 - p_{k-1})\lambda + p_{k-1}\lambda^{(k-1)}$$

(Remark: this was found to give better results than just putting $\lambda^{(k)} := \lambda^{(k-1)}$. The latter gave erratic performance, frequently throwing away good weight vectors in favour of inferior ones. Refer to our remarks above on the dangers of converging on a bad weight vector.)

4. Next Learning Iteration: $k := k + 1$.

6. Combining weight vectors: A final weight vector λ^* is chosen from all the $\lambda^{(k)}$ found at each of the successive learning iterations. Three methods were tried.

One only of the following is done:

(a) $\lambda^* =$ the $\lambda^{(k)}$ with the highest p_k (i.e. the best record).

(b) $\lambda^* = \sum_k p_k \lambda^{(k)}$.

(c) $\lambda^* = \sum_{k:p_k>1/2} p_k \lambda^{(k)}$. (I.e., only "winning" vectors — those whose average score per game is more than $1/2$ — are included in the weighted sum.)

A number of technical details should be mentioned.

Mathematically, the weight vectors do not need to be normalised, although no harm is done in doing so (and it may become necessary in practice if the weights get too large).

The value assigned to winning positions was simply 1.2 times the largest value previously occurring in the collected equations. This has the effect of giving a winning position a value higher than any other position encountered in the game, but not completely dominating the collected equations. It also works for different games where the highest position value during the game is unknown. This is similar in spirit to [2], where a win is one plus the total material value at the start of the game. Our choice of 1.2 is fairly arbitrary.

In order to ensure that, for any given SCL game, the games played were reasonably varied, a small random amount was added to position evaluations for the first few (typically, 10) moves of each game. This was done so as to affect choice of move without affecting the data used for the equations.

Draws can arise in any of three ways. Firstly, games are declared drawn after 200 moves. Secondly, draw by repetition: this was found to be important for the quality of equations generated. We curtail the game after two back-and-forth moves by both players so that repeated positions do not swamp and distort the data. Finally, a draw can occur when both players meet goals at the same time. An example of this could be when the white player meets his goal by taking the opponent's King (where there is an eradicate goal on that King), but at the same time lands on a square which meets an arrive goal of the opponent.

In Table 1 we give a brief description of the actual advisors used, which were the same as those of Pell [10,11,12]. All advisors are symmetric in the sense mentioned in the previous Section. Furthermore, where contributions (such as piece value, mobility, number of captures) from all pieces on the board are summed, the contributions are positive for the player's pieces and negative for the opponent's. Pell's work gives further details.

advisor	description
Material	Total value of pieces on board
	(individual piece values precomputed, similarly to [11])
Static mobility	Total empty-board single-move *moving* mobility of pieces in current position
Eventual mobility	Total empty-board multiple-move moving mobility of pieces currently on board (where the contribution due to a series of moves decays exponentially with number of moves)
Dynamic mobility	Total moving mobility with all pieces in current position
Capture mobility	Total number of captures available in current position
Possess	Sum of values (averaged over empty-board squares) of all possessed pieces (i.e. pieces in hand, as in Shogi)
Global threat	Value of player's best threat minus value of opponent's best threat
Arrive	Sum, over pieces with an **arrive** goal, of measure of difficulty of achieving the goal

Table 1. Advisors used (based on Pell [10, 11]).

3   Results

A number of experiments were run to test the performance of our learning methods.

The reader is reminded that our Metagame player, written in C by Powell, is not quite as general as Pell's in that it does not quite cover the whole SCL Metagame class. Some games in Pell's class are omitted from ours, simply because the extra generality required would have taken a disproportionate amount of time to implement for the benefit gained. Our class is still very general, and includes, for example, the following features: rectangular boards of any size; goals based on stalemating, arrival or eradication, either of the player's or opponent's pieces, and arbitrary disjunctions of such goals; leaping, riding and hopping pieces; pieces which capture differently to the way they move; different capture effects (removal from game, or possession by the player or the opponent); promotion (to either player's or opponent's piece); a possible must-capture constraint applying either to specific pieces or the whole game; similarly, a possible continue-captures constraint. The principal respects in which our class falls short of Pell's are: initial placement of pieces must be predetermined by the game definition, so cannot be done randomly or by the players; no cylindrical boards; the decision on which piece to promote to must be made by the player (never the opponent); no retrieval captures; each piece can only have one capture effect (even if it can capture in several different ways). We argue that these shortcomings are minor. Our class is broad enough to include, for example, approximations to the following chess variations: International Chess, Chaturanga (the first known form of Chess), Shatranj (an old Arabic variant), various forms of medieval chess (similar to Shatranj), Courier Chess, Turkish Great Chess, Shogi, Tsui Shogi (or Middle Shogi, not in Pell's SCL Metagame class (but we expect that could be easily changed)), Thai Chess, Capablanca's Chess and Losing Chess. It contains many other games as well, including Draughts.

3.1 Playing Performance

In the following tables we show the performance of our learning methods on Chess, Losing Chess, Draughts and five games which were randomly generated by Pell's game generator. These games may be reproduced from that generator using the seeds given in the following table:

game	seed
Game1	rand(12123,122,231)
Game2	rand(1938,13844,9541)
Game3	rand(19333,5115,4838)
Game4	rand(234,13,635)
Game5	rand(234,19,10)

In each case, the depth $d = 3$, the number of linear equations used per iteration was 1000, and the Black player was arbitrarily chosen to be the one to do the learning. The 'Baseline' column gives results when neither player did any learning. This column reveals that some games are inherently biased in favour of one or other of the players, which must be taken into account when assessing the results of learning.

Learning was performed by playing each game 1000 times. The number of positions (and hence equations) produced depends on the lengths of the games, and 1000 such positions were required for each learning iteration. Typically, playing a game 1000 times would produce around 20 learning iterations. After learning was completed, a single weight vector was produced using one of the three methods of combining weight vectors mentioned at the end of our description of the learning method. Then this learnt weight vector was used to play the game 1000 (or in some cases 500) times more to produce the final three columns of Table 2. This data indicates how well the learnt weight vector performs against the fixed, uniform-weights player.

Game	Result (for Learner)	Baseline (no learning)	Learning (by Black) with combining technique ...		
			1	2	3
game1	won	31.9	34.4	27.8	30.6
	drawn	46.2	41.4	53.8	46.4
	lost	21.9	24.2	18.4	23.0
	score:	*55.0*	*55.1*	*54.7*	*53.8*
game2	won	6.3	5.2	5.0	2.4
	drawn	88.2	93.4	94.2	96.2
	lost	5.5	1.4	0.8	1.4
	score:	*50.4*	*51.9*	*52.1*	*50.5*
game3	won	24.3	25.8*	25.4*	23.6*
	drawn	56.3	56.2*	56.6*	58.4*
	lost	19.4	18.0*	18.0*	18.0*
	score:	*52.5*	*53.9*	*53.7*	*52.8*
game4	won	32.2	38.2	44.8	47.0
	drawn	29.0	26.6	26.4	27.6
	lost	38.8	35.2	28.8	25.4
	score:	*46.7*	*51.5*	*58.0*	*60.8*
game5	won	29.4	41.4	39.8	40.8
	drawn	34.8	33.4	32.6	36.8
	lost	35.8	25.2	27.6	22.4
	score:	*46.8*	*58.1*	*56.1*	*59.2*
Chess	won	31.2	35.0	26.4	38.3
	drawn	38.3	40.6	41.8	39.2
	lost	30.5	24.4	31.8	22.5
	score:	*50.4*	*55.3*	*47.3*	*57.9*
Lose-chess	won	51.3	95.6	78.1	83.5
	drawn	4.8	2.2	7.6	5.5
	lost	43.9	2.2	14.3	11.0
	score:	*53.7*	*96.7*	*81.9*	*86.3*
Draughts	won	39.0			56.9
	drawn	13.9			24.0
	lost	47.1			19.1
	score:	*46.0*			*68.9*

Table 2. Results from learning with 1000 equations per iteration, depth $d = 3$, with Black Learning. Won/drawn/lost figures are percentages, from 1000 games (or 500, if starred). Scores: for each game, win/draw/loss = 1.0/0.5/0.0 points; total then scaled to 100.

These results show that learning produced a significantly better player for Game 4, Game 5, Lose-chess, and Draughts. For Chess, significant improvement was obtained with the third weight-combining technique, although the average performance over all three techniques is not signifcantly better. In Games 1, 2 and 3, the Learning Player's performance did not differ significantly from the baseline. Of the three weight-combining techniques considered, the third seemed to be the best, in that it always produced improved play (over baseline) whenever either of the other two did. Similar results, for the randomly-generated games, were obtained when we set the Learning Player to be White (instead of our usual choice of Black).

A further 12 random games were generated by Pell's system. Two were degenerate, in that one player always won. Of the other ten, there was very clear, significant improvement (over baseline play) in five, and no apparent improvement at all (but no worsening!) in the other five. Both these results, and the ones above, support the conclusion that our learning method produces significant improvement in play for about half the games generated randomly in Pell's SCL class, and appears to make no difference for the rest.

It is important for our learning methods that enough learning iterations are allowed. Results obtained using only 1/5 as many such iterations showed no evidence of learning, even though we were using ten times as many linear equations per learning iteration.

We used search depth 3 because it was the highest we could afford, given the computational resources available and the number of experiments. Some experiments were conducted for search depths other than 3. Depth 1 was clearly too small. Learning with depth 1 gave improved play for Chess and Draughts, but made play much worse for Lose-chess and Game 3. The picture for depth 2 was similar. Resource constraints did not permit much experimentation with depth 4, but learning did seem to improve play in Draughts.

One problem with our learning method is that it occasionally diverges for some games. Advisor weights become poor (perhaps through random noise), then get progressively worse because applying the evaluation function (with the bad weights) to the leaves of the search tree sometimes causes the backed-up value to become even worse. When this occurs, it is generally observed that one advisor weight becomes more and more negative until reaching -1. It is nearly impossible for the learning method to recover from this situation. While the technique for combining weight vectors at the end of learning ignores the poor weight vectors, increased learning time has no effect.

One possible remedy for this problem is to use the eventual outcome of a game to give an indication as to how reliable the backed up value is (suggested by C. S. Wallace (personal communication)). This could be done in a number of ways. It would appear that any method which assigns credit or blame for the outcome to earlier positions would need to take account of how far a position is from the end of the game. For example, in Tesauro's application [16] of Sutton's TD algorithm [15] to Backgammon, the credit due to a position for the result of a game decreases exponentially with distance from the end of the game. It is not clear how to do such credit assignment for general games in the SCL class, since a critical error could occur at any point in a game.

3.2 Advisor Weights

The advisor weights learnt for these games are of interest in themselves. It should be born in mind that, since the advisors return values on different "scales", their weights in a given game cannot be compared solely on the basis of their magnitude.

Table 3 gives examples of weights learned by our method. The tendency of one advisor to dominate is noted.

Game	Material	Static	Eventual	Dynamic	Capture	Possess	Gthreat	Arrive
Game1	0.11	0.10	0.08	0.10	-0.09	0.08	0.36	0.08
Game2	0.06	0.09	0.02	0.05	0.04	0.67	0.04	0.03
Game3	0.09	0.09	0.05	0.10	-0.26	0.22	0.11	0.07
Game4	0.02	0.02	0.04	0.04	0.00	0.52	0.02	0.33
Game5	0.06	-0.12	-0.09	0.06	0.12	0.47	0.07	0.00
Chess	0.11	0.18	-0.02	0.13	0.00	0.04	0.47	0.04
Lose-chess	-0.01	0.19	0.03	0.01	-0.67	0.01	0.07	0.01

Table 3. Examples of weights learned

It is evident that some advisor weights in the Table are negative. This stands in contrast to Pell's suggestion (see [11, 15.5.1.2] and [12, §2.3]) that weights should never be negative since advisors capture "...properties of a position which should be valuable to a player, other things being equal". Pell recognised [12] that some advisors may be negatively correlated with success for a player, which appears to be the case for the Capture advisor in Lose-chess. In that particular case, it is easy to see why that advisor should receive a negative weight, since threatening to capture would often help the opponent more than the player. Pell suggested that, when an advisor correlates negatively with success, another advisor should be sought which recognises why the opponent derives an advantage when the original advisor becomes more negative.

Not all negative weights correspond to advisors which are negatively correlated with success, however. It can be shown that if several advisors which are constructive (i.e. positively correlated with success) are also highly correlated with each other, then it is quite possible that some (but not all) should be negatively weighted. It is the weighted combination of such advisors that should always be positive, not the individual weight × advisor-value products, and this was indeed found to be the case. High correlation suggests that some of the advisors may be redundant or nearly so. It follows also that, if we are setting advisor weights ourselves, we cannot use a single advisor's weight, alone, to say how important that advisor is individually, independent of other advisors.

4   Conclusion

Our method of unsupervised learning in Metagame, which is a refinement of that used in [2] for Chess and Noughts-and-Crosses, has been shown to improve play significantly for many Symmetric Chess-like games in our minor restriction of Pell's class. For about as many games, however, it produces no discernible improvement with depth 3, though with that depth we find that it seldom makes things worse. Depth 3 appears to be the smallest depth at which our method produces improved play on average. It is of course likely that greater depth would produce more significant improvement. It would be interesting (although computationally expensive) to try this out, and see whether all SCL games can be learned with enough depth, or whether some games in the class are unlearnable by our methods, perhaps because our advisor set is not comprehensive enough. Another worthwhile extension to our approach would be to use a search method with nonuniform depth, such as quiescent search. This might give improved play without such a high computational cost.

The advisor weights learned for the different games are of interest in themselves. We have shed light on the appearance of negative advisor weights, which turns out not to be a problem after all, even when the advisor in question is constructive. In such cases negative weights are a manifestation of correlation of advisors, and weighted sums of correlated advisors will still be positive.

Some advisors were found to be mostly ignored after learning for most games, but occasionally were important. This leads to the idea of dynamic inclusions/exclusion of advisors during learning. If an advisor were found to be essentially useless for a particular game, then it could be removed to allow more time for learning the other advisors (if time limits were in effect).

As suggested by Pell, it would be desirable to allow somehow for the automatic construction and incorporation of new advisors and therefore for more of the actual game analysis to be performed by the machine. In [12], Pell discusses accumulating advice from elementary avisors (such as, for example, positional indicator functions which simply indicate, for a given piece and square, whether that piece is on that square), and calculating some advisor weights directly from the game description, using *subfeatures* (rather than learning the weights through play). (METAGAMER's automatic computation of piece values may be thought of as an example of this latter calculation.) These matters invite further exploration.

We have concentrated on learning advisor weights. It would be interesting to learn values for other parameters which influence play. For example, there are parameters in Metagame which give the rate at which certain types of reward (e.g. for possible promotion, or control of a square) decline with distance [11]. For another example, consider the search strategy. Cron [3] introduced *search advisors* to control search in Metagame, and studied the effect of such advisors' weights on play.

Acknowledgements

We thank Barney Pell and David Dowe for their helpful comments and suggestions.

References

1. Bruce Abramson, *The Expected-Outcome Model of Two-Player Games*, Research Notes in Artificial Intelligence, Pitman, London, 1992.
2. Jens Christensen and Richard E. Korf, A unified theory of heuristic evaluation functions and its application to learning, *AAAI'86* 148–152.
3. D. H. Cron, *Directing Search in Metagame*, M. Comp. thesis, School of Computer Science and Software Engineering, Monash University, to appear.
4. S. L. Epstein, The intelligent novice — learning to play better, in: D. N. L. Levy and D. F. Beal (eds.), *Heuristic Programming in Artificial Intelligence: The First Computer Olympiad*, Ellis Horwood, Chichester, 1989.
5. S. L. Epstein, J. Gelfand and J. Lesniak, Pattern-based learning and spatially oriented concept formation in a multi-agent, decision-making expert, *Computational Intelligence* **12** (1996) 198–221.
6. R. A. Levinson, Exploiting the physics of state-space search, in: S. Epstein and R. Levinson (eds.), *Games: Planning & Learning*, AAAI Technical Report FS-93-02, 1993, pp. 157–165.
7. R. A. Levinson, General game-playing and reinforcement learning, *Computational Intelligence* **12** (1996) 155–176. Also *Technical Report UCSC-CRL-95-06*, Department of Computer Science, Univeristy of California, Santa Cruz, May 1995.
8. B. Pell, Metagame: a new challenge for games and learning, in: H. van den Herik and V. Allis (eds.), *Heuristic Programming in Artificial Intelligence 3: The Third Computer Olympiad*, Ellis Horwood, Chichester, 1992. Also University of Cambridge Computer Laboratory Tech. Report No. 276.
9. B. Pell, Metagame in symmetric, chess-like games, in: H. van den Herik and V. Allis (eds.), *Heuristic Programming in Artificial Intelligence 3: The Third Computer Olympiad*, Ellis Horwood, Chichester, 1992. Also University of Cambridge Computer Laboratory Tech. Report No. 277.
10. B. Pell, A strategic Metagame player for general chess-like games, in: S. Epstein and R. Levinson (eds.), *Games: Planning & Learning*, AAAI Technical Report FS-93-02, 1993, pp. 148–156.
11. B. Pell, *Strategy Generation and Evaluation for Metagame Playing*, PhD Thesis, Computer Laboratory, University of Cambridge, Technical Report No. 315, 1993.
12. B. Pell, A strategic Metagame player for general chess-like games, *Computational Intelligence* **12** (1996) 177–198.
13. A. L. Samuel, Some studies in machine learning using the game of checkers, *IBM J. Res. Devel.* **3** (1959) 210-229.
14. C. E. Shannon, Programming a computer for playing chess, *Philos. Mag.* (Series 7) **41** (1950) 256–275.
15. R. S. Sutton, Learning to predict by the methods of temporal differences, *Machine Learning* **3** (1988) 9–44.
16. G. Tesauro, Practical issues in temporal difference learning, *Machine Learning* **8** (3/4) (1992) 257–277.
17. G. Tesauro, TD-Gammon, a self-teaching Backgammon program achieves Master-level play, *Neural Computation* **6** (2) (1993).

A Neural Networks Based Approach for Fast Mining Characteristic Rules

Monzurur Rahman[1], Xinghuo Yu[2], and Bala Srinivasan[1]

[1] Department of Computer Science and Software Engineering, Monash University,
Caufield Campus, Victoria 3145, Australia
{Monzur.Rahman,Bala.Srinivasan}@csse.monash.edu.au

[2] Faculty of Informatics and Communication, Central Queensland University,
Rockhampton, QLD 4702, Australia
X.Yu@cqu.edu.au

Abstract. Data mining is about extracting hidden information from a large data set. One task of data mining is to describe the characteristics of the data set using attributes in the form of rules. This paper aims to develop a neural networks based framework for the fast mining of characteristic rules. The idea is to first use the Kohonen map to cluster the data set into groups with common similar features. Then use a set of single-layer supervised neural networks to model each of the groups so that the significant attributes characterizing the data set can be extracted. An incremental algorithm combining these two steps is proposed to derive the characteristic rules for the data set with nonlinear relations. The framework is tested using a large size problem of forensic data of heart patients. Its effectiveness is demonstrated.

1. Introduction

Data mining has been a new and exciting research field receiving an increasing attention. As a multidisciplinary research field, it requires knowledge of many information technology areas such as database, artificial intelligence, networking, information retrieval, computational intelligence and statistics. For data mining, the first task is to construct a model that represents a huge data set of interest from a database. This enables data mining tasks to be done from top end by users without knowing details of the data. One common representation of data is by means of rules. There are mainly three kinds of rules; *association rules, classification rules* and *characteristic rules,* the latter is the one which is of interest to data miners [1,2]. The classification rules classify entities into groups by identifying common characteristics among the entities [8]. These common characteristics of a particular group are described by *characteristic rules.* A characteristic rule is an assertion that characterizes the concept satisfied by almost all the examples in the data set of concern.

Extracting characteristic and classification rules has been a very active research topic. AI techniques are often used for data mining modeling tasks, for example, the

N. Foo (Ed.): AI´99, LNAI 1747, pp. 36–47, 1999.

well known decision tree approach ID3 [15]. Decision trees are easy to construct and so is the rule extraction. However, its classification performance may be compromised because when the data set has complicated (nonlinear) domains and the mining goal is to assign each example in the data set to one of many categories, the decision tree approach has to generate many branches for each node which is computationally expensive and may result in a large mining error. Another emerging AI tool is the neural networks that have been proven to be better than the decision tree approach when dealing with complicated (nonlinear) data sets. Supervised multilayer neural networks based on the backpropagation have been an important tool for data mining. Although they are robust with respect to noise, they suffer from slow learning and convergence [10]. Nevertheless, it is much efficient especially in dealing with numeric data sets in comparison with ID3. Improving learning speed is crucial in effective use of neural networks for data mining.

The aim of this paper is to develop a neural networks based framework for mining characteristic rules with significantly improved learning and convergence speed. The framework contains a Kohonen map which will be used to decompose a large data set into a number of small-sized groups for fast mining. A single-layer neural network (SSNN) will be used to model each data group identified via the Kohonen map. It is well known that the SSNNs, although are simple to use, are poor in handling nonlinear and large data set. We will propose to use a set of SSNNs to model the data groups, each of which can be modeled as a linear model using the SSNN. We will then develop an incremental approach for mining characteristic rules (IAMCR) which combine the two steps mentioned above. Experimental study will be provided to show the effectiveness of the algorithms proposed.

This paper is organized as follows. Section 2 introduces the data mining problem statement, the Kohonen map and the SSNN, which we will use for data mining throughout the paper. Section 3 presents the incremental approach for mining characteristic rules. Experiments are illustrated to show the effectiveness of these algorithms in Section 4. Finally, Section 5 gives some concluding remarks.

2.   The Problem Statement and the Kohonen Map and the SSNNs

The problem of mining *characteristic rules* from a set of examples of the same class, denoted as G, can be formally stated as follows: Consider n attributes $(a_1, a_2, ..., a_n)$. Let D_i represent the set of possible values for attribute a_i. We are given a large data set or database D in which each example is a n tuple in the form $\langle v_1, v_2, \cdots v_n \rangle$ where $v_i \in D_i$ and $\langle v_1, v_2, \cdots v_n \rangle \in G$, i.e. each example belongs to the same class G. The problem is to obtain a set of characterizing rules in a conjunctive normal form

$$a_i \wedge \cdots \wedge a_j \Rightarrow G, \text{ where } i \neq j \text{ and } i, j \leq n.$$

The Kohonen map [17] will be used to group data initially. The Kohonen map describes a mapping from the input data space R^n onto a two dimensional array of neurons or nodes. A reference vector $m_i = (\mu_{i1}, \mu_{i2}, \cdots \mu_{in})^T$ is associated with each neuron where μ_{ij} are weights. The input vector, denoted as $x = (x_1, x_2, ..., x_n)^t$, where the superscript t denotes the transpose operation, is connected to all neurons. The teaching here is different from other neural networks in that it consists of choosing a winner neuron by means of similarity measure and updating the weights of neurons in the neighborhood of the winning neuron. The Euclidean distance is used as the similarity measure between the input vector and the neuron weight vector. The weight update rule for neuron is described as follows:

$$m_i^{k+1} = m_i^k + h_{ci}^k (x_i - m_i^k)$$

where k denotes time and h_{ci} is a non-increasing neighborhood function around the winner neuron m_c. The neighborhood function use is as follows:

$$h_{ci}^{k+1} = \beta^k \exp(-\frac{\|r_i - r_c\|^2}{2\sigma^2})$$

In this neighborhood function r_i and r_c are location vectors of the undergoing change of the neurons and the winning neuron. Two parameters β and σ are used here. The first one refers to the learning rate and the later to the neighborhood and both are decreasing functions in time, that is

$$\beta^k = \frac{\beta_0}{\sqrt{1+k}} \text{ and } \sigma = \frac{\sigma_0}{\sqrt{1+k}}$$

Where β_0 is the initial learning rate and σ_0 the initial neighborhood size chosen as the maximum radius of the Kohonen lattice. β_0 is usually between 0 and 1.

The SSNN we will use is the ADALINE (Adaptive Linear Neuron) which was developed by Widrow and Hoff [4]. The ADALINE, the building block for feed forward neural networks, is defined as

$$y = w^t x$$

where y is the output, with

$$w = (w_1, w_2, ..., w_n)^t$$

representing inputs and weights respectively. The learning algorithm, which is often referred to as the Widrow-Hoff delta rule [4], is

$$w^{k+1} = w^k + \alpha e_k x, \quad e_k = (d_i - (w^k)^t x)$$

or in a modified form [7]

$$w^{k+1} = \begin{cases} w^k + \dfrac{\alpha e_k x}{x^t x} & \text{if } x^t x \neq 0 \\ w^k & \text{if } x^t x = 0 \end{cases} \tag{1}$$

The learning rule (1) will be the main algorithm we use for training SSNN for data mining.

3. Using SSNNs for Mining Characteristic Rules

Consider a class, G, with n attributes $a = (a_1, a_2, ...a_n)$ where $a \in R^n$. For given examples of G, we want to find out the characteristic rules that can characterize G. Hence the n attributes of each example become the inputs to the SSNN and the output of the SSNN is an indicator of the degree of belonging to G. Assume each attribute takes value of either 1 or 0.

The characteristic rules can be found by selecting those attributes which have larger weights since the larger values indicate that these attributes have a more significant contribution towards the output than others. Since the SSNN does not use saturating functions, the weights truly reflect the characteristic nature of the particular attributes.

For our mining purpose, we set the output as $d_i=1$ as the desired output value. Our target is to train the SSNN so that it can approximate the given data set. We want to obtain the characteristic rules in the form of $a_i \wedge \cdots \wedge a_j \, (i \neq j \leq n)$.

We now develop the following mining algorithm for mining characteristic rules based on the SSNNs assuming the data set we are dealing with is linear so that it can be modeled by the SSNN. Given are P training pairs, $\{a^1, a^2, ..., a^P\}$, $a^i \in R^n$ and the desired output $d = 1$,

1. Initialize $iteration = 1$, $i = 0$, $sum\_error = 0$, $\Delta w = 0$ and the random weights $w \in R^n$. Set $\alpha, \varepsilon > 0$ and max_iteration;
2. The training cycle begins here. Input is presented and output computed:
$$y = w^t * a^i$$
3. Weights are updated as:

      If $(a^i)^t a^i > 0$ then $\Delta w = alpha * [d - y] * \left(\dfrac{a^i}{(a^i)^t a^i} \right)$

          Otherwise $\Delta w = 0$
$$w = w + \Delta w$$
  $sum\_error = sum\_error + (d - y)^2$

4. If $sum\_error > \varepsilon$ and $iteration <=$ max_iteraion , go back to step 2;
5. Select the weights which have a significant contribution to output d comparing to others;
6. Construct the input-output relationship with selected weights;
7. Extract rules from the input-output relationships by varying the value of input attributes. The combinations, which give an output close to 1 will be selected as characteristic rules;
8. Optimize the rules using the constrained defined by the user.

The algorithm can generate rules but it is not guaranteed that all the rules generated are strong and satisfy data mining requirements. Two concepts, Confidence and Support, are often used in the data mining literature for description of the strength of rules [5]. Since we have only a single class for the data set, the measure of confidence is not meaningful. Hence, we only use the concept of support to identify strong characteristic rules. The concept *Support* is defined as: The rule $x \Rightarrow y$ has a support of s in data set Ω if s percent of examples in Ω contain $x \cap y$ i.e. $s = \text{Pr} \, obablity(x \cap y)$. The level of support depicts the frequency of the rule found in the data set. Using this concept, the rules obtained in step 3 can be pruned using prescribed support measure to determine the dominant attributes of the class.

4.   Incremental Approach for Mining Characteristic Rules

Since the SSNN is incapable of handling large nonlinear data alone, an incremental approach will be proposed in this section. This approach makes use of piecewise local linearization idea in construction of a neural network model to handle the large nonlinear data set.

The SSNN model described in Section 3 is a single neuron structure, which can be considered as a local linear model for a nonlinear function. This model, in some sense, can only model a piece of the nonlinear function, which is, of course, insufficient to describe the entire nonlinear function. The piecewise local linearization idea has been used extensively in function approximation. Inspired by this idea, here we propose to use a set of SSNNs as local linear models to model "pieces" of the large nonlinear data set so that, as a whole, the entire large nonlinear data sets can be modeled and hence the characteristic rules can be extracted. It should be noted that such a structure for modeling a large nonlinear data set should give rise to a fast mining tool, evidenced by its simple structure, parallel implementation of SSNNs, and fast dynamic adjustments.

We now propose the incremental approach for mining characteristic rules (IAMCR). The algorithm contains three phases: Pattern Clustering, Constructing a Set of SSNNs, Extracting Rules, and Forming Rules. In the Pattern Clustering phase, the given data is subject to the Kohonen map so that they can be clustered into groups with similar common features. This will result in reduction of the number of SSNNs for approximation. In the construction phase, clustered data sets are inputted to a single SSNN at a time for training so that a given tolerance level of training is satisfied. The remaining data examples will be fed to another SSNN for training, so on and so forth, until all the data are approximated The extracting rule phase is done by using the algorithm developed in Section 3. Since there is no guarantee of having the rules which satisfy the user defined support level, the Forming Rules phase is ended by investigating combinations of attributes so that representative characteristic rules can be formed. Details of the phases are given below.

4.1   Pattern Clustering

To reduce the number of SSNNs for mining, the examples should be first preprocessed and clustered. We propose to use the two dimensional Kohonen map with an assumed maximum number of clusters, l. (For two-dimensional case, the index l is defined as $l = (number\, of\, rows) \times (number\, of\, columns)$. The training algorithm used is the one in [17], and the quantization error is used to measure the goodness of training. The neurons in the Kohonen map represent the centres of the cluster formed by the examples with some common features. All the examples are submitted again to the Kohonen map to determine grouping of examples, which can be ordered in a descending order of similarities between examples.

4.2   Constructing a Set of SSNNs

The construction of SSNNs for mining can be done as follows. With the P training pairs, $A = \{a^1, a^2, ..., a^P\}$, $a^i \in R^n$ and the desired output $d = 1$:

a) Initialize   the   set   of   SSNNs,   denoted   as   *SSSNN*,   to   *empty* and *Training Pattern Set* = A; Set   also   the   SSNN   parameters $\alpha, \varepsilon > 0$ and max_*iteration*;

b) Training SSNNs starts at here. Create a new SSNN with random weights $w \in R^n$ and put the SSNN into *SSSNN*;

c) Initialize *NonTrained Pattern Set* = *empty* and *Trained Pattern* Set = *empty*;

d) Take an example $a^i \in R^n$ from *Training Pattern Set* and set *sum_error* = 0;

e) Train the current *SSNN* with a^i using the learning algorithm in Section 3 until *sum_error* < ε or *iteration* > max_*iteraion*;

f) IF *sum_error* < ε Then put a^i into the *Trained Pattern Set*, Otherwise put a^i into the *NonTrained Pattern Set*;

g) If *Training Pattern Set* is not empty, go back to step d. Otherwise the training of the current SSNN terminates. *Trained Pattern Set* is the set trained by the current SSNN;

h) IF *Non Trained Pattern Set* is not empty, set *Non Trained Pattern Set* to *Training Pattern Set* and go back to step b for the next SSNN, Otherwise training session of the algorithm ends.

4.3   Extracting Characteristic Rules

Before going to the rule extraction phase from trained SSNNs, we need to define the mining requirement which has to be satisfied by all mined rules. We define *Local support* and *Global support* as a means to measure the support level of an individual SSNN performance as well as the overall performance over the entire data set. We use the following heuristics for extracting rules. We only consider the rules which has local and global support levels higher than the minimum desired support level. This will significantly reduce the numbers of rules to be dealt with and speed up the extracting speed. The algorithm for extracting characteristic rules is shown below:

a) Initialize *Char_Rule Set* = *empty* and *Desired_Support*;

b) Do the following steps until there is no *SSNN* in *SSSNN*;

c) Extract a *SSNN* from *SSSNN* and find the characteristic rule by inspecting significant weights;

d) Calculate $k = \sum w_j^i$ where w_j^i is j th significant weight of i th *SSNN*;

e) IF $|k-1| \le \varepsilon$ then mine a characteristic rule of the form $\{x_{i_1} \wedge x_{i_2} \cdots \wedge x_{i_m}\}$ where x_{i_j} denotes i_j th attribute;

f) Calculate the local support and global support of the rule found in step e. If both supports is equal or larger than the *Desired_Support* put it in to *Char _ Rule _ Set*, otherwise go to step e until all groups are considered.

g) The *Char_Rule_Set* contains the desired mining result for the problem stated in section 2.

5. Experimental Results

In order to test the algorithms developed, we conducted a series of experiments with a forensic data of heart patients [16]. The data set was replicated up to the size of 537 records, and each example has seven attributes: *age, sex, chest pain, blood pressure, cholesterol, sugar level in blood* and *heart beats*. We used a binary encoding system to code each attribute for use. The encoding scheme is summarized in Table 1. For all the experiments we trained the SSNNs to produce target output 1. The training parameters were $\alpha = 0.001$, $\varepsilon = 0.0001$, max_iteration $= 50000$ and minimum support $= 0.75$.

Input No.	Attribute	Coding rule	Symbol
1	Age	0 = age<40, 1=age>=40	a_1
2	Sex	0=female, 1=male	a_2
3	Chest pain	0=few times,1=many times	a_3
4	Blood pressure	0=low, 1=high	a_4
5	Cholesterol	0=low,1=high	a_5
6	Sugar	0=not significant in blood, 1=significant in blood	a_6
7	Heart beats	0=normal rate, 1=fast rate	a_7

Table 1: Coding of the attributes

We first mined the characteristic rules for heart patient data set using the algorithm discussed in section 3. It was found that a single SSNN modeled only 33 examples with weights $w = [0.1667,01.667,0.1667,0.1667,0.1667,0.0225,0.1667]$ and a training error 0.0001. From the weights we can construct the following rules:

Rule 1: $a_1 \wedge a_2 \wedge a_3 \wedge a_4 \wedge a_5 \wedge a_7 \Rightarrow G$ (Support 0.27374)

Rule 2: $a_1 \wedge a_2 \wedge a_3 \wedge a_4 \wedge a_5 \wedge a_6 \wedge a_7 \Rightarrow G$ (Support 0.04842)

It is obvious that above rules have a very low support level and no use in describing the example class.

This problem was solved successfully using the IAMCR that considered all the examples. We set same parameters as stated before. The experiments were conducted in two ways. First, the experiment was done without using any clustering technique. We call the data set used in this experiment as an unordered data set. The result of this experiment is reported in Table 2 and Appendix A, which list the set of rules constructed from the SSNNs and their support levels respectively. The minimum support was set to 0.75 and the following rule was found

$$a_3 \wedge a_4 \wedge a_5 \Rightarrow G$$

i.e. *chest pain*, *blood pressure* and *cholesterol* are the attributes as the main cause for the heart disease. In other words, the characteristic rule can be formulated as follows:

chest pain $\wedge$ blood pressure $\wedge$ cholesterol $\Rightarrow$ Heart patient

SSNN#	W(1)	W(2)	W(3)	W(4)	W(5)	W(6)	W(7)	Total	Error
1	0.1667	0.1667	0.1667	0.1667	0.1667	0.0225	0.1667	33	0.0001
2	0.2010	0.2119	0.1633	0.2119	0.1763	0.0527	0.2119	57	0.0001
3	0.1048	0.2000	0.2000	0.2000	0.2000	0.0196	0.2000	88	0.0001
4	0.2000	0.2000	0.2000	0.1017	0.2000	0.0076	0.2000	22	0.0001
5	0.2000	0.2000	0.2000	0.2000	0.0000	0.0423	0.2000	16	0.0001
6	0.2000	0.2000	0.0000	0.2000	0.2000	0.0000	0.2000	4	0.0001
7	0.0000	0.2000	0.2000	0.2000	0.2000	0.0000	0.2000	17	0.0001
8	0.0000	0.2500	0.0000	0.2500	0.2500	0.0000	0.2500	4	0.0001
9	0.0000	0.2500	0.2500	0.2500	0.0000	0.0000	0.2500	3	0.0001
10	0.2615	0.2431	0.2183	0.2771	0.1847	0.0320	0.0639	30	0.0000
11	0.1817	0.1592	0.3347	0.4743	0.2072	0.0803	0.3665	102	0.0001
12	0.1054	0.0000	0.2500	0.2500	0.2500	0.0536	0.2500	28	0.0001
13	0.2522	0.0290	0.2144	0.2522	0.2522	0.0000	0.2232	38	0.0001
14	0.0538	0.0000	0.3333	0.3333	0.1301	0.0000	0.3333	25	0.0001
15	0.2115	0.2031	0.4118	0.3834	0.2047	0.0000	0.1702	38	0.0000
16	0.2317	0.2211	0.3750	0.3467	0.1722	0.0668	0.0871	18	0.0001
17	0.1435	0.1125	0.3333	0.3333	0.3333	0.0000	0.0000	9	0.0001
18	0.3971	0.0000	0.3971	0.1915	0.2057	0.1915	0.0000	4	0.0001
19	0.3333	0.0000	0.3333	0.3333	0.0000	0.0000	0.0000	1	0.0001

Table 2. Results of IAMCR using unordered data sets.

Second, two experiments were done to investigate the effect of clustering on mining. The first experiment used the reasonably ordered data set formed from a 2x2 Kohonen map. The clustering result of this experiment is reported in Table 3. After training, the quantization error was found to be 0.652, which refers to the average difference between the example features and weights of cluster centroid. 333 examples were clustered in one Kohonen neuron and the rest 204 examples in the other neuron. The order of examples was arranged as being the 333 examples from the first neuron first, then followed by the 204 examples from the second neuron. We call this data set as a reasonably ordered data set as the clustering was done in a restricted size Kohonen map. The result using the IAMCR with this reasonably ordered data was reported in Table 4 and Appendix B. The mining result is the same.

Exp.	No. cluster	Quantization. Error	Cluster size in order
1	2	0.65236210	333,204
2	22	0.01686998	168,118,61,33,32,21,20,19,12,11,8,6,6,4,3,2,2,2,1,1,1

Table 3. Results of clustering.

The second experiment was done similarly except the size of Kohonen map was increased to (50x50) so that we form an almost ordered data set from groups. The result of this Kohonen clustering is shown in Experiment 2 in Table 3. It is obvious that it has a very small quantization error, indicating it clustered data well. The result of the experiment is reported in Table 5 and Appendix C. Nevertheless, We have the same mining result as before. The only difference is in the number of SSNNs used in the experiments and intermediate rules produced by them. From Table 2, 3 and 4, one can conclude that the almost ordered data set takes less number of SSNNs and hence the rule mining process is faster.

SSNN#	W(1)	W(2)	W(3)	W(4)	W(5)	W(6)	W(7)	Total	Error
1	0.1667	0.1667	0.1667	0.1667	0.1667	0.0180	0.1667	147	0.0001
2	0.0000	0.2000	0.2000	0.2000	0.2000	0.0070	0.2000	49	0.0001
3	0.2000	0.0000	0.2000	0.2000	0.2000	0.0357	0.2000	83	0.0001
4	0.0000	0.0000	0.2500	0.2500	0.2500	0.0039	0.2500	56	0.0001
5	0.2000	0.2000	0.2000	0.2000	0.2000	0.0064	0.0000	53	0.0001
6	0.0000	0.2500	0.2500	0.2500	0.2500	0.0000	0.0000	10	0.0001
7	0.2500	0.1143	0.2500	0.2500	0.0000	0.0226	0.2500	33	0.0001
8	0.0000	0.0369	0.3333	0.3333	0.0000	0.0000	0.3333	23	0.0001
9	0.2545	0.2228	0.0000	0.2545	0.1779	0.0586	0.2545	13	0.0001
10	0.1955	0.2909	0.0894	0.2576	0.2560	0.0274	0.3244	21	0.0001
11	0.2500	0.2500	0.2500	0.2500	0.0000	0.0000	0.0000	15	0.0001
12	0.0000	0.3333	0.3333	0.3333	0.0000	0.0000	0.0000	5	0.0001
13	0.2500	0.0000	0.2500	0.2500	0.0708	0.2500	0.0000	17	0.0001
14	0.2500	0.0000	0.2500	0.2500	0.2500	0.0000	0.0000	5	0.0001
15	0.3891	0.0946	0.2217	0.1674	0.3891	0.0000	0.0000	3	0.0000
16	0.0000	0.0000	0.3333	0.3333	0.3333	0.0000	0.0000	1	0.0001
17	0.3333	0.0000	0.3333	0.3333	0.0000	0.0000	0.0000	2	0.0001
18	0.0000	0.0000	0.5000	0.0000	0.0000	0.0000	0.5000	1	0.0001

Table 4. Results of IAMCR using reasonably ordered data sets.

SSNN#	W(1)	W(2)	W(3)	W(4)	W(5)	W(6)	W(7)	Total	Error
1	0.2345	0.2561	0.2500	0.2593	0.1780	0.0144	0.1305	262	0.0001
2	0.0934	0.2219	0.3571	0.3770	0.2659	0.0337	0.2124	136	0.0000
3	0.3151	0.1365	0.2399	0.2419	0.2810	0.0876	0.2029	30	0.0001
4	0.3163	0.1896	0.1842	0.2833	0.2492	0.0572	0.2833	13	0.0000
5	0.2962	0.0000	0.2962	0.2962	0.0553	0.1386	0.1115	22	0.0000
6	0.1068	0.1845	0.2233	0.4077	0.2233	0.0000	0.4077	32	0.0001
7	0.2691	0.0000	0.3135	0.4968	0.2341	0.0000	0.3135	21	0.0001
8	0.0000	0.0000	0.3333	0.3333	0.1175	0.0000	0.3333	19	0.0001
9	0.3333	0.0000	0.3333	0.0000	0.3333	0.0000	0.0000	1	0.0001
10	0.0000	0.0000	0.5000	0.0000	0.0000	0.0000	0.5000	1	0.0001

Table 5. Results of IAMCR using almost ordered data sets.

6. Conclusion

In this study, we have shown how to use single layered supervised neural networks to form an effective mining model for mining characteristic rules, so that the learning speed is much improved. The multi layer supervised neural networks based on the backpropagation is very powerful in solving many complex problems. But until today, it has not been widely used in data mining partly due to its time consuming training process. The algorithms proposed in this paper dose not suffer from this weakness

References

1. Cai, Y., Cercone, N., Han, J.: An Attribute-Oriented Approach for Learning Classification Rules from Relational Databases. Proceedings of 6th International Conference on Data Engineering (ICDE'90), Los Angeles, CA, (1990) 281-288
2. Cai, Y., Cercone, N., Han, J.: Learning Characteristic Rules from Relational Databases. Proceedings of International Symposium on Computational Intelligence 89, Elsevier Science, (1990) 187-196
3. Rosenblat, F.: The Perceptron: A Probabilistic Model for Information Storage and Organization in the Brain. Psychology Review, Vol 65, 1958(42-49)
4. Widrow, B.: Generalisation and Information Storage in Networks of Adaline 'Neurons' in self Organising Systems. Ed. Jovtz, M.C., Jacobi, G.T., Goldstein, G., Spartan Books (1962) 435-461
5. Piatetsky-Shapiro, G.: Discovery, Analysis, and Presentation of Strong Rules. Knowledge Discovery in Databases. AAAI/MIT Press (1991) 229-238
6. Refenes, A.N., Zapranis, A.D., Connor J.T., Bunn, D.W.: Neural Networks in Investment Management. In Intelligent Systems for Finance and Business, eds Goonatilake, S., Trelevan P., John Wiley & Sons (1995) 179-185
7. Kuschewski, J.G., Hui, S., Zak, S.H.: Application of Feedforward Networks to Dynamical System Identification and Control. IEEE Transactions on Control Systems Technology, Vol 1, (1993) 37-49
8. Agrawal, R., Imielinski, T., Swami, A.: Database Mining: A Performance Perspective. IEEE Transactions on Knowledge and Data Engineering,Vol. 5,No. 6, 1993 (914-925)
9. Chen, M.S., Han, J., Yu, P.S.: Data Mining: An Overview from a Database Perspective. IEEE Transactions on Knowledge and Data Engineering, Vol. 8, No. 6, (1996) 866-883
10. Lu, H., Setiono, R., Liu, H.: Effective data mining. IEEE Transactions on Knowledge and Data Engineering, Vol. 8, No. 6, (1996) 957-961
11. Agarwal, R., Ghosh, S., Imielinski, T., Lyer, B., Swami, A.: An Interval Classifier for Databse Mining Applications. Proceedings of International Conference on Very Large Data Bases (VLDB'92), Vancouver, British Columbia, Canada (1992) 560-573

12. Lubinsky, D.J.: Discovery from databases: A Review of AI and Statistical Techniques. IJCAI-89 Workshop on Knowledge Discover in Databases, Detroit (1989) 204-218

13. Piatetsky-Shapiro, G.: Knowledge Discovery in Databases. AAAI/MIT Press (1991)

14. Zurada, J.M.: Introduction to Artificial Neural Systems. West Publishing Co. (1992)

15. Quinlan, J.R.: Induction of Decision Trees. Machine Learning, Vol. 1, (1986) 81-106

16. Public domain STATLOG project data sets at http://www.ncc.up.pt/liacc/ML/statlog/datasets.html

17. Kohonen, T.: Self-Organizing Maps. Springer Series in Information Sciences (1995) 86-90

Appendix A: Rules by IAMCR Using the Unordered Data Set

Rule No	Rule Description	Produced By	Local Support	Global Support
1	A1^a2^a3^a4^a5^a7	SSNN#1	1.00000	0.27374
2	A1^a2^a3^a4^a7	SSNN#2	0.80702	0.31099
3	A1^a2^a4^a5^a7	SSNN#2	0.89474	0.29795
4	A2^a3^a4^a5^a7	SSNN#2	0.77193	0.36499
5	A2^a3^a4^a5^a7	SSNN#3	1.00000	0.36499
6	A1^a2^a3^a5^a7	SSNN#4	1.00000	0.28864
7	A1^a2^a3^a4^a7	SSNN#5	1.00000	0.31099
8	A1^a2^a4^a5^a7	SSNN#6	1.00000	0.29795
9	A2^a3^a4^a5^a7	SSNN#7	1.00000	0.36499
10	A2^a4^a5^a7	SSNN#8	1.00000	0.39665
11	a2^a3^a4^a7	SSNN#9	1.00000	0.40782
12	a1^a2^a3^a4	SSNN#10	0.76667	0.43762
13	a3^a4^a5^a7	SSNN#12	1.00000	0.62384
14	a1^a3^a4^a5	SSNN#13	0.97368	0.54749
15	a1^a3^a4^a7	SSNN#13	0.94737	0.48976
16	a1^a3^a5^a7	SSNN#13	0.94737	0.44320
17	a1^a4^a5^a7	SSNN#13	0.97368	0.45996
18	a3^a4^a5^a7	SSNN#13	0.94737	0.62384
19	a3^a4^a7	SSNN#14	1.00000	0.72812
20	a2^a3^a4	SSNN#16	0.77778	0.56238
21	a3^a4^a5 *****	SSNN#17	1.00000	0.76350
22	a1^a3^a4	SSNN#19	1.00000	0.66108

Appendix B: **Rules by IAMCR Using the Reasonably Ordered Data Set**

Rule No	Rule Description	Produced By	Local Support	Global Support
1	a1^a2^a3^a4^a5^a7	SSNN#1	1.00000	0.27374
2	a2^a3^a4^a5^a7	SSNN#2	1.00000	0.36499
3	a1^a3^a4^a5^a7	SSNN#3	1.00000	0.42831
4	a3^a4^a5^a7	SSNN#4	1.00000	0.62384
5	a1^a2^a3^a4^a5	SSNN#5	1.00000	0.37244
6	a2^a3^a4^a5	SSNN#6	1.00000	0.48231
7	a1^a3^a4^a7	SSNN#7	1.00000	0.48976
8	a3^a4^a7	SSNN#8	1.00000	0.72812
9	a1^a2^a4^a5	SSNN#9	0.76923	0.39851
10	a1^a2^a4^a7	SSNN#9	0.92308	0.33892
11	a1^a2^a5^a7	SSNN#9	0.76923	0.31285
12	a1^a4^a5^a7	SSNN#9	0.84615	0.45996
13	a2^a4^a5^a7	SSNN#9	0.76923	0.39665
14	a1^a2^a3^a4	SSNN#11	1.00000	0.43762
15	a2^a3^a4	SSNN#12	1.00000	0.56238
16	a1^a3^a4^a6	SSNN#13	1.00000	0.12849
17	a1^a3^a4^a5	SSNN#14	1.00000	0.54749
18	a3^a4^a5 *****	SSNN#16	1.00000	0.76350
19	a1^a3^a4	SSNN#17	1.00000	0.66108
20	a3^a7	SSNN#18	1.00000	0.74488

Appendix C: **Rules by IAMCR Using the Ordered Data Set**

Rule No	Rule Description	Produced By	Local Support	Global Support
1	a1^a2^a3^a4	SSNN#1	0.87405	0.43762
2	a1^a2^a4^a5	SSNN#1	0.77099	0.39851
3	a1^a3^a4^a5	SSNN#1	0.75191	0.54749
4	a2^a3^a4^a5	SSNN#1	0.82443	0.48231
5	a3^a4^a5 *****	SSNN#2	0.91176	0.76350
6	a3^a4^a7	SSNN#2	0.81618	0.72812
7	a3^a4^a7	SSNN#6	0.93750	0.72812
8	a4^a5^a7	SSNN#6	0.93750	0.66294
9	a3^a4^a7	SSNN#8	1.00000	0.72812
10	a1^a3^a5	SSNN#9	1.00000	0.56611
11	a3^a7	SSNN#10	1.00000	0.74488

***** Indicates mined characteristic rules.

FANRE: A Fast Adaptive Neural Regression Estimator

Zhihua Zhou, Shifu Chen, and Zhaoqian Chen

State Key Laboratory for Novel Software Technology
Nanjing University, Nanjing 210093, P.R.China
daniel@aiake1.nju.edu.cn, chensf@netra.nju.edu.cn, chenzq@netra.nju.edu.cn

Abstract. In this paper, a fast adaptive neural regression estimator named FANRE is proposed. FANRE exploits the advantages of both Adaptive Resonance Theory and Field Theory while contraposing the characteristic of regression problems. It achieves not only impressive approximating results but also fast learning speed. Besides, FANRE has incremental learning ability. When new instances are fed, it does not need retrain the whole training set. Instead, it could learn the knowledge encoded in those instances through slightly adjusting the network topology when necessary. This characteristic enable FANRE work for real-time online learning tasks. Experiments including approximating line, sine and 2-d Mexican Hat show that FANRE is superior to BP kind algorithms that are most often used in regression estimation on both approximating effect and training time cost.

1. Introduction

Adaptive Resonance Theory (ART) [1] is an important family of competitive neural learning model. Its memory mode is very similar to that of biological one, and memory capacity can increase while the learning patterns increase. It can perform real-time online learning, and can work under nonstationary world. Field Theory [2] is named from CPM (Coulomb Potential Model) [3]. It can perform real-time one pass supervised learning with fast speed, and no spurious responses will be produced regardless of the number of memories stored in the network. We have proposed a neural network classifier based on ART and Field theory, which achieved preferable results than several other neural algorithms [4].

There are lots of regression problems occurring in financial, decision and automation fields, such as the auto generating of stock price curvilinear, the predicting of the moving direction and extent of manipulator, etc. Preferably solving those problems will not only bring great economical benefit but also accelerate the technical progressing in those fields. However, although the neural algorithms designed to solve classification tasks have been deeply studied, the research on neural regression estimators is in deficiency. The output components of classification tasks are discrete, but that of regression tasks are continuous. Since the discrete nature, classification algorithms cannot get smooth approximating result while being applied to regression problems. Thus, devising effective neural regression estimator has become urgent affairs at present.

N. Foo (Ed.): AI'99, LNAI 1747, pp. 48–59, 1999.

In this paper, a neural regression estimator FANRE, which organically exploits the advantages of both ART and Field Theory while contraposing the characteristic of regression problems, is proposed. FANRE needs only one pass learning, and achieves not only impressive approximating effect but also fast learning speed. The learning of FANRE is performed in an incremental style. When new instances are fed, it does not retrain the whole training set as most feed-forward algorithms do. In stead, it could learn the knowledge encoded in the instances through slightly adjusting its topology, that is, adaptively appends one or two hidden units and some connections to the existing network when necessary. Moreover, since the network architecture of FANRE is adaptively set up, the disadvantage of manually determining the number of hidden units of most feed-forward networks is overcome. Experimental results show that FANRE is superior to BP kind algorithms that are most often used in regression estimation on both approximating effect and training time cost.

The rest of this paper is organized as follows. In Section 2, we detailedly describe and analyze the FANRE algorithm; in Section 3, we report on experimental results and comparisons on three function approximating problems against a BP kind algorithm; finally in Section 4, we conclude and indicate some directions for future work.

2. FANRE Algorithm

To feed forward neural networks, the hidden units in single hidden layer architecture are often too tightly coupled to make it possible that the improvement of the approximation on some points does not result in the deterioration on other ones. Comparatively, the hidden units in two hidden layer architecture are relatively loose coupled, and corresponding sub-regions could be adjusted independently. This enable the latter architecture achieves better results than the former while dealing with regression tasks. Considering that, FANRE adopts two hidden layers, which perform internal approximating corresponding to input and output patterns respectively. Fig.1 shows its architecture.

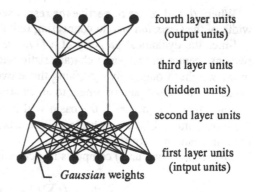

fourth layer units
(output units)

third layer units

(hidden units)

second layer units

first layer units
(intput units)

Gaussian weights

Fig. 1. The architecture of FANRE

Except the connections between the first and second layer units, all connections of FANRE are bi-directional. The feedback connections, whose function is just transmitting feedback signal to implement resonance, are always set to 1.0.

The initial network is composed of only input and output layers, whose unit number is respectively set to the number of components of the input and output pattern. In particular, the unit number of hidden layers is zero. This is different to some other neural algorithms that configure hidden units before the start of the learning course. When new instances are fed, FANRE will adaptively append hidden units and connections so that the knowledge encoded in those instances could be learned. The unit-appending process terminates after all the instances are fed. Thus, the topology of FANRE is always adaptively changing during the learning course.

When the first instance is fed, FANRE appends two hidden units to the network, one in the second layer and the other in the third layer. Those two units are connected with each other. The feed forward and feedback connections between them are all set to 1.0. The third layer unit is connected with all the output units, the feed forward connections are respectively set to the output components of current instance, the feedback connections are all set to 1.0. The second layer unit is connected with all the input units through *Gaussian* weights. The response-centers are respectively set to the input components of current instance, and the response-characteristic-widths are set to a default value.

FANRE introduces the notion of attracting basin, which is proposed in Field Theory [2]. Each second layer unit of FANRE defines an attracting basin by response-centers and response-characteristic-widths of *Gaussian* weights connecting with it. Thus, FANRE constructs its first attracting basin according to the first instance. And it will add or move basins according to the later instances.

Assuming that instances fed to the input units are $A_k\square(a_k^1\square a_k^2\square...\square a_k^n)$ $(k\square1\square2\square...\square m)$. Where k is the index of instance, and n is the number of input units. The value input to the second layer unit j from the first layer unit i is:

$$bIn_{ij} = e^{-\left(\frac{a_i^k-\theta_{ij}}{\alpha_{ij}}\right)^2} \tag{1}$$

Where θ_{ij} and α_{ij} are respective the response-center and the response-characteristic-width of the *Gaussian* weight connecting unit i with unit j.

Since the dynamical property of a *Gaussian* weight is entirely determined by its response-center and response-characteristic-width, learned knowledge can be encoded in the weight through only modifying those two parameters. Thus, during the training process, if the input pattern is near to an existing attracting basin that is determined by θ_{ij}'s and α_{ij}'s of Equation 1, the basin will be slightly adjusted so that it could cover the input pattern. Else a new basin will be established, whose θ_{ij}'s and α_{ij}'s ensure that the input pattern is covered.

The second layer unit j computes its activation value according to Equation 2:

$$b_j = f(\sum_{i=1}^{n} bIn_{ij} - \theta_j) \tag{2}$$

Where θ_j is the bias of unit j. f is *Sigmoid* function shown in Equation 3:

$$f(u) = \frac{1}{1+e^{-u}} \tag{3}$$

A leakage competition[1] is carried out among all the second layer units. The outputs of the winners are transferred to the related third layer units. The activation value of the third layer unit h is computed according to Equation 4:

$$c_h = f(\sum_{j=1}^{o} b_j v_{jh} - \theta_h) \tag{4}$$

Where b_j is the activation value of the second layer unit j, which is not only a winner in its competition but also connecting with unit h. o is the number of the second layer winners that connecting with unit h. v_{jh} is the feed forward weight connecting unit j to unit h. Attention should be paid to that v_{jh} is always 1.0. θ_h is the bias of unit h. f is still *Sigmoid* function.

Then, a leakage competition is carried out among all the third layer units that receiving inputs from the second layer units. Attention should be paid to that there might exist some units that are not qualified to attend the competition. The reason is that the attracting basins determined by the second layer units connecting with them are far from current instance. And there is no hope to cover the instance through only slightly adjusting those basins. In other words, the third layer unit connecting with no second layer winner is not qualified in the third layer competition.

The activation values of the third layer winners are enlarged to N times and transferred to the output units. The activation value of the output unit l is computed according to Equation 5:

$$d_l = \frac{1}{q} \sum_{h=1}^{q} (c_h \cdot N) w_{hl} \tag{5}$$

Where d_l is the activation value of the output unit l. c_h is the activation value of the third layer unit h, which is a winner in its competition. w_{hl} is the feed forward weight connecting unit h to unit l, q is the number of the third layer winners.

The reason that we enlarge the activation values of the third layer winners to N times is that the value of c_h which is attained through twice *Sigmoid* transforming is relatively small. If it is directly send to the output units, the difference between the real network output and expected output will be quite large, which will result in the appending of hidden units unnecessary. Experiments show that $N=10$ could generate satisfying results.

If the network is not in training, the approximation result is attained from Equation 5. Else three pre-set parameters are used, namely the maximum allowable error Err_{max}, the first-degree vigilance Vig_1 and the second-degree vigilance Vig_2. Vig_1 and Vig_2 are used to control the unit-appending process. Those parameters satisfy Equation 6:

$$Err_{max} < Vig_1 < Vig_2 \tag{6}$$

The error between real network output and expected output is computed. Here we use the average squared error as the measure, which is shown in Equation 7:

---

[1] In leakage competition, if the activation value of a unit is greater than a certain threshold, it will be a winner. So, there may exist more than one winner at the same time.

$$Err = \frac{1}{n}\sum_{l=1}^{n}\left(d_l - d_l^k\right)^2 \tag{7}$$

Where n is the number of the output units, d_l is the real output of the output unit l, d_l^k is its expected output.

If the error Err is less than Err_{max}, it means that an existing attracting basin covers current instance, and the approximating effect is satisfying. No adjustment is necessary in this situation.

If Err is beyond Err_{max}, it means that current instance is not covered by any existing attracting basins. Thus, the topology-adjusting phrase is encountered. In this phrase, we must find out whether current instance could be covered through slightly adjusting some basins, or it is necessary to construct a new basin according to the instance. Furthermore, if it is the latter situation, we must find out whether we could exploit existing internal output approximation represented by the existing third layer units or not.

If Err is beyond Err_{max} but less than Vig_1, it means that although the overall approximating performance is not satisfying, the internal approximations of current input and output pattern are still valid to some extent. In this situation, an existing basin could cover current instance through only fine adjustment. Thus, the third layer unit u that has the maximum activation value is found out according to Equation 8:

$$c_u = \underset{h=1}{\overset{q}{MAX}}\left(c_h\right) \tag{8}$$

Where c_h is the third layer unit activation value that computed according to Equation 4, q is the number of the third layer winners.

Unit u releases a stimulus signal and feeds it back through feedback connection to the second layer unit t that has the maximum activation value, which satisfies Equation 9:

$$b_t = \underset{j=1}{\overset{o}{MAX}}\left(b_j\right) \tag{9}$$

Where b_j is the second layer unit activation value that computed according to Equation 2, o is the number of the second layer winners that connecting with unit u.

The response-centers and response-characteristic-widths of the *Gaussian* weights connecting with unit t are repeatedly adjusted according to Equation 10 and 11 until Err is less than Err_{max}. The effect of Equation 10 is to move the center of the attracting basin toward current instance, and the effect of Equation 11 is to expend the verge of the basin toward current instance.

$$\theta_{ij}' = \begin{cases} \dfrac{\theta_{ij} + 0.3\alpha_{ij} + a_i^k}{2} & a_i^k \in \left(-\infty, \theta_{ij} - 0.3\alpha_{ij}\right) \\ \theta_{ij} & a_i^k \in \left[\theta_{ij} - 0.3\alpha_{ij}, \theta_{ij} + 0.3\alpha_{ij}\right] \\ \dfrac{\theta_{ij} - 0.3\alpha_{ij} + a_i^k}{2} & a_i^k \in \left(\theta_{ij} + 0.3\alpha_{ij}, +\infty\right) \end{cases} \tag{10}$$

$$\alpha'_{ij} = \begin{cases} \dfrac{3\alpha_{ij} - \left(10\alpha_i^k - 10\theta_{ij}\right)}{6} & a_i^k \in \left(-\infty, \theta_{ij} - 0.3\alpha_{ij}\right) \\ \alpha_{ij} & a_i^k \in \left[\theta_{ij} - 0.3\alpha_{ij}, \theta_{ij} + 0.3\alpha_{ij}\right] \\ \dfrac{3\alpha_{ij} + 10\alpha_i^k - 10\theta_{ij}}{6} & a_i^k \in \left(\theta_{ij} + 0.3\alpha_{ij}, +\infty\right) \end{cases} \qquad (11)$$

Attention should be paid to that the adjustment of the attracting basin is a resonant process, in which the second layer and the third layer of FANRE are respectively corresponding to the feature representation field and the category representation field of ART1 [5]. The analog of the ART1's top-down learned expectation in FANRE is the expected activation value of the third layer unit u. And the analog of the ART1's bottom-up information in FANRE is the feed forward value of the second layer unit t.

In the beginning of the adjustment, the attracting basin corresponding to unit t is adjusted according to Equation 10 and 11. After that, unit t transfers its activation value to unit u. Simultaneously, the output units provide unit u an expected activation value which enables Err less than Err_{max}. If the real activation value of unit u cannot match with the expected value, unit u releases a signal and feeds it back to unit t through feedback connection. Then, unit t performs another adjustment, and the resonance occurs. This resonant process terminates only when the real activation value of unit u matching with its expected value, that is, the bottom-up information matched with the top-down learned expectation.

The adjustment of attracting basin described above involves not only feedback signals but also iterative modulating. However, since the input pattern becomes more and more close to the selected attracting basin as adjusting continues, the adjusting resonance is due to stabilize at a point where the input pattern is covered by the basin. This stabilization property is an advantage that FANRE inherits from Adaptive Resonance Theory.

If Err is beyond Vig_1 but less than Vig_2, it means that the internal output approximation represented by unit u is applicable to current instance. And it is the internal input approximations represented by the existing second layer units unfit for current instance. Thus, a new unit is appended to the second layer. It is connected with not only unit u but also all the input units. The feed forward and feedback connections between the new unit and unit u are all set to 1.0. The response-centers of the *Gaussian* weights connecting with the new unit are respectively set to the input components of current instance. And the response-characteristic-widths are set to a default value. If Err is still beyond Err_{max} after the appending, it means that the basin is somewhat deviating from its typical attractor. The basin will be moved according to Equation 12 until Err is less than Err_{max} or a pre-set maximum moving step r is arrived.

$$\theta'_{ij} = \theta_{ij} + \delta\left(a_i^k - \theta_{ij}\right) \quad 0 < \delta < 1 \qquad (12)$$

Where δ is the response-center moving step. Experiments show that $\delta = 0.1$ and $r = 2$ could achieve satisfying results.

If Err is beyond Vig_2, it means that both the internal input approximation and the internal output approximation represented by the existing hidden units unfit for current instance. Thus, two units are appended to the hidden layers, one in the second layer, the other in the third layer. The new second layer unit is connected with all the input units. The response-centers of the *Gaussian* weights are respectively set to the input components of current instance. And the response-characteristic-widths are set to a default value. The new third layer unit is connected with all the output units. The feed forward connections are respectively set to the output components of current instance. And the feedback connections are all set to 1.0. Besides, the two new units are connected with each other. Both the feed forward and feedback connections between them are set to 1.0. If *Err* is still beyond Err_{max} after the appending, the corresponding attracting basin will be moved according to Equation 12 until *Err* is less than Err_{max} or a pre-set maximum moving step *r* is arrived.

The process of learning an instance fed to FANRE is accomplished hereunto. If there is instance that has not been fed, FANRE starts to deal with it. Or else the learning course terminates. Thus it can be seen that the learning of FANRE is performed in an incremental style, and the instances are fed in only one pass. Figure 2 shows the flowchart of the learning course.

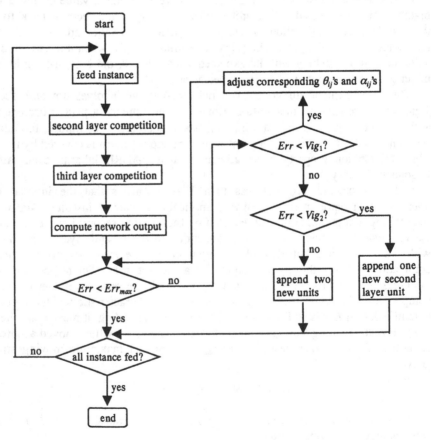

Fig. 2. Flowchart of the learning course of FANRE

3. Experimental Results and Comparisons

3.1 Methodology

We have performed some experiments to compare FANRE against a BP kind algorithm on three regression problems with ascending difficulty. The machine we used is Pentium MMX 200MHz, 32M RAM. The parameters of FANRE are set as follows. The default response-characteristic-width α_{ij} of *Gaussian* weight is set to 0.1. The bias of the hidden layer units is set to 0.01. The threshold of the leakage competition of the hidden units is set to 0.6. The response-center moving step δ is set to 0.1, and the maximum moving step r is set to 2. The maximum allowable error Err_{max} is set to 0.03. The first-degree vigilance Vig_1 is set to 0.04,.and the second-degree vigilance Vig_2 is set to 0.05.

Considering that Backpropagation is the most prevailing neural algorithm in dealing with regression tasks at present, an algorithm belonging to this kind is tested and compared against FANRE. The algorithm we selected is SuperSAB [6], which is a faster variation of Backpropagation. Tollenaere [6] reported that it is 10 to 100 times faster than standard BP [7]. In our experiments, the weight step η_{ij} of SuperSAB is set to 10; the weight increase factor η_{up} and the weight decrease factor η_{down} are respectively set to 1.05 and 0.2. In order to avoid overfitting, the training process is terminated after 500 epochs.

The measure we used in the comparison is the classical regression measure [8], that is, variance, which represent the average squared distance between the real point and the expected point. The mathematical form of variance is the same as Equation 7, where d_l denotes the real output and d_l^k denotes the expected output. The value range of variance is [0, 1], and the smaller the variance, the better the approximating result.

3.2 Approximating Line

In this experiment, we apply both FANRE and SuperSAB to approximate three lines, namely $y=x$, $y=0.5x$ and $y=0.3x$ while $x\square[0, 1]$. For each line, we uniformly sample 200 points, in which 50 points compose the training set and all the 200 points compose the test set. Table.1 shows the experimental results.

	Func	Training set Variance	Test set Variance	Training Time (second)
FANRE	$y=x$	0.000190	0.000278	0.020
	$y=0.5x$	0.000447	0.000492	0.020
	$y=0.3x$	0.000461	0.000465	0.020
SuperSAB	$y=x$	0.001330	0.001459	2,542
	$y=0.5x$	0.001344	0.001469	2,542
	$y=0.3x$	0.001283	0.001406	2,542

Table 1. Experimental result of *Line* approximation

From Table.1 we can see that both the test set variance and the training set variance of FANRE are less than 0.0005, which means the average absolute distance between the real point and the expected point is less than 0.023. Both the test set variance and the training set variance of SuperSAB are less than 0.0015, which means the average absolute distance between the real point and the expected point is less than 0.039. Thus, FANRE is slightly better than SuperSAB on the approximating effect although both algorithms achieve satisfying results. Moreover, the training time of FANRE is always about 5 magnitude less than that of SuperSAB. So, we conclude that FANRE is superior to SuperSAB on this problem. Fig.3 shows the approximating results on $y=x$ using 200 test instances, that is, the lines are depicted with 200 points.

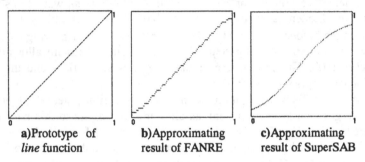

| a)Prototype of | b)Approximating | c)Approximating |
| *line* function | result of FANRE | result of SuperSAB |

Fig. 3. Comparison of the approximating results on $y=x$ while $x\square[0,1]$, using 200 test points

3.3   Approximating Sine

In this experiment, we apply both FANRE and SuperSAB to approximate the sine function $y=Sin(x)$, while $x\square[0, 2\pi]$. We uniformly sample 300 points from the curve, and construct 5 training sets respectively comprising 50, 100, 150, 200, 250 points while smaller one is the subset of bigger one. All the 300 points compose the test set. Table.2 shows the experimental results.

	Training set Size	Training set Variance	Test set Variance	Training time (second)
FANRE	50	0.000000	0.000244	0.030
	100	0.000167	0.000312	0.060
	150	0.000139	0.000147	0.120
	200	0.000201	0.000224	0.190
	250	0.000239	0.000241	0.270
SuperSAB	50	0.031475	0.031671	2,536
	100	0.026842	0.026926	5,045
	150	0.027568	0.027606	7,547
	200	0.027089	0.027115	10,053
	250	0.027019	0.027038	12,563

Table 2. Experimental results of *Sine* approximation

From Table.2 we can see that FANRE achieves better results than SuperSAB no matter what size the training set is. Both the test set variance and the training set variance of FANRE are less than 0.0025, which means the average absolute distance between the real point and the expected point is less than 0.05. Both the test set variance and the training set variance of SuperSAB are greater than 0.026, which means the average absolute distance between the real point and the expected point is greater than 0.162. Moreover, the training time of FANRE is always about 5 magnitude less than that of SuperSAB. So, we conclude that FANRE is superior to SuperSAB on this problem.

Attention should be paid to that the relatively worse result of SuperSAB is partially due to the training strategy we used, that is, we terminate the training course after 500 epochs in order to avoid overfitting. We believe that if we can continue its training and skillfully avoid overfitting, SuperSAB could attain better results. However, even if we can improve the approximating results of SuperSAB to the same level of that of FANRE, we still regard the latter superior to the former because the training time of the latter is far less than that of the former. Fig.4 shows the approximating results using 250 training instances and 300 test instances, that is, the curves are depicted with 300 points.

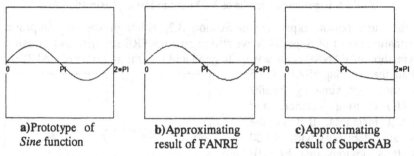

| a)Prototype of | b)Approximating | c)Approximating |
| *Sine* function | result of FANRE | result of SuperSAB |

Fig. 4. Comparison of the approximating results on $y=\sin(x)$ while $x\square[0,2\pi]$, using 300 test points

3.4 Approximating 2-d Mexican Hat

In this experiment, we apply both FANRE and SuperSAB to approximate the 2-d Mexican Hat function that is shown in Equation 13, while $x\square[-4\pi, 4\pi]$.

$$y = \sin c|x| = \frac{\sin|x|}{|x|} \tag{13}$$

We uniformly sample 1,000 points from the curve, and construct 5 training sets respectively comprising 100, 200, 400, 600, 800 points while smaller one is the subset of bigger one. All the 1,000 points compose the test set. Table.3 shows the experimental results.

From Table.3 we can see that approximating 2-d Mexican Hat is a somewhat difficult problem where SuperSAB achieves poor performance. Its test set variance is always greater than 0.125, which means the average absolute distance between the real point and the expected point is greater than 0.354, no matter what size the training set is. However, FANRE still achieves satisfying result on this problem. Its test set variance is always less than 0.0043, which means the average absolute distance between the real point and the expected point is less than 0.066. Moreover, the training time of FANRE is about 4 magnitude less than that of SuperSAB. So, we conclude that FANRE is superior to SuperSAB on this problem.

	Training set Size	Training set Variance	Test set Variance	Training time (second)
FANRE	100	0.002295	0.002375	0.091
	200	0.001883	0.002462	0.230
	400	0.003202	0.003474	0.751
	600	0.003875	0.004289	1.543
	800	0.002733	0.003107	2.634
SuperSAB	100	0.112657	0.142652	5,923
	200	0.099063	0.125969	10,055
	400	0.123704	0.153696	20,130
	600	0.145957	0.165955	30,186
	800	0.137124	0.151246	40,217

Table 3. Experimental results of 2-d Mexican Hat approximation

As the same reason expatiated in Section 3.3, although we may improve the approximating effect of SuperSAB, we still regard FANRE superior to it because the approximation of FANRE is already quite good and the training time of FANRE is far less than that of SuperSAB. Fig.5 shows the approximating results using 800 training instances and 1,000 test instances, that is, the curves are depicted with 1,000 points. It is obvious that FANRE approximates the prototype curve quite close while SuperSAB is nearly no use.

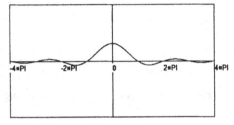

a)Prototype of 2-d Mexican Hat function

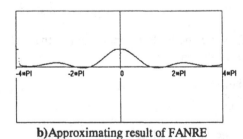

b)Approximating result of FANRE

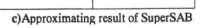

c)Approximating result of SuperSAB

Fig. 5. Comparison of the approximating result on $y=\text{sinc}|x|$ while $x\in[-4\pi,4\pi]$, using 1,000 test points

4.   Conclusions and Future Work

This paper proposes a fast neural regression estimator named FANRE, which exploits the advantages of both Adaptive Resonance Theory and Field Theory. It needs only one pass learning, and achieves not only impressive approximating effect but also fast learning speed. Besides, FANRE has incremental learning ability, which enables it fit for real-time online learning tasks. Moreover, FANRE can adaptively set up its topology so that the disadvantage of manually determining the number of hidden units of most feed-forward neural models is overcome. Experimental results show that FANRE is superior to SuperSAB on both approximating effect and training time cost.

Until now, FANRE has only been compared against BP kind algorithm. In order to exhibit its superiority, more comparisons should be done against other neural algorithms such as Fuzzy ARTMAP [9], Cascade-Correlation [10], et al. We plan to do this work in the near future. Moreover, FANRE has only been applied to artificial problems such as function approximating with single input and single output. Although some of them are quite difficult, they can not prove that FANRE is effective while facing real world tasks with multiple variables. In the future, we also plan to develop some neural regression estimation systems based upon FANRE that aims to solve real world problems.

Acknowledgements

The authors wish to thank Mr. Wenlong Wei and Mr. Dong Shao for their fruitful work. The National Natural Science Foundation of P.R.China and the Natural Science Foundation of Jiangsu Province, P.R.China, supported this research.

References

1. Grossberg S. Adaptive Pattern Classification and Universal Recoding, I: Parallel Development and Coding of Neural Feature Detectors. Biological Cybernetics, 23: 121-134, 1976.
2. Wasserman P D. Advanced Methods in Neural Computing. Van Nostrand Reinhold, New York, 1993.
3. Bachmann C M, Cooper L, Dembo A, et al. A Relaxation Model for Memory with High Storage Density. In: Proceedings of the National Academy of Science, USA, 21: 7529-7531, 1987.
4. Zhou Z, Chen S, Chen Z. FANNC: A Fast Adaptive Neural Network Classifier. Submitted to International Journal of Knowledge and Information Systems.
5. Carpenter G A., Grossberg S. A Massively Parallel Architecture for a Self-Organizing Neural Pattern Recognition Machine. Computer Vision, Graphics, and image Processing, 37: 54-115, 1987.
6. Tollenaere T. SuperSAB: Fast Adaptive Backpropagation with Good Scaling Properties. Neural Networks, 3: 561-573, 1990.
7. Rumelhart D, Hinton G, Williams R. Learning Representation by Backpropagating Errors. Nature, 323(9): 533-536, 1986.
8. Weiss S M, Indurkhya N. Rule-Based Regression. In: Proceedings of the 13th International Joint Conference on Artificial Intelligence, Chamborg, France, Morgan Kaufmann, 1072-1078, 1993.
9. Carpenter G A, Grossberg S, Markuzon N, et al. Fuzzy ARTMAP: A Neural Network Architecture for Incremental Supervised Learning of Analog Multidimensional Maps. IEEE Trans. on Neural Networks, 3(5): 698-713, 1992.
10. Fahlman S E, Lebiere C. The Cascade-Correlation Learning Architecture. In: Touretzky D ed., Advances in Neural Information Processing Systems 2, Mountain View, CA: Morgan Kaufmann, 524-5232, 1990.

Neural Networks for Defuzification of Fuzzy Rules: An Application in Macroeconomic Forecasting

Raouf Veliev[1], Alex Rubinov[1], and Andrew Stranieri[2]

[1] School of Information Technology and Mathematical Sciences, University of Ballarat, University drive, Mt Helen, P.O. Box 663 Ballarat, Victoria, 3353, Australia
[2] Donald Berman Laboratory for Information Technology and Law, Dept of Computer Science and Computer Engineering, La Trobe University, Bundoora, Victoria, Australia
imcu00rv@students.ballarat.edu.au, amr@ballarat.edu.au,
stranier@latcs1.cs.latrobe.edu.au

Abstract. Macroeconomic forecasting has traditionally been performed with the use of econometric tools though these methods necessarily make many theoretical assumptions that are not valid in all circumstances. The main advantage of the use of approaches that apply machine learning algorithms to economic data is that forecasts largely free of assumptions can be made. This study presents an approach to macro economic forecasting that generates fuzzy rules from data using a fuzzy control system architecture and evolutionary programming. However, the selection of a defuzification method is typically performed subjectively in fuzzy control systems. We demonstrate that the selection of defuzification method makes a substantial impact on forecasts. In order to overcome this subjectivity and further enhance our objectives of developing forecasting systems free of any technical or theoretical assumptions we introduce a neural network to perform the defuzification. The performance of our approach compares very favourably with other data mining techniques on cross validation tests with macro economic data.

1. Introduction

Macro economic modelling and forecasting has traditionally been performed with the exclusive use of mathematical and statistical tools. However, these tools are not always appropriate for economic modelling because of uncertainty associated with human decision making. The development of any economy is determined by a wide range of activities performed by humans as householders, managers, or government policy makers. Persons in each role pursue different goals and, more importantly, base their economic plans on decision-making in vague and often ambiguous terms. For example, a householder may make a decision on the proportion of income to reserve as savings according to the rule- {IF my future salary is likely to diminish, THEN I will save a greater proportion of my current salary}. Mathematical models of human decision-making impose precise forms of continuous functions and overlook the inherent fuzziness of the process.

In addition to imposing a crispness that may not be appropriate, mathematical and statistical models necessarily make assumptions that derive from economic theories. A large variety of sometimes conflicting models have emerged over the years as a

N. Foo (Ed.): AI´99, LNAI 1747, pp. 60-71, 1999.

consequence of this. Inferences drawn from a model hold only to the extent that the economic theoretical assumptions hold yet this is often difficult to determine. Macro economic researchers solely using mathematical or statistical models are compelled to make assumptions based on their own subjective view of the world or theoretical background and beliefs. For example, hypotheses generated by researchers who accept Keynesian assumptions are quite different from hypotheses from Classical theorists. Hypotheses are not only dependent upon the subjective beliefs of their creators but can easily become obsolete. Completely different economic systems can rise in different times in different countries and be described by different models [12].

We present a fuzzy system approach to macro economic modelling that better represents uncertainty caused by the prevalence of human factors in any economy. An evolutionary approach to building a fuzzy forecasting system can facilitate the design of a system that is largely free of subjective assumptions, and based only on patterns in the data.

In [17] we showed that fuzzy control systems can be successfully applied for macro economic forecasting tasks. Moreover, in investigated examples the results were found to compare favourably with those obtained using traditional statistical regression models or conventional neural network approximation techniques. In that work, the fuzzy sets and membership function were pre-set and defuzification method was predetermined. The main objective was to apply an evolutionary search in order to generate fuzzy rules that best describe macroeconomic data.

The search for a set of fuzzy rules that best describes macroeconomic data varies according to the different defuzification methods employed in a fuzzy control architecture. For example, we report differences in results between the *centre of gravity, area* and *maximal height* methods. However, there is no theoretical basis for preferring one method to another. Given that the choice of defuzification method is important for our work and for other applications of fuzzy control, we sought to identify a strategy for defuzzifying concepts that was not based on a subjective selection of one of the known methods. We summarise our motivation in the following way:

• To suggest an objective way of replacing a defuzification method in the fuzzy forecasting system's structure

• To improve performance of the fuzzy forecasting system on an example of macro economic modelling

In this paper we show that a neural network can be used to replace a predefined defuzification procedure in fuzzy logic reasoning. An application of this method to macroeconomic forecasting shows that the system performs favourably on evaluation trials. The system works with fuzzy sets of any shape and is more consistent with the fuzzy nature of macro economic modelling.

In the next section of this paper we briefly describe the method we used to generate fuzzy rules and highlight how results vary according to the defuzification method selected. This is included in order to provide the background and motivation for the work described in this paper. In the following section we describe the use of a neural network to perform the defuzification.

2. Generation of Fuzzy Rules Using Predefined Defuzification Methods

In [17] we used an evolutionary programming approach to generate fuzzy rules that best fit a given data set. We believe that fuzzy logic, though not normally used in macroeconomic modelling is suitable for capturing the uncertainty inherent in the problem domain. An evolutionary approach to building the system facilitates the design of a system that is free of subjective assumptions, and based only on patterns in the data.

Although genetic algorithms have been used to generate fuzzy rules by Rutkowska [13] and Karr [6] and Yuan and Zhuang [18] these approaches, in attempting to discover optimal rules and ideal membership functions, introduce theoretical and technical definitions and assumptions that we wish to avoid. A key assumption we make with macro-economic data is that the membership functions that map quantitative crisp values onto qualitative fuzzy values can be pre-set. With most macro economic indicators there seems to be general agreement about the mapping of quantitative terms onto qualitative terms though future research is planned to empirically verify this. In order to reduce complexity of the search problem and, in light of the nature of economic data, we do not search for near optimal membership functions but instead predetermine a membership function that seems reasonable.

Following positive results from artificially generated data where the functional dependence between input variables was known, we tested the rules generation with real economic data. We chose economic indicators with well-known interrelationships. The Keynesian General Theory is based on a fundamental assumption that the level of national income determines the level of consumption [7]. This hypothesis has been quite successfully tested in many developed countries. In contrast to this theory, according to classical economic theory, interest rates impact on the level of consumption. Classical theorists believe that if the level of interest rates rise, then people expect to earn more money in the future on each dollar saved in the present and will reduce present consumption.

We expected to generate fuzzy rules that depict well known associations depicted by both Keynesian and Classical theories and in addition, identify more accurately ways in which the theories conflict. Economic data, describing the dynamics of these indicators in the United States was obtained from The Federal Reserve Bank of St. Louis. The records were collected on a regular basis from 1960 till 1997. Fuzzy rules were generated and evaluated using cross validation by comparison with linear regression and a neural network trained with the same data. Results summarised in Table 1 indicate that the fuzzy rules generated demonstrate comparable predictive performance compared with the neural network and superior performance when compared with linear regression.

The fuzzy rules represented in tabular format are included in Table 2. Y is change from one quarter to the next in national income represented by fuzzy values PH, positive high; PL, positive low, NL negative low and NH negative high. I is the change in interest rates. The fuzzy rules predict change in consumption. The black box nature of neural networks is a distinct disadvantage for the analysis of macro-economic data. In contrast, as Table 2 illustrates, fuzzy rules generated without any theoretical assumptions can be used to explore patterns and to even assess the veracity of theories. For example, we see from this table that consumption rises (PH, PL) with a sharp drop in national income and a drop in interest rates. Keynesian economics predicts a drop in consumption in this case whereas Classical theory predicts a rise. The fuzzy rules indicate that a rise does occur but only when the national income drops dramatically. When the change in national income is still negative but small (Y=NL), consumption does not rise but displays behaviour predicted by Keynesian theory.

	Fuzzy rules	Neural network	Lin. regression
Mean	14.75	17.31	23.25
Std. Deviation	5.5	5.56	10.42
Median	13.59	15.4	21.98

Table 1. Comparison of fuzzy rules, neural network and linear regression

		I			
		NH	*NL*	*PL*	*PH*
Y	*NH*	PH	PL	NH	NL
	NL	NH	NL	NL	NL
	PL	NL	PL	PL	NL
	PH	PH	PH	PH	NL

Table 2. Fuzzy rules generated for the macroeconomic data.

Although results from fuzzy rules generation were promising we were concerned that the defuzification method used in that study, *centre of gravity*, may not have been the ideal method. We carried out a tenfold cross validation test over test data using three different defuzification methods: *Centre of gravity, Area* method and the *Maximal height* method. Table 3 summarises the evaluation results obtained.

	Centre of Gravity	*Area method*	*Maximal height method*
Mean	14.8	11.9	19.7
Median	13.6	9.2	16.8
Std. Dev.	5.8	7.7	11.8

Table 3. Prediction results of the generated fuzzy forecasting system using different defuzification methods.

Table 3 indicates that the performance on test data over each cross validation set varies substantially depending on the defuzification method used. In order to remain consistent with our objective of developing fuzzy rules that were independent of any theoretical or methodological biases we sought to derive a defuzification procedure that was based in some way only on the data in our training sets. In the next section we describes the use of a neural network to achieve this end.

3.   Neural Network Component of Fuzzy-Neural Hybrid Systems as an Objective Defuzification Procedure

The integration of fuzzy reasoning with neural networks has been fruitful [15], [3], [1] though the integration has been performed in many diverse ways. Many hybrid systems use a neural network to encode a fuzzy system. Each step in the fuzzy system process is equivalent to at least one layer of the neural network [5], [16], [11], [4], [10], [14]. Most of the architectures consistent with this approach have at least four layers corresponding to fuzzification, intersection, rule application and defuzification respectively. Furthermore, these architectures differ from conventional neural networks in terms of the uniformity of both the processing nodes and the interconnection strategy.

The main common disadvantage of these systems is a high dimensionality of the networks, which puts obvious limitations on an implementation. Maguire, McGinnity and McDaid introduced in [8] a hybrid system, which overcomes these limitations. But although the number of layers in their systems is three, the number of nodes in the hidden layer must be equivalent to the sum of numbers of fuzzy sets distributed over all input variables. However, this approach is restrictive in that only the bell-type membership function can be used for a chosen neural network activation function. Generating the output according to the Sugeno type fuzzy model finds a weighted average of rules' output and is not related to fuzzy representation of the output variable.

In our approach, we do not model the fuzzy system processes using layers of a neural network but instead take the outputs of the fuzzy system as inputs to a neural network. The neural network outputs are used to determine a crisp value. The neural network is not dependent on the vagaries of a defuzification method subjectively chosen. The defuzification method presented here can be used with fuzzy rules discovered from experts or with those generated from data using the evolutionary program outlined above.

There are two inputs to the neural network: 1) the label that represents a fuzzy set and 2) the height of membership function value. These are parameters that underpin the *centre of gravity, area* and *maximal height* defuzification methods. A brief survey of these defuzification methods will highlight the importance of the label and height as inputs into a neural network.

The majority of defuzification methods label each output fuzzy set inferred from a fuzzy rules table. The height of the set is important when performing a union of two or more sets. Defuzification methods differ on how labels and heights are combined to infer a crisp value. For example, in the *Area* method the crisp value is obtained according to the formula:

$$z_0 = \frac{\sum_{i=1}^{n} S_i \cdot z_i}{\sum_{i=1}^{n} S_i} \qquad (1)$$

In this formula z_0 is an output crisp value; S_i is an area of the output fuzzy set, which is inferred from the fuzzy rule table; z_i is a representative point, which is obtained using a height of the fuzzy set.

In a related vein, the *Maximal height* method uses a weighted average of height and the label of inferred fuzzy rules points, where weights are heights of the union of fuzzy sets. *Median* and *centre of gravity* methods use the properties of a united output fuzzy set, which, in turn, uses heights and labels of unionising fuzzy sets in its construction. According to these methods we find the centre of gravity point which divides the united output fuzzy set into two equal areas.

In contrast to all defuzzification methods, instead of using the labels and heights of inferred fuzzy rules in any rigid subjective way, we take them as inputs of the neural network. Fig. 1 illustrates the structure of the fuzzy-neural hybrid system.

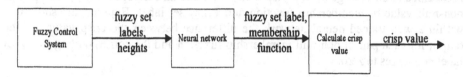

Fig. 1. Fuzzy-neural hybrid systems structure.

According to the procedure, reflected in Fig. 1 the first stage of the fuzzy-neural forecasting system involves the Fuzzy Control component.

Having determined a structure of the fuzzy control component of the hybrid system, we apply fuzzy reasoning for each record of the data set. In our case we use Mamdani's "min-max-gravity' fuzzy reasoning method [9] using the "AND" operator, with one exception that we stop the fuzzy control procedure on the unification stage and following defuzification stage. Thus, for example in two-input-one-output case each fact {x0, y0 -> z0, x0 $\in A_i$, y0 $\in B_i$, z0 $\in C_i$ with a degree $\mu_{B_i}(y0)$, $\mu_{B_i}(x0)$ and $\mu_{C_i}(z0)$, respectively, where A_i B_i C_i are fuzzy sets and $\mu(x)$ is a membership function} will produce the label of the output fuzzy set C_i' and a height for this set, which is calculated according to the formula below:

$$H_{C_i'} = \max_{z \in C_i'} \{\min\{\mu_{A_i}(x0), \mu_{B_i}(y0), \mu_{C_i}(z)\}\} \tag{2}$$

For each rule i, pairs of these labels and heights - {C_i' and $H_{C_i'}$} are obtained and form inputs for the feed-forward neural network. In order to reduce the number of input nodes for the neural network we take only those pairs that have non-null values of the output fuzzy set's height. Because the number of these pairs can vary, while the number of input nodes must be set invariant, we take the number of input nodes to be equal to the maximal possible number of non-null values for all input variables plus the same number of corresponding fuzzy set labels. The number of non-null values of a membership function equals the result of multiplication of the maximal numbers of overlapping fuzzy sets for each variable.

The output of the neural network can conceivably be either a crisp value or a non-null value of membership function and the corresponding label of each set it belongs to. We have implemented the second option because it is more consistent with the fuzzy nature of an output variable. If we change the fuzzy sets' shapes for output, the learning procedure and the system's properties will vary. If our network outputs a crisp value there will be no effect due to the fact that the crisp value stays the same.

A crisp value is calculated easily given a membership function and corresponding fuzzy set label as follows. We calculate the crisp values of the output for each pair of non-null values of the membership function and the corresponding fuzzy set label which are output by the neural network. Then, we take the average value of these crisp values as it is shown in Fig. 2. In Fig. 2 {n1, A, n2, B} are sample values for output nodes of the neural network and given fuzzy sets A and B. The crisp value x0 is obtained as an average of two crisp values - x1 and x2 corresponding to each pair of non-null value of membership function and fuzzy set label. Experiments show that within a well trained neural network the difference between the crisp values of the output for each pair of non-null membership function and the corresponding fuzzy set label converges to zero.

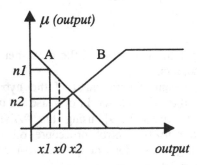

Fig. 2. Output crisp value determination in the fuzzy-neural system

In the next section we illustrate the use of a neural network for defuzzification with a conceptual example. Following that we apply the technique to macroeconomic data.

4.   A Conceptual Example

Figure 3 illustrates two sample fuzzyfied input variables - x and y and one output variable - z. A1, B1, C1 are fuzzy sets for variable x; A2, B2 are fuzzy sets for variable y; and A3, B3 are fuzzy sets for variable z - an output. Figure 4 illustrates a sample fuzzy rules table of the hybrid system.

Let's consider two facts given illustrated in Figure 3 for the training of the fuzzy-neural hybrid system: {x1, y1 - > z1} and {x2, y2 - > z2}. Figure 5 illustrates the values of membership function for each fuzzy variable from these two facts.

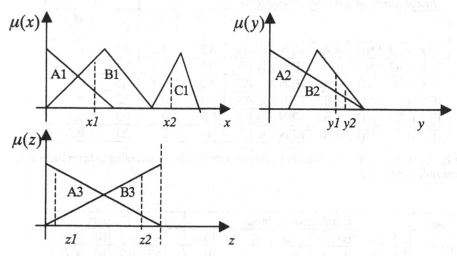

Fig. 3. Fuzzy variables x, y (inputs) and z (output)

		Y	
		A2	B2
X	A1	A3	B3
	B1	A3	A3
	C1	B3	B3

Fig. 4. Fuzzy rules table of the hybrid system

$\mu(x)$	x1	x2
A1	0.3	0
B1	0.7	0
C1	0	0.5

$\mu(y)$	y1	y2
A2	0.4	0.1
B2	0.6	0.2

$\mu(z)$	Z1	z2
A3	0.9	0.2
B3	0.1	0.8

Fig. 5. Membership function values for the facts - {x1, y1 -> z1} and {x2, y2 -> z2}

Fig. 6 illustrates the inferred fuzzy sets and their heights by applying the standard Mamdani's fuzzy reasoning procedure without the unification and subsequent defuzification stages. C_i' represents a fuzzy label and $H_{C_i'}$ represents the corresponding fuzzy sets' heights, which we obtain according to the Mamdani's procedure for the two given facts - {x1, y1 - > z1} and {x2, y2 - > z2}.

According to Figure 3 the maximal number of overlapping fuzzy sets is 2 for x1 (A1 and B1) and 2 for x2 (A2 and B2). Therefore the number of the input nodes for the neural network for this example is 2x2x2=8. Training data for the neural network are illustrated in Figure 7.

Fuzzy Rules form the fuzzy rules table	X1		X2	
	$C_i{}'$	$H_{c_i{}'}$	$C_i{}'$	$H_{c_i{}'}$
IF x is A1 AND y is A2 THEN z is A3	A3	0.3	A3	0
IF x is A1 AND y is B2 THEN z is B3	B3	0.3	B3	0
IF x is B1 AND y is A2 THEN z is A3	A3	0.4	A3	0
IF x is B1 AND y is B2 THEN z is A3	A3	0.6	A3	0
IF x is C1 AND y is A2 THEN z is B3	B3	0	B3	0.1
IF x is C1 AND y is B2 THEN z is B3	B3	0	B3	0.2

Fig. 6. Heights and the corresponding fuzzy set labels inferred according to Mamdani's fuzzy reasoning procedure

Case	Neural network Inputs								Outputs			
1	A3	0.3	B3	0.3	A3	0.4	A3	0.6	A3	0.9	B3	0.1
2	B3	0.1	B3	0.2	0	0	0	0	A3	0.2	B3	0.8

Fig. 7. Sample training for the example neural network

The next section describes an implementation of the proposed system for macro economic forecasting using US economic data.

5.   Implementation of the Fuzzy-Neural Hybrid System with Macro-economic Data

The use of a neural network to perform the defuzification was evaluated using macro economic data described in Section 2.   Fuzzy rules that predict national consumption, C from interest rates, I and national income, Y were generated using the evolutionary program cited in that section. The fuzzy rules obtained are illustrated in Table 2. The fuzzy sets negative high NH, negative low NL, positive high PH, and positive low PL refer to changes in interest rates over a quarter. Data representing consumption, interest rates and national income between 1960 and 1997 were collected by the Federal Reserve Bank of St Louis. Data transformation took the form of converting quarterly records to changes in those values from one quarter to the next.   150 records representing quarterly changes were collated. The interval of real values of inputs and outputs were set from minimum and maximum observed changes in each variable.

Tenfold cross-validation was used with hold out sets of size 15 and training sets of size 135. For each cross validation set, fuzzy rules were generated as described in Section 2, training sets for the defuzification neural network were created and a neural network was trained. The neural network has a feed-forward architecture consisting of three layers. The input layer had 8 nodes and the output layer had four nodes. The inputs were membership function values and labels as described in the conceptual example above. One hidden layer with 8 nodes was used and the network was trained using back propagation of errors with a learning rate of 0.2. A crisp value for consumption was calculated from the membership function value and fuzzy set label – outputs of the neural network. Each network was trained until the error rate on unseen test cases began to rise. Once trained, the network was applied to each record of the 135 training set records to defuzzify the outputs. The sum of square of differences between consumption predicted by the system and actual consumption on the test set of 15 was recorded for each cross validation set.

The performance of our fuzzy rules generator and neural defuzification approach was evaluated against other data mining techniques including a single feed forward neural network trained with back-propagation of errors (3 layer, learning rate = 0.2, no improvement in error rates after 40-55 epochs), log-linear regression, linear regression, and the same fuzzy rules defuzzified using the *Area* method. Table 4 illustrates the ranked results of the sum of square of the difference between predicted and actual change in consumption for each technique over the ten cross-validation sets.

	Neural network	Log-linear regression	Linear regression	Fuzzy system (area deffuz. method)	Fuzzy-neural hybrid system
1	14.0	2.6	11.4	3.1	3.7
2	14.4	8.1	11.6	5.8	4.8
3	14.7	8.8	13.7	7.0	7.3
4	15.1	9.2	15.1	7.8	7.5
5	15.4	9.4	21.5	8.1	8.9
6	16.1	10.2	22.4	10.3	9.5
7	16.6	11.6	26.0	11.0	11.3
8	17.2	15.0	29.8	18.3	13.1
9	18.4	19.4	40.0	24.3	14.6
10	19.1	32.0	41.1	25.1	14.9
Mean	*16.10*	*12.62*	*23.27*	*11.9*	*9.5*
Median	*15.74*	*9.78*	*21.98*	*9.2*	*9.2*
Std. Dev.	*1.71*	*8.11*	*10.99*	*7.76*	*3.9*

Fig 8. Comparison of the evaluation results of neural network, linera regression, log-linear regression, fuzzy system and fuzzy-neural hybrid system.

Figure 8 illustrates that mean error over cross-validation sets was lower for the fuzzy rules defuzzified using a trained neural network presented here than was the case for other techniques. As described in Section 2, defuzification using the *area* method provided fewer errors than defuzification using *centre of gravity* or the *maximal height method.* The neural defuzification presented here displayed the same median as the *area* method but a lower mean error and lower variation around the mean across cross-validation sets. This suggests that the objective of this study, to identify a defuzification method that was not based on a subjective choice but was tuned to empirical data, was realised.

The generated fuzzy rules defuzzified with the neural network performed very well compared with other data mining techniques. The poor performance of the linear regression model is consistent with the macroeconomic theory perspective that consumption is not best described as a simple linear relationship with interest rates or national income. Although the mean error for the single neural network was quite high, the variation over the cross validation sets was quite low. This may suggest that some improvement on neural network results may be noticed with more attention focused on adjusting learning rates, momentum and bias terms. However, it is also possible that contradictory records (i.e. same national income and interest rate inputs but different consumption outputs) in the data prohibit better performance no matter how much parameters are adjusted. This suggests that the fuzzy system proposed here can more adequately deal with contradictory data. Log-linear regression performed quite well and, if not for cross-validation set 10, would have indicated very good performance. However, this suggests that many data points can be described by a log-linear function but that some values will be very poorly described using this predefined function. The advantage of using the fuzzy rules generator and neural defuzification is that no assumptions about the functional form of the data are used at all. To a substantial degree, the data speaks for itself.

6. Further Research and Conclusions

We have developed an approach that applies fuzzy reasoning to macroeconomic forecasting, a field dominated by mathematical programming and statistical methods and riddled with a reliance on theoretical and technical assumptions that give rise to substantial variance in forecasts. As far as possible our approach must be free of assumptions so that forecasts can depend only on economic data input to the system. To realise this end we do not use fuzzy rules identified by experts but generate rules using evolutionary programs. Forecasts obtained were quite good but varied depending on the defuzification method selected. On our trials the *area* method outperformed *centre of gravity* or *maximal height* methods but this is unlikely to be the case with all data sets. Instead of selecting one defuzification method over another subjectively or engage in expensive empirical trials of each one with every new data set, we adapted a neural network for defuzification so as to avoid the use of standard methods entirely. Results suggest that our approach can be used for data mining and comparative studies with other techniques are favourable.

Future work will proceed in three directions. We aim to trial the method using incomplete and noisy data in order to simulate the economies of many nations where economic data is not collected reliably. Secondly, we aim to trial the method on data drawn from a variety of non-economic domains. Thirdly, we aim to trial the method in an application of game theory to model the behaviour of voters.

Freixas and Gambarelli [2] identify vastly different outcomes in voter predictions based on assumptions made in mapping the proportion of the votes an individual has to a measure of the degree of power the individual has in shaping the outcome of a decision. We expect that the subjectivity present in this mapping can be avoided by using the fuzzy-neural hybrid techniques presented here.

References

1. Brown M., Harris C., *Neurofuzzy adaptive modelling and control*, Prentice-Hall, 1994.
2. Freixas J., Gambarelli G., *Range of power indices*, Proc. of Third Spanish meeting on Game theory and applications, 28, June 1998.
3. Gupta M., Rao D., *On the principles of fuzzy neural networks*, Proc. Fuzzy sets and systems 61, 1-18, 1994.
4. Horikawa S., Furuhashi T., Uchikawa Y., *On fuzzy modelling using fuzzy neural networks with the back propagation algorithm*, IEEE trans. Neural nets 3:5, 801-806, 1992.
5. Jang, Roger J., *Predicting chaotic time series with fuzzy IF-THEN rules*, Proc. IEEE 2nd Int'l conference on fuzzy systems 2, 1079-1084, 1993.
6. Karr C.L., *Design of an adaptive fuzzy logic controller using a genetic algorithm*, Proc. 4th Int'l Conf. on genetic Algorithms 450-457, July 1991.
7. Keynes J., *The general theory of employment, interest and money*, MacMillan, NJ, 1961.
8. Maguire L., McGinnity T. M., McDaid L. J., *A fuzzy neural network for approximate fuzzy reasoning*, In intelegent hybrid systems, ed. Da Ruan, 35-58, 1997.
9. Mamdani E. H., *Application of fuzzy algorithms for conreol of a simple dynamic plant*, Proc. IEEE, 12 1, 1585-1588, 1974.
10. Mitra S., Pal S., *Logical operation based fuzzy MLP for classification and rule generation*, Neural networks 7:2, 353-373, 1994.
11. Nie J., Linkens D., *Neural network based approximate reasoning: principles and implementation*, Int'l journal of control 56:2, 399-413, 1992.
12. Rubinov A., Nagiyev A., *Elements of Economic Theory*, Baku, Bilik, 1992 (in Russian).
13. Rutkowska D., *On generating fuzzy rules by an evolutionary approach*, Cybernetics and Systems. 29, 391-407, 1998.
14. Simpson P., Jahns G., *Fuzzy min-max neural networks for function approximation*, Proc. IEEE int'l conference on neural networks 3, 1967-1972, 1993.
15. Takagi H., *Fusion Technology of fuzzy theory and neural networks: survey and future directions*, Proc. Int'l conference on fuzzy logic and neural networks, 13-26, July, 1990.
16. Takagi H., Hayashi I., *NN-driven fuzzy reasoning*, Int'l journal of approx. reasoning, 5, 191-212, 1991.
17. Veliev R., Rubinov. A., Stranieri A., *Generating a macroeconomic fuzzy forecasting system using evolutionary search*, to appear in The Seventh International Workshop on Rough Sets, Fuzzy Sets, Data Mining, and Granular-Soft Computing (RSFDGrC'99) Yamaguchi Resort Center, Ube, Yamaguchi, Japan, Nov. 9-11, 1999.
18. Yuan Y., Zhuang H., *A genetic algorithm for generating fuzzy classification rules*, Fuzzy sets and systems, 84, 1-19, 1996.

Semantic Integration of Databases Using Linguistic Knowledge

Jeong-Oog Lee and Doo-Kwon Baik

Software System Lab., Dept. of Computer Science & Engineering, Korea University,
1, 5-ka, Anam-dong, Sungbuk-gu, SEOUL, 136-701, KOREA
{ljo, baik}@swsys2.korea.ac.kr
http://swsys2.korea.ac.kr/index.html

Abstract. In order to give users integrated access to a large number of heterogeneous, autonomous information sources, we need an effective and efficient mechanism for enabling knowledge to be shared and exchanged. Sharing of knowledge, to be efficient and effective, must take account of semantic representation and semantic integration. In this paper, we provide a mechanism for knowledge sharing. We have made use of WordNet as linguistic knowledge to represent and interpret the meaning of the information, to integrate the information, and to give users efficient access to the integrated information.

1 Introduction

An information integration system provides a uniform interface to various information sources. Consider a user want to know those professors whose salary is over $50,000. This question might be answered using a specific university database. However, if the user issues the query with intent to retrieve all the professors whose salary is over $50,000 from all the accessible university databases, the question must be answered using integrated information rather than using a single source. In order to give users integrated access to those environments, we need an effective and efficient mechanism for enabling knowledge to be shared and exchanged. Exchange of knowledge, to be effective, must take place in an environment where it can be ensured that an information source interprets the information in exactly the same way as intended by the other sources. The information must also be easy to locate and retrieve. This is only possible where the meaning and method of representation of the information are known and agreed upon by the information sources.

In this paper, we introduce a mechanism for knowledge sharing among multiple information sources. For information sources, we focus on database systems, particularly relational database systems. A multidatabase system provides integrated access to heterogeneous, autonomous component databases in a distributed system. An essential prerequisite to achieving interoperability in multidatabase systems is to be able to identify semantically equivalent or related data items in component databases.

N. Foo (Ed.): AI'99, LNAI 1747, pp. 72–83, 1999.

While there is a significant amount of researches discussing schema differences, work on semantic issues in the multidatabase is insufficient. Because only schema considerations do not suffice to detect semantic heterogeneity [1], we have made use of linguistic knowledge from WordNet. WordNet is an on-line lexical dictionary and organized by semantic relations such as synonymy, antonymy, hyponymy, and meronymy [6]. The noun portion of WordNet is designed around the concept of synset which is a set of closely related synonyms representing a word meaning.

The rest of this paper is organized as follows. In section 2, we address some preliminaries to progress our approach. In section 3, we explain information integration process. An efficient access mechanism to an integrated environment shall be presented in section 4. After we review related works in section 5, we offer our conclusion in section 6.

2 Preliminaries

In this section, we briefly present several considerations for knowledge sharing and address the problem of semantic heterogeneity that must be detected and resolved for information integration. An overview of our approach for knowledge sharing will be outlined.

2.1 Considerations for Knowledge Sharing

In open and dynamic environments such as the Web, numerous information sources exist and new information sources can be created autonomously and continuously without formal control. In order to give a multidatabase system adaptability in those environments, we need a mechanism for enabling knowledge to be shared and exchanged. Sharing of knowledge, to be efficient and effective, must take account of several considerations;

1. The meaning of the information in each component database must be represented in a unified way (*semantic representation*)
2. A multidatabase system must interpret the meaning of the information in each component database (*semantic interpretation*)
3. A multidatabase system must integrate the information in all the component databases (*information integration*)
4. An efficient and effective access mechanism must be provided to retrieve desired information from the integrated information (*information access*)

2.2 Classification of Semantic Heterogeneity

Semantic heterogeneities include differences in the way the real world is modeled in the databases, particularly in the schemas of the databases [7]. Figure 1 shows an example to illustrate semantic heterogeneities.

Since a database is defined by its schema and data, semantic heterogeneities can be classified into schema conflict and data conflict [9]. Schema conflicts

Component Database 1 (CDB₁)

Undergraduate (sid, name, sex, address, advisor#)
Graduate (sid, name, sex, address, advisor#)
FullProfessor (pid, name, sex, office)
AssociateProfessor (pid, name, sex, office)
AssistantProfessor (pid, name, sex, office)

Component Database 2 (CDB₂)

Student (sid, nm, sex, advisor#)
Address (sid, street, city, state)
Professor (pid, nm, sex, salary, office)

Component Database 3 (CDB₃)

FemaleStudent (sid, name, street, city, state, advisor#)
MaleStudent (sid, name, street, city, state, advisor#)
FemaleProfessor (pid, name, salary, office)
MaleProfessor (pid, name, salary, office)

Component Database 4 (CDB₄)

Pupil (pid, nm, female, male, advisor#)
Teacher (tid, nm, office)

Fig. 1. Example database schemas

mainly result from the use of different structures for the same information and the use of different names for the same structures. For example, in figure 1, CDB_4 uses two attributes, **female** and **male**, for information on sex, while the same information is represented as values of the attribute **sex** in CDB_1. Data conflicts are due to inconsistent data in the absence of schema conflicts.

As our focus is only on the schema conflicts, we assume that data conflicts such as different representations for the same data are already conformed. Focusing on schema conflicts, we define the types of conflicts which are considered in this paper as follows.

- **Entity versus Entity Structure Conflicts (EESC)**
  These conflicts occur when component databases use different numbers of entities to represent the same information.
- **Entity versus Attribute Structure Conflicts (EASC)**
  This type of conflicts occurs if an attribute of some component databases is represented as an entity in others.
- **Entity versus Value Structure Conflicts (EVSC)**
  These conflicts occur when the attribute values in some component databases are semantically related to the entities in other component databases.
- **Attribute versus Attribute Structure Conflicts (AASC)**
  These conflicts occur when component databases use different numbers of attributes to represent the same information.
- **Attribute versus Value Structure Conflicts (AVSC)**
  These conflicts occur when the attribute values in some component databases are semantically related to the attributes in others.
- **Entity versus Entity Name Conflicts (EENC)**
  These conflicts arise due to different names assigned to the entities in different component databases.
- **Attribute versus Attribute Name Conflicts (AANC)**
  Attribute name conflicts are similar to the entity name conflicts.

2.3   An Overview of Our Approach for Knowledge Sharing

In our approach, we have made use of WordNet as linguistic knowledge to represent and interpret the meaning of the information, to integrate information, and to give users efficient access mechanism to the integrated system. The basic idea is to make a semantic network for each component database and to use WordNet to provide mapping between the semantic networks. Figure 2 shows an outline of out approach.

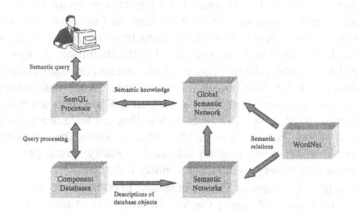

Fig. 2. An outline of our approach for knowledge sharing

Using WordNet and the descriptions of the database objects (entities and attributes), we construct a semantic network for each component database. Then, a global semantic network can be created with the semantic relations in Word-Net and the semantic networks. A global semantic network provides semantic knowledge about a distributed environment. Also, we provide a semantic query language, SemQL, to capture the concepts about what users want, which enables users to issue queries to a large number of autonomous databases without knowledge of their schemas.

3   Information Integration Process

As mentioned in section 2, to integrate information from multiple component databases, users must represent the meaning of the information in each component database in a unified way. At each component database (CDB), to represent the information, a local database administrator (DBA) makes descriptions of the database objects. In making descriptions, we make reference to ISO/IEC 11179 [10]. Using the descriptions and WordNet, users create a representation table. Then, a semantic network for the component database can be created according to the representation table. All the semantic networks in the component databases shall be integrated into a global semantic network for a multidatabase system.

3.1 Semantic Representation

The following are principles that must be used to make descriptions in order to represent the meaning of the information in a component database. A description can be formed with syntactic and semantic rules. Semantic rules govern the source and content of the words used in a description and enable meaning to be conveyed. Semantics concerns the meanings of description components. The components are entity terms, property terms, key terms, and qualifier terms. An entity term is a component of a description which represents an activity or object in real world. For example, in a description *Student Last Name*, the component *Student* is entity term. A set of property terms must consist of terms which are discrete(the definition of each does not overlap the definition of any other), and complete(taken together, the set represents all information concepts required for the specification of database objects). For example, in the description *Student Last Name*, the component *Last Name* is property. A key term is a component of a description for a database object, which describes the form of representation of the database object. For example, in *Student Last Name*, the component *Name* is key term. Qualifier terms may be attached to entity terms, property terms, and key terms if necessary to uniquely identify a description.

Syntactic principles specify the arrangement of components within a description. The entity term shall occupy the first (leftmost) position in the description. Qualifier terms shall precede the component qualified. The property term shall occupy the next position. And, the key term shall occupy the last position. No abbreviations are allowed. For example, a description *Student ID* is not allowed. It must be *Student Identification Number*. Furthermore, All descriptions shall be unique within a component database.

After descriptions are created according to the above rules, the descriptions are decomposed into unit terms. A unit term means a word or a phrase that can be found in WordNet. For example, as a compound noun, 'phone number', can be found in WordNet, it is treated as a unit term. The result for this decomposing process is a representation table. A representation table consists of object type, object name, data type, description, and a set of unit terms.

In making a representation table, the CDB administrator must cope with synonymy and polysemy. To identify unit terms related by synonymy automatically, we use synsets in WordNet. However, to acquire correct meaning of a unit term, the CDB administrator must deal with its polysemy manually, For example, when the local DBA inputs a unit term 'client' into WordNet, he/she must choose one among many different meanings.

Given a set of unit terms of a component database, each unit term is connected with a word(or a phrase) in WordNet. The output for this process is a semantic network. A semantic network provides mappings between words in WordNet and unit terms in a component database. Figure 3 shows a semantic network for CDB_2 of figure 1.

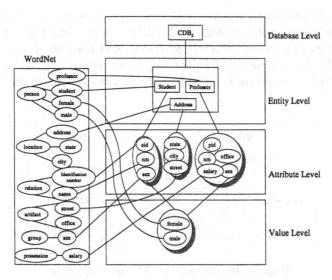

Fig. 3. A semantic network for CDB_2

3.2 Semantic Interpretation and Information Integration

A multidatabase system must interpret the meaning of the information and identify semantically equivalent or related objects. Once semantic networks are constructed, they are integrated into a global semantic network. In integrating semantic networks, a multidatabase system can detect and resolve semantic heterogeneity based on them.

The following are examples that show how we can detect semantic heterogeneity based on the semantic networks and the semantic relations in WordNet. The examples are explained with schemas in 2.2. The results of detection process can be used to resolve semantic heterogeneity in information access phase.

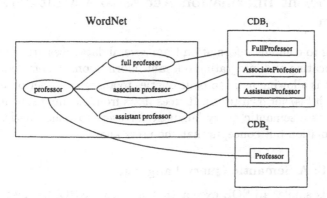

Fig. 4. Detection of EESC using hyponymy semantic relation

Figure 4 shows a partial state of merging two component databases. According to hyponymy semantic relation in WordNet, we can find that *professor* is a hypernym of *full professor*, *associate professor*, and *assistant professor*. Therefore, the entity **Professor** in CDB_2 is semantically equivalent to the set of entities, {**FullProfessor, AssociateProfessor, AssistantProfessor**}, in CDB_1.

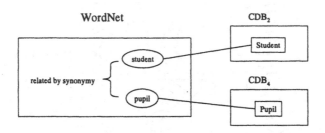

Fig. 5. Detection of EENC using synsets

Consider another example that shows the use of synsets in WordNet. Figure 5 depicts the detection of EENC using synsets. As *student* and *pupil* are synonymous in WordNet, we can interpret that the meaning of the two entities, **Student** in CDB_2 and **Pupil** in CDB_4, are the same.

The output for merging phase is a global semantic network. A global semantic network provides a multidatabase system with necessary knowledge for integrated access to component databases. The types of knowledge are as follows.

– A multidatabase system must know where to find the relevant information on the component databases (*access knowledge*).
– A multidatabase system must know which entities, attributes, or values in the component databases meet the semantics in the query (*semantic knowledge*).

4   An Efficient Information Access to a Multidatabase System

Users needing to combine information from several databases are faced with the problem of locating and integrating relevant information. An efficient and effective approach is allowing users to issue queries to a large number of autonomous databases with his/her own terms. It frees users from learning schema. We propose SemQL as a semantic query language for users to issue queries using not schema information but concepts that the users know.

4.1   SemQL: A Semantic Query Language

The SemQL is similar to SQL except that it has no FROM clause. The basic form of the SemQL is formed of the two clauses SELECT and WHERE and has the following form:

> SELECT ⟨concept list⟩
>
> WHERE ⟨condition⟩

Here ⟨concept list⟩ is a list of concepts whose values are to be retrieved by the query. The ⟨condition⟩ is a conditional search expression that identifies the tuples to be retrieved by the query.

The SemQL clauses specify not the entity or attribute names in component database schemas but the concept names about what users want. For example, suppose a user wants to find those professor whose salary is over $50,000. We assume that the user is familiar with SQL, but knows neither of the component database schemas. Then the user might issue a query in SemQL using the concepts that he/she knows;

> SELECT professor.name
>
> WHERE professor.salary > $50,000

4.2   Semantic Query Processing Procedure

The overall procedure of semantic query processing is shown in figure 6. The SemQL Processor consists of Query Parser, Resource Finder, Mapping Generator, Sub-query Generator, Query Distributor and Integrator.

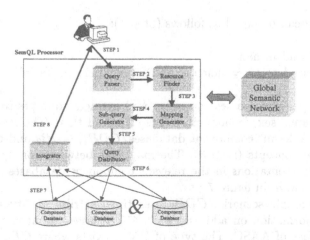

Fig. 6. The overall procedure of semantic query processing

Step 1: Users issue a semantic query with his/her own concepts to retrieve equivalent or related data items.

Step 2: The *Query Parser* parses the query and extracts entity, attribute and value concepts from the query.

Step 3: The *Resource Finder* identifies the relevant component databases where the concepts exist using a **global semantic network**.

Step 4: The *Mapping Generator* generates the mappings between concepts in original query and representations in component databases.

Step 5: The *Sub-query Generator* re-formulates the original query into multiple sub-queries for each component database schema according to the mappings. In this step, looking up the global semantic network, Sub-query Generator adds FROM clause to the sub-query.

Step 6: The *Query Distributor* submits the sub-queries to the component databases.

Step 7: The component databases receive the sub-query and execute it. And then return the result tuples to the **SemQL Processor**.

Step 8: The *Integrator* merges the intermediate results from various component databases and presents the integrated results to the users.

In this subsection, we introduce an example query scenario to demonstrate the procedure of semantic query process of our approach. Through the example scenario, we will also explain how the semantic conflicts can be resolved using the global semantic network. The example query is to find those female students who live in Seoul. We assume that the user who issues the query only knows the concepts about what he/she want. That is, the user does not know the detailed schema structure for each component database.

QUERY: Find those female students who live in Seoul.

The query can be posed as follows (Step 1):

SELECT student.name
WHERE student.sex = 'female' AND student.city = 'Seoul'

The *Query Parser* parses the query and extracts concepts from the query - {student, name, sex, female, city} (Step 2). And then, The *Resource Finder* identifies the relevant component databases, CDB_1, CDB_2 and CDB_3, which posses all the concepts (Step 3). The mappings between concepts in original query and representations in the relevant component databases are generated (Step 4) and shown in figure 7.

In this example scenario, CDB_3 uses three attributes, **street**, **city**, and **state**, for information on address, while CDB_1 uses one attribute, **address**. This is the case of AASC. The type of EASC exists where CDB_1 uses an attribute, **address**, in the **Student** entity to represent the student's address, and CDB_2 represents the same information in the **Address** entity. As CDB_3 uses the **FemaleStudent** entity for female students, and the same information for

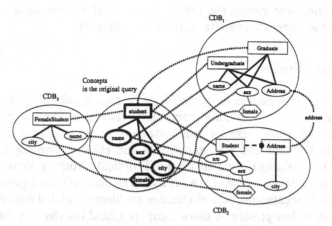

Fig. 7. The mappings between concepts and database objects for the example scenario

sex is represented as values of the **sex** attribute in CDB_1, the type of EVSC also occurs in the example scenario.

Now, the *Sub-query Generator* re-formulates the original query into three sub-queries for CDB_1, CDB_2 and CDB_3 according to the mappings (Step 5). Thus, the sub-query for CDB_1 might be;

    SELECT name
    FROM Undergraduate
    WHERE sex = 'female' AND address LIKE '%Seoul%'
    UNION
    SELECT name
    FROM Graduate
    WHERE sex = 'female' AND address LIKE '%Seoul%'

The original query might be re-formulated for CDB_2;

    SELECT Student.nm
    FROM Student, Address
    WHERE Student.sid = Address.sid AND Address.city = 'Seoul'

and for CDB_3;

    SELECT name
    FROM FemaleStudent
    WHERE city = 'Seoul'

After the *Sub-query Generator* re-formulates the original query into sub-queries, the *Query Distributor* sends them to CDB_1, CDB_2 and CDB_3, respectively (Step 6). The three component databases, CDB_1, CDB_2 and CDB_3, return the result tuples of the sub-queries to the **SemQL Processor** (Step 7).

Finally, the *Integrator* merges the results from the three component databases and presents the integrated results to the users (Step 8).

5   Related Works

Early researches on semantic heterogeneities in multidatabase systems focused on procedures to merge individual component database schemas into a single global schema. A global schema multidatabase supports a single, integrated global view to the user and provides simple and effective paradigm. However, creating and maintaining the global schema is difficult. Multidatabase languages are an attempt to resolve some of the problems associated with a global schema. Multidatabase language approach eliminates problems of global schema creation and maintenance, but presents a more complex global interface to the user.

In several researches [4][8], new approaches have been developed for integrating of information using new technological developments such as agent technology, domain ontologies, intelligent mediator, and high-level query languages, in dynamic and open environments. These approaches were designed to support flexibility and openness. A common assumption of these dynamic approaches is that users know pre-existing knowledge for integrating information, which might be a burden to the users.

Recent advances in online dictionaries and thesauruses make it possible to apply linguistic theory in an automated fashion, which enable users to perform integrating information more comfortably. The Summary Schemas Model (SSM) is proposed as an extension to multidatabase systems to aid in semantic identification [2]. The system uses the global data structure to match the user's terms to the semantically closest available system terms. However, this approach tends to centralize the search within a single logical index thereby introducing performance limitations for large networks.

As linguistic theories evolved in recent decades, linguists became increasingly explicit about the information a lexicon must contain in order for the phonological, syntactic, and lexical components to work together in the everyday production and comprehension of linguistic messages [6]. WordNet is an electronic lexical system developed at Princeton University. Several approaches [3][5] use WordNet as knowledge about the semantic contents of images to improve retrieval effectiveness. In particular, [3] uses WordNet for query and database expansion.

6   Summary and Conclusion

Using WordNet as linguistic knowledge, we have suggested a method for knowledge sharing among multiple databases. From the descriptions of database objects, we construct a semantic network to represent the meaning of the information in a component database. In merging semantic networks into a global semantic network, we can interpret the information in the same way as intended by a component database. A global semantic network provides a multidatabase system with necessary knowledge for integrated access to component databases, such as access knowledge and semantic knowledge. With the global semantic network and a semantic query language, SemQL, we give users an efficient and effective access mechanism to integrated information. SemQL captures the concepts about what users want, which enables users to issue queries to a large number of autonomous databases without knowledge of their schemas.

As it is not possible for any system to capture semantics without human interaction, creating a semantic network requires some initial input from users. So, user's descriptions for database objects are crucial for our approach. Weak and wrong descriptions may degrade the information integration system, which shall be drawback of our approach. However, if users make descriptions according to our guidelines, the information integration system let users focus on specifying what they want, rather than thinking about how to obtain the information. That is, our approach for the information integration system frees users from the tremendous tasks of finding the relevant information sources and interacting with each information source using a particular interface. Furthermore, in our approach, each information source needs no knowledge of other information sources for information integration, which diminishes a burden of the information source.

References

1. Amit Sheth, Vipul Kashyap: So Far(Schematically) yet So Near(Semantically), Proceedings, IFIP WG 2.6 Conference on Semantics of Interoperable Database Systems(Data Semantics 5) (1993) 283-312
2. A. R. Hurson, M. W. Bright: Global Information Access for Microcomputers, Journal of Mini and Micro Computer Applications (1991)
3. Aslandogan, Y. A., C. Thier, C. T. Yu, J. Zou and N. Rishe: Using semantic contents and WordNet in image retrieval, Proceedings of the 20th Annual ACM SIGIR Conference on Research and Development in Information Retrieval (1997)
4. Craig A. Knoblock, Yigal Arens, and Chun-Nan Hsu: Cooperating Agents for Information Retrieval, Proceedings of the second International Conference on Cooperative Information Systems (1994)
5. Eugene J. G. And Neil C. R.: Natural-Language Retrieval of Images Based on Descriptive Captions, In ACM Transactions on Information Systems 14(3) (1996)
6. G. A. Miller, R. Beckwith, C. Fellbaum, D.Gross, and K. Miller: Five Papers on WordNet, CSL Reort 43, Cognitive Systems Laboratory, Priceton Univ. (1990)
7. M. Garcia-Solaco, F. Saltor, and M. Castellanos: Semantic Heterogeneity in Multidatabase Systems, Object-Oriented Multidatabase Systems: A Solution for Advanced Applications, Edited by Orman A. Bukhres, Ahmed K. Elmagarmid, Prentice Hall Inc. (1996) 129-202
8. R. Bayardo, W. Bohrer, et al: InfoSleuth: agent-based semantic integration of information in open and dynamic environments, ACM SIGMOD Record, Vol. 26, No. 2 (1997)
9. W. Kim, J. Seo: Classifying Schematic and Data Heterogeneity in Multidatabase Systems, IEEE Computer, Vol. 24, No. 12 (1992) 12-18
10. Specification and standardization of data elements, ISO/IEC 11179

Representing 'Just Invalid' Knowledge

John Debenham

University of Technology, Sydney,
School of Computing Sciences,
PO Box 123, NSW 2007, Australia
debenham@socs.uts.edu.au

Abstract. Data, information and knowledge are all represented in a single formalism as "items". Items contain two types of acceptability measures that measure the invalidity of item instances. Objects are item building operators that also contain two types of acceptability measures. These acceptability measures define a graduated acceptability region for data, information and knowledge. This region represents 'just invalid' knowledge. A quantitative calculus estimates the extent to which a knowledge base may be expected to extend into this region as time passes. This calculus is simplified by the use of the unified knowledge representation. A single rule of knowledge decomposition simplifies the structure of the conceptual model. Expressions in this calculus are simplified if the knowledge has been decomposed.

Keywords: expert systems, knowledge representation.

1. Introduction

The terms 'data', 'information' and 'knowledge' are used here in a rather idiosyncratic sense [1]. The *data* in an application are those things that can be represented as simple constants or variables. The *information* is those things that can berepresented as tuples or relations. The *knowledge* is those things that can be represented either as programs in an imperative language or as rules in a declarative language. A unified knowledge representation for conceptual modelling is described in [2]. That representation is *unified* in the sense that no distinction is made between the knowledge, information and data throughout the design process. A conceptual model is expressed in terms of "items" and "objects" [3]; objects are item-building operators. A single rule for "knowledge decomposition" [4] simplifies the maintenance of the conceptual model and its implementation. Classical database normalisation [5] is a special case of that single rule. The conceptual model reported in [2] is extended here to describe 'just invalid' knowledge. This is achieved by introducing fuzzy functions to describe a graduated region of varying degrees of acceptability, and by introducing a calculus that estimates the extent to which a knowledge base may decay and extend into this graduated region as time passes. These fuzzy functions are generalisations of the knowledge constraints described in [6].

Approaches to the *preservation* of knowledge base integrity *either* aim to design the knowledge base so that it is inherently maintainable [2] *or* to present the knowledge in a form that discourages the introduction of inconsistencies [7].

N. Foo (Ed.): AI'99, LNAI 1747, pp. 84–95, 1999.

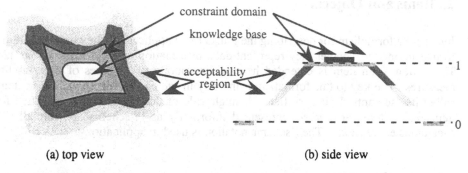

(a) top view   (b) side view

Fig. 1. Knowledge base, constraint domain and acceptability region

Constraints are seldom mentioned in connection with knowledge; they can play a useful role in preserving knowledge base integrity. An approach to specifying knowledge constraints is described in [6]. Those constraints are two-valued in the sense that either they are satisfied or they aren't. The *constraint domain* is the union of all knowledge base instances that satisfy a given set of knowledge constraints. The constraint domain can be visualised as an area within which a given knowledge base should reside, and outside which the integrity of chunks of knowledge should be questioned.

The two-valued division of knowledge by the constraint domain is too crude to describe 'just invalid' knowledge. But an "acceptability region" in which knowledge is "more acceptable" the "closer" it is to the constraint domain could make such a claim. Acceptability is defined in that sense here. A knowledge base's *acceptability region* is a graduated region which raises questions of integrity at differing degrees of confidence. This acceptability region may be visualised as "a halo surrounding" the knowledge base. This is illustrated in Fig. 1 where in (b) "1" means "true" and "0" means "false".

A calculus estimates the effects of knowledge decay. The definition of this calculus is simplified by the unified knowledge representation. Expressions in this calculus are simplified if the knowledge has been decomposed. The work described here has a rigorous, formal theoretical basis expressed in terms of the λ-calculus; the work may also be presented informally in terms of schema. Schema are used when the methodology is applied in practice.

[part/sale-price, part/cost-price, mark-up]

part/sale-price		part/cost-price		mark-up
part-number	dollar-amount	part-number	dollar-amount	factor-%
1234	1.48	1234	1.23	1.2
2468	2.81	2468	2.34	1.2
3579	4.14	3579	3.45	1.2
8642	5.47	8642	4.56	1.2
7531	6.80	7531	5.67	1.2
1470	8.14	1470	6.78	1.2

Fig. 2. Value set of the item *[part/sale-price, part/cost-price, mark-up]*

2. Items and Objects

Items are a formalism for describing the things in an application; they have a uniform format no matter whether they represent data, information or knowledge things [2]. The notion of an item is extended here to incorporate two classes of acceptability measures. The key to this formalism is the way in which the "meaning" of an item, called its "semantics", is specified. A single rule of decomposition is specified for items [8]. Items are *either* represented informally as "i-schema" *or* formally as λ-calculus expressions. The i-schema notation is used in applications.

2.1 The Value Set

The *semantics* of an item is a function that *recognises* the members of the "value set" of that item. The *value set* of an information item is the set of tuples that are associated with a relational implementation of that item. Knowledge items, including complex, recursive knowledge items, have value sets too [2]. For example, the item, which represents the rule "the sale price of parts is the cost price marked up by a universal mark-up factor", could have a value set as shown in Fig. 2.

The value set of an item will change in time τ, but an item's semantics should remain constant. The value set of a knowledge item at a certain time τ is a (possibly infinite) set of tuples such as the set illustrated in Fig. 2.

2.2 Item Acceptability Measures

Formally, given a unique name A, an n-tuple $(m_1, m_2, \ldots, m_n)$, $M = \Sigma_i \, m_i$, if:

• S_A is an M-argument expression of the form:

$$\lambda y_1^1 \ldots y_{m_1}^1 \ldots y_{m_n}^n \bullet [S_{A_1}(y_1^1,\ldots,y_{m_1}^1) \circ \ldots \circ S_{A_n}(y_1^n,\ldots,y_{m_n}^n) \circ J(y_1^1,\ldots,y_{m_1}^1,\ldots,y_{m_n}^n)]\bullet$$

where $\{A_1,\ldots, A_n\}$ is an ordered set of not necessarily distinct items, each item in this set is called a *component* of item A.

• V_A is an M-argument fuzzy expression [9] of the form:

$$\lambda y_1^1 \ldots y_{m_1}^1 \ldots y_{m_n}^n \bullet [V_{A_1}(y_1^1,\ldots,y_{m_1}^1) \circ \ldots \circ V_{A_n}(y_1^n,\ldots,y_{m_n}^n) \circ K(y_1^1,\ldots,y_{m_1}^1,\ldots,y_{m_n}^n)]\bullet$$

where $\{A_1,\ldots, A_n\}$ are the components of item A, K is a fuzzy predicate and $\circ$ is the fuzzy "min" conjunction.

• C_A is a fuzzy expression of the form:

$$[\, C_{A_1} \circ C_{A_2} \circ \ldots \circ C_{A_n} \circ (L)_A \,]$$

where $\circ$ is the fuzzy "min" conjunction and L is a fuzzy expression constructed as a logical combination of:

• $Card_A$ lies in some numerical range;
• $Uni(A_i)$ for some i, $1 \le i \le n$, and
• $Can(A_i, X)$ for some i, $1 \le i \le n$, where X is a non-empty subset of
$$\{A_1,\ldots, A_n\} - \{A_i\};$$

subscripted with the name of the item A,

then the named triple $A[\ S_A,\ V_A,\ C_A]$ is an M-adic *item* with *item name* A, S_A is called the *item semantics* of A, V_A is called the *item value acceptability measure* of A and C_A is called the *item set acceptability measure* of A. "Uni(A_i)" is a fuzzy predicate whose truth value is "the proportion of the members of the value set of item A_i that also occur in the value set of item A". "Can(A_i, X)" is a fuzzy predicate whose truth value is "in the value set of item A, the proportion of members of the value set of the set of items X that functionally determine members of the value set of item A_i,". "Card$_A$" means "the number of different values in the value set of item A". The subscripts identify the item's components to which that measure applies. Given an item A and tuple X, if $V_A(X) < 1$ but 'close' to 1 then X is *just invalid* in the value set of A. Also, if $C_A < 1$ but 'close' to 1 then A is *just invalid*.

For example, an application may contain an association whereby each *part* is associated with a *cost-price*. This association could be represented by the information item named *part/cost-price*; the λ-calculus form for this item is:

part/cost-price[

$\quad \lambda xy \bullet [\ S_{part}(x)\ \circ\ S_{cost\text{-}price}(y)\ \circ\ costs(x,\ y)\ ] \bullet$,

$\quad \lambda xy \bullet [\ V_{part}(x)\ \circ\ V_{cost\text{-}price}(y)\ \circ\ K_1(x,\ y)\ ] \bullet$,

$\quad [\ C_{part}\ \circ\ C_{cost\text{-}price}\ \circ\ (L_1)_{part/cost\text{-}price}\ ]\ ]$

for some fuzzy predicates K_1 and L_1, where costs(x, y) is a first-order predicate that means "x costs y". Rules, or knowledge, can also be defined as items. For example, the semantics of the *[part/sale-price, part/cost-price, mark-up]* item is:

$\lambda x_1 x_2 y_1 y_2 z \bullet [\ S_{part/sale\text{-}price}(x_1, x_2)\ \circ\ S_{part/cost\text{-}price}(y_1, y_2)$

$\quad \circ\ S_{mark\text{-}up}(z)\ \circ\ ((x_1 = y_1)\ \rightarrow\ (x_2 = z \times y_2))] \bullet$

The *semantics* of an item is a function that recognises the members of that item's value set. The *value acceptability* measure of an item is a fuzzy estimate of the likelihood that a given tuple is *not* in the item's value set. The value acceptability measure does not attempt to estimate the likelihood that a tuple *is* in the item's value set as that task is performed by the item's semantics. The *set acceptability* measure of an item is a fuzzy estimate of the likelihood that the general structure of the item's value set is invalid. So an item's semantics specifies what *should be* in an implementation, and the two acceptability measures are measures of invalidity of what *is* in an implementation. If an acceptability measure does *not* detect invalidity to any level of (fuzzy) significance then this does *not* imply that an implementation is valid.

For example, an application could contain a spare-part thing that is represented by the item *part*. If spare parts are identified by their part-number then the semantics of *part* is $\lambda x \bullet [is\text{-}a[x:part\text{-}number]] \bullet$ where the function ":" means "x *if* x is in P" and "undefined *otherwise*". Suppose that the generally expected range for part numbers is [0, 2 000]. Then the value acceptability measure for the item *part* could be $\lambda x \bullet [f(x)] \bullet$ where:

$$f(x) = \begin{cases} 0 & \text{if} & x < 0 \\ 1 & \text{if} & 0 \leq x \leq 2\,000 \\ 2 - \dfrac{x}{2\,000} & \text{if} & 2\,000 < x < 4\,000 \\ 0 & \text{if} & x \geq 4\,000 \end{cases}$$

Card_{part} is the number of *different* part-numbers. Suppose that the generally expected range for Card_{part} is less than 100. Then the set acceptability measure, C_{part}, for the item *part* is a fuzzy predicate; it could be:

$$C_{part} = \begin{cases} 1 & \text{if } \text{Card}_{part} \leq 100 \\ 2 - \dfrac{\text{Card}_{part}}{100} & \text{if } 100 < \text{Card}_{part} < 200 \\ 0 & \text{if } \text{Card}_{part} \geq 200 \end{cases}$$

In the *part/cost-price* example above, a simple expression for K_1 could be:

$$K_1(x, y) = \begin{cases} \dfrac{50}{y} & \text{if } 0 \leq x \leq 2 \quad 000 \text{ and } y \geq 50 \\ 1 & \text{otherwise} \end{cases}$$

and L_1 could be Can(*cost*, *part*); ie the proportion of part numbers that functionally determine their cost price in the association *part/cost-price*. In this way, value and set acceptability measures are developed for data items, and similarly for information and knowledge items.

Items make it difficult to analyse the structure of the whole application because, for example, two rules that share the same basic wisdom may be expressed in terms of quite different components; this could obscure their common wisdom. To make the inherent structure of knowledge clear 'objects' are introduced as item building operators [2].

2.3 Objects

Object names are written in bold italics. Suppose that the conceptual model already contains the item "*part*" which represents spare parts, and the item "*cost-price*" which represents cost prices; then the information "spare parts have a cost price" can be represented by "*part/cost-price*" which may be built by applying the "*costs*" object to *part* and *cost-price*:

part/cost-price = *costs* (*part*, *cost-price*)

Suppose that the conceptual model already contains the item "*part/sale-price*" which represents the association between spare parts and their corresponding selling price, and the item "*mark-up*" which represents the data thing a universal mark-up factor; then the rule "spare parts are marked up by a universal mark up factor" can be represented by *[part/sale-price,part/cost-price,mark-up]* which is built by applying the "*mark-up-rule*" object to the items "*part/sale-price*", "*part/cost-price*" and "*mark-up*":

[part/sale-price, part/cost-price, mark-up] =
    mark-up-rule (*part/sale-price*, *part/cost-price*, *mark-up*)

The conceptual model contains items.   A fundamental set of data items in the conceptual model is called the "basis". The remaining items in the conceptual model are built by applying object operators to the other items in the conceptual model.   As for items, objects may either be represented informally as "o-schema" or formally as typed λ-calculus expressions.

2.4 Decomposition

In [8] the decomposition of items and objects is described. Decomposition removes hidden relationships from the conceptual model. Hidden relationships can present a maintenance hazard. Here decomposition simplifies the estimation of knowledge base decay.

Item join provides the basis for item decomposition. Given the items A and B, the item with name $A \otimes_E B$ is called the *join* of A and B on E, where E is a set of components common to both A and B [8].   Using the rule of composition $\otimes$, knowledge items, information items and data items may be joined with one another regardless of type. For example, the knowledge item:

$[cost\text{-}price, tax]$ $[\lambda xy\bullet[\ S_{cost\text{-}price}(x) \circ S_{tax}(y) \circ (y = x \times 0.05)]\bullet,$

  $\lambda xy\bullet[\ V_{cost\text{-}price}(x) \circ V_{tax}(y) \circ K_2(x, y)\ ]\bullet,$

  $[\ C_{cost\text{-}price} \circ C_{tax} \circ (L_2)_{[cost\text{-}price, tax]}\ ]\ ]$

for some K_2 and L_2 can be joined with the information item *part/cost-price* on the set $\{cost\text{-}price\}$ to give the information item *part/cost-price/tax*. In other words:

$[cost\text{-}price, tax]$ $\otimes_{\{cost\text{-}price\}}$ *part/cost-price* =

  part/cost-price/tax$[\ \lambda xyz\bullet[\ S_{part}(x) \circ S_{cost\text{-}price}(y) \circ S_{tax}(z) \circ$

    $costs(x, y) \circ (z = y \times 0.05)]\bullet,$

  $\lambda xyz\bullet[\ V_{part}(x) \circ V_{cost\text{-}price}(y) \circ V_{tax}(z) \circ K_1(x, y) \circ K_2(y, z)\ ]\bullet,$

  $[\ C_{part} \circ C_{cost\text{-}price} \circ C_{tax} \circ (L_1 \circ L_2)_{part/cost\text{-}price/tax}\ ]\ ]$

In this way items may be joined together to form more complex items. Alternatively, the $\otimes$ operator may form the basis of a theory of decomposition in which each item may be replaced by a set of simpler items.   An item I is *decomposable* into the set of items $D = \{I_1, I_2,..., I_n\}$ if: I_i has non-trivial semantics for all i, $I = I_1 \otimes I_2 \otimes ... \otimes I_n$, where each join is *monotonic*; that is, each term in this composition contributes at least one component to I [8]. *If* item I is decomposable then it will not necessarily have a unique decomposition.

3. Estimating Knowledge Base Validity

The semantics of an item $A[\ S_A, V_A, C_A]$ is a function that recognises the members of its value set. The value set is a conceptual notion in the system design.

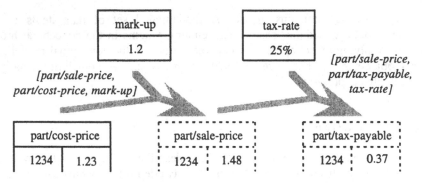

Fig. 3. Real and virtual items

So the value set of the item A—as in the definition of an M-adic item above—at time τ is:

$$\gamma^\tau(A) \;=\; \{\; y_1^1...y_{m_1}^1...y_{m_n}^n \;:\; S_A(y_1^1,..,y_{m_1}^1,..,y_{m_n}^n) \;\; \text{at time } \tau \;\}$$

A *knowledge base implementation* is a set of knowledge items and a set of stored relations and data domains representing some information and data items. Some information and data items are associated with actual stored data, and some are not. Knowledge items are not normally associated with actual stored data. If an item is associated with actual stored data then it is a *real item*; otherwise it is a *virtual item*.

The set of tuples in the implementation of the *real* item A is denoted by $\lambda^\alpha(A)$ where α is the time of the most recent modification to those tuples. Knowledge items may be used to derive tuples for virtual data and information items. For example, suppose that the real data item *mark-up* has a stored data value mark-up, and that the real information item *part/cost-price* has a stored relation part/cost-price. Then the knowledge item *[part/sale-price, part/cost-price, mark-up]*—or an "if-then" implementation of it—may be used to *derive* tuples in the relation for the virtual item *part/sale-price*. Further, the knowledge item *[part/sale-price, part/tax-payable, tax-rate]* could then enable the tuples in the relation for the virtual item *part/tax-payable* to be derived. This is illustrated in Fig. 3. If a virtual item A_i is a component of a knowledge item A where the tuples (or data values) associated with A_i are derived from $\{\; \lambda^{\alpha_j}(A_j) : A_j$ is a component of A, $j \neq i \;\}$ using the knowledge A then A_i is *derivable* and those tuples (or data values) are called the *derived set* which is denoted by $\lambda^\beta(A_i)$ where β is the time at which the derivation is performed. This definition is recursive. In Fig. 3 only part/cost-price, mark-up and tax-rate are stored. This example shows how the validity of the calculation of the tuples in the relation for the virtual item *part/tax-payable* relies on the validity of those three real items *and* on the validity of those two knowledge items. So if the validity of any of those three real items or either of those two knowledge items has "decayed" in some way then that calculation *may* yield an incorrect result.

For a knowledge base, its implementation may not be valid because *updates* that should have been performed were not, or *modifications* that should not have been performed were. The corruption of a knowledge base by such modifications is not considered here. The failure to perform updates is considered. So *updates* are changes

$\lambda^\alpha(part)$	$\Lambda^\tau(part)$	$\lambda^\alpha(part/cost\text{-}price)$		$\Lambda^\tau(part/cost\text{-}price)$	
part	*part*	*part/cost-price*		*part/cost-price*	
part-number	part-number	part-number	dollar-amount	part-number	dollar-amount
1234	1234	1234	1.20	1234	1.20
2345	2345	2345	2.40	2345	2.60
2468	2456	2468	3.60	2456	0.60
3456	2468	3456	4.80	2468	3.80
3579	3456	3579	5.10	3456	4.80
4567	3579	4567	6.30	3579	5.20
	4680			4680	0.80

Fig. 4. The implementation and the true set

that should have been performed on the implementation of real items or knowledge items. In addition, incorrect values may be attributed to a knowledge base implementation because the derived tuples for some virtual items were calculated prior to required updates being performed [10]. At time α the *true set* for a—real or virtual—item A is the set of tuples that should be associated with A at time α; it is denoted by $\Lambda^\alpha(A)$. In other words, the implementation is what *is* either stored or derived in the knowledge base, the true set is what *should be* either stored or derived.

Suppose that the implementation of the real data item *part* was stored at time α. Then at a subsequent time τ the implementation and the true set may be as shown on the left side of Fig. 4. In that Figure the implementation for the data item *part* contains the part number "4567" that should *not* be there, and does *not* contain two part numbers which *should* be there. Suppose that the implementation for the real information item *part/cost-price* was stored at time α. Then at a subsequent time τ the implementation and the true set may be as shown on the right side of Fig. 4. Likewise the implementation and the true set of a knowledge item may contain tuples that should not be there, and may not contain tuples that should be there.

Fig. 3 shows a knowledge base implementation consisting of two knowledge items, three information items and two data items. If the design and implementation are correct then the tuples associated with each real or virtual item will be the same as that item's true set.

3.1 Item and Object Validity

At time τ, the true set $\Lambda^\tau(A)$ and $\lambda^\alpha(A)$, $\alpha \le \tau$, of item A may not be the same. The implementation of a real item is "correct" as long as its tuples have been correctly stored and maintained [11]. The derived set of a virtual item is "correct" as long as the knowledge used to derive the tuples for that item has been correctly maintained *and* the stored data used by that knowledge has been correctly maintained. In reality we may hope that the implementation is correct, and expect that it is incorrect. To measure the extent that the implementation or the derived set are the same as the true set, let $p_{X/Y}$ be the proportion of those elements in set X that are also in set Y. Then the *difference measure*:

$$\Delta(A, B) = \sqrt{p_{A/B} \times p_{B/A}}$$

is unity if both sets are identical and is zero if one set contains no elements from the other; the square root ensures that this measure retains linearity with measured proportion. For example, if each set contains exactly half of the members of the other set then the value of this measure is 0.5. The value of the difference measure is *not* necessarily equal to the proportion of valid members in either set because the difference measure takes account of those elements that are not in each set but should be there. The *validity* of a real or virtual item A at time τ is:

$$\delta_A(\tau) = \Delta(\lambda^\tau(A), \Lambda^\alpha(A))$$

where $\tau \geq \alpha$ and the difference measure Δ is as defined above. $0 \leq \delta_A(\tau) \leq 1$. If $\delta_A(\tau) = 1$ then item A is *valid*. If $\delta_A(\tau) = 0$ then the set of tuples associated with item A contains no tuples that it should contain and A is *completely invalid*.

The knowledge item *[part/sale-price, part/cost-price, mark-up]* is built by applying the knowledge object **mark-up-rule** to the three items *part/sale-price*, *part/cost-price* and *mark-up*. That knowledge item may be used to derive tuples for the information item *part/sale-price*. The accuracy of these derived tuples relies on the implementation of the two real items *mark-up* and *part/cost-price* being accurate *and* on the knowledge object **mark-up-rule** being accurate. The integrity of these items and objects is expected to decay as time progresses.

If we know precisely what knowledge decay has occurred then we can usually rectify it [12]. In practice we tend to have some loose expectation ε of the validity δ. For example, we may expect that "within a year the whole part/cost-price relation will be out of date". So our expectation for the validity of the *part/cost-price* item may be represented by a function with a linear decay of one year's extent. Also, we may expect that "as the 'types' of parts are redesignated, the contents of the part/type relation will decay decreasingly over time so that in a year roughly half of the relation will be out of date and in a 'very long time' the whole relation will be out of date". So our expectation for the validity of the *part/type* item may be represented by a function with an exponential decay with a half-life of one year. The validity estimates for these two examples are:

$$\varepsilon_{part/cost-price}(\tau) = \begin{cases} 1 - \tau & \text{if } 0 \leq \tau \leq 1 \\ 0 & \text{otherwise} \end{cases}$$

$$\varepsilon_{part/type}(\tau) = 2^{-\tau} \text{ for } \tau \geq 0$$

The validity of an object will contribute to the validity of any item generated by that object. But objects do not have a value set or an implementation. The validity of the item A, generated using object B, $A = B(C, D, E, F)$ may be analysed completely in terms of the validity of items C, D, E and F and the validity of object B. In other words, if items C, D, E and F are valid then the validity of item A will be attributable entirely to the validity of object B. So the *validity* of an object is the validity of any item generated by that object when applied to a set of valid items.

3.2 Propagating Validity Estimates

It would be convenient if:

$$\varepsilon_{ob}(cc, dd)(\tau) = \varepsilon_{ob}(\tau) \times \varepsilon_{cc}(\tau) \times \varepsilon_{dd}(\tau)$$

but this product rule is *not* valid in general because the validity of the components—in the above example the components are *cc* and *dd*—may be logically dependent. This product rule is valid if the validity of the object *ob* and the validity of the two component items are all independent. If the validity of X is independent of the validity of Y then $(\varepsilon_X(\tau) \mid \varepsilon_Y(\tau)) = \varepsilon_X(\tau)$. If the validity of X is determined by the validity of Y then $(\varepsilon_X(\tau) \mid \varepsilon_Y(\tau)) = \varepsilon_Y(\tau)$.

Suppose that object *ob* is applied to a set of n component items $C = \{cc, D\}$ where *cc* is a component item and D is a set of n-1 component items. The general rule for propagating validity estimates through an object operator is:

$$\models \quad \varepsilon_{ob}(C)(\tau) = \varepsilon_{ob}(\tau) \times (\varepsilon_C(\tau) \mid \varepsilon_{ob}(\tau))$$
$$= \varepsilon_C(\tau) \times (\varepsilon_{ob}(\tau) \mid \varepsilon_C(\tau))$$

where $(\varepsilon_C(\tau) \mid \varepsilon_{ob}(\tau))$ is "an estimate of the validity of the set of n component items C at time τ given that the estimate of the validity of object *ob* at time τ is $\varepsilon_{ob}(\tau)$." If the conceptual model has been decomposed then $(\varepsilon_C(\tau) \mid \varepsilon_{ob}(\tau)) = \varepsilon_C(\tau)$. To propagate validity estimates across a set of component items, suppose that the set C is a set of n component items as above. The general recursive rule for propagating validity estimates over such a set is:

$$\models \quad \varepsilon_{\{cc, D\}}(\tau) = \varepsilon_{cc}(\tau) \times (\varepsilon_D(\tau) \mid \varepsilon_{cc}(\tau))$$

where $(\varepsilon_D(\tau) \mid \varepsilon_{cc}(\tau))$ is "an estimate of the validity of the set of n-1 component items D at time τ given that the estimate of the validity of the component item *cc* at time τ is $\varepsilon_{cc}(\tau)$." In general $(\varepsilon_D(\tau) \mid \varepsilon_{cc}(\tau)) \neq \varepsilon_D(\tau)$ even if the conceptual model has been decomposed. Now suppose that item *cc* is virtual and that it is derivable from the set of items D using knowledge item *ob*(*cc*, D), ie that Can(*cc*, D) = 1 in *ob*(*cc*, D). Then the validity of item *cc* depends on the validity of object *ob* and on the validity of the items in the set D. Estimates of these validities are propagated by:

$$\models \quad \varepsilon_{cc}(\tau) = \varepsilon_{ob}(\tau) \times (\varepsilon_D(\tau) \mid \varepsilon_{ob}(\tau))$$

If the conceptual model has been decomposed then $(\varepsilon_D(\tau) \mid \varepsilon_{ob}(\tau)) = \varepsilon_D(\tau)$.

The three rules above for propagating validity estimates follow from the definition of item validity. These three rules lead to complex expressions for validity estimates due to the quantity of conditional expressions—ie expressions involving "|". But the quantity of these conditional expressions may be reduced.

If the knowledge base has been decomposed [8] and if the sub-item relationships have been reduced to sub-type relationships between data items then the object operators and the basis items in the conceptual model are independent with the possible exception of sub-item relationships between data items [13]. So if the knowledge base has been decomposed and there are no sub-item relationships between data items then all the conditional expressions may be removed [14]. For example, if the knowledge base has been decomposed and there are no sub-item relationships between data items then the validity estimate for the virtual information item *part/tax-payable* is:

$$
\begin{aligned}
\varepsilon_{part/tax-payable}(\tau) &= \varepsilon_{tax-rule}(\tau) \\
&\quad \times \ (\ \varepsilon_{\{part/sale-price,\ tax-rate\}}(\tau) \mid \varepsilon_{tax-rule}(\tau)\ ) \\
&= \varepsilon_{tax-rule}(\tau) \ \times \ \varepsilon_{\{part/sale-price,\ tax-rate\}}(\tau) \\
&= \varepsilon_{tax-rule}(\tau) \ \times \ \varepsilon_{part/sale-price}(\tau) \\
&\quad \times \ (\ \varepsilon_{tax-rate}(\tau) \mid \varepsilon_{part/sale-price}(\tau)\ ) \\
&= \varepsilon_{tax-rule}(\tau) \ \times \ \varepsilon_{part/sale-price}(\tau) \ \times \ \varepsilon_{tax-rate}(\tau) \\
&= \varepsilon_{tax-rule}(\tau) \ \times \ \varepsilon_{mark-up-rule}(\tau) \\
&\quad \times \ (\ \varepsilon_{\{part/cost-price,\ mark-up\}}(\tau) \mid \varepsilon_{mark-up-rule}(\tau)\ ) \\
&\quad \times \ \varepsilon_{tax-rate}(\tau) \\
&= \varepsilon_{tax-rule}(\tau) \ \times \ \varepsilon_{mark-up-rule}(\tau) \\
&\quad \times \ \varepsilon_{part/cost-price}(\tau) \ \times \ \varepsilon_{mark-up}(\tau) \ \times \ \varepsilon_{tax-rate}(\tau)
\end{aligned}
$$

If sub-item relationships are present or if the conceptual model has not been decomposed then the calculations become more involved. For example, suppose the *supervisor* data item is a sub-item of the *person* data item. Consider the real *person/supervisor* item; the implementation of which is populated with 2-tuples (person-id, person-id) where the second person is the "supervisor" of the first. Suppose that this item is built by applying the *super* information object to the data items *person* and *supervisor*:

$$person/supervisor \ = \ super(\ person,\ supervisor\ )$$

then the validity estimate of the *person/supervisor* information item will be:

$$
\begin{aligned}
\varepsilon_{super(person,\ supervisor)}(\tau) \\
&= \varepsilon_{\{person,\ supervisor\}}(\tau) \ \times \ (\ \varepsilon_{super}(\tau) \mid \varepsilon_{\{person,\ supervisor\}}(\tau)\ ) \\
&= \varepsilon_{person}(\tau) \times (\ \varepsilon_{supervisor}(\tau) \mid \varepsilon_{person}(\tau)\ ) \ \times \ \varepsilon_{super}(\tau) \\
&= \varepsilon_{person}(\tau)^2 \ \times \ \varepsilon_{super}(\tau)
\end{aligned}
$$

where $(\ \varepsilon_{super}(\tau) \mid \varepsilon_{\{person,\ supervisor\}}(\tau)\ ) = \varepsilon_{super}(\tau)$ assuming that the knowledge base has been decomposed and the validity of the *super* operator is independent of the validity of the items to which it is applied; and where $(\ \varepsilon_{supervisor}(\tau) \mid \varepsilon_{person}(\tau)\ ) = \varepsilon_{person}(\tau)$ because the validity of *supervisor* is assumed, quite reasonably, to be determined by the validity of *person*.

4. Conclusion

A unified knowledge representation has been extended to represent "just invalid" knowledge. A quantitative calculus estimates the effect of knowledge decay on knowledge base validity. The estimate of validity in the calculus has been simplified by the use of the unified knowledge representation. Further simplification has been achieved by decomposing the knowledge in the conceptual model.

References

1. Tayar, N. "A Model for Developing Large Shared Knowledge Bases" in *proceedings Second International Conference on Information and Knowledge Management*, Washington, November 1993, pp717—719.
2. Debenham, J.K. "*Knowledge Engineering*", Springer-Verlag, 1998.
3. Debenham, J.K. "A Framework For Knowledge Reuse" in *proceedings 11th International FLAIRS Conference*, Florida, May 1998, pp199—203.
4. Debenham, J.K. "Knowledge Simplification", in *proceedings 9th International Symposium on Methodologies for Intelligent Systems ISMIS'96*, Zakopane, Poland, June 1996.
5. Date, C.J., "*An Introduction to Database Systems*" (4th edition) Addison-Wesley, 1986.
6. Debenham, J.K. "Constraints for Knowledge Maintenance", in *proceedings AAAI Spring Symposium in Artificial Intelligence in Knowledge Management*, Stanford, California, March 1997.
7. Kang, B., Gambetta, W. and Compton, P. "Validation and Verification with Ripple Down Rules", *International Journal of Human Computer Studies* Vol 44 (2) pp257—270 (1996).
8. Debenham, J.K. "Representing Knowledge Normalisation", *in proceedings Tenth International Conference on Software Engineering and Knowledge Engineering SEKE'98*, San Francisco, US, June 1998 pp132—135.
9. Emerson, E.A. "Temporal and Modal Logic" in Van Leeuwen, J. (Ed) "*Handbook of Theoretical Computer Science*", pp997-1072, MIT Press, 1994.
10. Katsuno, H. and Mendelzon, A.O., "On the Difference between Updating a Knowledge Base and Revising It", in *proceedings Second International Conference on Principles of Knowledge Representation and Reasoning, KR'91*, Morgan Kaufmann, 1991.
11. Debenham, J.K. "From Conceptual Model to Internal Model", in *proceedings Tenth International Symposium on Methodologies for Intelligent Systems ISMIS'97*, Charlotte, October 1997, pp227—236.
12. Walker, A., Kowalski, R., Lenat, D., Soloway, E. and Stonebraker, M., "Knowledge Management", in (L. Kerschberg, Ed.), "*Proceedings from the Second International Conference on Expert Database Systems*", Benjamin Cummings, 1989.
13. Debenham, J.K. "A Unified Approach to Requirements Specification and System Analysis in the Design of Knowledge-Based Systems", in *proceedings Seventh International Conference on Software Engineering and Knowledge Engineering SEKE'95*, Washington DC, June 1995, pp144—146.
14. Coenen F. and Bench-Capon, T. "Building Knowledge Based Systems for Maintainability", in *proceedings Third International Conference on Database and Expert Systems Applications DEXA'92*, Valencia, Spain, September, 1992, pp415-420.

Maximising Expected Utility for Behaviour Arbitration

Julio K. Rosenblatt

Australian Centre for Field Robotics
University of Sydney, NSW 2006, Australia
julio@mech.eng.usyd.edu.au

Abstract. Utility fusion is presented as an alternative means of action selection which ameliorates both the bottlenecks of centralised systems and the incoherence of distributed systems. In this approach, distributed behaviours indicate the utility of possible world states, along with their associated uncertainty. A centralised arbiter then combines these utilities and probabilities to determine a Pareto-optimal action based on the maximisation of expected utility. Utility theory provides a Bayesian framework for explicitly representing and reasoning about uncertainty within the action selection process. In addition, the construction of a utility map allows the arbiter to model and compensate for the dynamics of the system; experimental results verify that the resulting system provides significantly greater stability.

1. Introduction

In unstructured, unknown, and dynamic environments, such as those encountered by outdoor mobile robots, an intelligent agent must adequately address the issues of incomplete and inaccurate knowledge; it must be able to handle uncertainty in both its sensed and *a priori* information, in the current state of the agent itself, as well as in the effects of the agent's actions. In order to function effectively in such conditions, an agent must be responsive to its environment, as well as goal-oriented. When used appropriately, deliberative planning and reactive control complement each other and compensate for each other's deficiencies.

Centralised architectures provide the ability to coherently coordinate multiple goals and constraints within a complex environment, while decentralised architectures offer the advantages of reactivity, flexibility, and robustness. However, sensor fusion creates a bottleneck, and command arbitration runs the risk of losing information valuable to the decision-making process; therefore a careful balance must be struck between completeness and optimality on the one hand versus modularity and efficiency on the other. In addition, it is important to consider the agent's constraints.

The Distributed Architecture for Mobile Navigation (DAMN) achieves a symbiosis of deliberative and reactive elements; it consists of a group of distributed behaviours communicating with a centralised command arbiter, as shown in Figure 1 [16]. The arbiter is responsible for combining the behaviours' votes to generate the actions sent to the vehicle controller. A mode manager may also be used to vary these weights during the course of a mission. The distributed,

N. Foo (Ed.): AI'99, LNAI 1747, pp. 96 - 108, 1999.

asynchronous behaviours provide real-time responsiveness to the environment, while the centralised command arbitration provides a framework capable of producing coherent behaviour.

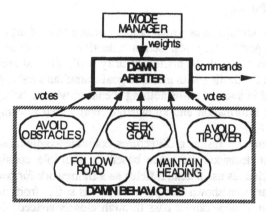

Fig. 1. DAMN framework: centralised arbitration of votes from distributed behaviours

2. Background

2.1. Centralised and Behaviour-Based Architectures

Centralised sensor fusion systems uses all available sensory data to create a complete model of its environment, plan a series of actions within the context of that model, and then execute that plan [10][11][21]. A complete plan to the goal may be constructed and followed in an open-loop fashion, or the agent may interleave planning and execution; this more closed-loop approach is better able to deal with uncertainty and incomplete knowledge. Sensor fusion is able to overcome ambiguity and noise inherent in the sensing process [6], but still has the disadvantage of creating a computationally expensive bottleneck, and a monolithic world model is also more difficult to develop and maintain. In addition to introducing delays, a centralised architecture is also more likely to fail entirely if any single part of it is not functioning properly, particularly when the real world deviates significantly from the models employed.

As a response to the inefficiencies of centralised systems in controlling autonomous robots, a new generation of architectures emerged which were designed in a bottom-up fashion to provide greater reactivity to the robot's surroundings. Rather than constructing the system with functional modules such as perception and planning, the system is composed of specialised task-achieving modules, or *behaviours*, that operate independently and asynchronously [4]. Each behaviour only receives that information specifically required for its task, thus avoiding the need for sensor fusion and its inherent bottlenecks. A behaviour encapsulates the perception, planning and task execution capabilities necessary to achieve one specific aspect of robot control. Behaviour-based systems tend to be *reactive*, i.e., maintain minimal internal state and respond directly to immediate stimuli. Such systems perform no lookahead, and do not represent or explicitly deal with uncertainty, in the belief that "the world is its own best model" [5], assuming that no benefit is to be gained from evidence combination and that all previous sensor data should be ignored.

2.2. Command Fusion

In behaviour-based architectures which employ priority-based arbitration such as the Subsumption Architecture [4], action selection is achieved by assigning control to the behaviour with the highest priority while the rest are ignored. This provides no means for dealing with multiple goals simultaneously. A compromise cannot be achieved in such an all-or-nothing scenario; when a behaviour's output is overridden, that information and knowledge represented is completely lost to the system [12].

In contrast, command fusion architectures combine commands from various behaviours so that decisions are made based on multiple considerations. For example, Motor Schemas use potential fields as a framework for command fusion [1]; however, it has been shown that potential fields suffer from oscillations and instability, and that a robot cannot pass through closely spaced obstacles [3]. In addition, vector addition results in an averaged command that may not be satisfactory to any of the contributing schemas. The root of these limitations is that, like with priority-based arbiters, each behaviour simply outputs a single command; in addition, they perform no lookahead and thus are subject to local minima.

In a DAMN "actuation-space" arbitration scheme used previously, each behaviour votes for or against various alternatives in the actuator command space. For example, a turn arbiter receives votes for turn commands from two behaviours (Figure 2a & b), computes a normalised weighted sum (Figure 2c), and the summed votes are smoothed and interpolated (Figure 2d); the resulting command with the maximum vote value is then sent to the vehicle controller [16].

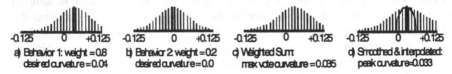

-0.125 0 +0.125	-0.125 0 +0.125	-0.125 0 +0.125	-0.125 0 +0.125
a) Behavior 1: weight = 0.8	b) Behavior 2 weight = 0.2	c) Weighted Sum	d) Smoothed & interpolated:
desired curvature = 0.04	desired curvature = 0.0	max vote curvature = 0.035	peak curvature = 0.033

Fig. 2. Command fusion in DAMN actuation-space arbiter.

This process is similar to fuzzy logic control systems, performing defuzzification using the maximum criterion, and in fact has been recast into a fuzzy logic framework [23]. Fuzzy logic has found many uses for mobile robot control, including command fusion systems (see [20] for a survey). Many use defuzzification strategies other than maximum, such as centre of mass, which assume a unimodal function, and in general this averaging of inputs will at times select inappropriate commands. In addition, these systems only deal with uncertainty implicitly.

These command fusion schemes provide mechanisms for the concurrent satisfaction of multiple goals as determined by independent behaviours, thus allowing incremental, evolutionary system development. However, command fusion in general still has shortcomings which reduce the system's overall effectiveness. A more complete overview of various types of architectures and their corresponding advantages and disadvantages can be found in [18].

3. Utility Fusion

A new means of action selection via *utility fusion* is introduced as an alternative to centralised sensor fusion architectures, as well as to priority-based arbitration and command fusion in distributed systems. Instead of expressing action preferences, behaviours indicate the utility of various possible world states, together with stochastic estimates of sensor uncertainty. Utility theory provides a unified conceptual framework for defining votes and weights and dealing with uncertainty. Because we are attempting to decide which among a set of possible actions to take, it is natural to make judgements on the usefulness of each action based on its consequences. If we assign a utility measure $U(c)$ for each possible consequence, and $P(c|a,e)$ is the probability that consequence c will occur given that we observe evidence e and take action a, then the expected utility $U(a)$ for a is given in equation 1:

$$U(a) = \sum_c U(c) \cdot P(c \mid a, e) \tag{1}$$

In the context of mobile robot navigation, for example, actions may be vehicle manoeuvring or sensor positioning, positive consequences staying on a road or reaching a goal, negative consequences colliding with an obstacle, and the evidence would be observations obtained by processing sensory data. The conditional probabilities $P(c|a,e)$ are determined by the uncertainty in the sensing process, in the vehicle position, and in vehicle control. The subjective utilities $U(c)$ are determined for each behaviour based on the relative importance of the consequence; for example, a collision would have a large negative utility, while the utility of following a pre-planned path may be small. Provided with these utilities and probabilities by the behaviours, an arbiter can then apply the *Maximum Expected Utility* criterion to select an optimal action based on all current information [13].

Utility fusion does not create a world model as sensor fusion systems do. The information combined and stored by the utility fusion arbiter does not represent sensed features of the world, as in certainty grids [10] for example, but rather the desirability of being in a particular state according to some criterion defined by the behaviour. The processing of sensory data is still distributed among behaviours, so the bottlenecks and brittleness associated with sensor fusion are avoided.

Unlike command arbitration or command fusion systems, the utility fusion arbiter does not select among or combine actions proposed by behaviours. Instead, the arbiter is provided with much richer evaluation information from behaviours, thus allowing for more complex decision-making. The arbiter accumulates utility and probability evaluations from the behaviours and bases its action selection on the combined evidence, so that the limitations of command fusion systems may be overcome.

Virtual sensors provide processed sensor data and uncertainty estimates to the behaviours. Uncertainty in the locations of objects, as well as in the position of the vehicle, can be generated by various means such as the covariance matrix of a Kalman filter [2] or the residual of a linear regression algorithm. Each behaviour then uses the output of its associated virtual sensors to determine the utility and probability of various world states, and passes these to the utility arbiter, which combines and maintains a map of this information and evaluates candidate actions within it. The action which maximises expected utility is then sent as a command to the controller.

For example, a utility arbiter has been developed for vehicle steering. Figure 3a shows an area of positive utility associated with a road and an area of negative utility associated with a detected obstacle, with the lighter polygons suggesting the reduced probabilities as distance increases. The arbiter evaluates the possible trajectories, shown in the figure as arcs emanating from the vehicle, by summing the expected utilities along them, and selects the one for which the total is greatest.

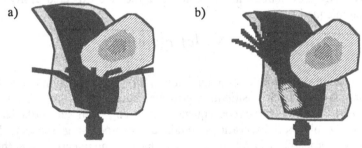

a)   b)

Fig. 3. Utility arbiter: a) evaluating arc trajectories - dark areas indicate high probability; b) evaluating clothoid-arcs originating from predicted vehicle position (lighter vehicle).

3.1. Advantages of Utility Fusion

Representation of Uncertainty. Uncertainties are often accounted for in an *ad hoc* manner, for example by "growing" the size of observed obstacles or by arbitrarily "fuzzifying" the inputs to a system to determine an approximately appropriate output. Similarly, potential fields implicitly deal with uncertainty with the field emanating from a point. Although the fuzzy behaviour blending described in [19] is formally defined as a logic of graded preferences [15], which is closely related to utilities, there is no objective measure and treatment of uncertainty based on probabilities.

Utility theory provides a Bayesian framework for reasoning about uncertainty, teasing apart the value of the consequence of an action from the probability it will occur [2]. Each behaviour votes for the subjective utility of being in the particular states of concern to that behaviour, e.g., obstacle or road locations, along with associated uncertainties expressed as covariances in a multi-dimensional normal distribution. The arbiter then applies the Maximum Expected Utility criterion to select an action that is Pareto-optimal [14]. Estimates of the uncertainties in the vehicle's position and control should also be taken into account when calculating expected utility; however, this has not yet been implemented. By casting the voting scheme within the framework of utility theory, uncertainty within the system is explicitly represented and reasoned about in the decision-making processes

System Model. Another advantage of map-based utility fusion over command fusion is that the dynamics of the system being controlled can be fully modelled and accounted for by the arbiter, providing greater control accuracy and stability. For example, a vehicle cannot change instantly from one turn to another, but follows a linear change in curvature, resulting in a clothoid path rather than a simple arc [7]. Another important difference between commanded and actual vehicle trajectories is due to system latencies. To maintain stability, the system must be able to anticipate latencies and determine which actions are achievable [8]. The evaluation of clothoid-arcs from the predicted vehicle state is illustrated in Figure 3b. The utility arbiter performs lookahead to consider the consequences of its actions in terms of predicted future states, but looks ahead only one step to determine the next immediate action, on the assumption that the large uncertainties in perception and action in a domain such as outdoor mobile robots renders further search futile. Thus, the system produces rational action while preserving responsiveness.

The utility arbiter can take all of this information into account and evaluate actions within a single interchangeable module; the behaviours simply express the utility of various world states independent of which actions would cause the robot to enter that state. This provides greater modularity and interchangeability of behaviours; for example, a behaviour developed for a vehicle with Ackerman steering could be reused as is for an omnidirectional robot.

Synchronisation. Allowing the behaviours in a distributed architecture to operate asynchronously, each at their greatest possible rate, maximises throughput and there-fore reactivity. However, without synchronisation, behaviour outputs are based on different system states, so that the semantics of combining votes from different behaviours is ill-defined and may yield unpredictable results. Command fusion involves combining behaviour outputs which are only valid for a brief interval, but the utility arbiter receives votes for external world states whose meaning is well-defined independent of the current vehicle state. The use of a map allows vote combination to occur within the arbiter without imposing timing constraints on the behaviours, while still maintaining a consistent interpretation of votes received at different times and from different locations, thus allowing reasoning to be coordinated and therefore coherent.

3.2. Implementation of Utility Arbiter

The utility arbiter for vehicle steering control maintains a local map of the utilities and associated uncertainties sent to it by the behaviours. The utilities may be represented by geometric constructs (points, lines, and polygons) with associated two-dimensional Gaussian distributions, or by a grid; behaviours may use whichever is more appropriate; the arbiter maintains the two representations independently and combines their utility estimates at the final stages.

For the sake of efficiency, the command choices to be evaluated are discretized; the results are smoothed and interpolated to avoid problems with bang-bang control, i.e., switching between discrete choices to achieve an intermediate value.

Initialise Vehicle Trajectories: Given N possible steering commands, create an NxN matrix A, with each element A_{ij} containing a trajectory corresponding to commanding curvature κ_i while the vehicle is currently executing an arc of curvature κ_j.

Collect Behaviour Utilities: Collect utilities, tagged by the sending behaviour with the position of the vehicle at the time the utilities were generated.

Predict Vehicle State: Get current vehicle state from controller, position (x_t, y_t, θ_t), speed v_t, and curvature κ_t. Compute predicted state based on estimated latency.

Transform Utility Coordinates: For each point, line, or polygon utility, transform the coordinates to the predicted vehicle reference frame. Let these coordinates be (x_u', y_u'). If any of these lies more than three standard deviations behind the vehicle, i.e., $(y_u' - y_n') > 3\sigma_y$ for all vertices, remove that utility object from the map.

Compute Expected Utilities: For each utility u and each point (x_n', y_n') along a candidate vehicle trajectory, determine the transformed coordinates $(x_u'^*, y_u'^*)$ of the point that is closest in Mahalanobis distance from (x_n', y_n'). Grid utilities are indexed by the vehicle position; zero is used if it is outside the bounds of the array.

The contribution $E(n',u)$ of utility u to the expected utility of point $n' = (x_n', y_n')$ is the product of the utility value υ and the probability as determined by the Mahalanobis distance between those two points in a bi-normal distribution:

$$\upsilon \cdot \frac{e^{-\left(\left(\left(x_u'^* - x_n'\right)/2\sigma_x^2\right) + \left(\left(y_u'^* - y_n'\right)/2\sigma_y^2\right)\right)}}{2\pi\sigma_x\sigma_y} \tag{2}$$

Sum Expected Utilities Along Trajectories: The total expected utility for taking action a, i.e., following arc A_{ij}, is then computed by summing the utilities at each of N points along the arc, multiplied by a discount factor λ ($0<\lambda<1$) used to account for the diminished expected returns of future actions, as in a POMDP:

$$U(a) = \sum_u \sum_{s=1}^{N} \lambda^s E(n',u) . \tag{3}$$

Maximise Expected Utility: Determine the maximum expected utility $U(\alpha)$ such that no other expected utility $U(a)$ has a greater value: $U(\alpha) | \forall \alpha : U(\alpha) \geq U(a)$.

Interpolate Commanded Curvature: Locally approximate the Gaussian distribution of votes around the selected action α by fitting a parabola to

$U(\alpha)$ and the utility values for the two adjacent commands, $U(\alpha-1)$ and $U(\alpha+1)$. The peak of this parabola is then chosen as the commanded action.

Send Controller Command: Send the steering command as determined in the previous step to the controller, and add it to a queue for use in feedforward prediction.

Repeat Loop: Return to Collect Behaviour Utilities step.

3.3. Utility-Based Behaviours

Within the framework of DAMN, behaviours must be defined to provide the task-specific knowledge for the domain. Each behaviour runs completely independently and asynchronously, using whichever sensor data and processing algorithms are best suited to the task at hand. Because behaviours operate asynchronously, each is allowed to perform as much or as little search as appropriate; for example, a reactive behaviour may perform no search while a deliberative behaviour may search all the way until the final goal and then vote for the next action in its constructed plan. DAMN has been used to construct several systems using many different behaviours [17]; some examples are provided below.

Obstacle Avoidance Behaviours: The *Avoid Obstacles* behaviour uses the SMARTY obstacle detection system [9], which processes laser range or stereo vision images to determine intraversable regions of terrain. For each obstacle detected, the behaviour reports to the arbiter a large negative utility with standard deviations representing the sensor uncertainty, as well as another negative utility with a smaller value and larger standard deviation due to the problems associated with getting too close to an obstacle, i.e., constrained mobility, occlusion of unknown areas, etc. The obstacle can be represented as either a point or as a polygon.

Goal Seeking Behaviours: While more reactive behaviours operate at a high rate to ensure safety and to provide functions such as road following and cross-country navigation, deliberative behaviours can process map-based or symbolic information at a slower rate, periodically issuing votes to the arbiter that guide the robot towards the current goal. These "high level" behaviours do not hand a plan down to a lower level for execution, but rather maintain an internal representation that allows them to participate directly in the control of the vehicle based on its current state [12].

For example, the *Follow Subgoals* behaviour associates a positive point utility with each of the subgoals to be reached by the vehicle. A line utility between subgoals is also defined so that a corridor is effectively created between consecutive goals to draw the vehicle back to the path when it strays, e.g., after avoiding an obstacle. The behaviour does not need to decide when a goal has been achieved or if it should be abandoned, each utility attracts the vehicle in turn as it gets closer;

More sophisticated map-based planning techniques which determine an optimal global path have also been used. For example, the *Follow Path* behaviour uses the D* planner [22], which creates a grid representing how to reach the goal from any location in the map, determined by using A*. The behaviour then sends a portion of its map around the current vehicle position to the arbiter.

4. Experimental Results

In this section, we present some results from experiments conducted on the Navlab II HMMWV outdoor mobile robot at Carnegie Mellon University (and in a simulation of that vehicle), as shown in Figure 4 in the environment in which the vehicle experiments took place; the terrain in the test area included many natural terrain features such as hills, rocks, and ditches.

Fig. 4. Vehicle in test area.

In order to demonstrate the advantages of utility fusion over command fusion, experiments were run comparing the utility arbiter against the "actuation-space" arbiter described briefly in Section 2, which accepted votes from the behaviours for and against various turn commands. Trials with the utility arbiter's predictive control capability turned off were also conducted so its effect could be observed independently. For experiments at low speeds, all arbiters successfully achieved their mission, both in actual vehicle experiments and in simulation. However, the effects of latency and dynamics became very apparent at higher vehicle speeds, and the utility arbiter with predictive control performed much better than the other arbiters.

4.1. Performance Metrics

Mean Obstacle Proximity. An important metric is the average distance from obstacles along a vehicle path. The distance to the closest obstacle provides a measure of safety clearance; when inverted, it provides a measure of proximity which is to be minimised. The mean obstacle proximity metric for a path is defined by the inverse square of the distance to the closest obstacle, integrated along the path and normalised by the total number of path points. A lower mean obstacle proximity means that the vehicle was on the average further away from the nearest obstacle, and therefore that the path was safer.

Roughness. Roughness is defined by the square of the change in vehicle curvature with respect to time, integrated along the path and normalised by the total time. A lower measure means that curvature either changed less or more gradually along the path, and therefore the vehicle path was smoother [7].

4.2. Utility Fusion vs. Command Fusion

In order to demonstrate the benefits of utility fusion in compensating for vehicle dynamics, a vehicle simulator was used for experiments where conditions could be carefully controlled and higher speeds could be used without risk of damage. The path arbiter with and without predictive control, in conjunction with the *Obstacle Avoidance* and *Follow Subgoals* behaviours (described above) were compared at various vehicle speeds and system latencies against the command fusion style turn arbiter and equivalent behaviours used in previous systems [9][16].

The graphs of mean obstacle proximity as a function of speed in Figure 5a and of path roughness vs. speed in Figure 5b show that the turn arbiter does very badly at higher speeds; these runs are shown in Figure 5c. The graphs also show that, at higher speeds, the utility arbiter without predictive control performed even worse than the turn arbiter, possibly due to the utility arbiter's greater complexity; these runs are shown in Figure 5d. However, when the utility arbiter made use of its predictive control capabilities, it was still able to go through this narrow corridor and reach the goal, in spite of the fact that a delay of 2 seconds at a speed of 6 m/s meant that the vehicle travelled 12m between the time that a command was issued and the time that it would actually be executed. These successful path traces are shown in Figure 5e, along with the trace of the position of the vehicle as predicted by the arbiter, which coincided well with the actual path.

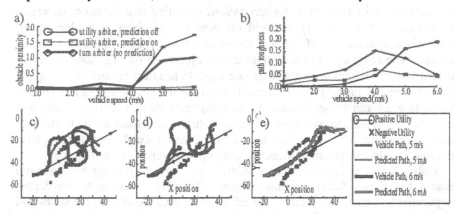

Fig. 5. (a-b) Path metrics as function of speed: a) mean obstacle proximity, b) roughness; (c-e) Paths at high speeds with large lag: c) turn arbiter, d) utility arbiter w/o and, e) with prediction.

4.3. Effect of Predictive Control in Utility Arbiter

The following tests were performed on the vehicle and environment shown above in Figure 4, operating at speeds of roughly 0.8 m/s. The utility arbiter was used both with and without predictive control in order to study its effect in isolation.

As can be seen in Figure 6, the vehicle oscillated quite a bit without predictive control, yielding a roughness measure of 4.3×10^{-3}, in contrast to the much more stable path generated using predictive control, with a roughness measure of 3.0×10^{-5}. The reduction in mean obstacle proximity, from 0.41 to 0.14, while not as dramatic, still represents a significant improvement in vehicle control afforded by utility fusion.

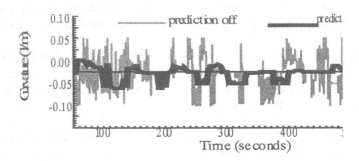

Fig. 6. Vehicle curvature vs. time, with and without prediction capabilities

5. Conclusion

Because reactivity is essential for any system operating in a dynamic, uncertain environment, it is necessary to avoid the sensing and planning bottlenecks of centralised systems, but if we are to avoid sensor fusion, the system must combine command inputs to determine an appropriate course of action. However, priority-based arbitration only allows one module to affect control at any given time. Command fusion provides a mechanism for the concurrent satisfaction of multiple goals and allows modules to be completely independent, thus allowing evolutionary system development. However, existing command fusion techniques deal with uncertainty in an *ad hoc* manner, and they do not take system constraints into consideration when deciding upon a proper course of action.

Utility fusion is introduced as a solution to the shortcomings of command fusion and sensor fusion systems. Instead of voting for actions, distributed, asynchronous behaviours indicate the utility of various possible world states and their probabilities based on domain-specific knowledge. The arbiter then evaluates various candidate actions, using system models to determine which actions can be taken without violating kinematic and dynamic constraints, and to provide greater stability. It then selects a Pareto-optimal action based on the maximisation of expected utility, thus providing a unified conceptual framework for defining the semantics of votes and for dealing with uncertainty. This new approach strikes a balance between action selection and sensor fusion and has been found to yield many benefits.

For example, a utility arbiter has been implemented for vehicle steering control. Behaviours indicate the relative desirability of various possible vehicle locations, and the arbiter maintains a local map of these utilities. The arbiter then evaluates candidate actions by summing the expected utilities along each trajectory, taking uncertainty into account. The arbiter then chooses that trajectory which maximises expected utility and sends that steering command to the vehicle controller.

The utility space is not time-dependent, so that an arbiter using such a representation is capable of effectively synchronising and maintaining a consistent interpretation of the votes received from asynchronous behaviours, thus providing coherent reasoning in a distributed system. Behaviours can function without knowledge of the system dynamics, thus increasing their reusability for other systems. The utility arbiter can use models of the system being controlled to determine which states are actually attainable, and to increase the accuracy and stability of control. In particular, the map-based path arbiter gathers information from behaviours about the desirability of possible vehicle locations and then evaluates candidate trajectories to determine appropriate actions. The arbiter can then use kinematic models of the robot to determine which actions can be commanded without violating non-holonomic constraints, and use of the system to provide greater stability. Thus, utility fusion provides coherent, optimal reasoning in a distributed, asynchronous system, combining the advantages of sensor fusion and command fusion while avoiding many of their drawbacks. It provides a well defined semantics of votes and uncertainty, and has been demonstrated experimentally to result in measurably better control.

DAMN has been used to combine various systems of differing capabilities on several mobile robots, at various sites; in addition to its use on the CMU Navlab vehicles, DAMN has also been used at the Lockheed Martin Corporation, the Hughes Research Labs, and the Georgia Institute of Technology. DAMN arbiters have been used to integrate navigation modules for the steering and speed control of single as well as multiple vehicles at these sites, and have also been used to select field of regard for the control of a pair of stereo cameras on a pan/tilt platform. Vehicles under the control of DAMN have driven at highway speeds, navigated across stretches of off-road terrain some kilometres in length, cooperated with other robotic vehicles, and performed teleoperation, all while providing for the safety of the vehicle and meeting mission objectives. Current work at the University of Sydney involves behaviour coordination for autonomous underwater vehicles.

Acknowledgements

This research was supported in part by grants from ONR (N00014-J-91-1451), ARL (DAAH049610297), ARPA (N00014-94-1090, DAST-95-C003, F30602-93-C-0039, DACA76-89-C-0014, DAAE07-90-C-R059), and NSF (BCS-9120655). The author was supported by a Hughes Research Fellowship.

References

1.   Arkin, R. Motor Schema-Based Mobile Robot Navigation. In *International Journal of Robotics Research*, Vol. 8(4), August 1989, pp. 92-112.

2.   Berger, J. Statistical Decision Theory and Bayesian Analysis, 2nd ed. New York: Springer, 1985.

3.   Borenstein, J. and Koren, Y. Potential Field Methods and Their Inherent Limitations for Mobile Robot Navigation. In *Proceedings of the International Conference on Robotics and Automation*, 1991.

4.   Brooks, R. A Robust Layered Control System for a Mobile Robot. In *IEEE Journal of Robotics and Automation*, vol. RA-2, no. 1, pp. 14-23, April 1986.

5.   Brooks, R. Intelligence Without Reason, in proceedings of *Twelfth International Joint Conference on Artificial Intelligence*, Sydney, Australia, pp. 569-595, August 1991.

6.   Durrant-Whyte, H. *Integration, Coordination, and Control of Multi-Sensor Robot Systems* (Ph.D.). University of Pennsylvania, Philadelphia, PA, 1986.

7.   Kanayama, Y. and. Miyake, N. Trajectory Generation for Mobile Robots. In *Proceedings of 3rd International Symposium on Robotics Research*, pp. 333-340, Gouvieux, France, 1985.

8.   Kelly, A. *An Intelligent Predictive Control Approach to the High-Speed Cross-Country Autonomous Navigation Problem* (Ph.D.). Carnegie Mellon University Robotics Institute Technical Report CMU-RI-TR-95-33, 1995.

9.   Langer, D., Rosenblatt, J., and Hebert, M. A Behavior-Based System For Off-Road Navigation. In *IEEE Journal of Robotics and Automation*, vol. 10(6), December 1994.

10.   Moravec, H. and Elfes, A. High Resolution Map From Wide-Angle Sonar. In *Proceedings of the IEEE International Conference on Robotics and Automation*, pp.116-121,1985.

11.   Nilsson, N. *Shakey the Robot*. SRI Tech. Note 323, Menlo Park, Calif., 1984.

12.   Payton, D., Rosenblatt, J., Keirsey, D. Plan Guided Reaction. In *IEEE Transactions on Systems Man and Cybernetics*, 20(6), pp. 1370-1382, 1990.

13.   Pearl, J. Probabilistic Reasoning in Intelligent Systems: Networks of Plausible Inference. Morgan Kaufmann, 1988.

14.   Pirjanian, P. The Notion of Optimality in Behavior-Based Robotics. To appear in *Journal of Robotics and Autonomous Systems*, 1999.

15.   Rescher, N. Semantic foundations for the logic of preference. In *The Logic of Decision and Action*, N. Rescher (ed.), Pittsburgh, PA, 1967.

16.   Rosenblatt, J. The Distributed Architecture for Mobile Navigation. In *Journal of Experimental and Theoretical Artificial Intelligence*, vol. 9(2/3), April-September, 1997.

17.   Rosenblatt, J. Utility Fusion: Map-Based Planning in a Behavior-Based System, in *Field and Service Robotics*, Springer-Verlag, 1998.

18.   Rosenblatt, J. and Hendler, J. Architectures for Mobile Robot Control, in *Advances in Computers* 48, M. Zelkowitz, Ed., Academic Press, London, 1999.

19.   Saffiotti, A., Konolige, K., and Ruspini, E. A multivalued-logic approach to integrating planning and control. In *Artificial Intelligence* 76(1-2), pp. 481-526, 1995.

20.   Saffiotti, A. The Uses of Fuzzy Logic in Autonomous Robotics: a catalogue raisonne, in *Soft Computing* 1(4):180-197, Springer-Verlag, 1997.

21.   Shafer, S., Stentz, A., and Thorpe, C. An Architecture for Sensor Fusion in a Mobile Robot. In *Proceedings of the IEEE International Conference on Robotics and Automation*, pp. 2002-2011, San Francisco, CA, April, 1986.

22.   Stentz, A. The Focussed D* Algorithm for Real-Time Replanning. In Proceedings of the International Joint Conference on Artificial Intelligence, 1995.

23.   Yen, J., Pfluger, N. A Fuzzy Logic Based Robot Navigation System. *Proceedings of AAAI Fall Symposium*, 1992.

Generating Natural Language Descriptions of Project Plans

Margaret Wasko and Robert Dale

Language Technology Group
Division of Information and Communication Sciences
Macquarie University, Sydney, nsw 2109 Australia
{mwasko,rdale}ics.mq.edu.au

Abstract. We often resort to graphical means in order to describe non-linear structures, such as task dependencies in project planning. There are many contexts, however, where graphical means of presentation are not appropriate, and delivery either via text or spoken language is to be preferred. In this work, we take some first steps towards the development of natural language generation techniques that seek the most appropriate means of expressing non-linear structures using the linear medium of language.

1   Introduction

Natural language generation—the use of natural language processing techniques to create textual or spoken output from some underlying non-linguistic information source—is an area of practical language technology that shows great potential. Various natural language generation (NLG) systems have been constructed which produce textual output from underlying data sources of varying kinds: for example, the FoG system [3] generates textual weather forecasts from numerical weather simulations; IDAS [5] produces online hypertext help messages for users of complex machinery, using information stored in a knowledge base that describes this machinery; MODELEXPLAINER [4] generates textual descriptions of information in models of object-oriented software; and PEBA [7] interactively describes entities in a taxonomic knowledge base via the dynamic generation of hypertext documents, presented as World Wide Web pages.

The present work represents the first steps in exploring how NLG techniques can be used to present the information in complex, non-linear data structures. In particular, we focus on project plans of the kind that might be constructed in an application such as Microsoft Project. These software tools make it easy to present the content of project plans via a number of graphical means, such as PERT and Gantt charts. However, they do not provide any capability for presenting the information in project plans via natural language. We pursue this possibility for two reasons.

Firstly, we are interested in exploring the extent to which language can be used to express complex non-linear structures. We might hypothesise that language is not a good means for expressing this kind of information, since language

N. Foo (Ed.): AI'99, LNAI 1747, pp. 109–121, 1999.

requires us to linearise the presentation of the material to be expressed. However, some recent work in NLG has explored the use of mixed mode output, where graphics and text are combined; see, for example, [1]. A key question, then, is how best to apportion material between the two modalities. We intend to build on some of this recent research to see what kinds of information are best conveyed using language, and what elements are best conveyed graphically. We also aim to explore how sophisticated use of typography—indented structures, graphs containing textual annotations, and so on—can overcome some of the inherent limitations in purely 'linear' text.

Secondly, we are interested in determining the extent to which the information in a project plan might be conveyed to a user via speech. Suppose a project manager is driving to a meeting, and needs a report on the current status of some project whose internal structure is complex. Assuming that we do not have sophisticated heads-up displays or other similar presentation technologies, there is no possibility here that the information can be presented visually. In such a context, speech is the most plausible medium for information delivery, and so we are particularly interested in how the information available in a non-linear structure can most effectively be presented in a linear speech stream. Similarly, speech may be the delivery medium of choice for users who are vision-impaired.

In this paper, we present some first steps towards achieving these goals. Our focus here is on a specific but particularly important sub-problem: how do we produce descriptions of parallel structures in such a way as to avoid ambiguity in interpretation? We have implemented a simple NLG system, PLANPRESENTER, that takes project plan information as input, and produces from this information a text that describes the dependencies between the project plan elements. Section 2 presents an overview of the system, describing the key components. Section 3 shows how PLANPRESENTER generates text from a simple input project plan, and Section 4 shows how a more complex example is dealt with using our intermediate level of representation to allow the required flexibility in the generation process. Section 5 summarises the state of the work so far and sketches our next steps in this research.

2   System Overview

The system we describe here takes as its starting point earlier work described in [6], but departs from the system described there by adopting more recent ideas regarding the decomposition of the natural language generation process and the intermediate levels of representation that are required, as described in [8]. The input to our system is approximately equivalent to the information that can be extracted from a combination of the interchange formats provided by Microsoft Project, and which is likely to be available for any such project management tool. More particularly, we assume that we will be provided with a set of constructs corresponding to the basic undecomposable tasks in the plan—we will call these ATOMIC ACTIONS—and a set of dependency links that indicate which tasks must be completed before other tasks.

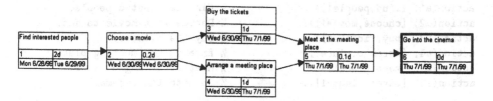

Fig. 1. A project plan for going to see a movie

It is likely that most project management systems will also make available information about other aspects of a project plan, such as the resources allocated to specific tasks, and hard constraints over temporal attributes such as start and end dates and task durations. In some contexts, we may also have access to information regarding the hierarchical relationships between plan components. We intend to make use of these elements of data as our work on project plan description proceeds; at this early stage, however, our primary concern is the linearisation of the information present in this essentially non-linear, networked structure.

The PLANPRESENTER system consists of three principal components:

- an INFORMATION STRUCTURER, which reconstructs the given plan information in a form more suited to textual description;
- a DESCRIPTION STRUCTURER, which assigns specific structural categories to all components of the plan; and
- a SURFACE REALISER, which works out how to express the content of the description structure linguistically.

The result is a set of English instructions instructions for performing that plan, written in such a way as to avoid ambiguities of understanding when parallelism occurs in the plan. The system is implemented in Prolog.

3 A Simple Worked Example

In this section we present a simple worked example that shows how PLANPRE-SENTER generates a description of a project plan from a symbolic representation of that plan.

3.1 The Project Plan

Figure 1 shows a PERT chart that indicates the relationships between a number of tasks within a larger project. In the example here, each task includes a start date, an end date and a duration; we will not make use of these for the moment, restricting ourselves to the standard elements of the temporal dependencies between the tasks.

```
action(a1, [find,people1]).        % Find interested people.
action(a2, [choose,movie1]).       % Decide what movie to see.
action(a3, [buy,tickets1]).        % Buy the tickets.
action(a4, [arrange,place1]).      % Arrange the meeting place.
action(a5, [meet,place1]).         % Meet at arranged place.
action(a6, [enter,cinema1]).       % Go into the cinema.


precedes(a1, a2).     precedes(a2, a3).     precedes(a2, a4).
precedes(a3, a5).     precedes(a4, a5).     precedes(a5, a6).
```

Fig. 2. The input representation corresponding to the project plan shown in Figure 1

The project is for a group of people to go to see a movie at the cinema together. The plan consists of six atomic actions, labelled here a1 through a6: first, we have to find the group of people who are interested in going, then we have to decide which movie to see, then we have to buy the tickets and arrange where to meet, and then we have to meet and go into the cinema. Note in particular that the actions of buying the tickets and of arranging a place to meet beforehand can be carried out in any order, or even in parallel.

The temporal dependencies here are indicated in the PERT chart by means of arrows. This information is presented to our system as a collection of symbolic constructs as shown in Figure 2. Here, for each action we have some additional information that will be used in describing this action: this is a pair of the form ⟨ActionType, Entity⟩, where the ActionType is drawn from an inventory of actions that the system knows how to express linguistically, and the Entity is a symbol that corresponds to some entity in the domain.[1] Given inputs of this kind, then, our goal is to generate a coherent text describing the plan in question.

3.2 Producing an Output Text

The present example is a very simple case of plan description; however, it allows us to demonstrate some of the essential elements of our method.

Building the Information Structure: First, we transform the given symbolic structures into a representation more suited to textual description. The key observation here is that language provides us with a variety of mechanisms for indicating both sequence and parallelism, so we re-express the input information

---

[1] There are clearly issues of specific versus non-specific reference here which complicate matters; however, our present focus is on describing the overall structure of a plan, so we will sidestep for the moment many of the issues regarding the fine-grained modelling of the entities that participate in the plan.

```
sequence([number_elements: 5],
[elements: [[1, atomic, a1],
           [2 ,atomic, a2],
           [3, simple_branch, [number_elements: 2],
               [elements: [[1, atomic, a3],
                           [2, atomic, a4]]]],
           [4, atomic, a5],
           [5, atomic, a6]]]).
```

Fig. 3. Representing sequence and simple parallelism

in a form that highlights these relationships. Applying this process to the input data shown in Figure 2 results in the following structure:[2]

```
sequence([a1, a2, parallel([a3, a4]), a5, a6]).
```

It is easy to see how, in general terms, such a structure might be mapped directly into a text:

– given a sequence of elements as in this case, we might simply express each element in the sequence by means of a sentence;
– if an element in the sequence is a parallel structure, then we might indicate explicitly that all the actions in this structure can be carried out in parallel.

Such a simple mapping mechanism will not, however, produce appropriate results in the case of more complex plans. In particular, if we have parallel structures that contain embedded parallelism or other complexities, then a direct mapping approach along the lines just sketched will result in unwieldy sentences.

Building the Initial Description Structure: In order to overcome this problem, instead of mapping the plan structure directly into text, we construct an intermediate representation which we call a DESCRIPTION STRUCTURE. This serves as an updateable repository for all the information we might need in making decisions as to how best to describe the plan. We can then perform reasoning operations over this structure to determine the best output, before committing ourselves to text. In the remainder of this section we show how the description structure is constructed and used in the present example; in Section 4 we show how this accommodates a more complex case of parallelism.

Figure 3 shows the initial description structure for our plan. Notice that here we have made explicit a number of properties of our original plan structure:

– We have explicitly indicated how many elements are present at each level in the plan structure.

---

[2] There exist plans whose structure does not readily map to the form described here. Consider for example Figure 7 with an arrow added from action 8 to action 5. Generating descriptions of plans such as these is a topic of future work.

- We have explicitly numbered each constituent element.
- We have explicitly indicated whether substructures in the plan are made up of atomic actions or are more complex in nature, as in the simple_branch element.

It is by virtue of this last step that our approach provides us with more sophisticated control over the description process. In essence, we identify different kinds of structural patterns in plans, where these different patterns correspond to different mechanisms for description. Thus, a simple branching structure is one where the elements within the parallelism are themselves atomic actions. Such a structure is amenable to the direct-mapping form of description suggested informally above, but more complex structures will require the use of more sophisticated linguistic mechanisms.

Determining Semantic Content: We now have to augment this description structure with additional information about the actions to be described. This is carried out as a sequence of two related processing steps. First, we incorporate information about how the actions themselves are to be described. The Action-Type in our input representation corresponds to the semantics of the predicate that will be used to describe that action, and the Entity serves as the index of the argument to the predicate. The next stage determines how the entities that participate in the plan will be referred to. For our present purposes, we do not make use of a sophisticated referring expression mechanism; essentially, we use simple table lookup to determine how a given entity should be described in a plan. At a later date we intend to incorporate more sophisticated algorithms for the generation of referring expressions along the lines described in [2]. The process of determining semantic content results in the output shown in Figure 4.

Applying Structure Realisation Strategies: Once we have determined the relevant aspects of the description of each of the actions in the plan, we are in a position to decide how to realise the overall description structure. We do this by means of STRUCTURE REALISATION STRATEGIES, which can be summarised in general terms as follows.[3]

- An action not immediately involved in a parallel description is described in a separate sentence, with appropriate adjuncts.
- Actions involved in simple parallelism are combined in a single sentence.
- actions involved in more complex parallelism are described in terms of the groupings assigned by the information structurer, with each group in a separate paragraph and signalled by appropriate adjuncts. See Section 4 for an example. Parallelism that is more embedded is signalled by means of the same strategy together with indentation.

---

[3] There are additional realisation strategies available, including textual ones such as numbered lists, and the use of multiple modalities. These topics are a subject of future work.

```
sequence([number_elements: 5],
[elements: [[1, atomic,
                [index: a1,
                 predicate: [sem: find],
                  argument: [index: people1,
                   syn: [category: np],
                   text: [some,interested,people]]]],
            [2, atomic,
                [index: a2,
                 predicate: [sem: choose],
                  argument: [index: movie1,
                             syn: [category: np],
                             text: [a,movie]]]],
            [3, simple_branch, [number_elements: 2],
                [elements: [[1, atomic,
                                [index: a3,
                                 predicate: [sem: buy],
                                  argument: [index: tickets1,
                                             syn: [category: np],
                                             text: [the,tickets]]]],
                            [2, atomic,
                                [index: a4,
                                 predicate: [sem: arrange],
                                  argument: [index: place1,
                                             syn: [category: np],
                                             text: [a,meeting,place]]]]]]],
            [4, atomic,
                [index: a5,
                 predicate: [sem: meet],
                  argument: [index: place1,
                             syn: [category: np],
                             text: [the,meeting,place]]]],
            [5, atomic,
                [index: a6,
                 predicate: [sem: enter],
                  argument: [index: cinema1,
                             syn: [category: np],
                             text: [the,cinema]]]]]])
```

Fig. 4. Adding semantic content and referring expressions to the description structure

```
sequence([number_elements: 5],
[elements: [[1, atomic,
                [index: a1,
                 syn: [category: s, pre_adjunct: [first,',']],
                 predicate: [sem: find,
                                syn: [category: v,
                                      vform: imperative]],
                   argument: [index: people1,
                              syn: [category: np],
                              text: [some,interested,people]]]]],
             [2, atomic,
                [index: a2,
                 syn: [category: s, pre_adjunct: [then,',']],
                 predicate: [sem: choose,
                                syn: [category: v,
                                      vform: imperative]],
                   argument: [index: movie1,
                              syn: [category: np],
                              text: [a,movie]]]]],
             [3, simple_branch, [number_elements: 2],
                [syn: [category: s],
                 pre_adjunct: [then,','],
                 conjunct: [and],
                 post_adj: [',',doing,these,in,any,order,you,like],
                 [elements: [[1, atomic,
                                [index: a3,
                                 syn: [category: s],
                                 predicate: [sem: buy,
                                                syn: [category: v,
                                                      vform: imperative]],
                                   argument: [index: tickets1,
                                              syn: [category: np],
                                              text: [the,tickets]]]]]
        [...]
```

Fig. 5. The result of applying realisation strategies to the description structure

```
[paragraph(1, [sentence([first,',',find,some,interested,people]),
              sentence([then,',',choose,a,movie]),
              sentence([then,',',buy,the,tickets,and,arrange,
                        a,meeting,place,',',doing,these,in,
                        any,order,you,like]),
              sentence([then,',',meet,at,the,meeting,place]),
              sentence([finally,',',go,into,the,cinema])])])]
```

Fig. 6. The final set of sentence specifications

The results of this process are shown in Figure 5. Here, we can see that the structure realisation rules for atomic actions have determined various aspects of the sentential forms to be used. By taking account of the number of the elements in the sequence, appropriate adjuncts for *first*, *then*, and *finally* are added; an alternative realisation rule might decide to use the adjuncts *second*, *third* and so on instead of *then*. The realisation rules have also determined that the imperative forms of the verbs should be used.

Surface Realisation Our description structure now contains enough information to be able to determine the final lexical content of our plan description. Information about the realisation of different verb forms is encoded in the system lexicon by means of entries like the following:

```
lex([category: verb, sem: find, vform:imperative,lex:find]).
lex([category: verb, sem: find, vform:progressive,lex:finding]).
```

The result of incorporating this information is a final specification for the text to be generated, as in Figure 6. These specifications are passed to a rendering module which, at present, simply uppercases the first character of the first word of each sentence and appends a full stop at the end of each sentence, and wraps the entire paragraph within appropriate HTML tags:

```
<p>
First, find some interested people.
Then, choose a movie.
Then, buy the tickets and arrange a meeting place,
doing these in any order you like.
Then, meet at the meeting place.
Finally, go into the cinema.
<\p>
```

Clearly, some improvements to the overall fluency are possible here, in particular with regard to the use of appropriate forms of subsequent. However, the key element of the system's behaviour we wish to focus on here is the use of the intermediate level of representation—the description structure—in enabling us to create textual realisations whose overall structure is coherent. In the next section we look at how this is used in a more complex example.

4 Dealing with Embedded Parallelism

4.1 The Project Plan

Figure 7 shows a PERT chart of a section of a plan dealing with housework. This part of the plan deals with cleaning the kitchen and dining area. After the task of ensuring that one has the required equipment, the tasks involved follow two main parallel branches. On one branch, we have the task of washing the

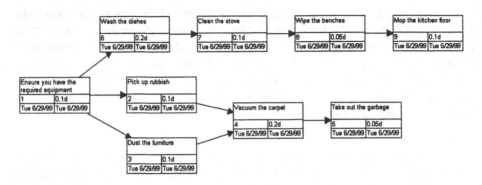

Fig. 7. A more complex plan fragment

dishes, followed by cleaning the stove, followed by wiping the benches, followed by mopping the kitchen floor. On the other branch we start with picking up rubbish and dusting the furniture, related to each other in simple parallelism. These two tasks are followed by vacuuming the floor, which is followed by taking out the garbage.

This plan provides an example of a structure we call EMBEDDED PARALLELISM: this occurs when the plan contains two or more collections of actions, where the ordering between these collections of actions does not matter, and where there is also parallelism within at least one of these collections of actions. The case shown here is also more complex than our first example above in that the two top-level parallel structures each contain more than one action in a sequence.

This plan information is provided to PLANPRESENTER in a form similar to that shown for our earlier example.

4.2   Producing an Output Text

Given the above input, PLANPRESENTER produces the following output text:

> First, ensure you have the required equipment. You are now ready for two main parts of the cleaning, which may be done in any order, or alongside each other.
> The first part is as follows. First, pick up any rubbish and dust the furniture, doing these in any order you like. Then, vacuum the carpet. Finally, take out the garbage.
> The second part is as follows. First, wash the dishes. Then, clean the stove. Then, wipe the benches. Finally, mop the kitchen floor.

Note that the parallel relationships that exist in the plan are preserved in the text.

As before, in order to generate this text we first construct an information structure as follows:

```
sequence([number_elements: 2],
[elements: [[1, atomic, a1],
            [2, complex_branch, [number_elements: 2],
             [elements:
              [[1, sequence, [number_elements: 3],
                [elements: [[1, simple_branch, [number_elements: 2],
                            [elements: [[1, atomic, a2],
                                        [2, atomic, a3]]]]
                           [2, atomic, a4],
                           [3, atomic, a5]]]]
               [2, sequence,[number_elements: 4]
                [elements: [[1, atomic, a6],
                            [2, atomic, a7],
                            [3, atomic, a8],
                            [4, atomic, a9]]]]]]]]])
```

Fig. 8. Representing sequence and embedded parallelism

```
sequence([a1,parallel([sequence([parallel([a2,a3]),a4,a5]),
                       sequence([a6,a7,a8,a9])])]).
```

Figure 8 shows part of the description structure that is then constructed from this representation. Note that this structure differs from our previous example in that, in building the description structure, we have recognised the presence of a COMPLEX BRANCH.

The realisation strategies then augment this structure with relevant syntactic and semantic information as before; in this case, the presence of the complex branch results in a realisation decision that the two parts of this branch should be realised by means of separate paragraphs, and that the entire text should be preceded by a sentence that indicates the overall structure of the plan.

Once complete, this description structure is then passed on to the surface realisation component, which produces the output specification shown in Figure 9.

5 Conclusions and Next Steps

In this paper, we have presented a NLG system that addresses the problem of generating English natural language descriptions of plans that contain non-linear elements. As a first step in this exercise, we have focussed on the problem of how to express parallelism at different levels of complexity. We have demonstrated how the use of an intermediate representation that encodes information about the overall structure of the plan can serve both as a updateable repository of information regarding the text to be generated, and as a structure that supports reasoning about the best ways to present that information. The resulting texts present instructions for performing the input plans in a way that makes attempts to remove potential ambiguities in the structures described.

```
[paragraph(1,  [sentence([first,ensure,you,have,the,required,equipment]),
                sentence([you,are,now,ready,for,two,main,parts,
                          of,the,cleaning,which,may,be,done,in,
                          any,order,or,alongside,each,other])]),
 paragraph(2,  [sentence([the,first,part,is,as,follows]),
                sentence([first,pick,up,any,rubbish,and,dust,the,
                          furniture,doing,these,in,any,order,you,like]),
                sentence([then,vacuum,the,carpet]),
                sentence([finally,take,out,the,garbage])]),
 paragraph(3,  [sentence([the,second,part,is,as,follows]),
                sentence([first,wash,the,dishes]),
                sentence([then,clean,the,stove]),
                sentence([then,wipe,the,benches]),
                sentence([finally,mop,the,kitchen,floor])])])]
```

Fig. 9. The final set of sentence specifications

So far we have only scratched the surface in this exploration of how to describe non-linear structures. There are three major directions in which we intend to extend the current work.

First, in many cases, a plan can be described hierarchically in terms of a number of high-level actions, each of which can consist of other high-level actions or atomic actions. We aim to incorporate this hierarchical information into our descriptions.

A second avenue of development concerns the means of expression that are available to PLANPRESENTER. So far we have only used simple typographic mechanisms, such as paragraph structuring, to indicate the underlying structure of the plan. We aim to extend the range of realisation strategies available to the system so that more sophisticated outputs can be achieved.

Finally, so far we do not make use of a significant amount of other information regarding durations and resources that is available to us; we intend to incorporate this information to provide more complete descriptions of plans.

References

1. Elizabeth André and Thomas Rist. Generating coherent presentations employing textual and visual material. *Artifical Intelligence Review*, 9:147–165, 1994.
2. Robert Dale. *Generating Referring Expressions: Constructing Descriptions in a Domain of Objects and Processes*. MIT Press, Cambridge, MA, 1992.
3. Eli Goldberg, Norbert Driedger, and Richard Kittredge. Using natural-language processing to produce weather forecasts. *IEEE Expert*, 9(2):45–53, 1994.
4. Benoit Lavoie, Owen Rambow, and Ehud Reiter. Customizable descriptions of object-oriented models. In *Proceedings of the Fifth Conference on Applied Natural-Language Processing (ANLP-1997)*, pages 253–256, 1997.

5. John Levine, Alison Cawsey, Chris Mellish, Lawrence Poynter, Ehud Reiter, Paul Tyson, and John Walker. IDAS: Combining hypertext and natural language generation. In *Proceedings of the Third European Workshop on Natural Language Generation*, pages 55–62, Innsbruck, Austria, 1991.
6. Chris Mellish and Roger Evans. Natural language generation from plans. *Computational Linguistics*, 15(4):233–249, 1989.
7. Maria Milosavljevic, Adrian Tulloch, and Robert Dale. Text generation in a dynamic hypertext environment. In *Proceedings of the 19th Australasian Computer Science Conference*, pages 417–426, Melbourne, Australia, 31 January–2 February 1996.
8. Ehud Reiter and Robert Dale. *Building Natural Language Generation Systems*. Cambridge University Press, 2000.

Categorizing Unknown Words: A Decision Tree-Based Misspelling Identifier

Janine Toole

Natural Language Lab, School of Computing Science, Simon Fraser University,
Burnaby, BC, Canada V5A 1S6
toole@cs.sfu.ca

Abstract. This paper introduces a robust, portable system for categorizing unknown words. It is based on a multi- component architecture where each component is responsible for identifying one class of unknown words. The focus of this paper is the component that identifies spelling errors. The misspelling identifier uses a decision tree architecture to combine multiple types of evidence about the unknown word. The misspelling identifier is evaluated using data from live closed captions - a genre replete with a wide variety of unknown words.

1 Introduction

In any real world use, a Natural Language Processing (NLP) system will encounter words that it does not recognize, what we term 'unknown words'. Unknown words are problematic because a NLP system will perform well only if it recognizes the words that it is meant to analyze or translate: the more words a system does not recognize the more the system's performance will degrade. Even when unknown words are infrequent, they can have a disproportionate effect on system quality. For example, Min [13] found that while only 0.6% of words in 300 e-mails were misspelled, this led to 12% of the sentences having errors (discussed in Min and Wilson [14]).

Words may be unknown for many reasons: the word may be a proper name, a misspelling, an abbreviation, a number, a morphological variant of a known word (e.g. *bigness*), or simply missing from the dictionary. The first step in dealing with unknown words is to identify the class of the unknown word; whether it is a misspelling, a proper name, an abbreviation etc. Once this is known, the proper action can be taken, misspellings can be corrected, abbreviations can be expanded and so on, as deemed necessary by the particular text processing application. In this paper we introduce a system for categorizing unknown words. The system is based on a multi- component architecture where each component is responsible for identifying one category of unknown words. The main focus of this paper is the component that identifies spelling errors. The misspelling identifier uses a decision tree architecture to combine multiple types of evidence about the unknown word. The misspelling identifier is evaluated using data from live closed captions - a genre replete with a wide variety of unknown words.

N. Foo (Ed.): AI'99, LNAI 1747, pp. 122–133, 1999.

This paper is organized as follows. In section 2 we outline the overall architecture of the unknown word categorizer (UWC). The misspelling identifier is introduced in section 3. Performance and evaluation issues are discussed in section 4. Section 5 compares the current system with relevant preceding research. Concluding comments can be found in section 6.

2   The Unknown Word Categorizer (UWC)

The goal of our research is to develop a system that automatically categorizes unknown words. According to our definition, an unknown word is a word that is not contained in the lexicon of an NLP system. As defined, 'unknown-ness' is a relative concept: a word that is known to one system may be unknown to another system.

Our research is motivated by the problems that we have experienced in translating live closed captions: live captions are produced under tight time constraints and contain many unknown words. Typically, the caption transcriber has a five second window to transcribe the broadcast dialogue. Because of the live nature of the broadcast, there is no opportunity to post-edit the transcript in any way.

As can be seen from Table 3, unknown words comprise about 2.3% of the words in our corpus of closed captions from business news programs. On average each caption line is 10.6 words (we translate captions line by line). Thus, on average every fourth line contains an unknown word. Table 4 provides insight into the distribution of unknown words in this corpus. The majority of unknown words in this sample are proper names. This is not surprising given the subject domain. However, there is also a large proportion of misspellings. This is primarily due to the constraints under which these captions are produced. As noted above, live captions are produced under strict time constraints and there is no time for post-editing. The data also contains examples of abbreviations, foreign words, and words missing from the lexicon. The thirty one numerical expressions that occur in this sample have been excluded from this list and from the calculations in Table 3 since our MT system includes a separate number parsing component.

Percentage of unknown words	2.33%
Average line length	10.6
Percentage of lines, on average, containing an unknown word	24.7%

Table 1. Data on unknown words from 5000 word sample

Although motivated by our specific requirements, the unknown word categorizer would benefit any NLP system that encounters unknown words of differing categories. Some immediately obvious domains where unknown words are frequent include e-mail messages, internet chat rooms, data typed in by call centre operators, etc. Any NLP system that needs to interpret, translate or text-mine

Name	62
Misspelling	24
Abbreviation	4
Foreign word	2
Missing from lexicon/morphological variant	25

Table 2. Distribution of unknown words from 5000 word sample

these types of data will need to deal with the problems posed by the many types of unknown words.

The environment in which we foresee using the unknown word categorizer imposes a further constraint: the system must be portable to different genres and languages, each of which may have different types and proportions of unknown words. To deal with these issues we propose a multi-component architecture where individual components specialize in identifying one particular type of unknown word. For example, the misspelling identifier will specialize in identifying misspellings, the abbreviation component will specialize in identifying abbreviations, etc. Each component will return a confidence measure of the reliability of its prediction (c.f. Elworthy [5]). The results from each component are evaluated to determine the final category of the word.

There are several advantages to this approach. Firstly, the system can take advantage of existing research. For example, the name recognition module can make use of the considerable research that exists on name recognition (e.g. McDonald [12], Mani et al. [11]). Secondly, this approach facilitates tuning for different domains. For example, some domains may have no unknown proper names. In these cases this component need not be included. For example, in their automatic spelling correction system integrated into an intelligent tutor for medical students, Elmi and Evens [4] assume that all unknown words are misspellings or abbreviations. In this case, all components except the misspelling and abbreviation components can be removed. Thirdly, individual components can be replaced when improved models are available, without affecting other parts of the system. Fourthly, this approach is compatible with incorporating multiple components of the same type to improve performance (cf. Van Halteren et al. [7] who found that combining the results of several part of speech taggers increased performance).

3   The Misspelling Identifier

The main purpose of this paper is to introduce the misspelling identifier. The goal of the misspelling identifier is to differentiate between those unknown words which are spelling errors and those which are not. We define a misspelling as an unintended, orthographically incorrect representation (with respect to an NLP system) of a word. A misspelling differs from the intended known word through one or more additions, deletions, substitutions, or reversals of letters, or the exclusion of punctuation such as hyphenation or spacing. Table 1 contains several examples of misspellings. 'Distincttion' differs from the known word 'distinction' by the addition of a letter. 'Laidup' differs from the known phrase 'laid up' by the deletion of a space. 'Foss' differs from the known word 'force' by the substitution and deletion of letters. Finally, the unknown word 'clamor' differs from the known word 'clamour' by the deletion of the vowel 'u'.

Misspelled unknown word	Correct Spelling
distincttion	distinction
laidup	laid up
foss	force
clamor	clamour

Table 3. Examples of Misspellings

Like the definition of 'unknown word', the definition of a misspelling is also relative to a particular NLP system. For example, a system that only includes British spellings like 'clamour' will not recognize American alternatives such as 'clamor', and vice versa. We consider these variants to be misspellings (from the system's perspective) since they differ from a known intended word by one or more substitutions, deletions, etc. Once identified as a misspelling such words can then be 'corrected' to the known spelling.

In order to identify those unknown words which are misspellings, we utilize a binary decision tree to model the characteristics of misspellings. Decision trees are automatically induced from a series of cases. A range of variables (or features) are specified for each case. The resulting decision tree consists of a series of zero or more internal decision nodes and terminal leaves. Each node represents a decision point. In order to classify a new instance, one starts at the root of the tree and follows the decision nodes to a terminal leaf.

The advantage of decision trees is that they are highly explainable: one can readily understand the features that are affecting the analysis (Weiss and Indurkhya [17]). They are fast, and the purity of individual nodes provides a measure of reliability for individual predictions. Furthermore, decision trees are well-suited for combining a wide variety of information. Hence, it is particularly suited to an explorative investigation such as this paper describes. For this project, we made use of the Decision Tree that is part of IBM's Intelligent Miner suite for data mining.

The features we use are intended to capture the characteristics of misspellings. These are predominantly derived from previous research. However, we also include some more exploratory features. The features fall into two categories: (i) lexical features: characteristics of the unknown word, and (ii) contextual features: characteristics of the context in which the unknown word occurs. An abridged list of the features that are used in the training data is listed in Table 2 and discussed below. We exemplify the discussion using data from our training corpus: live closed captions from business news broadcasts. The effectiveness of the various features is discussed more fully in the section on evaluation.

Characteristics of the Word	Characteristics of the Context
Corpus frequency	Distance to next unknown
Word length	Part of speech
Edit distance	Suggestion in context
Ispell information	Local frequency
Character sequence frequency	Name in vicinity
Non-English characters	

Table 4. Features used in decision tree

Corpus frequency Vosse [16] differentiates between misspellings and neologisms (new words) in terms of their frequency. His algorithm classifies unknown words that appear infrequently as misspellings, and those that appear more frequently as neologisms. Our corpus frequency variable specifies the frequency of each unknown word in a 2.6 million word corpus of business news closed captions.

Word length Agirre et al. [1] note that their predictions for the correct spelling of misspelled words are more accurate for words longer than four characters, and much less accurate for shorter words. This observation can also be found in Kukich [10]. Our word length variables measures the number of characters in each word.

Edit Distance Edit-distance is a metric for identifying the orthographic similarity of two words. Typically, one edit-distance corresponds to one substitution, deletion, reversal or addition of a character. Damerau [3] observed that 80% of spelling errors in his data were just one edit-distance from the intended word. Similarly, Mitton [15] found that 70% of his data was within one edit-distance from the intended word. We implement this feature as follows. We use the unix ispell program to generate spelling suggestions for each unknown word. We then calculate three different distance measures for each suggestion and select the measures for the ispell suggestion that is most similar to the unknown word. The first distance measure is the simple edit-distance metric introduced above; the number of substitutions, insertions, deletions, reversals required to convert from one word to the other. The other distance measures we use are the score and percentage returned by the 'lalign' program (Huang and Miller [8]). The lalign program was originally developed for aligning DNA sequences, but it is equally effective for aligning character sequences, and returns two scores representing their similarity.

Ispell Information Unix ispell is a spell-checking program that returns a variety of information about the words it checks. There are five different return codes that indicate the status of the word; correctly spelled, incorrectly spelled with suggestions, incorrectly spelled without suggestions, etc. A categorical variable captures this information.

Character sequence frequency A characteristic of some misspellings is that they contain character sequences which are not typical of the language, e.g. *tlted, wful.* Exploiting this information is a standard way of identifying spelling errors when using a dictionary is not desired or appropriate. The best results reported are obtained using positional binary tri- grams (e.g. Hull and Srihari [9]). A positional binary tri-gram array contains information about the existence/non-existence of a tri-gram *abc* occurring in position *ijk*. Recent work records the frequency of trigrams, rather than just (non-) existence.

The disadvantage of positional binary tri-grams is that they require a large number of parameters. In this paper we use an alternate approach that requires fewer parameters. Before calculating character sequence frequency, we append an identifier, such as '#' to the beginning and end of each word. These identifiers are included in determining the character n-grams. For example, the word 'house' consists of the following tri-grams: *#ho, hou, ous, use, se#*. These tri-grams are sensitive to character sequences at the beginning and end of a word but do not differentiate where a sequence occurs within a word. Hence, fewer parameters need to be stored.

Having determined which tri-grams to consider, the next question that arises is what source to use to determine frequencies. Early work calculated character sequence frequencies from lexicons. However, Zamora [18] obtain better results by using a corpus rather than a dictionary. Since our corpus is very noisy, i.e. it contains many unknown words, it is not clear whether this corpus would obtain the same results. For this reason we hedge our bets and obtain frequency data from a range of sources: the Oxford Advanced Learners Dictionary; a 2.6 million word corpus of business news closed captions; an 11 million word corpus of non-live closed captions (less noisy); and the approximately one million word Lund-Oslo-Bergen corpus. The frequencies for each corpus are represented by separate features, two for each corpus. The two features contain the frequencies of the two lowest frequency tri-grams found in each word.

The features discussed to this point have been well-motivated by previous research. In the following we outline some of the more exploratory features which we have included in the current version of the misspelling identifier.

Non-English Characters This binary feature specifies whether a word contains a character that is not typical of English words, such as accented characters, etc.

Distance to next unknown This feature identifies the distance, in number of words, to the next unknown word.

Part of Speech (POS) The tagset we used is a reduced version of the tags used in the Oxford Advanced Learners Dictionary.

Suggestion in context As described above, the unix ispell program returns a list of possible spellings for the unknown word. This feature specifies whether any of these spellings occur in the nearby context. This feature is motivated by the characteristics of live closed captions: captioners occasionally follow a misspelling with the correct form of the word.

Local frequency This feature specifies whether the unknown word itself occurs in the local context. Local context in this case is defined as plus or minus twenty words.

Name in Vicinity We include two features identifying whether this word is a name or is adjacent to a word identified as a name. We make use of a simple proper name recognizer that we have available. This name recognizer cues off titles and other easy to determine information since captions do not include case information (the main information source for most proper name recognizers).

All of the features that we have included have at least one thing in common: they are extremely portable. Each of them can be readily re-calculated for a new domain, or even a new language. Apart from a corpus of the new domain and language, the only other requirements are some means of generating spelling suggestions (ispell is available for many languages), some type of proper name recognizer, and optionally, a part of speech tagger (although we are not yet convinced of the usefulness of this feature). If more information sources are available, such as the results of morphological, syntactic, or semantic analysis, then these can readily be included in the decision tree training corpus. For our purposes, where portability is an important criteria, we avoid the use of such application-specific information sources.

4   Evaluation

In this section we evaluate the misspelling identifier introduced above.

The training data for the decision tree consists of 1350 cases of unknown words extracted from a 2.6 million word corpus of live business news captions. The relatively small size of the training data was partly motivated by the portability requirement: for training and testing it is necessary to manually identify the unknown words that are misspellings, (all the other features can be automatically generated). Hence, a system that requires only a small training set is more portable than one that requires a large training set.

The data was split into ten training/test sets. The test set contains ten percent of the data. The training set contains the remaining ninety percent. Each test set covers a different ten percent of the data. The results reported below are for the average over the ten tests. Given the small size of the test and training sets, this is a more reliable approach than simply splitting the data into a single training set.

The average precision and recall data for the ten tests are given in Table 5, together with two base-line cases. The first base-line case assumes that we categorize all unknown words as misspellings. Tthe second base-line case assumes that all unknown words are not misspellings. As can be seen, the current state of the system is a significant improvement over the baseline cases. The baseline case for predicting spelling errors is 39.6% precision. In contrast, the decision tree approach obtains 71.8% precision and 71.2% recall.

	Baseline Precision	Precision	Recall
Predicting Misspellings	39.6%	71.8%	71.2%
Predicting Non-misspellings	60.4%	81.2%	81.2%

Table 5. Precision and recall for baseline and initial decision tree

The above results assume that both types of possible errors are weighted equally. (The two types of errors are: classifying a misspelling as correct, and classifying a correct word as a misspelling.) However, since the misspelling identifier is the only opportunity in the system for identifying spelling errors, the system should emphasize recall over precision. That is, it is more important that the misspelling identifier identify all spelling errors, at the cost of including some correctly spelled words. Since the misspelling identifier is embedded in a larger system where the results from all components are combined, there is the opportunity for those words that are incorrectly deemed to be spelling errors to be re-classified.

Hence, we include results in Table 6 for a weighted tree which emphasizes recall over precision. The tree is weighted so that the cost of predicting that a misspelling is correct is six times the cost of predicting that a correct spelling is a misspelling. (The weighting factor of six was obtained empirically through manual manipulation of the weighting factor). Using this approach increases the recall to 91.4% with a loss of precision to 57.3%. In the remainder of this section, we explore these results in more detail to determine which features are most influential in identifying spelling errors and which cases are most resistant to correct classification.

	Precision	Recall
Predicting Misspellings: weighted by 6.	57.3%	91.4%

Table 6. Precision and recall for weighted tree

Evaluation of our feature set reveals that several rely on the ispell program to predict possible correct alternatives. Features which rely on this information include all three edit distance measures and the 'suggestion in context' feature. This suggests that we may do best in those cases where possible spellings exist and less well in those cases where ispell could not provide alternative suggestions. Indeed this is the case. If we include only those cases where ispell can provide a suggestion, then our test results improve considerably even though the training set is reduced by 35%. These results can be found in Table 7. Unweighted results are given in the first entry. Recall has increased to 75.9% and precision has increased to 74.9%. Weighting these results also gives significantly increased recall, as indicated by the second line of Table 7. 97.0% recall of these examples can be achieved with 61.0% precision. (Again, the weighting factor was determined empirically by manual adjustment of the weighting factor). This indicates that we will have to focus more attention on developing features which are less reliant on the information provided by ispell in order to increase the accuracy of the decision tree on all the examples.

	Precision	Recall
Predicting Misspellings	74.9%	75.9%
Predicting Misspellings: weighted by 10	61.0%	97.0%

Table 7. Precision and recall for reduced training data

Analysis of the ten trees produced by the training process also provides interesting insight into the strengths and weaknesses of the current approach. In the following discussion we evaluate the decision trees produced by reduced training/test data. Although each tree was trained on a small training corpus, there is considerable similarity between the trees. Three of the features are found in each of the trees. These are listed in Table 8, together with the node level at which they first appear in each of the ten trees. This table indicates that the first three levels of the decision trees are quite similar. Each tree uses the frequency of the unknown word in the corpus as the first feature on which to branch the tree. Similarly, each tree makes use of edit distance as one of the features on which to make the secondary split. Thirdly, the name feature is common to all trees at the third level, except for tree5 where it appears at the second level.

Trees	tree1	tree2	tree3	tree4	tree5	tree6	tree7	tree8	tree9	tree10
Frequency	1	1	1	1	1	1	1	1	1	1
Edit Distance	2	2	2	2	2	2	2	2	2	2
Name	3	3	3	3	2	3	3	3	3	3

Table 8. Features common to all trees and the level at which they first occur in each tree

All but three of the remaining features found in the trees are character sequence features. Recall, we extracted character sequence frequencies from a range of corpora. For each unknown word we extract the two lowest frequency character tri-grams found in the unknown word. No one frequency feature was definitive enough to be found in all of the trees. However, the fact that at least one such feature was found in every tree indicates that this type of information has predictive value. One of our next steps will be to explore different ways of exploiting this information in a way that can be more consistently predictive.

The three remaining features which occur in the trees are word length, lalign percent, and the non-English feature. Table 9 indicates the relative usefulness of these features. Word length was used in nine out of the ten trees and hence is a valuable feature. In contrast, lalign percent and the feature identifying words with non-English characters occur only one or two times. The infrequency of the lalign percent feature and the total absence of the lalign score feature are no doubt due to the superior predictive value of the simple edit-distance feature. As we noted in Table 8, edit-distance occurs uniformly in every tree at the second branching level. This indicates that the simpler edit distance measure may be sufficient for the purposes of detecting misspellings, and that the more sophisticated approaches, as represented by the lalign features, are essentially redundant.

Trees	tree1	tree2	tree3	tree4	tree5	tree6	tree7	tree8	tree9	tree10
Word length	5			4	4	3	4	7	3	6	4
Lalign percent	4	5								
Non-English		3								

Table 9. Features common to all trees and the level at which they first occur in each tree

This discussion provides excellent insight into productive directions for future research. Our first step will be to experiment with the character sequence features in order to identify features that will lead to more stable trees, i.e. we need to find one or two such features that can be found across all trees rather than the diverse range of character sequence features that we have now which all appear inconsistently. Secondly, our best results have been with misspellings for which ispell can provide alternate suggestions. We need to evaluate means by which we can improve our accuracy on the remaining unknown words. Thirdly, we plan to increase the size of the training corpus to determine the possible benefits to be gained from a larger training and test set.

Further, one of our primary goals has been to develop a system that could rapidly be tuned for a new domain or language. An immediate goal is to tune the system for the domain of e-mail messages and evaluate its performance. Like the domain of closed caption, e-mail messages also contain many unknown words. However, unlike closed captions, e-mail messages usually contain case information, thus making the differentiation between misspellings and proper names an easier task.

5 Related Research

There is little research that has focused on differentiating misspellings from other rtpes of unknown words. For example, research on spelling error detection and correction for the most part assumes that all unknown words are misspellings and make no attempt to identify other types of unknown words (e.g. Elmi and Evens [4]). Naturally, these are not appropriate comparisons for the work reported here. However, as is evident from the discussion above, previous spelling research does provide an important role in suggesting productive features to include in the decision tree.

Research that is more similar in goal to that outlined in this paper is Vosse [16]. Vosse uses a simple algorithm to identify three classes of unknown words: misspellings, neologisms, and names. Capitalization is his sole means of identifying names. However, capitalization information is not available in closed captions. Hence, his system would be ineffective on the closed caption domain with which we are working. Granger [6] uses expectations generated by scripts to analyze unknown words. The drawback of his system is that it lacks portability since it makes use of scripts.

Research that is similar in technique to that reported here is Baluja et al. [2]. Baluja and his colleagues use a decision tree classifier to identify proper names in text. Their motivation for using this approach reflects our own: decision tree classifiers are effective at combining different types of information.

6   Conclusion

In this paper we have introduced the misspelling identifier component of the unknown word categorizer. The purpose of the misspelling identifier is to identify those unknown words that are misspellings. Because of the requirements of the unknown word categorizer in which this component is embedded, the spelling identifier must be readily tunable to different domains and languages. To this end, we introduced a decision tree-based system which combines multiple types of information about the unknown word. The types of features used to characterize misspellings are readily recalculated for new domains and languages. The system provides encouraging results when evaluated against a particularly challenging domain: transcripts from live closed captions. Evaluation of the results indicates several productive directions for future work. Further, although this system has been motivated by the demands of the closed caption domain in which we are working, the unknown word categorizer will be useful in any domain that contains different types of unknown words. Relevant domains which we identified include e-mail, internet chat, and call-centre data.

References

1. Agirre, E. Gojenola, K., Sarasola, K., and Voutilainen, A. (1998). Towards a single proposal in spelling correction. In the Proceedings of the 36th Annual Meeting of the ACL and the 17th International Conference on Computational Linguistics, Montreal 1998: 22-28.
2. Baluja, S., Mittal, V., and Sukthankar, R. (1999). Applying machine learning for high performance named-entity extraction. In the Proceedings of the Conference of the Pacific Association for Computational Linguistics, Waterloo 1999: 365-378.
3. Damerau, F. (1964). A technique for computer detection and correction of spelling errors. Communications of the ACM 7, 3: 171-176.

4. Elmi, M., and Evens, M. (1998). Spelling correction using context. In the Proceedings of the 36th Annual Meeting of the ACL and the 17th International Conference on Computational Linguistics, Montreal: 360-364.

5. Elworthy, D. (1998). Language identification with confidence limits. In Charniak (ed.) Proceedings of the 6th Workshop on Very large Corpora. August 15-16, Montreal.

6. Granger, R. (1983). The NOMAD system: expectation-based detection and correction of errors during understanding of syntactically and semantically ill-formed text. American Journal of Computational Linguistics, 9: 188-198.

7. van Halteren, H., Zavrel, J., and Daelemans, W. (1998). Improving data driven word class tagging by system combination. In the Proceedings of the 36th Annual Meeting of the ACL and the 17th International Conference on Computational Linguistics, Montreal 1998: 491-497.

8. Huang, X. and Miller, W. (1991). Advanced Applied Mathematics, 12: 337-57.

9. Hull, J., and Srihari, S. (1982). Experiments in text recognition with binary n-gram and Viterbi algorithms. IEEE Trans. Patt. Anal. Machine Intell. PAMI-4, 5: 520-530.

10. Kukich, K. (1992). Techniques for automatically correcting words in text. ACM Computing Surveys, vol 24 No 4: 377-439.

11. Mani, I., McMillan, R., Luperfoy, S., Lusher, E., and Laskowski, S. (1996). Identifying unknown proper names in newswire text. In Bran Boguraev and James Pustejovsky (eds.) Corpus Processing for Lexical Acquisition. MIT Press, Cambridge.

12. McDonald, David. (1996). Internal and external evidence in the identification and semantic categorization of proper names. In Bran Boguraev and James Pustejovsky (eds.) Corpus Processing for Lexical Acquisition. MIT Press, Cambridge.

13. Min, K. (1996). Hierarchical Error Recovery Based on Bidirectional Chart Parsing Techniques. Ph.D. Dissertation, University of NSW, Sydney, Australia.

14. Min, K. and Wilson, W. (1998). Integrated control of chart items for error repair. In Proceedings of the 36th Annual Meeting of the Association for Computational Linguistics and the 17th International Conference on Computational Linguistics, August 10-14, Montreal, Canada.

15. Mitton, R. (1987). Spelling checkers, spelling correctors, and the misspellings of poor spellers. Inf. Process. Manage., 23, 5: 495-505.

16. Vosse, T. (1992). Detecting and correcting morpho-syntactic errors in real texts. In Proceedings of the 3rd Conference on Applied Natural Language Processing, Trento Italy: 111-118.

17. Weiss, S. and Indurkhya, N. (1998). Predictive Data Mining. San Francisco, Morgan Kauffman Publishers.

18. Zamora, E., Pollock, J., and Zamora, A. (1981). The use of tri-gram analysis for spelling error detection. Inf. Process. Manage. 17, 6: 305-316.

Sync/Trans: Simultaneous Machine Interpretation between English and Japanese

Shigeki Matsubara[1], Katsuhiko Toyama[2,3], and Yasuyoshi Inagaki[2]

[1] Faculty of Language and Culture, Nagoya University
matubara@lang.nagoya-u.ac.jp
[2] Department of Computational Science and Engineeering, Nagoya University
[3] Center for Integrated Acoustic Information Research, Nagoya University
Furo-cho, Chikusa-ku, Nagoya 464-8601, Japan

Abstract. This paper describes Sync/Trans, an incremental spoken language translation system. The system has been being developed for efficiently translating a spontaneous speech dialogue between an English speaker and a Japanese speaker. Its purpose being to behave as a simultaneous interpreter, the system produces the target output synchronously with the source input. Sync/Trans has the following features: (1) the system consists of modules that work in a synchronous fashion, (2) the system translates the source language possibly word-by-word according to the appearance order, (3) the system utilizes grammatically ill-formed expressions for the speech output, and (4) the system corrects the grammatical ill-formedness of the speech input at a pretty early stage. An experimental system for translating English speech into Japanese speech has been implemented. A few experimental results have shown Sync/Trans to be a promising system for simultaneous interpretation.

1 Introduction

Immediate speech comprehension and production are essential to a smooth interaction in a spoken dialogue. A spontaneously spoken dialogue through interpretation systems thus demands that they should also participate in the dialogue without preventing the coherence.

Our intuitions suggest that efficient speech dialogue translation strongly requires a simultaneous interpretation which is one of the ambitious applications in artificial intelligence [10]. As an example, let us consider a dialogue between an English speaker and a Japanese speaker through an English-Japanese interpretation system and a Japanese-English interpretation system. Figure 1 shows a comparison with the dialogue using a conventional machine translation system. Since the conventional system cannot start the translation processing until the input of an entire Japanese/English sentence finishes, the waiting time [1] of the

---

[1] This means the time from the end of an utterance by the English/Japanese speaker to the start of the utterance by the Japanese-English/English-Japanese interpretation system.

N. Foo (Ed.): AI'99, LNAI 1747, pp. 134–143, 1999.

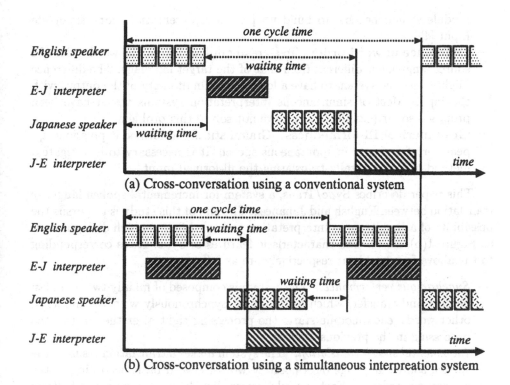

(a) Cross-conversation using a conventional system

(b) Cross-conversation using a simultaneous interpreation system

Fig. 1. Comparison between a dialogue through conventional systems and a dialogue through simultaneous interpretation systems

English/Japanese speaker is long. Therefore, the time required for one cycle [2] necessarily becomes long. On the other hand, since the simultaneous interpretation system can start translating it right after the start of the input, the waiting time is reduced. As a result, the time of one cycle also becomes shorter.

The following enumerates several problems that should be solved in the development of a simultaneous interpretation system.

- **Architecture** A machine translation system is usually composed of modules such as parsing, transfer and generation, which work sequentially in a compositional way [11]. That is to say, each module cannot start the processing until the previous module finishes processing an entire sentence. It is practically impossible for such the system to behave as a simultaneous interpreter.
- **Incrementality** Current most techniques for parsing, transfer and generation process a natural language on a sentence-by-sentence basis. Each

---

[2] This means the time from the start of an utterance to the start of the next utterance by the English/Japanese speaker.

module should be able to build up partial representations for incomplete input [4].

- **Difference in word-order** To a greater or less degree, the word-order of a source language is different from that of the target language. The difference might cause the system to have a loss to the simultaneity of the output with the input. Most of simultaneous interpretation systems which have been proposed so far (e.g., [6,7,1,2]), have not solved this problem.
- **Grammatical Ill-formedness** Grammatically ill-formed expressions appear very frequently in spontaneous speech. It is necessary to investigate a method of incrementally translating the ill-formed input.

This paper describes Sync/Trans, a system for incremental spoken language translation between English and Japanese. The aim of this study is to pursue the possibility of a simultaneous interpretation and to realize a speech dialogue on it as Figure 1(b) shows. The characteristic features of Sync/Trans corresponding to the above four problems respectively are as follows:

- *Synchronous performance:* The system is composed of mainly two modules: parsing and transfer, which work almost synchronously with the input. In other words, each module starts the processing right after the start of the processing in the previous module.
- *Incremental speech translation:* The system makes a translation result of the spoken source language on a possibly word-by-word basis according to the appearance order [3]. Each module can predict the precessing result halfway through the input. The next module performs the processing using the result at any time.
- *Utilization of grammatically ill-formed expressions:* The system utilizes grammatically ill-formed expressions characterizing spoken language for the translation results [8,9]. This is a key to the success of translating between English and Japanese, which are different in word-order, in an exceedingly incremental way.
- *Correction of grammatical ill-formedness at an early stage:* Finding out grammatical ill-formedness in an input sentence, the system corrects it immediately. This enables the system to robustly proceed with the translation processing.

This paper reports on the evaluation of Sync/Trans through a few translation experiments. However, we will concentrate on the evaluation of the English-to-Japanese translation part of Sync/Trans, because the current implementation is restricted on the translation of English into Japanese.

2   English-Japanese Translation

2.1   Overview

We have developed a system for translating English speech into Japanese speech incrementally. Figure 2 shows the configuration of the system. The system is

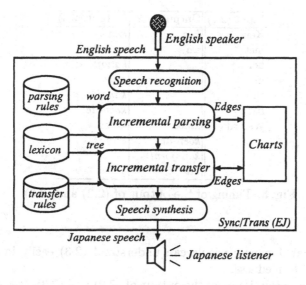

Fig. 2. Configuration of the English-Japanese part of Sync/Trans

composed of eight components: speech recognition, speech synthesis, incremental parsing, incremental transfer, parsing rules, transfer rules, a lexicon and a chart. The chart component is the data structure which represents the possible phrase structures of the source language halfway through the input. Executing incremental parsing and transfer sequentially for each word, as a consequence, the system can translate a spoken English sentence synchronously with the appearance.

2.2 Production of Grammatically Ill-formed Sentences

The expressions such as repetitions, inversions, ellipses, repairs and hesitations are grammatically ill-formed but natural in Japanese daily conversations. In order to incrementally and synchronously translate between English and Japanese which are different in word-order, the system utilizes these expressions in an effective way.

For example, although the standard Japanese translation of an simple English sentence (2.1) is (2.2), the system generates (2.3) synchronously with the input of (2.1).

(2.1) Ken met her in the park yesterday.

(2.2) *ken-wa* (Ken) *kinoo* (yesterday) *koen-de* (in the park) *kanojo-ni* (her) *atta* (met).

(2.3) *ken-wa* (Ken) *atta* (met) *kanojo-no, anoo, kanojo-ni* (her) *koen-de* (in the park) *kinoo* (yesterday) *atta* (met).

Input (2.1)	Output (2.2)	Output (2.3)
Ken	*ken*	*ken*
met	*wa*	*wa atta*
her		*kanojo-no*
in		*anoo*
the		*kanojo-ni*
park		*koen-de*
yesterday	*kinoo*	*kinoo*
	koen-de	*atta*
	kanojo-ni	
	atta	

Fig. 3. Timing of the output of (2.2) and (2.3)

We can say that Japanese people can understand (2.3) easily in spite of the grammatical ill-formedness.

Figure 3 shows the timing of the output of (2.2) and (2.3). It is obvious that the system can output (2.3) synchronously with (2.1).

2.3   Chart-Based Framework

To represent incomplete structures gained on incremental parsing, we have adopted a chart-based framework in both parsing and transfer [9].

Incremental chart parsing produces edges labeled the term whose category is a sentence. The edges represent the possible structures of the entire source language inputed up to the point of time. The altering point for the orthodox bottom-up chart parsing method [5] is that the operations of applying a parsing rule to an active edge and replacing the leftmost undecided term in an active edge with the term labeling another active edge are introduced. On the other hands, the incremental transfer produces the Japanese expressions by applying transfer rules to an edge in a top-down fashion. How the system utilizes grammatically ill-formed expressions is described as the transfer rules.

2.4   Translation of Grammatically Ill-formed Sentences

The system can translate grammatically ill-formed source sentences incrementally by correcting the error immediately after the parsing fails. Correctly constructing the structure for the well-formed part in the ill-formed sentence, the system can reproduce it as the translation result to some extent.

For example, an English sentence (2.4) can be considered as one in which a word "going" of the part "going by train" is omitted.

(2.4) I think by train is best.

The system inserts a category, e.g. gerund, immediately after "by" is inputed. The Japanese people can understand correctly the semantic contents of (2.5) which is the translation result of (2.4).

Table 1. Translation result of 278 sentences

type	sentences	rate(%)
A) correct (no repair)	96	34.5
B) correct (repairs)	132	47.5
C) unnatural	33	11.9
D) incorrect	16	5.7
E) failed	1	0.4

(2.5) *watashi-wa* (I) *omoimasu* (think) *densya-de-ga* (by train) *ichiban-ii* (is best) *to-omoimasu* (think).

3 Evaluation

An experimental system has been implemented in GNU Common Lisp 2.2 on a workstation. We have made a few experiments with the dialogues in ATR Dialogue Databse, whose task is the application of travels.

3.1 Basic Experiment

To evaluate the effectiveness of the system, to begin with, we have made a translation experiment using 4 dialogues. The dialogues consist of 278 spoken English sentences, the average length of which is 6.8 words. The system has been implemented in the scale of 476 English words and 204 grammar rules. In order to enhance only the real-time processing of the system, the English input was restricted to grammatically well-formed sentences. To satisfy this requirement, we have excluded extra-grammatical phenomena such as hesitations and errors from the source sentences in advance.

The success rate was examined. As Table 1 shows, we have classified the source sentences according to the translation results. 228 sentences classified into (A) or (B) are translated correctly, providing a success rate of 82.0%. The result shows the system to be available for spoken language translation. Although the successful Japanese sentences gained on the system are different from those on a conventional system in the sense that they include much ill-formedness, they represent the semantic contents of the source sentences correctly.

3.2 Translation Processing Unit

Many causes of the translation failure in the above experiment is that many repairs appear too frequently in the translation results (33 sentences classified into (C), accounting for 11.9%). In particular, the longer the source sentence becomes, the more repairs appear in the translation. In order to solve the problem, we can consider to relax the restriction of the word-by-word basis.

Table 2. Translation results on a delay of one word

type	sentences	rate (%)
A) correct (no repair)	122	43.9
B) correct (repairs)	113	40.6
C) unnatural	27	9.7
D) incorrect	15	5.4
E) failed	1	0.4

Table 3. Translation results of 278 sentences without error correcting

type	sentences	rate (%)
A) correct (no repair)	21	7.6
B) correct (repairs)	106	38.1
C) unnatural	9	3.2
D) incorrect	45	16.2
E) failed	97	34.9

We have tried to make an experiment on a system translating with a delay of one word. We have used the same 4 dialogues. Table 2 shows the success rate. 235 sentences (accounting for 84.5%) are translated correctly. Although the frequency of the repairs averaged 1.07 times a sentence in the above experiment, the one word delay reduces the frequency to 0.74 times. In general, there exists a trade-off between the translation unit and the translation accuracy. This result shows that it is important to pursue an effective translation unit for simultaneous interpretation.

3.3 Translation of Grammatically Ill-formed Sentences

In Section 3.1, we have made the experiment on the assumption that all input is well-formed. However, such an assumption is not realistic for spontaneously spoken language translation.

We have made an experiment with the same 4 dialogues consisting well-formed 181 sentences and ill-formed 97 sentences on the system having 391 English words and 94 grammar rules. Figure 3 and 4 show the results of the translation without error correcting and with error correcting. As a result of introducing error correcting, 27 sentences providing a rate of 9.7% are newly added to the correct translation results. This result shows the error correcting method to be effective for the spontaneous speech translation.

Table 4. Translation results of 278 sentences with error correcting

type	sentences	rate (%)
A) correct (no repair)	21	7.6
B) correct (repairs)	133	47.8
C) unnatural	15	5.4
D) incorrect	100	36.0
E) failed	9	3.2

4 Japanese-English Translation

This section describes the Japanese-English translation part of Sync/Trans briefly. There exist some difficulties which should be overcome in developing a system of incremental Japanese-English translation. One of the difficulties is as follows:

- In spite that the system should output the English verb at an early stage, the verb usually appears in the end of a Japanese sentence.

As an example, let us consider translating the following Japanese sentence into English incrementally.

(4.1)   *kinoo* (yesterday) *ken-wa* (ken) *mado-wo* (the window) *hanma-de* (with an hammer) *watta* (broke).

The standard translation of (4.1) is (4.2).

(4.2)   Ken broke the window with a hammer yesterday.

It is impossible in principle to output the English verb phrase "broke the window with a hammer" before the Japanese verb "*watta*" appears.

To overcome the difficulty, we are investigating to predict a English verb at an early stage. In the dialogue task restricted to some extent, it might be possible to predict the appearing verb from the other noun phrases in the sentence. If the verb "broke" can be predicted from "Ken" and "the window", the system can product an English sentence (4.3) synchronously with (4.1).

(4.3)   Yesterday, Ken broke the window with a hammer.

Figure 4 shows a comparison between the timing of the output of (4.2) and (4.3).

5 Concluding Remarks

This paper has described Sync/Trans, an speech-to-speech translation system which we have been studying. Sync/Trans has the features: synchronous architecture, incremental translation, utilization of grammatical ill-formedness and early error correcting.

Input (4.1)	Output (4.2)	Output (4.3)
kinoo		yesterday
ken-wa	Ken	Ken
mado-wo		broke
hanma-de		the window
watta	broke	with a hammer
	the window	
	with a hammer	
	yesterday	

Fig. 4. Timing of the output of (4.2) and (4.3)

This paper has provided a few experimental results on the English-Japanese part which we have implemented as a first step towards simultaneous interpretation. From the results, we have found that incrementally translating the source language in an appropriate unit and correcting the errors in the source sentence at an early stage, are effective for speech-to-speech translation. In the near future, as soon as the Japanese-English translation part is implemented, we are planning to evaluate Sync/Trans on a speech dialogue between an English speaker and a Japanese speaker. We might be able to confirm the effectiveness of Sync/Trans as a spontaneous dialogue interpreter through the evaluation. To this end, high-accuracy speech recognition and real-time language processing are essential.

Acknowledgements

The authors would like to thank Satoru Asai for his valuable contributions on an earlier version of this study. The authors are also deeply indebted to Yoshihide Kato and Yoshiyuki Watanabe for their considerable assistance with the experiments. This research has been supported in part by The Hori Information Science Promotion Foundation.

References

1. Amtrup J.W.: Chart-based Incremental Transfer in Machine Translation, *Proceedings of the 6th International Conference of Theoretical and Methodological Issues in Machine Translation*, pp. 188-195 (1995).
2. Furuse, O. and Iida, H.: Incremental Translation Utilizing Constituent Boundary Patterns, *Proceedings of the 16th International Conference on Computational Linguistics*, pp. 412–417 (1996).
3. Iida, H., and Sumita, E. and Furuse, O.: Spoken-Language Translation Method Using Examples, *Proceedings of the 16th International Conference on Computational Linguistics*, pp. 1074–1077 (1996).

4. Inagaki Y. and Matsubara S.: Models for Incremental Interpretation of Natural Language, *Proceedings of the 2nd Symposium on Natural Language Processing*, pp. 51–60 (1995).
5. Kay M.: Algorithm Schemata and Data Structures in Syntactic Processing, *Technical Report CSL-80-12*, Xerox PARC (1980).
6. Kitano, H.: Incremental Sentence Production with a Parallel Marker-Passing Algorithm, *Proceedings of the 13th International Conference on Computational Linguistics*, pp. 217–222 (1990).
7. Kitano, H.: *Speech-to-Speech Translation: A Massively Parallel Memory-based Approach*, Kluwer Academic Publishers (1993).
8. Matsubara S. and Inagaki Y.: Utilizing Extra-Grammatical Phenomena in Incremental English-Japanese Machine Translation, *Proceedings of the 7th International Conference on Theoretical and Methodological Issues in Machine Translation*, pp. 138–145 (1997).
9. Matsubara S., Asai S., Toyama K. and Inagaki Y.: Chart-based Parsing and Transfer in Incremental Spoken Language Translation, *Proceedings of the 4th Natural Language Processing Pacific Rim Symposium*, pp. 521–524 (1997).
10. Menzel, W.: Parsing of Spoken Language under Time Constraints, *Proceedings of the 11th European Conference of Artificial Intellingence*, pp. 560–564 (1994).
11. Landsbergen J. and Jong F.: *Compositional Translation*, Rosseta M. (Ed.), pp. 57–84 (1994).

Minimal Belief Change and Pareto-Optimality

Oliver Schulte

Department of Computing Science, University of Alberta
Edmonton, AB T6G 2H1, Canada
oliver.schulte@ualberta.ca

Abstract. This paper analyzes the notion of a minimal belief change
that incorporates new information. I apply the fundamental decision-
theoretic principle of *Pareto-optimality* to derive a notion of minimal
belief change, for two different representations of belief: First, for beliefs represented by a *theory*—a deductively closed set of sentences or
propositions—and second for beliefs represented by an axiomatic *base*
for a theory. Three postulates exactly characterize Pareto-minimal revisions of theories, yielding a weaker set of constraints than the standard
AGM postulates. The Levi identity characterizes Pareto-minimal revisions of belief bases: a change of belief base is Pareto-minimal if and only
if the change satisfies the Levi identity (for "maxichoice" contraction operators). Thus for belief bases, Pareto-minimality imposes constraints
that the AGM postulates do not.

Keywords: belief revision, decision theory

1 Minimal Theory Change

New information changes our beliefs continually. How should we incorporate new
assertions into a body of existing ones? This question arises in many situations of
practical interest. For example, if the new assertion describes new data, incorporating the evidence into current beliefs is an essential part of learning systems.
If the new assertion is a datum presented to a database system, we face the
question of how to update a database, and the same goes for knowledge bases.

In the last two decades or so, the following principle has attracted much
interest among computer scientists and logicians [3,8,6,10,2]: Revise your beliefs so as to *minimize the extent of change* from the original beliefs. The aim
of this paper is to analyze the notion of minimal belief change. I derive axioms for minimal belief change from basic principles of *decision theory*. The
same decision-theoretic principles lead to different results for different ways of
formally representing beliefs. Specifically, I consider two such representations:
Belief modeled as a deductively closed set of sentences (or propositions), and
belief modeled by an axiomatic "belief base". For each of these representations
of belief, I consider the consequences of using the fundamental decision-theoretic
principle of *Pareto-Optimality* to define minimal belief changes.

Roughly, Pareto-minimal belief revisions are those that cannot be improved
by adding fewer beliefs without giving up more, or by giving up fewer beliefs

N. Foo (Ed.): AI'99, LNAI 1747, pp. 144–155, 1999.

without adding more. As it turns out, there is a purely set-theoretic definition of Pareto-minimal belief revisions in terms of the symmetric set differences between the current theory and alternative revisions. The main theorem of this paper establishes that certain axioms for belief revision characterize Pareto-minimal theory changes, in the sense that a theory change is Pareto-minimal if and only if the change satisfies these axioms. The chief difference between Pareto-minimality and the standard AGM postulates [3] arises in the case in which the current theory neither entails the new information nor its negation. In that case, the AGM revision is the result of adding the new information to the current theory. Pareto-minimal revisions, however, may be logically *weaker* than the AGM revision.[1]

Pareto-optimality leads to different results for minimal revisions of *belief bases*, sets of sentences that need not contain all of their logical consequences. The well-known *Levi identity* characterizes Pareto-minimal changes of belief bases: I prove that they are *exactly* those that result from, first, retracting just enough basic beliefs to make the agent's basic beliefs consistent with the new information (technically, a "maxichoice contraction" [3, Ch. 4.2]), and second, adding the new information to the basic beliefs contracted in this manner. Since AGM revisions may give up more beliefs than maxichoice contraction permits, this characterization shows that Pareto-minimality yields some constraints on the revision of belief bases that the AGM axioms do not require (cf. [1]).

2   Theories

Following much of the belief revision literature, I employ a syntactic representation of an agent's beliefs. However, all the developments to follow are valid for a semantic approach based on propositions (sets of models) as well. I assume that some language L has been fixed, and take a theory to be a deductively closed set of formulas from L. In Section 5 I considers belief sets that are not deductively closed.

As is usual in belief revision theory, my assumptions about the structure of the language in which an agent formulates her beliefs are sparse; essentially, all I assume is that the language features the usual propositional connectives. I take as given a suitable consequence relation between sets of formulas in the language, obeying the standard Tarskian properties. The formal presuppositions are as follows.

A **language** L is a set of formulas satisfying the following conditions. (1) L contains a **negation operator** $\neg$ such that if p is a formula in L, so is $\neg p$. (2) L contains a **conjunction connective** $\wedge$ such that if p and q are formulas in L, so is $p \wedge q$. (3) L contains an **implication connective** $\rightarrow$ such that if p and q are formulas in L, so is $p \rightarrow q$.

A **consequence operation** $Cn : 2^L \rightarrow 2^L$ represents a notion of entailment between sets of formulas from a language L. A set of formulas Γ **entails** another

---

[1] In this respect, Pareto-minimal revisions agree with Katsuno and Mendelzon's approach to "belief update" [6]; see Section 4.

set of formulas Γ', written $\Gamma \vdash \Gamma'$, iff $Cn(\Gamma) \supseteq \Gamma'$. A set of formulas Γ entails a formula p, written $\Gamma \vdash p$, iff $p \in Cn(\Gamma)$. I assume that Cn satisfies the following properties, for all sets of formulas Γ, Γ': **Inclusion**: $\Gamma \subseteq Cn(\Gamma)$; **Monotonicity**: $Cn(\Gamma) \subseteq Cn(\Gamma')$ whenever $\Gamma \subseteq \Gamma'$; and **Iteration**: $Cn(Cn(\Gamma)) = Cn(\Gamma)$.

A **theory** is a deductively closed set of formulas. That is, a set of formulas $T \subseteq L$ is a theory iff $Cn(T) = T$. The entailment relation $\vdash$ is related to the propositional connectives as follows.

Modus Ponens If $\Gamma \vdash p$, $(p \to q)$, then $\Gamma \vdash q$.
Implication If $\Gamma \vdash q$, then $\Gamma \vdash (p \to q)$.
Deduction $\Gamma \cup \{p\} \vdash q$ iff $\Gamma \vdash (p \to q)$.
Conjunction $\Gamma \vdash (p \wedge q)$ iff both $\Gamma \vdash p$ and $\Gamma \vdash q$.
Consistency Suppose that $\Gamma \not\vdash p$. Then $\Gamma \cup \{\neg p\} \not\vdash p$.
Inconsistency $\{p \wedge \neg p\} \vdash L$.
Double Negation $\Gamma \vdash p$ iff $\Gamma \vdash \neg\neg p$.

Classical propositional logic satisfies these assumptions. Belief revision theorists usually assume that the consequence relation Cn is compact; none of the results in this paper require compactness.[2] For the remainder of this paper, assume that a language L and a consequence relation Cn (and hence an entailment relation $\vdash$) have been fixed that satisfy the conditions laid down above.

3   Theory Change: Additions and Retractions

My approach to defining minimal belief change is to seek a *partial order* $\prec_T$ where we read $T_1 \prec_T T_2$ as "T_1 is a smaller change from T than T_2 is". Since this ordering is partial, there may be possible changes that are incomparable. As far as a given partial order among theory changes goes, if two changes are incomparable, we should view neither as a smaller change than the other. However, a theory change T_2 from an old theory T is *not* minimal if there is another, comparable, new theory T_1 such that $T_1 \prec_T T_2$. Thus I shall take minimal changes from a current theory T to be the minimal elements in the given partial order $\prec_T$.

I make use of decision-theoretic principles to define partial orders among theory changes. Let's begin by distinguishing two kinds of change: A *retraction* in which the old theory entails a formula that the new theory does not entail, and an *addition*, in which the new theory entails a formula that the old theory does not entail. Thus T' **retracts** the formula p from T iff $T \vdash p$ and $T' \not\vdash p$, and T' **adds** the formula p to T iff $T \not\vdash p$ and $T' \vdash p$.

Next, I define two partial orders among theory changes. The first partial order defines a notion of a new theory T_1 "retracting more" from a previous theory T than another new theory T_2, namely if T_1 retracts all the formulas from T that T_2 retracts from T, and T_1 retracts at least one formula from T that T_2 does not retract. The second partial order defines a notion of a new

---

[2] A consequence relation Cn is compact iff for all formulas p and sets of formulas Γ, we have that $p \in Cn(\Gamma)$ only if $p \in Cn(\Gamma')$ for some *finite* subset Γ' of Γ.

theory T_1 "adding more" to a previous theory T than another new theory T_2, namely if T_1 adds all the formulas from T that T_2 adds to T, and T_1 adds at least one formula to T that T_2 does not add to T. It is not difficult to see that these notions can be expressed in terms of set inclusions as follows ($\subset$ denotes proper set inclusion).

Definition 1. *Let* T, T_1, T_2 *be three theories.*

1. T_1 **retracts more** *formulas from* T *than* T_2 *does* $\Longleftrightarrow T - T_2 \subset T - T_1$.
2. T_1 **adds more** *formulas to* T *than* T_2 *does* $\Longleftrightarrow T_2 - T \subset T_1 - T$.

We may think of the addition partial order and the retraction partial order as defining two distinct dimensions of "cost" in theory revision. If additions and retractions were linked such that minimizing one minimizes the other, this distinction would have no interesting consequences for the question of how to minimize theory change: we would just minimize both additions and retractions at once. What makes the distinction important is the fact that in general, additions and retractions *trade off* against each other. Typically, avoiding retractions entails adding more sentences than necessary, and avoiding additions entails retracting more sentences than necessary. An example will clarify this point.

Example. Imagine a cognitive scientist who believes that a certain AI system, say SOAR, is the only candidate for machine intelligence. This scientist believes that "if SOAR is not intelligent ($\neg s$), there is no intelligent machine ($\neg m$)". Thus the scientist believes the sentence $p = \neg s \rightarrow \neg m$. Suppose that the scientist believes only the consequences of p, that is, her current theory is $T = Cn(\{p\})$. In particular, the scientist neither believes that there is an intelligent machine (m), nor does she believe that there is no intelligent machine ($\neg m$). Now the scientist receives new information to the effect that SOAR is not intelligent. She has to revise her theory T on evidence $\neg s$. Let us consider two possible revisions, T_1 and T_2. Revision T_1 adds the new information $\neg s$ to T and accepts the deductive consequences of this addition; thus $T_1 = Cn(\{p\} \cup \{\neg s\})$. This revision T_1 is logically stronger than T and hence retracts nothing from T. However, the revision adds the sentence $\neg m$ ("there is no intelligent machine"), since p and $\neg s$ entail $\neg m$.

Contrast this with a different revision T_2 that retracts the scientist's initial belief that SOAR is the only road to machine intelligence, and adds the new information that SOAR is not intelligent. That is, $T_2 = Cn(\{\neg s\})$. This revision T_2 retracts more from T than T_1 does. On the other hand, T_2 adds less to T than T_1 does, since T_2 is strictly weaker than T_1. In particular, T_2 continues to reserve judgment about whether machine intelligence is possible or not, whereas T_1 concludes that it is impossible ($\neg m$).

As the results below show, this example illustrates a general tension between avoiding additions and avoiding retractions; essentially, additions and retractions trade off against each other unless the current theory already entails the new information. When additions and retractions stand in conflict, how shall we make trade-offs between them? This is the topic of the next section.

4   Pareto-Minimal Theory Change

When a conflict arises between avoiding additions and avoiding retractions in belief revision, an agent may strike a subjective balance between them, as in any case of conflicting aims. She may assign one kind of change more subjective weight than the other, or favour some beliefs as more "entrenched" than others.[3] But before we resort to subjective factors, we can look to decision theory for an objective constraint that applies to all agents seeking to minimize theory change. If avoiding changes is our aim, then we should avoid revisions that make more additions than necessary without avoiding retractions, and we should avoid revisions that make more retractions than necessary without avoiding additions. This is an instance of the following uncontroversial principle for rational choice under certainty between objects with multiple relevant attributes: If A is at least as desirable as B with respect to all relevant attributes, and A is strictly better than B with respect to at least one attribute, choose A over B. The decision-theoretic term for this principle is *Pareto-optimality*.[4] For minimal theory change, we can render it as follows.

Definition 2. *Let T, T_1, T_2 be three theories. T_1 is a **greater change** from T than T_2 is $\Longleftrightarrow$*

1. *T_1 retracts more formulas from T than T_2 does, and for all formulas p, if T_2 adds p to T, then T_1 adds p to T; or*
2. *T_1 adds more formulas to T than T_2 does, and for all formulas p, if T_2 retracts p from T, then T_1 retracts p from T.*

An equivalent purely set-theoretic definition is: T_1 is a greater change from T than T_2 is iff $T_2 \triangle T \subset T_1 \triangle T$, where $\subset$ denotes proper inclusion and $\triangle$ is symmetric difference $(A \triangle B = A - B \cup B - A)$.[5] (I owe this definition to an anonymous referee.)

Thus the principle of Pareto-Optimality defines a partial relation $\prec_T$ between theories: $T_2 \prec_T T_1$ iff T_1 is a greater change from T than T_2 is. It seems that we can now take a minimal change from T to be a minimal theory in the

---

[3] Many investigators assume that a relation of "epistemic entrenchment" guides belief revision (e.g., Gärdenfors and Nayak [3, Ch.4], [8]). They typically take epistemic entrenchment to be subjective in the sense that different rational agents may view the same belief as entrenched to different degrees.

[4] Social choice theorists often use Pareto-optimality as a principle for comparing social states. The Pareto principle applies both to social choice and to choice between objects with multiple attributes because these two choice situations are formally equivalent (identify the set of "attributes" with the set of individual members of society).

[5] Chou and Winslett too define a partial order among (first-order) models of the form "N is closer to M than N'" in terms of symmetric difference [2]. From the perspective of this paper, their definition is a special case of Definition 2, namely Pareto-minimality applied to models rather than theories.

$\prec_T$-ordering. But on that definition, the only minimal change from T is T itself! Of course, it is generally true that the smallest change is no change, on any acceptable notion of "small change". What we want is a minimal change that satisfies *additional constraints*. In the case of belief update, the additional constraint is that the minimal theory change should incorporate the new information. Accordingly, I define a Pareto-minimal theory change from T, given new information p, as a theory that is minimal in the $\prec_T$-ordering among the theories that entail p.

Definition 3. *Let T, T_1 be two theories, and let p be a formula. Then T_1 is a* **Pareto-minimal change** *from T that incorporates p $\Longleftrightarrow$*

1. *$T_1 \vdash p$, and*
2. *there is no other theory T_2 such that $T_2 \vdash p$ and T_1 is a greater change from T than T_2 is.*

Now we are ready for the main result of this paper: Necessary and sufficient conditions for a theory revision to be a Pareto-minimal change.

Theorem 1. *Let T be a theory and let p be a formula. A theory revision $T * p$ is a Pareto-minimal change from T that incorporates p $\Longleftrightarrow$*

1. *$T * p \vdash p$, and*
2. *$T \cup \{p\} \vdash T * p$, and*
3. *if $T \vdash p$, then $T * p = T$.*

The theorem shows that the tension between additions and retractions arises whenever the agent's current theory does not already entail the new information. When this is the case, the revisions that make Pareto-acceptable trade-offs run in strength from adding the evidence to the current theory ($T \cup \{p\}$) to entailing nothing but the evidence and its consequences ($\{p\}$). This account of minimal change distinguishes sharply between the case in which the current theory already entails the new information and the case in which it does not. The standard AGM axioms [3, Ch.3.3] also make a sharp distinction, but along a different line: They distinguish between the case in which the evidence is consistent with the current theory (but not necessarily already part of it) and the case in which the evidence is inconsistent with the current theory. Specifically, the AGM axiom K*3 requires that $T \cup p \vdash T * p$, which is the characteristic axiom of Pareto-minimal theory change. The postulate K*4 posits that if $T \cup p$ is consistent, then $T * p \vdash T \cup p$. Thus the AGM axioms require the revised theory to be $Cn(T \cup \{p\})$ whenever p is consistent with T. In that case, the revision $Cn(T \cup \{p\})$ is a Pareto-minimal theory change, but it is just one of many possible Pareto-minimal revisions, namely the logically strongest one.

Another theory of belief change that endorses K*3 but not K*4 is the "updating" approach [6]. Intuitively, the connection between Pareto-minimality and the Update operator is this: Katsuno and Mendelzon postulate that "an update method should give each of the old possible worlds [in which the previous theory is true] equal consideration" [5, p.4]. Translating from possible worlds to sets of sentences, this means that Update treats adding new beliefs (removing possible worlds) as a "cost" in belief change, which can justify retracting previous beliefs (adding new possible worlds), even when the new information is consistent with the agent's current theory (for an example, see [5, p.7]).

Katsuno and Mendelzon argue that giving equal consideration to each of the old possible worlds is appropriate when an agent learns how the world has changed (update) rather than new facts about a static world (revision). This suggests that an agent's attitude towards the relative importance of additions and retractions may depend on the context and content of her beliefs. Pareto-minimality weights additions and retractions equally; in other contexts we may wish to give priority to minimizing retractions.[6] In the limiting case, we give absolute priority to minimizing retractions first, and only then consider avoiding additions. It can be shown that an agent's theory revision satisfies K*4 if and only if the agent makes the trade-off between additions and retractions in this way.

5   Pareto-Minimal Revision of Belief Bases

So far I have treated all of an agent's beliefs as equally important. A more refined representation of the agent's epistemic state may distinguish between a "basic" set of beliefs B, and the consequences of B that the agent might be said to hold because he believes B.[7] Hansson endorses the distinction between a basic set of beliefs and their consequences as a "small step toward capturing the justificatory structure" of an agent's beliefs [4]. I shall take a **base** for a theory T to be a set of formulas B, which may or may not be deductively closed, such that $B \vdash T$. (For more on belief bases, see [9,10] and the references therein).

To define Pareto-minimal revision of belief bases, I begin again with two ways of making a change to a belief base. If B, B' are two bases, I say that B' **retracts** the formula p from B iff $p \in B$ and $p \notin B'$, and that B' **adds** the formula p to B iff $p \notin B$ and $p \in B'$. The definition of "adding more" and "retracting more" from a base is just like that for theories (cf. Definition 1). Thus B_1 **retracts more** formulas from B than B_2 iff $B - B_2 \subset B - B_1$, and B_1 **adds more** formulas to B than B_2 iff $B_2 - B \subset B_1 - B$.

As with Definition 3, we can apply the principle of Pareto-optimality to define a partial comparison of base revisions with respect to the extent of change that they induce.

Definition 4. *Let* B, B_1, B_2 *be three bases. Then* B_1 *is a **greater change** from* B *than* B_2 *is* $\Longleftrightarrow$

---

[6] Levi presents a theory of how an agent may minimize the loss of "damped informational value" [7, Ch.2.1]. In my terms, this is advice for how to retract some beliefs to avoid adding too many.

[7] A paradigm example is a database, where we may distinguish between the records that are explicitly stored in the database and what follows from the explicitly stored information.

1. B_1 retracts more formulas from B than B_2 does, and for all formulas p, if B_2 adds p to B, then B_1 adds p to B; or
2. B_1 adds more formulas to B than B_2 does, and for all formulas p, if B_2 retracts p from B, then B_1 retracts p from B.

As with Definition 2, an equivalent set-theoretic definition is that B_1 is a greater change from B than B_2 is iff $B_2 \bigtriangleup B \subset B_1 \bigtriangleup B$.

When we consider the extent of change of a belief base, it is natural to take into account only changes in basic beliefs, not changes in the logical consequences of the basic beliefs that "just follow" from them. My definition of retracting and adding to a belief base expresses this view of minimal belief change by considering only which sentences are added to or retracted from the set of basic beliefs. For example, there may be a sentence q such that $B * p \vdash q$ and $B \not\vdash q$ but $q \notin B * p$. In that case the revision $B * p$ adds q to the logical consequences of the agent's beliefs, but does not add q to her basic beliefs. In effect, Definition 4 does not count such additions to the consequences of the agent's basic beliefs as an addition, unless they are also additions to the agent's basic beliefs themselves. Discounting changes in the logical consequences of basic beliefs in this way gives rise to a fundamental difference between the Pareto-minimal revision of basic beliefs and Pareto-minimal theory change: Pareto-minimal base revisions never add basic beliefs to the previous ones other than the new information. For suppose that a revision $B * p$ adds a belief q to a base B; then $B * p - \{q\}$ adds less to B and retracts no more. Hence $B * p$ is not a Pareto-minimal change of B. In contrast, a theory revision $T * p$ will typically add many beliefs to T, namely logical consequences of previous beliefs conjoined with the new information p. Another way to put the point is that for bases a conflict between additions and retractions does not arise: it is possible to minimize both additions and retractions at the same time. In the case in which the new information contradicts the current basic beliefs, this will lead an agent to hold inconsistent beliefs. Since many researchers accept as a general norm of epistemic rationality that an agent ought to avoid inconsistent beliefs, I shall restrict Pareto-minimal revisions to consistent bases.

Definition 5. *Let B, B_1 be two bases, and let p be a formula. Then B_1 is a* **Pareto-minimal consistent change** *from B that incorporates p* $\Longleftrightarrow$

1. $p \in B_1$, and
2. B_1 is consistent, and
3. there is no other consistent base B_2 such that $p \in B_2$ and B_1 is a greater change from B than B_2 is.

What are the characteristic properties of Pareto-minimal base revisions? It turns out that a version of a proposal originally due to Levi amounts to necessary and sufficient conditions for a base revision to be Pareto-minimal and consistent. The proposal is to think of a Pareto-minimal revision of a belief base B on new information p as proceeding in two steps: First, remove just enough beliefs from B to obtain a belief base B' that is consistent with p; then add p to B'. Formally, we require that B' be a belief base that is consistent with p—thus $B' \not\vdash \neg p$—and removes as few beliefs from B as possible. Hence I define a retraction-minimal *contraction* of a belief base as follows.

Definition 6. *Let* B, B_1 *be two bases, and let* p *be a formula. Then* B_1 *is a* **retraction-minimal contraction** *from* B *on* $p \Longleftrightarrow$

1. $B_1 \subseteq B$, *and*
2. $B_1 \not\vdash p$, *and*
3. *there is no other base* B_2 *such that* $B_2 \not\vdash p$ *and* B_1 *retracts more from* B *than* B_2 *does.*

Retraction-minimal contractions of a base B on new information p have a simple characterization: They are exactly those subsets of B that cannot be expanded without entailing p. (The proof is left to the reader.)

Lemma 1. *Let* B, B_1 *be two bases such that* $B_1 \subseteq B$, *and let* p *be a formula. Then* B_1 *is a* **retraction-minimal contraction** *from* B *on* $p \Longleftrightarrow$ *for all formulas* q, *if* B_1 *retracts* q *from* B, *it is the case that* $B_1 \cup \{q\} \vdash p$.

Thus retraction-minimal contractions are those that belief revision theorists refer to as "maxichoice contractions" [3, Ch.4.2]. The **Levi identity** says that minimal revisions of a belief set K given new information p are the result of adding p after contracting K on $\neg p$ (see [3, Ch.3.6]). The next proposition shows that the Levi identity for retraction-minimal (maxichoice) contractions characterizes Pareto-minimal revisions of belief bases that lead to consistent belief bases.

Theorem 2 (The Levi Identity for Belief Bases). *Let* B *be a base and let* p *be a formula. Suppose that a revision* $B * p$ *contains* p. *Then* $B * p$ *is a Pareto-minimal consistent change from* B *that incorporates* $p \Longleftrightarrow$ *there is a retraction-minimal contraction* B' *from* B *on* $\neg p$ *such that* $B * p = B' \cup \{p\}$.

I omit the proof for space reasons. In view of Theorem 2, it is not difficult to see that Pareto-minimal consistent revisions of belief bases satisfy the AGM axioms K*1–K*5 (interpreted for base revisions with $\supseteq$ in place of $\vdash$; see also [1, Part II]).[8] The converse is not true, however: Pareto-minimality places more constraints on the revision of belief bases than K*1–K*5, since AGM revisions need not be the result of maxichoice contractions and hence may give up more beliefs than Pareto-minimal revisions.

---

[8] For K*2 I require that $p \in B * p$. For K*5 we must assume that the underlying consequence relation $\vdash$ is consistent in the sense that $\emptyset \not\vdash L$; otherwise there is no consistent base. When the new information p is inconsistent, there is no consistent revision on p; in that case I require that $B * p$ is an inconsistent base in accordance with K*5.

Alchourrón and Makinson conjectured that "when applied to bases that are irredundant, choice contraction and revision functions serve as good formal representations of the corresponding intuitive processes" [1, p.21]. Theorem 2 establishes a formal version of this conjecture, in which Pareto-minimality takes the place of "intuition".[9]

6 Conclusion

The principle of minimal belief change is an important and influential idea in several areas of computer science such as artificial intelligence and database theory. This paper showed a method for rigorously deriving axioms for minimal belief change from fundamental decision-theoretic principles. This approach clarifies the foundations of belief revision postulates; and it allows us to distinguish universally valid postulates from those whose applicability depend to a larger extent on the details of how we represent beliefs and the relative weight we assign to retractions and additions in a given application domain.

Specifically, with regard to beliefs represented by deductively closed theories, Theorem 1 shows that the AGM axiom K*3 is universally valid for Pareto-minimal belief change, whereas the axiom K*4 is not.

With regard to beliefs represented by belief bases—which need not be deductively closed—Pareto-minimality validates K*4 and other staples of belief revision theory such as the Levi identity. In fact, Pareto-minimal base revision obeys constraints that go beyond the AGM postulates. Thus the results of my analysis of base revision largely agree with previous work; however, my method is different: I do not appeal to intuition, or even representation theorems, for justifying belief revision maxims, but instead *derive* them from fundamental decision-theoretic principles.

Altogether, the results in this paper show that Pareto-minimality provides a fruitful and principled decision-theoretic foundation for postulates guiding minimal belief revision.

7 Proof of Theorem 1

Theorem 1. *Let T be a theory and let p be a formula. A theory revision $T * p$ is a Pareto-minimal change from T that incorporates p $\Longleftrightarrow$*

1. *$T * p \vdash p$, and*
2. *$T \cup \{p\} \vdash T * p$, and*
3. *if $T \vdash p$, then $T * p = T$.*

Proof. ($\Rightarrow$) Part 1: Immediate from Definition 3. Part 2: I show the contrapositive. Suppose that $T \cup \{p\} \not\vdash T * p$. Then there is a formula q in $T * p$ such that

---
[9] Nebel also argues for constructing minimal base revisions from maxichoice contractions followed by adding the new information [9, Secs. 7, 8].

$T \cup \{p\} \not\vdash q$. So (a) $T \not\vdash q$ by Monotonicity. Now consider $T' = (T * p) \cap Cn(T \cup \{p\} \cup \{\neg q\})$. First I note that T' is closed under deductive consequence. For let $r \in Cn((T*p) \cap Cn(T \cup \{p\} \cup \{\neg q\}))$. Then by Monotonicity, $r \in Cn(T*p)$ and $r \in Cn(Cn(T \cup \{p\} \cup \{\neg q\}))$. We assumed that $T*p$ is closed under consequence, and Iteration implies that $Cn(Cn(T \cup \{p\} \cup \{\neg q\})) = Cn(T \cup \{p\} \cup \{\neg q\})$; thus $r \in T * p \cap Cn(T \cup \{p\} \cup \{\neg q\})$. This shows that $Cn(T') = T'$.

Next, note that (b) $T' \not\vdash q$ because $Cn(T \cup \{p\} \cup \{\neg q\}) \not\vdash q$ by Consistency (applied to $T \cup \{p\}$) and Iteration; thus from Monotonicity and the fact that $T' \subseteq Cn(T \cup \{p\} \cup \{\neg q\})$, it follows that $T' \not\vdash q$. Moreover, we have from Monotonicity and the fact that $T' \subseteq T * p$ as well that (c) if T' adds a formula to T, so does $T * p$. From (a), (b) and (c) it follows that (d) $T * p$ adds more formulas to T than T'.

Now I show that (e) T' retracts from T exactly the formulas that $T*p$ retracts from T. Monotonicity implies immediately that if $T*p$ retracts a formula from T, so does T'. For the converse, suppose that T' retracts a formula r from T. Since $Cn(T \cup \{p\} \cup \{\neg q\}) \vdash T$, this implies that $r \notin (T*p)$. And that means that $T*p$ retracts r from T as well.

Finally, we have that (f) $T' \vdash p$, since $T * p \vdash p$ by Part 1 and clearly $Cn(T \cup \{p\} \cup \{\neg q\}) \vdash p$. Together, (a)–(f) establish that T' incorporates p and $T * p$ is a greater change from T than T' is. Hence $T * p$ is not a Pareto-minimal change.

Part 3: Immediate, since every theory other than T retracts or adds more formulas to T than T itself does.

($\Leftarrow$) Suppose that $T * p$ satisfies conditions 1, 2 and 3. Then the claim is immediate if $T \vdash p$ and $T * p = T$; suppose that $T \not\vdash p$. I show that $T * p$ is not a greater change from T than any other change T' that incorporates p.

First, suppose that $T * p$ retracts a formula q from T but T' does not, such that $T' \vdash q$. Then $T' \vdash (p \wedge q)$ by Conjunction, whereas $T * p \not\vdash (p \wedge q)$ by Conjunction as well. Since we supposed that $T \not\vdash p$, it follows that $T \not\vdash (p \wedge q)$ by Conjunction once more. So T' adds a formula to T—namely $p \wedge q$—that $T * p$ does not add to T, and hence $T * p$ is not a greater change from T than T' is.

Second, suppose that $T * p$ adds a formula q to T, but $T' \not\vdash q$. Condition 2 asserts that $T \cup \{p\} \vdash T * p$ and hence $Cn(T \cup \{p\}) \vdash q$. By Deduction, we have that (a) $T \vdash p \to q$. Moreover, Implication implies that (b) $T * p \vdash p \to q$. Also, (c) $T' \not\vdash p \to q$. For suppose that on the contrary, $T' \vdash p \to q$. Then since $T' \vdash p$, it follows from Modus Ponens that $T' \vdash q$, contrary to assumption. From (a), (b) and (c) we have that T' retracts a formula from T—namely $p \to q$—that $T * p$ does not retract from T. Thus $T * p$ is not a greater change from T than T' is.

These arguments establish that if $T * p$ satisfies conditions 2 and 3, then there is no theory T' incorporating p such that $T * p$ is a greater change from T than T' is. From Condition 1 it follows that $T * p$ is a Pareto-minimal change from T that incorporates p.   □

References

1. Alchourrón, C.E. and Makinson, D.: 1982, 'The logic of theory change: Contraction functions and their associated revision functions', *Theoria* 48:14–37.
2. Chou, T. and Winslett, M.: 1994, 'A Model-Based Belief Revision System', in *Journal of Automated Reasoning* 12:157–208.
3. Gärdenfors, P.: 1988, *Knowledge In Flux: modeling the dynamics of epistemic states.* MIT Press, Cambridge, Mass.
4. Hansson, S.O.: 1998, 'Editorial: Belief Revision Theory Today', *Journal of Logic, Language and Information*, Vol.7(**2**):123–126.
5. Katsuno, H. and Mendelzon, A.O. 1990: *On the difference between updating a knowledge base and revising it*, Technical Report on Knowledge Representation and Reasoning, KRR-TR-90-6, University of Toronto, Department of Computer Science.
6. Katsuno, H. and Mendelzon, A.O. 1991: 'On the difference between updating a knowledge base and revising it', in *Proceedings of the Second International Conference on Principles of Knowledge Representation and Reasoning*, Cambridge, Mass., pp.387–394, Morgan Kaufmann.
7. Levi, I.: 1996, *For the sake of the argument: Ramsey test conditionals, Inductive Inference, and Nonmonotonic Reasoning*, Cambridge University Press, Cambridge.
8. Nayak, A.: 1994, 'Iterated Belief Change Based on Epistemic Entrenchment', *Erkenntnis* 41: 353-390.
9. Nebel, B.: 1989, 'A Knowledge Level Analysis of Belief Revision', in: R. J. Brachman, H. J. Levesque, and R. Reiter (eds.), *Proceedings of the First International Conference on Principles of Knowledge Representation and Reasoning* (KR'89), Toronto, Canada, pp. 301–311, Morgan Kaufmann.
10. Nebel, B.: 1994 'Base Revision Operations and Schemes: Representation, Semantics and Complexity', in: *Proceedings of the 11th European Conference on Artificial Intelligence* (ECAI'94), Amsterdam, Netherlands, pp. 341–345, Springer Verlag.

Basic Infobase Change

Thomas Meyer

Department of Computer Science, School of Information Technology,
University of Pretoria, Pretoria, 0002, South Africa
tmeyer@cs.up.ac.za
http://www.cs.up.ac.za/~tommie

Abstract. Generalisations of theory change involving arbitrary sets of wffs instead of belief sets have become known as base change. In one view, a base should be thought of as providing more structure to its generated belief set, and can be used to determine the theory change operation associated with a base change operation. In this paper we extend a proposal along these lines by Meyer et al. [12]. We take an infobase as a finite *sequence* of wffs, with each element in the sequence being seen as an independently obtained bit of information, and define appropriate infobase change operations. The associated theory change operations satisfy the AGM postulates for theory change [1]. Since an infobase change operation produces a new infobase, it allows for iterated infobase change. We measure iterated infobase change against the postulates proposed by Darwiche et al. [2,3] and Lehmann [10].

1 Introduction

It is generally accepted that belief sets do not have a rich enough structure to serve as appropriate models for epistemic states [8], [6], and theory change is therefore regarded as an elegant idealisation of a more general theory of belief change, involving arbitrary sets of wffs known as bases. In one view, a base should be thought of as providing more structure to its associated belief set. The added structure of the base can be used, in one way or another, to pick an appropriate associated theory contraction operation. This, in turn, can be used to aid in the process of constructing a range of suitable base contraction operations. Recently, Meyer et al. [12] proposed a form of base change along these lines. They regard an infobase as a finite set of wffs consisting of independently obtained bits of information. Taking AGM theory change [1] as the general framework in which to operate, they present a method that uses the structure of an infobase to determine which AGM theory change operation to associate with the infobase change operation to be constructed. In this paper we improve on the proposal by Meyer et al. [12] in two ways. Firstly, and in line with the claim by Meyer et al. [12] that the definition of an infobase as a finite *set* of wffs is in conflict with the intuition of independently obtained wffs,[1] we view an infobase as a finite *sequence* of wffs. This has a number of favourable consequences. Secondly,

---

[1] See [11,12] for a justification of this claim.

N. Foo (Ed.): AI'99, LNAI 1747, pp. 156–167, 1999.

the approach of Meyer et al. [12] associates a unique infobase contraction and revision operation with every infobase. We generalise this approach by allowing for a whole spectrum of infobase contraction and revision operations obtained from a given infobase, ranging from a "foundational" approach at one extreme to a "coherentist" approach at the other.

2   Preliminaries

For the rest of this paper L denotes a finitely generated propositional language, closed under the usual propositional connectives, and with a classical model-theoretic semantics.[2] The set of interpretations of L is denoted by U. For every $X \subseteq L$, we denote the set of models of X by $M(X)$, and for $\alpha \in L$ we write $M(\alpha)$ instead of $M(\{\alpha\})$. Classical entailment is denoted by $\vDash$. Closure under entailment is denoted by Cn. A *theory* or a *belief set* is a set $K \subseteq L$ closed under entailment. For every $V \subseteq U$, we let $Th(V)$ denote the *theory determined by* V. For every $V \subseteq U$, we let F_V denote some wff for which $M(F_V) = V$. It is well-known that such a finite axiomatisation exists for every $V \subseteq U$.

An infobase will be represented as a finite sequence of wffs enclosed by square brackets. Although infobases are sensitive to the order in which wffs occur, as well as to their syntactical form, we shall see that these superficial qualities can be done away with by employing the notion of element-equivalence. Two infobases IB and IC are *element-equivalent*, written as $IB \approx IC$, iff for every β occurring in IB such that $\nvDash \beta$, there is a unique logically equivalent wff γ occurring in IC, and for every γ occurring in IC such that $\nvDash \gamma$, there is a unique logically equivalent wff β occurring in IB. We shall sometimes abuse notation slightly by applying the notion of element-equivalence to sets instead of infobases. For a finite sequence σ of wffs, we use the symbol $\bullet$ to denote concatenation by a single wff. The converse of concatenation (removing the last wff from a finite sequence σ) will be denoted by $\overline{\sigma}$. For a finite sequence σ of wffs, the *set* of wffs occurring in σ is denoted by $S(\sigma)$. That is, $S(\sigma) = \{\beta \mid \beta \text{ occurs in } \sigma\}$. We say that an infobase IB is *associated* with a belief set K (and K is *associated* with IB) iff $Cn(S(IB)) = K$.

Formally, we consider infobase change operations(which include contraction and revision operations) as functions from $\mathcal{IB} \times L$ to $\mathcal{IB}$, where $\mathcal{IB}$ is the set of all infobases. We shall also frequently assume the existence of a fixed infobase IB, and consider infobase IB-change operations as functions from L to $\mathcal{IB}$.

From results by Grove [7] and Katsuno et al. [9], AGM theory change can be characterised by a set of total preorders (i.e. connected, reflexive, transitive relations) on U. For a total preorder $\preceq$ on U, we say that $x \in V \subseteq U$ is $\preceq$-*minimal* in V iff for every $y \in V$, $x \preceq y$, and we denote the set of $\preceq$-minimal elements of $M(\phi)$ by $Min_{\preceq}(\phi)$. For $X \subseteq L$, $\preceq$ is X-*faithful* iff $x \prec y$ for every $x \in M(X)$ and $y \notin M(X)$, and $x \preceq y$ for every $x, y \in M(X)$. The required results are obtained in terms of the following two identities:

---

[2] Meyer et al. [11] provides a treatment of basic infobase change involving a larger class of logics.

(Def − from $\preceq$) $K - \alpha = Th(M(K) \cup Min_{\preceq}(\neg\alpha))$
(Def ∗ from $\preceq$) $K * \alpha = Th(Min_{\preceq}(\alpha))$

Theorem 1. *1. Every K-faithful total preorder defines an AGM theory contraction using (Def − from $\preceq$). Conversely, every AGM theory contraction can be defined in terms of a K-faithful total preorder using (Def − from $\preceq$).*
2. Every K-faithful total preorder defines an AGM theory revision using (Def ∗ from $\preceq$). Conversely, every AGM theory revision can be defined in terms of a K-faithful total preorder using (Def ∗ from $\preceq$).

The following two identities can be used to define AGM theory revision and theory contraction in terms of one another.

(Harper Identity) $K - \phi = K \cap (K * \neg\phi)$
(Levi Identity) $K * \phi = (K - \neg\phi) + \phi$

With the exception of theorem 1, which is a well-known result by now, the proofs of the results in this paper can all be found in [11].

3 Infobase Change

To construct an infobase contraction, we first use the structure of the infobase IB to obtain an $S(IB)$-faithful total preorder. The theory contraction obtained from the $S(IB)$-faithful total preorder is taken to be the theory contraction associated with the infobase contraction that we aim to construct.

Definition 1. *For every infobase IB, a theory contraction − is associated with an infobase IB-contraction $\ominus$ iff $Cn(S(IB)) - \alpha = Cn(S(IB \ominus \alpha))$ for every $\alpha \in L$.*

Using the intuition associated with an infobase, we order the interpretations in U according to the number of wffs of IB they satisfy; the more they satisfy, the "better" they are deemed to be, and the lower down in the ordering they will be.

Definition 2. *For $u \in U$, we define u_{IB}, the IB-number of u, as the number of wffs β in IB such that $\not\vDash \beta$ and $u \in M(\beta)$.*

This ordering is used to obtain an appropriate $S(IB)$-faithful total preorder in terms of IB as follows:

(Def $\preceq$ from IB) $u \preceq v$ iff $v_{IB} \leq u_{IB}$

Definition 3. *We refer to the faithful total preorder $\preceq_{IB}$ defined in terms of an infobase IB using (Def $\preceq$ from IB) as the IB-induced faithful total preorder.*

The IB-induced faithful total preorder is used to construct a theory contraction as follows:

(Def $-_{IB}$ from IB) $Cn(S(IB)) -_{IB} \alpha = Th(M(S(IB)) \cup Min_{\preceq_{IB}}(\neg\alpha))$

Definition 4. *The theory contraction $-_{IB}$ defined in terms of an infobase IB using (Def $-_{IB}$ from IB) is referred to as the IB-induced theory contraction.*

Clearly the IB-induced theory contraction is an AGM theory contraction. Associating the IB-induced theory contraction with the infobase IB-contraction allows us to determine which wffs in IB should be retained, and which cannot be retained, after a contraction of IB.

Definition 5. *The set of α-discarded wffs (of an infobase IB) is defined as $IB^{-\alpha} = \{\beta \in S(IB) \mid \beta \notin Cn(S(IB)) -_{IB} \alpha\}$. We refer to $S(IB) \setminus IB^{-\alpha}$ as the set of α-retained wffs (of IB).*

The α-retained wffs are precisely the wffs in IB that should be retained when contracting IB by α, while the α-discarded wffs are replaced with appropriately weakened wffs. In deciding on an appropriate method for the weakening of the α-discarded wffs, it is necessary to strike the right balance between what we tentatively refer to as a *coherentist* approach, emphasising knowledge level matters, and a *foundationalist* approach, emphasising the independence of the wffs occurring in IB. The following example serves to make these matters concrete.

Example 1. Consider the infobase $IB = [p, q, r]$. Figure 1 gives a graphical representation of the IB-induced faithful total preorder $\preceq_{IB}$. The wffs p, q and r each represents independently obtained information. So, when contracting IB by $p \wedge q$, the resulting infobase should contain weakened versions of the two $(p \wedge q)$-discarded wffs p and q, and should contain the $(p \wedge q)$-retained wff r itself. But what should the weakened versions of p and q look like? An application of the coherentist approach on a local level suggests that, in order to minimise the loss of information, one should add only the minimal models of $\neg(p \wedge q)$ to the models of both p and q, and let the corresponding wffs be the appropriate weakened versions. The weakened version of p would be logically equivalent to $p \vee (q \wedge r)$ and the weakened version of q would be logically equivalent to $q \vee (p \wedge r)$. On the other hand, the foundationalist approach, which stresses the independence of the wffs in IB, suggests that the presence of r should have no effect on the weakened versions of p and q. In this view, the wff $p \vee q$ (or any wff logically equivalent to it) would be a suitable choice for the weakened versions of both p and q.

There does not seem to be a definite answer to the question of which one of these two approaches to infobase change is the "correct" one. They should rather be seen as opposites on a whole spectrum of possibilities. The coherentist approach can be described as the case where *all* the wffs in IB play a role in determining the weakened versions of the α-discarded wffs, while the foundationalist approach ensures that only the set of α-discarded wffs themselves is involved in the construction of their weakened versions. Given these two opposites, it also seems perfectly reasonable to allow for *any* set of wffs in between (i.e., containing the α-discarded wffs and included in $S(IB)$) to be involved in the construction of the weakened versions of the α-discarded wffs.

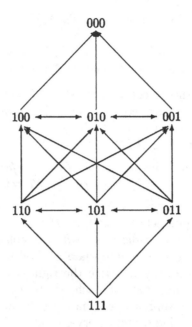

Fig. 1. A graphical representation of the IB-induced faithful total preorder $\preceq_{IB}$, with $IB = [p,q,r]$. For every $u, v \in U$, $u \preceq_{IB} v$ iff (u,v) is in the reflexive transitive closure of the relation determined by the arrows. Interpretations are represented as ordered triples of 0s and 1s, 0 representing falsity and 1 representing truth. The first digit in a triple represents the truth value of p, the second the truth value of q and the third the truth value of r

Definition 6. *Given an infobase IB and a wff α, a set R is said to be (IB, α)-relevant iff $IB^{-\alpha} \subseteq R \subseteq S(IB)$.*

Our goal is to ensure that, in the process of obtaining the weakened versions of the α-discarded wffs, the effect of the wffs *not* in the (IB, α)-relevant set R are neutralised. To do so, we should not just add the $\preceq_{IB}$-minimal models of $\neg\alpha$, but also any other models of $\neg\alpha$ that behave exactly like the $\preceq_{IB}$-minimal models with respect to the wffs in R, but that might differ from the $\preceq_{IB}$-minimal models on the truth value of the wffs in $S(IB) \setminus R$.

Definition 7. *For $X \subseteq L$ and $u, v \in U$, u is X-equivalent to v, written $u \equiv_X v$, iff for every $\chi \in X$, $u \in M(\chi)$ iff $v \in M(\chi)$.*

In general, we obtain the weakened version of every α-discarded wff β as follows. We need some appropriate set of interpretations that can be added to the models of β to obtain the set of models of its weakened version. Once we have decided on an (IB, α)-relevant set R, we use the set of minimal models of $\neg\alpha$ as our starting point and then try to expand it so that only elements in R have any influence, thus neutralising the possible influence of any of remaining wffs in IB.

This is accomplished by including all the models of $\neg\alpha$ that are R-equivalent to some minimal model of $\neg\alpha$.

Definition 8. *Let R be any (IB, α)-relevant set. For $u \in Min_{\preceq_{IB}}(\neg\alpha)$, let $N_u^R(\neg\alpha) = \{v \in M(\neg\alpha) \mid v \equiv_R u\}$ and $N_{IB}^R(\neg\alpha) = \bigcup_{u \in Min_{\preceq_{IB}}(\neg\alpha)} N_u^R(\neg\alpha)$. We refer to $N_{IB}^R(\neg\alpha)$ as the (R, α)-neutralised models of IB.*

We take the (R, α)-neutralised models as the set of interpretations to be added to the models of each α-discarded wff. We can think of the (R, α)-neutralised models as a set of interpretations in which the influence of the wffs not in R has been removed, but in which the wffs in R have the same impact as on the minimal models of $\neg\alpha$.

It turns out that there is an elegant way to provide a uniform description of infobase contraction. We can describe it as a process in which *all* the wffs in the current infobase are replaced with weaker versions, but where the "weaker" version of every α-retained wff turns out to be logically equivalent to the wff itself.

Definition 9. *Let R be any (IB, α)-relevant set. For every $\beta \in S(IB)$, we let $N_\beta^R(\neg\alpha) = \bigcup_{u \in Min_{\preceq_{IB}}(\neg\alpha) \setminus M(\beta)} N_u^R(\neg\alpha)$. We refer to $N_\beta^R(\neg\alpha)$ as the (R, α, β)-neutralised models of IB.*

The next proposition shows that an α-retained wff β has no (R, α, β)-neutralised models, and that, for an α-discarded wff β, adding the (R, α, β)-neutralised models to the models of β, has the same effect as adding the (R, α)-neutralised models.

Proposition 1. *Let R be any (IB, α)-relevant set.*

1. *If $\beta \in S(IB) \setminus IB^{-\alpha}$ then $N_\beta^R(\neg\alpha) = \emptyset$.*
2. *If $\beta \in IB^{-\alpha}$ then $M(\beta) \cup N_\beta^R(\neg\alpha) = M(\beta) \cup N_{IB}^R(\neg\alpha)$.*

We are now almost in a position to define *basic* infobase contraction.

Definition 10. *A function $rs : IB \times \wp L \to \wp\wp L$ is a relevance selection function iff*

1. *$IB^{-\alpha} \subseteq rs(IB, \alpha) \subseteq IB$,*
2. *if $\alpha \equiv \beta$ then $rs(IB, \alpha) = rs(IB, \beta)$, and*
3. *if $IB \approx IC$ then $rs(IB, \alpha) \approx rs(IC, \alpha)$.*

Intuitively, a relevance selection function indicates which of the wffs in IB should play a role in determining the weakened versions during a contraction. Observe that $rs(IB, \alpha)$ is (IB, α)-relevant.

Definition 11. *1. An infobase change operation $\ominus$ is a basic infobase contraction iff there is a relevance selection function rs such that, for every $IB \in \mathcal{IB}$ and every $\alpha \in L$, $IB \ominus \alpha$ is obtained by replacing every wff β in IB with $F_{M(\beta) \cup N_\beta^{rs(IB,\alpha)}(\neg\alpha)}$.*

2. *For every* $IB \in \mathcal{IB}$, *an infobase* IB-*change operation* $\ominus_{IB}$ *is a basic infobase* IB-*contraction iff it can be obtained from a basic infobase contraction* $\ominus$ *by fixing the infobase* IB. *That is, iff* $IB \ominus_{IB} \alpha = IB \ominus \alpha$ *for every* $\alpha \in L$.

It can be verified that for the infobase $IB = [p, q]$, for example, there is at least one basic infobase contraction $\ominus$ such that $IB \ominus p \approx [\top, q]$ and $IB \ominus (p \wedge q) \approx [p \vee q, p \vee q]$, and at least one basic infobase contraction $\ominus'$ such that $IB \ominus' p \approx [p \vee q, q]$ and $IB \ominus' (p \wedge q) \approx [p \vee q, p \vee q]$.

Basic infobase revision is defined by an appeal to the following infobase analogue of the Levi Identity:

(Def ⊛ from ⊖) $IB \circledast \alpha = (IB \ominus \neg \alpha) \bullet \alpha$

Definition 12. *An infobase change operation is a basic infobase revision iff it is defined in terms of a basic infobase contraction using (Def ⊛ from ⊖).*

4   Properties of Basic Infobase Change

Given the intuition associated with infobase change, it is to be expected that the IB-induced theory contraction is the theory contraction associated with every basic infobase IB-contraction. The next result shows that this is indeed the case, and that a similar result holds for basic infobase revision.

Definition 13. *A theory revision* $*$ *is associated with an infobase* IB-*revision* $\circledast$ *iff* $Cn(S(IB)) * \alpha = Cn(S(IB \circledast \alpha))$ *for every* $\alpha \in L$.

(Def $*_{IB}$ from IB) $Cn(S(B)) *_{IB} \alpha = Th(Min_{\preceq_{IB}}(\alpha))$

Definition 14. *The theory revision* $*_{IB}$ *defined in terms of an infobase* IB *using (Def $*_{IB}$ from IB) is referred to as the* IB-*induced theory revision.*

For the remainder of this section we assume $\ominus$ be a basic infobase contraction, and we let $\circledast$ be the basic infobase revision defined in terms of $\ominus$ using (Def ⊛ from ⊖).

Proposition 2. $Cn(S(IB)) -_{IB} \alpha = Cn(S(IB \ominus \alpha))$ *and* $Cn(S(IB \circledast \alpha)) = Cn(S(IB)) *_{IB} \alpha$.

The next result, which follows straightforwardly from the construction, shows that the syntactic form of the wffs in an infobase, as well as the form of the wff with which to contract or revise, are irrelevant.

Proposition 3. *If* $IB \approx IC$ *and* $\alpha \equiv \beta$ *then* $IB \circledast \alpha \approx IC \circledast \beta$ *and* $IB \ominus \beta \approx IC \ominus \gamma$.

We regard this property of infobase change as an advantage over some of the other, more syntactically-oriented, approaches to base change.

In the context of infobase change, reason maintenance [4] amounts to ensuring that the contraction of IB by a wff α in IB results in the removal of all the wffs that are dependent on α for being in $Cn(S(IB))$. Fuhrmann [5] has given a precise meaning to the idea of a wff being dependent on α (for being in $Cn(S(IB))$).

Definition 15. *A wff $\beta \in L$ is IB-dependent on α iff $\alpha \in S(IB)$ and $\beta \in Cn(S(IB))$, but $\beta \notin Cn(S(IB) \setminus \{\alpha\})$.*

The next result shows that basic infobase change incorporates reason maintenance.

Proposition 4. *If β is IB-dependent on α then $\beta \notin Cn(S(IB \ominus \alpha))$ and $\beta \notin Cn(S(B \circledast \neg \alpha))$.*

A related question is whether, if α is in IB and $\alpha \notin Cn(S(IB \ominus \gamma))$, it will be the case that $\beta \notin Cn(S(IB \ominus \gamma))$ for every β that is IB-dependent on α. This property is known as Fuhrmann's *filtering condition* [5]. It is easy to see that basic infobase contraction can violate the filtering condition. But, given the intuition associated with infobases, the filtering condition is clearly too strong a requirement to impose. For it requires that for any infobase contraction $\ominus$, $Cn(S(IB \ominus \gamma)) = Cn(\top)$ for any singleton infobase IB and any $\gamma \in Cn(S(IB))$ (where $\nvdash \gamma$), thus leaving no room for weakening the wff in IB to anything but a logically valid wff.

Finally, it is also possible to provide a result for infobase change which is reminiscent of the Harper Identity.

Proposition 5. *Let $\circledast$ be a basic infobase revision, and let $\ominus$ be an infobase change operation such that $IB \ominus \alpha \approx \overline{IB \circledast \neg \alpha}$. Then $\ominus$ is a basic infobase contraction.*

5   Iterated Infobase Change

Although an infobase IB induces the unique theory contraction $-_{IB}$, infobases do not contain enough information to determine a basic infobase contraction or revision. To do that, we also need a relevance selection function rs. Once rs is fixed, though, we are dealing with a specific basic infobase contraction and revision, which allows for the possibility of iterated infobase change. In this section we investigate whether iterated infobase change measures up to the postulates supplied by Darwiche et al. [2,3] and Lehmann [10]. To do so, we have to work on the level of *epistemic states*.[3] Following Darwiche and Pearl we assume that every epistemic state Φ has associated with it a belief set $K(\Phi)$ and a $K(\Phi)$-faithful total preorder $\preceq_{\Phi}$. To bring infobase change into this framework, we

---

[3] The use of epistemic states have been advocated by a number of authors, including Darwiche and Pearl [3] and Lehmann [10].

assume that it is possible to extract a unique infobase IB_Φ from every epistemic state Φ. This implies that $K(\Phi) = Cn(S(IB_\Phi))$ and that $\preceq_\Phi$ is identical to the IB_Φ-induced faithful total preorder $\preceq_{IB_\Phi}$. Note, however, that infobases contain more information than such ordered pairs. For example, letting $IB = [p, q]$ and $IC = [p \wedge q, p \vee q]$, it is easy to check that $Cn(S(IB)) = Cn(S(IC))$, and that $\preceq_{IB}$ and $\preceq_{IC}$ are identical. Furthermore, it is also easy to establish that every ordered pair of this kind can be obtained from some infobase. (See p. 26 of [11]) More importantly, perhaps, is the fact that the extra information contained in infobases plays an important role in the process of infobase change, as the next example shows.

Example 2. Let $\ominus$ be the basic infobase contraction obtained from the relevance selection function rs, where $rs(IB, \alpha) = IB^{-\alpha}$, for every $IB \in \mathcal{IB}$ and every $\alpha \in L$, and let $\circledast$ be the basic infobase revision defined in terms of $\ominus$ using (Def $\circledast$ from $\ominus$). Let $IB = [p, q]$ and let $IC = [p \wedge q, p, q, p \vee q, p \to q, q \to p]$. Clearly $Cn(S(IB)) = Cn(S(IC))$ and it is easily established that $\preceq_{IB}$ and $\preceq_{IC}$ are identical. Yet, it can be verified that $IB \circledast (p \wedge \neg q) \approx [p, \top, p \wedge \neg q]$ and that $IC \circledast (p \wedge \neg q) \approx [p, p, p \vee q, p \vee q, \top, q \to p, p \wedge \neg q]$. It can then also be verified that $IB \circledast (p \wedge \neg q)$ and $IC \circledast (p \wedge \neg q)$ induce different faithful total preorders.

Having established that epistemic states need to have a richer structure than ordered pairs of the form $(K(\Phi), \preceq_\Phi)$, we now turn to the definition of revision on epistemic states in terms of basic infobase revision.

$$
\textbf{(Def } * \textbf{ from } \circledast\textbf{)} \quad \begin{bmatrix} K(\Phi * \alpha) = Cn(IB_\Phi \circledast \alpha) \\[2mm] \preceq_{\Phi * \alpha} \;=\; \preceq_{(IB_\Phi \circledast \alpha)} \end{bmatrix}
$$

Definition 16. *We refer to the revision on epistemic states defined in terms of a basic infobase revision $\circledast$ using (Def $*$ from $\circledast$) as the $\circledast$-associated revision on epistemic states.*

5.1   DP-Revision

In two influential papers, Darwiche et al. [2,3] argue that belief change ought to be conducted on the level of epistemic states and, in addition to modifying the AGM postulates appropriately, propose the following additional four postulates for iterated revision:

(DP1) If $\alpha \vDash \beta$ then $K((\Phi * \beta) * \alpha) = K(\Phi * \alpha)$
(DP2) If $\alpha \vDash \neg\beta$ then $K((\Phi * \beta) * \alpha) = K(\Phi * \alpha)$
(DP3) If $\beta \in K(\Phi * \alpha)$ then $\beta \in K((\Phi * \beta) * \alpha)$
(DP4) If $\neg\beta \notin K(\Phi * \alpha)$ then $\neg\beta \notin K((\Phi * \beta) * \alpha)$

When placed in this framework, basic infobase revision yields favourable results. The revisions on epistemic states associated with basic infobase revisions satisfy all but the first one of the four DP-postulates. This is in marked contrast with the version of infobase revision described in [12] which does not satisfy any of these postulates.

Proposition 6. *Let ⊛ be a basic infobase revision, and let ∗ be the ⊛-associated revision on epistemic states. Then ∗ satisfies (DP2)–(DP4), but does not necessarily satisfy (DP1).*

It is our contention that the violation of (DP1) by basic infobase revision is an indication that this postulate is perhaps too restrictive to accommodate a wide range of rational forms of revision. Below we give a realistic example in support of this claim.[4]

Example 3. I have a circuit containing two components; an adder and a multiplier. I have made three independent observations about these components: (1) The adder is working, (2) the multiplier is working, and (3) if the adder doesn't work then the multiplier also doesn't work. Another observation now indicates that at least one of the two components is not working. In trying to incorporate this new information, we have to discard (or weaken) at least one of the first two observations. Moreover, we cannot retain both observations (2) and (3), for they imply observation (1). So it seems reasonable to retain the belief that the adder is working and the belief that a broken adder implies a broken multiplier. Together with the new information that at least one of the components is broken, it then follows that it is the multiplier that is broken.

This line of reasoning can be formalised by using the two atoms a (indicating that the adder is working) and m (indicating that the multiplier is working). My initial infobase then looks like this: $IB = [a, m, \neg a \rightarrow \neg m]$. It is easily verified that for any basic infobase revision ⊛, $Cn(S(IB \circledast \neg(a \wedge m))) = Cn(a \wedge \neg m)$, which means that m should be discarded and that a and $\neg a \rightarrow \neg m$ should be retained. But what should the weakened version of the discarded wff m look like? One reasonable option is to discard it completely, or, what amounts to the same thing, to weaken it so that it becomes logically valid. Formally, this can be accomplished as follows. Let rs be a relevance selection function such that $rs(IB, a \wedge m) = IB^{-(a \wedge m)} = \{m\}$. Since $IB^{-(a \wedge m)}$ is $(IB, \alpha \wedge m)$-relevant, there is such an rs. Now consider the basic infobase contraction $\ominus$ which is obtained using rs. It can be verified that $IB \ominus \neg\neg(a \wedge m) \approx IB \ominus (a \wedge m) \approx [a, \top, \neg a \rightarrow \neg m]$ and therefore $IB \circledast \neg(a \wedge m) \approx [a, \top, \neg a \rightarrow \neg m, \neg(a \wedge m)]$, where ⊛ is the basic infobase revision defined in terms of $\ominus$ using (Def ⊛ from $\ominus$).

To see that the revision ∗ defined in terms of ⊛ using (Def ∗ from ⊛) violates (DP1), observe that $Cn(S(IB \circledast \neg a)) = Cn(\neg a)$, but that $Cn(S((IB \circledast \neg(a \wedge m)) \circledast \neg a)) = Cn(\neg a \wedge \neg m)$. So $K((\Phi \ast \neg(a \wedge m)) \ast \neg a) \neq K(\Phi \ast \neg a)$ even though $\neg a \vDash \neg(a \wedge m)$ where Φ is an epistemic state such that $IB_\Phi = IB$.

There is a form of basic infobase revision which always satisfies (DP1). It corresponds to the coherentist approach to infobase change.

Definition 17. *A coherentist basic infobase revision ⊛ is a basic infobase revision such that $rs(IB, \alpha) = IB$ for every $\alpha \in L$, for the relevance selection function rs from which ⊛ is obtained.*

---

[4] The example was inspired by a similar example of Darwiche et al. [3].

Proposition 7. *Let $\circledast$ be the coherentist basic infobase revision and let $*$ be the revision on epistemic states defined in terms of $\circledast$ using (Def $*$ from $\circledast$). Then $*$ satisfies (DP1).*

5.2   L-Revision

Lehmann [10] considers iterated belief revision in the context of finite sequences of revisions. He extends the notion of a revision $*$ on epistemic states to a revision by a finite sequence of wffs. $\Phi * \sigma$ then refers to the iterated revision of Φ by the wffs in σ, and if σ is the empty sequence, $\Phi * \sigma$ is just the epistemic state Φ. A wff α is identified with a sequence of length one. Considering only sequences of *satisfiable* wffs, Lehmann proposes the following postulates for iterated revision.

(L$*$1) $K(\Phi) = Cn(K(\Phi))$
(L$*$2) $\alpha \in K(\Phi * \alpha)$
(L$*$3) $K(\Phi * \alpha) \subseteq K(\Phi) + \alpha$
(L$*$4) If $\alpha \in K(\Phi)$ then $K(\Phi * \sigma) = K(\Phi * (\alpha \bullet \sigma))$
(L$*$5) If $\alpha \vDash \beta$ then $K(\Phi * (\beta \bullet \alpha \bullet \sigma)) = K(\Phi * (\alpha \bullet \sigma))$
(L$*$6) $K(\Phi) \neq Cn(\bot)$
(L$*$7) $K(\Phi * (\neg\alpha \bullet \alpha)) \subseteq K(\Phi) + \alpha$
(L$*$8) If $\neg\beta \notin K(\Phi * \alpha)$ then $K(\Phi * (\alpha \bullet \beta \bullet \sigma)) = K(\Phi * (\alpha \bullet \alpha \wedge \beta \bullet \sigma))$

It is easily verified that the revision $*$ on epistemic states obtained in terms of a basic infobase revision using (Def $*$ from $\circledast$) satisfies (L$*$1), (L$*$2), (L$*$3) and (L$*$6). It can also be verified that (L$*$7) is a weakened version of (DP2) and it thus follows from proposition 6 that $*$ also satisfies (L $*$7). It does not necessarily satisfy (L$*$4), (L$*$5) and (L$*$8), though, as the following example shows.

Example 4. Let $\circledast$ be the basic infobase revision obtained from the relevance selection function rs for which $rs(IB, \alpha) = IB^{-\alpha}$ for every $IB \in \mathcal{IB}$ and every $\alpha \in L$.

1. Let $IB = [p \wedge \neg q, p \vee q]$. Clearly $IB \circledast p \approx [p \wedge \neg q, p \vee q, p]$. It can be verified that $Cn(S((IB \circledast p) \circledast q)) = Cn(p \wedge q)$, but that $Cn(S(IB \circledast q)) = Cn(q)$. Taking p as α and q as the sequence of wffs σ, this is a violation of (L$*$4).
2. Let $IB = [p \leftrightarrow q, p \vee \neg q, \neg p \vee \neg q, \neg q]$. It can be verified that $IB \circledast q \approx [p \leftrightarrow q, p \vee \neg q, p \vee \neg q, q]$, $IB \circledast p \vee q \approx [p \vee \neg q, \neg p \vee \neg q, \neg q, p \vee q]$, $(IB \circledast p \vee q) \circledast q \approx [p \vee q, q]$, $Cn(S(((IB \circledast p \vee q) \circledast q) \circledast \neg q)) = Cn(p \wedge \neg q)$, and $Cn(S((IB \circledast q) \circledast \neg q)) = Cn(\neg p \wedge \neg q)$. Taking $p \vee q$ as β, q as α, and $\neg q$ as the sequence of wffs σ, this constitutes a violation of (L$*$5).
3. Let $IB = [p \vee q, p \vee \neg q]$. Clearly $IB \circledast p \approx [p \vee q, p \vee \neg q, p]$, $(IB \circledast p) \circledast q = [p \vee q, p \vee \neg q, p, q]$, and $(IB \circledast p) \circledast p \wedge q = [p \vee q, p \vee \neg q, p, p \wedge q]$. It can be verified that $Cn(S(((IB \circledast p) \circledast q) \circledast \neg p)) = Cn(\neg p \wedge q)$, and $Cn(S(((IB \circledast p) \circledast p \wedge q) \circledast \neg p)) = Cn(\neg p)$. With p as α, q as β, and $\neg p$ as the sequence of wffs σ, it follows that (L$*$8) is violated.

An examination of this example suggests that, unlike the DP-postulates, (L$*$4), (L$*$5) and (L$*$8) are fundamentally incompatible with basic infobase revision.

6   Conclusion

We have extended the initial infobase proposal of Meyer et al. [12], but much still needs to be done. Two obvious extensions that still needs to be developed has already been hinted at by Meyer et al. [12]. Both involve the introduction orderings of epistemic relevance in the spirit of Nebel [13,14,15]. And finally, it remains to be seen how baisc infobase change fits into a more general theory of base change.

References

1. Carlos E. Alchourrón, Peter Gärdenfors, and David Makinson. On the logic of theory change: Partial meet functions for contraction and revision. *Journal of Symbolic Logic*, 50:510–530, 1985.
2. Adnan Darwiche and Judea Pearl. On the logic of iterated belief revision. In Ronald Fagin, editor, *Theoretical Aspects of Reasoning about Knowledge*, pages 5–23, Pacific Grove, CA, 1994. Morgan Kaufmann.
3. Adnan Darwiche and Judea Pearl. On the logic of iterated belief revision. *Artificial Intelligence*, 89:1–29, 1997.
4. Jon Doyle. Reason maintenance and belief revision: Foundations versus coherence theories. In Peter Gärdenfors, editor, *Belief Revision*, volume 29 of *Cambridge Tracts in Theoretical Computer Science*, pages 29–51. Cambridge University Press, Cambridge, 1992.
5. André Fuhrmann. Theory contraction through base contraction. *Journal of Philosophical Logic*, 20:175–203, 1991.
6. Peter Gärdenfors. *Knowledge in Flux : Modeling the Dynamics of Epistemic States*. The MIT Press, Cambridge, Massachusetts, 1988.
7. Adam Grove. Two modellings for theory change. *Journal of Philosophical Logic*, 17:157–170, 1988.
8. Sven Ove Hansson. In defense of base contraction. *Synthese*, 91:239–245, 1992.
9. H. Katsuno and A.O. Mendelzon. Propositional knowledge base revision and minimal change. *Artificial Intelligence*, 52:263–294, 1991.
10. Daniel Lehmann. Another perspective on Default Reasoning. *Annals of Mathematics and Artificial Intelligence*, 1995.
11. Thomas A. Meyer. *Semantic belief change*. PhD thesis, Department of Computer Science and Information Systems, University of South Africa, Pretoria, South Africa, 1999.
12. Thomas A. Meyer, Willem A. Labuschagne, and Johannes Heidema. Infobase Change: A First Approximation. *Journal of Logic, Language and Information (to appear)*, 1999.
13. Bernhard Nebel. *Reasoning and Revision in Hybrid Representation Systems*, volume 422 of *Lecture Notes in Artificial Intelligence*. Springer-Verlag, Berlin, 1990.
14. Bernhard Nebel. Belief revision and default reasoning: Syntax-based approaches. In James Allen, Richard Fikes, and Erik Sandewall, editors, *Principles of Knowledge Representation and Reasoning: Proceedings of the Second International Conference KR '91*, pages 417–428. Morgan Kaufmann, San Francisco, California, 1991.
15. Bernhard Nebel. Syntax-based approaches to belief revision. In Peter Gärdenfors, editor, *Belief Revision*, volume 29 of *Cambridge Tracts in Theoretical Computer Science*, pages 52–88. Cambridge University Press, Cambridge, 1992.

A Framework for Multi-Agent Belief Revision
Part I: The Role of Ontology

Wei Liu and Mary-Anne Williams

Information Systems, School of Management, The University of Newcastle
Callaghan, NSW 2308, Australia
mgwl@infosystems.newcastle.edu.au

Abstract. In this paper, we identify that failure to cater for the various forms of heterogeneity is one of the major drawbacks of the previous research on multi-agent belief revision(MABR). Three major categories of heterogeneity, namely social, semantic and syntactic heterogeneity are clarified. Several issues posed by such heterogeneities are addressed in the context of BR. The use of ontology is proposed as a powerful tool to tackle the heterogeneity issues so as to achieve the necessary reliable communication and system interoperability required by MABR. The question of what kind of ontology would be suitable to support MABR in a heterogenous setting is answered in Part I. In its sequel, Part II, a general framework for MABR is presented based on a shared knowledge structure which serves as the theoretical basis for ontology design.

1 Introduction

Belief Revision(BR) is a ubiquitous process underlying many forms of intelligent behaviour[33]. An essential skill an autonomous agent should possess is the ability to revise its beliefs in a coherent and rational fashion when it receives new information. Most BR research, however, has been developed with a single agent in mind, ie, only one problem solver using the BR service. SATEN[1] - a web based BR system which incorporates several revision strategies is a good example of a single BR agent. Although it is able to clone its current state, the clones and their ancestors can not communicate. In other words, they act independently as single agents without awareness of other's existence.

Multi-Agent Systems (MASs) are distributed computing systems composed of a number of interacting computational entities (possibly from various vendors). One important characteristic distinguishing MASs from traditional distributed systems is that both MAS and its components(agents) are intelligent[29]. As MASs become increasingly attractive for solving larger and more complex problems, the need for adequate BR technology in the MAS paradigm arises. Only a few BR frameworks are known that claim to be suited for MAS applications. In section 2, a BR hierarchy is suggested to clarify the terminologies adopted in resent research on *Multi-Agent Belief Revision*(MABR). Section 3 reviews the evolution of various frameworks for MABR.

---

[1] http://infosystems.newcastle.edu.au/webworld/saten

N. Foo (Ed.): AI'99, LNAI 1747, pp. 168–179, 1999.
© Springer-Verlag Berlin Heidelberg 1999

An enormous number of forms of heterogeneity exist in MASs because of the flexibility and complexity of agent interaction and organisation, in addition, agents might be developed by different vendors[9][27]. Current frameworks do not sufficiently support BR which requires and is affected by interagent communication and interoperation in a heterogeneous environment. This functionality is highly desirable in many domains, such as *electronic commerce, group decision making* and *cooperative information systems.* In section 4, we describe different forms of heterogeneity and emphasize the issues raised by it in BR systems.

The development of ontologies is becoming widely accepted as a powerful methodology for bridging the gap between legacy systems, to enable communication and interoperability within a heterogeneous system[17]. In section 5, basic concepts of ontology are briefly introduced and the types of ontology needed for developing a general MABR system are identified.

The paper concludes in section 6 by stating the current and future research problems to be solved so as to develop sound ontology support for the construction of a MABR test bed based on the single agent implementation SATEN.

2 BR in MASs - Concepts and Terminologies

A variety of notations have been adopted by researchers investigating BR of MASs. A good understanding of the relationships between these approaches is essential before carrying out any further research. To clarify the terminologies for BR of MASs, let us revisit the definition of "agent". Generally, an *agent* implies a problem solving entity that both *perceives* and *acts* upon the environment in which it is situated, applying its individual knowledge, skills and other resources to accomplish high-level *goals.* By employing various algorithms and processes, agents are capable of taking various actions to achieve their individual goals or interacting with other agents to achieve mutual goals. According to whether BR is involved in individual goals or mutual goals, previous research efforts in BR of MAS can be classified into two categories, ie, *BR using information from Multiple Sources*(MSBR) and MABR.

On one hand, BR could be considered as part of the agent's skills to maintain the consistency of its own epistemic state. In this case, an *individual* BR process is carried out in a multi-agent environment, where the new information may come from multiple sources and maybe conflict. BR in this sense is called MSBR by Dragoni et al[3][7][4]. Cantwell[2] tries to resolve conflicting information by ordering the information sources on the basis of their trustworthiness. This could be served as a rational way of generating the new information credibility based on the source reliability using the terms of MSBR. Benferhat *et. al.*[1] investigate revision of information from multiple sources in face of uncertainty as *data fusion,* using possibilistic logic; Liberatore and Schaef[23] treat the MSBR process as intelligent merging of knowledge bases, which they call *Arbitration.*

On the other hand, BR could also be used to achieve a society's or team's mutual belief goals(e.g. reaching consensus before carrying out plans). In this setting, more than one agent takes part in the process. In order to pursue the mutual goal, agents involved need to communicate, cooperate, coordinate and negotiate with one another. A MABR system is a MAS whose mutual goal involves BR. Since an MAS is actually an intelligent distributed system, an alternative name for MABR could be *intelligent Distributed Belief Revision*(DBR). MABR is the terminology adopted by Kfir-dahav and Tennenholtz[22]. Dragoni et al prefer DBR[6] based on the comparison with *Distributed Truth Maintenance*(DTM). Van der Meyden's semantical theory of BR in synchronous MAS, namely, Mutual Belief Revision, also falls into the same category as MABR.

MSBR studies individual agent revision behaviours, ie, when an agent receives information from multiple agents towards whom it has social opinions. MABR investigates the overall BR behaviour of agent teams or a society. MSBR is one of the essential components of MABR.

The AGM paradigm[12] has been widely accepted as a standard framework for BR. But it is only capable of prescribing revision behaviours of a single agent. The BR process is more complex in multiple agent case. Besides the *Principle of Minimal Change*, there exist other requisites due to the sophisticated agent interactions. Therefore, the AGM framework is not rich enough to prescribe a satisfactory revision operator for MABR. In this paper and its sequel[2], we develop a general framework based on ontology to capture the necessary heterogenous properties so as to enable the sophisticated agent interactions.

As a result, BR can be thought of in a narrow sense, which encompasses all previous work in AGM. It can be considered in a wider sense, taking into account MASs, from the viewpoint of an agent and an agent society. An agent is capable of carrying out *Individual Belief Revision*(IBR), while an agent society or team is capable of MABR. IBR in a single agent environment(*Single Belief Revision*, SBR) could be achieved using classical BR satisfying AGM postulates. IBR in a multiple agent environment is MSBR, ie, a single agent will have to process information coming from more than one source. After obtaining the new credibility of the new information on evaluating the multiple sources using some techniques(e.g.[2][4]), MSBR turns to SBR. We can classify the types of BR using the hierarchy in Fig.1.

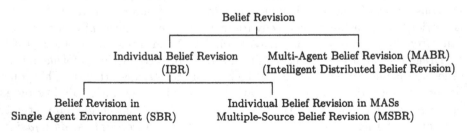

Fig. 1. Belief Revision Hierarchy

---

[2] A Framework for Multi-Agent Belief Revision (Part II: Shared Knowledge Structure)

3 Evolution of MABR Frameworks - A Review

3.1 Mutual Belief Revision of Van der Meyden

Mutual Belief Revision is a nested process during which an agent must revise not only its own beliefs about the world, but also its beliefs about other agents' beliefs about the world and moreover about other agents' beliefs about its own beliefs, and so on. A multi-agent version of *perfect introspection logic* $K45_n$ is employed to model the so-called *mutual belief*[3].

The theory of mutual belief revision ends up with a unique operator which satisfies the following four assumptions: **[I]** Agents have perfect introspection[4], but maybe inconsistent; **[II]** Agents revise their beliefs synchronously, in response to an event ϵ whose occurrence is common knowledge; **[III]** The world is static; **[IV]** Each agent's revision method is common knowledge. III simplifies the problem so that there is no need to consider the temporal factor. But the other three assumptions limit the proposed theory's capability of handling heterogenous multi-agent environment. The inability of modelling incompetent or stupid agents is the major drawback associated with the perfect introspection assumption I. II confines this theory to the simple environment of broadcasting and synchronizing. Actually, IV and II together assumes each agent's revision process is common knowledge, that is, transparent to other agents.

In the given "scientist in conference" example[26], all the agents work faithfully, broadcasting what they know and what they do not know. Considering a distributed knowledge base system, where an agent represents a local *Knowledge Base*(KB). Based on the above four assumptions, the agent should store its own knowledge about the world. Meanwhile, it has full accessibility to all the remote KBs of other agents. Therefore, every agent knows what the others know and what they do not know. On the receipt of new information, first the agent revises its own beliefs, then because the revision method is common knowledge, it could readily and successfully predict what all the other agents will do with their beliefs. In fact, mutual belief revision can be thought of as a set of single BR processes carried out uniformly in a parallel but decentralized manner.

3.2 MABR of Kfir-dahav and Tennenholtz

In contrast to Van der Meyden, Kfir-dahav and Tennenholtz[22] initiate research on MABR in the context of *heterogeneous* systems. The Private Domains (PD_i) and the Shared Domain (SD) of the agent knowledge base are defined in order to capture a general setting where each agent has private beliefs as well as beliefs shared with other agents. Under such knowledge structure, each agent may have its own perspective of the world but needs to coordinate (ie agree on) its belief on shared elements. The shared domain also defines the communication language for the agents.

---

[3] Roughly, a set of agents mutually believe φ iff each of them believes φ, and each of them believes that each of them believes φ, and so on, *ad infinitum*[10].

[4] Perfect introspection assumes a considerable degree of self-knowledge, [11] has detail.

One important question to this scenario is how do we manage the knowledge in PD_i and SD? By definition[22], SD is just the intersection of each agent's KB. Although it is not explictly stated, the authors assume the $agent_i$ is aware of (knows) its own knowledge in PD_i and the existence of SD. Since an agent does not know other agents' PD, what happens if after several sequences of revision, the intersection of PD_is is not empty? For example, consider the situation in which two agents(A_1, A_2) engage in revision, Φ_i stands for the KB of A_i, i=1,2. $\Phi_1 = \{\gamma, \phi, \psi\}$, $\Phi_2 = \{\alpha, \beta, \phi\}$. Then according to the definition, $SD = \{\phi\}; PD_1 = \{\psi, \gamma\}; PD_2 = \{\alpha, \beta\}$. If A_2 receives a piece of new information, say, $\alpha \rightarrow \psi$, then by Modus Ponens, ψ should be in PD_2. Thus,$PD_1 \cap PD_2 = \{\psi\} \neq \emptyset$. A_2 will only expand PD_2 but not SD providing that nobody telling that ψ is also believed by A_1. The authors did not tell us what to do with this ψ. If $\psi \in SD$, it seems to be implicitly assumed that there exists a super agent who knows all the agents' private knowledge and the society's shared knowledge, so that the intersection of private knowledge can always be upgraded to the shared domain. If $\psi \notin SD$, the definition of SD has been violated.

3.3   MSBR and DBR of Dragoni et al.

MSBR. Recognizing that agents may join the network with low degrees of competence or non-cooperative intentions, Dragoni et al states that the *reliability* of the source affects the *credibility* of the information and vice-versa[5]. Neglecting the "priority to the incoming information principle"is thus proposed and implemented by considering $\langle informant, information \rangle$ rather than just *information*.

In the AGM paradigm, priority is given to the incoming information. For instance, the new information will be accepted using an expansion if it is consistent with the current belief sets. In the sense of transmutation[32], or possibility theory[8] or other revision schemes, the new information is allowed to come with a certain rank and to be accepted at this prescribed level. In this case although you don't necessarily totally accept the new information, you do need to respect the incoming rank. There is no explicit rational step to change the rank. While the non-priority of or in the extreme case, neglecting incoming information is thus a two step procedure, first, revise the rank according to the reliability of the informant and then incorporate the information with the new rank. Therefore, by evaluating the source reliability, the receiver agent has the flexibility of deciding whether to take the impinging information into account or not.

DBR. In DTM[19], all the agents are both individually and mutually consistent with any other agent with whom they exchanged knowledge. While in DBR[5][6], the "Liberal Belief Revision Policy"is adopted, that is, to let all the agents stand by their own beliefs based on their own view of the evidence. Therefore, the local consistency is considered as a prerequisite, but the global consistency is only considered as an end point which is eventually reached through some selection strategies. Every node (agent) in the DBR system is able to carry out MSBR as well as communicate with each other.

As to the knowledge structure, local knowledge has been distinguished from global knowledge. By using some *voting* functions[5], the local knowledge can be selected to become global knowledge. Compared to Kfir-dahav and Tennenholtz's terminology, Dragoni et al's local and global knowledge could be seen as the counterparts to the knowledge in PD_i and SD, respectively. But a subtle improvement is made by Dragoni et al that certain *voting* function is employed to generate global knowledge rather than simply taking the intersection of PD_is. Actually, private or local knowledge as defined here are not private in the real sense, in other words, it is implicitly assumed some super agent, at least a human developer, exists in the system to supervise the *knowledge upgrade*[5]. Private knowledge should be confidential, ie, invisible to all the outsiders. To classify agent knowledge in these ways is still too simple to some extent. For example, in an agent society housing multiple agents, some agents might wish to form small groups or teams to accomplish goals. Therefore, *shared knowledge* (or team knowledge) rather than global knowledge is sometimes prefered.

3.4 Summary

To summarize, mutual belief revision is only capable of revising *knowledge*, but not graded *belief*. Kfir-dahav and Tennenholtz's MABR and Dragoni et al's DBR have overcome this by discussing revision in the broad sense of knowledge system transmutation. The social behaviour that might affect the information credibility has been discussed by Dragoni et al in the context of MSBR. This is a great advance over other studies based on reliable, faithful and mutually trustworthy communication. The knowledge structures proposed by Kfir-dahav and Tennenholtz and Dragoni et al initiate the effort of classifying knowledge. But they are not rich enough to eliminate some ambiguity as well as offer some essential flexibility. It will be shown in section 4 that finding a feasible way of classifying knowledge is an important step towards modelling *social heterogeneity* from the viewpoint of KB. For all schemes discussed above, none address the issues might arise from multiple revision strategies, while this could be highly desired in a heterogenous revision system. Although MABR and DBR's communication mode is not restricted to broadcast as mutual belief revision does, the underlying heterogeneity issues which might inhibit efficient and reliable communication has not been addressed to any depth. Since the heterogeneity exists elsewhere in MASs, special issues arise in MABR, which must be discussed.

---

[5] Knowledge upgrade is one phase of *knowledge migration*, which also encompasses the dual phase of upgrade, ie *knowledge degrade*. Upgrade refers to the process that local knowledge is selected to become global knowledge, while degrade is the opposite process. Knowledge migration will be fully discussed in Part II of this paper.

4   Heterogeneity of Multi-Agent Systems

Much of the conceptual power of the MAS paradigm arises from the flexibility and sophistication of the agent interactions and organisations. As the basic skill for both individual agents and agent societies to maintain consistency, the BR process and result will highly depend on the way agents communicate, cooperate, coordinate and negotiate with one another. Heterogeneity is the one of the basic originations of such flexibility but it also causes complexity. Taking the opportunities as well as solving the difficulties could lead to a more dynamic and versatile BR perspective. Therefore, it is necessary to study how the heterogeneities might affect BR behaviours in MASs.

Heterogeneities in a MAS could have many forms ranging from the hardware and software platform that each agent is based on, to the organisation schema that relate individual agents socially to others forming teams and societies, to the basic knowledge representation structure and reasoning strategy that makes the agent intelligent, to the problem domain that an agent specialised in. This paper focuses on the issues raised by heterogeneities in the knowledge systems, which includes the last two cases. Following is a brief classification according to the source (ie level) of these knowledge system heterogeneities.

- Social Character Heterogeneity(social-level): Within the MAS paradigm, an agent is socially situated in a particular environment with other agents. As a problem solving entity, an agent is also defined as software that acts on behalf of the user to accomplish a task assigned by the user. Therefore, just as human could behave in a *benevolent* or *malicious* way, there is no reason to forbid agents from possessing such characters. In the context of *modelling trust*[21], "free will "has been defined to describe the mental process that decides between benevolent and malicious behaviour. Agents possessing free will of this type are designated as *passionate*. However, an agent, such as algorithms, protocols, software and hardware which could hardly be characterized as having a free will is classified as *rational*. On the other hand, due to technical or other possible reasons (e.g. hardware quality), the agent could either be *competent* or *incompetent*. Combining these characteristics, agents could be roughly classified into four categories: competent rational, competent passionate, incompetent rational and incompetent passionate agent.
- Semantic or Logical Heterogeneity(meta-level): Borrowing terms from *cooperative information systems*(CIS)[20], semantic heterogeneity results when different conceptualisations and different database schemas are used to represent the same or overlapping data which is replicated in two or more databases. A simple real world example could be the various grading techniques in an educational system such as percentage or letter grade[18]. A generalisation of such heterogeneity also occurs in the agent KBs. For example, the knowledge could be represented using different logics, in favour of agent's problem solving capability with respect to certain problem domain.
- Syntactic Heterogeneity(content-level): This is a domain specific heterogeneity which arises from the fact that in many cases the same letters or words

are used to represent different concepts or objects by different agents and vice versa. This happens during the process of building knowledge into autonomous agents to enhance their intelligence. Natural language is commonly transformed into a simple logical form. Developers have the freedom to name things as they wish. For example, some agent may choose the letter "a" for describing an apple, while some other agents might prefer the whole word "apple" or something else. This is also a common phenomenon in all the emerging research areas, different terminologies have been used to describe the same concept, or vice versa. While a research area matures, general terms and frameworks will be proposed to serve as a specification.

It can be seen from the previous study in MABR, researchers have progressively put more accent on the heterogeneity existing in agent knowledge bases. In the early 1990's, Fagin et al[10] semantically defined *mutual belief* and *common knowledge*. Van der Meyden extended this modal logic approach into MABR in 1994. Malheiro[25] in the same year defined *private* and *shared belief* to model the BR process in a DTM system. Similarly, Kfir-dahav and Tennenholtz claimed in 1996 that their work[22] is more amenable to solve the heterogeneity problem than Van der Meyden's by stating that agent knowledge could fall into *private* and *shared* domains. Recently, other researchers[24][30], following Fagin et al's approach, defined various concepts such as *team knowledge* and *shared knowledge*. Dragoni et al also distinguishes *global knowledge* from *local knowledge*[5].

Actually, defining shared, common and private knowledge paved the way for modelling the *social character heterogeneity*, in other words, the diversity of different kinds of knowledge is the reflection of social heterogeneity in agent KBs. Private knowledge is needed by a passionate agent to keep confidential information. Such privacy enables the possibility of malicious behaviour which is sometimes needed for an agent to maximize its own or group utility in a competitive environment. On the other hand, common or shared knowledge is essential to establish cooperation-oriented communication and commitment. For example, incompetent agents could carry out teamwork by sharing knowledge so as to achieve high-level goals which could not be accomplished by any individual. Understanding the similarities and distinctions among these conceptualisations of agent knowledge poses a serious challenge when trying to integrate systems based on different knowledge structures.

Semantic and syntactic heterogeneity have not yet been studied in the context of MABR.

Various BR strategies are examples of *semantic heterogeneities* that exist in MABR. For BR within AGM paradigm, many revision schemes have emerged during the past decade, such as numerical revision using probabilistic[28] or possibilistic logic[8], sentence-based revision using various transmutations[32] and so on. Because a variety of ranking mechanisms[6] might be used when employing various revision strategies, special communication and interoperability issues arise. How does an agent communicate with each other in terms of the informa-

---

[6] Ranging from ordinal natural numbers(ie $\{0, 1, 2, ..., \infty\}$) to unit interval (ie $[0, 1]$).

tion credibility? In other words, how does an agent incorporate new information from another ranking system?

Communication and interoperability difficulties are associated with *syntactic heterogeneity* too. How could the information reliability be guaranteed during the information passing process in a system with such low-level heterogeneity that same letter means something different?

5   Ontology - A Solution to the Heterogeneity Issues

Recently, it has become more and more widely accepted that *ontologies* are efficient approaches to solve the problems involved in the generalization of low-level heterogenous data to relatively high-level concepts for the purposes of communication, system interoperability and software reusability. To solve heterogeneity issues in MABR different types of ontology are needed.

The basic idea of *conceptualisation* needs to be clarified first before introducing ontology. According to Guarino[16], a conceptualisation is a set of informal rules that constrain the structure of a piece of reality. A conceptualisation may be implicit, e.g. exist only in someone's head, or embodied in a piece of software. An explicit account or representation of some part of a conceptualisation is usually called an *ontology*[15].

Uschold's review paper on *knowledge level modelling*[31] has an excellent treatise on ontology related terms and concepts. Following is some of the key dimensions along which ontology may vary adapted from this review.

  – Formality: An ontology is *highly informal* if expressed loosely in natural language; *structured informal* if in a restricted and structured form of natural language; *Semi-formal* if in an artificial formally defined language such as Ontolingua and Knowledge Interchange Format(KIF)(links in [14]) and etc; *rigorously formal* if in meticulously defined terms with formal semantics, theorems and proofs of such properties as soundness and completeness.
  – Purpose: There are three main categories of use of ontologies: for the purpose of *communication* between people and organisations, of *inter-operability* between systems and of *system engineering benefits*.
  – Subject matter: *Domain ontology* is for special subjects such as medicine, finance and etc. *Upper model* is general world knowledge. *Task, method or problem solving ontology* is for the subject of problem solving. *Representation ontology* is for the subject of a knowledge representation language.

To enable various degrees of sharing among agent knowledge bases, it is necessary to establish a general knowledge structure which could capture not only the property of shared knowledge/belief but also that of private knowledge/belief. The main purpose of this general framework is to enable interoperability within a *heterogenous society* and communication across society boundaries. A heterogenous society is an agent society populated with both rational and passionate agents who might be competent or incompetent in a certain domain. An ontology for this purpose serves as an interchange format to translate between different modelling methods and paradigms. Ontolingua or KIF would be suitable for designing a computer executable semi-formal ontology. Therefore, considering the general framework nature, the ontology needed here could be seen as a *semi-formal upper model* for the classification of agent knowledge base. The upper model here bridges the gap between rational and passionate society. It also establishes a foundation for modelling heterogenous society. An implemental proposal for modelling the agent heterogenous behaviour could be based on whether the agent will release its true opinion on the credibility of the information it passes to others. Rational agents will never deliver information which is not believed or with wrong credibility. Passionate agents will pass information with wrong rank occasionally. It is more complicated when trying to model the agent competency. Many aspects are involved. Suppose agent qualification is evaluated by the adequacy of its knowledge with regard to some special domain, the model should be able to reasoning about *ignorance*. If an agent is evaluated by the reliability of its revision skill, competency could be judged by whether there is inconsistency in its knowledge base. In this sense, an inconsistent local knowledge base is allowed in order to capture the behaviour of stupid agents(i.e. faulty reasoners), who believe in sentences inconsistent with their knowledge bases. Detailed discussion of the upper model will appear in Part II.

Similarly, according to the classification criteria above, on the semantic heterogeneity of ranking system, a problem solving ontology is needed to transform one ranking system to another. While as to the syntactic heterogeneity, a specific domain ontology need to be developed. To be computer executable, normally, semi-formal and rigorously formal format would be preferable or required.

6 Future Work

Ontologies can be both constructive and destructive. Information distortion could occur during the generalisation process of ontology design. Many criteria exist to prescribe a good ontology[13] and more are still under investigation. Essentially, the key is to thoroughly understand the problem domain.

To design the upper model of knowledge structure, both philosophical and psychological investigations into the nature of shared/common and private knowledge would be a good start. Currently, a general knowledge structure, which encompasses private, shared and accessible knowledge, is proposed along the way to our model (described in Part II of this paper). Many interesting features about this structure are still under investigation, e.g. *knowledge migration*, *speech act generation* and *exception tolerant nature*. In the knowledge migration phase, a proper revision operator on a shared domain poses a great challenge due to the fact that BR in this case is a mixed process composed of traditional BR, communication and other interactions. Sophisticated decision making techniques are required of such BR operator, because the revision process could branch according to communication mode and social intension. Therefore in certain circumstances, the revision result might not be easily predicted. The implementation of such idea to a multi-agent version of SATEN is the focus of our current research.

The possibility of translating among various ranking systems is another challenge. It is important to note that not all ranking systems are equally expressive, hence information will be lost when one translates ranks from a rich ranking system such as [0,1] to an ordinal one. Determining the appropriate translation may require substantial communication between agents to clarify the intended meaning of their ranking. This determination is to be supported by the ontology.

Finally, the established system will be tested by applying it to special domains such as electronic commerce and group decision support systems.

References

1. Salem Benferhat, Dider Dubois, and Henri Prade. From semantic to syntactic approaches to informtion combination in possibilistic logic. In B. Bouchon-Meunier, editor, *Aggregation and Fusion of Imperfect Information, Studies in Fuzziness and Soft Computing*, pages 141–161. Physica Verlag, 1997.
2. John Cantwell. Resolving conflicting information. *Journal of Logic, Language, and Information*, 7:191–220, 1998.
3. A.F. Dragoni. Belief revision under uncertainty in a multi-agent environment. In S.Tzafestas, editor, *Knowledge-Based Systems: Advanced Concepts, Techniques and Applications*, pages 191–215. World Scientific, 1997.
4. A.F. Dragoni and Paolo Guorgini. Revising beliefs received form multiple sources. In Mary Anne Williams and Hans Rott, editors, *Frontiers of Belief Revision*. 1999.
5. A.F. Dragoni, Paolo Guorgini, and Marco Baffetti. Distributed belief revision vs. belief revision in a multi-agent environment: First result of a simulation experiment. In *Multi-Agent Rationality, Proc. of MAAMAW'97*, LNAI, pages 45–62, Ronneby, Sweden, 1997. Springer-Verlag.
6. A.F. Dragoni, Paolo Guorgini, and Paolo Puliti. Distributed belief revision versus distributed truth maintenance. In *Proc. of 6th IEEE conf. on Tools with A.I.* IEEE computer Press, 1994.
7. A.F. Dragoni and P.F. Guorgini. Belief revision through the belief function formalism in a multi-agent environment. In *Third International Workshop on Agent Theories, Architectures and Languages*. Springer-Verlag, 1997.
8. Dider Dubois and Henri Prade. Belief change and possibility theory. In Peter Gärdenfors, editor, *Belief Revision*, pages 142–182. Cambridge University Press, Cambridge, 1992.
9. Eithan Ephrati and Jeffrey S. Rosenschein. Deriving consensus in multiagent systems. *Artificial Intelligence*, 87:21–74, 1996.
10. Ronald Fagin, Joseph Y. Halpern, Yoram Moses, and Moshe Y. Vardi. *Reasoning about Knowledge*. The MIT Press, London, 1 edition, 1995.
11. Dov M. Gabbay, C.J. Hogger, and J. A. Robinson, editors. *Handbook of Logic in Artificial Intelligence and Logic Programming*, volume 1. Oxford University Press Inc., New York, 1993.
12. Peter Gärdenfors. *Knowledge in Flux - Modeling the Dynamics of Epistemic States*. The MIT Press, London, 1988.
13. Thomas R. Gruber. Toward principles for the design of ontologies used for knowledge sharing. Technical Report KSL 93-04, Knowledge Systems Laboratory, Stanford University, 1993.
14. Tom Gruber. Welcome to the srkb working group. *SRKB mailing list, http://www-ksl.stanford.edu/email-archives/srkb.messages/0.html*, 1994.
15. N. Guarino and P. Giaretta. Ontologies and knowledge bases - towards a terminological clarification. In NJ Mars, editor, *Towards Very Large Knowledge Bases-Knowledge Building and Knowledge Sharing*, pages 25–32. IOS Press, 1995.

16. Nicola Guarino. Understanding, building and using ontologies - a commentary to 'using explicit ontologies in kbs development'by van heijst, schreiber and wielinga. *International Journal of Computer Studies*, 46(3/4):293–310, 1997.

17. Nicola Guarino. Formal ontology and information systems. In Nicola Guarino, editor, *1st International Conf. on Formal Ontology in Information Systems(FOIS'98)*, Trento, Italy, 1998. Amsterdam, IOS Press.

18. Jiawei Han, Raymond T. Ng, Yongjian Fu, and Son K. Dao. Dealing with semantic heterogeneity by generalization-based data mining techniques. In Gunter Schlageter Michael P. Papazoglou, editor, *Cooperative Information Systems - Trends and Directions*, pages 207–232. Academic Press, San Diego, 1998.

19. M. N. Huhns and D. M. Bridgeland. Distributed truth maintenance. In S. M. Dean, editor, *Cooperating Knowledge Based Systems*, pages 133–147. Springer-verlag, 1990.

20. Richard Hull. Managing semantic heterogeneity in databases. In *Proceedings of the Sixteenth ACM SIGACT-SIGMOD-SIGART Symposium on Principles of Database Systems (Invited tutorial)*, pages 51–61, Tucson, Arizona, 1997. ACM.

21. Audum Jøsang. Prospectives for modeling trust in information security. In Vijay Varadharajan, Josef Pieprzyk, and Yi Mu, editors, *Information Security and Privacy, ACISP'97*, volume 1270 of *LNCS*, pages 2–13, Sydney, Australia, 1997. Spinger-Verlag.

22. Noa E. Kfir-dahav and Moshe Tennenholtz. Muti-agent belief revision. In *6th Conf. on Theoretical Aspects to Rationality and Knowledge*, pages 175–194, 1996.

23. Paolo Liberatore and Marco Schaerf. Arbitration (or how to merge knoweledge bases). *IEEE Trans. on Knowledge and Data Engineering*, 10(1):76–90, 1998.

24. Alessio Lomuscio and Mark Ryan. Ideal agents sharing (some!) knowledge. In Henri Parade, editor, *13th European Conf. on AI, ECAI'98*, pages 557–561. John Wiley & Sons, Ltd, 1998.

25. Benedita Malheiro, N.R. Jennings, and Eugénio Oliveira. Belief revision in multi-agent systems. In A. G. Cohn, editor, *11th European Conferece on Artificial Intelligence*, pages 294–298, Amsterdam, The Netherlands, 1994. John Wiley & sons, Ltd.

26. Ron van der Meyden. Mutual belief revision. In *the Fourth International Conference on Principles of Knowledge Representation and Reasoning (KR'94)*, 1994.

27. Michael P. Papaxoglou and Gunter Schlageter, editors. *Cooperative Information Systems*. Academic Press Limited, San Diego, California, 1998.

28. J. Pearl. *Probabilistic Reasoning for Intelligent Systems*. Morgan Kaufmann Publishers, 1988.

29. Munindar P. Singh. *Muti-Agent systems - A theoretical framework for intentions, know-how, and communications*. LNAI. Springer-Verlag, Berlin Heidelberg, 1994.

30. Gil Tidhar, Elizabeth A. Sonenberg, and Anand S. Rao. On team knowledge and common knowledge. In Yves Demazeau, editor, *Third International Conference on Multi-Agent Systems*, pages 301–308, Paris, France, 1998. IEEE Computer Society.

31. Mike Uschold. Knowledge level modeling: concepts and terminology. *The Knowledge Engineering Review*, 13(1):5–29, 1998.

32. Mary Anne Williams. Transmutation of knowledge systems. In J. Doyle, E. Sandewall, and P. Torasso, editors, *4th International Conf. on Principles of Knowledge Representation and Reasoning*, pages 619 – 629. Morgan Kaufmann Publishers, 1994.

33. Mary Anne Williams. Anytime belief revision. In *International Joint Conference on Artificial Intelligence*, pages 74 – 80. Morgan Kaufmann Publishers, 1997.

Genetic Programming for Multiple Class Object Detection

Mengjie Zhang and Victor Ciesielski

Department of Computer Science, Royal Melbourne Institute of Technology
GPO Box 2476V, Melbourne Victoria 3001, Australia
{mengjie,vc}@cs.rmit.edu.au
http://www.cs.rmit.edu.au/~{mengjie,vc}

Abstract. We describe an approach to the use of genetic programming for object detection problems in which the locations of small objects of multiple classes in large pictures must be found. The evolved programs use a feature set computed from a square input field large enough to contain each of objects of interest and are applied, in moving window fashion, over the large pictures in order to locate the objects of interest. The fitness function is based on the detection rate and the false alarm rate. We have tested the method on three object detection problems of increasing difficulty with four different classes of interest. On pictures of easy and medium difficulty all objects are detected with no false alarms. On difficult pictures there are still significant numbers of errors, however the results are considerably better than those of a neural network based program for the same problems.

Keywords: Machine learning, Genetic algorithms, Neural networks, Vision

1 Introduction

As more and more images are captured in electronic form the need for programs which can find objects of interest in a database of images is increasing. For example, it may be necessary to find all tumors in a database of x-ray images, all cyclones in a database of satellite images or a particular face in a database of photographs. The common characteristic of such problems can be phrased as "Given $subpicture_1, subpicture_2...subpicture_n$ which are examples of the object of interest, find all pictures which contain this object and its location(s)". Figure 4 shows examples of problems of this kind. Figure 4c shows a human retina. We are required to find all of the micro aneurisms and haemorrhages, as indicated by the white squares. Figure 5 shows an enlarged view. Examples of other problems of this kind include target detection problems [5,17,19] where the task is to find, say, all tanks, trucks or helicopters in a picture. Unlike most of the current work in the object recognition area, where the task is to detect only objects of one class [5,11,12], our objective is to detect objects from a number of classes.

N. Foo (Ed.): AI'99, LNAI 1747, pp. 180–192, 1999.

Several approaches have been applied to automatic object detection and recognition problems. Typically, they use multiple independent stages, such as preprocessing, edge detection, segmentation, feature extraction and object classification[4,10], which often results in some efficiency and effectiveness problems. The final results rely too much upon the results of each stage. If some objects are lost in one of the early stages, it is very difficult or impossible to recover them in the later stage. To avoid these disadvantages, this paper introduces a single stage approach.

There have been a number of reports on the use of genetic programming in object detection and classification [13,15]. [18] describes a genetic programming system for object detection in which the evolved functions operate directly on the pixel values. [16] describes a genetic programming system and a face recognition application in which the evolved programs have a local indexed memory. All of these approaches are based on two class problems, that is, objects vs everything else.

Performance in object detection is measured by detection rate and false alarm rate. The detection rate is the number of objects correctly reported as a percentage of the total number of real objects and false alarm rate is the number of objects incorrectly reported as a percentage of the total number of real objects. For example, a detection system looking for grey squares in figure 4a may report that there are 25. If 9 of these are correct the detection rate will be $(9/18) * 100 = 50\%$. The false alarm rate will be $(16/18) * 100 = 88.9\%$. It is important to note that finding objects in pictures with very cluttered backgrounds is an extremely difficult problem and that false detection rates of 200-2,000% (that is the detection system suggests that there are 20 times as many objects as there really are) are common [12,14].

1.1   Outline of the Approach to Object Detection

A brief outline of the method is as follows:

1. Assemble a database of pictures in which the locations and classes of all of the objects of interest are manually determined. Reserve some of the pictures as 'unknowns' for measuring detection performance.
2. Determine an appropriate size (n) of a square which will cover all objects of interest and form the input field.
3. Invoke an evolutionary process to generate a program which can determine the class of an object in its input field.
4. Apply the generated program as a moving window template [1] to the pictures reserved with step 1 and obtain the locations of all the objects of interest in each class. Calculate the detection rate and the false alarm rate on the test set as the measure of performance.

1.2 Goals

Our overall goal is to determine whether programs evolved by genetic programming can do a good enough job of finding the objects of interest in pictures such as those shown in figure 4. Specifically we are interested in:

- What image processing features would make useful terminals?
- Whether the four standard arithmetic operators will be sufficient for the function set?
- How can the fitness function be constructed given that there are several classes of interest?
- How will performance vary with increasing difficulty of image detection problems?
- Will the performance be better than a neural network approach [22] on the same problems.

2 Genetic Programming

Genetic programming is a relatively recent technology based on the use of Darwinian evolution in the generation of computer programs. Developed and first published by John Koza in[7], it has been successfully applied in areas such as pattern recognition[13], control[9], robocup[20] and modelling[6]. The process starts with a randomly generated population of programs. Each program is executed and its degree of success in achieving its task is measured and assigned as its fitness. Programs with high fitness are then selected for mating. In the mating process two parents are chosen and randomly selected sub-trees are swapped giving two children of a new population. In general, individuals in the new generation will be fitter than those in the current generation. The process terminates when the best individual does not improve over the course of a few generations.

The programs are constructed from *a terminal set* and *a function set* which will vary according to the problem domain. Functions form the root and the internal nodes of the parse tree representation of a program. Terminals have no arguments and form the leaves of the parse tree. Terminals represent the inputs to the program. Assuming that one has available a generalized genetic programming 'engine' to perform the evolutionary processes, the task of using genetic programming for any given problem becomes one of determining the appropriate set of functions and terminals and a suitable fitness function. It is important to note that the selection of the functions and terminals is critical to success. A bad selection could result in very slow convergence or to not being able to find a solution at all. More details of genetic programming and its applications can be found in [2,8].

2.1 Genetic Programming Adapted to Object Detection

As noted above the main tasks in using genetic programming in some problem domain are (1)Determine the terminal set, (2)Determine the function set, and (3)Determine the method of measuring fitness.

2.2 The Terminal Set

For object detection problems terminals correspond to image features. In our case twenty features, *F1 to F20* in figure 1, are extracted from a square input field, which is large enough to contain all objects of interest. In figure 1a, the grey circle is an object of interest, the filled square A1-B1-C1-D1-A1 represents the square input field. Other squares represent regions for which features will be computed. The mean and standard deviation of the pixels comprising each of these regions are used as two separate features. There are 6 regions giving 12 features, *F1 to F12*. Also we use pixels along the main axes of the input field as shown in figure 1b, giving features *F13 to F20*.

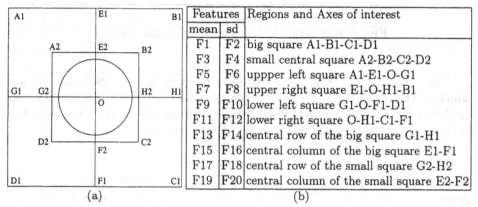

Features		Regions and Axes of interest
mean	sd	
F1	F2	big square A1-B1-C1-D1
F3	F4	small central square A2-B2-C2-D2
F5	F6	uppper left square A1-E1-O-G1
F7	F8	upper right square E1-O-H1-B1
F9	F10	lower left square G1-O-F1-D1
F11	F12	lower right square O-H1-C1-F1
F13	F14	central row of the big square G1-H1
F15	F16	central column of the big square E1-F1
F17	F18	central row of the small square G2-H2
F19	F20	central column of the small square E2-F2

(a)   (b)

Fig. 1. Feature extraction based on local image region intensities. Note: sd – standard deviation

In addition to these features we have a terminal which generates a random number in the range [0,255]. This corresponds to the number of grey levels in the images.

These features have the following characteristics:

- They are symmetrical and contain some information of object translation and rotation invariance.
- Local region features are included. This assists the finding of object centres in the sweeping procedure – if the evolved program is considered as a moving window template, the match between the template and the sub image forming the input field will be better when the moving template is close to the centre of an object.
- They are domain independent and easy to extract.

2.3 The Function Set

We use the function set: $F = \{+, -, *, /\}$ which represents four arithmetic operations that form the second order nodes (i.e. 2 arguments). The +, -, and * operators have their usual meanings while / represents "protected" division which is the usual division operator except that a divide by zero gives a result of zero. A generated program that performed particularly well is shown in figure 2.

```
(+ (- (+ (+ (/ f16 f14) f5) (+ (/ (/ f11 (* f14 f20)) f11) (- f12
f14))) (- (* ( - (* (* (* f9 f11) f1) f10) (* f9 f17)) (/ f5 f18))
(- (+ (+ f17 (* (+ f11 f12) f20)) (* (- (+ f2 145.765) (/ f6 f11))
(- 133.082 f17))) (/ f11 (* f14 f20)))))) (* (- (* (- (- f6 f5) (*
f3 f6)) (/ (+ (+ f1 145.765) (* f16 f10)) f18)) f12) (+ (+ f17 (*
(+ f17 f12) f20)) (* (+ f14 f12) (- (+ f1 f12) f17))))))
```

Fig. 2. A generated program for the coins problem

The output of any program is a floating point number which must indicate which of the objects of interest is currently in its input field. This is achieved as shown in figure 3 where n is the number of classes of interest, *ProgOut* is the output value of the evolved program and T is a constant.

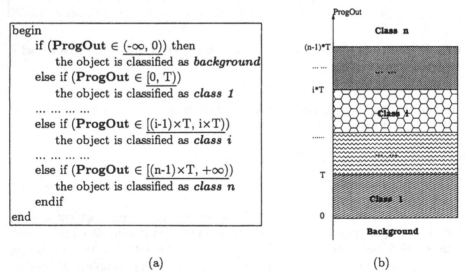

(a)   (b)

Fig. 3. Mapping of program output to an object classification

2.4   The Fitness Function

The fitness of a program in the population is calculated by using its detection rate and false alarm rate on the training images and is obtained as follows:

1. Apply the program as a moving $n \times n$ (n is the size of the input field) window template to each of the full training images and obtain the output values of the program at each pixel position. Label each pixel position with the 'detected' object according to the algorithm described in figure 3. Call this data structure a detection map.

2. Find the centres of *objects of interest only*. This is done as follows:
   - Scan the detection map for an object of interest. When one is found mark this point as the centre of the object and continue the scan $n/2$ pixels later.

3. Match these 'detected' objects with the known locations of each of the 'true' objects and their classes. A match is considered to occur if the detected object is within TOLERANCE pixels of its known true location. The detection rate Dr and the false alarm rate Fr are then computed.

4. Compute the fitness as shown in equation 1.

$$fitness(Fr, Dr) = A * Fr + B * (1 - Dr) \tag{1}$$

where A and B are constants which reflect the relative importance of false alarm rate versus detection rate.

With this design, it is clear that the smaller the fitness, the better the performance. Zero fitness is the ideal case, which corresponds to the situation in which all of the objects of interest in each class are correctly found by the evolved program without any false alarms.

2.5 Genetic Programming Parameters

The values for the various system parameters used in the experiments are shown in table 1. POPULATION_SIZE is the number of individuals in the population, ELITISM_PCNT gives the percentage of the best individuals in the current population that are copied unchanged to the next generation, CROSS_RATE is the percentage of individuals in the next generation that are to be produced by crossover, MUTATION_RATE is the percentage of individuals in the next generation that are to be produced by mutation (thus ELITISM_PCNT + CROSS_RATE + MUTATION_RATE = 100%), CROSS_CHANCE_TERM is the probability that, in a crossover operation two terminals will be swapped, CROSS_CHANCE_FUNC is the probability that in a crossover operation random subtrees will be swapped (thus CROSS_CHANCE_TERM + CROSS_CHANCE_FUNC = 100%), INITIAL_MAX_DEPTH is the maximum depth of the randomly generated programs in the initial population, MAX_DEPTH is the maximum depth permitted for programs resulting from crossover and mutation operations, MAX_GENERATIONS gives the stopping condition, T, A, B and TOLERANCE are as described above.

Table 1. Parameters used for GP training in the three databases

Parameters	Easy Pictures	Coin Pictures	Retina Pictures
POPULATION_SIZE	100	500	500
ELITISM_PCNT	10%	1%	2%
CROSS_RATE	65%	74%	73%
MUTATION_RATE	25%	25%	25%
CROSS_CHANCE_TERM	15%	15%	15%
CROSS_CHANCE_FUNC	85%	85%	85%
INITIAL_MAX_DEPTH	5	5	5
MAX_DEPTH	8	12	20
MAX_GENERATIONS	100	200	250
T	100	100	100
A	50	50	50
B	1000	1000	3000
TOLERANCE (pixels)	2	2	2

3   The Image Databases

We used three different databases in the experiments. Example pictures and key characteristics are given in figure 4. The pictures were selected to provide problems of increasing difficulty. Database 1 (Easy) was generated to give well defined objects against a uniform background. The pixels of the objects were generated using a Gaussian generator with different means and variances for each class. The coin pictures (database 2) were intended to be somewhat harder and were taken with a CCD camera over a number of days with relatively similar illumination. In these pictures the background varies slightly in different areas of the image and between images and the objects to be detected are more complex, but still regular. The retina pictures (database 3) were taken by a professional photographer with special apparatus at a clinic and contain very irregular objects on a very cluttered background. The objective is to find two classes of retinal pathologies – haemorrhages and micro aneurisms. Note that in each of the databases the background counts as a class. The objective is to find the locations (centres) of all the objects of interest in each class.

4   Results

This section presents a series of the experiments on detection problems of increasing difficulty with different classes of interest. The results are compared with those obtained using a neural network approach for object detection on the same databases [21,22]. The method used was the same as that shown in section 1.1, except that step 3 was replaced by a neural network.

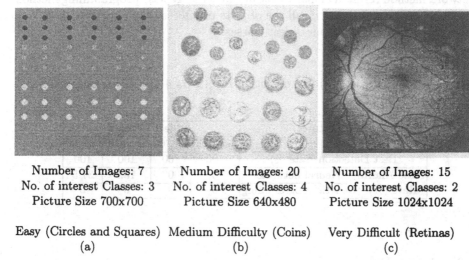

Number of Images: 7   Number of Images: 20   Number of Images: 15
No. of interest Classes: 3   No. of interest Classes: 4   No. of interest Classes: 2
Picture Size 700x700   Picture Size 640x480   Picture Size 1024x1024

Easy (Circles and Squares) Medium Difficulty (Coins)   Very Difficult (Retinas)
          (a)   (b)   (c)

Fig. 4. Object Detection Problems of Increasing Difficulty

4.1 Easy Pictures

Table 2 shows a comparison of the results between the two methods. For Class1 (black circles) and Class3 (grey circles) both methods achieved a 100% detection rate with 0% false alarms. For Class2 (grey squares) the genetic programming system also achieved 100% detection rate with 0% false alarms. However the neural network system had a false alarm rate of 92% at a detection rate of 100%.

Table 2. Comparison of object detection results on 3-class *easy* pictures. Input field size: 14×14

Easy Pictures		Object Classes		
		Class1	Class2	Class3
Best Detection Rate(%)		100	100	100
False Alarm	Neural network	0	92	0
Rate (%)	Genetic programming	0	0	0

4.2 Coin Pictures

Experiments with coin pictures gave similar results which are shown in Table 3. Detecting the heads and tails of 5 cents is relatively straight forward, where the neural network approach led to 100% of detection rate without any false alarms. Detecting heads and tails of 20 cent coins is a difficult problem, where the neural network method resulted in many false alarms. The genetic programming method gave the ideal results, that is, all the objects of interest were found without any false positives for all the four object classes.

Table 3. Comparison of object detection results on 4-class *coin* pictures. Input field size: 24×24

Coin Pictures		Object Classes			
		head005	tail005	head020	tail020
Best Detection Rate(%)		100	100	100	100
False Alarm	Neural network	0	0	182	37.5
Rate (%)	Genetic programming	0	0	0	0

4.3   Retina Pictures

The results for the retina pictures are summarised in Table 4. Compared with the results for the previous image databases the results are disappointing. However, the false alarm rate is greatly improved over the neural network method.

The results over the three data bases show similar trends: the genetic programming method always gives a lower false alarm rate for the same detection rate.

Table 4. Comparison of object detection results on retina pictures. Input field size: 16×16

Retina Pictures		Object Classes	
		haem	micro
Best Detection Rate(%)		70	100
False Alarm	Neural network	2698	10104
Rate (%)	Genetic programming	1357	588

4.4   Summary and Analysis

Summary We have tested the new genetic programming based approach on multi-class object detection problems of increasing difficulty: a three-class easy detection problem, a four-class medium difficulty coin detection problem and a very difficult two-class retinal pathology detection problem. In all cases on easy and medium difficulty detection problems the new approach produced the ideal results, that is, all the objects of interest in every class were found without any false alarms. For "micro" and "haem" detection in the very difficult retina pictures, the new method resulted in much better performance than the neural network approach.

Analysis of Results of Retina Picture We found three main reasons why the results on retina pictures are not as good as those on easy and coin pictures. Firstly, in easy and coin pictures the background is relatively uniform, whereas in the retina pictures it is highly cluttered. Secondly, in the retina pictures, there are only two classes of interest, that is, "micro" and "haem", but there are also several other classes such as veins and other eye anatomy. Thus the objects of non-interest are classified background. It appears that this makes the background too complex to be considered as a single class. Thirdly, in the easy and coin pictures all of the objects in a class are the same size whereas the sizes of the objects in each class in the retina pictures are quite different. The sizes of "micro" vary from 3×3 to 5×5 pixels and the sizes of "haem" vary from 7×7 to 16×16 pixels. Thus the sizes of "micro" are still similar, but this is not the case for the "haem". This might be the main reason that the results for detecting "micro" are much better than that of "haem". This suggests that the current set of functions and terminals cannot be successfully applied to detecting objects in the same class with a large variation in size.

Further Experiments We experimented with an alternative set of terminals based on a circular set of features. The features were computed based on a series of concentric circles centred in input field. This terminal set focused on boundaries rather than regions. In the coin and retina pictures, the results based on this terminal set are slightly worse than those with the square region feature set. This suggests that the local region features are better for these detection problems.

We also experimented with a different function set. We hypothesised that convergence might be quicker if the function values were close to the range $(-1, 1)$. We used *dabs, sin* and *exp*, (absolute value, sine and exponent to base e) in addition to the four arithmetic operators $(+, -, *$ and $/)$. The detection results are similar to those based on the function set of only the four arithmetic operators. Convergence was slightly faster training the coin and retina pictures, but slightly slower for easy pictures. This suggests that *dabs, sin* and *exp* may be useful for more difficult problems, however considerably more experimentation is required.

5   Conclusions

The goal of this paper was to develop a general, single stage method for detecting small objects of multiple classes in large pictures based on genetic programming. A secondary goal was to compare the performance of this method with a neural network based method. The results show that genetic programming can be used to generate programs for object detection. The method appears to be applicable to detection problems of varying difficulty. The genetic programming method also gives better detection performance than a neural network based approach for the same problem set.

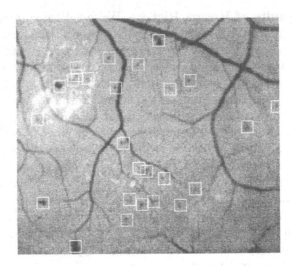

Fig. 5. Enlargement of retina picture

The genetic programming approach has the following limitations:

- The training times for the coin problem and the retina problem are quite long. Some of the runs took longer than 48 hours on a 4 processor ULTRA-SPARC4. We are investigating ways of shortening the training times.
- The method is not particularly effective in detecting objects with different sizes which are in the same class, for example the haemorrhages in the retina pictures. This might be related to the simple pixel-based image features used. High level image features which contain size invariant information need to be investigated.
- The classification strategy employed in the generated programs is not easy to determine. However, if a particular feature does not appear in a program that works well, it can be inferred that that feature is not important.
- Some experimentation is required to find good values of the various parameters for each different problem.
- A threshold T (figure 3) was used to give "fixed" size ranges for determining the class of the object from the output of the program. We are investigating ways of finding individual thresholds for each class.

Acknowledgements

We would like to thank Dr. James Thom and Dr. Zhi-Qiang Liu for useful discussions on image processing and retrieval, Peter Wilson whose basic genetic programming package was used in the project and Chris Kamusinski who provided and labelled the retina pictures.

References

1. Ballard, D.H., Brown, C.M.: Computer Vision. Englewood Cliffs, N.J: Prentice-Hall, Inc.(1982)
2. Banzhaf, W., Nordin, P., Keller, R.E. and Francone, F.D.: Genetic Programming: An Introduction on the Automatic Evolution of Computer Programs and Its Applications. Morgan Kaufmann, Inc. San Francisco, California(1998)
3. Bernardon, A., and Carrick, J.E.: A neural system for automatic target learning and recognition applied to bare and camouflaged sar targets. Neural Networks, Vol.8. 7/8 (1995) 1103–1108
4. Casasent, D.P., Neiberg, L.M.: Classifier and Shift-invariant Automatic Target Recognition Neural networks. Neural Networks, Vol.8. 7/8 (1995) 1117–1129
5. Gader, P.D., Miramonti, J.R., Won Y., Coffield P.: Segmentation free shared weight neural networks for automatic vehicle detection. Neural Networks, Vol.8. 9 (1995)1457–1473
6. Greeff, D.J., Aldrich, C.: Evolution of empirical models for metallurgical process system. In: Koza, J.R., Deb, K., Dorigo, M., Fogel, D.B., Garzon, M., Iba, H., Riolo, R.L. (eds.): Genetic Programming 1997: Proceedings of the Second Annual Conference, Stanford University,Morgan Kaufmann (1997) 138-146
7. Koza, J.R.: Genetic programming : on the programming of computers by means of natural selection. Cambridge, Mass. : MIT Press, London, England(1992)
8. Koza, J.R.: Genetic programming II: Automatic Discovery of Reusable Programs. Cambridge, Mass.: MIT Press, London, England(1994)
9. McKay, B., Willis, M., Barton, G.W.: On the application of genetic programming to chemical process system. In: 1995 IEEE Conference on Evolutionary Computation, Vol. 2. Perth, Australia. IEEE Press, New York (1995) 701-706
10. Rogers, S.K., Colombi, J.M., Martin, C.E., Gainey, J.C., Fielding, K.H., Burns, T.J., Ruck, D.W., Kabrisky, M., Ocley, M.: Neural networks for automatic target recognition. Neural Networks, Vol.8. 7/8 (1995)1153–1184
11. Roitblat, H.L., Au, W.W.L., Nachtigall, P.E., Shizumura,R., Moons, G.: Sonar Recognition of Targets Embedded in Sediment. Neural Networks, Vol. 8. 7/8 (1995) 1263–1273
12. Roth, M.W.,: Survey of neural network technology for automatic target recognition. IEEE Transactions on neural networks, Vol. 1. 1 (1990) 28–43
13. Sherrah, J.R., Bogner, R.E., Bouzerdoum, A.: The evolutionary pre-processor: Automatic feature extraction for supervised classification using genetic programming. In: Koza, J.R., Deb, K., Dorigo, M., Fogel, D.B., Garzon, M., Iba, H., Riolo, R.L. (eds.): Genetic Programming 1997: Proceedings of the Second Annual Conference, Stanford University,Morgan Kaufmann (1997) 304-312
14. Shirvaikar, M., Trivedi, M.,: A network Filter to detect small targets in high Clutter backgrounds. IEEE Transactions on Neural Networks, Vol. 6. 1 (1995) 252–257
15. Tackett, W.A.: Genetic Programming for Feature Discovery and Image Discrimination. In: Forrest S. (ed.): Proceedings of the 5th International Conference on Genetic Algorithms(ICGA-93), Morgan Kaufmann, University of Illinois at Urbana-Champaign(1993) 303–309
16. Teller A., Veloso, M.: A controlled experiment : Evolution for learning difficult image classification. In: Pinto-Ferreira, C., Mamede, N.J. (eds): Proceedings of the 7th Portuguese Conference on Artificial Intelligence, Berlin, Springer Verlag, LNAI, vol.990. (1995)165–176

17. Waxman, A.M., Seibert, M.C., Gove, A., Fay, D.A., Bernandon, A.M., Lazott, C., Steele, W.R., Cunningham, R.K.: Neural Processing of Targets in Visible, Multi-spectral IR and SAR Imagery. Neural Networks, Vol. 8. **7/8** (1995)1029-1051
18. Winkeler, J.F., Manjunath, B.S.: Genetic Programming for Object Detection. In: Koza, J.R., Deb, K., Dorigo, M., Fogel, D.B., Garzon, M., Iba, H., Riolo, R.L. (eds.): Genetic Programming 1997: Proceedings of the Second Annual Conference, Morgan Kaufmann, Stanford University, (1997) 330-335
19. Won,Y., Gader, P.D., Coffield, P.C.: Morphological shared-weight networks with applications to automatic target recognition. IEEE Transactions on Neural Networks, Vol.8., **5**(1997)1195-1203
20. Wilson, P.: Development of Genetic Programming Strategies for use in the RoboCup Domain. Honours Thesis, RMIT, Department of Computer Science (1998)
21. Zhang, M.: A pixel-based approach to recognising small objects in large pictures using neural networks. In: Proceedings of the Annual RMIT Computer Science Postgraduate Students' Conference, Department of computer science, RMIT. TR 97-51, Melbourne (1997) 57-68. Also in: http://goanna.cs.rmit.edu.au/~mengjie/papers.html
22. Zhang, M., Ciesielski, V.: Centred Weight Initialization in Neural Networks for Object Detection. In: Proceedings of the Twenty Second Australasian Computer Science Conference, Auckland (1999) 39-50. Also in: http://goanna.cs.rmit.edu.au/~vc/papers/vc-conf.html

A Simulated Annealing-Based Learning Algorithm for Boolean DNF*

Andreas Albrecht[1] and Kathleen Steinhöfel[2]

[1] Univ. of Hertfordshire, Dept. of Computer Science,
Hatfield, Herts AL10 9AB, UK
[2] GMD - National Research Center for IT,
Kekuléstr. 7, 12489 Berlin, Germany

Abstract. We describe a stochastic algorithm learning Boolean functions from positive and negative examples. The Boolean functions are represented by disjunctive normal form formulas. Given a target DNF F depending on n variables and a set of uniformly distributed positive and negative examples, our algorithm computes a hypothesis H that rejects a given fraction of negative examples and has an ε-bounded error on positive examples. The stochastic algorithm utilises logarithmic cooling schedules for inhomogeneous Markov chains. The paper focuses on experimental results and comparisons with a previous approach where all negative examples have to be rejected [4]. The computational experiments provide evidence that a relatively high percentage of correct classifications on additionally presented examples can be achieved, even when misclassifications are allowed on negative examples. The detailed convergence analysis will be presented in a forthcoming paper [3].

1 Introduction

The learnability of disjunctive normal forms (DNF) has been studied intensely over the past decade in the context of VALIANT's PAC learning model [22]. For the general case of DNF, the learnability from positive and negative examples is still an open problem. Therefore, various subclasses have been studied within different modifications of the PAC learning model. Positive results on PAC learnability could be obtained for relatively restricted subclasses of DNF only, such as DNF formulae consisting of terms with a constant number of literals or a constant number of terms, respectively; see [12,22,23]. Another example of PAC learnable problem classes are constant-depth decision lists [20], which include the above-mentioned subclasses of DNF. In [21], the learnability of visual concepts has been investigated, which is closely related to the learning problem of DNF. The approach has been extended in [15] to a wider class of digital pictures and the authors obtained that DNF are PAC learnable as long as the set of terms

---

* Research partially supported by the AIF Research Programme under Grant No. FKV 0352401N7. Part of the research was done while the first author was visiting the CUHK within the SRP under Grant No. 9505.

N. Foo (Ed.): AI'99, LNAI 1747, pp. 193–204, 1999.

satisfying a given example can be characterised in polynomial time. Thus, the number of terms as well as the number of literals are not bounded by a constant. In [2], it has been shown that learning all but an exponentially small fraction of DNF formulas is possible when the average term size is at most a constant, or at least a constant fraction $\Omega(n)$ of the variables. Another line of research is dealing with various extensions of VALIANT's learning model, e.g., by equivalence and membership queries; see [5,17,19]. For an overview on DNF learnability and the discussion of different learning models, including a comprehensive list of references, we refer to [2].

In the PAC learning model, the probability distributions $D(\tilde{\sigma})$ of positive and negative examples $\tilde{\sigma} \in \{0,1\}^n$ are not specified and the hypothesis has to be found in polynomial time, i.e., the learning algorithm has to provide with probability at least $1 - \delta$ a hypothesis with an error of at most ε, regardless of $D(\tilde{\sigma})$. In some papers, this condition has been weakened, i.e., subexponential algorithms have been designed for special classes of DNF under the uniform probability distribution $D(\tilde{\sigma}) = 2^{-n}$. In [24], DNF consisting of $n^{O(1)}$ terms are ε-approximated with confidence $1 - \delta$ from positive and negative examples in time $n^{O(\log(n/(\varepsilon \cdot \delta)))}$ under the uniform probability distribution. The learning procedure employs a greedy algorithm that originally was designed for approximate solutions of $\mathcal{NP}$-complete set-theoretic problems [13]. The time bound has been improved in [16] to $n^{O(\log\log(n/(\varepsilon \cdot \delta)))}$, however, by using the membership query model. Within the same model, JACKSON [11] proved the existence of a polynomial time algorithm. For a uniform probability distribution $D(\tilde{\sigma}) = 2^{-n}$, the sum of probabilities of tuples accepted by a polynomial number of terms of size $\Omega(n)$ is exponentially small, i.e., the algorithm described in [2] is not applicable and the learnability problem remains open for polynomial DNF which accept a constant fraction of all 2^n input tuples.

In the present paper, we consider essentially the same problem as in [16,24], and our algorithm is very similar to VERBEURGT's approach [24], but the complete search for conjunctive terms of length $O(\log n)$ maximising the number of satisfied positive examples is replaced by a simulated annealing search for a conjunction that satisfies at least a fixed positive example and rejects a pre-defined fraction $f \leq 1$ of all negative examples. The search is performed for any positive example separately, and after all positive examples have been processed, the conjunctive terms with the largest number of satisfied positive examples which cover the entire set of positive examples are taken together. A good classification rate could be obtained if both the ratio of training examples per conjunction and the number of repeated trials to enhance the coverage of positive training examples were sufficiently large. In particular, the correct classification of previously unknown negative examples depends significantly on the "multiplicity" of conjunctions of the hypothesis on the set of positive training examples.

The present paper is a continuation of [4], where the special case $f = 1$ has been considered. A detailed convergence analysis of the underlying simulated annealing-based procedure is performed in [3].

2 Basic Definitions

2.1 The Approximation Problem

We consider Boolean functions F of n variables which can be represented by disjunctive normal forms containing at most $s = n^{O(1)}$ conjunctive terms. The corresponding class of Boolean functions is denoted by $\mathcal{F}_s := \{ F : F = \bigvee_{i \in I} t_i, |I| \leq s \}$, where the $t_i \neq 0$ are conjunctions of literals $x^\sigma \in \{x_1, \cdots, x_n, \overline{x_1}, \cdots, \overline{x_n}\}$. For the number $l(t_i)$ of literals we have $1 \leq l(t_i) \leq n$. We denote by NEG, POS $\subset \{0,1\}^n$ negative and positive examples of F, i.e., $\tilde{\sigma} \in$ NEG $\Leftrightarrow F(\tilde{\sigma}) = 0$ and $\tilde{\sigma} \in$ POS $\Leftrightarrow F(\tilde{\sigma}) = 1$.

We assume a uniform distribution $D(\tilde{\sigma}) := 2^{-n}$ on the entire set of inputs $\tilde{\sigma} \in \{0,1\}^n$. The uniform distribution $D(\tilde{\sigma})$ makes it possible to consider only relatively small values of $l(t)$: If $l(t) \geq \log k$, where $1 \leq k \leq n$, then $t(\tilde{\sigma}) = 1$ on $2^{n-l(t)} < 2^{n-\log k} = k^{-1} \cdot 2^n$ tuples $\tilde{\sigma}$. Thus, if we try to approximate $F \in \mathcal{F}_s$ and all terms t' with $l(t') > \log(s/\varepsilon)$ are deleted from F, then the error is smaller than $s \cdot \varepsilon/s = \varepsilon$. We note that the error caused by deleting terms of a certain length may occur only for "positive examples" of the original disjunctive normal form. Thus, it is sufficient to take into account only terms t of length $\leq \lceil \log(s/\varepsilon) \rceil$. Furthermore, it is assumed that all terms of the target DNF are extended to the length $l_0 := \lceil \log(s/\varepsilon) \rceil$. The corresponding increase of the number of terms is upper bounded by $O(s^2/\varepsilon) = n^{O(1)}/\varepsilon$, i.e., instead of s one can consider $s' = O(s^2/\varepsilon)$. The corresponding set of DNFs is denoted by

$$\mathcal{F}_s^\varepsilon := \left\{ F' : F' = \bigvee_{i \in I} t_i, |I| = O(s^2/\varepsilon), l(t) = \lceil \log(s/\varepsilon) \rceil \right\}. \quad (1)$$

We suppose that information about an element of $\mathcal{F}_s^\varepsilon$ is provided by m examples, $|\text{NEG}| + |\text{POS}| = m$.

2.2 General Structure of Simulated Annealing

Our stochastic approximation algorithm is based on the general framework of simulated annealing which was introduced in [8,14] as a new approach to calculate approximate solutions of combinatorial optimisation problems, where the underlying framework was based on METROPOLIS' method [18] of computing equilibrium states for substances consisting of interacting molecules. Detailed information about this method and applications in different areas can be found in [1,7,10]. We will consider simulated annealing procedures for the special type of logarithmic cooling schedules for inhomogeneous Markov chains.

Simulated annealing algorithms are acting within a configuration space in accordance with a certain neighbourhood structure, where the particular transitions between adjacent elements of the configuration space are controlled by the value of an objective function. Now, we are going to introduce these notions for the *basic step* of approximations of DNF $F \in \mathcal{F}_s^\varepsilon$ which is related to the search for terms of length $\lceil \log(s/\varepsilon) \rceil$ rejecting all negative examples.

To simplify notations, we consider the configuration space for each positive example $\tilde{\sigma} \in \text{POS}$ particularly, i.e., we are concentrating on a single term as part of the entire hypothesis H for $F \in \mathcal{F}_s^e$. The underlying configuration space is defined by

$$C_n^{\tilde{\sigma}} := \left\{ t : t(\tilde{\sigma}) = 1; \, l_0 \leq l(t); \, |\{\tilde{\eta} : \tilde{\eta} \in \text{NEG} \, \& \, t(\tilde{\eta}) = 0\}| \geq f \cdot |\text{NEG}| \right\}, (2)$$

where $f \leq 1$ is a global parameter.

For the definition of the neighbourhood relation, we consider $t, t' \in C_n^{\tilde{\sigma}}$: The two terms $t, t' \not\equiv 0$, $t \neq t'$ are called *neighbouring*, if t' can be generated from t by deleting a literal in t or adding $x_i^{\sigma_i}$ to t, where σ_i is the ith position of $\tilde{\sigma}$. The set of neighbours of t is denoted by $\mathcal{N}_t$, including t itself. Thus, we have

$$l_0 \quad \leq \quad |\mathcal{N}_t| \leq n + 1. \tag{3}$$

The lower bound follows from the fact that at any step the l_0 critical variables can be added if they have been deleted at previous steps.

The value $l_0 = \lceil \log(s/\varepsilon) \rceil$ is the length of terms for hypotheses H related to $F \in \mathcal{F}_s^e$. Therefore, the objective function can be defined by

$$\mathcal{Z}(t) := l(t)/l_0. \tag{4}$$

The set of terms $t \in C_n^{\tilde{\sigma}}$ minimising $\mathcal{Z}$ is denoted by $C_n^{l_0}$.

We denote by $G[t, t']$ the probability of generating $t' \in \mathcal{N}_t$ from t and by $A[t, t']$ the probability of accepting t' once it has been generated from t. Since we consider a single step of transitions, the value of $G[t, t']$ depends on the set $\mathcal{N}_t$. We choose the uniform probability

$$G[t, t'] := \begin{cases} \frac{1}{|\mathcal{N}_t|}, & \text{if } t' \in \mathcal{N}_t, \\ 0, & \text{otherwise.} \end{cases} \tag{5}$$

As for $G[t, t']$, there are different possibilities for the choice of acceptance probabilities $A[t, t']$. A straightforward definition related to the underlying analogy to thermodynamic systems is the following:

$$A[t, t'] := \begin{cases} 1, & \text{if } \mathcal{Z}(t') - \mathcal{Z}(t) \leq 0, \\ e^{-(\mathcal{Z}(t') - \mathcal{Z}(t))/c}, & \text{otherwise,} \end{cases} \tag{6}$$

where c is a control parameter having the interpretation of a *temperature* in annealing procedures.

Finally, the probability of performing the transition between t and t' is defined by

$$\mathbf{Pr}\{t \to t'\} = \begin{cases} G[t, t'] \cdot A[t, t'], & \text{if } t' \neq t, \\ 1 - \sum_{t' \neq t} G[t, t'] \cdot A[t, t']. \end{cases} \tag{7}$$

By definition, the probability $\Pr\{t \to t'\}$ depends on the control parameter c.

Let $a_t(k)$ denote the probability of being in the configuration t after k steps performed for the same value of c. The probability $a_t(k)$ can be calculated in accordance with

$$a_t(k) := \sum_{t'} a_{t'}(k-1) \cdot \Pr\{t' \to t\}. \tag{8}$$

The recursive application of (8) defines a *Markov chain* of probabilities $a_t(k)$, where $t \in \mathcal{C}_n^{\tilde{\sigma}}$ and $k = 1, 2, \dots$. When the parameter $c(k)$ is a constant $c = c(k)$, the chain is said to be a *homogeneous* Markov chain; otherwise, if $c(k)$ is lowered at any step, the sequence of probability vectors $a(k)$ is an *inhomogeneous* Markov chain.

We briefly recall HAJEK's result [10] on logarithmic cooling schedules for inhomogeneous Markov chains, which can be easily verified for our specific minimisation problem. Moreover, the parameters which are significant for the cooling schedules can be chosen in a straightforward way for the elements of $\mathcal{C}_n^{\tilde{\sigma}}$.

First, we need to introduce some parameters characterising local minima of the objective function:

Definition 1 *A configuration $t' \in \mathcal{C}_n^{\tilde{\sigma}}$ is said to be reachable at height h from $t \in \mathcal{C}_n^{\tilde{\sigma}}$, if $\exists t_0, t_1, \dots, t_r \in \mathcal{C}_n^{\tilde{\sigma}}\left(t_0 = t \wedge t_r = t'\right)$ such that $G[t_u, t_{u+1}] > 0, u = 0, 1, \dots, (r-1)$ and $\mathcal{Z}(t_u) \le h$, for all $u = 0, 1, \dots, r$.*

We use the notation $height(t \Rightarrow t') \le h$ for this property. The configuration t is a *local minimum*, if $t \in \mathcal{C}_n^{\tilde{\sigma}} \setminus \mathcal{C}_n^{lo}$ and $\mathcal{Z}(t') > \mathcal{Z}(t)$ for all $t' \in \mathcal{N}_t \setminus t$.

Definition 2 *Let $t_{\min}$ denote a local minimum, then the depth $depth(t_{\min})$ is the smallest h such that there exists a $t' \in \mathcal{C}_n^{\tilde{\sigma}}$ satisfying $\mathcal{Z}(t') < \mathcal{Z}(t_{\min})$ that is reachable at height $\mathcal{Z}(t_{\min}) + h$.*

We will use the following result obtained by B. HAJEK:

Theorem 1 [10] *Given a cooling schedule defined by*

$$c(k) = \frac{\Gamma}{\ln(k+2)}, \ k = 0, 1, \dots, \tag{9}$$

the asymptotic convergence $\sum_{t \in \mathcal{C}_n^{lo}} a_t(k) \xrightarrow[k \to \infty]{} 1$ of the simulated annealing algorithm, using (5), (6), and (7), is guaranteed if and only if

(i) $\forall t, t' \in \mathcal{C}_n^{\tilde{\sigma}} \exists t_0, t_1, \dots, t_r \in \mathcal{C}_n^{\tilde{\sigma}}\left(t_0 = t \wedge t_r = t'\right):$
   $G[t_u, t_{u+1}] > 0, u = 0, 1, \dots, (r-1);$

(ii) $\forall h : height(t \Rightarrow t') \le h \iff height(t' \Rightarrow t) \le h;$

(iii) $\Gamma \ge \max_{t_{\min}} depth(t_{\min}).$

3   The DNF Approximation Algorithm

3.1   The Search Algorithm for Conjunctive Terms

Given a positive example $\tilde{\sigma}$ of a function $F \in \mathcal{F}_s^{\varepsilon}$ and a polynomial set NEG of negative examples, we employ a simulated annealing procedure to find a conjunctive term of length l_0 that satisfies $t(\tilde{\sigma}) = 1$ as well as $t(\tilde{\eta}) = 0$ for $f \cdot |\text{NEG}|$ negative examples $\tilde{\eta}$. The algorithm works on the set of parameters $\text{PAR} := [n, s, f, \varepsilon, c(k)]$ and the input $\text{IN} := [\tilde{\sigma}, \text{POS}, \text{NEG}]$, where $c(k)$ denotes the logarithmic cooling schedule (9) of the underlying inhomogeneous Markov chain.

The algorithm can be described as follows: From n literals defined by $\tilde{\sigma}$, an initial hypothesis $t_{\text{init}} := x_1^{\sigma_1} \cdots x_n^{\sigma_n}$ which rejects all negative examples. Then, we perform a simulated annealing procedure which is based on an inhomogeneous Markov chain. Thus, the structure of our algorithm **term_approx**(PAR,IN) approximating a $\lceil \log(s/\varepsilon) \rceil$-term can be described as shown in Fig. 1. For our

> procedure **term_approx**(PAR,IN) :
> $k := 0$; *generate* $t_{\text{init}} := \bigwedge_{i=1}^{n} x_i^{\sigma_i}$; $t := t_{\text{init}}$;
> repeat
> $\mathcal{Z}(t) := l(t)/\lceil \log(s/\varepsilon) \rceil$;
>   repeat
>   *generate uniformly* $u \in \{1, \dots, n\}$;
>   if ($x_u^{\sigma_u}$ *not in* t) then $t' := t \wedge x_u^{\sigma_u}$
>   else
> $t' := t \setminus x_u^{\sigma_u}$;
>   until $|\{\tilde{\eta} : \tilde{\eta} \in \text{NEG} \,\&\, t'(\tilde{\eta}) = 0\}| \geq f \cdot |\text{NEG}|$;
> $\mathcal{Z}(t') := l(t')/\lceil \log(s/\varepsilon) \rceil$;
>   if $\mathcal{Z}(t') \leq \mathcal{Z}(t)$ then $t := t'$;
>   else
> $c := c(k)$; *generate uniformly* $\eta \in [0, 1]$;
>   if $\exp\big((\mathcal{Z}(t) - \mathcal{Z}(t'))/c\big) \geq \eta$ then $t := t'$;
>   if $l(t) = l_0$ goto FIN;
> $k := k + 1$;
> until $k > k_{(\varepsilon, \delta)}$;
> FIN: *output* $t_{\text{fin}} := t$.

Figure 1

simulated annealing procedure, we have chosen the cooling schedule (9), and we suppose that Γ is a sufficiently large value (see (12)). From the definition of the learning procedure and Theorem 1 we obtain:

Theorem 2 *The inhomogeneous Markov chain, which realises* **term_approx** *and is based on (5) till (7) and (9), tends to the distribution* $\lim_{k \to \infty} \sum_{t \in \mathcal{C}_n^{l_0}} \mathbf{a}_t(k)$.

In our algorithm, we are searching for a representation by conjunctive terms of length l_0, and therefore we obtain from the defining equation (4) of the objective function:

$$1 \leq \mathcal{Z}(t) \leq n/\lceil \log(s/\varepsilon) \rceil. \tag{10}$$

By definition $\big($see (1) and (2)$\big)$, any positive example $\tilde{\sigma}$ can be represented by a conjunctive l_0-term, i.e., when the current hypothesis t does not contain a subset of l_0 literals rejecting $f \cdot |\text{NEG}|$ negative examples, the term t has to be extended by at most l_0 literals to a new hypothesis t' satisfying the necessary condition. Thus, we have

$$\mathcal{Z}(t') \leq \frac{l(t) + l_0}{\lceil \log(s/\varepsilon) \rceil} = \mathcal{Z}(t) + 1. \tag{11}$$

From t' to $t' \in C_n^{l_0}$, which represents $\tilde{\sigma}$, There exists a sequence of transitions from t' to $t' \in C_n^{l_0}$ that decreases the length at any step. Therefore, according to Definition 2 and Theorem 1, condition (iii), we obtain in our case the lower bound

$$\Gamma \geq 1. \tag{12}$$

3.2   Approximations of DNF

The procedure **term_approx**(PAR,IN) (see Fig. 1) has to be performed for a polynomial number of positive examples. Since the outcome might be the same for different $\tilde{\sigma} \in \text{POS}$, it remains only to collect all pairwise different conjunctive terms.

The entire procedure **dnf_approx**(PAR,M,POS,NEG) can be described as shown by the simple structure from Fig. 2. The new parameter M defines the number of repeated trials for a given $\tilde{\sigma} \in \text{POS}$. The aim is to enhance the number of positive examples which are satisfied by t_i in addition to $\tilde{\sigma}_i$, i.e., M affects the "multiplicity" of t_i on POS. At the end of the procedure, only the terms with the highest multiplicity which cover the entire set POS are taken for the final hypothesis.

Based on HAJEK's theorem [10] (see Theorem 1), we can prove the following result about the convergence speed [3]:

Theorem 3 *Given the minimal length of conjunctive terms* $l_0 = \lceil \log(s/\varepsilon) \rceil$, *the condition*

$$k > \log^{O(1)} (1/\delta) + n^{O(l_0)}$$

implies for $\delta > 0$ *and arbitrary initial probability distributions* $\mathbf{a}(0)$ *the relation*

$$\sum_{t \notin C_n^{l_0}} \mathbf{a}_t(k) < \delta, \quad \text{and therefore} \quad \sum_{t' \in C_n^{l_0}} \mathbf{a}_{t'}(k) > 1 - \delta.$$

We note that the time complexity of basic operations performed in **term_approx** and **dnf_approx** can be estimated roughly by n^2.

4 Computational Experiments

Both procedures **term_approx**(PAR,IN) and **dnf_approx**(PAR,M,POS,NEG) have been implemented and tested for a number of parameter settings. The implementation was running on a ACERALTOS 500 machine.

The target DNF F was generated randomly for given values of n, s, and ε. The value $\varepsilon = 1/n$ was chosen, and l_0 was calculated according to $l_0 = \lceil \log(s/\varepsilon) \rceil$; see (1). Then, for F and a given total number m of examples, an equal number of $m/2$ positive and $m/2$ negative examples was generated. We are presenting the outcome of computational experiments for two values of n: $n = 32$, $n = 64$, and s taking three values 8, 16, and 32. The two values of n and the number of conjunctive terms are larger than the corresponding numbers considered, e.g., in [9] (see Section 4.3 there).

procedure **dnf_approx**(PAR,M,POS,NEG)
begin
    enumerate POS *from 1 till* $p := |\text{POS}|$; $i := j := 1$;
    $H := H' := Empty\ DNF$;
    repeat
        m := 0;
            $t_i := $ **term_approx**(PAR,$[\tilde{\sigma}_i$,NEG]);
            $m'(t_i) := |\{\tilde{\sigma} \mid \tilde{\sigma} \in \text{POS} \& t_i(\tilde{\sigma}) = 1\}|$;
            if $m' > m$ then $m = m'$;
            $j := j + 1$; until $j > M$;
        if $\forall t \left(t \text{ from } H' \rightarrow t_i \neq t \right)$ then $H' := H' \vee t_i$;
        $\tilde{m}(t_i) := m$; $i := i + 1$;
    until $i > p$;
    repeat
        if $\forall t' \left(t, t' \text{ from } H' \rightarrow \tilde{m}(t) \geq \tilde{m}(t') \right)$
        then *delete* t in H' and $H := H \vee t$;
    until $\forall \tilde{\sigma} \exists t \left(\tilde{\sigma} \in \text{POS} \& t \text{ from } H \rightarrow t(\tilde{\sigma}) = 1 \right)$;
    output H;
end.

Figure 2

The hypotheses were computed using **term_approx** and **dnf_approx**. For each hypothesis H, additional m examples were generated randomly from the corresponding F (different from the examples used for the computation of the hypothesis) and H was evaluated on these sets of $m/2$ positive and $m/2$ negative examples.

4.1 The Case of f = 1

The test procedure has been repeated up to five times, and the average evaluation results are shown in Table 1 till Table 3 for the case of $f = 1$. As can be seen from Table 1 and Table 2, the error on additionally generated examples becomes smaller with an increasing number M of repeated trials to enhance the

$n = 32$ $s = 8$ $f = 1$ $\varepsilon = 1/n = 0.03125$ $l_0 = 9$ $|POS| + |NEG| = 512$

M	Examples per Term of F	Evaluation of $H(\tilde{\sigma})$ and $H(\tilde{\eta})$ for $F(\tilde{\sigma})=1$	$F(\tilde{\eta})=0$	Number of Terms in H	Average Multiplicity of Terms	Run-Time (Seconds)
128	64	69.2%	93.4%	77	6.9	190
256	64	73.2%	92.4%	76	7.8	366
512	64	75.7%	95.1%	68	8.3	674

Table 1

multiplicity of conjunctions from the hypothesis. However, the average multiplicity increases only within a small margin even by taking a larger value, which is four times of M. Furthermore, the correct classification increases significantly in case of a larger number of examples per conjunctive term of the target DNF.

A smaller number of conjunctive terms in F and therefore a smaller l_0 (for a fixed ε) implies an increase of the computation time because the search for a shorter conjunction rejecting all elements of NEG becomes more difficult. However, the number of accepted positive examples increases for shorter conjunc-

$n = 32$ $s = 8$ $f = 1$ $\varepsilon = 1/n = 0.03125$ $l_0 = 9$ $|POS| + |NEG| = 1024$

M	Examples per Term of F	Evaluation of $H(\tilde{\sigma})$ and $H(\tilde{\eta})$ for $F(\tilde{\sigma})=1$	$F(\tilde{\eta})=0$	Number of Terms in H	Average Multiplicity of Terms	Run-Time (Seconds)
128	128	89.8 %	91.2 %	102	10.9	785
256	128	89.6 %	92.3 %	96	12.5	1385
512	128	92.3 %	95.8 %	79	13.9	2820

Table 2

tions, i.e., the entire hypothesis becomes shorter which leads to better classifications on NEG. With a decreasing average ratio of examples per conjunction of

$n = 64$ $s = 16$ $f = 1$ $\varepsilon = 1/n = 0.015625$ $l_0 = 11$

$|POS| + |NEG|$	M	Examples per Term of F	Evaluation of $H(\tilde{\sigma})$ and $H(\tilde{\eta})$ for $F(\tilde{\sigma})=1$	$F(\tilde{\eta})=0$	Number of Terms in H	Average Multiplicity of Terms	Run-Time (Seconds)
1024	512	64	22.7 %	92.0 %	185	4.8	6131
2048	128	128	43.0 %	89.3 %	411	5.2	5927
4096	16	256	64.2 %	79.5 %	697	6.1	5712

Table 3

the target DNF F, the classification becomes rapidly worse, although the average multiplicity does not differ significantly. Therefore, to obtain a good classification rate for large values of n and s, a very large number of training examples is required; see Table 3. On the other hand, it remains open to investigate the performance of our algorithm on more specific data with a nonuniform generation probability, i.e., if the training data carry more information about the structure of the problem instance.

The algorithm has been applied to large problem instances as well, e.g., $n = 1024, s = 128, m = 1024$, but only for small values of M and therefore a small resulting average multiplicity.

As can bee seen from Table 1 till Table 3, the representation of the information about the target function (i.e., l_0 multiplied by the number of terms of the hypothesis H) is significantly smaller compared to the trivial disjunction of all positive examples.

4.2   The Case of f < 1

We performed a number of runs in order to investigate the impact of the test $t(NEG) \equiv 0$. Due to the uniform generation probability of negative examples, the hypotheses derived from a positive example reject with a high likelihood a large fraction of all negative examples. The comparison with Table 1 shows that there

$n = 32$ $s = 8$ $M = 128$ $\varepsilon = 1/n = 0.03125$ $l_0 = 9$ $|POS| + |NEG| = 512$

f	Evaluation of $H(\tilde{\sigma})$ and $H(\tilde{\eta})$ for $F(\tilde{\sigma})=1$ $F(\tilde{\eta})=0$		Number of Terms in H	Average Multiplicity of Terms	Run-Time (Seconds)
0.75	66.8%	92.2%	89	6.8	178
0.50	71.5%	89.8%	85	6.7	179
0.25	72.7%	93.4%	92	6.6	215

Table 4

is no significant difference to the case when $f = 1$ is chosen, even for only 256 negative examples. The average rejection rate is very high and close to 256. We think that an impact of the test $t(NEG) \equiv 0$ might be expected for large values of the ratio n/l_0, when the number of negative examples increases correspondingly. In Table 5, the length $l_0 = \log n$ has been taken, i.e., $n/l_0 = 6.4$, whereas

$n = 32$ $s = 8$ $M = 128$ $l_0 = \log n = 5$ $|POS| + |NEG| = 512$

f	Evaluation of $H(\tilde{\sigma})$ and $H(\tilde{\eta})$ for $F(\tilde{\sigma})=1$ $F(\tilde{\eta})=0$		Number of Terms in H	Average Multiplicity of Terms	Run-Time (Seconds)
0.75	94.1 %	66.1%	56	22.7	539
0.50	87.1%	63.3%	68	23.9	491
0.25	85.9%	59.4%	57	21.8	467

Table 5

$n/l_0 = 3.6$ in Table 4. As can be seen, the correct classification on untrained negative examples becomes worse compared to the smaller ratio of Table 4. The results on negative examples are to be expect worse also due to the short length l_0 itself, not only due to the larger ratio n/l_0.

5   Concluding Remarks

A simulated annealing-based learning algorithm has been presented that generates hypotheses about Boolean functions from positive and negative examples alone. The algorithm utilises HAJEK's Theorem on the convergence of logarithmic cooling schedules. The convergence speed of inhomogeneous Markov chains depends on the maximum value of the minimum escape depth from local minima of the underlying energy landscape. The algorithm has been implemented and tested on a number of small examples. Our computational experiments have shown that a relatively high percentage of correct classifications on additionally presented examples can be achieved, even in the case when misclassifications up to a certain degree are allowed on negative examples. The complexity of the hypotheses is significantly smaller than the trivial disjunction of all positive examples. Further research will concentrate on nonuniform generation probabilities of examples, i.e., when more information is available about the structure of the problem instance.

References

1. E.H.L. Aarts and J.H.M. Korst. *Simulated Annealing and Boltzmann Machines: A Stochastic Approach* (Wiley & Sons, New York, 1989).
2. H. Aizenstein and L. Pitt. On the Learnability of Disjunctive Normal Form Formulas. *Machine Learning*, 19:183 – 208, 1995.
3. A. Albrecht and C.K. Wong. A DNF Approximation Algorithm Based on Inhomogeneous Markov Chains (submitted for publication, 1999).
4. A. Albrecht, R. Müller, and M. Patze. A Stochastic Learning Procedure for Boolean Functions. In: Derek Bridge et al., editors, *Proc. 10th Annual Irish Conference on Artificial Intelligence & Cognitive Science*, pp. 65 – 71, 1999.
5. D. Angluin. Queries and Concept Learning. *Machine Learning*, 2:319 – 342, 1988.
6. O. Catoni. Rough Large Deviation Estimates for Simulated Annealing: Applications to Exponential Schedules. *The Annals of Probability*, 20(3):1109 – 1146, 1992.
7. O. Catoni. Metropolis, Simulated Annealing, and Iterated Energy Transformation Algorithms: Theory and Experiments. *Journal of Complexity*, 12(4):595 – 623, 1996.
8. V. Černy. A Thermodynamical Approach to the Travelling Salesman Problem: An Efficient Simulation Algorithm. Preprint, Inst. of Physics and Biophysics, Comenius Univ., Bratislava, 1982 (see also: *J. Optim. Theory Appl.*, 45:41 – 51, 1985).
9. P. Clark and T. Niblett. The CN2 Induction Algorithm. *Machine Learning*, 3:261 –283, 1989.
10. B. Hajek. Cooling Schedules for Optimal Annealing. *Mathem. Oper. Res.*, 13:311 – 329, 1988.
11. J. Jackson. An Efficient Membership-Query Algorithm for Learning DNF with Respect to the Uniform Distribution. In *Proc. of the 35th Annual Symposium on Foundations of Computer Science*, pp. 42 – 53, 1994.
12. M. Kearns, M. Li, L. Pitt, and L.G. Valiant. Recent Results on Boolean Concept Learning. In *Proc. 4th Int. Workshop on Machine Learning*, pp. 337 – 352, 1987.
13. M. Kearns and M. Li. Learning in the Presence of Malicious Errors. In *Proc. of the 20th Annual Symposium on the Theory of Computations*, pp. 267 – 279, 1988.

14. S. Kirkpatrick, C.D. Gelatt, Jr., and M.P. Vecchi. Optimization by Simulated Annealing. *Science*, 220:671 – 680, 1983.
15. E. Kushilevitz and D. Roth. On Learning Visual Concepts and DNF Formulae. *Machine Learning*, 24:65 – 85, 1996.
16. Y. Mansour. An $n^{O(\log \log n)}$ Learning Algorithm for DNF under the Uniform Distribution. In *Proc. of the 5th Annual Workshop on Computational Learning Theory*, pp. 53 – 61, 1992.
17. H.D. Mathias. DNF - If You Can't Learn 'em, Teach 'em: An Interactive Model of Teaching. In *Proc. of the 8th Annual Workshop on Computational Learning Theory*, pp. 222 – 229, 1995.
18. N. Metropolis, A.W. Rosenbluth, M.N. Rosenbluth, A.H. Teller, and E. Teller. Equation of State Calculations by Fast Computing Machines. *The Journal of Chemical Physics*, 21(6):1087 – 1092, 1953.
19. K. Pillaipakkamnatt and V. Raghavan. On the Limits of Proper Learnability of Subclasses of DNF Formulas. In *Proc. of the 7th Annual Workshop on Computational Learning Theory*, pp. 118 – 129, 1994.
20. R.L. Rivest. Learning Decision Lists, *Machine Learning*, 2(3):229 – 246, 1987.
21. H. Shvaytser. Learnable and Nonlearnable Visual Concepts. *IEEE Transactions on Pattern Analysis and Machine Intelligence*, 12(5):459 – 466, May 1990.
22. L.G. Valiant. A Theory of the Learnable. *Comm. ACM*, 27(11):1134 – 1142, 1984.
23. L.G. Valiant. Learning Disjunctions of Conjunctions. In *Proc. of the 9th International Joint Congerence on Artificial Intelligence*, pp. 560 – 566, 1985.
24. K. Verbeurgt. Learning DNF under the Uniform Distribution in Quasi-Polynomial Time. In *Proc. of the 3rd Annual Workshop on Computational Learning Theory*, pp. 314 – 326, 1990.

MUTANT: A Genetic Learning System

Stéphane Calderoni and Pierre Marcenac

IREMIA - Université de la Réunion
F-97715 Saint-Denis - La Réunion - France
calde@univ-reunion.fr

Abstract. This paper presents MUTANT, a learning system for autonomous agents. MUTANT is an adaptive control architecture founded on genetic techniques and reinforcement learning. The system allows an agent to learn some complex tasks without requiring its designer to fully specify how they should be carried out. An agent behavior is defined by a set of rules, genetically encoded. The rules are evolved over time by a genetic algorithm to synthesize some new better rules according to their respective adaptive function, computed by progressive reinforcements. The system is validated through an experimentation in collective robotics.

Keywords: control, genetic algorithms, reinforcement learning, multiagent systems.

1 Introduction to Multiagent Learning

1.1 The Viability Concept

Learning theory in multiagent domain essentially comes from artificial life. Indeed, this emerging research area focuses on behavioral aspects of agent architectures, including autonomy and self-adaptation, founded on the *viability* problematic. The notion of viability could be transposed, in multiagent domain, as a satisfaction function. Robots, animats or agents, in order to satisfy their objectives during their evolution f, have to keep their state σ within a sphere of viability K in such a way that: $\sigma(t+1) = f(\sigma(t))$ to the extent that $\forall \sigma, f(\sigma) \in K$.

Therefore, they need to be equipped with sensors and effectors suitable for the constraints induced by their environment, as well as a control system responsible for selecting a satisfying action to execute, at the good time, in accordance with their goals. The sensors provide the agent with the capability to intercept sensorial information from its external environment or its internal state, while the effectors afford the agent the means to act within its environment. The control system coordinates perceptions and actions. The behavior of an agent may be qualified as adaptive while its control system is able to keep $f(\sigma)$ in K. The figure 1 represents a robot moving on a ground scattered with holes. Suppose it has to learn to move in this environment by avoiding the holes. Its state $\sigma(t)$ may be expressed in terms of two variables $\varepsilon_1(t)$ and $\varepsilon_2(t)$ that vary over time. The sphere of viability K may be considered as the region of the states space

N. Foo (Ed.): AI'99, LNAI 1747, pp. 205–217, 1999.

where σ should be kept. The outer side of K corresponds to states that may endanger the survival or the goal of this robot. The sensors of the robot should indicate to itself that there is a hole in front of it, and its control system then has to choose which action to accomplish. Thus, at point P, $\sigma(t)$ risks of leaving K in $\sigma'(t + \Delta t)$ if the agent moves towards the hole. An adaptive behavior would be the one that performs a corrective action on this state transition so as to transform σ in $\sigma(t + \Delta t)$, which is inside of K, by passing round the hole.

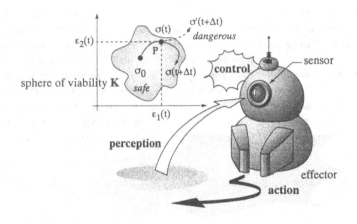

Fig. 1. an adaptive perception-control-action triad

1.2 Hard-Wired Architectures

A preliminary approach to design animats consists in coupling filtered sensors directly to the appropriate action. The hard problem lies neither at the sensor nor at the integration level, but at the level of arbitrating among potentially many actions and selecting one [Bro91a]. In the majority of behavior-based systems the solution is a built-in, fixed control hierarchy imposing a priority ordering on the behaviors. It ensures that only one of the behaviors can have control over the effectors, and that control is always appropriated to the behavior with the highest priority within the given context. Many of those are based on selecting an action by computing a multivariable function implicitly encoded in behavior activation levels. By spreading activation throughout the behavior networks and using carefully chosen thresholds for triggering actions, action selection can be tuned and even learned [Bro91b].

Nevertheless, the main weakness of this kind of architectures lies on their inefficiency to cope with unexpected situations, namely those which have not been planned by the designer. However, it may be imperative to exhibit robust behavior in complex and highly dynamic environment, and to be capable of reacting in case of non-hardwired situation. Furthermore, it may be salutary to be inventive ! It is obvious that fixed approaches do not cope with such capabilities. In addition, the design process often implies long adjustment phases to identify, define, add and tune required skills to implement in the system. Thus it may be very useful to rely on generic methods that can be adapted in various domains and does not make any assumptions on the tackled problem. In such a way, the design process can be significantly reduced by taking advantage of the reusability of such methods. In other respect, multidisciplinary research repeatedly involves similar but not identical design to adapt a system from a domain to another. A generic approach is then strongly recommended, especially if we consider the increasing complexity of tasks that autonomous systems have to face nowadays, that prohibits more and more built-in approaches.

1.3 Reinforcement Learning

The most employed techniques for adaptive coordination of perception and action in autonomous agents design are usually based on reinforcement learning. Reinforcement is used by agents to improve their performance at reaching their goals by practice or experience [Kae96]. A weight factor is assigned to each condition-action pair of the agent's repertory, and constitutes the discriminator in the action selection process, since the behavioral control mechanism select the pair with an applicable condition that has the highest weight. The values of weights fluctuate over time, in accordance with some rewards and punishments, reflecting a credit assignment to the current behavior coming from the environment.

These techniques allow to not freeze the coupling between the environmental context and the way the agent may react. [Mat97] proposes a table-based learning system which updates a condition-action reinforcement matrix over time. Each entry $R(c, a)$ reflects the propensity for the action a to be performed in the context c. R is computed as an heterogeneous reinforcement function combining immediate and delayed payoffs. The immediate payoffs correspond to immediate (un)satisfactions, whereas the delayed ones are computed from some progress estimators. In this way, she manages to progressively contract the links between suitable conditions and actions. Figure 2 illustrates this kind of learning system. The reinforcement matrix can be expressed as an oriented graph where each edge $c_i \rightarrow a_j$ is weighted by the reinforcement value $R(c_i, a_j)$.

One of the famous extension of this kind of reinforcement is those known as Q-Learning [WD92]. The Q-Learning algorithm is a type of reinforcement learning in which the value of taking each possible action a in each situation c is represented as a utility function $Q(c, a)$. Watkins proved its algorithm converges to the optimal policy under the conditions that all $Q(c, a)$ values are computed in a table, and the learning set includes an infinite number of episodes for each state c and action a.

This kind of approaches is highly limited by the size of the search space. Indeed, the learning system has to maintain the weight of all potential combinations between each condition c and each action a. Then, in order to reduce

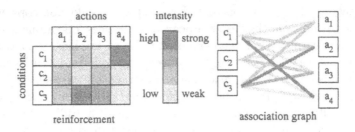

Fig. 2. reinforcement learning

the complexity of the search space, both the implemented conditions and actions must be of high abstraction level. Additionally, it may be crucial to trigger an action if more than one of the implemented conditions are gathered. In this case, the designer must adds new entries in the matrix for new conditions that implement the combinations of some others. Considering the whole of possible combinations, it seems obvious that the amount of knowledge the agent must update over time may become very huge. Nevertheless, large parts of it becomes progressively totally unuseful as the learning advances.

Consequently, we propose an adaptive control architecture able to shape the agent behavior according to its environmental context. Instead of being omniscient and rapidly swamped with the size of the search space, as those of Mataric, our architecture has been designed to handle a reasonable amount of knowledge in the same time, and to be able however to broaden its knowledge, by exploring the search space. This architecture, named MUTANT, is founded on the selective exploration mechanisms of genetic techniques and is detailed in the next section.

2   MUTANT: A Cyber(ge)netic Model

2.1   Genes of the Behavior

An important stage in autonomous agent design consists in listing the set of basis behaviors to implement. A basis behavior set should contain only behaviors that are necessary in the sense that each either achieves, or help achieve, a relevant goal that cannot be achieved with other behaviors in the set and cannot be reduced to them. Furthermore, a basis behavior set should be sufficient for accomplishing the goals in a given domain so no other basis behaviors are necessary. The construction of such a set highly depends on the tackled domain, and furthermore on both the perceptual and active capabilities of the agents, namely on the kind of both sensors and effectors they are equipped with.

By another way, we have to keep in mind that the lack of accurate and reliable sensors is arguably the most common complaint of researchers in situated agent control and learning. In robotics, in particular, sensors have been targeted as one of the limiting factors in the way of progress towards more complex autonomous behavior. Most of the commonly used sensors provide noisy data and are difficult to accurately characterize and model, presenting a major challenge for real-time robot learning [Mat97]. These constraints must be considered in order to provide researchers with reusable techniques. That's why we assume, in our work, that agents are provided with sensors that only perceive low-level information, like distance towards objects, or contact with obstacles, etc. This may be considered as an heavy disadvantage, especially from the multiagent perspective where the ability to sense and correctly distinguish members of one's group from others, from obstacles and from various features in the environment is crucial for most tasks. Actually, the lack of sophisticated perceptual discrimination is a critical limitation in multi-robot work. Non-visual sensors such as infra-red, contact sensors and sonars are all of limited use in the social recognition task. This kind of difficulties is termed as the hidden state problem [WB91]. If viewed as a form of sensing, communication in multiagent systems can be used to effectively deal with the hidden state problem. Like other sensors, radio transceivers perceives signals and pass those on for further processing [Mat98]. Specific properties of sensors vary greatly, and these differences can be usefully exploited: some information that is very difficult to directly sense can be easily communicated.

Anyway, when a sensor catch a signal from the environment, the resulting quantum of information is digitalized in a raw state. As shown in figure 3, it must be filtered and read with others, then compiled into high-level informative cells. These cells constitute the interpretable information for the agent. Actually, they play the role of excitating elements able to sollicitate the control system and to trigger actions. In other words they play the role of stimuli. The whole of such stimuli thus constitutes the substrate of prerequesite conditions for action triggerring in the behavior control system.

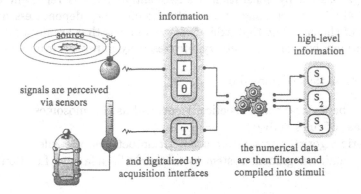

Fig. 3. from perception to stimuli synthesis

Once the set of relevant stimuli has been identified, the basis actions set can be determined on its turn. The actions to implement strongly depends on available effectors. On the opposite to sensors, the effectors allow to act on the environment. Thus, basis actions should trigger the effectors by sending them some suitable impulse signals. That is the sum of such simultaneous impulses which conditions the resulting behavior of the agent. If the control system of a robot sends uniform impulses both to its engine and to its rotator, then the robot will move by describing an arc of a circle.

The sets of stimuli and basis actions thus constitute the repertory of elementary bricks available to build the global behavior of the agent. In other words, these bricks are the elementay units of its behavioral program, exactly as the genes are the bricks of the genetic program of living beings. The simple combination of these primitives then allow an agent to develop some complex behavior.

The main difficulty being the way of connecting these genes. How to associate some sensorial genes with the suitable actions, and how to coordinate these stimuli-action pairs in a good policy, and in an adaptive way? To respond to these issues, MUTANT is defined as a genetic classifier system.

The classifiers have been introduced by John Holland as the theoretical foundations of learning with genetic algorithms. They are programs able to learn rules to optimize the performance of a system or reinforce its autonomy. A genetic classifier is composed of three main elements: a rules system, a credit assignment system and a genetic algorithm [Hol92]. Both the rules and the credit assignment systems are domain dependant, whereas the genetic algorithm is generic. The efficiency of a genetic algorithm is not magic. John Holland has proposed an interpretation based on the notion of schemes. A scheme is a mathematical object able to express the similarities between genetic codes. It's a genetic pattern. Individuals, be they good (*adapted*) or not, are generally unstables since they may disappear from a generation to another under the application of the genetic crossing-over. A good algorithm will thus be the one that save the best schemes, generation by generation. Consequently, schemes represent the substance on which a genetic algorithm works. Its efficiency depends essentially on the choice of the encoding that exhibits some schemes that are not destroyed by recombinations, but, on the contrary, progressively improved from a generation to the next.

MUTANT is thus composed of:

- a set of behavioral rules, genetically encoded as chromosomes,
- a system of rules activation,
- a genetic algorithm to set up a competition between the rules,
- and a credit assignment system to measure the adaptive function of each rule.

Let us focus, in the next section, on the genetic encoding of behavioral rules.

2.2   The Chromosome: A Genetic Encoding of the Behavior

Each rule R_i is defined as a combination of a predicate P_i and an action A_i in such a way that, if P_i is true, then A_i is considered as applicable. A predicate P_i

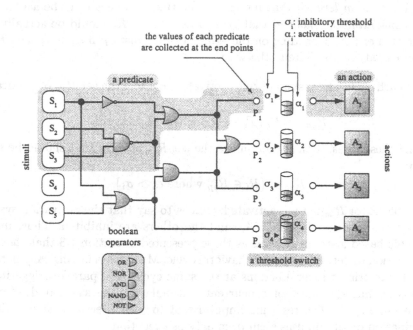

Fig. 4. the genetic structure of behavioral rules

is a multivariable boolean function that combines the stimuli perceived from the environment in a tree where nodes are boolean operators and leaves are stimuli. In such a way, complex environmental situations may be expressed, even from a reduced set of recognizable stimuli. When stimuli are sensed from the environment, they are propagated through the boolean tree, from the leaves, and filtered by the boolean operators so as to be collected as a single boolean value at the root of P_i. This value then makes the corresponding actions A_i applicable or not, depending on its value.

The action A_i corresponds to a basis skill of the agent, namely a behavioral primitive. The implementation of this primitive indicates which effectors of the agent should be activated, and how. For instance, if the action is to turn around in the case of a robot, then both its engine and its rotator will be activated with uniform signals. We argue that such a set of rules is sufficient to express a wide variety of complex behaviors by combination.

The structure of these rules is shown in figure 4.

P_i constitutes a necessary precondition for the application of the rule R_i. However, we will see in the next section that, even if it is a necessary condition for the actual triggering of actions, this notion of applicability is not sufficient, and the system of rules activation requires further features.

2.3   The System of Rules Activation

Each rule R_i is provided with two factors for the determination of its activation:

- an *activation level* α_i that represents the rule's propensity to be activated,
- an *inhibiting threshold* σ_i that determines wether R_i should be actually activated or not, depending on the value of α_i against σ_i: if $\alpha_i > \sigma_i$ then R_i is activated, and inhibited otherwise.

At each cycle, the system of rules activation collects the set R_{ap} of applicable rules:

$$R_{ap} = \{R_i : P_i \rightarrow A_i, \text{ where } P_i \text{ is } \mathbf{true}\}$$

Among these rules, it then determines the set R_{ac} of rules that should be activated:

$$R_{ac} = \{R_i \in R_{ap} \text{ where } \alpha_i > \sigma_i\}$$

Each rule R_i of R_{ac} is then activated, that is to say that the activation system triggers the associated actions A_i, and the others are inhibited. Thus, unlike the table-based learning systems as those presented in section 1.3 that choose a single action to perform at each behavioral cycle, MUTANT is intrinsically parallel and able to trigger several actions at the same cycle. The parallel triggering of actions A_i has the effect of concurrently stimulating the associated effectors in the same cycle. The resulting impulse sent to each effector is thus a signal combination of all impulses stem from actions execution.

In the case of none rule may be activated, then the activation system chooses a random rule to be activated.

When a rule is activated, its activation a_i level is decreased by a factor da_i. By this way, a single rule cannot be triggered indefinitely, and lets the opportunity, after a sufficient time, to others to be activated at their turn. This corresponds, in such a way, to an accustoming phenomenon, that progressively inhibits the response to a same stimulus.

Symetrically, the da_i factor is split up into equal parts da_i^j and shared among all the inhibited rules $R_j \notin R_{ac}$. This phenomenon corresponds to a progressive increasing of the motivation of inactive rules. Accustoming and motivation are thus opposite phenomena that regulate the equilibrium between the rules for the activation process. Although being stem from apart considerations, this algorithm presents some likeness with the *Bucket Brigade*, proposed by Holland in [Hol92].

2.4   The Genetic Algorithm

The genetic algorithm is used to impose an evolutionary competition among the rules, and to synthesize some new rules from the best ones available. Actually, each rule R_i is weighted by an adaptive function ω_i that indicates its efficiency for the agent evolution. In other words, ω_i reflects the propensity of R_i to maintain the state of the agent within its sphere of viability (*see* section 1.1). This function is computed as the difference between α_i and σ_i:

$$\omega_i = \alpha_i - \sigma_i$$

Initially, each agent is provided by a set of random rules, where each factor is randomly generated. At each genetic cycle, the genetic algorithm selects the best adapted rules (those with highest weights). These rules are proposed to the reproduction system to generate some clones of them that will replace the bad rules. Then, in accordance with the rank selection method, proposed in [Bak85], that determines the number of clones that each rule should provide, the rules proposed for reproduction are cloned in correlation with their respective weight. The new set of rules is then processed by the genetic operators: crossing-over and mutation.

The crossing-over operator is applied on the respective predicates P_i and P_j of two rules R_i and R_j with the same action part A. It extracts two sub-trees π_i and π_j from P_i and P_j and swap them. The number of pairs $[R_i, R_j]$ which participates to a crossing-over depends on a crossing-rate τ_c.

The mutation operator allows to obtain some randomly variations on the selected rules in order to avoid a premature convergence. The operator works by randomly selecting a subtree in the predicate part of a rule, and by replacing it by another subtree, generated by a stochastic process, whose depth is controlled by a limiting factor.

The figure 5 shows the techniques of these two genetic operators. The genetic paradigm which is utilized here has been introduced by John Koza and is better known as *genetic programming* [Koz89].

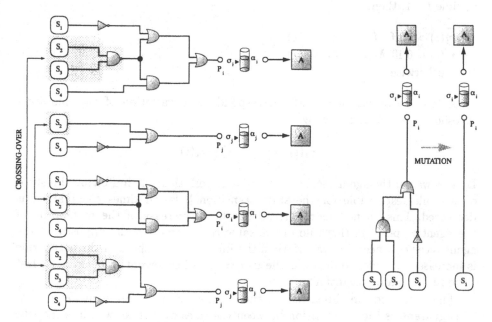

Fig. 5. the genetic operators

The final step in the adaptive control system designing concerns the credit assignment. This is the process by which the rules may be rewarded or punished in accordance with the benefits they bring about to the agents.

2.5   The Credit Assignment System

The credit assignment system of MUTANT is a reinforcement algorithm. A potential problem in traditionnal reinforcement learning is that the payoffs are generally delayed. The agent must successfully complete a sequence of steps before receiveing a reward. This makes credit assignment in the intervening steps more difficult. To address this issue, we propose a alternate reward scheme where the agent is provided intermediate rewards as it carries out the task.

We consider that, rather than coming from the environment, as implemented in many programs, the reinforcement must be intrinsically deduced by the agent itself, from satisfaction or disapointment indicators. It then should be able to evaluate something like a progress, stationary or regression estimation after a state transition, in accordance with its goals. This evaluation is highly domain dependant. For instance, a robot trying to reach a target in the environment will evaluate an increase if it gets closer to this target, or a decline if it moves away from it, or a stagnation otherwise.

The difficulty for the designer is thus to indentify the set of reinforcements associated to each relevant event that may indicate a state variation that is useful for the improvement of the behavior. In a general way, if $M(t)$ is a measure of the state at time t, and $r_i(t)$ the payoff attributed at time t to the rule R_i triggered at time $t-1$, then:

- $r_i(t) > 0$ iff $M(t) > M(t-1)$
- $r_i(t) < 0$ iff $M(t) < M(t-1)$
- 0 otherwise.

Actually, this payoff directly corresponds to a variation of the inhibiting threshold σ_i of R_i as following:

$$\sigma_i(t) = \sigma_i(t-1) - r_i(t)$$

By this way, if the agent receives a positive payoff, then the inhibiting threshold of the rule responsible for the state transition between times $t-1$ and t is decreased. This phenomenon corresponds to an increase of the motivation of the agent to perform this rule in the same conditions. On the opposite, if the agent receives a negative payoff, then the inhibiting threshold of the active rule is increased, in order to decrease the motivation of the agent to perform its last action in the same conditions.

The fluctuation in thresholds σ_i then causes the fluctuation in weights ω_i. This guarantees the competition between the rules over time, which is the *sine qua non* feature for the adaptability of the agent behavior.

3   Experiments and Results

We chose, in the scope of this paper, to experiment the MUTANT architecture in collective robotics domain, through a foraging robots system. We thus have developed a simulator for autonomous robots. This simulator has been implemented using JAAFAAR: a kernel we have developed for generic multiagent simulation.

Table 1. parameters of the simulation

stimuli	actions	payoffs	events
is_base_visible?	wander	1	puck delivered
is_puck_visible?	move_forward	1	puck picked-up
is_close_to_puck?	turn_on_left	-3	puck dropped outside
is_close_to_base?	turn_on_right	0.5	puck pushed to base
is_puck_within_base?		-0.5	puck pushed away from base

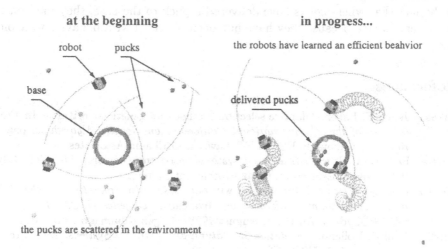

at the beginning   in progress...

robot   pucks   the robots have learned an efficient beahvior

base   delivered pucks

the pucks are scattered in the environment

Fig. 6. simulation snapshots

Four robots are equipped with a vision sensor, able to discriminate a home region (their base) and some pucks, scattered in the environment. Each robot is also equipped with both an engine to move forward and a rotator to turn. The task this group of robots has to learn is to wander in the environment until finding a puck, then pushing the puck into the base. At the beginning of the simulation, the set of behavioral rules of each robot is generated randomly, that

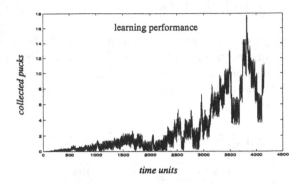

Fig. 7. simulation results

is to say that their knowledge is totally flimsy. The table 1 lists the parameters of the simulation: the set of basis behaviors, the payoffs and corresponding events. The figure 6 shows some snapshots of the simulation. And the figure 7 presents how performance improves as the agents learn over time (about 1000 simulations have been averaged). The sudden drops in curves is a parasite phenomenon due to the fact that when agents have delivered a puck to the base, they may push the others outside because they have not been provided with behavior to avoid this.

References

Bak85.   James E. Baker. Adaptive selection methods for genetic algorithms. In *Proceedings of the 1st International Conference on Genetic Algorithms*, pages 101–111, Pittsburgh, USA, 1985. Lawrence Erlbaum Associates.

Bro91a.   Rodney A. Brooks. Integrated systems based on behaviors. *SIGART*, July 1991. Special issue on Integrated Intelligent Systems.

Bro91b.   Rodney A. Brooks. Intelligence without reason. In *Proceedings of the 12th International Joint Conference on Artificial Intelligence (IJCAI-91)*, pages 569–595, Sydney, Australia, August 1991. Morgan Kaufmann Publishers.

Hol92.   John H. Holland. *Adaptation in Natural and Artificial Systems*. MIT Press, Cambridge, MA, USA, 2nd edition, 1992.

Kae96.   Leslie P. Kaelbling, editor. *Recent Advances in Reinforcement Learning*. Kluwer Acadcemic Publishers, 1996. Reprinted from Machine Learning, 22(1,2,3), January, February, March 1996.

Koz89.   John R. Koza. Hierarchical genetic algorithms operating on population of computer programs. In *Proceedings of the 11th International Joint Conference on Artificial Intelligence (IJCAI-89)*, San Mateo, 1989. Morgan Kaufmann Publishers.

Mat97.   Maja J. Mataric. Reinforcement learning in the multi-robot domain. *Autonomous Robots*, 4(1):73–83, March 1997.

Mat98.   Maja J. Mataric. Using communication to reduce locality in distributed multi-agent learning. *Journal of Experimental and Theoretical Artificial Intelligence*,

10(3):357–369, 1998. special issue on Learning in DAI Systems, Gerhard Weiß, ed.

WB91.   S. D. Whitehead and D. H. Ballard. Active perception and reinforcement learning. *Neural Computation*, 2(4):409–419, 1991.

WD92.   C. Watkins and P. Dayan. Technical note: Q-Learning. *Machine Learning*, 1992.

Computing Least Common Subsumers in Expressive Description Logics

Thomas Mantay

Artificial Intelligence Laboratory, University of Hamburg,
mantay@informatik.uni-hamburg.de

Abstract. Computing least common subsumers in description logics is an important reasoning service useful for a number of applications. As shown in the literature, this reasoning service can be used for the approximation of concept disjunctions in description logics, the "bottom-up" construction of knowledge bases, learning tasks, and for specific kinds of information retrieval. So far, computing the least common subsumer has been restricted to description logics with rather limited expressivity. In this article, we continue recent research on extending this operation to more complex languages and present a least common subsumer operator for the expressive description logic $\mathcal{ALENR}$.

1 Introduction

Knowledge representation languages based on description logics (DLs) have proven to be a useful means for representing the terminological knowledge of an application domain in a structured and formally well understood way [6]. In DLs, knowledge bases are formed out of *concepts* representing sets of individuals. Complex concepts are built out of atomic concepts and atomic roles (representing binary relations between individuals) using the concept constructors provided by the DL language. For example, the set of *grandmothers* can be described using the atomic concepts woman and parent and the atomic role has-child: woman $\sqcap \exists$ has-child.parent.

A central feature of knowledge representation systems based on DLs is a set of reasoning services with the ability to deduce implicit knowledge from explicitly represented knowledge. For instance, the subsumption relation between two concepts can be determined. Intuitively speaking, a concept C *subsumes* a concept D if the set of individuals represented by C is a superset of the set of individuals represented by D, i.e., if C is more general than D.

As another reasoning service, the *least common subsumer* (LCS) operation, applied to concepts C and D, computes the most specific concept (from the infinite set of all concepts) which subsumes C and D. The LCS is an important reasoning service useful for a number of applications. Cohen et al. consider an LCS operator for learning tasks [4] and in order to approximate a disjunction operator in the DL $\mathcal{ALN}$ with feature chain equality because the disjunction operator is not explicitly present. Baader et al. use the LCS for the "bottom-up"

N. Foo (Ed.): AI'99, LNAI 1747, pp. 218–230, 1999.

construction of KBs based on the DLs $\mathcal{ALN}$ [1] and $\mathcal{ALE}$ [2]. In [8], Möller et al. apply the operator to similarity-based information retrieval where the LCS formalizes the notion of "similarities" of concepts. As recent literature shows, there is a tendency to extend this reasoning service to more and more expressive DL languages.

The main contribution of this paper is the proposal of an LCS operator for the expressive DL $\mathcal{ALENR}$ consisting of the top and bottom concept, atoms, negations of atoms, concept conjunctions, $\exists$-, $\forall$-quantifications, role conjunctions, and number restrictions. The constructors offered by $\mathcal{ALENR}$ have proven to be useful in our similarity-based information retrieval applications.

Cohen, Borgida, and Hirsh [3] showed that if a unique least upper bound operation on the set of arguments of each concept forming operator is available and subsumption between two concepts can be computed structurally, their LCS can be determined by a simple recursive algorithm. The first task can be accomplished rather easily, whereas great efforts are necessarily in order to transform an $\mathcal{ALENR}$ concept into structural subsumption normal form. Therefore, the main object of this article is to give a definition of such a normal form and provide an algorithm to compute it for $\mathcal{ALENR}$ concepts. Technical details of the presented work including complete proofs are available in [7].

2 Preliminaries

In this section, we review the definition and some properties of the DL $\mathcal{ALENR}$ (e.g., considered in [5,6]).

Definition 1. *Let C be a set of atomic concepts and $\mathcal{R}$ a set of atomic roles disjoint from C. ($\mathcal{ALENR}$-) concepts are recursively defined as follows:*

- *The symbols $\top$ and $\bot$ are concepts (top concept, bottom concept).*
- *A and $\neg A$ are concepts for each $A \in C$ (atomic concept, negated atomic concept).*
- *If C and D are concepts, $R \in \mathcal{R}$ is an atomic role, and $n \in I\!N \cup \{0\}$, then*
  - *$C \sqcap D$ (concept conjunction),*
  - *$\exists R.C$ (existential role quantification),*
  - *$\forall R.C$ (universal role quantification),*
  - *$(\geq n\,R)$ ($\geq$-restriction), and*
  - *$(\leq n\,R)$ ($\leq$-restriction)*
  are also concepts.
- *If R and S are roles, then $R \sqcap S$ is a role (role conjunction).*

A *subexpression* of a concept C is a substring of C that qualifies as a concept. The semantics of a concept is defined in terms of an interpretation.

Definition 2. *An interpretation $\mathcal{I} = (\Delta^{\mathcal{I}}, \cdot^{\mathcal{I}})$ of a concept consists of a non-empty set $\Delta^{\mathcal{I}}$ (the domain of $\mathcal{I}$) and an interpretation function $\cdot^{\mathcal{I}}$. The interpretation function maps every atomic concept A to a subset $A^{\mathcal{I}} \subseteq \Delta^{\mathcal{I}}$ and every role R to a subset $R^{\mathcal{I}} \subseteq \Delta^{\mathcal{I}} \times \Delta^{\mathcal{I}}$. The interpretation function is recursively extended to a complex concept as follows. Assume that $A^{\mathcal{I}}, C^{\mathcal{I}}, D^{\mathcal{I}}$ and $R^{\mathcal{I}}, S^{\mathcal{I}}$ are already given and $n \in I\!N \cup \{0\}$. Then*

- $\top^{\mathcal{I}} := \Delta^{\mathcal{I}}, \bot^{\mathcal{I}} := \emptyset, (\neg A)^{\mathcal{I}} := \Delta^{\mathcal{I}} \setminus A^{\mathcal{I}},$
- $(C \sqcap D)^{\mathcal{I}} := C^{\mathcal{I}} \cap D^{\mathcal{I}}, (R \sqcap S)^{\mathcal{I}} := R^{\mathcal{I}} \cap S^{\mathcal{I}},$
- $\exists R.C^{\mathcal{I}} := \{a \in \Delta^{\mathcal{I}} | \exists b : (a, b) \in R^{\mathcal{I}} \wedge b \in C^{\mathcal{I}}\},$
- $\forall R.C^{\mathcal{I}} := \{a \in \Delta^{\mathcal{I}} | \forall b : (a, b) \in R^{\mathcal{I}} \Rightarrow b \in C^{\mathcal{I}}\},$
- $(\geq n R)^{\mathcal{I}} := \{a \in \Delta^{\mathcal{I}} | \sharp\{b | (a, b) \in R^{\mathcal{I}}\} \geq n\},$ and
- $(\leq n R)^{\mathcal{I}} := \{a \in \Delta^{\mathcal{I}} | \sharp\{b | (a, b) \in R^{\mathcal{I}}\} \leq n\}.$

An interpretation $\mathcal{I}$ is a model of a concept C iff $C^{\mathcal{I}} \neq \emptyset$. If C has a model, C is called consistent. A role R is a subrole of a role S iff, for all interpretations $\mathcal{I}$, $R^{\mathcal{I}} \subseteq S^{\mathcal{I}}$. A concept C is subsumed by a concept D ($C \sqsubseteq D$) iff $C^{\mathcal{I}} \subseteq D^{\mathcal{I}}$ holds for all interpretations $\mathcal{I}$ of C and D. C is equivalent to D ($C \equiv D$) iff $C \sqsubseteq D \wedge D \sqsubseteq C$.

Note that both constructors $\top$ and $\bot$ are expressible by ($\geq 0 R$) and $A \sqcap \neg A$, respectively. For some explanations of the algorithms presented subsequently, we introduce the concept depth.

Definition 3. *The* depth *of a concept C is recursively defined over its structure.*

- If $C = \exists R.C'$ or $C = \forall R.C'$, then $depth(C) = 1 + depth(C')$.
- If $C = C_1 \sqcap \cdots \sqcap C_n$, then $depth(C) = \max(\{depth(C_i) | 1 \leq i \leq n\})$.
- In all other cases, $depth(C) = 0$.

A *depth n subexpression* of a concept C is a subexpression of C that occurs on depth n of C. Furthermore, for a consistent concept C in which a role R occurs as a substring, we say that C has an R-successor if, in every model of C, there is an individual which functions as an R-successor.

Definition 4. *Given a consistent concept C and a role R occurring in C, we say that C has an R-successor iff, for all models $\mathcal{I}$ of C, there are individuals i, j such that $(i, j) \in R^{\mathcal{I}}$.*

The LCS of two concepts C and D is defined as the set of most specific concepts which subsume both C and D.

Definition 5. *Let C and D be concepts. Then we define the set of* least common subsumers *as:*

$$lcs(C, D) := \{E \mid C \sqsubseteq E \wedge D \sqsubseteq E \wedge$$
$$\forall E' : C \sqsubseteq E' \wedge D \sqsubseteq E' \Longrightarrow E \sqsubseteq E'\}.$$

From this definition it follows immediately that, for concepts C and D, all pairs of elements of $lcs(C, D)$ are equivalent. Due to this uniqueness property, we will consider $lcs(C, D)$ as a concept rather than a set of concepts in the following. Definition 5 can straightforwardly be extended to n arguments. In this case, lcs is associative and commutative and $lcs(C_1, \ldots, C_n) = lcs(C_1, lcs(C_2, \ldots lcs(C_{n-1}, C_n) \ldots))$. In our analysis, it will be convenient to define the most specific role of two role conjunctions.

Definition 6. *Let $R = \sqcap_{1 \leq i \leq n} R_i$ and $S = \sqcap_{1 \leq j \leq m} S_j$ be roles, $\mathfrak{R} = \{R_1, \dots, R_n\}$, and $\mathfrak{S} = \{S_1, \dots, S_m\}$. Then we define the most specific role of R and S as a partial function:*

$$msr(R, S) := \begin{cases} \sqcap_{T \in \mathfrak{R} \cap \mathfrak{S}} T & \text{if } \mathfrak{R} \cap \mathfrak{S} \neq \emptyset, \\ \text{undefined} & \text{otherwise.} \end{cases}$$

Definition 6 can easily be extended to more than two role arguments. In the next section, we will define a normal form for concepts with which the subsumption problem for $\mathcal{ALENR}$ can be decided by a structural subsumption algorithm.

3   Structural Subsumption Normal Forms

We are interested in a normal form with which the subsumption relation between pairs of concepts can be decided by structural comparisons. It will be convenient to order the concept components w.r.t. the concept forming operators.

Definition 7. *An concept C is in sorted normal form (SNF) iff $C = \top$ or $C = \bot$ or*

$$C = A \sqcap E \sqcap F \sqcap L \sqcap M \text{ with} \tag{1}$$
$$E = \sqcap_{1 \leq i \leq n} \exists R_i.C_i,$$
$$F = \sqcap_{1 \leq i \leq m} \forall R_i'.C_i',$$
$$L = \sqcap_{1 \leq i \leq p} (\geq n_i \, S_i), \text{ and}$$
$$M = \sqcap_{1 \leq i \leq q} (\leq m_i \, S_i')$$

where A is an arbitrary conjunction of atomic and negated atomic concepts and C_i and C_i' are also in SNF. Furthermore, we assume all nested conjunctions to be flattened, i. e., $A \sqcap (B \sqcap C) \rightarrow A \sqcap B \sqcap C$, conjunctions of $\forall$-quantifications to be factorized, i.e., $\forall R.C \sqcap \forall R.D \rightarrow \forall R.(C \sqcap D)$, $\forall$-quantifications to be spread over other $\forall$-quantifications, i.e., $\forall R.C \sqcap \forall S.D \rightarrow \forall R.C \sqcap \forall S.(C \sqcap D)$ if S is a subrole of R, and $\forall$-quantifications to be spread over $\exists$-quantifications, i.e., $\exists R.C \sqcap \forall S.D \rightarrow \exists R.(C \sqcap D) \sqcap \forall S.D$ if R is a subrole of S.

We will now give an algorithm with which subsumption between concepts can be computed by structural comparisons. In Algorithm 1, the test if $C \equiv \top$

Algorithm 1 structural-subsumption(C, D)

Let $C = C_1 \sqcap \cdots \sqcap C_n$ and $D = D_1 \sqcap \cdots \sqcap D_m$. Then $D \sqsubseteq C$ iff $C \equiv \top$ or $D \equiv \bot$ or, for all C_i:

1. if C_i is an atomic concept, then there exists a D_j such that $C_i = D_j$,
2. if C_i is of the form $\exists R.C'$ ($\forall R.C'$), then there exists a D_j of the form $\exists S.D'$ ($\forall S.D'$) such that S (R) is a subrole of R (S) and $D' \sqsubseteq C'$,
3. if C_i is of the form $(\geq n \, R)$ $[(\leq n \, R)]$, then there exists a D_j of the form $(\geq m \, S)$ $[(\leq m \, S)]$ such that $n \leq m$ ($m \leq n$) and S (R) is a subrole of R (S).

($C \equiv \bot$) can be performed by the subsumption (satisfiability) algorithm for the DL $\mathcal{ALCNR}$ [5]. Note that the Algorithm does not necessarily return the correct result for *arbitrary* $\mathcal{ALENR}$ concepts. In the sequel, we will define a normal form for concepts C and D such that *structural-subsumption*(C, D) returns *true* iff $D \sqsubseteq C$. We will motivate the definition by an example.

When determining the subsumption relationship between concepts, several kinds of possible "interactions" between concept forming operators must be considered. These interactions are pointed out by the following example. Let $X_1 := \exists R.(A \sqcap B)$, $X_2 := \forall R.(A \sqcap B)$, $X_3 := (\geq 1\,R)$, and $Y := \exists R.A \sqcap \exists R.B \sqcap (\leq 1\,R)$. Then, the invocations *structural-subsumption*(X_1, Y), *structural-subsumption* (X_2, Y), and *structural-subsumption*(X_3, Y) all return *false*, even though $Y \sqsubseteq X_1$, $Y \sqsubseteq X_2$, and $Y \sqsubseteq X_3$ hold. The reason is that Y implies the $\exists$-quantification $\exists R.(A \sqcap B)$, the $\forall$-quantification $\forall R.(A \sqcap B)$, and the $\geq$-restriction $(\geq 1\,R)$. These concepts are not explicitly present as subexpressions of Y, but their existence would be relevant for the structural subsumption algorithm to work correctly.

As a consequence, in order to transform a concept C into a normal form $\hat{C}$ such that subsumption can be decided by structural comparisons, the idea is to make the relevant implicitly contained information explicit and conjunctively add it to C in the form of additional concept components. Since $\hat{C}$ contains no "new" information w.r.t. C, semantical equivalence between C and $\hat{C}$ is guaranteed. For instance, if we define $\hat{Y} := Y \sqcap \exists R.(A \sqcap B) \sqcap \forall R.(A \sqcap B) \sqcap (\geq 1\,R)$, $\hat{X}_1 := X_1 \sqcap (\geq 1\,R)$, $\hat{X}_2 := X_2$, and $\hat{X}_3 := X_3$, the invocations *structural-subsumption*$(\hat{X}_1, \hat{Y})$, *structural-subsumption*$(\hat{X}_2, \hat{Y})$, and *structural-subsumption*$(\hat{X}_3, \hat{Y})$ all returns *true* as desired. Obviously, atomic concept components do not influence the process of computing the structural subsumption normal form of a concept and there are no relevant $\leq$-restrictions that need to be made explicit.

We will now generalize the ideas pointed out by the above example in order to get a definition of a structural subsumption normal form of a concept. For a set of concepts $\mathcal{S}$, we define $\mathcal{S}^{\neq}$ as the largest subset of $\mathcal{S}$ in which no pair of equivalent concepts occurs.

Definition 8. *Let C be a concept in SNF given by (1). Then, we first define*

$$\mathcal{E}_C := \{\exists\,R.D \mid C \sqcap \exists\,R.D \equiv C \land \forall(\exists\,R.D') : C \sqcap \exists\,R.D' \equiv C \Rightarrow D \sqsubseteq D'\},$$

$$\mathcal{L}_C := \{(\geq n\,R) \mid C \sqcap (\geq n\,R) \equiv C \land C \sqcap (\leq n-1\,R) \text{ is inconsistent}\}, and$$

$$\mathcal{A}_C := \{\forall\,R.D \mid C \sqcap \forall\,R.D \equiv C \land \forall D' : C \sqcap \forall\,R.D' \equiv C \Rightarrow D \sqsubseteq D'\}.$$

A concept $\hat{C}$ is in structural subsumption normal form *(SSNF) w.r.t. C iff*

$$\hat{C} = A \sqcap \hat{E} \sqcap \hat{F} \sqcap L \sqcap M \sqcap \bigsqcap_{D' \in \mathcal{E}_C^{\neq} \cup \mathcal{L}_C^{\neq} \cup \mathcal{A}_C^{\neq}} \hat{D}'$$

where $\hat{E}, \hat{F}, \hat{D}'$ is in SSNF w.r.t. E, F, D. SSNF(C) denotes the set of all concepts in SSNF w.r.t. C.

Intuitively, for a concept C, the sets $\mathcal{E}_C, \mathcal{L}_C$, and $\mathcal{A}_C$ contain the most specific $\exists$-quantifications, $\geq$-restrictions, and $\forall$-quantifications following from C which are relevant for structural subsumption computation but possibly not explicitly represented as conjuncts in C. These sets are used for the definition of a new concept $\hat{C}$ in which the additional $\exists$-quantifications, $\geq$-restrictions, and

∀-quantifications are made explicit. By construction it is clear that $\mathcal{E}_C^{\neq}$, $\mathcal{L}_C^{\neq}$, and $\mathcal{A}_C^{\neq}$ are finite and, thus, $\hat{C}$ is well defined. In general, an SSNF of a concept C need not be unique. Therefore, we collect all concepts in SSNF w.r.t. C in the set $SSNF(C)$. Later we will sketch an algorithm for computing one element of this set. As an obvious consequence of Definition 8, we can state the following proposition.

Proposition 1. *Let C be a concept and $\hat{C} \in SSNF(C)$. Then $C \equiv \hat{C}$.*

Proof. (sketch) The proposition holds because C is a subexpression of $\hat{C}$ and the additional constraints in $\hat{C}$ are logical consequences of C.

As a consequence of Proposition 1 and Definition 8, we get the following theorem.

Theorem 1. *Let C and D be concepts and $\hat{C} \in SSNF(C)$ and $\hat{D} \in SSNF(D)$. Then* structural-subsumption$(\hat{C}, \hat{D})$ *returns* true *iff $D \sqsubseteq C$.*

Proof. (sketch) Theorem 1 holds since, by Proposition 1, we have $C \equiv \hat{C}$ and $D \equiv \hat{D}$ and in the concepts $\hat{C}$ and $\hat{D}$, all ∃-, ∀-quantifications, and ≥-restrictions relevant for structural subsumption computation are made explicit.

When determining the subsumption relationship between two concepts C and D we first compute concepts $\hat{C} \in SSNF(C)$ and $\hat{D} \in SSNF(D)$ and invoke Algorithm 1 on $\hat{C}$ and $\hat{D}$. Theorem 1 guarantees that the subsumption relationship $D \sqsubseteq C$ holds if and only if *structural-subsumption*(C, D) returns *true*. In the next section, we will develop an algorithm for computing $\hat{C} \in SSNF(C)$ for a concept C.

4   Computing Structural Subsumption Normal Forms

The preceding section showed that in order to compute a concept $\hat{C}$ in SSNF w.r.t. a concept C, we must make information explicit which is only implicitly contained in C. The difficulty is to capture exactly those ∃-, ∀-quantifications, and ≥-restrictions which are induced by *every* model of C. Therefore, the algorithm is closely related to the functioning of a tableaux prover for $\mathcal{ALENR}$ [5]. Since tableaux provers aim at creating a constraint system representing only *one* possible model of C, our algorithm will create a finite set of (partial) constraint systems representing the set of *all* (partial) models of C. Each constraint system of this set induces a concept and, by considering the commonalities of these concepts, the sets $\mathfrak{E}_C^{\neq}$, $\mathfrak{L}_C^{\neq}$, and $\mathfrak{A}_C^{\neq}$ in Definition 8 can be obtained. In order to keep the presentation of the algorithm simple, we will only consider consistent concepts C with $C \not\equiv \top$. This can be done without loss of generality since subsumption between concepts C and D can easily be determined by Algorithm 1 if C or D (or both) are equivalent to $\top$ or $\bot$.

We first introduce some helpful notation. Throughout the rest of this section, for a concept C in SNF given by (1), let

$$\mathfrak{E}_C := \{\exists R_1.C_1, \dots, \exists R_n.C_n\}, \mathfrak{A}_C := \{\forall R_1'.C_1', \dots, \forall R_m'.C_m'\},$$
$$\mathfrak{L}_C := \{(\geq n_1\, S_1), \dots, (\geq n_p\, S_p)\}, \mathfrak{M}_C := \{(\leq m_1\, S_1'), \dots, (\leq m_q\, S_q')\}.$$

We assume that there exists an alphabet of variable symbols. A *constraint* is a syntactic object of the form (x, R, C) where x is a variable, R is a role and C is a concept. Intuitively, (x, R, C) says that x has to be interpreted as an R-successor in the interpretation of C. A constraint system CS is a finite, non-empty set of constraints.

Definition 9. *Let C be a concept in SNF given by (1) and $\mathfrak{A}_C|_R := \{\forall S.D \in \mathfrak{A}_C|R$ is a subrole of $S\}$. Then we define the function*

$$cs(C) := \{(x, R, D)|\ \text{there exists } \exists R.D \text{ in } \mathfrak{E}_C\} \cup$$
$$\{(x, R, D)^1, \dots, (x, R, D)^r|\ \text{there exists } (\geq r\ R) \text{ in } \mathfrak{L}_C \text{ and } D = D_1 \sqcap$$
$$\cdots \sqcap D_k, \text{ if } \mathfrak{A}_C|_R = \{\forall S_1.D_1, \dots, \forall S_k.D_k\}, D = \top \text{ if } \mathfrak{A}_C|_R = \emptyset\}.$$

Intuitively, the function $cs(C)$ returns the constraint system induced by $\mathfrak{E}_C$ and $\mathfrak{L}_C$. Our intention is to successively modify $cs(C)$ into a new constraint system CS' such that the sets $\mathcal{E}_C^{\neq}$, $\mathcal{L}_C^{\neq}$, and $\mathcal{A}_C^{\neq}$ can easily be derived from CS'. As the example in Section 3 shows, it may be necessary to "merge" constraints due to the existence of $\leq$-restrictions in C. We will model the merging process as a result of repetitive applications of a merging rule to $cs(C)$ yielding a new constraint system CS'.

For a concept C and a constraint system CS, we say that CS is *compliant with $\mathfrak{L}_C$* iff, for all $(\geq n\ R) \in \mathfrak{L}_C$, there exist at least n constraints in CS involving subroles of R. CS is *compliant with $\mathfrak{A}_C$* iff, for all $\forall R.D \in \mathfrak{A}_C$, there exists no constraint (x, S, D') in CS such that S is a subrole of R and $D \sqcap D'$ is inconsistent. Finally, CS is *compliant with $\mathfrak{M}_C$* iff, for all $(\leq n\ R) \in \mathfrak{M}_C$, there exist at most n constraints in CS involving subroles of R.

Definition 10. *Let $CS = \{(x, R_1, C_1), \dots, (x, R_n, C_n)\}$ be a constraint system and $\mathfrak{L}_C$ and $\mathfrak{M}_C$ be given for a concept C. Then we say that CS' emerges from CS by application of the $\exists$-merging rule ($CS \longrightarrow_\exists CS'$) iff $\exists k, k' \in \{1, \dots, n\}, k \neq k'$, such that*

(i) $CS' = \{(x, R_i, C_i)|i \in \{1, \dots, n\} \setminus \{k, k'\}\} \cup \{(x, R_k \sqcap R_{k'}, C_k \sqcap C_{k'})\}$,
(ii) *CS' is compliant with $\mathfrak{L}_C$ and $\mathfrak{A}_C$ but not with $\mathfrak{M}_C$*,
(iii) *$msr(R_k, R_{k'})$ is defined, and*
(iv) *$C_k \sqcap C_{k'}$ is consistent.*

CS' emerges from CS by successive applications of the $\exists$-merging rule iff $\exists CS_1, \dots, CS_r, r \in \mathbb{N} \cup \{0\}$, such that $CS = CS_1 \longrightarrow_\exists \cdots \longrightarrow_\exists CS_r = CS'$. CS' is $\exists$-merging rule complete w.r.t. CS iff CS' emerges from CS by successive applications of the $\exists$-merging rule and $\neg \exists CS'' : CS' \longrightarrow_\exists CS''$. In this case, CS' is called an $\exists$-merging rule completion of CS. Furthermore, we define the set of $\exists$-merging rule completions of CS as

$$M_{CS}^\exists := \{CS'|CS' \text{ is an } \exists\text{-merging rule completion of } CS\}.$$

Intuitively, by applying the $\exists$-merging rule to a constraint, we yield a new constraint in which the role components and the concept components of two constraints are conjunctively combined, respectively. According to Definition 10, we can apply the $\exists$-merging rule if the resulting constraint system is compliant with $\mathcal{L}_C$ and $\mathfrak{A}_C$ but not with $\mathfrak{M}_C$. For the new constraint to be able to represent the two merged constraints, the msr of the roles of the two merged constraints must be defined and the conjunction of their concept components must be consistent.

Let us apply the $\exists$-merging rule to our example concept Y. We have $cs(Y) = \{(x, R, A), (x, R, B)\}$ and, by two alternative applications of $\longrightarrow_\exists$, we get $M^\exists_{cs(Y)} = \{\{(x, R, A \sqcap B)\}, \{(x, R, B \sqcap A)\}\}$.

In the next step, we will show how to compute $\mathcal{E}^{\neq}_C$ and $\mathcal{A}^{\neq}_C$ (see Definition 8) from $M^\exists_{cs(C)}$ for a concept C. We introduce two functions $somes(CS)$ and $alls(CS, \mathfrak{M}_C)$ which extract the $\exists$- and $\forall$-quantifications induced by the constraint system CS.

Definition 11. *Let CS be a constraint system and $CS|_R := \{(x, S, C) \in CS | S$ is a subrole of $R\}$ and*

$$E_{CS} := \{\exists\, R.D | (x, R, D) \in CS\} \text{ and}$$
$$A_{CS, \mathfrak{M}_C} := \{\forall\, R.D | \text{ there exists } (\leq n\, S) \text{ in } \mathfrak{M}_C \text{ such that } \sharp CS|_S = n \text{ with}$$
$$CS|_S = (x, R_1, C_1), \ldots, (x, R_n, C_n)\} \text{ and } D = lcs(C_1, \ldots, C_n)$$
$$\text{and} \quad R = msr(R_1, \ldots, R_n)\}.$$

Then we define the following functions:

$$somes(CS) := \sqcap_{E \in E_{CS}} E \text{ and}$$
$$alls(CS, \mathfrak{M}_C) := \sqcap_{A \in A_{CS, \mathfrak{M}_C}} A. \tag{2}$$

For each constraint (x, R, C) in CS, $somes(CS)$ contains a conjunct $\exists\, R.C$. The function $alls(CS, \mathfrak{M}_C)$ contains a $\forall$-quantification of the form $\forall\, msr(R_1, \ldots, R_n).lcs(C_1, \ldots, C_n)$ if there is an $\leq$-restriction in $\mathfrak{M}_C$ involving a number n which is equal to the number of constraints $(x, R_1, C_1), \ldots, (x, R_n, C_n)$ in CS involving a subrole of R. The set $A_{CS, \mathfrak{M}_C}$ is well defined since the LCS operation used in (2) is applied to concepts of depth smaller than the original concept C. Hence, no cyclic definition is present. Considering $\mathfrak{M}_Y = \{(\leq 1\, R)\}$, we get $somes(\{(x, R, A \sqcap B)\}) = \exists\, R.(A \sqcap B), somes(\{(x, R, B \sqcap A)\}) = \exists\, R.(B \sqcap A), alls(\{(x, R, A \sqcap B)\}, \mathfrak{M}_Y) = \forall\, R.(A \sqcap B)$, and $alls(\{(x, R, B \sqcap A)\}, \mathfrak{M}_Y) = \forall\, R.(B \sqcap A)$.

Each single conjunction $SA_i := somes(CS_i) \sqcap alls(CS_i, \mathfrak{M}_C)$ characterizes properties of a specific class of partial[1] models of the depth 0 components of C. Since we are interested in a characterization of the properties of *all* partial models of the depth 0 components of C, we compute the commonalities of $SA_1, \ldots, SA_n$ by means of the LCS operation defined in Section 2.

---

[1] We use the expression "partial models" because atomic and negated atomic concept components are not considered in the constraint systems.

Definition 12. *Let C be a concept, $M^\exists_{cs(C)} = \{CS_1, \ldots, CS_n\}$ be the set of $\exists$-merging rule completions of $cs(C)$. Then we define*

$$\exists\forall\text{-}completion(C) := lcs(somes(CS_1) \sqcap alls(CS_1, \mathfrak{M}_C), \ldots,$$
$$somes(CS_n) \sqcap alls(CS_n, \mathfrak{M}_C)).$$

Since we compute the LCS of conjunctions of $\exists$- and $\forall$-quantifications which do not interact with each other, the computation can be restricted to an LCS operation on concepts with depth smaller than the original concept C. Hence, no cyclic definition is present and $\exists\forall\text{-}completion(C)$ is well defined. Let us compute $\exists\forall\text{-}completion(Y)$ for our example concept Y. We have $lcs(\exists R.(A \sqcap B) \sqcap \forall R.(A \sqcap B), \exists R.(B \sqcap A) \sqcap \forall R.(B \sqcap A)) \equiv \exists R.(A \sqcap B) \sqcap \forall R.(A \sqcap B)$. We can now state the following proposition.

Proposition 2. *Let C be a concept. Then $\exists\forall\text{-}completion(C) \equiv \sqcap_{E \in \mathcal{E}^{\neq}_C} E \sqcap \sqcap_{A \in \mathcal{A}^{\neq}_C} A$.*

Proof. (sketch) Each $\exists$-merging rule completion CS of $cs(C)$ induces a partition of the set of all partial models of the depth 0 components of C. For each CS, $somes(CS)$ and $alls(CS, \mathfrak{M}_C)$ represent the $\exists$- and $\forall$-quantifications induced by CS and $\mathfrak{M}_C$. Hence, $\exists\forall\text{-}completion(C)$ represents the conjunction of $\exists$- and $\forall$-quantifications induced by all $\exists$-merging rule completions of $cs(C)$ which is equivalent to $\sqcap_{E \in \mathcal{E}^{\neq}_C} E \sqcap \sqcap_{A \in \mathcal{A}^{\neq}_C} A$.

From Proposition 2 it follows that, for a concept C, we can compute the sets $\mathcal{E}^{\neq}_C$ and $\mathcal{A}^{\neq}_C$ in Definition 8 as follows. We first generate the constraint system $cs(C)$. By successive $\exists$-merging rule applications we construct the set of $\exists$-merging rule completions $M^\exists_{cs(C)} = \{CS_1, \ldots, CS_n\}$ from $cs(C)$. Then, for each CS_i, we construct $somes(CS_i) \sqcap alls(CS_i, \mathfrak{M}_C)$. Eventually, by means of the LCS operation, we can compute the $\exists$- and $\forall$-quantifications in $\mathcal{E}^{\neq}_C$ and $\mathcal{A}^{\neq}_C$.

In order to compute $\mathcal{L}^{\neq}_C$ in Definition 8, we make use of a merging rule similar to the one in Definition 10. Starting from a concept C, our intention is to obtain a set of constraint systems $M^{\geq}_{cs(C)}$ from which the $\geq$-restrictions in $\mathcal{L}^{\neq}_C$ can be derived in a similar way than $\mathcal{E}^{\neq}_C$ and $\mathcal{A}^{\neq}_C$ can be obtained from $M^\exists_{cs(C)}$. Definition 10 cannot be used for this since the merging process terminates as soon as the constraint system is compliant with $\mathfrak{M}_C$. As explained by the following example, it is necessary to continue the merging process as long as the constraint system is compliant with $\mathcal{L}_C$ and $\mathfrak{A}_C$. Let $X := \exists R.A_1 \sqcap \exists R.A_2 \sqcap \exists R.A_3 \sqcap (\leq 2R)$. Then, $cs(X) = \{(x, R, A_1), (x, R, A_2), (x, R, A_3)\}$ and $M^\exists_{cs(X)} = \{\{(x, R, A_1 \sqcap A_2), (x, R, A_3)\}, \{(x, R, A_1 \sqcap A_3), (x, R, A_2)\}, \{(x, R, A_2 \sqcap A_3), (x, R, A_1)\}\}$. From $M^\exists_{cs(X)}$ it follows that X has at least two R-successors. However, as can be easily seen, there are models of X with only one R-successor. Therefore, we change the condition for stopping the merging process such that the termination criterion is independent on $\mathfrak{M}_C$.

Definition 13. *Let $CS = \{(x, R_1, C_1), \ldots, (x, R_n, C_n)\}$ be a constraint system and $\mathcal{L}_C$ be given for a concept C. Then we say that CS' emerges from CS by* *application of the $\geq$-merging rule $(CS \longrightarrow_\geq CS')$ iff $\exists k, k' \in \{1, \dots, n\}, k \neq k'$, such that*

  (i) $CS' = \{(x, R_i, C_i) | i \in \{1, \dots, n\} \setminus \{k, k'\}\} \cup \{(x, R_k \sqcap R_{k'}, C_k \sqcap C_{k'})\}$,
  (ii) CS' is compliant with $\mathfrak{L}_C$ and with $\mathfrak{A}_C$,
  (iii) $msr(R_k, R_{k'})$ is defined, and
  (iv) $C_k \sqcap C_{k'}$ is consistent.

CS' emerges from CS by successive applications of the $\geq$-merging rule iff $\exists CS_1$, $\dots, CS_r$, $r \in \mathbb{N} \cup \{0\}$, such that $CS = CS_1 \longrightarrow_\geq \cdots \longrightarrow_\geq CS_r = CS'$. CS' is $\geq$-merging rule complete w.r.t. CS iff CS' emerges from CS by successive applications of the $\geq$-merging rule and $\neg \exists CS'' : CS' \longrightarrow_\geq CS''$. In this case, CS' is called an $\geq$-merging rule completion of CS. Furthermore, we define the set of $\geq$-merging rule completions of CS as

$$M_{CS}^\geq := \{CS' | CS' \text{ is an } \geq\text{-merging rule completion of } CS\}.$$

As an example, after repetitive $\geq$-merging rule applications on $cs(X)$, we get $M_{cs(X)}^\geq = \{\{(x, R, A_1 \sqcap A_2 \sqcap A_3)\}, \{(x, R, A_1 \sqcap A_3 \sqcap A_2)\}, \{(x, R, A_2 \sqcap A_1 \sqcap A_3)\}\{(x, R, A_2 \sqcap A_3 \sqcap A_1)\}, \{(x, R, A_3 \sqcap A_1 \sqcap A_2)\}, \{(x, R, A_3 \sqcap A_2 \sqcap A_1)\}\}$.

    The final step for computing $\mathcal{L}_C^{\neq}$ is similar to the one for computing $\mathcal{E}_C^{\neq}$ and $\mathcal{A}_C^{\neq}$.

Definition 14. *Let CS be a constraint system, $\mathfrak{R} := \{R | (x, R, C) \in CS\}$, $CS|_R := \{(x, S, C) \in CS | S \text{ is a subrole of } R\}$, and*

$$L_{CS} := \{(\geq n\, R) | \exists \mathfrak{R}' \subseteq 2^{\mathfrak{R}} \text{ with } \mathfrak{R}' = \{R_1, \dots, R_t\} \text{ and } R = msr(R_1, \dots, R_t)$$
$$\text{is defined and } n = \sharp CS|_R\}.$$

Then we define the function: $at\text{-}leasts(CS) := \sqcap_{L \in L_{CS}} L$.

The function $at\text{-}leasts(CS)$ computes the $\geq$-restrictions induced by the constraint system CS. For example, if $CS = \{(x, R \sqcap S, A), (x, R \sqcap T, B)\}$, we get $at\text{-}leasts(CS) = (\geq 1\, (R \sqcap S)) \sqcap (\geq 1\, (R \sqcap T)) \sqcap (\geq 2\, R)$.

Definition 15. *Let C be a concept, $M_{cs(C)}^\geq = \{CS_1, \dots, CS_n\}$ be the set of $\geq$-merging rule completions of $cs(C)$. Then we define*

$$\geq\text{-}completion(C) := lcs(at\text{-}leasts(CS_1), \dots, at\text{-}leasts(CS_n)).$$

With this definition we can state the following proposition.

Proposition 3. *Let C be a concept. Then, $\geq\text{-}completion(C) \equiv \sqcap_{L \in \mathcal{L}_C^{\neq}} L$.*

The proof of Proposition 3 is analogeous to the proof of Proposition 2. We can now combine the results of Proposition 3 and Proposition 2.

Theorem 2. *Let C be a concept in SNF given by (1), $\exists \forall\text{-}completion(C) = \exists T_1.E_1 \sqcap \cdots \sqcap \exists T_r.E_r \sqcap \forall U_1.F_1 \sqcap \cdots \sqcap \forall U_s.F_s$, compute-ssnf$(C) := \exists \forall\text{-}completion(C)$*

$\sqcap \geq$ -completion(C), and $D := \exists\, T_1.compute\text{-}ssnf(E_1) \sqcap \cdots \sqcap \exists\, T_r.$
$compute\text{-}ssnf(E_r) \sqcap \forall\, U_1.compute\text{-}ssnf(F_1) \sqcap \cdots \sqcap \forall\, U_s.compute\text{-}ssnf(F_s)$, and

$$\hat{C} := A \sqcap \hat{E} \sqcap \hat{F} \sqcap L \sqcap M \sqcap D \text{ with}$$
$$\hat{E} = \sqcap_{1 \leq i \leq n} \exists\, R_i.compute\text{-}ssnf(C_i)$$
$$\hat{F} = \sqcap_{1 \leq i \leq m} \forall\, R'_i.compute\text{-}ssnf(C'_i).$$

Then, $\hat{C} \in SSNF(C)$.

Theorem 2 states that we obtain a concept $\hat{C}$ which is in SSNF w.r.t. C if we apply the procedure described in this section on every depth of C and on each $\exists$- and $\forall$-quantification in $\exists\forall$-completion(C). In our initial example, we get $compute\text{-}ssnf(Y) = \exists\, R.(A \sqcap B) \sqcap \forall\, R.(A \sqcap B) \sqcap (\geq 1\, R)$ and, thus, $\hat{C} = C \sqcap \exists\, R.(A \sqcap B) \sqcap \forall\, R.(A \sqcap B) \sqcap (\geq 1\, R)$ as desired.

In this section, we presented an algorithm to compute a concept $\hat{C} \in SSNF(C)$. We will now use this result for computing the LCS of two concepts.

5 LCS Computation

Given concepts C and D and $\hat{C} \in SSNF(C)$ and $\hat{D} \in SSNF(D)$, $lcs(C,D)$ can straightforwardly be implemented into an algorithm taking $\hat{C}$ and $\hat{D}$ as arguments. Algorithm 2 recursively computes $lcs(C,D)$ with arguments $\hat{C}$

Algorithm 2 compute-lcs (C, D)

> **if** $D \sqsubseteq C$ **then** C **else if** $C \sqsubseteq D$ **then** D
> **else if** $(C = A \vee C = \neg A)$ and $(D = B \vee D = \neg B)$ for atomic concepts A and B
> **then if** $C = D$ **then** C **else** $\top$
> **else if** $C = \exists\, R.C'$ and $D = \exists\, S.D'$ **then**
>   **if** $msr(R, S)$ is undefined **then** $\top$
>   **else** $\exists\, msr(R, S).compute\text{-}lcs(C', D')$
> **else if** $C = \forall\, R.C'$ and $D = \forall\, S.D'$ **then** $\forall\, (R \sqcap S).compute\text{-}lcs(C', D')$
> **else if** $C = (\geq n\, R)$ and $D = (\geq m\, S)$ **then**
>   **if** $msr(R, S)$ is undefined **then** $\top$
>   **else** $(\geq \min\{n, m\}\, msr(R, S))$
> **else if** $C = (\leq n\, R)$ and $D = (\leq m\, S)$ **then** $(\leq \max\{n, m\}\, R \sqcap S))$
> **else if** $C = C_1 \sqcap \cdots \sqcap C_n$ **then** $\sqcap_{1 \leq i \leq n} compute\text{-}lcs(C_i, D)$
> **else if** $D = D_1 \sqcap \cdots \sqcap D_n$ **then** $compute\text{-}lcs(D, C)$
> **else** $\top$ **endif**

---

and $\hat{D}$. The invocations $compute\text{-}lcs(\hat{X}_i, \hat{Y})$, $i \in \{1, 2, 3\}$, yield respectively $\exists\, R.(A \sqcap B)$, $\forall\, R.(A \sqcap B)$, and $(\geq 1\, R)$ as desired.

Theorem 3. *Let C and D be concepts and $\hat{C} \in SSNF(C)$, and $\hat{D} \in SSNF(D)$. Then compute-lcs($\hat{C}, \hat{D}$) returns a concept which is equivalent to $lcs(C, D)$.*

Proof. (sketch) By Theorem 1 we know that subsumption between C and D can be computed structurally by applying Algorithm 1 to $\hat{C}$ and $\hat{D}$. Now Theorem 3 is a consequence of Theorem 3 in [3] which states that the LCS of concepts C

and D can be computed according to Algorithm 2 if, for each language constructor, a least upper bound operation on the arguments of the constructor is present and the input concepts are in structural subsumption normal form. The least upper bound operations are implicitly given by Algorithm 2.

6 Conclusion

We have presented an LCS operator for the expressive DL $\mathcal{ALENR}$. Computing the LCS for concepts is a very important inference service applicable to a number of applications. This article contributes to recent research on extending the LCS to more and more expressive DLs. As shown in the literature, the LCS can be computed by a simple algorithm if, for each language constructor, a unique least upper bound operation on the space of the arguments of this constructor can be provided and the concepts are first transformed into a normal form with which subsumption between the concepts can be decided by a structural subsumption algorithm. The special challenge one faces is that interactions between different concept constructors imply relevant implicit information that must be made explicit. Based on the least upper bound operations, we extended the LCS computation algorithm for the description logics $\mathcal{ALN}$ and $\mathcal{ALE}$ to the new language constructs included in $\mathcal{ALENR}$. Future research should include the extension of the LCS operation to more complex DLs. Moreover, it would be interesting to extend the notion of concept commonalities to description logics including a disjunction operator. The LCS operator does not seem to be useful for this because the LCS of two concepts would just be their disjunction which we found to not express meaningful commonalities in our similarity-based information retrieval application.

References

1. F. Baader and R. Küsters. Computing the Least Common Subsumer and the Most Specific Concept in the Presence of Cyclic $\mathcal{ALN}$-concept Descriptions. In O. Herzog and A. Günter, editors, *Proceedings of the 22nd German Conference on Artificial Intelligence, KI'98*, volume 1504, pages 129–140, 1998.
2. F. Baader, R. Küsters, and R. Molitor. Computing Least Common Subsumer in Description Logics with Existential Restrictions. In T. Dean, editor, *Proceedings of the 16th International Joint Conference on AI (IJCAI'99)*, pages 96–101. Morgan Kaufmann, 1999.
3. W. W. Cohen, A. Borgida, and H. Hirsh. Computing Least Common Subsumers in Description Logics. In *Proceedings of the International Conference on Fifth Generation Computer Systems*, pages 1036–1043, Japan, 1992. Ass. for Computing Machinery.
4. W.W. Cohen and H. Hirsh. The learnability of description logics with equality constraints. *Machine Learning*, 17:169–199, 1994.
5. F. M. Donini, M. Lenzerini, D. Nardi, and W. Nutt. The Complexity of Concept Languages. *Information and Computation*, 134(1):1–58, April 1997.
6. F. M. Donini, M. Lenzerini, D. Nardi, and A. Schaerf. *Principles of Knowledge Representation*, chapter Reasoning in Description Logics, pages 191–236. CSLI Publications, 1996.

7. T. Mantay. Computing Least Common Subsumers in Expressive Description Logics. TR FBI-HH-M-286/99, Dep. of CS, University of Hamburg, 1999.
8. R. Möller, V. Haarslev, and B. Neumann. Semantics-based Information Retrieval. In *International Conference on Information Technology and Knowledge Systems*, Vienna, Budapest, 1998.

E-SETHEO: Design, Configuration and Use of a Parallel Automated Theorem Prover

Gernot Stenz and Andreas Wolf

Institut für Informatik, Technischen Universität München
80290 München, Germany
{stenzg,wolfa}@in.tum.de

Abstract. One of the key issues in Automated Theorem Proving is the search for optimal proof strategies. Since there is not one uniform strategy which works optimally on all proof tasks, one is faced with the difficult problem of selecting a good strategy for a given task. Strategy parallelism, where a proof task is attempted in parallel by a set of strategies with distributed resources, is a way of circumventing this strategy selection problem. However, the problem of selecting the parallel strategies and distributing the available resources among them still remains. Therefore we have developed a method for automatic strategy and resource configuration based on the combination of a genetic algorithm and a gradient procedure. For the effective use of this method it is necessary to be able to automatically gather large amounts of experimental data. We present an environment for such large scale data collection that has been used by us in preparation of the CADE-16 automatic system competition. In order to evaluate the potential of the method experimentally, we have implemented the strategy parallel theorem prover e-SETHEO. The experimental results obtained with the system already justify our approach while showing substantial potential for future development.

1 Introduction

Automated Theorem Proving (ATP) is the subfield of computer science dealing with the automatic verification of the validity of logical formulae. Attempting to prove the validity of such formulae automatically, particularly beyond simple textbook examples, typically results in a tremendously large search space. Such a search problem is usually solved by a uniform search procedure. In automated deduction, different search strategies may behave significantly different on a given problem. Unfortunately, in general, it cannot be decided in advance which strategy is the best for a given problem. This motivates the competitive use of different strategies, especially when the available resources are restricted. In order to be successful with such an approach, the strategies must satisfy the following two conditions. *Sub-linearity:* Let $sol(s,t)$ denote the set of problems solved with a strategy s in time t. Then, for a typical set of problems, the function $\frac{|sol(s,t)|}{t}$ must be sub-linear, i.e., with each additional time interval fewer new problems are solved. *Complementarity:* The competing strategies must be

N. Foo (Ed.): AI'99, LNAI 1747, pp. 231–243, 1999.

complementary w.r.t. a given problem set, i.e., the sets of problems solved in a certain time limit by two different strategies should differ significantly. If both conditions are satisfied, then a competitive use of different strategies can be more successful than the best single strategy.

The selection of more than one search strategy in combination with techniques to partition the available resources in a manner dependent on the task defines the parallelization method *strategy parallelism*: distributed competitive agents attempt to solve the same problem, but with different strategies. It is intended that these strategies should traverse the search space such that, in practice, the repeated consideration of identical parts is largely avoided. In this paper we address some aspects of strategy parallelism, such as search space partitioning, strategy selection and resource allocation. We also describe the design of a strategy parallel theorem prover and give some experimental results which justify our approach. According to our experiments, even simple forms of strategy parallelism can yield super-linear speedups.

The paper is organized as follows. In the next section, we give a brief overview on Automated Theorem Proving. Section 2 relates strategy parallelism with other parallelization methods in automated deduction and discusses problems like partitioning, schedule computation, and scalability. Furthermore, in this Section we give an outline of the design and the implementation of our strategy parallel theorem prover e-SETHEO. Then, in Sections 3 and 4 we briefly describe our prover configuration method. Section 5 presents some experimental results obtained with this system. We conclude the paper with an outlook on future development and an assessment of our current work.

2   Strategies and Strategy Parallelism, a Framework for a Strategy Parallel Prover

For us, a strategy is one particular way of traversing the search space. We are now looking for a way of efficiently combining and applying different strategies in parallel. Many ways of organizing parallel computing have already been studied. However, many of these methods do not apply to automated theorem proving, since it is generally impossible to predict the size of each of the parallelized subproblems and it is therefore very hard to create an even workload distribution among the different agents. Here, we cite some of the successful examples. An example can be found in the *nagging* concept [SS94a]: dependent subtasks are sent by a master process to the naggers, which try to solve them and report on their success. The results are integrated into the main proof attempt. A combination of different strategies is used within the teamwork concept [Den95] of DISCOUNT [DKS97] for unit equality problems. These strategies periodically exchange intermediate results and work together evaluating these intermediate results and determining the further search strategies. A simple but effective combination of different theorem provers is applied in SSCPA [SS99]. Strategy selection techniques are applied even in systems with finite search spaces like EUREKA [CV98]. Partitioning of the search space [SS94b] is done. e. g. in

PARTHEO [SL90]. Some of these approaches are very good in certain aspects. Partitioning, for example, can guarantee that no part of the search space is considered twice, therefore providing an optimal solution for the problem of generating "significantly" differing search strategies. The fundamental weakness of partitioning, however, is that it needs a tight and extensive communication between the agents. Therefore, we have investigated a competition approach. Different strategies are applied to the same problem and the first successful strategy stops all others. However, not all strategies are equally promising or require equal effort. It is therefore advisable to divide the available resources in an adequate way.

The selection of more than one search strategy in combination with techniques to partition the available resources such as time and processors is called *strategy parallelism* [WL99]. Different, competitive agents traverse the same search space via different, ideally non-overlapping paths. Such a selection of strategies together with a resource allocation for the strategies is called a *schedule*. One of the key problems of strategy parallelism is the strategy allocation problem. We capture this problem by using a set of training examples from the given domain and optimizing the admissible strategies for this training set. The training phase, however, is extensive, as can be seen from the following consideration. Given a set of training problems, a set of usable strategies, a time limit, and a number of processors, we want to determine an optimal distribution of resources to each strategy, i.e., a combination of strategies which solves a maximal number of problems from the training set within the given resources. Unfortunately, even the single processor decision variant of this problem is strongly NP-complete [WL99]. In practice, we therefore use suboptimal schedules whose generation will be described in Section 3.

Using SETHEO as the basic underlying inference machine, we have developed p-SETHEO, a prototypical implementation of a strategy parallel theorem prover. This system in the meanwhile has been further developed into e-SETHEO, the most important improvements being the augmentation by the new E prover, a superposition calculus equality prover [Sch99] and the employment of FLOTTER [WL99] as a conversion procedure from full first order logic to conjunctive normal form (CNF). The inclusion of E as an important strategy has cured SETHEO's weakness in the equality domain. We have used e-SETHEO to collect experimental data and will participate with that system in the ATP system competition at the CADE-16 conference. Our implementation had initially been written in C, Perl and PVM, and currently consists of about 1500 lines of code without the basic SETHEO prover. While in the early stages of development nearly all stages had been variants of SETHEO (that is, e-SETHEO would invocate different instantiations of SETHEO with different parameterizations), in the meanwhile we have begun to incorporate a much wider variety of different strategies covering special problem classes. Often, certain characteristics of a proof task that are generally easy to recognize imply a special treatment of this task with a special strategy. For example, if the problem is either ground or can be grounded, it is possible to apply a propositional theorem prover to that problem, which is not only very fast but additionally implements a *decision procedure* for this kind of problem, allowing fast detection of non-theorems as well. Watching the current development it can be said that e-SETHEO is moving from a parallel version of the SETHEO prover to a general platform for parallel theorem proving able to incorporate all state of the art ATP systems, provided these ATP systems adhere to minimum standards regarding issues such as resource allocation or input-output behavior.

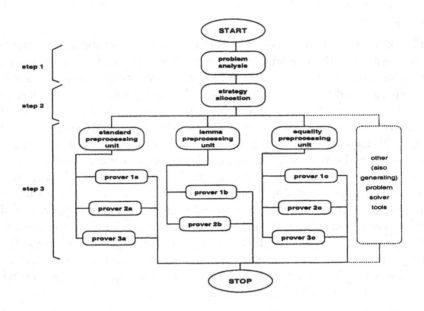

Fig. 1. Schematic view of the functionality of e-SETHEO.

E-SETHEO performs its proof tasks in a number of distinguishable steps, as is depicted in Figure 1. The first step that is done upon invocation is *problem analysis*. The problem analysis provides e-SETHEO with the most important syntactic problem statistics such as the number of clauses and literals, the number of variables or the number of equality predicates. From our experimental experience it became evident that the greatest improvements in prover performance are not to be gained in the inference machine (which in itself has been refined and optimized over a period of several years), but in the analysis of the proof task and the subsequent choice of strategies. This first step also performs the CNF conversion if necessary.

This analysis is the basis for step two of the proof task, the *strategy allocation* by schedule selection. A schedule is defined for that proof task according to criteria based on the problem statistics. This schedule is chosen from a schedule set generated during the prover configuration, which is explained in Section 3. Basically, a schedule is a list of strategies with resources assigned to each strategy.

Each strategy is a list of steps to be performed by the prover system. But as certain subparts, such as basic preprocessing steps, can often be shared among the strategies that make up the schedule, the schedules can also be seen as a *program execution tree* or as a set of *program execution trees*. The selected schedule is then written to a configuration file. After the configuration, the final step is executed, the actual *parallel prover runs*. At that stage e-SETHEO hands over control to a utility called *WRAPPER* that executes the selected schedule and watches the progress of the parallel subtasks, terminating the entire schedule when a strategy has been successful.

3 Prover Configuration

The multitude of settings of the basic SETHEO inference machine and the considerable number of additional prover tools employed by e-SETHEO result in a vast number of different configurations in which the prover system can be used. It is obvious that it is not feasible to test all these possible configurations for their performance on a given problem domain. However, using heuristics, intuition and experience, a number of about one hundred of these configurations has been identified as potentially useful and implemented as strategies. Still, having a hundred different strategies to choose from (and to distribute resources among), trying to obtain an optimal solution for resource allocation would be futile. Therefore we choose our schedule from a number of pseudo-optimal solutions we acquire in a three-phased process.

In the first phase, all given problems are divided into a small number of classes according to some very simple discrimination criteria, such as Horn or non-Horn formulae with or without equality. In the second phase, for each of these classes a set of schedules is evaluated by the genetic algorithm described in [SW99]. The best of these schedules are selected for refinement in the third phase by applying the gradient method explained in [Wol98b]. This process results in a set of pseudo-optimal schedules, one for each class, that are then used for configuring e-SETHEO. It can easily be seen that this entire configuration process can be done automatically, the one task remaining for the user being the selection of a suitable subset of the problem domain to be used for training. The experiments described in the next section showed among other things that the genetic algorithm generates decent results in a very short time. Several refinements of the process could only slightly enhance the results, but could ensure a better convergence of these results. This is a direct consequence of the first required strategy property as postulated in Section 1.

4 Data Generation

We capture the schedule determination problem by using a set of training examples from the given domain and optimizing the admissible strategies for this training set using the genetic gradient method[1]. Providing the necessary training data, however, is a very extensive task. Given a set of training problems, a set of usable strategies, a time limit t, and a number of processors, we want to determine a combination of strategies which solves a maximal number of problems from the training set within the given resources. To compute this combination, we have to determine for all admissible strategies S the solution times (within t) on all problems P from the training set. In our experiment, we employed 50 workstations for some weeks CPU time to determine all necessary data on a training set of about 4000 problems and a set of 110 strategies. The workstations were organized in a loosely connected cluster with shared disk memory. Additionally, we used a controller workstation separated from the cluster.

We do not have exclusive access to the workstation cluster, and because of the large amount of work to be done and because of the (in general) considerable resources required by theorem prover programs, the data generation system needs to have some means of balancing and limiting the load produced by our experimental setup, so the interactive users of the workstation cluster and the connecting network will not be needlessly encumbered. Therefore we employ an Performance Evaluator. This Performance Evaluator is responsible for the generation and maintenance of a data base containing all data necessary for the evaluation of the expected performance and the expected free resources on all involved machines. We limit the number of prover processes running simultaneously on the same processor as well as the maximum load and the minimum amount of free memory allowed before starting a new prover task.

The Task Generator maintains a list of tasks to be treated. Using inquiries on the available strategies, on the available problems, and on the strategy-problem-pairs which already have been finished properly, Task Generator generates a To-do-List which is given to the Task Scheduler component. This Task Scheduler launches all the tasks from the To-do-List as soon as the Performance Evaluator provides usable hosts. If a certain task finished correctly, i. e., without errors caused by the operation system or other users, this fact and the generated data is recorded and used for the generation of the data matrices required for the genetic gradient algorithm as well as for providing re-entry points necessary when the whole data generation system has to be restarted, e. g., after re-booting the controller workstation or a general network failure. An abstract view of the data generation system can be seen in Figure 2.

5   Experimental Results

Our experiments were conducted in two phases. First we intended to verify the feasibility of the approach described in Section 3 with reduced problem and strategy sets. Therefore we used the 547 eligible TPTP problems [SSY94] of the theorem prover competition at the 15th Conference on Automated Deduction in 1998 to be our training data set. Our participating prover p-SETHEO [Wol98a]

---

[1] The genetic gradient algorithm is the genetic algorithm followed by the application of the gradient procedure to the best individuals.

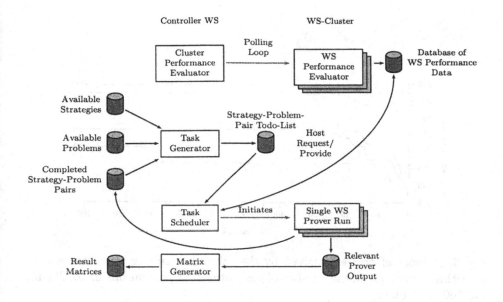

Fig. 2. Schematic view of the data generation system.

system employed 91 different strategies, these formed our strategy set. We extracted all these strategies and ran each strategy on all problems using the standard sequential SETHEO [MIL+97]. The successful results of all those runs were collected in a single list that became the database for our genetic gradient algorithm. 398 problems can be solved by at least one of the strategies in at most 300 seconds. Then we ran the genetic gradient algorithm on the collected data. The success of each of the schedules, as the individuals of our genetic algorithm, was evaluated by looking up the list entries for the problems and respective strategies and time resources.

In all experiments we used the gradient procedure and the genetic algorithm[2] described above. The attributes of the initial generation that are selected at random strongly influence the overall results of the experiment. The deficiencies of an unfit initial generation can not be wholly remedied by the subsequent optimizations. Therefore all experiments were repeated at least ten times. The curves and tables depicted in this section represent the median results. Figure 3 shows the number of problems solved after 0 to 100 generations for 10, 20, 40, and 160 individuals (numbers at the curves) in 300 seconds on a single processor system. The next Figure 4 displays the number of problems solved on a single processor system with 100 individuals after 0, 10, and 50 generations (numbers at the curves) in the time interval from 0 to 1000 seconds. The behavior is compared with the best single strategy (denoted by bs). Note, that the strategy parallel system proved 378 problems within 1000 seconds, the best

---

[2] The fixed parameters have been a kill-off rate of 0.6, a mutation rate of 0.1, and a mutation probability for each strategy of 0.2.

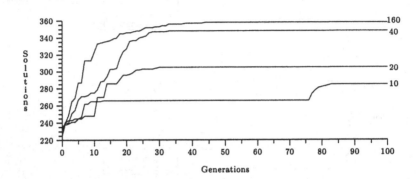

Fig. 3. Number of problems solved by the schedule resulting from the genetic algorithm depending on the number of generations for populations of 10, 20, 40, and 160 individuals.

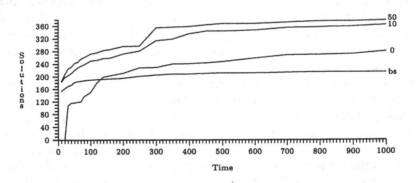

Fig. 4. Number of problems solved by the schedule resulting from the genetic algorithm depending on the consumed time on a single processor system with 100 individuals after 0, 10, and 50 generations, compared with the best single strategy (bs).

processors	1	2	4	8
gradient procedure (solutions)	355	361	374	382
genetic algorithm (solutions)	352	369	381	388

Table 1. Solutions found by the gradient and the genetic method on systems with 1, 2, 4, and 8 processors.

single strategy only 214, that is 57% of the strategy parallel version. These 214 problems have already been solved by the strategy parallel system after 25 (!) seconds. Figure 5 illustrates the number of problems solved for 100 individuals

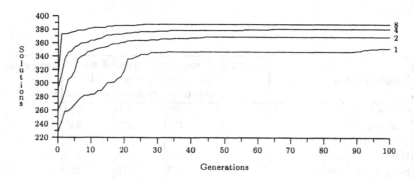

Fig. 5. Number of problems solved by the schedule resulting from the genetic algorithm depending on the number of generations for populations of 100 individuals each on systems with 1, 2, 4, and 8 processors and a time limit of 1000 seconds.

and 0 to 100 generations with a timeout value of 1000 seconds on systems with 1, 2, 4, and 8 processors (numbers at the curves). Finally, we compare the results of both (single) methods, the gradient method and the genetic algorithm on 1, 2, 4, and 8 processors with 300 seconds each (see Table 1). We see the slightly better results of the gradient procedure on one processor. In all other cases, the genetic algorithm performs better.

Our experimental results show only a poor scalability for our actual prover system. That is due to the very limited number of training problems. Furthermore, many of the used strategies *overlap* one another (see [WL99]). Still, all the above figures indicated that the genetic gradient approach is extremely useful for automatically configuring a strategy parallel theorem prover, and therefore we started the data generation for the entire problem and strategy sets. We tested each of the 110 strategies on all 4004 problems of the latest version of the TPTP problem library [SSY94]. These test runs were conducted on the workstation cluster as described in Section 4 with a time limit of 300 seconds per problem and strategy and took about two months; the results of these tests can be seen in the second and third columns of Table 2. Using the data from these runs we generated a set of pseudo-optimal schedules for the different problem classes. After having configured e-SETHEO with these schedules, we tested e-SETHEO on the TPTP problems again, the number of problems solved by the strategy parallel prover is shown in the fourth column of Table 2 with the fifth column giving the number of strategies contained in the respective schedules. Even if the relative increases gained by our process may not seem excessively high, it has to be noted that the TPTP library as a whole contains many trivial problems as well which can also be solved by brute force strategies in very short time. Additionally, as has been explained in Section 1, due to the highly sub-linear nature of strategy performance over time, large gains in the number of problems solved become ever more unlikely with increasing problem difficulty. So the results obtained by our automatic prover configuration can actually be considered a success.

Problem Class	problems in class	# solved by some strategy	# solved by best strategy	# solved by schedule	strategies in schedule
Groundable	753	685	410	682	4
Unit Equality	446	365	330	341	5
Pure Equality	132	96	85	93	6
Horn w. Equality	226	183	175	183	3
Horn w/o Equality	373	293	275	291	3
non-Horn w/o Eq. (large)	268	98	74	96	6
non-Horn w/o Eq. (small)	266	227	191	227	6
non-Horn w. Eq. (large)	841	140	78	132	9
non-Horn w. Eq. (small)	699	445	317	416	12
TOTAL	4004	2532	2201	2461	-

Table 2. Results in number of proofs found for TPTP v2.2.0 (1 processor, 300 seconds)

6   Future Work: Beyond Syntactic Problem Classification

In this section we want to address an issue that has not (at least up to now) been sufficiently treated by ATP researchers. Strategy parallelism has eliminated the necessity to choose a suitable search strategy in advance. Yet, given the large number of different strategies or even only the comparably small number of different schedules, it is still necessary to choose the proper way of solving the proof problem. In e-SETHEO, this choice is based solely on the syntactic characteristics of the problem clauses. In many cases this is a very efficient approach, as in the case of groundable formulae, where the absence of function symbols strongly suggests grounding the formula and subsequently using a semantic tree procedure. Yet, there remain large formula classes without an apparent inner structure implied by syntactic characteristics. A typical example for such a formula class is the class of non-Horn problems with equality, the class containing the most general problems available. Different attempts to divide this class, such as according to the specific number of function symbols or predicates, have all failed as it turned out that syntactically very similar problems caused widely differing search space behavior.

As the next step in our research we intend to tackle this problem using a genetic algorithm. Given a set of schedules (such as the ones we are currently using), we employ such a genetic algorithm to define a schedule selection function using the syntactic data as input. Such a function would be a weighted sum over the syntactic values, the coefficients the sub-terms forming the chromosomes. A set of such chromosomes representing the function as a whole would constitute an individual. Given these individuals, we can use the genetic algorithm to produce a function that provides a nearly optimal problem classification.

7 Conclusion

In this paper we have demonstrated how the performance of automated theorem provers can be improved by the introduction of strategy parallelism. Our experiments demonstrate that it is possible to significantly increase this performance even with a simple strategy allocation algorithm and a non-optimized set of available strategies. While in theorem proving the system developer or advanced user often can tune the system by a suitable selection of parameters, this is not possible if the theorem prover is to be integrated into a larger proof environment like ILF. In this case the configuration of the theorem prover must be done automatically and strategy parallelism is a good solution of this problem.

It can be said that our implementation of e-SETHEO has moved away from a parallel framework for SETHEO towards a generic tool for parallel theorem proving, able to incorporate practically any state-of-the-art theorem prover.

In this paper we did not address a variety of issues of considerable importance that will be the subject of future research: Often, strategies are successful for a certain problem class, like the use of a special prover for unit equality or ground problems. The identification of such features can make the selection of strategies more specific and hence more successful. Currently we identify such features by purely syntactic means. Can we advance to an improved way of feature detection that involves semantic analysis? The success of the selected strategies depends on the training set of problems used for learning about the efficiency of strategies. How do we obtain a training set which is representative for the considered domain of problems? The number of sensible strategies for SETHEO, which are successful and maximally orthogonal seems to be bounded. This restricts the scalability to large platforms of parallel processors. Can we find a systematic method for producing an arbitrary number of successful and orthogonal strategies? It is very likely that in order to overcome this problem random elements such as the ones mentioned in Section 2 have to be employed. Furthermore, possible improvements of the strategy allocation algorithm should be investigated. Up to now e-SETHEO employs a non-communicating variety of cooperation. Yet it can be imagined that the strategies periodically report on their proof status, inference rate, host processor performance etc., information that could be used for online strategy evaluation. This might allow the replacement of badly performing strategies or the migration of strategies from badly performing processors.

Finally, we have to face the objection that e-SETHEO is excessively tuned to perform well on the TPTP, a collection of mostly very theoretical problems. We admit to that. We think, however, that this is not the point. If ATP systems want to be of practical use in fields such as verification, then the adaption of the prover system to the respective problem domain will be a basic necessity. We have shown our ability to adapt in such a way in the case of the TPTP, and as our tuning and configuration mechanism is entirely generic, we are optimistic that we are able to adapt our system to perform reasonably well on any problem domain.

References

CV98.   D. J. Cook and R. C. Varnell. Adaptive Parallel Iterative Deepening Search. *JAIR*, 9:139–165, 1998.

Den95.   J. Denzinger. Knowledge-Based Distributed Search Using Teamwork. *ICMAS-95*, pp. 81–88. 1995.

DF96.   J. Denzinger and M. Fuchs. Experiments in Learning Prototypical Situations for Variants of the Pursuit Game. *ICMAS-96*, pp. 48–55. 1996.

DGHW97. B. I. Dahn, J. Gehne, T. Honigmann, and A. Wolf. Integration of Automated and Interactive Theorem Proving in ILF. *CADE-14*, LNAI 1249, pp. 57–60. 1997.

DKS97.   J. Denzinger, M. Kronenburg, and S. Schulz. DISCOUNT. A Distributed and Learning Equational Prover. *JAR*, 18(2):189–198, 1997.

FSS98.   B. Fischer, J. Schumann, and G. Snelting. Deduction Based Software Retrieval. *Automated Deduction. A Basis for Applications. Volume III*, pp. 265–292. Kluwer, 1998.

Hol92.   J. H. Holland. *Adaptation in Natural and Artificial Systems*. MIT Press, 1992.

Kor90.   R. E. Korf. Depth-First Iterative-Deepening: An Optimal Admissible Tree Search. *Expert Systems, A Software Methodology for Modern Applications*, pp. 380–389. IEEE Computer Society Press, 1990.

Koz92.   J. R. Koza. *Genetic Programming*. MIT Press, 1992.

LMG94.   R. Letz, K. Mayr, and C. Goller. Controlled Integration of the Cut Rule into Connection Tableau Calculi. *JAR*, 13(3):297–338, 1994.

Lov78.   D. W. Loveland. *Automated Theorem Proving: a Logical Basis*. North-Holland, 1978.

MIL+97.   M. Moser, O. Ibens, R. Letz, J. Steinbach, C. Goller, J. Schumann, and K. Mayr. SETHEO and E-SETHEO. The CADE-13 Systems. *JAR*, 18(2):237–246, 1997.

Sch95.   J. Schumann. Using SETHEO for Verifying the Development of a Commu-
            nication Protocol in Focus – A Case Study. *TABLEAUX-95*, LNAI 918,
            pp. 338–352. 1995.

Sch99.   S. Schulz. System Abstract: E 0.3. *CADE-16*, LNAI 1632, pp. 297–60.
            1999.

SL90.   J. Schumann and R. Letz. PARTHEO: A High-Performance Parallel The-
            orem Prover. *CADE-10*, LNAI 449, pp. 40–56. 1990.

SW99.   G. Stenz and A. Wolf. Strategy Selection by Genetic Programming.
            FLAIRS-12, pp. 346–350. 1999.

SS94a.   D. B. Sturgill and A. M. Segre. A Novel Asynchronous Parallelism Scheme
            for First-Order Logic. *CADE-12*, LNAI 814, pp. 484–498. 1994.

SS94b.   C. Suttner and J. Schumann. Parallel Automated Theorem Proving. *PPAI-
            94*, pp. 209–257. 1994.

SS99.   G. Sutcliffe and D. Seyfang. Smart Selective Competition Parallelism ATP.
            FLAIRS-99, pp. 341–345. 1999.

SSY94.   G. Sutcliffe, C. Suttner, and T. Yemenis. The TPTP Problem Library.
            CADE-12, LNAI 814, pp. 252–266. 1994.

WL99.   C. Weidenbach, B. Gaede and G. Rock. SPASS & FLOTTER version 0.42.
            CADE-13, LNAI 1104, pp. 141–145. 1996.

WL99.   A. Wolf and R. Letz. Strategy Parallelism in Automated Theorem Proving.
            IJPRAI, 13(2):219–245, 1999.

Wol98a.   A. Wolf. p-SETHEO: Strategy Parallelism in Automated Theorem Proving.
            TABLEAUX-98, LNAI 1397, pp. 320–324. 1998.

Wol98b.   A. Wolf. Strategy Selection for Automated Theorem Proving. *AIMSA-98*,
            LNAI 1480, pp. 452–465. 1998.

PTTP+GLiDeS:
Guiding Linear Deductions with Semantics

Marianne Brown and Geoff Sutcliffe

Computer Science, James Cook University
{marianne,geoff}@cs.jcu.edu.au

Abstract. Using semantics to guide automated theorem proving systems is an under-utilised technique. In linear deduction, semantic guidance has received only limited attention. This research is developing semantic guidance for linear deduction in the Model Elimination paradigm. Search pruning, at the possible loss of some refutation completeness, and search guidance, are being considered. This paper describes PTTP+GLiDeS, a PTTP style prover augmented with a semantic pruning mechanism, GLiDeS. PTTP+GLiDeS combines a modified version of Stickel's PTTP prover with the model generator MACE.

1 Introduction

Automated theorem proving (ATP) aims to use computer technology to solve problems that require logical reasoning. Applications for ATP systems include logic circuit design validation, software verification, mathematical and logical research [18].

Resolution [9] was developed in 1965 and has formed the basis of much of the research undertaken in the field since. Resolution uses 'proof by contradiction' in its search for a proof. Assumptions (axioms) about the problem and the negated conjecture are expressed in the clause normal form of first order logic. The naïve resolution approach takes the input clause set, S_0, and generates the set of all possible resolvents, R_0. If the empty clause is a member of R_0, a contradiction has been found and the problem solved. Otherwise, a new set S_1 is created, $S_1 = S_0 \cup R_0$, and the process continues. If set S_n contains the empty clause, S_n forms the search space for a minimal length proof. A large search space means the time taken to find a proof can be long. In order to find proofs quickly, both the size of the search space and the path the prover takes through the search space needs to be controlled in an intelligent manner.

To control the search of a resolution based system, ordering and pruning strategies are used. Ordering strategies control the order in which resolvents are generated by giving preference to certain clauses and literals. Pruning strategies prevent certain combinations of clauses and also discard clauses, preventing them from taking any further part in the deduction. While ordering strategies attempt to guide the search along paths that may be more likely to produce the empty clause, pruning strategies reduce the search space.

N. Foo (Ed.): AI'99, LNAI 1747, pp. 244–254, 1999.

Search control may utilise syntactic or semantic methods. Syntactic methods use some physical feature of the clauses to determine which clauses will be resolved together and on which literals. Semantic methods use interpretations to give information about the clauses. This information is then used in choosing the clauses and literals to resolve. Semantic methods have the potential to perform much better than syntactic ones [16]. Semantic search control for forward chaining resolution strategies has been in use for some time. Set of support (SoS) [17], model resolution [6], and semantic resolution [10] are all forward chaining resolution strategies. Two systems that employ semantic guidance are CLIN-S [2] and SCOTT [11]. SCOTT is a resolution based prover that uses an interpretation to weight clauses and thus give preference to those clauses that are FALSE in the interpretation. CLIN-S is an instantiation based prover, and uses an interpretation to guide the generation of ground clauses, which are then examined for unsatisfiablity.

Incorporating semantic methods into backward chaining resolution strategies is not as easy as for forward chaining ones. Semantic guidance for linear-input resolution is well understood [1], as described in Section 3. This research aims to incorporate semantic guidance into general linear resolution [5,7], primarily considering pruning strategies.

The next section contains a brief explanation of the Model Elimination (ME) paradigm and introduces some terminology. Section 3 describes the architecture of PTTP+GLiDeS and explains the way in which semantic guidance has been incorporated into the ME based system. Implementation and performance are discussed in Sections 4 and 5 respectively. Further enhancements are being explored and these are outlined in Section 6.

2   Model Elimination

ME is a chain format linear resolution procedure for first order logic, first proposed in [4]. A chain is an ordered list of A- and B-literals, with the disjunction between the literals being implicit. Chains generated from the input clauses are called input chains and are composed entirely of B-literals. The chains that form the linear path in the refutation are called the centre chains. The input chains that are resolved with the centre chains are called the side chains. A-literals are those literals in a centre chain that have been resolved upon. A-literals are indicated by a frame, e.g., $\boxed{p}$. The first centre chain is called the top chain. One of the input chains is chosen to be the top chain; a chain generated from the negated conjecture is the usual choice. All input chains are potential side chains.

In ME there are two deduction operations, extension and reduction, and one book-keeping operation, truncation. The extension operation is a binary resolution between a centre chain and a side chain. The resolution takes place between the rightmost B-literal in the centre chain and a complimentary (after unification) B-literal in the side chain. The B-literal in the centre chain then becomes an A-literal, and the B-literal in the side chain is removed. The remaining B-literals in the side chain are added to the right of the newly created A-literal in the centre chain. A reduction operation is a unification between the rightmost B-literal in the centre chain and an A-literal. The new centre chain is formed by removing the B-literal. Reduction implements ancestor resolution and factoring. Truncation is the removal of A-literals from the right-hand end of a centre chain. See Figure 1 for an example of an ME refutation.

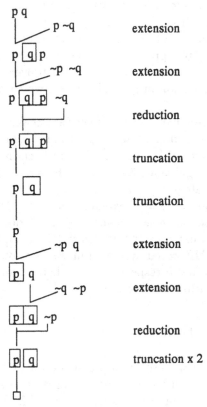

Fig. 1. An ME refutation of the set { p ∨ q, p ∨ ~q, ~p ∨ q, ~p ∨ ~q }

One method of implementing ME is using the Prolog Technology Theorem Prover (PTTP) [12] principle. The idea here is to have the theorem prover rewrite the input clause set into Prolog procedures that implement ME deduction for the clauses. The procedures are then compiled and executed on a Prolog engine (see Figure 2). Prolog is based on linear-input deduction for Horn clauses and has an incomplete search strategy and unsound unification algorithm. A PTTP style system overcomes these issues by using a bounded depth first search and unification with an occurs check.

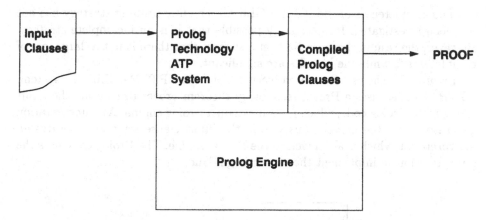

Fig. 2. Architecture of PTTP-based ATP systems

3   Architecture

The PTTP+GLiDeS semantic pruning strategy is based upon the strategy that can be imposed on linear-input deductions, as follows: If there exists a linear-input refutation, the last centre clause is the empty clause. The empty clause has the interpretation of FALSE in every interpretation. A FALSE resolvent must have one or more FALSE parents. If there is a model M of the side clauses, then this implies that the second last centre clause must be FALSE in M, and so on up to the top clause. So, if the side clauses are known and a model of them, M, can be found, then any centre clause that is TRUE in M can be rejected. A simple possibility is to choose a negative top clause from a set of Horn clauses, in which case the non-negative clauses are the potential side clauses. More sensitive analysis is also possible [3,14]. Linear-input resolution is complete for Horn clauses only.

Unfortunately, the extension of the linear-input semantic pruning strategy to linear deduction is not direct. For the non-Horn case, ancestor resolution is required for refutation-completeness. The possibility of ancestor resolutions means that centre clauses may be TRUE in a model of the side clauses. Investigation of how to allow for centre clauses that are TRUE in the model of the side clauses is a focus of this research.

In PTTP+GLiDeS, rather than placing a constraint on entire centre clauses, a semantic constraint is placed on selected literals of the centre clauses as follows: The input clauses other than the chosen top clause of a linear deduction are named the *model clauses*. In a completed linear refutation, all centre clause literals that have resolved against input clause literals are required to be FALSE in a model of the model clauses. TRUE centre clause literals must be resolved against ancestor clause literals. This leads to a semantic pruning strategy for ME deductions that at every stage requires all A-literals in the deduction so far to be FALSE in a model of the model clauses. The result is that only FALSE B-literals are extended upon, and TRUE B-literals must reduce.

The completeness of the PTTP+GLiDeS semantic pruning strategy has not yet been investigated. It is certainly possible that it is an incomplete strategy. However, the results shown in Section 5 suggest that there is not a 'large loss of completeness', while the benefits are significant.

Figure 3 shows the architecture of the PTTP+GLiDeS system. PTTP+GLiDeS uses a Prolog technology theorem prover to compile the input clauses into Prolog code, which is then run on a Prolog engine. An interpretation generator takes the model clauses from the input clause set and generates an interpretation which is also given to the Prolog engine. The Prolog code uses the interpretation to implement the semantic guidance.

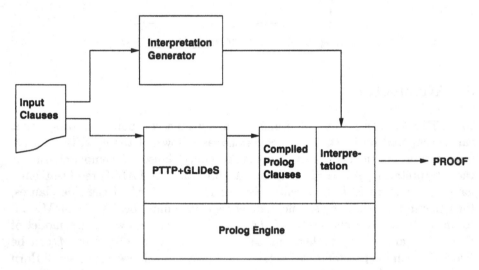

Fig. 3. Architecture of the PTTP+GLiDeS system.

4   Implementation

PTTP+GLiDeS consists of modified versions of PTTP (Prolog version 2e) [13] and MACE (v1.3.2) [8], combined by a csh script. PTTP+GLiDeS takes problems in TPTP [15] format as input. The tptp2X utility is used to transform the input problem to PTTP and MACE formats. The transformation to PTTP format selects the first conjecture clause as the top chain for the linear deduction.

A perl script is used to remove the first conjecture clause from the MACE format file, and MACE is called to generate a model of the remaining clauses. MACE is capable of generating many models, but in this experiment the first model generated is used. If MACE is unable to generate a model then PTTP+GLiDeS terminates. Otherwise MACE outputs its model in the form of Prolog facts, e.g.,

```
eval(functor,a,0).
eval(predicate,p(0,0),true).
```

The modified PTTP is then started.

The modified PTTP produces Prolog procedures that i) maintain a list of all A-literals that have been produced in the deduction so far, and ii) call a semantic checking procedure after each extension and reduction operation. The facts produced by MACE are used to interpret the A-literals. If the semantic checking procedure finds an A-literal that is TRUE then the extension or reduction is rejected.

5 Performance

Testing has been carried out using 541 "difficult, unbiased" problems from the TPTP library v2.1.0. The testing was done on a SUN sparc20, with a CPU time limit of 600 seconds. Table 1 gives an overall summary of the results.

Total number of problems:	541		
Number of models generated:	260		
Number of problems solved from 260:	PTTP	PTTP+GLiDeS	
	68	54	
Number of useful models generated:	144		
Number of problems solved from 144:	PTTP	PTTP+GLiDeS	
	21	19	

Table 1. Summary of experimental data.

For PTTP+GLiDeS, MACE produced models for only 260 of the 541 problems, and thus PTTP+GLiDeS could attempt only those problems. Of the 260 problems for which models were generated, plain PTTP solved 68 and PTTP+GLiDeS solved 54. Altogether, there were 69 problems that had models generated and were solved by either system. Of the 260 models, only 144 proved to be useful in that they provided guidance that pruned the search space of PTTP+GLiDeS. Of these 144 problems, PTTP solved 21 and PTTP+GLiDeS solved 19. In total, there were 22 problems that had useful models generated and were solved by either system.

For the 22 problems solved, Table 2 shows the CPU times taken, the number of inferences made, and the number of inferences rejected during the search. The "CPU time" column for PTTP+GLiDeS includes the time taked for preprocessing the MACE input file to exclude the choosen top clause leaving only the model clauses, model generation and output time, writing of the Prolog procedures, and the Prolog search time. For PTTP, the CPU time includes the time for writing the Prolog procedures, and the Prolog search time. The "Inferences" columns give the total number of extension and reduction operations performed during the search for a solution. The "Rejected Inferences" are the numbers of inference operations that were rejected by the semantic pruning routine. The

"Inference Ratio" shows the number of inferences made by PTTP+GLiDeS relative to PTTP.

The number of inferences made during the search gives an indication of the search space being covered during the search. A smaller inference count on the same problem does not necessarily indicate that the proof itself was any smaller. Instead, it shows that less of the search space was covered before the proof was found.

Table 2. Results for problems where semantic guidance rejected some inferences

Problem	PTTP		PTTP+GLiDeS			Inference
	CPU time (sec)	Inferences	CPU time (sec)	Inferences	Rejected Inferences	Ratio
B00004-1	11.0	10515	19.5	9355	365	0.89
B00012-1	392.8	1579178	TIMEOUT			
CAT001-4	108.5	427522	549.0	376020	37716	0.89
CAT002-4	23.9	84480	87.6	80428	5220	0.95
CAT003-3	TIMEOUT		230.2	217996	34840	
CAT003-4	8.6	11077	16.7	10816	585	0.98
CAT012-3	84.5	175367	49.1	49150	4124	0.28
CAT018-1	73.0	226900	343.2	183518	19806	0.81
GRP012-3	362.8	1282139	TIMEOUT			
HEN003-3	17.2	47136	50.5	44322	1093	0.94
HEN008-1	17.7	72068	65.9	69959	803	0.97
HEN008-3	7.7	11524	17.7	10905	308	0.95
HEN012-3	25.2	85312	101.1	80481	1857	0.94
PUZ032-1	15.4	26947	19.8	18629	4427	0.69
RNG002-1	13.7	27867	36.9	27313	756	0.98
RNG003-1	14.3	31150	38.0	23867	1412	0.77
RNG040-1	9.0	563	11.9	533	67	0.95
RNG041-1	11.1	8826	16.8	4859	824	0.55
ROB016-1	8.0	4546	22.8	3738	92	0.82
SET008-1	7.4	276	9.2	370	56	1.34
SYN071-1	411.8	832600	53.3	84908	27653	0.10
SYN310-1	438.0	1476442	TIMEOUT			
Average	87.25	254354.80	91.54	71545.11	7868.83	0.82

PTTP+GLiDeS solved one problem, CAT003-3, that PTTP failed to solve, but timed out on three that PTTP did solve. In all but one case PTTP+GLiDeS took less inferences than PTTP, and in many cases significantly less. The times taken by PTTP+GLiDeS are higher than for PTTP in most cases. Two interesting cases to note are CAT012-3 and SYN071-1. These are non-Horn problems, and have the best reduction in inference counts and less CPU time than PTTP. Of the 22 problems, 7 are non-Horn and it is in these cases that PTTP+GLiDeS performs best on average for CPU time and inference counts, as shown in Table 3.

Table 3. Results for non-Horn problems

Problem	PTTP		PTTP+GLiDeS			Inference
	CPU time (sec)	Inferences	CPU time (sec)	Inferences	Rejected Inferences	Ratio
CAT003-3	TIMEOUT		230.2	217996	34840	
CAT012-3	84.5	175367	49.1	49150	4124	0.28
PUZ032-1	15.4	26947	19.8	18629	4427	0.69
RNG040-1	9.0	563	11.9	533	67	0.95
RNG041-1	11.1	8826	16.8	4859	824	0.55
SET008-1	7.4	276	9.2	370	56	1.34
SYN071-1	411.8	832600	53.3	84908	27653	0.10
Average	89.87	174097	55.76	53778	10284	0.65

There were 15 problems out of the group of 260 problems that were solved by PTTP and not PTTP+GLiDeS. Of these, 12 were Horn problems that had models generated where the positive literals were TRUE, i.e., the models were trivial. PTTP+GLiDeS performed badly on these 12 problems as semantic checking was done when it was not going to have any effect on the search for a solution other than to slow its progress. It is a simple matter to check for this situation and omit the semantic guidance. Future implementations of PTTP+GLiDeS will have this feature. Of course, a better solution is to not generate trivial models in the first place. MACE is capable of producing many models for a given set of model clauses. In this experiment, the first model generated was used for the interpretation. A better approach may be to generate more than one model and select the 'best' one for use, or at least select a non-trivial model, as discussed in Section 7.

6   Using Multiple Models

Work is currently under way on two different multiple model versions of PTTP+GLiDeS. Version 1 generates several different models for a problem and perform the semantic checking using all models, i.e., the A-literals must be acceptable to all models before an inference operation is accepted. By using more than one model it is hoped that greater pruning will be achieved. Preliminary testing has shown that while some extra pruning is achieved, the time taken to perform the semantic checking is greatly increased. For this approach to be practical a much more efficient implementation of the semantic checking routine needs to be written.

Version 2 runs PTTP+GLiDeS in parallel with different models; the first one to find a solution kills the others. It has been observed that in some cases one model results in a timeout and another produces a solution for the same problem. By running in parallel with different models, it is hoped that one of the models will be a 'good' model and produce a solution. It may also assist in overcoming any incompleteness problems.

Table 4 shows data for PTTP+GLiDeS using the different multiple model versions and the data for PTTP. The models were hand coded rather than generated by MACE. The parallel approach of version 2 was simulated - PTTP+GLiDeS was run with each of the eight different models, then the best time was selected and multiplied by eight. The number of inferences was also multiplied by eight, but the rejected inferences count was not.

Table 4. Results for PTTP and multiple model versions of PTTP+GLiDeS

Problem	PTTP CPU time (sec)	Inferences	8 Models Version 1 CPU time (sec)	Inferences	Rej. Inf.	8 Models Version 2 CPU time (sec)	Inferences	Rej. Inf.
LCL007-1	3.7	3	4.3	3	0	34.4	24	0
LCL010-1	4.5	1349	672.4	1321	11	374.4	10584	7
LCL118-1	4.7	1897	532.9	1392	64	327.2	11136	64

Version 1 can produce greater pruning than using a single model. However, this is at the cost of greatly increase CPU time, greater than for version 2 where the best CPU time was multiplied by 8.

Version 2 is of no benefit when all models result in solutions being found, as in the problems shown in Table 4. Its usefulness is more apparent in cases where one of the models does not produce a solution but another does. In such a case, version 1 would timeout but version 2 would not.

7   Conclusion

The preliminary experiments are encouraging. In the cases where both PTTP and PTTP+GLiDeS find a solution, PTTP+GLiDeS makes fewer inferences on average. This indicates that the semantic guidance is successfully pruning the search space. A side effect of the pruning may be a loss of refutation completeness. Further work needs to be done to assess the extent of this. The time taken by PTTP+GLiDeS is greater than PTTP in the majority of cases where both systems find a solution. It may be possible to improve the time taken by PTTP+GLiDeS by making the semantic checking code more efficient.

Currently the tptp2X utility chooses the first conjecture clause in the problem as the top centre chain for PTTP. The failure to generate models in some cases is due to this unintelligent selection of the top chain. The performance of both PTTP and PTTP+GLiDeS are likely to be improved if this selection is done more intelligently. In particular, it is hoped that MACE will be able to produce models for many more problems, hence giving PTTP+GLiDeS an opportunity to attempt more problems.

Trivial model generation is another problem that needs to be overcome. It is possible to examine the model generated by MACE and determine if it is unlikely to be of use, as in the case of a trivial model, and reject it. It would be preferable to prevent generation of such a model in the first place. Further examination of this issue is needed.

Using multiple models should enable PTTP+GLiDeS to achieve greater pruning of the search space. Preliminary results show that this is the case but the increase in CPU time is currently too high.

References

1. A. Bundy. *The Computer Modelling of Mathematical Reasoning*. Academic Press, 1983.
2. H. Chu. *CLIN-S User's Manual*. Chapel Hill, USA, 1994.
3. D.A. de Waal and J.P. Gallagher. The Applicability of Logic Programming Analysis and Transformation to Theorem Proving. In A. Bundy, editor, *Proceedings of the 12th International Conference on Automated Deduction*, number 814 in Lecture Notes in Artificial Intelligence, pages 207–221. Springer-Verlag, 1994.
4. D.W. Loveland. Mechanical Theorem Proving by Model Elimination. *Journal of the ACM*, 15(2):236–251, 1968.
5. D.W. Loveland. A Linear Format for Resolution. In Laudet M. et al., editor, *Proceedings of the IRIA Symposium on Automatic Demonstration*, pages 147–162. Springer-Verlag, 1970.
6. D. Luckham. Some Tree-paring Strategies for Theorem Proving. *Machine Intelligence*, 3:95–112, 1968.
7. D. Luckham. Refinement Theorems in Resolution Theory. In Laudet M. et al., editor, *Proceedings of the Symposium on Automatic Demonstration*, pages 163–190. Springer-Verlag, 1970.
8. W.W. McCune. A Davis-Putnam Program and its Application to Finite First-Order Model Search: Quasigroup Existence Problems. Technical Report Technical Report ANL/MCS-TM-194, Argonne National Laboratory, Argonne, USA, 1994.
9. J.A. Robinson. A Machine-Oriented Logic Based on the Resolution Principle. *Journal of the ACM*, 12(1):23–41, January 1965.
10. J.R. Slagle. Automatic Theorem Proving with Renamable and Sematic Resolution. *Journal of the ACM*, 14:687–697, October 1967.
11. J.K. Slaney. SCOTT: A Model-Guided Theorem Prover. In R. Bajcsy, editor, *Proceedings of the 13th International Conference on Artificial Intelligence*, pages 109–114. Morgan-Kaufman, 1993.
12. M.E. Stickel. A Prolog Technology Theorem Prover. In *Proceedings of the 1st International Symposium on Logic Programming*, pages 211–217. IEEE Computer Society Press, 1984.
13. M.E. Stickel. A Prolog Technology Theorem Prover: A New Exposition and Implementation in Prolog. Technical Report Technical Note 464, SRI International, Menlo Park, USA, 1989.
14. G. Sutcliffe. Linear-Input Subset Analysis. In D. Kapur, editor, *Proceedings of the 11th International Conference on Automated Deduction*, number 607 in Lecture

Notes in Artifical Intelligence, pages 268–280, Saratoga Springs, NY, USA, June 1992. Springer-Verlag.

15. G. Sutcliffe and C.B. Suttner. The TPTP Problem Library: CNF Release v1.2.1. *Journal of Automated Reasoning*, 21(2):177–203, 1998.
16. L. Wos. *Automated Reasoning - 33 Basic Research Problems*. Prentice-Hall, 1988.
17. L. Wos, D. Carson, and G.A. Robinson. The Unit Preference Strategy in Theorem Proving. In *Proceedings of the AFIPS 1964 Fall Joint Computer Conference* , pages 615–621. Spartan Books, 1964.
18. L. Wos, R. Overbeek, E. Lusk, and J. Boyle. *Automated Reasoning Introduction and Applications*. Prentice-Hall, Englewood Cliffs, New Jersey, 1984.

Neural Network Learning Using Low-Discrepancy Sequence

Ivan Jordanov and Robert Brown

Design Engineering Research Centre, University of Wales Institute,
Cardiff, Western Avenue, Llandaff, Cardiff CF5 2YB, UK
IJordanov@uwic.ac.uk,
RBrown@uwic.ac.uk

Abstract. Backpropagation, (BP), is one of the most frequently used practical methods for supervised training of artificial neural networks. During the learning process, BP may get stuck in local minima, producing suboptimal solution, and thus limiting the effectiveness of the training. This work is dedicated to the problem of avoiding local minima and introduces a new technique for learning, which substitutes gradient descent algorithm in the BP with an optimization method for a global search in a multi-dimensional parameter (weight) space. For this purpose, a low-discrepancy LP_τ sequence is used. The proposed method is discussed and tested with common benchmark problems at the end.

Keywords – Neural networks, NN learning.

1. Introduction

Backpropagation [14] is still one of the most widely used methods for supervised training of neural networks by minimizing an *error* function (*cost*), that represents the difference between the desired and obtained output, with respect to the weights of the network. Because the different techniques (*gradient descent, line search, conjugate gradients, Newton's and quasi-Newton's*) used in BP depend strongly on the initial conditions [2, 9, 12], there is always danger of getting stuck in local minima during the learning (theoretically even in a saddle point [1]) and this way obtaining sub-optimal training [2, 8, 19]. Bianchini *et al.* [2] reviewed some theoretical contributions to the optimal learning, focusing on the problem of local minima. Another useful survey of the problems of supervised and unsupervised learning is given in [1].

One conventional approach is to consider the learning as an *error function* minimization problem. For this reason, investigation of the structure and landscape of the *error surface* is a related topic of continuous interest. Its detailed analysis and study [7, 11, 18] could reveal features and properties of the *error function* behavior, thus giving orientation where and how to search for a global minimum, and helping to define local minima free conditions [2, 8, 10, 17, and 19].

N. Foo (Ed.): AI´99, LNAI 1747, pp. 255 - 267, 1999.

In summary, a general viewpoint can be made that convergence of the BP learning algorithms is guaranteed only in the vicinity of a minimum, and during the iterative process of *error function* minimization, can become entrapped in wrong extreme, thus providing suboptimal learning.

In this work, a method for modified BP supervised learning is reported, in which the BP *backward pass* (adjusting the weights) is substituted with a technique for global search in the weight space, using LP_τ low-discrepancy sequence of points.

2. LP_τ LP_t Search

We use an efficient technique for searching in a multi-dimensional bounded space, which uses the LP_τ low-discrepancy sequence of points. Comprehensive description of this method can be found in [16]. Here we describe it very briefly.

2.1 Uniformly Distributed Sequence of Points in an Arbitrary Domain G

Let $P_1, P_2, ..., P_i, ...$ be a sequence of points belonging to a unit n-dimensional cube C^n. If G denotes an arbitrary domain in C^n, with volume $V_G > 0$, and $S_N(G)$ denotes the number of points $P_i, 1 \le i \le N, P_i \in G$, then the sequence of points P_i is said to be uniformly distributed in C^n if

$$\lim_{N \to \infty} \frac{S_N(G)}{N} = V_G . \tag{1}$$

It is obvious from (1) that when N is large enough, the number of points of a given sequence from an arbitrary domain G is proportional to its volume, $S_N(G) \sim N V_G$. Fig.1 shows two different uniformly distributed sequences [16].

2.2 LP_τ Net in a Multi-Dimensional Unit Cube

Any point P_i from an n-dimensional unit cube C^n (Fig. 1, $n=2$) has Cartesian coordinates $P_i = (x_{i,1}, x_{i,2}, ..., x_{i,n})$, that satisfy the inequalities..., $F(P_N)$ $0 \le x_{i,j} \le 1$, for $j = 1, 2, ..., n$, and $i = 1, 2, ..., N$. It is usually assumed that a cubic net of $N = M^n$ points (Fig. 1(a)) best represents such a cube. Nevertheless, this is true only in the linear case, when $n=1$, and with the increase of n, its "uniformity" decreases quickly. To prove that, let us compare the 2D nets from Fig. 1. They both consist of 16 points and any of the 16 small squares contains one and only one point of a net. It seems that both nets have nearly the same uniform distribution. However, this impression will be changed if we consider a function $f(x_1, x_2)$, defined in C^2, which is extremely sensitive to small changes in one of the variables (x_1), while large changes in the other one do not affect a significant change in the function value. In the extreme, if we assume $f = f(x_1)$, and calculate the function for all points from the *cubic* net (Fig. 1(a)), we would receive four different values only, each of them repeated four times. If we do the same with the points from the LP_τ net (Fig. 1(b)), we would receive 16 values that give much better description of the function behavior in that domain. In a multi-dimensional case (which is more common, when function as $f(x_1, x_2, ..., x_n)$ depends strongly on some variables and weakly on the rest), the distribution of the *cubic* net becomes worse, because the lost information increases.

Now, if we go back for a moment to the neural networks, the *cost* is a function of the weights and it is well known that there is a redundant information, contained in the weights of a fully connected network [7, 11]. Different *pruning* algorithms are used for eliminating the "weak" weights, for which the *cost* is less sensitive. As will be seen later, the use of the LP_τ sequence for searching the *error surface* could be very effective in cases, where we do not know *a priori* how many of the parameters (weights) act strongly on the optimized function (*cost*), and how many act weakly.

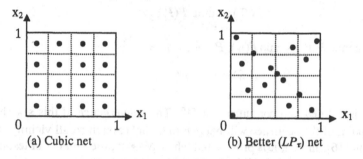

(a) Cubic net   (b) Better (LP_τ) net

Fig. 1. Two nets (n=2, M=4, N=16)

In the next section we bound the weight space by a hyper parallelepiped Π. In order to transfer the co-ordinates of the uniformly distributed points in C^n to those in Π, we give the following two lemmas (their proofs can be found in [16]).

Lemma 1: If a sequence of points Q_i with Cartesian co-ordinates $(q_{i,1}, ..., q_{i,n})$ is uniformly distributed in C^n, then a sequence of points $W_i, 1 \le i \le N$ with Cartesian coordinates $(w_{i,1}, ..., w_{i,n})$, where

$$w_{i,j} = w_j' + (w_j'' - w_j')\, q_{i,j}, \; j = 1, 2, ..., n \tag{2}$$

is a uniformly distributed sequence in parallelepiped Π, whose Cartesian co-ordinates of points satisfy the inequalities

$$w_j' \le w_{i,j} \le w_j'', \tag{3}$$

where, as in (2), the superscripts ' and " denote lower and upper bounds respectively.

Lemma 2: Let $w_1, ..., w_i, ...$ be a sequence of points uniformly distributed in Π, and $G \subset \Pi$ be an arbitrary domain with volume $V_G > 0$. If among the points w_i we choose those belonging to G, we obtain a sequence of points uniformly distributed in G.

The LP_τ sequence of points is one of the best low-discrepancy sequences known so far (for example, comparing with an r-nary LP_o sequence, a (τ, s) - sequence in base b [4], or a P_τ - sequence [16]). Below we give three examples of effective use of this sequence when searching for a global minimum (GM) difficult to optimize functions (with many local minima (LM), plateaus and very steep regions).

Usually, an optimization problem is defined as minimization (maximization) of objective function(s) $F(w)$ with respect to a vector (w), which components are n unknown design variables, or parameters $w_i, 1 \le i \le n$. The parameters are usually bounded by physical realizability criteria, so that the optimization is subject to constrains (3). These bounds determine an n dimensional hyper parallelepiped Π^n in the parameter space. In this parallelepiped we generate LP_τ sequence of points $P_1, P_2, ..., P_N$, using formulae (2) and (3) (for calculation of (2), so called direction constants given in a table from [16] are used), and from the values $F(P_1), F(P_2), ..., F(P_N)$ we found the minimum one

$$F(P_i) = \min_{1 \le i \le N} F(P_i) . \tag{4}$$

We assume that $F(P_i) \approx \min F(w)$, $P_i \approx \hat{w}$, where

$$F(\hat{w}) = \min_{w \in \Pi^n} F(w) , \tag{5}$$

and $F(w)$ is defined and continuous in Π^n. The convergence of this search, that at least one point of the sequence will happen to be in "enough small vicinity" of a GM is proved in [16]. In fact, it is proved that when $N \to \infty$, the number of testing points from the vicinity of a global minimum is much greater.

Below, we list three functions that we used to test the LP_τ search for finding a GM.

Function 1. Two-dimensional *Waves* test function (many LM and one GM (5, 2)):

$$f(x, y) = 1 - \sin(z)/z, \quad z = \sqrt{(x-5)^2 + (y-2)^2} + \varepsilon .$$

Function 2. Two-dimensional *Shubert* test function (760 LM and 18 GM):

$$f(x, y) = \left\{ \sum_{i=1}^{5} i \cos[(i+1)x + i] \right\} \left\{ \sum_{i=1}^{5} i \cos[(i+1)y + i] \right\} .$$

Function 3. Two-dimensional *Rastrigin* test function (50 LM and 1 GM (0, 0)):

$$f(x, y) = x^2 + y^2 - \cos(18x) - \cos(18y) .$$

In Table 1 relevant parameters of the carried out test search for a GM of the listed above functions are given (with 2^{16} LP_τ points for all intervals). The optimization was done in several passes, which means starting with initially "wide" search intervals (3), and subsequently narrowing the intervals before each successive pass. Bottom three rows of Table 1 shows three search intervals and co-ordinates of three successive points found in the vicinity of a GM for the third function. For the other two functions just the result of the last pass is given. The search interval (third column) is the same for both parameters. Obtained GM values for each function show very good agreement with the results given in [5], where they use the same functions to test their subenergy tunneling method (TRUST) for fast global optimization.

Table 1. GM found for the test functions

Function	GM found	Interval
Waves	(5.0008, 2.0005)	[0.0, 10.0]
Shubert	(-7.7069, -7.0841)	[-10, 0]
Rastrigin	(0.01525, 0.01525)	[-500, 1000]
	(0.00152, 0.00152)	[-50, 100]
	(0.00015, 0.00015)	[-5, 10]

3. Network Learning

Despite the variety of gradient descent methods used in BP learning, it still holds two major weaknesses – slow convergence and presence of local minima. In this paper we concentrate mainly on the problem of avoiding local minima. One conventional approach, adopted in [16], is to consider learning as a surface-fitting problem. We consider learning as a non-linear optimization problem in which the goal is to find a set of values for the network weights which minimizes an objective function that represents the deviation between the actual and desired network output.

The network under consideration is a fully connected (between adjacent layers) static network, consisting of L layers denoted with index l, $0 \leq l \leq L$, where for the input layer $l=0$, for the hidden layers $0<l<L$, and for the output layer $l=L$. Each layer of the network consists of units which number is denoted by n_l, and each unit in layer l is indexed with i_l, $i_l = 1, 2,..., n_l$.

We assume $\bar{x}_0^p$ and $\bar{t}_0^p$, $p=1,2,...,P$ to be the input and target patterns respectively. For a given pattern p, the activation of a unit i from the l-th layer, is

$$a_i^p = g(\bar{w}_i, \bar{x}_{l-1}^p) = \sum_{j=0}^{n_{l-1}} w_{i,j} x_j^p,$$

(6)

where $w_{i,j}$ is the weight associated with the connection between unit j from the $(l-1)$-th layer and unit i from the l-th layer. The bias is defined by $x_0^p = 1$ with corresponding bias weight $w_{i,0}$. The output produced of unit i from the l-th layer is related to its activation as $x_i = f(a_i)$, where $f(\cdot)$ is a standard sigmoidal non-linear function. It has a useful for the BP property:

$$f'(\cdot) = f(\cdot)[1 - f(\cdot)]: \; x_i = f(a_i) = (1 + e^{-\beta a_i})^{-1},$$

(7)

where β is the gain (in our case $\beta = 1$).

For a given experiment with P learning samples, the difference between the produced and desired output data is estimated by means of a *cost* function $E_P = \sum\limits_{p=1}^{P} E_p = \sum\limits_{p=1}^{P} d(\overline{x}_L^p - \overline{t}_L^p)$, where $d(\cdot)$ is a distance in $\mathfrak{R}^n$. Most frequently this distance is an L_2 norm which is given by

$$E_P = \frac{1}{2}\sum_{p=1}^{P}\sum_{i=1}^{n_L}(x_i^p - t_i^p)^2 = \frac{1}{2}\sum_{p=1}^{P}\sum_{i=1}^{n_L}(e_i^p)^2. \tag{8}$$

The choice of the *cost* function is important and as pointed out in [2], different choices might lead to optimization problems with different minima. It could also give rise to spurious and structural local minima [17].

Usually, the weight adjustment (in *pattern* mode) is given by the well-known gradient descent technique

$$\Delta w_{i,j}(k+1) = -\eta\frac{\partial E_P}{\partial w_{i,j}} + \alpha\,\Delta w_{i,j}(k), \quad w_{i,j}(k+1) = w_{i,j}(k) + \Delta w_{i,j}(k+1), \tag{9}$$

where η and α are non-negative parameters called learning *rate* and *momentum*, and the iteration index is denoted with k.

BP minimizes the *cost (error energy)* function (8) through adjusting the weights with (9). The objective *cost* function, represents the network mapping errors and describes an error surface in the weight space. In many cases this surface can be highly convoluted and nonconvex, with many plateaux and long narrow troughs, and can encounter many saddle points and LM [11]. This can make learning very difficult and can fail BP to find optimal solution in reasonable time.

With our method of learning, while keeping the forward pass of the BP, we modify the backward pass, substituting gradient descent with the LP_τ search for a global minimum of the *cost* function (8). Initially, we create the network weight vector as a q-dimensional real Euclidean vector $\overline{W}$, whose components consist of all weights of the network,

$$q = \sum_{l=1}^{L}(n_{l-1} + 1)n_l . \tag{10}$$

The associated with l-th layer matrix of weights $W_l \in \mathfrak{R}^{n_l, n_{l-1}+1}, 0 < l \le L$ we represent with a layer vector by concatenating its rows. Then, concatenating all layer vectors, we receive the network weight vector $\overline{W}$. This vector is defined in the weight space Ω^q, in which we define a q-dimensional hyper parallelepiped Π^q, $(\Pi \subset \Omega)$ with the constrains (3). The objective is to find a point $\overline{W}^*$ from Π^q, which minimizes the *error* function $E(\overline{W})$,

$$E\left(\overline{W}^*\right) = \min\left\{E\left(\overline{W}\right) | \overline{W} \in \Pi^q\right\} \tag{11}$$

The weight space Π^q is assumed compact and the *cost* function $E(\overline{W})$ continuous in it, which guarantees that its values are limited away from infinite magnitude. Clearly, the network weight vector determines the input-output transfer function of the network as stated in [7].

The proposed algorithm can be summarized as follows:

1. Define the number of elements q (10) of the network weight vector $\overline{W}$ and the weight limit intervals (3), that define Π^q;

2. Give the number of testing points N for the LP_τ low-discrepancy sequence;

3. Using LP_τ sequence technique, calculate a point from Π^q which defines the designed network weight vector $\overline{W}^*$;

4. Propagate the network using formulae (6) and (7);

5. Calculate the *error* function (8);

6. Repeat steps 3-5 and save the better from the two points (if $E(\overline{W}^*) > E(\overline{W}_{new})$, then $\overline{W}^* \Leftarrow \overline{W}_{new}$);

7. Exit if $E(\overline{W}^*) < \varepsilon$, where ε is initially given "sufficiently small" value, or if the number of iterations is greater then N; if not, continue to repeat steps 3-7;

8. If after exiting step 7, condition $E(\overline{W}^*) < \varepsilon$ is still not satisfied, then change the intervals (3) considering the values of the recent best point $\overline{W}^*$; $\overline{W}^* \in \Pi^q$, and if necessary, change the number of testing points N (usually increasing).

If there exists an exact solution of the mapping problem, such as $E(\overline{W}) = 0$ (input patterns can be successfully separated), then this could be the ideal situation. However, more common case is when such a solution does not exist, and then we consider a global minimum of $E(\overline{W}) < 0$ as $E(\overline{W}^*)$. We accept it as the optimal solution of the problem, and the whole process as optimal training of the network. It is also possible that after several executions of step (8), the condition $E(\overline{W}^*) < \varepsilon$ still not to be satisfied. In this case, either the best point $(\overline{W}^*)$ can be taken as the optimal one, or alternatively, it may be necessary to redefine the problem (for example, changing the dimensionality q, respectively changing the number of hidden units of the network, etc.), and repeating the whole procedure again.

4. Computer Simulated Tests and Discussion

In this section, we present network training with the proposed technique on benchmark test problems and compare the obtained results with those of the standard BP. In all examples, activation function (7) is used and considered ANN include biases. For the third problem, ANN with continuous output is also employed. For comparison, a standard BP with a learning rate of 0.1, a momentum of 0.9, and initial weights in the interval (–0.5, 0.5) was performed for all cases.

4.1   Classification of the XOR Problem

Many authors use XOR as a benchmark problem when investigating error surfaces with local minima free conditions [3, 6, 10, 13, 15, and 18]. We also chose this problem and employed appropriate neural network with minimal architecture, consisting of two inputs, two units in the hidden layer and one output. Such network contains 9 connection weights and defines a 9-dimensional ($q=9$) learning problem.

Table 2. Optimal weight vectors for standard BP and LP_τ learning (XOR problem).

j	W^*_{BP}	$W^*_{LP_\tau}$	j	W^*_{BP}	$W^*_{LP_\tau}$
1	2.9467	-5.1365	6	-5.6204	8.9520
2	-6.9569	9.7997	7	-5.8389	-5.2562
3	-6.9556	-7.7755	8	-12.325	9.4496
4	8.3925	-2.0289	9	12.146	9.4316
5	-5.6207	-9.4904			

We carried out the proposed in the previous section learning procedure on three passes, starting with intervals (13) (Fig. 2), with $N=2^{18}$ points from the LP_τ sequence. For every point we calculate the *cost* for each pattern from the batch (P=4) using (8), and choose the worst error as a batch error for that point (12). Then, from all (N) such batch errors, we found the minimal one with (14), and consider $\overline{W}^*$ as the weight global minimum point for the training:

$$F_i = \max\{E_{i,p}(\overline{W}) \mid \overline{W} \in \Pi^q; \ p = 1, ..., 4\}, \tag{12}$$

$$\Pi^q = \{w_j \mid -20 \le w_j \le 20; \ j = 1, 2, ..., q\}, \tag{13}$$

$$E(\overline{W}^*) = \min\{F_i; \ i = 1, 2, ..., N\}. \tag{14}$$

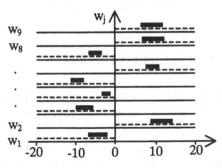

Fig. 2. Weight histograms of narrowing search intervals for XOR problem (—— first pass, - - - - second pass, ▬▬ third pass).

In [6], 50% success (failure) rate of the run simulations with gradient descent are reported to get stuck in LM, where their tunneling method (its convergence is not guaranteed for a multidimensional case) managed to escape local minima. BP training with much higher successful percentage of 91.3% is reported in [15] after 10000 trials, but they consider a GM reached when the summed squared error is less than 2.5% per pattern. In our case, we received 0.0047% error for the BP learning and 0.013% error for the LP_τ learning.

Table 3. Test with noisy input, and output results for BP local minimum (LM), LP_τ global minimum (GM), and Global Descent (GD) minimum for XOR problem.

Pattern	Target	LM BP	GM LP_τ	GD
0.15 0.08	0.0	0.030	0.010	0.030
0.92 0.12	1.0	0.995	0.976	0.964
0.09 0.91	1.0	0.995	0.984	0.963
0.93 0.95	0.0	0.010	0.016	0.031
0.50 0.50	0.0	0.995	0.014	

We trained the network with an additional pattern (0.5, 0.5) and target 0 (so-called XOR5 problem in [8]). Obtained nine weights with the two methods are given in Table 2. BP weights define a LM solution that separates XOR task, but fails to separate the additional pattern of XOR5. It is seen from the last row of Table 3 that the network trained with our method succeeded. In the same time BP is quicker, our method lasted 23 and 5 seconds for the last two passes with $N=2^{14}$ and $N=2^{12}$ points, respectively (Table 4). However, it is worth finding a global minimum even at the expense of more training time. In the last column of Table 3, results obtained by Cetin et al. with their *TRUST* technique, named *Global Descent* (GD) in [6], are given. It is seen that their results are worse than ours are, and should also be noted that they are obtained for the correspondent noisy-free patterns from the first column. Table 4 shows the necessary time when different number of points N is chosen for the training.

Table 4. Necessary time for different number of searching points (XOR problem).

N [x1024]	1	2	4	8	16	32	64	128	256
Time [sec]	1	2	5	11	23	53	119	265	614

4.2   Classification of K-Input Parity Problem

When solving the K-input parity problem, the network must produce a *one* if the input has an odd number of *one* inputs, and a *zero* otherwise. It is considered a good benchmark problem for evaluation of network training methods, since the output is sensitive to every single input change. The XOR is a special case ($K=2$) of the input parity problem. We consider the problem when $K=4$. The network architecture is 4-4-1 (four inputs, four hidden units, one output, and a bias). This architecture contains 25 connection weights and thus defines a 25-D learning problem (q=25). There are P=16 input-target patterns for the training set. We performed the learning in a similar manner with the only difference that instead (12) we used

$$F_i = \min \{ \frac{1}{2} \sum_{p=1}^{P} E_{i,p}^2(\overline{W}) \mid \overline{W} \in \Pi^q; P = 16 \}. \tag{15}$$

Again, we carried out the proposed learning algorithm in several passes, starting with intervals (-15, 15) for all weights, with $N=2^{18}$ points from the LP_τ sequence, and subsequently narrowing the intervals and decreasing the number of points.

Table 5. Optimal weight vector for the LP_τ training (K-input parity problem).

j	$W_{LP_\tau}^*$	j	$W_{LP_\tau}^*$	j	$W_{LP_\tau}^*$	j	$W_{LP_\tau}^*$
1	2.597	8	4.783	15	-6.785	22	2.973
2	-0.196	9	-4.920	16	8.641	23	-9.997
3	-0.644	10	4.958	17	-5.489	24	-11.25
4	1.885	11	3.435	18	-5.194	25	12.581
5	-0.921	12	-6.294	19	5.431		
6	2.612	13	-6.364	20	-5.086		
7	5.040	14	6.690	21	0.462		

The obtained 25 optimal weights with the LP_τ learning are given in Table 5. With these weights, the produced training error (15) is 0.005% and the error for a test with noisy input is 0.021%. The values for the BP are 0.14% and 0.78% correspondingly.

Table 6. Necessary time for different number of points (K-input parity problem).

N [x1024]	1	2	4	8	16	32	64	128
Time [sec]	2	5	12	29	67	146	334	753

The time for BP in the above case was 4 sec. The necessary time for our training, using a different number of testing points is given in Table 6. Comparing the errors given in [6] for this case, ours are considerably smaller (they reported global solution with 0.22% error for noisy-free input). We were not able to compare the times, because the authors do not report such. Our optimal result does not depend on the initial conditions, as [13] reported multiple entrapment of BP in local minima (initial random weights in (–0.5, 0.5)), and relatively low success rate (32%) after 30000 iterations (initial random weights in (–1.5, 1.5)), for the same network architecture.

4.3   Classification of Lenses Problem

We obtained the database for this small, fitting contact lenses benchmark problem from the UCI repository of databases. The task is whether to fit a patient with hard, soft or no contact lenses at all. The data set is composed of 24 instances, and each of them features four attributes. Three of the attributes (spectacle prescription, tear rate, and astigmatic) have binary values, and one (age) is ternary-valued. The data is distributed between three classes as follows: hard lenses – 4 instances (16.7%), soft lenses – 5 (20.8%), and neither – 15 (62.5%). We trained two different networks to recognize this problem. One, producing binary output, with architecture 4-4-3 (one hidden layer with 4 units), with the three output classes coded as (1, 0, 0), (0, 1, 0), and (0, 0, 1), respectively. This architecture contains 35 connection weights and thus defines a 35-dimensional learning problem (q=35). The other network with architecture 4-3-1 (three hidden layer units) produces continuous output with the three classes coded as 0.9 (hard), 0.5 (soft), and 0.1 (neither). This architecture defines a 19-dimensional learning problem (q=19). We combined two sets of data (one for training and one for testing) with 12 instances in each, having in both nearly the same class distribution. We used (15) again for optimal learning, starting with initial intervals (13) for all weights, with $N=2^{18}$ points from the LP_τ sequence, and P=12 patterns.

Table 7. Obtained errors in % for the two trained architectures (Lenses problem).

Size	BP train	BP test	LP_τ train	LP_τ test
4-4-3	0.13%	17.5%	0.47%	0.92%
4-3-1	0.35%	3.10%	0.40%	0.42%

Using the proposed algorithm, we received optimal solution with errors (15), given in Table 7. As it can be seen from Table 7, the obtained errors from the BP are smaller for the training set, but poorer for the testing set where it failed to separate three of the patterns. The time for BP in that case was 3 and 2 seconds, respectively. The necessary time for our training, using different number of testing points N is given in Table 8.

Table 8. Necessary training time in seconds for the two architectures (Lenses problem).

N [x1024]	1	2	4	8	16	32	64	128
Time (4-4-3)	4	7	17	41	94	215	488	1101
Time (4-3-1)	2	4	9	23	51	114	262	589

The computational time depends on the number of testing points, and the number of patterns (instances). The number of testing points depends on the size of parameter intervals (parameter space), and on the error threshold ε. Of course, the iterative narrowing of intervals could lead to decreasing the number of searching points, whether decreasing the value of the error threshold ε would increase their number, respectively increasing the search time. Not always all the searching points are computed. If the minimum error (step 7) is reached, the training process stops.

5 Conclusion

The introduced method for modified feed-forward optimal learning is presented with results on standard benchmark problems and proved as an efficient and reasonably simple technique for a small size ANN. It does not depend on the initial conditions and compared to the standard BP, it has the advantage to avoid local minima and to produce optimal learning. However, it is more time consuming, especially in the initial passes of the proposed procedure. With the increase of dimensionality, the number of testing points should be increased which, in turn, increases the computational load. Future directions for this work will concentrate on this problem. One of the advantages of our method is that it does not make assumptions for the transfer functions to have continuous and differentiable first and second derivatives, and solves the original learning problem - finding a global minimum of the *error* function, not a system of derivative equations.

References

1. Baldi, P., Hornik, K.: Learning in Linear Neural Networks: a Survey, IEEE Trans. Neural Networks **6** (1995) 837-858
2. Bianchini, M., Gori, M.: Optimal Learning in Artificial Neural Networks: A Review of Theoretical Results. Neurocomputing **13** (1996) 313-346
3. Blum, E.K.: Approximation of Boolean Functions by Sigmoidal Networks: Part I: XOR and Other Two-variable Functions. Neural Computation **1** (1989) 532-540
4. Bratley, P., Fox, B., Niederreiter, H.: Implementation and Tests of Low-discrepancy Sequences. ACM Trans. on Modeling and Computer Simulation **2** (1992) 195-213
5. Cetin, B., Barhen, J., Burdick, J.: Terminal Repeller Unconstrained Subenergy Tunneling (TRUST) for Fast Global Optimization. J. Opt. Theory and Appl. **77** (1993) 97-126
6. Cetin, B., Burdick, J., Barhen, J.: Global Descent Replaces Gradient Descent to Avoid Local Minima Problem in Learning with Artificial Neural Networks. In: Proc. of the IEEE Conf. on Neural Networks, Vol. 2. (1993) 836-842
7. Chen, A.M., Lu, H., Nielsen, R.H.: On the Geometry of Feedforward Neural Network Error Surfaces. Neural Computation **5** (1993) 910-927
8. Gori, M., Tesi A.: On the Problem of Local Minima in Backpropagation. IEEE Trans. on Pattern Analysis and Machine Intelligence **14** (1992) 76-85
9. Gustafson, K.: Internal Sigmoid Dynamics in Feedforward Neural Networks. Connection Science **10** (1998) 43-73
10. Hamey, L.G.: XOR Has no Local Minima: A Case Study in Neural Network Error Surface Analysis. Neural Networks **11** (1998) 669-681
11. Hush, D.R., Horne, B., Salas, J.: Error Surfaces for Multilayer Perceptrons. IEEE Trans. Systems, Man, and Cybernetics **22** (1992) 1152-1161
12. Kolen, J.F., Pollack, J.B.: Backpropagation is Sensitive to Initial Conditions. Complex Systems **4** (1990) 269-280
13. Lisboa, P.G., Perantonis, S.J.: Complete Solution of the Local Minima in the XOR Problem. Network **2** (1991) 119-124

14. Rumelhart, D.E., Hinton, G.E., Williams, R.J.: Learning Internal Representation by Error Propagation. In: Parallel Distr. Proc., Vol. 1. Cambridge, MA: MIT Press (1986) 318-362

15. Smagt, P.: Minimization Methods for Training Feedforward Neural Networks. Neural Networks 7 (1994) 1-11

16. Sobol', I.M., Statnikov, P.B.: Choosing Optimal Parameters in Multicriteria Problems. Nauka, Moscow (1981)

17. Sontag, E.D., Sussmann, H. J.: Back Propagation Separates Where Perceptrons Do. Neural Networks 4 (1991) 243-249

18. Sprinkhuizen-Kuyper, I.G., Boers, E.J.: The Error Surface of the Simplest XOR Network Has Only Global Minima. Neural Computation 8 (1996) 1301-1320

19. Yu, X.H., Chen, G.A.: On the Local Minima Free Condition of Backpropagation Learning. IEEE Trans. Neural Networks 6 (1995) 1300-1303

An Investigation into the Effect of Ensemble Size and Voting Threshold on the Accuracy of Neural Network Ensembles

Robert Cox, David Clark, and Alice Richardson

Division of Management and Technology,
University of Canberra,
ACT, 2601, Australia
mithril@ozemail.com.au,
{davidc,alicer}@ise.canberra.edu.au

Abstract. If voting is used by an ensemble to classify data, some data points may not be classified, but a higher proportion of those which are classified are classified correctly. This trade off is affected by ensemble size and voting threshold. This paper investigates the effect of ensemble size on the proportions of decisions made and correct decisions. It does this for majority voting and consensus voting on ensembles of neural network classifiers constructed using bagging. It also models the relationships in order to estimate the asymptotic values as the ensemble size increases.

1   Introduction

Using the results of several classifiers is a technique which has been shown to give more accurate classification than a single classifier [1], [2], [3]. The resulting classifier is known as an ensemble.

The most popular methods of constructing ensembles are *bagging* [4] and *boosting* [5]. Both methods generate multiple classifiers by resampling the training data. Bagging (bootstrapping aggregates) trains the component classifiers using independent samples drawn with replacement from the training data. Boosting creates a succession of classifiers by giving greater weight to data points misclassified by previous classifiers.

In an ensemble constructed by bagging, the ensemble may classify a data point by *averaging* or *voting*. When averaging is used, the predictions of the component classifiers are averaged to make the ensemble classification. With voting, each component classifier votes for a category and the ensemble category is the category with the most votes. These methods may be modified by weighting the classifiers according to their individual accuracy.

The most popular method for ensemble classification is unweighted averaging [4], [6], typically with the outputs of each component classifier being normalized.

N. Foo (Ed.): AI'99, LNAI 1747, pp. 268-277, 1999.

Part of the reason that voting is not as popular is that it does not use all of the information available. It does not distinguish between a weak and a strong preference by the component classifier. Voting, however, does give the opportunity not to make decisions where there is insufficient agreement. This can increase the accuracy of classification where a decision has been made. There is thus a trade off between the proportion of data points for which a decision is made and the proportion of those data points which are correctly classified. As the threshold of agreement is raised, fewer data points are classified, but a higher proportion of those are classified correctly. Similarly, as the number of classifiers in the ensemble is increased, fewer data points may be classified, but again a higher proportion of those are classified correctly.

1.1 The Effect of Misclassification

For some classification problems, every data point must be classified. In that case, the best classifier is the classifier with the highest proportion of correct classifications. For other problems, it is more important to reduce the number of misclassifications by not making decisions for some data points in order to increase the proportion correct when a decision is made.

An example is in recognizing postcodes. If an error is made and the article is sent to the wrong area, recovery is expensive. It is better to make fewer decisions and rely on manual sorting for the remaining articles. When recognizing postcodes, any classification error is expensive. In other problems, a classification error in one category may be more serious than in another. For example, Smith et al [7] report on a neural network which predicts post-operative bleeding. The aim of their study was to enable medical staff to start treatment earlier and to reduce the amount of drugs administered. In this case the effect of incorrectly predicting that a patient is not at risk of post-operative bleeding is more serious than of incorrectly predicting that a patient is at risk. In the latter case, the patient may be given unnecessary treatment. In the former case, an untreated patient may die.

This study does not differentiate between false positives and false negatives when a binary classification is made.

1.2 The Aim of this Study

The aim of this study is to investigate the effect of ensemble size and voting threshold on the proportion of decisions made and the classification accuracy of those decisions. The voting thresholds considered are *consensus* (all classifiers must agree) and *majority* voting (over half of the classifiers must agree). We use feedforward neural networks trained by backpropagation as our component classifiers and bagging as our method of constructing ensembles.

2 Methodology

Each data set is divided into three parts, a training set, a classifiers testing set and an ensemble testing set. Each classifier is trained on a set drawn with replacement from the training set and of the same size as the training set. The classifiers testing set is used to test each classifier. The ensemble testing set is used to determine the classification accuracy of the ensemble.

Majority voting is reported on for ensembles with an odd number of classifiers, We choose odd ensemble size because an even size gives the possibility of half of the votes being given for one category and half for another. The ensemble makes a decision if $(n+1)/2$ component classifiers agree. For consensus voting, all classifiers must agree. The ensemble sizes tested are from 3 to either 39 or 49 depending on the data set. The details for each data set are given in Figure 1.

Figure 1. Sizes of data sets and ensembles

Data set	size of training set	size of classi- fier testing set	size of ensem- ble testing set	largest ensemble
Abalone	2177	1000	1000	49
Cancer	483	100	100	49
Card	350	170	170	39
Diabetes	388	190	190	39
Heart	460	230	230	39
Weedseed	198	100	100	39

3   Data Sets

We have used the Abalone, Cancer, Card, Diabetes, Heart and Weedseed data sets in our study.

In the Abalone data set [8], [9], abalone shellfish are classified into one of three aged-related groups according to eight measurements made on abalone collected by divers in a survey. The set contains 4177 samples. The proportion of data which is correctly classified by a single backpropagation classifier is moderate (64%).

In the Cancer data set [9], [10] nine measurements are used to classify tumors as benign or malignant. There are 683 samples. The proportion of data which is correctly classified by a single backpropagation classifier is high (94%).

In the Card data set [9], 51 measurements are used to determine whether approval should be given of issuing a credit card to a customer. The proportion of data which is correctly classified by a single backpropagation classifier is high (86%).

In the Diabetes data set [9], 8 measurements are used to predict whether a Pima indian individual is diabetes positive. The proportion of data which is correctly classified by a single backpropagation classifier is high (78%).

In the Heart data set [9], 35 measurements are used to determine whether one or more of four major vessels is reduced in diameter by 50% or more. The proportion of data which is correctly classified by a single backpropagation classifier is high (80%).

In the Weedseed data set [11], weed seeds are classified into one of ten types, based on seven measurements of dimensions of the seeds. The data consists of measurements of 398 different seeds, giving 39 or 40 examples of each seed type. The proportion of data which is correctly classified by a single backpropagation classifier is only moderate (63%).

4   Results

We will first consider the heart data. Figure 2 shows the proportion of times that a decision was made using consensus voting for different ensemble sizes, along with the proportion of those decisions that were correct. Thus the solid line gives the probability of an ensemble of a given size making a decision, and the dashed line gives the conditional probability of an ensemble of a given size making a correct decision, given that a decision was made. Figure 3 shows the same information for majority voting on the heart data.

Figure 2. Results of consensus voting on the heart data.

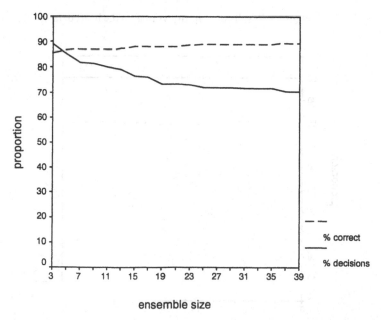

As expected, under consensus voting, the probability of making a decision decreases slowly as the ensemble size increases. But given that a decision has been made, the probability that it is the right decision increases as the ensemble size increases. This implies that although decisions will be made less often with large ensembles, the decisions made are more likely to be right.

In order to estimate the asymptotic value of the proportions of decisions made and correct decisions made as n increases, non-linear functions of the form $y = a + bc^n$ were fitted to the data shown in Figure 2. The variable y is the percentage of decisions made and the percentage of correct decisions made; n is the ensemble size; and a, b and c are parameters requiring estimation . The statistical package SPSS was used to carry out the estimation, and the following functions were obtained.

Percentage of decisions made = $69.82 + 24.16(0.92)^n$
Percentage of correct decisions made = $90.04 - 4.91(0.95)^n$

The first function suggests that as the ensemble size increases, the percentage of decisions made follows a power law that starts at about 90% for an ensemble of size 1 and reaches an asymptote at about 70%. The second function suggests that as the ensemble size increases, the percentage of correct decisions made follows a power law that starts at about 85% for an ensemble of size 1 and reaches an asymptote at about 90%. These functions together could be used to predict both the percentage of decisions made and the percentage of correct decisions before embarking on construction of a neural network, thus allowing researchers to consider where effort is best spent in order to achieve aims.

Figure 3. Results of majority voting on the heart data.

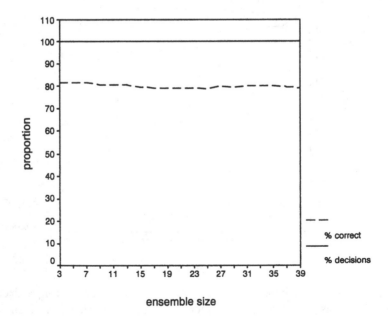

Under majority voting, the pattern is slightly different. The probability of making a decision is 1. Then given that a decision was made, the conditional probability that the decision is correct decreases slightly as the ensemble size increases. No modeling of proportions was therefore carried out for majority voting because the relationship between ensemble size and proportion of decisions or correct decisions made was much more predictable, with no power law required.

This pattern of decision making is similar for the abalone data, the card data and the diabetes data. The cancer data is similar as well except that under consensus voting the probability of making a correct decision is 1 for all ensemble sizes. This can be regarded as the ideal situation that the other four data sets aim to achieve but do not quite do so.

The percentages of correct decisions when a decision is made using majority voting are given in Figure 4. The single classifier results are included for comparison. The results show very little movement as the ensemble size is increased except in the case of weedseed data. The percentage of decisions made is not shown as it is close to 100% for all ensemble sizes for all data sets except weedseed where it reduces from 96% for ensemble size of 3 to 92% for ensemble size of 39.

Figure 4. Percentage correct vs ensemble size, majority voting

Data set	1	3	9	39
Abalone	64.1	63.8	63.6	63.7
Cancer	94.3	96.0	96.0	95.0
Card	86.4	86.5	87.0	86.5
Diabetes	78.5	78.4	78.4	80.0
Heart	80.4	81.7	80.4	79.1
Weedseed	63.2	67.7	71.7	76.1

The percentages of correct decisions when a decision is made using consensus voting are given in Figure 5. The percentage of decisions made is also shown. They demonstrate the trade off expected between increasing the percentage of correct decisions at the expense of fewer decisions being made as the ensemble size increases. In most data sets the trade off is reasonable. The cost of improved accuracy is a moderate reduction in the proportion of decisions made. Again weedseed is atypical.

Figure 5. Percentage correct and decisions made vs ensemble size, consensus voting

Data set	1	3	9	39
Abalone	64.1	68.3	69.0	73.3
		86.0	78.2	65.9
Cancer	94.3	100.0	100.0	100.0
		93.0	88.0	80.0
Card	86.4	88.6	90.0	92.1
		92.9	88.2	81.8
Diabetes	78.5	83.3	84.7	87.0
		88.4	79.0	69.0
Heart	80.4	85.4	87.2	89.5
		89.1	81.3	70.4
Weedseed	63.2	71.5	79.3	90.0
		52.0	29.0	10.0

As indicated in Figures 4 and 5, the weedseed data is a severe test for the ensemble, and the results reflect the difficult in carrying out the classification. Figure 6 shows the results under consensus voting, and Figure 7 shows the results under majority voting. Here we see that under consensus voting, the probability of making a decision decreases not just slowly, but sharply, as the ensemble size increases. Indeed by the time the ensemble contains about 30 classifiers, the probability of making a consensus decision has sunk to about 10%. On the other hand the conditional probability of making a correct decision takes similar values to those observed in the other data set. This probability starts at about 70% and increases slowly as the ensemble size increases.

When non-linear functions of the form $y = a + bc^n$ were fitted to the data shown in Figure 6, the following estimates were obtained.

Percentage of decisions = $9.64 + 56.15(0.89)^n$
Percentage of correct decisions = $92.01 - 27.74(0.899)^n$

The first function suggests that as the ensemble size increases, the percentage of decisions made follows a power law that starts at about 60% for an ensemble of size 1 and reaches an asymptote at about 10%. The second function suggests that as the ensemble size increases, the percentage of correct decisions made follows a power law that starts at about 67% for an ensemble of size 1 and reaches an asymptote at about 92%. As before, these models could be used for prediction of success rates in a neural network and decision-making about the number of classifiers required to achieve stated aims.

Figure 6. Results of consensus voting on the weedseed data.

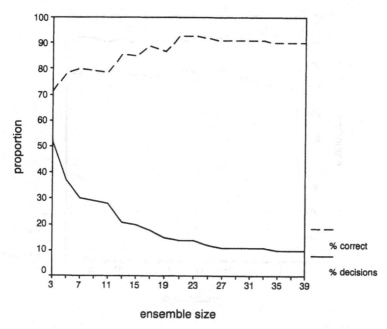

ensemble size

Under majority voting the effects are similar, but less dramatic. The proportion of decisions made falls from 96% with an ensemble of size 3 to 92% for an ensemble of size 39. At the same time the percentage of correct decisions made increases form 63% to 76%. Weedseed thus shows a more improvement in classification accuracy than the other data sets when majority voting is used. This is in agreement with the findings of Maclin and Opitz [12] who report that the gains in performance of bagging over a single classifier is greater on data sets where there more than two categories. (It should be noted that they use averaging rather than voting and they also report that in these data sets boosting is more effective than bagging.)

It appears therefore that the weedseed data follows a pattern that is atypical. We speculate that the large number of categories in the weedseed data (10 compared to 2 or 3 in the other data sets) contributes to the difficulty of decision making both by consensus and majority voting. Other factors which may contribute to fewer decisions being made are that weedseed is a relatively noisy data and there are only about 20 points in each category in the training set. For weedseed, the standard deviation of the individual classifiers was 4%, compared to 1% for each of the other data sets.

Figure 7. Results of majority voting on the weedseed data.

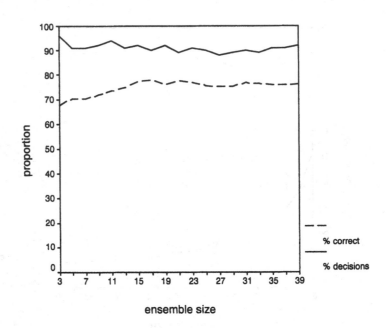

5   Conclusion

The above results and discussion are consistent with the following conclusions.

1. The proportion of correct decisions made can be significantly improved by using consensus voting.
2. For most data sets the penalty in the reduction in the proportion of decisions made is moderate.
3. In the weedseed data under consensus voting the proportion of decisions made drops so sharply that the technique is not useful. This may be due to the large number of categories, noisy data and / or relatively few points in the data set.
4. Majority voting is not as effective as consensus voting in increasing the proportion of correct decisions made except in the case of the weedseed data. This may also be true in other data sets which share weedseed's characteristics of being noisy, small and multi-categoried.

References

1. Brieman, L.: Bagging predictors. Machine Learning 24(2) (1996) 123-140
2. Clemen, R.: Combining forecasts: A review and annotated bibliography. Journal of forecasting 5 (1989) 559-583
3. Wolpert, D.: Stacked generalization. Neural Networks 5 (1992) 241-259
4. Brieman, L.: Stacked regressions. Machine Learning 24(1) (1996) 49-64
5. Freund, Y. and Schapire, R.: Experiments with a new boosting algorithm. Proceedings of the Thirteenth International Conference on Machine Learning (1996) Morag Kaufmann 148-156
6. Alpaydin, E.: Multiple networks for function learning. Proceedings of the 1993 IEEE International conference on Neural Networks, I (1993) 27-32
7. Smith, I., Lister, R., May, R.: A Multi-Layer Perceptron for Predicting Post-Operative Bleeding, and Issues in Representing Analog Input-Output Values. Proceedings of the Fifth Australian Conference on Neural Networks, (1994) 234-237
8. Nash, W. J., Sellers, T. L., Talbot, S. R., Cawthorn, A. J. Ford, W. B., "The Population Biology of Abalone (*Haliotis* species) in Tasmania. I. Blacklip Abalone (*H. rubra*) from the North Coast and Islands of the Bass Strait, SFD, Tasmania. Technical Report # 48 (1994)
9. UCI machine learning repository at http://www.ics.uci.edu/~mlearn/MLRepository.html
10. Mangasarian, W. L., Wolberg, W. H. Cancer diagnosis via linear programming. SIAM News, 23 5 (Sept. 1990) 1 & 18
11. Weedseed data. Obtained from the Scottish Crop Research Centre, in private communication, Collier, P.A., Dept. of Computer Science, Univ. of Tasmania.
12. Maclin, R., Opitz, D.: An Empirical Evaluation of Bagging and Boosting. Proceedings of the Fourteenth National Conference on Artificial Intelligence (1997)

Neurofuzzy Learning of Mobile Robot Behaviours

Richard Willgoss and Javaid Iqbal

School of Mechanical & Manufacturing Engineering,
The University of New South Wales, Sydney 2052, Australia.
{r.willgoss, j.iqbal} @unsw.edu.au

Abstract. The era of mobile robotics for use in service and field applications is gaining momentum. The need for adaptability becomes self evident in allowing robots to evolve better behaviors to meet overall task criteria. We report the use of neuro-fuzzy learning for teaching mobile robot behaviors, selecting exemplar cases from a potential continuum of behaviors. Proximate active sensing was successfully achieved with infrared in contrast to the usual ultrasonics and viewed the front area of robot movement. The well-known ANFIS architecture has been modified compressing layers to a necessary minimum with weight normalization achieved by using a sigmoidal function. Trapezoidal basis functions (*B splines of order 2*) with a partition of 1 were used to speed up computation. Reference to previous reinforcement learning results was made in terms of speed of learning and quality of behavior. Even with the limited input information, appropriate learning invariably took place in a reliable manner.

1   Introduction

There are many ways in which a learning phase for machine intelligence can now be arranged with fuzzy, neural, genetic and reinforcement algorithms [1],[2],[3] including combinations like neuro-fuzzy systems [4],[5]. The test bed of mobile robots is a suitable environment to evaluate the worth of each paradigm since direct comparisons of performance for exemplar problems can be made. It is also recognized that mobile robotics is the fastest growing area of robotic innovation at present leading to robots useable in service and field applications from hospital gofors [6], to organizing themselves in a factory situation [7]. A large body of theoretical work is now slowly being matched by experimental verification as a range of versatile platforms become available such as Nomad, Kepera, Rug Warrior, Pioneer and Helpmate, details of which are accessible on the web.

The theory of machine learning reaches back some 50 years. Practical uses have gained prominence in the last 10 years. The concept of defining a suite of behaviors has received attention recently [8],[9],[10],[11],[12]. Kelly & Keating [13], have investigated the reinforcement learning algorithm for a fleet of mobile robots and shared learning over radio links using ultrasonic sensing of proximity. Simulation [14][15] has helped to evaluate a range of interaction scenarios.

Song & Sheen [16], have obtained neuro-fuzzy obstacle avoidance in the context of indoor navigation and concluded that smooth operation was possible. They used a ring of 16 ultrasonic sensors providing very rich information upon which to work in a

N. Foo (Ed.): AI'99, LNAI 1747, pp. 278–290, 1999.

cycle time of 250ms. Tsoukalas et al [17], devised neuro-fuzzy motion planners for mobile robots using an idealised model called MITOS. Their model predicts that smooth motion is possible even for rudimentary sensor input. Tschichold-Gurman [18], attempted to combine the best of processing strategies such as neural networks, fuzzy logic and classical control theory to achieve mobile robot navigation. A basic feedforward neural network has a usual fuzzy input attached to it. A set of IF-THEN rules are used to shape the net. It is claimed the learning time is much reduced over other classifiers. Aycard et al [19], used a fuzzy controller for reactive navigation of a mobile robot in an unknown environment. A two layer system corresponded to local and global behaviors. Experiments with a NOMAD robot showed navigation and avoidance could be simultaneously achieved but there was no learning. Gaussier et al [20], have taken an interesting approach in employing a neural net structure to learn by imitation. The perception-action (PerAc) architecture is very similar to a neuro-fuzzy one where the basis functions have been tailored to give temporal and spacial discrimination. Vision analysis formed the basis of sensor input. Rylatt et al [21], recently surveyed the field as connectionist research. They emphasize the importance of rich environments if learning is to take place and conclude, perhaps pessimistically, that connectionist architectures may never provide the key to generating cognitive capacities similar to the human brain. On the other hand, they feel there is some hope in hand-crafting architectures such as subsumption. Kim & Trivedi [22], very recently reported similar work to that presented here. In their case, the learning was supervised via the back propagation algorithm and the extent of the fuzzy rule set was predetermined. This essentially makes the learning significantly dependant on the teacher for sensible choice of rules.

We present findings on the determination of learning in a continuum of potential behaviors. The neuro-fuzzy calculations are similar to the ANFIS model [2], but incorporate least mean squares (LMS) analysis without the need to invoke back propagation or be selective on rule choice. The work reported here is part of an investigation into devising parametric ways to evaluate learning paradigms. To that end, a consistent mobile robot platform was created that had a range of sensing and movement capabilities backed by computation. The ideal platform should consist of life-size devices but the cost when dealing with a fleet of five upwards is high. A similar result can be obtained at a lower level of expenditure giving good relative quantitative results.

Of general interest has been learning rates and how they are affected by the richness of the environment, the need for normalising to keep function surfaces within bounds, annealing to avoid local minimums, the overall specification of desired behavior and platform programming environment. Present results indicate that learning for behaviors such as avoidance can be achieved in periods of a few minutes with rudimentary sensors at the 68HC11 computing power level chosen to work at. A scaling to the computational speed of a target system is easily achieved. Infra red is used as the sensing medium relying on strength of return signals from robot on-board emitters to be a measure of the closeness to objects around the robot. Whilst infrared is a noisy medium and can be subject to interference from a wide range of extraneous sources such as daylight, hot bodies and artificial lighting, it makes for a realistic platform in testing learning algorithms.

2   Platform

As mentioned, the platform (Rug Warrior Pro) was chosen to keep costs within reasonable limits. The infrared sensors of the Rug Warrior were modified to sense either side of and directly in the forward aspect with good directionality to the return signals to the mobile robot. The sensors can be clearly seen in Fig. 1. Infrared filters were also incorporated to reduce the interference from daylight and nightlight spectrums. Two different techniques were used. Firstly, pulsed emission from a standard infrared emitter/photodiode pair was used to increase noise immunity. Secondly, a proprietary small infrared range finder (SHARP GP2D02) operating in the range 70mm to 800mm was used instead to check on how the accuracy of distance measurement affected learning quality. The operating environment enabled programs to be written subsumptively. Radio communication transceivers were available to exchange learning data when working in a multi-robot scenario.

Fig. 1. The Rug Warrior Pro platform is available in kit form already incorporating infrared sensing as well as the capability of using light and sound. The left image shows the simple sensing and the right image shows mounting of the proprietary infrared range finder.

3   Theory

The neuro-fuzzy algorithm was based on modifying the ANFIS model of learning incorporating the standard LMS analysis for a system of linear equations containing errors [2]. A system of linearly seperable equations related to some form of MISO causal system can be represented by

$$A(u).c = y. \tag{1}$$

where $A(u)$ is the matrix of known functions f on u, the vector of inputs, c is the vector of the regression coefficients, and y is the vector of outputs.

Hence a_{ij} equates to $f_i(u_j)$ in a matrix of i columns and j rows. For a MIMO system, c and y become matrices. In equation (1), for a neuro-fuzzy system, the column components of A are the membership function values of the full set of inputs whilst the rows are repetitions of any experiment or exemplar data that is used to evaluate c. c now becomes synonymous with the weights in a neural net leading to the output nodes. In practice, the system has noise present and (1) has to be rewritten to give

$$A(u).c + e = y. \tag{2}$$

where e is an error vector.

It is now not possible to find an exact solution to (1) but we can obtain the best estimate

$$E(c) = \Sigma(y_i - a_i^T c)^2 = (y - A.c)^T(y - A.c). \tag{3}$$

It can further be shown that, instead of attempting to obtain the direct inverse of A by keeping the dimensions of A square, it is better to allow for a variable number of input/output pairs and solve for the pseudo-inverse, such that

$$\hat{c} = (A^T.A)^{-1}A^Ty. \tag{4}$$

where $\hat{c}$ is a least mean squares estimator and A^{-1} is replaced by $(A^T.A)^{-1}A^T$ to make $A^T.A$ square.

If the computations of the pseudo-inverse are made as shown above to determine $\hat{c}$, the scalar values within $\hat{c}$ can be essentially unbounded. Therefore, as the stages for computing the pseudo-inverse are completed, a sigmoidal function is applied to the $(A^T.A)^{-1}$ term to normalize before the final multiplication. It then remains to apply a scaling function to adjust weight values to suit the range of motor velocities that were used to obtain the exemplar data in the first place.

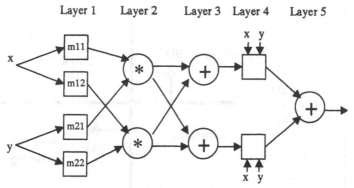

Fig. 2. The Generalised ANFIS Architecture. In general, Layer 1 refers to fuzzification, Layer 2 enacts the AND or min function, Layer 3 normalises, Layer 4 gives options for implementing a Sugeno, Tsakamoto or like consequent result for an output and Layer 5 is the usual neural summation term.

In Fig. 2, it is possible to compress the architecture into three layers retaining Layer 1 that fuzzifies, omitting Layer 2, normalising in Layer 3, omitting Layer 4 and retaining a general neural summation in Layer 5. In this way, the fuzzification is virtually transparent to the analysis as long as the membership functions give a partition of unity on each input. In a sense, they act as linear separators of the magnitude of each input into the member function categories.

The question then arises as to what constitutes input and output for the mobile robots. In our experiments, state space is quantised (see Fig. 3) so that movement is divided into eight quadrant parts, the stand still movement being excluded because it always generates a zero differential. Thus output y corresponds to two-off angular velocities for each of two motors making y dimensions 2*n i.e. a matrix, where n is the number of results taken per calculation. Input comes from two sensors each of which has three membership functions to fuzzify into the nil, far and near categories. Thus two inputs become six categories in the A matrix giving it dimensions 6*n.

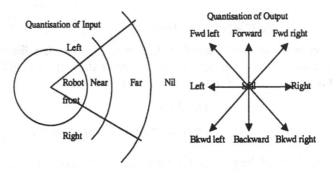

Fig. 3. The Robot Quantisation of State Space. The potential behavior of the robot was quantized for the benefit of allocating membership functions to input values and output motor movement.

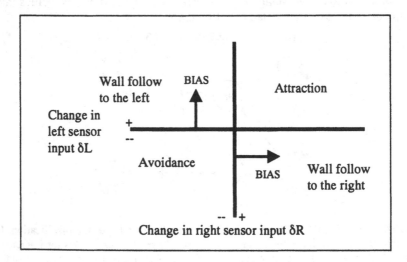

Fig. 4. A set of behaviors is really a continuum depending on sensor input interpretation.

The avoidance behavior is one among a suite of behaviors derived from the definition of how the strength of return signals from sensors should correlate to the motion control. If attraction is required, then the detected relationship is used unmodified. If avoidance is required, then the relationship is inverted. It is also possible to bias the relationship in such a way that a continuum of behaviors can be learnt. Fig. 4 illustrates the fundamental modes to be expected.

There still remains the overall interpretation of sensor input. It transpires that it is possible to detect the proximity of obstacles or objects by noticing that the function determining their distance away is close to an exponential decay. Theoretically, an inverse square law may prevail but is practically dependent on target size as a function of distance from the robot. A test was made of sensor signal strength as a function of distance to see how close the approximation desired was. Fig. 5 shows the relationship obtained for a constant size target being offered normal to the propogation direction of the infrared signals.

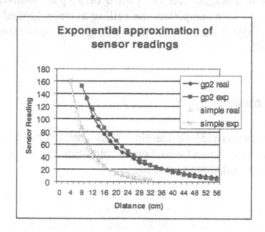

Fig. 5. The sensor functions differentiate to themselves with a scaling factor added. Simple refers to using an emitter/sensor photodiode pair. GP2 refers to a proprietary infrared range finder. This is useful in that it is now possible to interrogate the environment by determining the differential of sensor input and treat it as distance information via scaling.

The approximation of the sensor function to a decaying exponential is remarkably close. A look-up table is normally needed to obtain real distance and is based on a stereotyped target held normal to the robot.

4   Experiments

Avoidance is a part of a spectrum of generic behaviors depending upon the interpretation of what sensor inputs mean. Attraction is the converse and wall following is a band pass version of them both. Hence avoidance has been used here to demonstrate learning rates for comparison purposes. The environment also plays a key role in affecting learning rates. Exposure to both rich and sparse environments has shown an obvious effect on learning convergence rates such that the richer the environment, the faster the learning.

The mobile robots were programmed so that calculation of the LMS estimator, ĉ, containing the desired weights for driving the motors, was repeated over the same repertoire of movements covering all possible ways the robot could move. This amounted to using a block of 24 separate movements, repeating each of the eight possible moves thrice. On this basis, it was possible to watch the robot move around sensing proximate objects and then for the experimenter to rearrange the objects from time to time as the actions were repeated. An action consisted of moving motors set distances in combination to achieve small changes in both direction and position. Sensor input was measured before and after movement, the difference, as explained in section 3, being used as the scaled distance and location of the object from the robot.

Bearing in mind the potential noisiness of the system sensors, a rolling average routine was then applied to the blocks of 24 results as they were obtained. Hence it was possible to see how stable the weight values were between blocks of data and to note any longer term changes. Sets of upward of 30 pseudo-inverse calculations on each block of 24 data were completed, the rolling average applied and the changes to weights observed. Robots were then able to change to a non-learning mode and their behavior to be fixed.

5   Reinforcement Results

Some previous results [23] on learning with reinforcement using a modified Q-learning algorithm, have been obtained on the platform in use here. Here, the standard pulsed emitter/sensor technique was used.

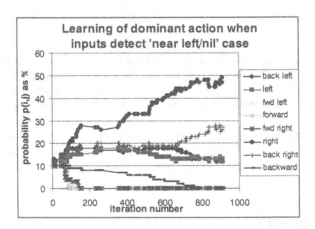

Fig. 6. Reinforcement learning times on the target mobile robot showing retention of some multi-mode behavior.

For the purposes of comparison, Fig. 6 shows the resolution to a near-dominant choice of action when detecting an obstacle in the near left/nil position, nil meaning that on the right sensor, essentially very little incremental change in the return signal was detected. The learning has been terminated at around 900 iterations and shows clearly the iteration points when each reinforcement took place. Actions 'right' 'back right', 'left' and 'back left' are all still retained as significant with a tendency for 'right' to become the dominant result given enough time. The roulette wheel method of choosing the next action clearly shows there is scope for non-optimum actions to be tested long after a more successful action has developed a high probability of choice.

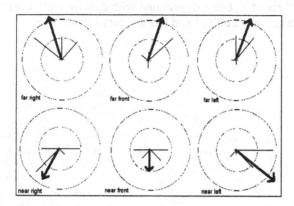

Fig. 7. Net vectoral movement of the mobile robot after reinforcement learning is complete. The legends *near right etc.* refer to the categorization of sensor input.

Fig. 7 shows all the reinforcement learning results, except for the input duple (nil/nil), expressed as net vectoral movement based on the learning that had taken place after 900 iterations, equivalent to approximately 7 minutes of running time, an update rate of 2Hz. Much of this time is devoted to actually moving the robot in order to get a difference input. Hence the speed of learning is not computationally bound. The results indicate the robot would move in a sensible direction to avoid obstacles detected all around the forward-looking aspect. It should also be noted that the resultant avoidance behavior automatically obtains to movement forward if no obstacle is in the way.

6 Neurofuzzy Results

As outlined in Section 4, the experimental procedure in a neuro-fuzzy system used the LMS method for obtaining learned weights. Energizing motor movement to obtain a particular behavior relies on the accumulation of at least one block of 24 exemplar data before a result is possible. This is in contradistinction to the incremental method used in Q-learning reinforcement where improvement is seen to be gradual and evolves at every interrogation of the environment.

Fig. 8 shows a series of independent results. Calculations using the pseudo-inverse formula, equation (4), revealed that some results were sensitive to rounding errors in the evaluation of the inverse $(A^T.A)^{-1}$ obtained by a standard Gauss-Jordon elimination method. It can be seen that the prediction of weights is variable across all results, sometimes with good reproducibility. Fig. 9 shows the effect of incorporating past results to improve the estimate of the weights with a running average.

The equation for the running average is

$$\hat{c}_k = \gamma \hat{c}_k + (1-\gamma)\hat{c}_{k-1} \tag{5}$$

where $\hat{c}_k$ is the kth result, $\hat{c}_1$ being determined with $\hat{c}_0$ identically 0 and γ set to 1, γ is normally in the range of 0.1 to 0.25 and k is the iteration number.

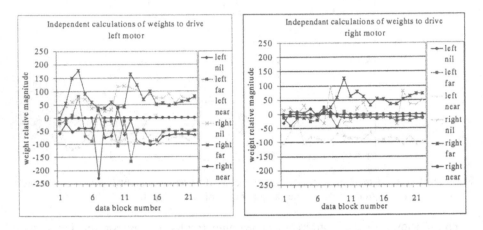

Fig. 8. Neuro-fuzzy learning of *left motor* and *right motor* weights with the proprietary infrared range finder. There was a small improvement in the quality of results when using the range finders instead of the standard sensors. No running average has been applied, therefore each result is independent of all others.

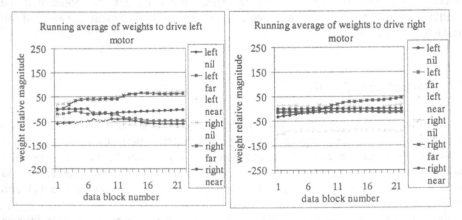

Fig. 9. The same results as in Fig. 8 but with a *running average* applied obeying the relationship as in equation (5) where γ is 0.1.

In order to see the significance of the results in Fig. 8 and Fig. 9, a visualization of behavior is shown in Fig. 10. Each horizontal bar has two arrows attached to either end that represent motor speeds. The bar/arrow combinations have been placed at various places where an obstacle is detected. Any combination of obstacles can lead to a superposed result for the motor speeds. The general fields of view of each sensor are qualitatively marked in along with the ranges where the fuzzy membership functions near/far/nil cross over. An omission of an arrowhead means that the speed was virtually zero.

The behavior of the mobile robot using the learned results lead to very little movement if the obstacle was far away in the nil/nil range. As the obstacle comes nearer, the mobile robot will back away from it in a balanced manner. This is in contradistinction to reinforcement learning where learning gives forward movement if no obstacles are detected. The time to complete the movements and calculations of weights from one block of data to the next was approximately 20 seconds. Given the inclusion of the benefit of the running average over ten iterations, the time to learn was estimated to be just over 3 minutes. It should be noted that environment interrogation via mechanical movement dominates the learning time once again since the final calculation of the weights involving a Gauss-Jordon inverse takes less than 4% of the single iteration time.

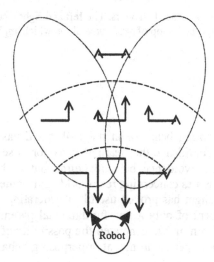

Fig. 10. A representation of the learned neurofuzzy behavior by reference to the magnitude of motor speed at various places where the obstacle is detected.

Fig. 11 displays a set of three neurofuzzy learning outcomes where a forward bias has been introduced to either motor control for the left and right results. The nature of the results shifted such that the behaviors *avoidance* and *seek right/left* were superposed. For the left forward motor bias, the change from zero bias appears more modest than for the right. Both biased results show less tendency to avoid than in the zero bias condition (center result) for objects that are near front. Observance of behavior after learning showed a mobile robot seeking left/right or virtually still in the absence of obstacles and then proceeding right/left in avoidance preference. Bearing in mind the highly non-linear characteristics of the sensor detection lobes and their idyosynchratic shapes, the results are best evaluated by observing behavior. It must be noted that the result is particular to one mobile robot in one chosen environment of a given richness. Having said that, the learning of appropriate behavior for such an unique scenario is now practically possible and reduces much of the uncertainty of calibrating in the absence of knowing the target environment.

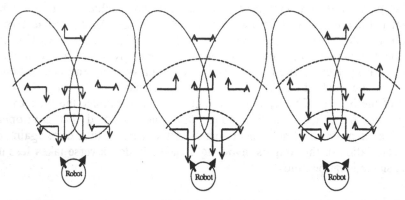

Fig. 11. An illustration of superposed behaviors. The left and right results are for *seek right* and *seek left* respectively superposed on top of *avoidance* alone which applies to the center result.

7   Conclusions

The mobile robot learning behavior in the real world has been characterized in such a way as to have confidence that learned behavior is sensible and robust even with noisy sensors. The avoidance behavior turns out to be a good vehicle for evaluating a number of issues concerning real world environmental uncertainty.

The neurofuzzy paradigm has proved useful in generating a spectrum of possible behaviors from adjustment of only a few fundamental parameters in the algorithm. The use of neurofuzzy learning has generated the possibility of tailoring behavior of a mobile robot to suit the target environment superposing behavior traits into the one learning phase.

Whilst there are a number of ways the platform can be improved such as using more powerful emitters, modulation to reduce noise and employing highly directional emission, the relatively slow computational speed of the platform has not been on the critical path. Rather, it is the mechanical movement in the real world that ultimately limits speed of learning. Hence the cost benefit of the small mobile robot platform is very high.

8   Future Work

At present, further paradigms are being loaded into the platform to build a parametric data base on learning technique. The results will be blended into the multi-mobile robot scenarios to enable them to reliably identify and move with respect to each other, communicating both by radio link and by infrared emission signal coding.

References

1. Zurada, J., Marks II, R., Robinson, C. eds: Computational Intelligence. IEEE Press No. PC04580 New York 1994.
2. Jang, J.S.R., Sun, C.T., Mitzutani, E.: Neuro-fuzzy and Soft Computing, Prentice Hall, 1997.
3. Sutton, R., Barto, A.: Reinforcement Learning. MIT Press Bradford Books USA 1998.
4. Brown, M., Harris, C.: Neuro-fuzzy Adaptive Modelling and Control. Pren. Hall UK 1994.
5. Harris, C.J., Brown, M., Bossley, K.M., Mills, D.J., Feng, M.: Advances in neuro-fuzzy algorithms for real-time modeling and control. J. Eng. Appl. of AI, Vol. 9(1) (1996) 1-16.
6. Evans, J.M.: Helpmate: an autonomous mobile robot courier for hospitals. Proceedings IEEE/RSJ Int. Conf. on Intelligent Robots & Systems, Munich Germany, (1994) 1695-1700.
7. Wallace, A.: Flow control of mobile robots using agents. 29th International Symposium on Robotics 97 BRA, Birmingham UK April 27-May 1 (1998).
8. Mataric, M.: Behavior based robotics as a tool for synthesis of artificial behavior and analysis of natural behavior. J. Experimental & Theoretical AI Vol. 9, (1997) 323-336.
9. Mataric, M.: Reinforcement learning in a multi-robot domain. Autonomous Robots, Vol. 4 No 1 (1997) 73-83.
10. Mataric, M.: Studying the role of embodiment in cognition. Cybernetics & Systems, Vol. 28 No 6 (1997) 457-470.
11. Mataric, M.: Learning social behaviors. Robot. & Auton. Systems, Vol 20 (1997) 191-204.
12. Michaud, F., Mataric, M.: Learning from history for behavior-based mobile robots in non-stationary conditions. Autonomous Robots/Machine Learning (Joint Issue Feb 1998) 1-29.
13. Kelly, I.D., Keating, D.: Increased learning rates through the sharing of experiences of multiple autonomous mobile robot agents. IEEE World Congress on Computational Intelligence Alaska USA (1998).
14. Habib, M.K., Asama, H., Ishida, Y., Matsumoto A., Endo I.: Simulation environment for an autonomous and decentralized multi-agent robotic system. Proceedings IEEE/RSJ International Conf. on Intelligent Robots & Systems Rayleigh NC USA 1992) 1550-1557.
15. Willgoss, R. The simulation of multiple mobile robot task assignments. 29th International Symposium on Robotics 97, BRA, Birmingham UK April 27-May 1 (1998) 127-130.
16. Song, K.T., Sheen, L.H.: Fuzzy-neuro control design for obstacle avoidance of a mobile robot. Joint Conf. 4th IEEE Int. Conf. on Fuzzy Systems and 2nd Int. Fuzzy Engineering Symp. Vol. 1 (1995) 71-76.
17. Tsoukalas, L.H., Houstis, E.H., Jones, G.V.: Neuro-fuzzy motion planners for intelligent robots. Journal of Intelligent and Robotic Systems Vol. 19 (1997) 339-356.

18. Tschishold-Gurman, N.: The neural network model RuleNet and its application to mobile robot navigation. Fuzzy Sets and Systems Vol. 85 (1997) 287-303.
19. Aycard, O., Charpillet, F., Haton, J-P.: A new approach to design fuzzy controllers for mobile robots navigation. Proc. IEEE Int. Symp. Computational Intelligence in Robotics and Automation (1997) 68-73.
20. Gaussier, P., Moga, S., Quoy, M., Banquet, J.P.: From perception-action loops to imitation processes: a bottom-up approach of learning by imitation. Applied Artificial Intelligence, Vol. 12 (1998) 701-727.
21. Rylatt, M., Czarnecki, C. & Routen, T.: Connectionist Learning in Behavior-Based Mobile Robots. Artificial Intelligence Review Vol. 12 (1998) 445-468.
22. Ng, K.C., Trivedi, M.M.: A Neuro-Fuzzy Controller fro Mobile Robot Navigation and Multirobot Convoying. IEEE Trans. SMC Part B: Cybernetics, Vol. 28 (6) (1998) 829-840.
23. Willgoss, R.A., Iqbal, J.: Reinforcement Learning of Behaviors in Mobile Robots Using Noisy Infrared Sensors. Proc. Australian Conference on Robotics and Automation. Brisbane ARAA (1999) 119-125.

$\mathcal{INDU}$: An Interval & Duration Network

Arun K. Pujari, G. Vijaya Kumari, and Abdul Sattar

[1] Department of C. I. S., University of Hyderabad, Hyderabad, 500 046, INDIA
[2] J. N. Technological University, Kukatpally, Hyderabad, INDIA
[3] School of C.I.T., Griffith University, Nathan, QLD 4111, Brisbane, AUSTRALIA

Abstract. The significance of representing duration information along with the qualitative information of the time intervals is well argued in the literature. A new framework $\mathcal{INDU}$ (**IN**terval and **DU**ration) network consisting of 25 basic relations, is proposed here. $\mathcal{INDU}$ can handle qualitative information of time interval and duration in one single structure. It inherits many interesting properties of Allen's Interval Algebra (of 13 basic relations) but it also exhibits several interesting additional features. We present several representations of $\mathcal{INDU}$ (ORD-clause, Geometric and Lattice) and characterise its tractable subclasses such as the Convex and Pre-convex classes. The important contribution of the current study is to show that for the tractable subclasses (Convex as well as Pre-convex) 4-consistency is necessary to guarantee global consistency of $\mathcal{INDU}$-network.

1 Introduction

The field of temporal reasoning has been a central research topic in AI since many years. It has been studied in a wide range of areas such as knowledge representation, natural language understanding, commonsense reasoning, qualitative reasoning, plan generation, scheduling etc.. Temporal information is typically represented in terms of a collection of qualitative and metric relations constraining time points or intervals. The main reasoning tasks are concerned with determining the consistency of such a collection, deducing other implied relations from the given set of relations, and finding the instantiation of the point and interval variables satisfying the set of constraints imposed by the set of relations. Allen [1] proposed an algebraic framework named Interval Algebra (IA), for qualitative reasoning with time intervals where the binary relationship between a pair of intervals is represented by a subset of 13 atomic relations. Vilain and Kautz [13] proposed a sub-algebra, Point Algebra (PA), on the set of time points with three atomic relations between a pair of points as $<, =$ and $>$. The origin of the 13 atomic relations can be traced back to the philosophical analysis presented by C.D. Broad in 1938 [3]. Broad holds the view that the temporal characteristics of experience fall into three different sets. (i) temporal relations (ii) duration and (iii) transitive aspects of temporal facts. Broad also mentions that two of the above aspects, namely duration and temporal relations, are very closely interconnected and they can be grouped under the heading of extensive

N. Foo (Ed.): AI'99, LNAI 1747, pp. 291–303, 1999.

aspect of temporal facts. Since 1983 when IA was proposed, though a substantial amount of work have been carried out on the topic by many researchers, the importance on qualitative information on duration has been ignored except for a few isolated cases. Though IA and PA are popularly used for representing temporal information they cannot specify qualitative information of interval duration. Allen observes that in order to encode duration information a separate system, orthogonal to the IA system, is necessary. In the same spirit, some recent work proposed bi-network based approaches to represent information about duration [2], [8] and [14]. These recent works and the philosophical analysis by C. D. Broad inspired us to revisit the IA. The significance of representing information about durations is well argued in the literature.

Example 1. Let us consider the following narration. *John and Mary are doctors and work in the same hospital. Today, they arrived at their work at the same time and they immediately started examining their respective patients without rest. They examined a patient together later in the day. By then, John has finished with 3 patients whereas Mary has examined only 2 patients.* One can easily infer that the John and Mary were examining the patient either *'During the office hour'* or, *'they started examining during office hour but stayed late to finish the work'* or *'they started the work only after the day is over'.*

The similar story can be told in another context. *John and Mary are students in the same Department. Today they arrived at the department at the same time and immediately went to their respective classes. Sometime later in the day they attended the same class. But by then John had attended 3 classes without any gap and Mary had attended two lectures without rest.* One can see that the IA-network for both these stories is the same. But there is some implicit information in the second one. That is, the duration of all the classes are of same length. If we incorporate this information about duration, the given information becomes inconsistent.

Example 2. Let us consider the scheduling of concurrent processes where each process is comprised of certain atomic transactions. In a database environment, each atomic transaction can be visualised as a *seek* operation. Depending on the hardware and the file size the actual seek time can be calculated. This information may not be available at the time of scheduling. On the other hand, based on the number of atomic transactions in a process, we can always determine the relative duration of each of the processes.

In the foregoing discussion, we make two major observations:

- There are instances when the duration information is implicit, but should not be ignored. If it is ignored, it may lead to wrong conclusion.
- There are instances where the relative duration instead of the absolute length of the interval, is more relevant.

The existing frameworks of Temporal CSP do not model this aspect. The expressive power of IA and PA is limited, as it is not possible to represent qualitative information of interval duration along with other relations. The bi-network based approaches put unnecessary burden on computational resources. Keeping these in mind, we attempt to answer the question that whether an IA-like framework can be designed to represent qualitative information of intervals and duration. Of course, we expect such a system to preserve the simplicity and elegance of the IA. We also hope that the specialised algorithms (computationally efficient) developed over the years for IA based reasoning systems (in various domains) could be easily adapted for the proposed extended framework of temporal reasoning,

In this paper, we gracefully extend the IA to model qualitative information about intervals and durations in a single binary constraint network and we term this network as $\mathcal{INDU}$-**IN**terval and **DU**ration network. $\mathcal{INDU}$ comprises of 25 basic relations between a pair of two intervals. We discuss various representations (ORD Clause, Geometric and Lattice) of $\mathcal{INDU}$ and characterise its subclasses, namely, convex and pre-convex classes. Our main result is to show that this network exhibits similar characteristics as the IA network in the sense that for the pre-convex classes consistency checking can be carried out by polynomial algorithm. But the level of local consistency necessary for the global consistency of $\mathcal{INDU}$-network is 4 contrary to the 3-consistency in the case of IA network. We prove that if the network is strongly 4-consistent and the relations are in Pre-convex class, then the network is globally consistent. Hence, the feasible schedule of the network can be found in a polynomial algorithm for these classes.

2   Extension of Interval Algebra: $\mathcal{INDU}$

We begin with 13 basic relations of IA [1], $I = \{b, bi, m, mi, o, oi, s, si, d, di, f, fi, eq\}$. Intuitively, 7 of these 13 relations between any two intervals implicitly represent relations between their corresponding durations. These include $\{eq, s, si, d, di, f, fi\}$. However, in case of 6 remaining relations, i.e., $\{b, bi, m, mi, o, oi\}$, nothing is known about durations of the respective intervals. There are only three possible ways durations of these intervals can be related, $\{<, =, >\}$. Therefore, we need 18 (6×3) relations to express relationships between intervals and durations with respect to the above six relations. Hence, we need a total of 25 basic relations to adequately model qualitative information about intervals and durations. These relations have an important property that they integrate the qualitative information of interval duration along with its relative position on time scale. The relations are denoted as

$$E = \{b^<, b^=, b^>, bi^<, bi^=, bi^>, m^<, m^=, m^>, mi^<, mi^=, mi^>, o^<, o^=, o^>, oi^<, oi^=, oi^>, s^<, si^>, d^<, di^>, f^<, fi^>, eq^=\}.$$

For any two intervals, there can be exactly one of the set of 25 atomic relations. Let X^b, X^e, and X^d denote the start point, the endpoint and the duration, respectively, of any interval X. Then, these relations can also be expressed as set of inequalities in terms of the end points and duration. For example, $Xb^<Y \equiv X^e < Y^b \wedge X^d < Y^d$ (see Table 1). The indefinite qualitative temporal information can be expressed as disjunction of the atomic relations and can be represented as a subset of E. For example, The expression $X\{b^<, o^>\}Y$ means that $Xb^<Y \lor Xo^<Y$. Thus, there can be $2^{25} = 33554432$ possible binary relations between any pair of time intervals. This set of relations is denoted by $\mathcal{INDU}$, a rich language for representing temporal knowledge.

Basic Interval Relation	Converse Relation	Schematic Representation	End-point relations & relative duration
$b^<$	$bi^>$	xxx yyyy	$X^b < Y^b, X^b < Y^e,$ $X^e < Y^b, X^e < Y^e, X^d < Y^d$
$b^=$	$bi^=$	xxx yyy	$X^b < Y^b, X^b < Y^e,$ $X^e < Y^b, X^e < Y^e, X^d = Y^d$
$b^>$	$bi^<$	xxxx yyy	$X^b < Y^b, X^b < Y^e,$ $X^e < Y^b, X^e < Y^e, X^d > Y^d$
$m^<$	$mi^>$	xxx yyyy	$X^b < Y^b, X^b < Y^e,$ $X^e = Y^b, X^e < Y^e, X^d < Y^d$
$m^=$	$mi^=$	xxx yyy	$X^b < Y^b, X^b < Y^e,$ $X^e = Y^b, X^e < Y^e, X^d = Y^d$
$m^>$	$mi^<$	xxxx yyy	$X^b < Y^b, X^b < Y^e,$ $X^e = Y^b, X^e < Y^e, X^d > Y^d$
$o^<$	$oi^>$	xxx yyyy	$X^b < Y^b, X^b < Y^e,$ $X^e > Y^b, X^e < Y^e, X^d < Y^d$
$o^=$	$oi^=$	xxx yyy	$X^b < Y^b, X^b < Y^e,$ $X^e > Y^b, X^e < Y^e, X^d = Y^d$
$o^>$	$oi^<$	xxxx yyy	$X^b < Y^b, X^b < Y^e,$ $X^e > Y^b, X^e < Y^e, X^d > Y^d$
$d^<$	$di^>$	xxx yyyyyyy	$X^b > Y^b, X^b < Y^e,$ $X^e > Y^b, X^e < Y^e, X^d < Y^d$
$s^<$	$si^>$	xxx yyyyy	$X^b = Y^b, X^b < Y^e,$ $X^e > Y^b, X^e < Y^e, X^d < Y^d$
$f^<$	$fi^>$	xxx yyyyy	$X^b < Y^b, X^b < Y^e,$ $X^e > Y^b, X^e = Y^e, X^d < Y^d$
$eq^=$	-	xxxx yyyy	$X^b = Y^b, X^b < Y^e,$ $X^e > Y^b, X^e = Y^e, X^d = Y^d$

Table 1: 25 basic relations and the schematic diagram

3   Different Representations of $\mathcal{INDU}$

There have been many different methods of visualising the qualitative relationships of intervals as proposed in IA. These include (i) expressing the relations in $\mathcal{INDU}$ as ORD-clause form [9]; (ii) geometrically representing the intervals in two-dimensional planes and considering the relations as admissible regions in this plane [6], [10] and (iii) representing the relations as a lattice [6]. These interpretation provide a rich insight and better understanding of the expressive power of the language.

3.1   ORD-Clause Form

Nebel et al. [9] introduce ORD clauses and show that all interval formulas of IA can be translated into their equivalent ORD-clause form. In the similar line, the relations in $\mathcal{INDU}$ can be equivalently expressed as ORD-clause where the literals involve not only the end point parameters but also the duration variables X^d and Y^d. We give below the relevant concept as introduced in [9] but suitably modified for the present context.

Similar to the traditional definition, by a *clause* we mean a disjunction of literals. However, by a *literal* in this case we mean an atomic formula of one of the following forms: $a = b, a \leq b, a \neq b, a \nleq b$, where a and b are X^b, X^e or X^d for some time interval X. The literals, $a = b$ and $a \leq b$ are termed as *positive literals* and the other two literals $a \neq b$ and $a \nleq b$ are *negative literals*. It may be noted that the relation $a \nleq b$ can be equivalently written as two clauses $a \neq b$ and $b \leq a$. A formula is essentially a conjunction of set of ORD clauses.

Definition 1 (ORD-Clause Form). *The ORD-clause is a clause containing literals of the following forms, $a = b, a \leq b, a \neq b$, where a and b are X^b, X^e or X^d for some time interval X. ORD-clause form of an interval relation is the the clause form containing only ORD-clauses. ORD Horn clause formula are the ORD clause forms admitting at most one positive literal.*

The following result can be inferred directly from definitions.

Theorem 1. *Any relation in $\mathcal{INDU}$ can be equivalently represented in ORD-clause form.*

Example 3. Though every relation can be equivalently expressed as ORD-Clause form, it is not possible to express every relation in ORD-Horn form. For instance, the relation $X(bi^<, oi^>)Y$ cannot be represented as ORD-Horn form. Its equivalent expression is $(X^d \leq Y^d \vee Y^e \leq X^b) \wedge (Y^d \leq X^d \vee X^b \leq Y^e) \wedge (X^d \neq Y^d) \wedge (X^b \neq Y^e)$. On the other hand, the relation $X(bi^<, bi^>, oi^<, oi^=, oi^>)Y$ can be represented as ORD-Horn clause as the following:

$$(Y^e \leq X^e) \wedge (Y^b \leq X^b) \wedge (Y^e \neq X^e) \wedge (Y^b \neq X^b) \wedge (Y^e \neq X^b) \wedge$$
$$(X^b \leq Y^e \vee X^d \neq Y^d).$$

3.2 Geometric Representation of $\mathcal{INDU}$

It is useful to visualise the relations of $\mathcal{INDU}$ as regions in the Euclidean plane. An interval which is an ordered pair of real numbers (X^b, X^e) can be represented as points in $\Re^2$. Since $X^b < X^e$ holds for an interval (X^b, X^e), the space of all time intervals can be identified with the half plane $\mathcal{H}$ defined as the upper half of $\Re^2$ to the left of the line $X^b = X^e$. Let $A = (A^b, A^e)$ be a fixed interval with the duration A^d. Then for each atomic relation $r \in E$, there is a well-defined region in the half plane $\mathcal{H}$ which consists of points $X = (X^b, X^e)$ related by r to A. The regions associated with all atomic relations are shown in the Figure 1. More generally, the region associated with a non-atomic relation is the union of the regions associated with each of the constituent atomic relations. Dimension of a relation is defined as the dimension of the associated region. The relations $b^<, b^>, o^<, o^>, oi^<, oi^>, bi^<, bi^>, d^<$ and $di^>$ are of dimension 2. The relations $m^<, m^>, s^<, fi^>, f^<, si^>, o^=, oi^=, mi^<, mi^>, bi^=$ and $b^=$ are of dimension 1. The relations $eq^=, m^=, mi^=$ are 0 dimensional regions. We shall be making use of this representation throughout the work.

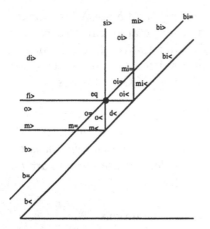

Fig. 1. The admissible regions of Y for a given X when $Y r X$.

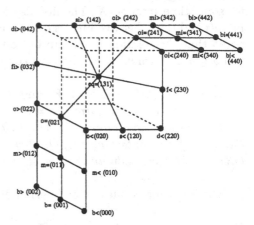

Fig. 2. Lattice Representation

3.3   Lattice Representation of $\mathcal{INDU}$

The relations in IA are represented in the form of a lattice to provide a different insight [7] and it helps in defining convex, pre-convex and other relations. These relations possess some interesting computational properties. In the similar line, we represent the atomic relations in $\mathcal{INDU}$ as a lattice. Any atomic relation r between interval variables X and Y is given by a triple of numbers (m_1, m_2, m_3) as follows. If $Y^b < X^b$, then $m_1 = 0$; If $Y^b = X^b$, then $m_1 = 1$; If $X^b < Y^b < X^e$, then $m_1 = 2$; If $Y^b = X^e$ then $m_1 = 3$; and If $Y^b > X^e$ then $m_1 = 4$;

The m_2 is similarly, 0, 1, 2, 3 or 4 depending on whether the relation corresponds to $Y^e < X^b, Y^e = X^b, X^b < Y^e < X^e, Y^e = X^e$ or, $Y^e > X^e$, respectively and the m_3 is 0, 1, or 2 depending on whether $Y^d < X^d, Y^d = X^d$, or $Y^d > X^d$, respectively. Thus for each of the 25 relations in E, coded as a triplet, is a point in the lattice and the lexicographic ordering of these triplets induces a partial order in the lattice. (see Figure 2) Precedence in the lattice is defined component-wise: $(m_1, m_2, m_3) < (n_1, n_2, n_3)$ if and only if $m_1 < n_1 \vee m_2 < n_2 \vee m_3 < n_3$. A non-atomic relation can be represented as a subset of the lattice.

4   Subclasses of $\mathcal{INDU}$

We use the lattice representation of $\mathcal{INDU}$ to define convex, pre-convex and other relations. The motivation behind identifying these relation is that the similar relations in IA provide insight into understanding of tractable classes [7]. For any two atomic relations r and s such that $r \leq s$ in the lattice, $[r, s]$ denotes the set of all relations which are between r and s in the lattice. For instance, $[b^<, o^=]$ represents the set of relations between $b^<$ and $o^=$ in the lattice. $b^<$ has the lattice code $(0,0,0)$ and $o^=$ corresponds to the code $(0,2,1)$. Hence the elements which are between these two elements in the lattice are (000),(001), (010), (011), (020),and (021). The corresponding relation in $\mathcal{INDU}$ is $\{b^<, b^=, m^<, m^=, o^<, o^=\}$. We call this as an interval in the lattice.

Definition 2 (Convex Relation). *A relation in $\mathcal{INDU}$ is said to be a convex relation if it corresponds to an interval in the lattice and is of the form $[r, s]$ for some $r, s \in E$.*

In geometric interpretation, a convex relation is a convex region in $\mathcal{H}$. The convex relations when translated into ORD-clause form, yield formulas containing only unit clauses. Define $\mathcal{C} \subset \mathcal{INDU}$ as the set of all convex relations. Enumeration reveals that there are 227 convex relations in $\mathcal{INDU}$, that is $|\mathcal{C}| = 227$.

Theorem 2. *For an interval relation $c \in \mathcal{INDU}$ between any two intervals X and Y following are equivalent.*

1. *c is a convex relation.*
2. *The restriction imposed by X on the domain of Y is a convex region in $\mathcal{H}$.*
3. *The equivalent ORD Clause form of c in terms of the endpoints and durations of X and Y contains only unit clauses.*

Definition 3 (Pre-convex Relation). *Pre-convex relations are those relations which are obtained from a convex relation by removing zero or more number of atomic relations of lower dimensions.*

In other words, if the convex relation corresponds to a region of dimension 2, then the pre-convex relations are obtained by removing atomic relations of dimensions 1 and 0, but if the convex relation is of dimension 1, then we obtain the pre-convex relations by removing only atomic relations of dimension 0. Obviously, any convex relation is a pre-convex relation. Geometrically, the region of a pre-convex relation is a convex shape with linear or point discontinuities. Define $\mathcal{PC} \subset \mathcal{INDU}$ as the set of all pre-convex relations. Enumeration reveals that there are 77223 pre-convex relations in $\mathcal{INDU}$.

Definition 4 (Convex Closure). *For a $\mathcal{INDU}$-relation r, a convex closure is the smallest (in terms of set inclusion) convex relation that contains r.*

From any pre-convex relation, we can obtain its convex closure by restoring the smaller dimensional elements that are deleted to get the relation.

Theorem 3. *For an interval relation $c \in \mathcal{INDU}$ between any two intervals X and Y following are equivalent.*

1. *c is a pre-convex relation.*
2. *The restriction imposed by X on the domain of Y is a convex region in $\mathcal{H}$ with linear or point discontinuities.*
3. *The equivalent ORD Clause form of c in terms of the endpoints and durations of X and Y contains only ORD-Horn clauses.*

Example 4. The relation $X(bi^<, bi^>, oi^<, oi^=, oi^>)Y$ is a pre-convex relation. Its clause representation is $(Y^e \leq X^e) \wedge (Y^b \leq X^b) \wedge (Y^e \neq X^e) \wedge (Y^b \neq X^b) \wedge (Y^e \neq X^b) \wedge (X^b \leq Y^e \vee X^d \neq Y^d)$. It is obtained from the lattice interval $[oi^<, bi^>]$ by removing the elements $bi^=, mi^<, mi^=$ and $mi^>$, out of which $mi^=$ is 1-dimensional and others are 2-dimensional. In $\Re^2$ the admissible domain of Y for a fixed instantiantiation of X is the region shown Figure 3. On the other hand, $\{b^<, b^=, m^<, o^<, s^<, eq^=\}$ is not a pre-convex relation.

5　Reasoning in $\mathcal{INDU}$

Constraint network is a simple way of representing the set of variables with specified domains and the constraints between them. Hence, any temporal information with interval variables and the binary relations as elements of $\mathcal{INDU}$ can be represented as a constraint network to facilitate reasoning with intervals and duration. The main reasoning problem of a constraint network is to determine whether the network is consistent and if consistent, then to determine the feasible relations and the minimal network. We study this aspect of $\mathcal{INDU}$ in this section.

Definition 5 ($\mathcal{INDU}$-Network). *$\mathcal{INDU}$-network is a binary constraint network consisting of a set of n interval variables $I_1, I_2, \ldots, I_n$ and a set the binary constraints between variables. These binary constraints are the interval relations in $\mathcal{INDU}$. A convex $\mathcal{INDU}$-network is a $\mathcal{INDU}$-network having all its relations in C. Similarly, a pre-convex $\mathcal{INDU}$-network has all its relations in $\mathcal{PC}$.*

An *instantiation* of an interval X is an assignment of X to a point in $\mathcal{H}$. A consistent instantiation of X and Y is the instantiation of X and Y such that the binary relations between them is satisfied. In a network, the consistent instantiation of the all interval variables is called a *solution*. Local consistency has proven to be an important concept in the area of constraint network. A local consistency algorithm helps in a sort of pre-processing the network for a efficient running of the backtracking algorithm. Moreover, for certain subclasses of the problem, local consistency suffices to determine global consistency. We analyze below such properties for convex and pre-convex class of $\mathcal{INDU}$- network

Definition 6 (k-consistency [4], [12]). *A network is said to be k-consistent if and only if for any instantiation of any $k - 1$ variables satisfying all the direct relations among those variables, there exists an instantiation of the kth variable such that the k values taken together satisfy all the relations among them. A network is strongly k-consistent if and only if it is j-consistent for all $j \leq k$.*

We call the network to be globally consistent when it is strongly n-consistent. Any globally consistent network is necessarily minimal, but minimal network need not be globally consistent.

Theorem 4. *Consider a convex $\mathcal{INDU}$-network with n interval variables such that the intervals $I_1, I_2, \ldots, I_{(n-1)}$ be consistently instantiated as*

$A_1, A_2, \ldots, A_{(n-1)}$. *If for all $1 \leq p, q, r \leq (n-1)$ the given instantiation A_p, A_q and A_r can be extended consistently to an instantiation of I_n, then the instantiation $A_1, A_2, \ldots, A_{(n-1)}$ can be extended to a n-tuple of consistent instantiation of all the n intervals.*

Proof. The binary relations r_{jn}, restrict the permissible domain of I_n for the given instantiation A_j. Since the relations are convex, these admissible domains, R_{jn}, are convex sets in $\Re^2$. As a direct consequence of Helly Theorem, if any three of these convex regions have non-empty intersection then all the $(n-1)$ regions have a common non-empty region. Hence, the given instantiation can be extended to a n-tuple which is a consistent instantiation of all the n variables.

Theorem 5. *A convex 4-consistent $\mathcal{INDU}$-network is globally consistent and minimal.*

Proof. The theorem is proved by showing that if the network is strongly 4-consistent and all of constraints are convex constraints then the network is k-consistent for all $k \leq n$. Hence the network is strongly n-consistent and therefore, minimal. This is straight forward from the above theorem.

Interestingly, Theorem 4 can be extended to the pre-convex relations. The main result of this work is to establish that for pre-convex $\mathcal{INDU}$-network, the network is globally consistent if the network is strongly 4-consistent. The proof is based on some of the following smaller results.

Lemma 1. *If for two intervals I_1 and I_2 in $\mathcal{INDU}$-network, such that the relations r_{1k} and r_{2k} are 1-dimensional and their corresponding linear regions R_{1k} and R_{2k} are contained in the same line (they may not be same line segments, but they are portions of the same straight line), then the A_1 and A_2 satisfy a 1-dimensional or 0-dimensional relation in r_{12}.*

Proof. (sketch) The proof is straight forward once we graphically interpret the statement. In Figure 4, if for a given instantiation A_1, the region R_{in} is a line segment P and similarly, for the given A_2, the region R_{2n} is a line segment Q such that both R_{1n} and R_{2n} are parts of the same straight line UV, then A_2 must lie on the vertical line UV or the horizontal line UW.

Corollary 1. *If for two intervals I_1 and I_2 in $\mathcal{INDU}$-network, such that the relations r_{1k} and r_{2k} are 0-dimensional and their corresponding regions R_{ik} and R_{2k} are points, then the A_1 and A_2 satisfy r_{12} such that $A_1^d = A_2^d$.*

Theorem 6. *For a path consistent convex $\mathcal{INDU}$-network, such that for the given consistent instantiation A_1 and A_2, the regions $R_{1n} \cap R_{2n} = P$ where P is a line segment then r_{12} is a 2-dimensional non-atomic relation or both R_{1n} and R_{2n} are lines.*

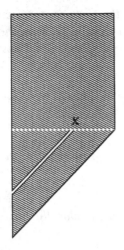

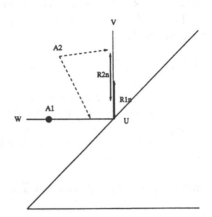

Fig. 3. The admissible region of Y when $X(bi^<, bi^>, oi^<, oi^=, oi^>)Y$.

Fig. 4. A_2's admissible domain falls on a line (horizontal or vertical) when R_{1n} and R_{2n} are on the same line

Proof. For the given instantiation, A_1 and A_2, if $R_{1n} \cap R_{2n} = P$, then P lies in the boundary line where both the regions meet. This is possible only when there is an atomic relation in r_{1n} (and in r_{2n}) which corresponds to a line segment colinear with P. By the above theorem, A_1 and A_2 instantiate a 1- or, 0- dimensional relation. Unless both R_{1n} and R_{2n} are lines, for a (x, y) in P, we can always select a point $B = (x', y')$ in neighbourhood of (x, y) such that $B \in R_{1n}$, but not in R_{2n}. Thus, A_1 and B are consistent instantiation of I_1 and I_n. But if I_2 is to be consistent with these then it has an instantiation A_2' satisfying all the direct relations with I_1 and I_n. This can happen only when the relation r_{12} is necessarily two-dimensional.

Definition 7 (Maximal instantiation). *The interval variables I_i and I_j are said to maximally instantiated to A_i and A_j, if A_i and A_j satisfy the relation of maximal dimension of non-atomic relation r_{ij} between I_i and I_j.*

Theorem 7. *If r is a strongly 4-consistent $\mathcal{INDU}$-network such that all the relations are pre-convex then it is globally consistent.*

Proof. (sketch) Let us take any k intervals $I_1, I_2, \ldots, I_k$ and let the intervals $I_1, I_2, \ldots, I_{(k-1)}$ be maximally and consistently instantiated as A_i, $1 \leq i \leq (k-1)$. The main line of argument is directed towards reaching a contradiction on maximality. Assume that R_i, $1 \leq i \leq (k-1)$, be the pre-convex admissible domains of I_k associated with r_{ik}, $1 \leq i \leq (k-1)$. 4-consistency ensures that for any three, p, q, s such that $1 \leq p < q < s \leq (k-1)$, we have $R_p \cap R_q \cap R_s \neq \emptyset$. Assume that $\bigcap_{i=1}^{k-1} R_i = \emptyset$. Let $\bar{R}_i$ denote the convex closure of R_i. Clearly,

$$R_p \cap R_q \cap R_s \neq \emptyset \ \forall \ 1 \leq p < q < s \leq (k-1) \Rightarrow$$

$$\bar{R}_p \cap \bar{R}_q \cap \bar{R}_s \neq \emptyset \ \forall 1 \leq p < q < s \leq (k-1) \Rightarrow \bigcap_{i=1}^{k-1} \bar{R}_i \neq \emptyset .$$

Let the common region of $\bar{R}_i$, $1 \leq i \leq (k-1)$ be P. Since P is not in all of R_i, but is common to all $\bar{R}_i$'s, P is part of the additional region that is added to obtain the convex closure for some pre-convex relation. Hence, P is of dimension 1 or 0. We can consider the two cases separately, namely, (i) P is a line segment and (ii) P is a point. If P is a line segment then the maximal relations are necessarily 2-dimensional but these are not instantiated. Hence a contradiction. Similarly if P is a point, the maximal relations are 1-dimensional, but the given instantiation for which P is the common regions requires that these are 0-dimensional instantiation. Thus in either case we reach contradiction on maximality to complete the proof. Hence, the network is k-consistent.

Thus the consistency of an $\mathcal{INDU}$-network can be checked in polynomial time.

6   Algebraic Properties

We discuss in the earlier section that if the network is 4-consistent then it is globally consistent and is also minimal. In order to have a reasoning system in the present framework, it is necessary to have a method of deciding whether a network is 4-consistent and if not, to enforce 4-consistency by the process of constraint tightening. In order to accomplish this task, we need certain algebraic operation for $\mathcal{INDU}$. The atomic relation in E can also be viewed as an ordered pair (r, ℓ) where $r \in I$ and $\ell \in D$. Thus $E \subset I \times D$ where $D = \{<, >, =\}$. Three atomic operations, namely, unary converse (denoted by $\smile$). binary intersection (denoted by $\cap$) and relational composition (denoted by $\otimes$) can be defined on $\mathcal{INDU}$ as follows:

Definition 8 (Converse). *For any atomic relation $\xi = (r, \ell)$, the converse of ξ denoted by $\xi^{\smile}$ is given by $\xi^{\smile} = (r^{\smile}, \ell^{\smile})$. The $r^{\smile}$ and $\ell^{\smile}$ have the usual meaning of converse as in IA and PA.*

For any non-atomic relation $r = \{\xi_1, \xi_2, \ldots, \xi_n\}$ in $\mathcal{INDU}$, the converse of r is $r^{\smile} = \{\xi_1^{\smile}, \xi_2^{\smile}, \ldots, \xi_n^{\smile}\}$, The intersection of any two relations r and s in $\mathcal{INDU}$ can be expressed as the set-theoretic intersection of the set of atomic relations.

Definition 9 (Intersection). *If $r = \{\xi_1, \xi_2, \ldots, \xi_n\}$ and $s = \{\rho_1, \rho_2, \ldots, \rho_n\}$ then $r \cap s$ is the set intersection $\{\xi_1, \xi_2, \ldots, \xi_n\} \cap \{\rho_1, \rho_2, \ldots, \rho_n\}$.*

Definition 10 (Composition). *For any two atomic relations $\xi_1 = r_1^{\ell_1}$, and $\xi_2 = r_2^{\ell_2}$, the composition $r = \xi_1 \otimes \xi_2$, is given by the set of ordered pairs in the cartesian product $((r_1 \otimes_I r_2) \times (\ell_1 \otimes_P \ell_2)) \cap E$, where $(r_1 \otimes_I r_2$ and $\ell_1 \otimes_P \ell_2$ are the compositions in IA and in PA, respectively.*

Theorem 8. *$\mathcal{INDU}$ is closed under converse, intersection and composition.*

Proof is straight forward from the definition. $\mathcal{INDU}$ is an algebra with these operations.

7   Conclusion

In the original proposal of IA [1] suggested that duration information can be encoded in a network orthogonal to the interval relationships network. Allen called this a *duration reasoning system*. There are other works PDN [8] and APDN [14]. The PDN is a bi-network framework, representing qualitative information points and durations. It can only handle pointisable (SIA) relations and to represent the interval information, PDN translates it to equivalent point information. This increases the complexity of the problem. APDN follows the same structure but extends PDN to represent quantitative information as well. Koubarakis [5] also attempts to represent relations between durations of intervals. However, this work addresses a restricted class of temporal constraints. Recently, a unified framework for quantitative and qualitative reasoning is proposed as PIDN [11]. PIDN handles the interval and duration information in a much more general sense. But it does not possess the elegant computational properties of $\mathcal{INDU}$. The $\mathcal{INDU}$ elegantly extends IA, and all existing efficient methods for IA can easily be extended for $\mathcal{INDU}$. In a forthcoming paper, the authors propose to report on algorithmic characteristics of $\mathcal{INDU}$.

References

1. J. Allen. Maintaining knowledge about temporal intervals. *Communication of the ACM*, 26(11):832–843, 1983.
2. F. Barber. A metric time-point and duration-based temporal model. *SIGART Bulletin*, 4(3):30–49, 1993.
3. C. D. Broad. Ostensible temporality. In G. M. Richard, editor, *The Philosophy of Time: A collection of essays*. Macmillan, 1968.
4. E.C. Freuder. A sufficient condition for backtrack-free search. *Journal of ACM*, 29:24–32, 1982.
5. M. Koubarakis. Dense time and temporal constraints with $\neq$. In *Proceedings of the 3rd International Conference on Principles of Knowledge Representation and Reasoning (KR-92)*, pages 24–35, 1992.
6. G. Ligozat. A new proof of tractability of ord-horn relations. In *Proceedings of the 9th National Conference in Artificial Intelligence (AAAI-96)*, pages 395–401, Anaheim, CA, 1996.
7. G. Ligozat. "corner" relation in allen's algebra. *Constraints: An International Journal*, 3:165–177, 1998.
8. I Navarrete and R. Marin. Qualitative temporal reasoning with points and durations. In *Proceedings of the 15th International Joint Conference on Artificial Intelligence (IJCAI-97)*, pages 1454–1459, Nagoya, Japan, 1997.
9. B. Nebel and H. Bürckert. Reasoning about temporal relations: A maximal tractable subclass of allen's interval algebra. *Journal of the ACM*, 42(1):43–66, 1995.
10. Arun K. Pujari. Neighbourhood logic and interval algebra. Technical report, International Institute of Software Technology, United Nations University, Technical Report No 116, Macau, 1997.

11. Arun K. Pujari and A. Sattar. A new framework for reasoning about points, intervals and durations. In *Proceedings of the 16th International Joint Conference on Artificial Intelligence (IJCAI-99)*, pages 1259–1264, 1999.
12. P. van Beek. Reasoning about qualitative temporal information. *Artificial Intelligence*, 58:297–326, 1992.
13. M. Vilain and H. Kautz. Constraint propagation algorithms for temporal reasoning. In *Proceedings of the 5th National Conference in Artificial Intelligence (AAAI-86)*, pages 377–382, Philadelphia, PA, 1986.
14. R. Wetprasit and A. Sattar. Temporal reasoning with qualitative and quantitative information about points and durations. In *Proceeding of the 15th National Conference on Artificial Intelligence (AAAI-98)*, pages 656–663, Madison, Wisconsin, 1998.

A Logical Framework for Inductive Inference and Its Rationality

Wei Li

Beijing University of Aeronautics and Astronautics
Beijing 100083, China
liwei@cs.sebuaa.ac.cn

Abstract. The rules of inductive inference are formalized using a transition rules. The rejection of a consequence obtained by inductive inference is formalized by a revision rule. An inductive process is defined as a sequence of versions of a theory generated by alternatively applying the inductive inference rules and the revision rule. An inductive procedure scheme is constructed. It takes a sequence $\mathcal{E}_M$ of instances of a given model M and a given formal theory Γ as its inputs, and generates the inductive processes. It is proved that if $\mathcal{E}_M$ contains all instances of the model M, then every inductive sequence generated by the procedure scheme is convergent. Its limit is the set of all true statements of the model M.

Keywords: inductive reasoning, belief revision, knowledge representation and reasoning, inductive process

1 Deduction and Induction

It is well known that inductive inference is different from deductive inference. Generally speaking, deductive inference deals with how to get a particular consequence from a general statement while the concern of inductive inference is how to obtain regularities from a particular result or instance or obtain a sufficient condition from the necessary conditions.

A rigorous mathematical theory of inductive inference and their rationality is set up. It is based on the classical proof theory and model theory within the scope of first order language. The basic ideas of this paper in dealing with inductive inference can be expressed as follows:

1. The sequences of versions of formal theories. One of the fundamental differences between inductive inference and deductive inference is that inductive inference promotes the evolution of a theory and involves the growth of knowledge, while deductive inference is essentially the transformations of tautology, or, in other words, the conclusion deduced is implied in the premises, hence no substantial growth of knowledge is incurred. Let $\vdash$ denote deductive relation, Γ denote a formal theory, and $Th(\Gamma)$ denote the theoretical closure of Γ under the rules of deductive inference (for example, Gentzen rules). Let $\Longrightarrow$ denote

N. Foo (Ed.): AI'99, LNAI 1747, pp. 304–315, 1999.

inductive relation (or evolutionary relation). This difference can be described by the following forms: For the deductive inference, we have

If $\Gamma \vdash A$,   then $Th(\Gamma) = Th(\{A\} \cup \Gamma)$.

But in the case of inductive inference, the information is increasing. That is to say:

If $\Gamma \Longrightarrow A$,   then $Th(\Gamma) \subseteq Th(\{A\} \cup \Gamma)$

A new formal theory is generated after a rule of inductive inference is applied. To put it more precisely, a new version of the theory is generated after a rule of inductive inference is applied[1]. If Γ_n is used to denote the nth version of a given formal theory Γ, then an inductive process can be naturally described by the sequence of the versions of the theory according to the order of their appearance.

$$\Gamma_1, \Gamma_2, \cdots \Gamma_n, \cdots$$

Where $\Gamma_i \Longrightarrow \Gamma_{i+1}$, i.e., Γ_{i+1} is obtained by applying a rule of inductive inference to Γ_i.

In "Topica" of his famous "Organon", Aristotle stressed: *"induction is a passage from individuals to universals"* [2]. This statement has a dual implication. One is that the inductive inference proceeds from a particular fact to a universal statement, and the other is that the induction is a **sequence** which describes the growth of knowledge from individuals to universals.

2.The orthogonality of decuctivity and inductivity. If we use tree structures to denote the theoretical closure of a theory under the deduction. The relation between inductive inference and deductive inference can be expressed by the following diagram:

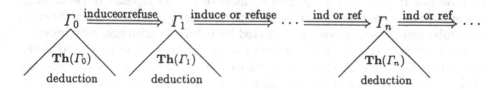

The above simple diagram describes a certain "orthogonality" of the inductive inference and deductive inference. It is the starting point for this paper to set up the theory of inductive inference. The similar diagram was used by Plotkin [3]to describe the relation between program executions and their proofs in structured operational semantics.

3. The refutations of inductive consequences. Another fundamental difference between inductive inference and deductive inference lies in the fact that deductive inference is sound, i.e., the consequence obtained by applying some rules of deductive inference is always true provided the premises are true. But it is not the case with inductive inference. The inductive consequence may not necessarily be true, it can wrong in many cases.

As a matter of fact, the truth or falsity of a consequence derived by inductive inference can only be examined by the presence or absence of counter-examples, which run against the consequence. An inductive consequence is false if it is refuted by some counter-examples. Therefore, in no sense can inductive inference be independent of refutation. Inductive inference and refutation are opposite and complementary to each other. Since the word "refutation" is used in many publications to denote different things, in this paper, we use "the rejection by facts" to avoid confusion [4].

4. The context sensitive character of inductive inference. We use the following form:

$$\Gamma \Longrightarrow \Gamma'. \tag{1}$$

where Γ' is a new version of Γ after a certain rule of inductive inference is applied. In order to make the inductive inference meaningful, the consistency between the inductive consequence and its premise is required. Thus, Γ' should be consistent with Γ. This means that the rules of inductive inference are formed by the context-sensitive grammar.

5. The rationality of inductive inference. The paradigm of inductive inference given above is the followng: Suppose that the world which we study is described by a model $\mathbf{M}$, and that $\mathcal{E}_M$ is a set of instances of $\mathbf{M}$ and Γ_0 is the initial version of a theory. The goal is to induce a theory from $\mathcal{E}_M$ using inductive inference, and to guarantee that this theory takes all true statements of the model $\mathbf{M}$ as its logical consequences.

We reach this goal by the following approach: We begin with Γ_0, and repeat the following operations: At each time, we pick one instance A from $\mathcal{E}_M$, and then check the current version Γ_n using A; and generate a new version Γ_{n+1} either by applying some inductive inference rules if A is a positive instance or by applying revision rule if A denotes a rejection by facts of Γ_n. By repeatedly performing the operations, a sequence of versions of the theories is produced. Since, for each particular time, the new version generated by inductive inference, may rejected by some instance later, it is hard to say the rationality at that particular time. The rationality is meaningful only in the case that the sequence of the versions of the theory is convergent, and its limit is the set of all true statements of the model $\mathbf{M}$.

2   The Rules of Inductive Inference

A first order language L is assumed, which is formally defined, for example, in [7]. CN, FN and PN are used to denote the sets of constants, functions and predicates of L respectively, and CN is a countably infinite set. A, Γ and $Th(\Gamma)$ are used to denote a formula, a set of formulas and the theoretical closure of Γ under the deduction (for example, Gentzen style) rules. $CN(\Gamma), FN(\Gamma)$, and $PN(\Gamma)$ are the sets of constants, functions, and predicates of Γ. $\Gamma \vdash A$ is called a sequent and denotes the A is deduced from Γ according to Gentzen style deduction rules [11]. Here, Γ is a sequence, similarly, $A(t), \forall x.A(x), \Gamma$ and $A, A \supset B, B, \Gamma$ are formal theories and are sequences. They are also taken as a set of formulas when it is required [11].

A model $\mathbf{M}$ is a pair of $< M, I >$, where M is a domain, I is an interpretation. Sometimes, $\mathbf{M}_\wp$ is used to denote a model for a particular problem $\wp$. $\mathcal{T}_{M_\wp}$ denotes the set of all true sentences of $\mathbf{M}_\wp$ and is a countable set. To simplify the proofs, it is assumed that $\mathcal{T}_{M_\wp}$ has the built-in Skolem functions [8]. $\Gamma \models A$ is used to mean that A is a semantic (or logical) consequence of Γ [7]. The validity, satisfiability, and falsifiability of deduction of the first order logic are defined as in [7]. Therefore the deduction rules are sound and complete.

To formalize the rules of inductive inference, we need the Herbrand universe defined below [7]: Let

$$\mathbf{H}_0 = \{a_0, \cdots, a_n, \cdots | a_n \in CN\}$$
$$\mathbf{H}_{i+1} = \mathbf{H}_i \cup \{f^n(t_1, \cdots, t_n) | t_j \in \mathbf{H}_i, f^n \in FN\}$$
$$\mathbf{H} = \bigcup_{i=0}^{\infty} \mathbf{H}_i$$

$\mathbf{H}$ is called a Herbrand universe of L. The transition:

$$\frac{cond(\Gamma, \Gamma')}{\Gamma \Longrightarrow \Gamma'}$$

is used to represent the rules of inductive inference, where Γ and Γ' are formal theories. $cond(\Gamma, \Gamma')$ is a condition that Γ and Γ' must satisfy. The rule can be informally interpreted as: If the $cond(\Gamma, \Gamma')$ holds, then Γ becomes Γ' after a rule of inductive inference is applied. The inductive inference rules are given below:

Definition 1. Inductive inference rules
Inductive Extension

$$\frac{P \notin PN(\Gamma) \quad t \in \mathbf{H}}{\Gamma \Longrightarrow P(t), \Gamma}$$

$$\frac{P \notin PN(\Gamma) \quad t \in \mathbf{H}}{\Gamma \Longrightarrow \neg P(t), \Gamma}$$

Inductive Generalization

$$\frac{\neg A(t') \notin Th(\Gamma) \quad t' \in \mathbf{H}}{A(t), \Gamma \Longrightarrow A(t), \forall x.A(x), \Gamma}$$

Inductive sufficient Condition

$$\frac{\neg A \notin Th(\{B\} \cup \Gamma)}{A \supset B, B, \Gamma \Longrightarrow A, A \supset B, B, \Gamma}$$

Informally, the inductive extension rule means that a new predicate can be added in a theory; the inductive generalization rule says that a particular instance can be generalized to a universal statement; the inductive sufficient condition rules allows to obtain a sufficient condition from a necessary condition.

Lemma 1. If Γ' is obtained from Γ by applying an inductive inference rule given in definition 2.1, then Γ' is consistent with Γ.

Proof: Straightforward from the the definition of the rules. □

The lemma shows that the rules of inductive inference are in the category of context sensitive grammars. Γ_n and Γ' are called a version of theory Γ. A version of a theory is usually viewed as a consistent set of non-logical axioms of a particular problem.

3   Rejetion by Facts and Revision Rule

Definition 2. *Rejection by facts*

Let $\Gamma \models A$. The model $\mathbf{M}$ is called a rejection by facts of Γ of A, if $\mathbf{M} \models \neg A$ holds.

Let $\Gamma_{M(A)} \equiv \{A_i \mid A_i \in \Gamma, \ \mathbf{M} \models A_i, \ \mathbf{M} \models \neg A\}$.

$\mathbf{M}$ is called an *ideal* rejection by facts of A iff $\Gamma_{M(A)}$ is *maximal* in the sense that there does not exist another rejection by facts of A, $\mathbf{M}'$, such that $\Gamma_{M(A)} \subset \Gamma_{M'(A)}$. An ideal rejection by facts of A is denoted by $\overline{\mathbf{M}}(A)$. Let

$$\mathcal{R}(\Gamma, A) \equiv \{\Gamma_{\overline{M}(A)} \mid \overline{\mathbf{M}} \text{ if an ideal rejection by facts of } A\}$$

The ideal rejection by facts satisfies the Occam's razor, which says: "*Entities are not to be multiplied beyond necessity*[4,6]."

Definition 3. Ideal revision

Let $\Gamma \vdash A$. A theory Λ is called an ideal revision of Γ by $\neg A$, if it is a maximal subset of Γ and is consistent with $\neg A$.

Let $\mathcal{A}(\Gamma, A)$ be the set of all ideal revisions of Γ by $\neg A$.

Theorem 1. $\mathcal{A}(\Gamma, A) = \mathcal{R}(\Gamma, A)$.

Proof: Straightforward. □

Example 1. Let $\Gamma \equiv \{A, A \supset B, B \supset C, E \supset F\}$. Obviously, $\Gamma \vdash C$ holds. According to the definition, $\mathcal{A}(\Gamma, C)$ consists of the following three maximum subsets of Γ:

$$\{A, A \supset B, E \supset F\}, \quad \{A, B \supset C, E \supset F\}, \quad \{A \supset B, B \supset C, E \supset F\}.$$

A revision rule can be described as follows:

Revision rule

$$\frac{A \in Th(\Gamma) \quad \Lambda \in \mathcal{A}(\Gamma, A)}{\Gamma \Longrightarrow^r \Lambda}$$

The rule means that when a consequence deduced from theory Γ meets a rejection by facts $\neg A$, a new version of Γ is an ideal revision of Γ by $\neg A$. The concept of reconstruction tells how a new version of a theory can be constructed:

Definition 4. Reconstruction

Given a theory Γ and a sentence A, a theory Γ' is called a reconstruction of Γ for A, if Γ' is defined as below:

If $\Gamma \models A$, then Γ' is Γ itself; if $\Gamma \models \neg A$ ($\neg A$ meets a rejection by facts), then Γ' is Δ, $\Delta \in \mathcal{R}(\Gamma, A)$; otherwise, Γ' is obtained from Γ by applying a rule of inductive inference to Γ and A. For the sake of simplicity, they are called E-reconstruction, R-reconstruction, and I-reconstruction of Γ respectively.

If Δ is an R-reconstruction of Γ for A, then Δ is a maximum subset of Γ and is consistent with $\neg A$. Therefore, R-reconstruction is not unique. The similar idea of R-reconstruction is given in [5], where it is called the maxichoice contraction. The minor difference is that the maxichoice contraction is defined for the theoretical closure $Th(\Gamma)$ in propositional logic, and focused on its proof-theoretic aspects called postulates. In this paper, we are interested in its model-theoretic aspects and the interaction between a theory and its environments. We will focus our attention on the convergent sequences of versions of a theory[10].

4   Sequences and Limits

Definition 5. Sequence

A sequence $\Gamma_1, \Gamma_2, \cdots \Gamma_n, \cdots$ is called a sequence of theories, or sequence for short, if Γ_n is a theory for all $n \geq 1$. It is increasing if $\Gamma_n \subseteq \Gamma_{n+1}$ for all n; it is decreasing if $\Gamma_n \supseteq \Gamma_{n+1}$ for all n; otherwise, it is non-monotonic.

It is assumed that P and Q are the same sentence if $P \equiv Q$ i.e., $(P \supset Q) \wedge (Q \supset P)$ is a tautology.

Definition 6. Limit of a sequence

Let $\{\Gamma_n\}$ be a sequence. The set of sentences:

$$\Gamma^* \equiv \bigcap_{n=1}^{\infty} \bigcup_{m=n}^{\infty} \Gamma_m$$

is called the upper limit of $\{\Gamma_n\}$. The set of sentences:

$$\Gamma_* \equiv \bigcup_{n=1}^{\infty} \bigcap_{m=n}^{\infty} \Gamma_m$$

is called the lower limit of $\{\Gamma_n\}$.

A sequence is convergent if and only if $\Gamma_* = \Gamma^*$. Its limit is lower (upper) limit of the sequence and is denoted as $\lim_{n \to \infty} \Gamma_n$.

The following lemma tells the meaning of the lower and upper limits

Lemma 2.   1. $A \in \Gamma_*$ if and only if there exists $N > 0$ such that $A \in \Gamma_m$ holds for $m > N$.

2. $A \in \Gamma^*$ if and only if there exists a sub-sequence $\{k_n\}$, such that $A \in \Gamma_{k_n}$ holds for $1 \leq n < \infty$.

Proof. Straightforward from the definition. □

Lemma 3. Every increasing sequence $\{\Gamma_n\}$ is convergent. Its limit is $\bigcup_{n=1}^{\infty} \Gamma_n$. Every decreasing sequence $\{\Gamma_n\}$ is also convergent. Its limit is $\bigcap_{n=1}^{\infty} \Gamma_n$.

Example 2. **Increasing sequences**
    The increasing sequences play an important rule in the proofs of some theories of mathematical logic. For example, Lindenbaum theorem says: "Any formal theory of the language L can be extended to be a maximum theory." Its proof is as follows: Since the set of sentences of L is countable, it can be given in the order: $A_1, A_2, \cdots, A_n, \cdots$. Let $\Gamma_0 = \Gamma$,

$$\Gamma_{n+1} = \begin{cases} \Gamma_n \bigcup \{A_n\} & \text{if } \Gamma_n \text{ and } A_n \text{ are consistent} \\ \Gamma_n & \text{if } \Gamma_n \text{ and } A_n \text{ are not consistent} \end{cases}$$

Here, $\{\Gamma_n\}$ is an increasing sequence, its limit $\bigcup_{n=0}^{\infty} \Gamma_n$ is a maximum theory.

Example 3. **Divergent sequence**

$$\Gamma_n = \begin{cases} \{A\} & n = 2k + 1 \\ \{\neg A\} & n = 2k \end{cases}$$

We have $\Gamma^* = \{A, \neg A\}$ and $\Gamma_* = \emptyset$. $\{\Gamma_n\}$ is divergent.

Example 4. **Random sequence**
    Let A be: "*Tossing a coin, and getting a tail*" and Γ_n denote the result of the nth toss. $\{\Gamma_n\}$ is a random sequence of A and $\neg A$, and is divergent.

5 Complete Inductive Processes and Their Limits

Definition 7. Inductive processes
    The sequence $\Gamma_1, \Gamma_2, \cdots, \Gamma_n, \cdots$ is called an inductive process or inductive sequence if Γ_{i+1} is a reconstruction of Γ_i, where $i \geq 1$.

Theorem 2. 1. An inductive process $\{\Gamma_n\}$ is strictly increasing if and only if for every $n \geq 1$, Γ_{n+1} is an I-reconstruction of Γ_n for some A.
  2. An inductive process $\{\Gamma_n\}$ is strictly decreasing if and only if for every $n \geq 1$, Γ_{n+1} is a R-reconstruction of Γ_n for some A.
  3. An inductive process $\{\Gamma_n\}$ is non-monotonic if and only if I-reconstructions and R-reconstructions appear alternatively.

Proof: Straightforward from the definition. □

It is assumed that one is always able to decide whether an instance is true or false. Thus, the instances can be described using the Herbrand universe [7] discussed in section 2:

Definition 8. Complete instance sequence of a model M

Let $\mathbf{P}_0 \quad = \{P_0, \cdots, P_n, \cdots | P_n$ is a 0-ary predicate or its negation$\}$

$\quad \mathbf{P}_{i+1} = \mathbf{P}_i \cup \{P^n(t_1, \cdots, t_n) | t_j \in \mathbf{H}_i, P^n$ is n-ary predicate or its negation$\}$

$\quad \mathbf{P} \quad = \bigcup_{i=1}^{\infty} \mathbf{P}_i$

An enumeration of the set is called a Herbrand sequence of L.

Let $M_\wp$ be a given model of a particular problem $\mathcal{P}$. The interpretation of the Herbrand universe of L under $M_\wp$ is called the Herbrand universe of $M_\wp$, and is denoted by $\mathbf{H}_{M_\wp}$. The interpretation of a Herbrand sequence of L of $M_\wp$ is called a complete instance sequence of $M_\wp$, it is denoted by $\mathcal{E}_M$, sometimes by $\{A_m\}$ if no confusion can occur. A sub-sequence of a complete instance sequence of $\mathbf{M}$ is called a sample sequence of $\mathbf{M}$.

For a given model $\mathbf{M}$, the interpretation of every complete instance sequence is determined. On the contrary, when any complete instance sequence is determined, the model is determined. The following lemma will be used latter.

Lemma 4. $(Th(\Gamma))_* \equiv Th((Th(\Gamma))_*)$

Proof: Straightforward from the definition.

Suppose that we know $\mathcal{E}_M \equiv \{A_m\}$ which is a complete instance sequence of a given model $\mathbf{M}$, and it is the only thing which we know about $\mathbf{M}$. Suppose that Γ is an initial version of a theory. Our goal is to obtain all true sentences of $\mathbf{M}$ by using an inductive procedure which takes $\mathcal{E}_M$ and Γ as its inputs. The basic idea of this procedure is the following:

Let $\Gamma_1 = \Gamma$. Γ_{n+1} will be defined as follows:

1. If $\Gamma_n \vdash A_i$ for some i, then $\Gamma_{n+1} = \Gamma_n$;
2. If $\Gamma_n \vdash \neg A_i$, Γ_{n+1} is a R-reconstruction of Γ_n by $\neg A$. In this case, $\neg A_i$ has met a rejection by facts A_i, and A_i must be accepted.
3. If neither 1 nor 2 can be done, then Γ_{n+1} is defined by the induction rules given in section 2 as below:
   (a) If $A_i = B(t)$ and the inductive generalization rule can be applied, then Γ_{n+1} is $\{A_i, \forall x.B(x)\} \cup \Gamma_n$;
   (b) Otherwise, if $A_i = B$ and exists A, such that $\Gamma_n \vdash A \supset B$, and the inductive sufficient condition rule can be applied for A, then Γ_{n+1} is $\{A, A \supset B, B\} \cup \Gamma_n$;
   (c) If neither case (a) nor case (b) can be done, then Γ_{n+1} is $\{A_i\} \cup \Gamma_n$. □

In the above procedure scheme, for every case, Γ_{n+1} (or Γ_{n+2}) contains A_i. This is because that $A_i \in \mathcal{E}_M \subseteq \mathcal{T}_M$, and it is necessary that the inductive sequence $\{\Gamma_n\}$ will converge to $\mathcal{T}_M$. The following example shows its necessity: Assume that $\mathcal{E}_M \equiv \{A(c_1), \neg A(c_2)\}$ is a complete instance sequence of a given model $\mathbf{M}$. Let $\Gamma \equiv \emptyset$. If we do not allow that Γ_{n+1} must contain A_i, then according to the above procedure scheme, the generalization rule is applied to $A(c_1)$, and Γ_1 becomes $\{\forall x.A(x)\}$. But then, $\neg A(c_2)$ becomes a rejection by facts of Γ_1. Since the R-reconstruction of Γ_1 by $\neg A(c_2)$ is the empty set. Thus, $A(c_1)$ is lost.

When an R-reconstruction is taken in response to a rejection by facts in the nth stage of an inductive process, there are two things which we should deal with:

1. Any R-reconstruction selected should contain all instances accepted in the first the $(n-1)^{th}$ stages. To do so, we introduce a sequence Δ to store these accepted instances.

2. If an R-reconstruction is not selected properly, some information may still be lost. For example, consider $\Gamma = \{A \wedge B\}$, both $\Gamma \vdash A$ and $\Gamma \vdash B$ are provable. Assume that A has met a rejection by facts, then the maximal subset of Γ which is consistent with $\neg A$ is the empty set. Thus, the R-reconstruction (of Γ for A) is the empty set. B does not meet a rejection, but is missing after the revision rule is applied to A! In order to avoid this to happen, we introduce a sequence Θ to collect those instances A_m which are taken to be as logical consequences in case 1. After each R-reconstruction is taken, the procedure checks all A_m contained in Θ, and picks up the lost ones back. Since, at any evolution stage, Θ is always finite, the checking will be terminated.

The above procedure scheme can be specified by a Pascal-like procedure. In the procedure, $*$ is used to denote the concatenation or union of two sequences. The procedure can also be specified by using some transition systems which can be found from [10].

Definition 9. An inductive procedure

Let $\mathbf{M}$ be a given procedure and $\mathcal{E}_M \equiv \{A_i\}$ be a complete instance sequence of $\mathbf{M}$, Γ be a theory. Let $\Gamma_1 = \Gamma$, Γ_{n+1} is defined by the following procedure declaration (see next page):

A sequence $\{\Gamma_n\}$ generated by the procedure GUINA is called a complete inductive process (or sequence) of $\mathcal{E}_M$ and Γ, if the complete instance sequence $\mathcal{E}_M$ of the model $\mathbf{M}$ and theory Γ are taken to be the actual parameters of the the procedure GUINA,

In the this procedure scheme declaration, a composition of inductive inference rules are used in some cases. For example, in the third case (the second *else if*), when the condition $head(\mathcal{T}_n) \equiv P(t)$ and $\Gamma_n \not\vdash \exists x.\neg P$ are satisfied, the procedure will execute as follows:

1. If $P \notin PN(\Gamma_n)$, then the inductive extension rule is applied first, and $\Gamma_n \Longrightarrow P(t), \Gamma_n$ is obtained, and then, since $\Gamma_n \not\vdash \exists x.\neg P$, the inductive generalization rule is further applied to $P(t)$ and Γ_n, that is $P(t), \Gamma_n \Longrightarrow P(t), \forall x.P(x), \Gamma_n$.

procedure GUINA($\mathcal{T}$: F-seq: *var* Γ: F-seq);
    var $\Theta = \emptyset$: F-seq; % F-seq denoted a sequence of sentences
    var $\Delta = \emptyset$: F-seq;
    begin
       loop do
          begin
            if $\Gamma_n \vdash head(\mathcal{T}_n)$
              then begin
                  $\Gamma_{n+1} := \Gamma_n; \mathcal{T}_{n+1} := tail(\mathcal{T}_n);$
                  $\Delta_{n+1} := \Delta_n; \Theta_{n+1} := \Theta_n * \{head(\mathcal{T}_n)\} ;$
              end
            else if $\Gamma_n \vdash \neg head(\mathcal{T}_n)$
                then begin
                $\Gamma_{n+1} := \Lambda,$ where $\Lambda \in \mathcal{A}(\Gamma_n, \neg head(\mathcal{T}_n))$ and $\Delta_n \subset \Lambda;$
                $\mathcal{T}_{n+1} := head(\mathcal{T}_n) * \Theta_n * tail(\mathcal{T}_n);$
                $\Theta_{n+1} := \Theta_n; \Delta_{n+1} := \Delta_n$
                end
              else if $head(\mathcal{T}_n) \equiv P(t)$ and $\Gamma_n \not\vdash \exists x. \neg P$
                then begin
                  $\Gamma_{n+1} := \{P(t), \forall x.P(x)\} * \Gamma_n;$
                  $\mathcal{T}_{n+1} := tail(\mathcal{T}_n);$
                  $\Theta_{n+1} := \Theta_n; \Delta_{n+1} := \{P(t)\} * \Delta_n$
                end
              else if $head(\mathcal{T}_n) \equiv B$ and there is A such that
                  $\Gamma_n \vdash A \supset B$ and $\Gamma_n \not\vdash \neg A$
                then begin
                  $\Gamma_{n+1} := \{A, B\} * \Gamma_n; \mathcal{T}_{n+1} := tail(\mathcal{T}_n);$
                  $\Theta_{n+1} := \Theta_n * \{B\}; \Delta_{n+1} := \Delta_n$
                end
              else begin
                $\Gamma_{n+1} := \{head(\mathcal{T}_n)\} * \Gamma_n;$
                $\mathcal{T}_{n+1} := tail(\mathcal{T}_n);$
                $\Theta_{n+1} := \Theta_n; \Delta_{n+1} := \Delta_n * \{head(\mathcal{T}_n)\}$
              end
        end
       end loop
    end

2. If $P \in PN(\Gamma_n)$, since $\Gamma_n \not\vdash \exists x. \neg P$, we have

$$\Gamma_n \Longrightarrow P(t), \Gamma_n.$$

and then, the inductive generalization rule is applied to $P(t), \Gamma_n$, and $P(t), \Gamma_n \Longrightarrow P(t), \forall x.P(x), \Gamma_n$ is obtained. In the second case, the rule:

$$\frac{P \in PN(\Gamma) \quad \Gamma \text{ and } P(t) \text{ are consistent}}{\Gamma \Longrightarrow P(t), \Gamma}$$

is used. We did not define this rule as a basic inductive rule since it seems trivial. It can be derived from the sufficient condition rule. Let us see how the procedure works through the following example:

Example 5. Let $\mathbf{H} = \{a, b\}$, $\mathbf{P} = \{P(a), P(b), Q(a), Q(b)\}$, under the model$\mathbf{M}$ the interpretation of $\mathbf{P}$is $\varepsilon_M = \{P(a), \neg P(b), Q(a)\}$. The procedure scheme 5.3 can inductively produce $\forall x P(x) \supset Q(x)$.

1. The first step: $\Gamma_1 = \{\}$, $\varepsilon_M = \{P(a), \neg P(b), Q(a)\}$, $T_1 = \varepsilon_M$, $\Theta_1 = \Delta_1 = \emptyset$.
2. The inductive generalization Using the rule of inductive generalization,

$$\frac{\exists x \neg P(x) \notin Th(\Gamma_1)}{P(a), \Gamma_1 \Rightarrow P(a), \forall x P(x), \Gamma_1} \ ,$$

   we obtain $\Gamma_2 = \{P(a), \forall x P(x)\}$, $T_2 = \{\neg P(b), Q(a)\}$, $\Theta_2 = \emptyset$, $\Delta_2 = \{P(a)\}$.
3. Using the revision rule:

$$\frac{P(b) \in Th(\Gamma_2) \ \ \{P(a)\} \in \mathcal{A}(\Gamma_2, P(b))}{\Gamma_2 \Rightarrow^r \{P(a)\}} \ ,$$

   we obtain $\Gamma_3 = \{P(a)\}$, $T_3 = \{\neg P(b), Q(a)\}$, $\Theta_3 = \emptyset$, $\Delta_3 = \{P(a)\}$.
4. Using the inductive extension rule, we obtain: $\Gamma_4 = \Gamma_3 \cup \{\neg P(b)\}$, thus $\Gamma_4 = \{P(a), \neg P(b)\}$, $T_4 = \{Q(a)\}$, $\Theta_4 = \emptyset$, $\Delta_4 = \{\neg P(b), P(a)\}$.
5. Using the inductive generalization again

$$\frac{\exists x \neg Q(x) \notin Th(\Gamma_4)}{Q(a), \Gamma_4 \Rightarrow Q(a), \forall x Q(x), \Gamma_4} \ ,$$

   we obtain $\Gamma_5 = \{P(a), \neg P(b), Q(a), \forall x Q(x)\}$, $T_5 = \emptyset$, $\Theta_5 = \emptyset$, $\Delta_5 = \{Q(a), \neg P(b), P(a)\}$.
   When $n > 5$, $\Gamma_n \equiv \Gamma_5 = \{P(a), \neg P(b), Q(a), \forall x Q(x)\}$.
6. Deductive inference: Since $\Gamma_n \vdash \neg P(b)$, by $\exists$ rule, we have: $\Gamma_n \vdash \exists x \neg P(x)$. Using $\vee$ rule we obtain $\Gamma_n \vdash \exists x \neg P(x) \vee Q(x)$. But $\exists x \neg P(x) \vee Q(x) \equiv \neg \forall x P(x) \vee Q(x) \equiv \forall x P(x) \supset Q(x)$. Therefore, when $n \geq 5$ $\forall x P(x) \supset Q(x) \in Th(\Gamma_n)$ can be derived, that is

$$\forall x P(x) \supset Q(x) \in (Th(\Gamma_n))_*.$$

$\square$

For the inductive procedure scheme 5.3, the following theorem holds:

Theorem 3. Let $\mathbf{M}_\wp$ be a model for a specific problem $\wp$, $T_{M_\wp}$ be the set of its all true sentences, $\mathcal{E}_{M_\wp}$ be its complete instance sequence, and Γ be a theory. If $\{\Gamma_n\}$ is an inductive process of $\mathcal{E}_{M_\wp}$ and Γ, and is generated by the inductive procedure 5.3, then $\{\Gamma_n\}$ is convergent, and

$$\lim_{n \to \infty} Th(\Gamma_n) = T_{M_\wp}.$$

Proof. By structured induction (see Appendix) □

The meaning of theorem 5.2 can be understood as follows: For a particular problem $M_\wp$, one does not know all its laws at the outset of his studying of the problem. As a matter of fact, his knowledge of the problem is being constantly improved and deepened throughout the inductive process. An instance sequence $\mathcal{E}_{M_\wp}$ serves as the criteria upon which to test the inductive inference; one instance of $\mathcal{E}_{M_\wp}$ is examined each time; if it is a logical consequence of the current version of a theory, then it is taken to be an evidence of the theory; if it is a rejection by facts of the current version, then the new version of the theory is an ideal revision of the current version; otherwise, the new version is induced from the instance in accordance with the inductive inference rules given in section 2. If $\mathcal{E}_{M_\wp}$ is a complete instance sequence of $M_\wp$, then the sequence of the versions of the theory is convergent, its limit is $\mathcal{T}_{M_\wp}$. In fact, this can be seen as the rationality of the inductive inference rules.

Finally, the inductive procedure 5.3 is just a simple strategy to generate convergent inductive processes. In fact, one can construct many procedure schemes this kind. It is a major objective of research of "machine learning" to look for the efficient inductive algorithms which generate fast convergent inductive processes.

Acknowledgements

The author expresses his thanks to Zhang Yuping, Wang Ju, Liang Dongmin and Ma Shilong for their helpful discussions and comments.

References

1. Mo, S., Some thoughts on Inductive Inference, The supplement of Logic, Studies of Philosophy, (in Chinese), 1993.
2. McKeon, R., The Basic Works of Aristotle, Random House, New York, 1941, pp 198.
3. Plotkin, G., A structural approach to operational semantics, Lecture notes, Aarhus University, Denmark, September, 1981.
4. Li, W., An Open Logic System, Science in China, Series A, Vol.36, No.3, March, 1993.
5. Alchourrón, C.E., Gärdenfors, R. and Makinson, D., On the logic of theory change: partial meet contraction and revision functions, The Journal of Symbolic Logic, Vol.50, No.2, June, 1985.
6. Flew, A., A Dictionary of Philosophy, Pan Books Ltd, 1979.
7. Gallier, J.H., Logic for Computer Science, foundations of automatic theorem proving. John Wiley & Sons, 1987, 147-158, 162-163, 197-217.
8. C.C Chang & H.J.Keisler , Model Theory , North–Holland , 1990.
9. Hume, D., Theory of knowledge, "An Enquiry Concerning Human Understanding, University of Texas Press, Austin, 1953.
10. Li, W., A logical framework for evolution of specifications, Programming Languages and Systems, (ESOP'94), LNCS 788, Sringer-Verlag, 1994.
11. Paulson, L., Logic and Computations, Cambridge University Press, 1987, 38-50.

Semantics for Pollock's Defeasible Reasoning*

Quoc Bao Vo and Joe Thurbon

Knowledge Systems Group, School of Computer Science and Engineering,
University of New South Wales
{vqbao,joet}@cse.unsw.edu.au

Abstract. Many researchers have proposed argumentation-based reasoning as a viable alternative to reasoning systems with a flat epistemological structure. Perhaps one of the longest standing approaches has been in the Oscar project, led by John Pollock. Unfortunately, without a formal semantics, it is often difficult to evaluate the various incarnations of defeasible reasoning. We provide a semantics for Pollocks defeasible reasoning in terms of Bondarenko *et al.*'s unified framework for default reasoning. We also indicate some internal inconsistencies between the motivation behind and definition's governing Pollock's system.

1   Introduction

The OSCAR system is the implementation of a combination of many theories of rationality, and is probably most completely described in [7]. One major component, which is of particular interest to those researching commonsense and non-monotonic reasoning, is based around defeasible or argumentation based reasoning. It is this component with which we will be solely concerned. Pollock argues for this type of structure sensitive approach as a basis for epistemological theories, which he contrasts with the more traditional approach of logic based theories. In particular [6] he argues that his formalism captures aspects of reasoning which have resisted logic based approaches, using as examples situations in which default logic [9] and circumscription [5] fail to deliver answers which he considers appropriate. However, as it is presented in [6], the rules which define defeasible reasoning in Oscar fail to capture the intuitions which were employed to motivate them. We present two examples (self-defeat and cycles of defeat - both of which were presented in [6]) that are handled in a manner contrary to our expectations.

No formal semantics has been defined for Pollock's system thus far. This causes two problems: (i) it becomes difficult to carry out a systematic study and/or extend Pollock's system (e.g. to specialise it to fit into some specific formalism or a special domain); and more importantly, (ii) it is not always clear whether this system will give sound conclusions. A well-defined semantics is thus desirable, especially in light of the examples presented herein.

---

* An extended version of this paper with full proofs of all theorems is also available. The reader should feel free to contact the authors for a copy.

N. Foo (Ed.): AI'99, LNAI 1747, pp. 316–327, 1999.

1.1 Outline

First, we present Bondarenko *et al.*'s system, then re-express the argument structure proposed by Pollock [6] in terms of algebraic expressions so that it becomes comparable to other frameworks in default reasoning, in particular, Bondarenko *et al.*'s.

We also rectify some limitations in Pollock's representation of argument structures to guarantee the integrity of the representation and note some internal inconsistencies in it as presented in [6]. Finally, we provide a semantics for Pollock's system in terms of Bondarenko *et al.*'s.

2   Bondarenko *et al.*'s System

The original approach as presented by Dung in [4] is an abstract and general framework for argumentation which is independent of any system defined on top of this formalism. It defines an *argumentation framework* as a pair $\langle AR, attacks \rangle$ consisting of a set AR of arguments and the attack relationship between arguments, i.e., $attacks \subseteq AR \times AR$.

Further refinement led by Bondarenko *et al.* results in a unified framework for default reasoning [1]. A close examination of Pollock's and Bondarenko *et al.*'s approaches shows some intimate connections between the two formalisms. We reproduce the relevant definitions from Bondarenko's work for completeness.

A *deductive system* is a pair $\langle \mathcal{L}, \mathcal{R} \rangle$ where
-$\mathcal{L}$ is a formal language consisting of countably many sentences, and
-$\mathcal{R}$ is a set of inference rules of the form

$$\frac{\alpha_1, \ldots, \alpha_n}{\alpha}$$

where $\alpha, \alpha_1, \ldots, \alpha_n \in \mathcal{L}$ and $n \geq 0$.

- Any set of sentences $T \subseteq \mathcal{L}$ is called a *theory*. A *deduction* from a theory T is a sequence $\beta_1, \ldots, \beta_m$, where $m > 0$, such that, for all $i = 1, \ldots, m$,
  - $\beta_i \in T$, or
  - there exists $\frac{\alpha_1, \ldots, \alpha_n}{\beta_i}$ in $\mathcal{R}$ such that $\alpha_1, \ldots, \alpha_n \in \{\beta_1, \ldots, \beta_{i-1}\}$.
- $T \vdash \alpha$ means that there is a deduction from T whose last element is α. $Th(T)$ is the set $\{\alpha \in \mathcal{L} \mid T \vdash \alpha\}$.

Definition 1 [1] Given a deduction system $\langle \mathcal{L}, \mathcal{R} \rangle$, an *assumption-based framework* with respect to $\langle \mathcal{L}, \mathcal{R} \rangle$ is a tuple $\langle T, Ab, {}^- \rangle$ where
-$T, Ab \subseteq \mathcal{L}$ and $Ab \neq \emptyset$,
-$^-$ is a mapping from Ab into $\mathcal{L}$, where $\overline{\alpha}$ denotes the contrary of α.

Definition 2 [1] Given an assumption-based framework $\langle T, Ab, {}^- \rangle$ and $\Delta \subseteq Ab$,
-Δ is *conflict-free* iff for all $\alpha \in Ab, T \cup \Delta \not\vdash \alpha, \overline{\alpha}$,
-Δ is *maximal conflict-free* iff Δ is conflict-free and there is no conflict-free $\Delta' \supset \Delta$.

Definition 3 [1] Given an assumption-based framework $\langle T, Ab, {}^- \rangle$,

-a set of assumptions $\Delta \subseteq Ab$ *attacks* an assumption $\alpha \in Ab$ iff $T \cup \Delta \vdash \bar{\alpha}$,

-a set of assumptions $\Delta \subseteq Ab$ attacks a set of assumptions $\Delta' \subseteq Ab$ iff $\Delta \subseteq Ab$ attacks some assumption $\alpha \in \Delta'$.

If Δ attacks α (respectively Δ'), we also say that Δ is an *attacker against* α (resp. Δ'), or α-attacker (resp. Δ'-attacker). Notice the deviation from the notation of the original in [1].

Definition 4 [1] Given an assumption-based framework $\langle T, Ab, ^- \rangle$, and a set of assumptions $\Delta \subseteq Ab$: Δ is *closed* iff $\Delta = \{\alpha \in Ab \mid T \cup \Delta \vdash \alpha\}$.

Definition 5 [1] A set of assumptions Δ is *stable* iff

-Δ is closed,

-Δ does not attack itself, and

-Δ attacks each assumption $\alpha \notin \Delta$.

Definition 6 [1] 1. An assumption $\alpha \in Ab$ is said to be *defendeded* with respect to a set $\Delta \subseteq Ab$ iff for each closed set of assumptions $\Delta' \subseteq Ab$, if Δ' is a minimal α-attacker then Δ attacks Δ'.

2. A closed set of assumptions $\Delta \subseteq Ab$ is *admissible* iff

- Δ does not attack itself, and

- each α in Δ is defended with respect to Δ.

Definition 7 [1] A set of assumptions $\Delta \subseteq Ab$ is *preferred* iff Δ is maximal (with respect to set inclusion) admissible.

3   Pollock's System

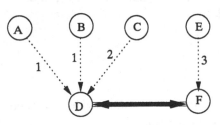

Fig. 1. A simple inference graph

In Pollock's system, one represents an argument as a graph in which the nodes represent steps of inference in the argument. The directed edges in the graph are of three types. The first, *conclusive reasons*, represent deductive links or logical entailment from one node to another. The second, *prima facie reasons*, represent defeasible reasons to conclude one node given another. The third, *defeaters*, represent reasons not to accept a node that was only defeasibly concluded. In this paper, we limit our discussion to graphs that have no conclusive reasons, since the intended resolution of a situation in which a node is both conclusively deduced and also defeated is not clear in Pollock's work. We follow Pollocks conventions, representing prima-facie or defeasible reasons with dashed arrows, and defeaters with filled arrows.

As presented in [6], at most one justification is allowed for each node. That is, all of the prima facie reasons for a node in a graph are required, under conjunction, to justify a conclusion together. To represent multiple justifications[1] we

---

[1] which Pollock does by variously appealing to the use of multiple graphs, or modifying the graphs to be AND/OR graphs

introduce the concept of *labelled inference links* so that different justifications of a node can be identified with different labels, not multiple graphs. For example, in figure 1, node D is justified either throuh justification 1 (requiring support from both node A and node B) or through justification 2, requiring support only from node C. Node F has only one justification, namely 3. Nodes D and F defeat each other.

Definition 8 An *inference graph* is a labelled directed graph $\langle V, L, \mathcal{I}, \mathcal{D} \rangle$ consisting of a finite set of nodes V representing the *steps of inference* (or *arguments*), and L is a set of labels which gives each justification of a node a unique name. Furthermore,

- $\mathcal{I} \subseteq V \times V \times L$ is the set of *labelled inference links* (also called *reasons*); and
- $\mathcal{D} \subseteq V \times V$ is the set of *defeat links* (also called *defeaters*).

Let α be a node of an inference graph $\langle V, L, \mathcal{I}, \mathcal{D} \rangle$, we will denote

- the set of labels that denotes the justifications of α as α-*bases*,
- the set of nodes that are connected to α through a defeat link as α-*defeaters*.
- each $\lambda \in \alpha$-bases is associated with a set of nodes which are required to fulfill the justification labelled λ. We denote this set by λ-*root*.

- In a graph Γ a node α is initial iff α-defeaters $= \emptyset$ and for every β in every λ-root of α, β is initial. We call the set of initial nodes in the graph Γ-*initial*

For instance, in the example in Figure 1, we have:
- D-base $= \{1, 2\}$,
- D-defeaters $= \{E\}$,
- The 1-root of D is $\{A, B\}$, and the 2-root of D is $\{C\}$.

Definition 9 A *status assignment* σ of an inference graph $\Gamma = \langle V, L, \mathcal{I}, \mathcal{D} \rangle$ is a function $V \rightarrow \{defeated, undefeated\}$ which indicates the status of nodes in V. A status assignment must also abide by the restrictions which amend those in [6] to admit multiple justifications.

An assignment σ of *defeated* and *undefeated* to a subset of the nodes of an inference graph is a *partial status assignment* iff for all $\alpha \in V$,

(1) $\sigma(\alpha) = undefeated$ if $\alpha \in \Gamma$-initial

(2) $\sigma(\alpha) = undefeated$ iff $\sigma(\beta) = undefeated$ for all β in some λ-root of α, and $\sigma(\gamma) = defeated$ for all $\gamma \in \alpha$-defeaters

(3) $\sigma(\alpha) = defeated$ iff $\sigma(\beta) = defeated$ for some β in every λ-root of α, or $\sigma(\gamma) = undefeated$ for some $\gamma \in \alpha$-defeaters

σ is a status assignment iff σ is a partial status assignment and σ is not properly contained in any other status assignment.

We use *Status Assignment* (i.e. with capital letters) to refer to the intersection of all status assignments of a single graph V.

There are two possible interpretations of this definition. The first corresponds σ being a total function over some sub-set of V, with all nodes not in the domain of σ being removed from the graph. The second corresponds to σ being a partial function over the entire graph V. It is Pollock's intention that the first of these interpretations be used [personal correspondence].

In situations where there are more than one status assignment, one takes the skeptical approach, giving the following definition:

Definition 10. [6][7] A node is considered undefeated iff every status assignment assigns *undefeated* to it; otherwise it is defeated. Of the defeated nodes, a node is defeated outright iff no status assignment assigns *undefeated* to it, otherwise it is provisionally defeated.

We introduce a fourth definition, for clarity.

Definition 11. A *total status assignment* σ of a graph $\Gamma = \langle V, L, \mathcal{I}, \mathcal{D} \rangle$ is a status assignment and is total over V.

For the intended interpretation of status assignment to give the proper results, it must be the case that a partial status assignment can only be admitted if it is maximal in two senses: (i) that it not be properly contained in any other status assignment, as per Definition 9, and (ii) it also must come from a sub-graph which is maximal in the following sense. A sub-graph of Γ, say Γ', is maximal with respect to status assignments on Γ iff Γ' has a total status assignment and no graph $\Gamma'' \supset \Gamma'$, where $\Gamma'' \subseteq \Gamma$, has a total status assignment.

Without this addition, the system as originally presented by Pollock must consider any node with incident defeaters as provisionally defeated[2], and hence only initial nodes could ever be considered undefeated.

3.1 Provisional and Outright Defeat

In Definition 10, Pollock draws the distinction between the provisional and outright defeat of a node. Although they do not figure directly in any of his more formal definitions, they form the basis of the motivation for these definitions [6] and [7]. From [6], a provisionally defeated node should be *infectious*; that is, unable to support any inference, but able to defeat another node. An outright defeated node should not be able to do either. Although the formal definitions capture Pollock's intentions in graphs that have total status assignments, they fail to do so in graphs that have only partial status assignments. That is, the motivations behind the definitions are inconsistent with the definitions themselves.

In particular, cases of so-called *self-defeat*, where a node defeats one of its (possibly indirect) ancestors, were one of the primary motivators for the notion of outright defeat[6]. However, a self defeating node results in only the provisional defeat of that node. The admission of partial status assignments recognises that there can be arguments, for a node which are inconsistent. However, the manner in which they are handled essentialy involves hoping that the Status Assignment generated by taking the intersection of all status assignments captures the intended meaning of the original graph. The example of a self-defeating argument for a node, which should result in the that node's outright defeat, shows that

---

[2] This follows immediately from allowing σ to be defined over arbitrary subsets of V. For instance, consider the status assignment for the graph in Figure 1 containing only four nodes A, B, C and E. If this were admitted, then E would be considered provisionally defeated in the Status Assignment of V.

this is not always the case. A similar argument can be made regarding defeat cycles of odd length.

4 Relationships between Pollock's and Bondarenko *et al.*'s Frameworks

Despite the similar appearance of the two frameworks proposed by Pollock and Dung (in the most straightforward way, one would think about an equivalence between the attacks relationship in [4] and the defeat links in [6]), there are no obvious ways to subsume one under another or to prove their equivalence. This is due to differences underlying the basic structures of the two frameworks.

From the above re-formalisation of Pollock's system in terms of algebraic expressions, however, one can see resemblances with Bondarenko *et al.*'s system. However, some minor differences include: (i) the structure of the arguments are not restricted in Pollock's system while Bondarenko *et al.* require the elements of an assumption-based framework to be logical sentences and the links among them to be inference rules; (ii) in Pollock's system the defeating relationships are explicitly represented, where in Bondarenko *et al.*'s they must be derived through the derivation of the contrary of assumptions.

Despite the above differences, there seem to be many commonalities between the two frameworks. Firstly, the central notions of the two systems model both the reasoning process as arguments and the defeat (or, attack) relationships between the basic elements of each system. Secondly, the intuitions behind the semantics (resp. status assignments) of assumption-based frameworks (resp. inference graphs) seem to be closely related. For instance, the stable model semantics [1] requires a stable extention to attack every assumption which does not belong to it. There is an analogous requirement for status assignments: that the accepted nodes be assigned undefeated, while the rest are assigned defeated. Further, if a status assignment assigns defeated to a node, it must assign defeated to one of its ancestors, or undefeated to one of its defeaters: this is similar to being attacked. A similar correspondence between preferred extensions and partial status assignment can also be observed.[3] In light of these similarities, one may ask: Are these two systems actually equivalent in some sense, especially from a semantic point of view, i.e., will they produce the same answer for every problem domain?

In general these two systems don't produce exactly the same results as each other, in particular when there are no stable extensions or total status assignments for the given problem. This should also be expected because of the different motivations behind each system: The credulous semantics play an important part in [1], [4], whereas Pollock's system maintains a sceptical approach. Notice also that the sceptical versions of the semantics proposed in [1] do not correspond exactly to the assignment of *defeated* and *undefeated* to the nodes of inference

---

[3] Part of this result is reported in this paper (Theorem 2 and Corollary 2). The other part appears in an extended version of this paper.

graphs. However, since both approaches have their own suitable applications, a further study to combine the merits of both of them into a single system is desirable. That is the main aim of this paper.

The first observation is that a common language is necessary to compare the results of both systems. On the surface, Pollock's system seems more general than Bondarenko *et al.*'s system since no restrictions are imposed on the internal structures of the arguments or the nodes in an inference graph. However, we will embed Pollock's system into the formalism proposed in [1]. There are two reasons that we wish to do so: (i) it has been argued elsewhere [10], Pollock has taken his research in a direction which is too general for AI's uses; and (ii) Bondarenko *et al.*'s system has several well-defined (and well understood) semantics and has close connections with most major frameworks in non-monotonic reasoning .

4.1   The Translation

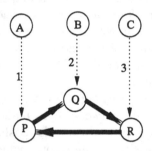

Fig. 2. A simple inference graph

To define the transformation of an inference graph to an assumption-based framework, we introduce the function Υ defined as follows: let S be a set of symbols, $\Upsilon(S) = \{\Upsilon(\theta) \mid \theta \in S\}$. Intuitively, elements of the set $\Upsilon(S)$ play a similar role to the justifications in default rules as defined in [9], $\Upsilon(\theta)$ is read as "it is consistent to assume that θ does not hold".

Given an inference graph $\Gamma = \langle V, L, \mathcal{I}, \mathcal{D} \rangle$, for convenience, we define Γ-*defeaters* $= \{\delta \in V \mid \text{for some } \alpha \in V, (\delta, \alpha) \in \mathcal{D}\}$.

Definition 12 Let $\Gamma = \langle V, L, \mathcal{I}, \mathcal{D} \rangle$ be an inference graph, the translation of Γ to an assumption-based framework, denoted as $ABF(\Gamma)$, is defined as follows: $ABF(\Gamma) = (\langle \mathcal{L}, \mathcal{R} \rangle, \langle T, Ab, - \rangle)$, where

- $\mathcal{L} = V \cup \Upsilon(\Gamma\text{-defeaters})$,
- $\mathcal{R}$ is the smallest set such that for each node α in V: let α-defeaters $= \{\delta_1, \ldots, \delta_m\}$ and if $\lambda \in \alpha$-bases and λ-root $= \{\alpha_1^\lambda, \ldots, \alpha_n^\lambda\}$ then

$$\frac{\alpha_1^\lambda, \ldots, \alpha_n^\lambda, \Upsilon(\delta_1), \ldots, \Upsilon(\delta_m)}{\alpha} \in \mathcal{R},$$

- $T = \Gamma\text{-initials}$,
- $Ab = \Upsilon(\Gamma\text{-defeaters})$, and
- for each $\alpha \in Ab$, if $\alpha = \Upsilon(\theta)$ then $\overline{\alpha} = \theta$.

Example 1 Consider the inference graph in figure 1:
$$\Gamma_1 = \langle \{A, B, C, D, E, F\}, \{1, 2, 3\}, \{(A, C, 1), (B, C, 1), (D, C, 2), (E, F, 3)\},$$
$\{(D, F), (F, D)\}\rangle$, which will be translated to an assumption-based framework as follows:

$ABF(\Gamma_1) = \langle\langle\{A,B,C,D,E,F\}, \{\frac{A,B,\Upsilon(F)}{D}, \frac{C,\Upsilon(F)}{D}, \frac{E,\Upsilon(D)}{F}\}\rangle,$
$\langle\{A,B,C,E\}, \{\Upsilon(D),\Upsilon(F)\}, ^-\rangle\rangle$, where $\overline{\Upsilon(D)} = D$ and $\overline{\Upsilon(F)} = F$.

Example 2 Consider the inference graph in figure 2:

$\Gamma_2 = \langle\{A,B,C,P,Q,R\}, \{1,2,3\}, \{(A,P,1),(B,Q,2),(C,R,3)\}, \{(P,Q),$
$(Q,R),(R,P)\}\rangle$, which will be translated to an assumption-based framework as follows:

$ABF(\Gamma_2) = \langle\langle\{A,B,C,P,Q,R\}, \{\frac{A,\Upsilon(R)}{P}, \frac{B,\Upsilon(P)}{Q}, \frac{C,\Upsilon(Q)}{R}\}\rangle,$
$\langle\{A,B,C\}, \{\Upsilon(P),\Upsilon(Q),\Upsilon(R)\}, ^-\rangle\rangle$, where $\overline{\Upsilon(\mu)} = \mu$ for each $\mu \in \{P,Q,R\}$.

There are several semantics proposed for assumption-based frameworks as has been mentioned above. Also, Pollock introduces a semi-formal system for inference graphs in which the notions of status assignments and partial status assignments have been employed to give the acceptability (or alternatively defeat) status for each node in the graph. In addition, an algorithm has also been provided.[4] The interesting question is: *Do the notions of status assignments and partial status assignments correspond to any of the formal semantics introduced by Bondarenko et al.?*

Before we answer, we make two notes. Firstly, in Pollock's work, the notions of "defeated" and "undefeated" have been used throughout while Bondarenko *et al.* use the notion of "acceptability" in most cases. There is an obvious correspondence between the two notions of "undefeated" and "acceptability". We will use "undefeated" in contexts which are more or less involved with inference graphs while "acceptability" will be used more often when we talk about assumption-based frameworks. Secondly, we will only consider stratified inference graphs in the sense that: (i) nodes are finitely reachable from the initial nodes; and (ii) no cycles that involve only inference links are allowed[5]. We give the formal definition for stratified inference graphs:

Definition 13 Let $\Gamma = \langle V, L, \mathcal{I}, \mathcal{D}\rangle$ be an inference graph, Γ is said to be *stratified* if and only if it contains no infinite path of the form $\alpha_1, \ldots, \alpha_n, \ldots$, where for each $i \geq 1$, there exists a $\lambda \in L$ such that $(\alpha_i, \alpha_{i+1}, \lambda) \in \mathcal{I}$.

---

[4] Whether or not the algorithm does correspond exactly to the definitions and the definitions correctly reflect the intuitions motivating Pollock's framework is another story. Certainly, it is unclear whether the algorithm presented in [6] captures the definitions presented therein.

[5] In this case, there are at most two ways to assign statuses to the nodes involved in the cycle regardless of the assignment given for other nodes, namely all of them are assigned either defeated or undefeated. It boils down to the following three cases: two trivial cases in which (*a*) all nodes must have the defeated status; and (*b*) all nodes must have the undefeated status. The only non-trivial case arises when both status assignments are consistent with the given graph. In this case none of these nodes will be accepted in a sceptical extension of the given inference graph which takes the intersection of all assignments. Though it is not impossible to obtain the results below with the presence of cycles of inference links (the obvious way is to expand the set of assumptions to include all elements of the set V as well), this restriction will significantly simplify the presentation and concentrate on the essence of the results rather than getting bogged down with unnecessary details.

Notice that our notion of stratification of inference graphs as defined in the above definition has no correspondence with the notion of stratified assumption-based framework as defined by Bondarenko *et al.* The key difference is that we try to avoid the cycles of inference links for the sake of simplicity whereas stratified assumption-based framework is defined on the basis of so-called *attack relationship graphs*. Say in other words, by stratified assumption-based frameworks, Bondarenko *et al.* rule out infinite chains of attack links[6] (including cyclic chains of attack links) in assumption-based frameworks. It is obvious that in most applications, the arguments, and thus the assumptions, would usually attack each other. Therefore, Bondarenko *et al.*'s stratified assumption-based frameworks are not very useful for general real-world applications.

Henceforth, when there is no possible confusion, we will refer to stratified inference graphs simply as inference graphs.

4.2   The Correspondence

We show that the above translation captures exactly the intuitive meaning of the defeat links within the *attacks* relationships. The following theorem shows that, under the above translation, the stable model semantics corresponds exactly to the status assignments as defined by Pollock.

Lemma 1 Let $\Gamma = \langle V, L, \mathcal{I}, \mathcal{D} \rangle$ be an inference graph and Δ a set of assumptions of $ABF(\Gamma)$.

$T \cup \Delta \vdash \Upsilon(\alpha)$ if and only if $\Upsilon(\alpha) \in \Delta$.

The proof for the above lemma is trivial according to the fact that the consequents of the inference rules in $\mathcal{R}$ can only be members of the set V. This lemma implies that every set of assumptions $\Delta \subseteq Ab$ of $ABF(\Gamma)$ is closed. Those assumption-based frameworks that enjoy this property are said to be *flat* following Bondarenko *et al.* (1997).

We now proceed to the main lemma of this paper.

Lemma 2 Let $\Gamma = \langle V, L, \mathcal{I}, \mathcal{D} \rangle$ be an inference graph and σ a status assignment for Γ. Let $\Delta_\sigma = \{\Upsilon(\delta) \in Ab \,|\, \sigma(\delta) = defeated\}$ be a set of assumptions of $ABF(\Gamma)$. $\alpha \in Th(T \cup \Delta_\sigma)$ iff $\sigma(\alpha) = undefeated$, where T is the theory of $ABF(\Gamma)$.

Then part (a) of the following theorem is an immediate corollary of the above lemma. For the converse, we introduce the notion of a status assignment associated with a set of assumptions with respect to the translated assumption-based framework of a given inference graph. Let $\Gamma = \langle V, L, \mathcal{I}, \mathcal{D} \rangle$ be an inference graph and Δ a set of assumptions in $ABF(\Gamma)$, the mapping σ_Δ which assigns the "undefeated" and "defeated" status to elements of V, defined as follows: for each $\alpha \in V$,

$$\sigma_\Delta(\alpha) = \begin{cases} undefeated, & \text{iff } \alpha \in Th(T \cup \Delta) \\ defeated, & \text{otherwise.} \end{cases}$$

---

[6] Bondarenko *et al.*'s attack links are similar to defeat links in Pollock's terms under our translation. The difference is that a defeat link connects between two nodes of an inference graph whereas the attack links connect betweeen assumptions. The essential details make no difference since both kinds of links play the same role.

is called the Δ-assumption assignment.

Theorem 1 Let $\Gamma = \langle V, L, \mathcal{I}, \mathcal{D} \rangle$ be an inference graph.

(a) If σ is a status assignment for Γ then the set of assumptions Δ_σ is stable in $ABF(\Gamma)$.

(b) If Δ is a stable set of assumptions in $ABF(\Gamma)$ then σ_Δ is a status assignment for Γ.

Example 1 (*continued.*) In Pollock's framework, there are two total status assignments for Γ_1, denoted as σ_1^1 and σ_2^1 which are defined as follows:

$\sigma_1^1(A) = \sigma_1^1(B) = \sigma_1^1(C) = \sigma_1^1(D) = \sigma_1^1(E) = undefeated$ and $\sigma_1^1(F) = defeated$, and

$\sigma_2^1(A) = \sigma_2^1(B) = \sigma_2^1(C) = \sigma_2^1(E) = \sigma_2^1(F) = undefeated$ and $\sigma_2^1(D) = defeated$.

On the other hand, we have the following two stable set of assumptions in $ABF(\Gamma_1)$: $\Delta_1^1 = \{\Upsilon(F)\}$ and $\Delta_2^1 = \{\Upsilon(D)\}$ which respectively correspond to the following two extensions of $ABF(\Gamma_1)$: $\{A, B, C, E, D, \Upsilon(F)\}$ and $\{A, B, C, E, F, \Upsilon(D)\}$.

One thus can observe the correspondence between the notions of status assignments and stable extensions in this example.

Corollary 1 Let $\Gamma = \langle V, L, \mathcal{I}, \mathcal{D} \rangle$ be an inference graph.

(a) If σ is a (total) status assignment for Γ then $\sigma_{\Delta_\sigma} = \sigma$,

(b) If Δ is a stable set of assumptions in $ABF(\Gamma)$ then $\Delta_{\sigma_\Delta} = \Delta$.

Notice also that there are no (total) status assignment for the inference graph Γ_2. This is the case for self-defeating arguments and odd length cycles of defeat links (which is the case for Γ_2) as has been pointed out by Pollock [6]. On the other hand, the assumption-based framework $ABF(\Gamma_2)$ does not possess any stable set of assumptions since any set of assumptions that contains at least two of the assumptions $\Upsilon(P), \Upsilon(Q)$, and $\Upsilon(R)$ should attack itself and any set of assumptions that contains at most one of the assumptions does not attack some other assumption, e.g. the set $\Delta = \{\Upsilon(P)\}$ does not attack $\Upsilon(R)$.

It is not surprising that (total) status assignments in Pollock's system exactly correspond to the stable model semantics of Bondarenko *et al.*'s framework, and therefore also fit into the standard semantics of most non-monotonic reasoning formalisms including default logic, non-monotonic modal logic, autoepistemic logic, logic programming and some fragments of circumscription as has been shown by Bondarenko *et al.* But it is well-known that the more important features in both frameworks proposed by Pollock and Bondarenko *et al.* lie in the extensions of their frameworks - the partial status assignments, and the preferred and admissible semantics respectively. These extensions allow their systems to cope with some interesting problems which can not be solved by many traditional non-monotonic formalisms. We now investigate the the relationships between these notions more closely.

Theorem 2 Let $\Gamma = \langle V, L, \mathcal{I}, \mathcal{D} \rangle$ be an inference graph. If σ is a partial status assignment for Γ then the set of assumptions Δ_σ is admissible in $ABF(\Gamma)$.

Corollary 2 Let $\Gamma = \langle V, L, \mathcal{I}, \mathcal{D} \rangle$ be an inference graph. If σ is a maximal partial status assignment for Γ then the set of assumptions Δ_σ is preferred in $ABF(\Gamma)$.

Example 2 (*continued.*) In Pollock's framework, there is a single partial status assignment for Γ_2 (which is also maximal), denoted as σ^2, defined as follows:

$$\sigma^2(A) = \sigma^2(B) = \sigma^2(C) = undefeated \text{ and } \sigma^2(P) = \sigma^2(Q) = \sigma^2(R) = unassigned.$$

This allows us to compute the following preferred set of assumptions in $ABF(\Gamma_2)$ (following the definition given above): $\Delta^2 = \Delta_{\sigma^2} = \emptyset$. This set of assumptions is associated with the preferred extension consisting of only A, B and C.

It is obvious that the converse of Theorem 2 does not hold. That the converse of Corollary 2 holds is reported in the extended version of this paper.

5 Discussion

As has been discussed throughout this paper, the argumentation systems as proposed by Pollock and Bondarenko *et al.* have some important strengths in comparison to other frameworks in defeasible and non-monotonic reasoning. Among the significant advantages of these approaches is their generality. Both are abstract argumentation frameworks which in general do not depend on a particular underlying logic or language. This feature allows both systems to capture most reasoning facilities sanctioned by well-known non-monotonic reasoning mechanisms. In particular, as it has been proved in [1], most non-monotonic reasoning mechanisms can be expressed in terms of assumption-based frameworks.

While Pollock's system is presented with some seemingly natural representations of argument structures (inference graphs), this system suffers from its lack of a well-defined formal semantics. As has been shown in this paper, some notions which seem to be intuitive at first sight may not turn out to be captured by the definitions. To rectify this shortcoming of Pollock's system and at the same time, provide an insight into the two systems and their relationships, we introduced a translation which has been proved to be sound and complete with respect to the stable semantics in terms of assumption-based frameworks [1]. Furthermore, we also examined the aspects of this relationship when the standard semantics of default logic, logic programming, autoepistemic logic, etc. does not exist.

The subsumption of Pollock's systems under Bondarenko *et al.*'s framework suggests that the assumption-based framework is very powerful. However, it seems that the generality and expressiveness of assumption-based frameworks are not always desirable. Firstly, certain peculiarities may arise when arbitrary relationships are allowed in an assumption-based framework.[7] More seriously, Bondarenko *et al.*'s system does not provide any way to detect and avoid such situations. Secondly, there has always been a trade-off between expressiveness

---

[7] an example of these situations is presented in the extended version of the present paper.

and computation. As has been shown in [3], except for the case of skeptical admissible semantics which comes down to trivial monotonic reasoning, computing preferred semantics is in general harder than computation of stable model semantics in logic programming.

5.1 Future work

We would like to provide a set of definitions in Pollock's framework which properly capture the notion of outright and provisional defeat, but maintain the elegant locality of the rules that currently define his system, or prove that you cannot. We hope to extend the results in this work further and in more detail to shed light on the significance of argumentation-theoretic approaches in AI and, in particular, reasoning.

Acknowledgements

This work would not have been possible without the support of the Knowledge Systems Group, in particular, Allen Courtney, Norman Foo, Rex Kwok and Yusuf Pisan were motivating forces behind this paper. The anonymous referees provides some insightful comments that help improve both the content and presentation of this paper. Joe Thurbon is partially supported by an APA research scholarship. Quoc Bao Vo is partially supported by an OPRS scholarship.

References

1. Bondarenko, A., Dung, P.M., Kowalski, R.A., Foni, F. (1997) An Abstract, Argumentation-theoretic Approach to Default Reasoning. *Artificial Intelligence* (93) pp63-101
2. Doerpmund, J. (1997) Limitations of Skeptical Default Reasoning; in *Procedings of International Conference on Uncertainty in Artificial Intelligence*
3. Y. Dimopoulos, B. Nebel, F. Toni, (1999) Preferred Arguments are Harder to Compute than Stable Extensions, in: *Proceedings of the 16th International Joint Conference on Artificial Intelligence* (IJCAI'99), Stockholm, Sweden
4. Dung, P.M. (1995) The Acceptability of Arguments and its Fundamental Role in Nonmonotonic Reasoning, Logic Programming and n-person games *Artificial Intelligence*, (77) pp321-357
5. Lifschitz, V. (1987) Pointwise Circumscription, in Ginsberg, M. (ed) *Readings in Nonmonotonic Reasoning.* Morgan Kauffman, Los Altos
6. Pollock, J. (1994) Justification and Defeat *Artificial Intelligence* (67) pp377-408
7. Pollock, J. (1995) *Cognitive Carpentry: A Blueprint for How to Build a Person.* MIT Press, London
8. Pollock, J. (1996) Implementing Defeasible Reasoning *Workshop on Computational Dialectics, International Conference on Formal and Applied Practical Reasoning.* Bonn, Germany
9. Reiter, R. (1980) A Logic for Default Reasoning. *Artificial Intelligence* (13) pp81-132
10. Simari, G.R., Loui, R.P. (1992) A Mathematical Treatment of Defeasible Reasoning and its Implementation *Artificial Intelligence* (53) pp125-157

Feasibility of Optimised Disjunctive Reasoning for Approximate Matching

Ian Horrocks[1], Lin Padgham[2], and Laura Thomson[2]

[1] Dept. of Computer Science
University of Manchester, UK
horrocks@cs.man.ac.uk
[2] Dept. of Computer Science
Royal Melbourne Institute of Technology
Melbourne, VIC 3001, Australia
{linpa, laura}@cs.rmit.edu.au

Abstract. Description logics are powerful knowledge representation systems providing well-founded and computationally tractable classification reasoning. However recognition of individuals as belonging to a concept based on some approximate match to a prototypical descriptor has been a recurring application issue as description logics support only strict subsumption reasoning. Expression of concepts as a disjunction of each possible combination of sufficient prototypical features has previously been infeasible due to computational cost. Recent optimisations have greatly improved disjunctive reasoning in description logic systems and this work explores whether these are sufficient to allow the heavy use of disjunction for approximate matching. The positive results obtained support further exploration of the representation proposed within real applications.

1 Introduction

Description Logic systems are knowledge representation systems based on First Order Logic or a subset of FOL chosen specifically for computational reasons. They have a Tarski-style semantics and a syntax which is particularly well suited to an object-oriented approach to describing concepts (classes) and individuals. Key functionality of DL systems is based on the notion of subsumption testing which is used both in building the class hierarchy and in recognising which concepts individuals belong to. This class of systems have been successfully used in a range of applications (e.g. [5]). However a number of other applications have experienced difficulty due to the fact that recognition of individuals as belonging to a concept is done on the basis of the individuals having all characteristics defined for that concept. There is no notion in DLs of exceptions or of default or typical characteristics.[1]

We argue that in many applications what one wants is a notion of individuals being recognised as members of a concept, based on having a sufficient number of a cluster of

---

[1] Some work has been done on extending DLs to include defaults (e.g. [3, 17, 18]) but this is primarily directed towards default reasoning, rather than the issue of using defaults for recognition as is being explored here.

N. Foo (Ed.): AI'99, LNAI 1747, pp. 328–339, 1999.

typical characteristics (plus possibly some necessary characteristics), rather than simply a fixed set of characteristics.

For example Coupey and Fouquere describe how for recognising faults in a telecommunications application it is absolutely necessary to be able to take account of default characteristics [6]. However they take an approach of requiring that individuals explicitly have an exception to a default characteristic to allow recognition. This can be awkward, and is not always even possible. A medical diagnosis application [18] similarly needs to use typical symptoms to describe diseases, but does not want an individual presentation not to be recognised because it does not have *all* typical symptoms.

In order to meet the needs of the many applications similar to these it is necessary to be able to define a set of typical characteristics associated with a concept. An individual belonging to the concept is required to have some "critical mass" of these characteristics, and *should be recognised as belonging to the concept on this basis*. The most obvious way to achieve this within the semantics of first order logic (and Description Logics) is to define the concept as a disjunction of all the combinations of sufficiently many typical characteristics.

In an example from [18], chronic pyelonephritis is described as having the characteristics urine.dysuria, urine.casts, fatigue and urine.bacteria. Defining the concept on the basis of 75% of these characteristics would give us:

$$CPN \doteq (urine.dysuria \sqcap urine.casts \sqcap fatigue) \sqcup$$
$$(urine.casts \sqcap fatigue \sqcap urine.bacteria) \sqcup$$
$$(fatigue \sqcap urine.bacteria \sqcap urine.dysuria) \sqcup$$
$$(urine.bacteria \sqcap (urine.dysuria \sqcap urine.casts).$$

Previously the intractability of the algorithms used for reasoning with disjunctions has meant that heavy usage of disjunctions is not a viable option computationally for real application systems.

For example, KRIS [2], one of the first DL systems that included principled reasoning with disjunction at all, exhibits very poor performance when reasoning with knowledge bases (KBs) containing significant numbers of disjunctive concepts.

Optimizations of KRIS that allowed it to obtain similar performance characteristics to CLASSIC [1] (the most efficient of the set of tested DL systems [10]), did not address optimisations for disjunctive concepts (which cannot be represented in CLASSIC).

The new algorithms and optimisation techniques recently developed allow the typical case reasoning performance of DL systems to be radically improved [14]. These optimisations are particularly effective with respect to disjunctive reasoning. However there has been no experimentation which pushes the limits of these new algorithms, or examines whether they are adequate for particular application oriented needs which require heavy use of disjunction.

The work presented in this paper explores whether these techniques are in fact sufficiently powerful to support the routine use of disjunctive concepts to address the application issue of approximate matching to a prototype for recognition of individuals. Section 2 describes a representational model for defining concepts; section 3 describes in some detail the problem with disjunctive reasoning and the optimisations used in the FaCT system, which we hope will make the proposed representation viable. Section 4 describes the experiments done to investigate this viability and the results obtained.

The results appear promising and we are building a bibliographic database application based on the techniques described, to further investigate the mechanisms within a genuine application.

2 Representation of Concepts

Literature from cognitive psychology supports the idea that when people think in terms of concepts, they actually think in terms of prototypical descriptions, rather than in terms of strictly necessary characteristics [19]. However using a prototypical description for a concept descriptor in description logic systems (or any other system based on first order logic) will cause problems, as some sub-concepts as well as individuals will not have all characteristics of the prototype. In terms of recognising individuals, or automatically classifying sub-concepts, the prototypical description of the concept is over-defined. On the other hand, use of only necessary characteristics in defining a concept results in concepts being under-defined, with consequent lack of discrimination.

Earlier work by Padgham and others [16, 18] has explored describing concepts using two descriptors - a *core descriptor* for defining the strictly necessary characteristics and a default descriptor, (which we will call the *prototype descriptor*) which is subsumed by the core and in addition defines the prototypical characteristics. However this mechanism does not explicitly offer any assistance in recognising the specific concept an individual belongs to in cases where the core is under-defined and the individual does not fit the full prototype descriptor.

We build on this work by also defining a *basic descriptor* which explicitly captures the space of concept descriptions which are sufficiently close to the prototype descriptor that individuals subsumed by the basic descriptor should be recognised as instances of the concept.

The form of the basic descriptor is an "or" statement which defines any combination of 70% of the "features"[2] used in the prototype descriptor. The basic descriptor thus subsumes the prototype descriptor and an individual should be recognised as being an instance of a concept X based on subsumption by the basic descriptor for X.

Once users or application developers have defined the core and prototype descriptors the definition of basic descriptors can be automated. It would also be possible to generate descriptors capturing varying levels of agreement with the prototype (e.g. 90%, 70%, 50%) in different structures, allowing applications to attempt instance inference, or recognition of individuals at various levels of closeness to the prototype descriptor.

Further extensions where characteristics within a prototype can be grouped, requiring some critical mass in each group, can also be envisaged. However all these refinements rely on the adequacy of the optimisations being explored to provide computational viability when relatively large 'or' clauses are routinely used.

---

[2] Further investigation is needed regarding constraints that may need to be placed on the form of prototype descriptors. However this is outside the scope of the initial explorations presented in this paper. The agreement level of 70% may also be subject to variation.

3   Subsumption Involving Disjunction

Description Logic systems provide a range of automated reasoning services, in particular inferring subsumption and instantiation (instance-of) relationships. Subsumption is the class/super-class relationship between concepts, while instantiation is the relationship between individuals and those concepts of which they are instances. The use of subsumption inference to build a concept hierarchy (partial order) is known as *classification* and the use of instantiation inference to determine the classes each individual belongs to is known as *recognition*.

A standard Tarski style model theoretic semantics is used to interpret descriptions and to justify inferences. The meaning of concepts and roles is given by an interpretation $\mathcal{I}$ which is a pair $(\Delta^{\mathcal{I}}, \cdot^{\mathcal{I}})$, where $\Delta^{\mathcal{I}}$ is the domain (a set) and $\cdot^{\mathcal{I}}$ is an interpretation function. The interpretation function maps each concept to a subset of $\Delta^{\mathcal{I}}$, each role to subset of $\Delta^{\mathcal{I}} \times \Delta^{\mathcal{I}}$, and each individual to a unique element of $\Delta^{\mathcal{I}}$. More complex descriptions can be built up by combining descriptions using a variety of operators, with the semantics of the resulting description being derived from its components.

A concept C is subsumed by (is more specific than) a concept D (written $C \sqsubseteq D$) if it can be inferred that $C^{\mathcal{I}} \subseteq D^{\mathcal{I}}$ for all possible interpretations $\mathcal{I}$. The result of classification procedures based on the subsumption relation is typically cached in the form of a directed acyclic graph called the concept hierarchy or taxonomy.

An individual x is an instance of a concept C (written $x \in C$) if it can be inferred that $x^{\mathcal{I}} \in C^{\mathcal{I}}$ for all possible interpretations $\mathcal{I}$. In many cases, instantiation reasoning, (or recognition), can be reduced to subsumption reasoning using either precompletion [11] or encoding [8] techniques; for this reason most recent studies have concentrated on subsumption reasoning. We follow this tradition and explore the tractability of recognition by obtaining experimental results for appropriate subsumption tests.

Most modern DL systems[3] perform subsumption reasoning by transforming the subsumption problem into an equivalent satisfiability problem: $C \sqsubseteq D$ if and only if the concept description $(C \sqcap \neg D)$ is *not* satisfiable. The satisfiability problem can then be solved using a provably sound and complete algorithm based on the tableaux calculus [20]. This approach was first described for the $\mathcal{ALC}$ DL and its practical application was demonstrated by the KRIS system.

The FaCT system uses an optimised implementation of a tableaux algorithm to perform subsumption reasoning. Like other tableaux algorithms it either proves the satisfiability of a concept C by constructing an example interpretation in which $C^{\mathcal{I}}$ has at least one member, or proves its unsatisfiability by demonstrating that all attempts to construct an example must lead to a contradiction. When C contains disjunction, trying to construct an example interpretation is non-deterministic. Earlier DLs dealt with this non-determinism by naively performing an exhaustive depth first search, and it is this which leads to the poor performance of the KRIS system with highly disjunctive concepts. Although it still performs an exhaustive search, the FaCT system includes a range of optimisations which can dramatically reduce the size of the search space—these include the normalisation and encoding of concept descriptions, an improved search al-

---

[3] At least those which provide sound and complete reasoning.

gorithm, the use of heuristics to guide the search, dependency directed backtracking, and the caching and re-use of partial results.

3.1 Example

A simple example illustrates the vital importance of optimisation techniques with the kinds of basic concept descriptors that will be generated using the representation discussed in section 2.

We will take a simple prototypical concept description consisting of only four "features" $\exists f_1.C_1 \sqcap \exists f_2.C_2 \sqcap \exists f_3.C_3 \sqcap \exists f_4.C_4$, where each of the C_i is a conjunction of three primitives such as $P_{i1} \sqcap P_{i2} \sqcap P_{i3}$, and generate a basic descriptor C_v that will subsume any conjunction containing at least two of the $\exists f_i.C_i$ terms:

$$C_v \doteq (\exists f_1.C_1 \sqcap \exists f_2.C_2) \sqcup (\exists f_1.C_1 \sqcap \exists f_3.C_3) \sqcup$$
$$(\exists f_1.C_1 \sqcap \exists f_4.C_4) \sqcup (\exists f_2.C_2 \sqcap \exists f_3.C_3) \sqcup$$
$$(\exists f_2.C_2 \sqcap \exists f_4.C_4) \sqcup (\exists f_3.C_3 \sqcap \exists f_4.C_4)$$

When classifying a concept $D \doteq \exists f_1.C_1 \sqcap \exists f_2.C_2$, it will be necessary to determine if C_v subsumes D. As described above, this will be transformed into a satisfiability test: C_v subsumes D iff $D \sqcap \neg C_v$ is not satisfiable. As a result of its being negated, the C_v part of this description becomes a conjunction of disjunctive clauses:

$$(\exists f_1.C_1 \sqcap \exists f_2.C_2) \sqcap$$
$$(\forall f_1.\neg C_1 \sqcup \forall f_2.\neg C_2) \sqcap (\forall f_1.\neg C_1 \sqcup \forall f_3.\neg C_3) \sqcap$$
$$(\forall f_1.\neg C_1 \sqcup \forall f_4.\neg C_4) \sqcap (\forall f_2.\neg C_2 \sqcup \forall f_3.\neg C_3) \sqcap$$
$$(\forall f_2.\neg C_2 \sqcup \forall f_4.\neg C_4) \sqcap (\forall f_3.\neg C_3 \sqcup \forall f_4.\neg C_4)$$

To test the satisfiability of this concept, a naive tableau algorithm would try to build an example interpretation by proceeding roughly as follows:

1. Initialise the interpretation to contain a single individual x_0 which satisfies the concept. Expand all of the conjunctions, making it explicit that x_0 satisfies each of $\exists f_1.C_1, \ldots, (\forall f_3.\neg C_3 \sqcup \forall f_4.\neg C_4)$.
2. Search for a consistent expansion of the disjunctive concepts. Expand each unexpanded disjunction by selecting one of the disjuncts, backtracking and trying the other disjunct if that fails (leads to a contradiction). Typically, $\forall f_1.\neg C_1$ would be chosen from the first disjunction, $\forall f_2.\neg C_2$ from the fourth disjunction (disjunctions 2 and 3 are satisfied by the first choice), and $\forall f_3.\neg C_3$ from the last disjunction.[4]
3. Expand the $\exists f_i.C_i$ terms one at a time. For $\exists f_1.C_1$, this means creating a new individual x_1 satisfying the concept C_1 and related to x_0 by the role f_1. Due to the $\forall f_1.\neg C_1$ chosen from the first disjunction, x_1 must also satisfy $\neg C_1$. This seems to be an obvious contradiction, but as C_1 is actually the conjunction $P_{11} \sqcap P_{12} \sqcap P_{13}$, and $\neg C_1$ is the disjunction $\neg P_{11} \sqcup \neg P_{12} \sqcup \neg P_{13}$, discovering the contradiction in x_1 will mean expanding the conjunction and then searching the terms in the disjunction to discover that each choice leads to a contradiction with one of the expanded conjuncts.

---

[4] Completing all propositional reasoning before expanding $\exists R.C$ terms minimises space requirements [12].

4. Having discovered this contradiction, the algorithm will backtrack and continue searching different expansions of the conjunctions which x_0 must satisfy until it discovers that all possibilities lead to contradictions. It is then possible to conclude that $D \sqcap \neg C_v$ is not satisfiable, and that C_v thus subsumes D.

There are several obvious inefficiencies in this procedure, and some not so obvious. In the first place, there is the problem of the late discovery of "obvious" contradictions, for example when a complete (non-deterministic) expansion of C_1 and $\neg C_1$ is performed in order to discover the contradiction in x_1. This is a consequence of the fact that most tableaux algorithms assume the input concept to be fully *unfolded* (all defined concepts are substituted with their definitions), and in *negation normal form* (NNF), with negations applying only to primitive concepts [12]. Arbitrary $\mathcal{ALC}$ concepts can be converted to NNF by internalising negations using DeMorgan's laws and the identities $\neg \exists R.C = \forall R.\neg C$ and $\neg \forall R.C = \exists R.\neg C$.

The KRIS system uses *lazy unfolding* to deal with the problem of late discovery, only unfolding and converting to NNF as required by the progress of the algorithm. Thus if C_1 were a named concept (introduced by a concept definition statement of the form $C_1 \doteq P_{11} \sqcap P_{12} \sqcap P_{13}$), then its unfolding would be postponed and the contradiction between C_1 and $\neg C_1$ immediately discovered. FaCT takes this idea to its logical conclusion by giving unique system generated names to all compound concepts. Moreover, the input is lexically analysed to ensure that the same name is given to lexically equivalent concepts. This means that the concepts $\exists f_1.C_1$ and $\forall f_1.\neg C_1$ would be named A and $\neg A$ respectively (for some system generated name A), and a contradiction would be detected without the need to create x_1.

Another problem with the naive search is that the same expansion can be explored more than once. For example, after some backtracking the algorithm will determine that choosing $\forall f_2.\neg C_2$ from the fourth disjunction always leads to a contradiction and will try the second choice, $\forall f_3.\neg C_3$. Expanding the fifth disjunction will then lead to $\forall f_2.\neg C_2$ being chosen, an identical solution to the first one. FaCT avoids this problem by using a *semantic branching* search technique adapted from the Davis-Putnam-Logemann-Loveland procedure (DPL) commonly use to solve propositional satisfiability (SAT) problems [7, 9]. Semantic branching works by selecting a concept C such that C is an element of an unexpanded disjunction and $\neg C$ is not already in the solution, and searching the two possible expansions obtained by adding either C or $\neg C$. Wasted search is avoided because the two branches of the search tree are strictly disjoint. For example, when the choice of $\forall f_1.\neg C_1$, $\forall f_2.\neg C_2$ and $\forall f_3.\neg C_3$ leads to a contradiction, subsequent backtracking will cause the choice of $\forall f_2.\neg C_2$ to be changed to $\neg \forall f_2.\neg C_2$, so the first solution can never be repeated.

Finally, after the discovery of the contradiction in x_1, the naive search continues with *chronological* backtracking in spite of the fact that the contradiction was caused by $\forall f_1.\neg C_1$, the first choice made. FaCT deals with this problem by using *backjumping*, a form of dependency directed backtracking adapted from constraint satisfiability problem solving [4]. Each concept is labelled with a dependency set indicating the branching choices on which it depends, and when a contradiction is discovered the algorithm can jump back over intervening choice points without exploring alternative choices.

4 Empirical Investigations

An empirical evaluation was performed in order to determine the viability of using a
real knowledge base developed using the representational model described in section 2.
This evaluation used synthetically generated data in order to evaluate the performance
of FaCT and to determine if the optimisation techniques described in Section 3.1 would
be sufficiently powerful to permit empirically tractable reasoning with respect to the
kinds of subsumption problem that would be encountered. The tests were also run using
KRIS in order to identify levels which have previously caused problems, and as a way
of identifying cases where FaCT may involve extra cost.

The testing used a variation of a random concept generation technique first described by [9] and subsequently refined by
[15]. The generated concepts are of the form $\exists f_1.C_1 \sqcap \ldots \sqcap \exists f_\ell.C_\ell$, where each f_i is
an attribute (single valued role) and each C_i is a conjunction of n primitive concepts
chosen from N possibilities.

For a given concept C and an approximation value V in the range 0–100, a concept
C_v is formed, as in Section 3.1, consisting of a disjunction of all possible conjunctions
containing $V\%$ of the $\exists f_i.C_i$ terms in C.[5] To represent the (hardest) kind of subsumption test that would be involved in the recognition process, a second concept C_r is
formed from C by changing elements of the C_i from each $\exists f_i.C_i$ term so that C_r is
subsumed by C_v with a probability P, and the time taken to test if C_v does in fact subsume C_r is measured. Varying ℓ (the number of "features") and V gives disjunctions of
varying size, and varying P allows performance to be measured for tests ranging from
"obvious" subsumption to "obvious" non-subsumption.

Initial explorations indicate that for a variety of applications the number of default
features is likely to be in the range of 10–15, while the percentage match required is
likely to be about 70%. Tests were performed for the 9 sets of values given in Table 1,
with $n = 4$ and $N = 6$ in all cases. For each test, P was varied from 0–1 in steps of 0.05,
with 10 randomly generated subsumption problems being solved at each data point,
giving a total of 210 subsumption problems in each test. All the tests were performed
on 300MHz Pentium machines, with Allegro CL 5.0 running under Linux, and in order
to keep the CPU time required within reasonable limits a maximum of 1,000s was
allowed for each problem.

Table 1. Parametric values for tests

Test	T1	T2	T3	T4	T5	T6	T7	T8	T9
ℓ	5	5	5	10	10	10	15	15	15
$V(\%)$	90	70	50	90	70	50	90	70	50

Tests T1–T3 proved relatively easy for both FaCT and KRIS, with both systems
able to solve any of the problems in less than 0.1s of CPU time. This is not particularly

---

[5] The number of terms is rounded down to the nearest integer.

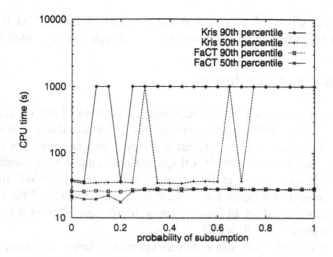

Fig. 1. Percentile times for T9 with KRIS and FaCT

surprising as, even for T3, C_v will be a disjunction of only 10 conjuncts, each of which is of size 2. Tests T4 and T7 also proved relatively easy, with both systems able to solve any problem in less than 0.3s of CPU time. This is again due to the small size of the disjunctions, resulting in this case from the 90% approximation value.

For tests T5 and T6 the difference between FaCT and KRIS became more evident. For T5, FaCT is able to solve >90% of problems in less than 0.3s, while for T6 this increases to 0.4s. With KRIS, the time taken to solve a problem critically depends on whether C_v subsumes C_r (i.e., $C_r \sqcap \neg C_v$ is unsatisfiable) or not. For T5 most non-subsuming (satisfiable) problems are solved in less than 0.1s whereas subsuming problems take more than 3.5s, while for T6 these values are 0.1s and 21s respectively. KRIS's faster time for non-subsuming problems is due to the fact that, in most cases, a solution can quickly be found regardless of the search strategy; FaCT, on the other hand, still has the overhead of its more sophisticated search techniques, and in particular of the lexical analysis and naming of sub-concepts.

For tests T8 and T9, KRIS's difficulty with subsuming problems becomes critical and it proved unable to solve any such problem within the 1,000s of CPU time allowed. FaCT remained consistent with respect to both subsuming and non-subsuming problems, solving >90% of problems in less than 9s for T8 and less than 28s for T9, with FaCT's worst time in all tests being 31s. Figure 1 shows the 50th percentile (median) and 90th percentile[6] times for T9 with KRIS and FaCT plotted against the probability of generating subsuming concepts. Note that where the CPU time is shown as 1,000s no solution was found, and the time which would be required in order to find a solution could be ≫1,000s.

KRIS's poor performance is easily explained by the fact that for T8, C_v will be a disjunction of 3,003 conjuncts, each of which is of size 10. When C_v is negated in the subsumption test this becomes a conjunction of disjuncts which, using a naive strategy,

---

[6] The 90th percentile is the maximum time taken to solve all but the hardest 10% of problems.

leads to a search of 10^{3003} possible expansions (although only 2^{10} of these can be unique); for T9 C_v will be a disjunction of 6,435 conjuncts, each of which is of size 7.

5   Discussion and Conclusions

Clearly the results using FaCT on the larger disjuncts (in tests T8 and T9) are encouraging compared to KRIS, indicating that frequent use of optimised disjunctive reasoning is potentially viable. To ascertain whether the very significant gains are sufficient to justify the proposed representation in real applications, some further questions should be considered: At what rate do individuals need to be categorised? Will one instance inference, or recognition process, lead to further instance inferences? How many subsumption tests are needed for an instance recognition? How likely is it that the more difficult subsumption tests will occur?

An additional question also has to do with space complexity. The naive representation of the conceptual representation described results in exponential increase in space requirements. However we would expect to adapt existing techniques which only require keeping part of the concept hierarchy in memory, and to expand concepts to their full representation only at run-time. The exponential space increase will not result in exponential time increase using the described optimisations, due to the fact that most of the increase is in equivalent concepts which are pruned away.

The rate at which instance inference needs to be done can vary widely depending on the application. In a real-time telecommunications fault diagnostic system, individual descriptors needing to be classified as normal, or as a particular category of fault, may arrive at several per second. On the other hand a support system for medical diagnosis, being used by an individual doctor, could reasonably expect a descriptor of patient symptoms every 10 minutes. The rate for a bibliographic or travel KB, responding to user queries probably lies somewhere between these two. The experimental response times we have established are clearly adequate for some applications, but possibly inadequate for others.[7]

Applications with highly interrelated individuals can result in significant propagation when a single individual is modified. Consequently one recognition process can trigger several other such processes. Some applications (such as a bibliographic database or a travel information database) rely on a large set of individuals many of which may be interrelated. However, other applications (such as the medical diagnostic support described in [18], where individuals are descriptions of a set of patient symptoms) mostly deal with individuals which have no effect on other individuals and thus can only result in the subsumption tests necessary for a single recognition problem.

The number of subsumption tests required for a particular instance recognition task depends on both the number of concepts and the form of the hierarchy. Assuming that the hierarchy is close in form to a tree, and that individuals typically belong to only one sub-class at each level (at least until the bottom levels of the hierarchy are reached), then the number of subsumption tests needed at each level will be equal to the fan-out of the

---

[7] Although if inadequate response times occur relatively infrequently it may be possible to achieve usability by supplementing the optimisation techniques with special purpose heuristics.

hierarchy at that level. Consequently, the total number of subsumption tests required will be roughly the average fan-out multiplied by the depth of the tree. Moreover, FaCT uses a caching optimisation to facilitate the quick discovery of non-subsumption, and this will typically work for all but one test at each level [13]. This effectively reduces the number of "full" subsumption tests to be equal to the depth of the tree.

The form of the hierarchy generated using the representation described in Section 2, with 3 descriptors per concept, obviously increases the number of nodes in the hierarchy by a factor of 3. It is also possible that the form of the hierarchy differs from concept hierarchies with which we are familiar, due to the various nuances of A is-a B which become available. For example in Figure 2 the hierarchy on the left represents the case where As are typically Bs, whereas the hierarchy on the right represents the case where As are always Bs. Further work is needed to determine the form of application taxonomies using this representation, but it is unlikely that the number of hard subsumption tests required per recognition task will change significantly: only the basic descriptors are highly disjunctive, and the caching optimisation should still allow "full" tests to be avoided in most cases. It is also likely that further optimisations can be developed, based on the particular representations we are using.

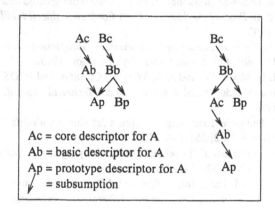

Fig. 2. Two nuances of A is-a B with 3 descriptors

The experimental subsumption problems generated were deliberately designed to be difficult, and it is unclear how often such problems would be encountered in a KB using the representation proposed (it is likely they would be more common than is usual for difficult subsumption problems in KBs not routinely using this representation). The best case would be that such difficult subsumption tests would be encountered only very occasionally, and never more than one per individual recognition process. Given that ontologies tend to be much broader than they are deep, typically with a depth in the range of 7 to 14, this would give (for the T9 situation) a response time which occasionally peaked at around 30s; the worst case would be that all "full" subsumptions for a given individual were difficult, giving a response time of 7 minutes for a typical hierarchy of depth 14. This may still be acceptable for an application such as that described in [18] where the system is being used as a diagnostic support tool for medicine.

To sum up, even making very pessimistic assumptions leads to a predicted worst-case response time of 7 minutes per recognition process. This is clearly within the range of useful response times for some applications. As a result of these explorations we are convinced that the recent optimisations make routine disjunctive reasoning feasible and thus justify using a representational approached based on disjunction. We are in the process of building a bibliographic KB application to further explore the representation of concepts as described and the associated computational properties.

References

1. F. Baader, E. Franconi, B. Hollunder, B. Nebel, and H.-J. Profitlich. An empirical analysis of optimization techniques for terminological representation systems or: Making KRIS get a move on. In *Proc. of the 3rd Int. Conf. on the Principles of Knowledge Representation and Reasoning (KR-92)*, pages 270–281, 1992.
2. F. Baader and B. Hollunder. KRIS: Knowledge representation and inference system. *SIGART Bulletin*, 2(3):8–14, 1991.
3. Franz Baader and Bernhard Hollunder. How to prefer more specific defaults in terminological default logic. In *Proc. of the 13th Int. Joint Conf. on Artificial Intelligence (IJCAI-93)*, pages 669–674, 1993.
4. A. B. Baker. *Intelligent Backtracking on Constraint Satisfaction Problems: Experimental and Theoretical Results*. PhD thesis, University of Oregon, 1995.
5. J. I. Berman, H. H. Moore IV, and J. R. Wright. CLASSIC and PROSE stories: Enabling technologies for knowledge based systems. *AT&T Technical Journal*, pages 69–78, January/February 1994.
6. P. Coupey and C. Fouquere. Extending conceptual definitions with default knowledge. *Computational Intelligence*, 13(2):258–299, 1997.
7. M. Davis, G. Logemann, and D. Loveland. A machine program for theorem proving. *Communications of the ACM*, 5:394–397, 1962.
8. G. De Giacomo and M. Lenzerini. TBox and ABox reasoning in expressive description logics. In *Proc. of the 5th Int. Conf. on the Principles of Knowledge Representation and Reasoning (KR-96)*, pages 316–327, 1996.
9. F. Giunchiglia and R. Sebastiani. A SAT-based decision procedure for $\mathcal{ALC}$. In *Proc. of the 5th Int. Conf. on the Principles of Knowledge Representation and Reasoning (KR-96)*, pages 304–314, 1996.
10. J. Heinsohn, D. Kudenko, B. Nebel, and H.J. Profitlich. An empirical analysis of terminological representation systems. In *Proc. of the 10th Nat. Conf. on Artificial Intelligence (AAAI-92)*, pages 676–773, 1992.
11. B. Hollunder. *Algorithmic Foundations of Terminological Knowledge Representatin Systems*. PhD thesis, Universität des Saarlandes, 1994.
12. B. Hollunder and W. Nutt. Subsumption algorithms for concept languages. In *Proc. of the 9th European Conf. on Artificial Intelligence (ECAI-90)*, pages 348–353, 1990.
13. I. Horrocks. *Optimising Tableaux Decision Procedures for Description Logics*. PhD thesis, University of Manchester, 1997.
14. I. Horrocks. Using an expressive description logic: FaCT or fiction? In *Proc. of the 6th Int. Conf. on the Principles of Knowledge Representation and Reasoning (KR-98)*, pages 636–647, 1998.

15. U. Hustadt and R. A. Schmidt. On evaluating decision procedures for modal logic. In *Proc. of the 15th Int. Joint Conf. on Artificial Intelligence (IJCAI-97)*, volume 1, pages 202–207, 1997.

16. Lin Padgham. Defeasible inheritance: A lattice based approach. *Computers and Mathematics with Applications*, 23(6-9):527–541, 1992. Special Issue on Semantic Nets.

17. Lin Padgham and Bernhard Nebel. Combining classification and non-monotonic inheritance reasoning: A first step. In *Proc. of the 7th Int. Sym. on Methodologies for Intelligent Systems (ISMIS-93)*, pages 132–141, 1993. LNAI 689.

18. Lin Padgham and Tingting Zhang. A terminological logic with defaults: A definition and an application. In *Proc. of the 13th Int. Joint Conf. on Artificial Intelligence (IJCAI-93)*, volume 2, pages 662–668, 1993.

19. E. Rosch. Cognitive representations of semantic categories. *Journal of Experimental Psychology*, 104, 1975.

20. R. M. Smullyan. *First-Order Logic*. Springer-Verlag, 1968.

An Examination of Probabilistic Value-Ordering Heuristics

Matt Vernooy and William S. Havens

Intelligent Systems Lab, School of Computing Science, Simon Fraser University
Burnaby, B.C., Canada V5A 1S6
{mvernooy,havens}@cs.sfu.ca

Abstract. Searching for solutions to constraint satisfaction problems (CSPs) is NP-hard in general. Heuristics for variable and value ordering have proven useful in guiding the search towards more fruitful areas of the search space and hence reducing the amount of time spent searching for solutions. Static ordering methods impart an ordering in advance of the search and dynamic ordering methods use information about the state of the search to order values or variables during the search. A well-known static value ordering heuristic guides the search by ordering values based on an estimate of the number of solutions to the problem. This paper compares the performance of several such heuristics and shows that they do not give a significant improvement to a random ordering for hard CSPs. We give a dynamic ordering heuristic which decomposes the CSP into spanning trees and uses Bayesian networks to compute probabilistic approximations based on the current search state. Our empirical results show that this dynamic value ordering heuristic is an improvement for sparsely constrained CSPs and detects insoluble problem instances with fewer backtracks in many cases. However, as the problem density increases, our results show that the dynamic method and static methods do not significantly improve search performance.

1 Introduction

Constraint satisfaction problems [16] consist of a set of variables, a domain of values for each variable and a set of constraints between variables representing mutually permissive value assignments. A CSP admits a solution when there exists a value for each variable such that all the constraints are satisfied. Many problems in artificial intelligence can be modeled as CSPs. Some examples include scheduling, machine vision, planning, image recognition, scene analysis and configuration. The constraints in a CSP can be over one or more variables however, we restrict our study to CSPs with binary constraints where all constraints are between two variables without loss of generality [10].

Constructive search algorithms such as backtracking [5], maintain a set of assigned variables which are a partial solution satisfying all of the constraints. At each iteration, a variable which is not currently assigned is chosen and a value from its domain assigned. If no values in the domain are consistent with the

N. Foo (Ed.): AI'99, LNAI 1747, pp. 340–352, 1999.

partial assignment, the previous assignment is redone. The algorithm proceeds in this manner until a solution is found or all possible assignments have been visited unsuccessfully. In general searching for solutions to CSPs in NP-hard, so it is of great interest to explore heuristics that guide the search towards areas of the search space that are likely to contain solutions. Such guides can be incorporated into a backtracking algorithm by advising on the next variable to instantiate or by ordering the values in a variable's domain. The order in which the variables and their values are considered can be decided prior to searching (static ordering) or during the search (dynamic ordering). This paper examines the utility of both static and dynamic value-ordering heuristics in search.

Estimates of the number of solutions to a CSP, originally introduced in [6], can be used as value-ordering heuristics by advising on the next move in the search. The idea of using an estimate of the number solutions in the subtree rooted at a particular instantiation was later applied as a static value-ordering heuristic by Dechter and Pearl [2]. Their estimation method reduces the complexity of a CSP by removing constraints until a spanning tree remains and values are then ordered according to the estimated number of solutions. Meisels et al. [7] describe another method, based on probabilistic updating in Bayesian networks, which was shown to be more accurate on average than the spanning tree method. Their estimates were used to derive global solution probabilities for each variable-value instantiation. Each variable's domain is ordered based on an approximation to the probability that the instantiation is part of a global solution.

We introduce a new static value-ordering heuristic, called the *Multiple Spanning Tree method* (MST), which approximates the probability that a CSP is satisfiable. The multiple spanning tree method preserves the constraints in the network by reducing the complete CSP to a disjoint set of decomposed subproblems. We then show how it can be extended by incorporating Bayesian networks to give a dynamic value-ordering heuristic.

The remainder of this paper is organized as follows: Section 2 gives a description of existing probabilistic static value-ordering methods. The first, called the *Single Spanning Tree method* (SST), is based on a decomposition of the CSP into a representative spanning tree. The second method is the *Uniform Propagation method* which is an improvement on SST and gives more accurate approximations on average. In Section 3 we introduce the multiple spanning tree method (MST) which is an extension to Dechter and Pearl's SST method. However, instead of maintaining a single spanning tree from the original CSP, our method preserves the complete CSP in the form of a disjoint set of spanning trees. The MST method can be used to order values in advance of the search (static MST) and we describe a dynamic value-ordering heuristic (dynamic MST) which combines the multiple spanning tree method with Bayesian networks to approximate solution probabilities for branching choices based on the current configuration of the search. Section 4 compares the search performance of three static value-ordering heuristics and our dynamic one. We compare the methods on problems with varying degrees of difficulty and measure their performance in terms of the number of consistency checks in search. Our empirical results show that the static value-ordering methods are of marginal utility as they tend to perform as poorly as a random ordering as problem hardness increases. The dynamic ordering detects insoluble problems with fewer backtracks and gives an improvement on hard CSPs that are sparsely constrained but the performance degrades as problems become more dense.

2   Previous Work

A binary CSP is defined by a set of n variables $\{X_1, ..., X_n\}$ each having a domain D_i of m possible values $\{v_1, ..., v_m\}$. C is a set of binary constraints between variables where each constraint is denoted as a set C_{jk} of consistent value pairs for constrained variables X_j and X_k respectively. A CSP is satisfiable if there exists a set of values $\{v_1, ..., v_n\}$ corresponding to variables $\{X_1, ..., X_n\}$ such that $(v_j, v_k) \in C_{jk}$ for all constrained variables (X_j, X_k). The number of solutions to a CSP consists of the total number of such unique value sets.

Dechter and Pearl [2] introduce a single spanning tree approximation heuristic (SST) which estimates the number of solutions to a CSP and use it as an advising technique for value ordering. Their method relaxes the constraint network of the CSP by extracting a spanning tree of the tightest constraints and computes the exact number of solutions for the spanning tree as an estimate of the total number of solutions to the complete CSP. The algorithm orders values for a variable X_j by considering the subproblem rooted at X_j (denoted G_j). Each arc in G_j is assigned a weight representing the number of compatible value pairs for that binary constraint. The constraints are then relaxed to form a maximum-weighted spanning tree which is used as an approximation to G_j. Once the spanning tree has been established, the algorithm computes the number of solutions for each of the possible value assignments for the current variable. An estimate of the number of solutions with variable X_j (the root node of the spanning tree) instantiated to value v_t is computed recursively as:

$$N(X_j = v_t) = \prod_{C'} \sum_{D'} N(X_c = v_l)$$

where

$$C' = \{c | X_c \, is \, a \, child \, of \, X_j\}$$

$$D' = \{v_l \in D_c | (v_t, v_l) \in C_{jc}\}$$

The algorithm computes the number of solutions starting from the leaves and working towards the root. The spanning trees for each level in the complete search tree are computed prior to searching and thus value-orderings for each variable are determined statically.

The decomposition method of Dechter and Pearl has several identifiable shortcomings that affect the accuracy of the approximations. One problem is that when the constraints of a given CSP of are equally tight, SST fails to use any criteria for selecting constraints for the decomposed CSP and thus the representative spanning tree is chosen arbitrarily. Another problem with SST is that tightly constrained problems with many variables may suffer from a lack of accuracy in their approximation. For example, consider a CSP having constraints of equal tightness between each variable. Such a CSP has $\frac{n(n-1)}{2}$ constraints. A spanning tree consists of $n-1$ arcs, thus Dechter and Pearl's decomposition method only preserves $\frac{2}{n}$ of the constraints from the original CSP.

Meisels *et al.* [7] describe a method called *Uniform Propagation* which approximates the number of solutions to a CSP without relaxing the constraint network to form a spanning tree. Their approximation method formulates a CSP as a Bayesian network and uses an algorithm based on probability updating to estimate the number of solutions to the CSP. It approximates for each variable-value assignment the probability of being part of a global solution to the CSP. This is represented as $P(X_i = v_j)$ for a variable X_i and a value v_j. In effect, this is an approximation of the ratio of the number of complete solutions that include these particular assignments.

The constraint network for a CSP is converted into a directed acyclic graph (DAG) where an edge (X_j, X_i) between constrained variables X_j and X_i is defined when $i < j$. Thus, X_j is a predecessor of X_i and X_1 is the designated *sink node* which has no successors. The marginal probabilities for each variable represents the corresponding success probabilities for the domain values conditioned on all of the predecessor nodes in the network. To compute the probabilities for an arbitrary variable X_i, the network must be organized such that X_i is the sink node (ie. $X_i = X_1$)

Starting at a node X_n in the network (called the *root node*) and considering every node towards the designated sink node X_1, the marginal probabilities for each node in the network are conditioned on its predecessors. Predecessors of a node X_i are nodes connected through a constraint and whose marginal probabilities have already been computed. To ensure that the marginal probabilities for each node will be considered either directly or indirectly at the sink node, *vacuous constraints* are added to the network which permits any pair of values between X_j and X_1. Vacuous constraints are added between the sink and every other node in the network that does not have any successors.

Once the constraint network of the CSP has been converted into a DAG with an appropriate ordering, the approximation algorithm is applied to determine the probabilities of the designated sink node X_1. The marginal probability of a variable instantiation $X_j = v_t$ being part of a global solution where $\pi(X_j)$ denotes the predecessor of node X_j is denoted $P(X_j = v_t)$ and computed recursively as:

$$\frac{1}{|D_{X_j}|} \prod_{\{c | X_c \in \pi(X_j)\}} \sum_{\{v_l \in D_c | (v_t, v_l) \in C_{jc}\}} P(X_c = v_l)$$

This algorithm assumes conditional independence between predecessors of node X_j. This assumption temporarily removes edges causing cycles between X_j

and its immediate predecessors and allows the probabilistic approximations to be computed in polynomial time. The effect of this independence assumption is that a margin of error is introduced into the probabilities. The probabilistic approximation method is used as a static value-ordering heuristic by imparting an ordering on the domain of each variable. The probabilities for each variable-value combination are computed in advance of the search by making each variable in turn the sink node and running the uniform propagation algorithm. This ordering heuristic was found to perform slightly better than the SST method on an experimental set of problems (as discussed later).

3   Multiple Spanning Tree Method

As previously mentioned, one of the major limitations of the approximation method of Dechter and Pearl is that the decomposition is generally not an accurate representation of the original CSP. It was shown that their method gives estimates that are over-optimistic for non-tree CSPs [7] and performs quite poorly in practice [13]. The Uniform Propagation method of Meisels et $al.$ is an improvement. Their method maintains the topology of the constraint network and gives more accurate approximations by preserving all the constraints.

We introduce a new approximation method which decomposes the constraint network of a CSP into a set of spanning trees of subproblems. Contrary to the decomposition method of Dechter and Pearl, our Multiple Spanning Tree (MST) method maintains all of the constraints from the original CSP. Approximations are computed for each of the subproblems and are then composed giving approximations to the complete CSP. Our approximation algorithm is composed of two components: Decomposition and Approximation.

Decomposition Given a CSP C and its corresponding constraint graph $\mathcal{G}$, our algorithm first decomposes $\mathcal{G}$ into a set of N spanning trees. The decomposition algorithm extracts at each iteration i, a minimum spanning tree C_i from the constraint graph $\mathcal{G}$ in the same way as the SST method of Dechter and Pearl by choosing first those constraints which are tightest. The constraints chosen for S_i are then removed from $\mathcal{G}$ before the next iteration. This decomposition thus preserves all of the constraints of the original network. That is,

$$\mathcal{G} = C_1 \cup C_2 \cup ... \cup C_N \tag{1}$$

where

$$C_1 \cap C_2 \cap .. \cap C_N = \phi \tag{2}$$

Approximation Once the CSP C has been decomposed, we compute the probabilities for each C_i. It was shown by Meisels et $al.$ [7] that the SST and Uniform Propagation methods compute probabilities exactly and equivalently for trees in polynomial time. Bayesian networks are also known to admit these exact probabilities for trees in linear time [11], [8]. We represent each subproblem (C_i) as a Bayesian network and compute their exact probabilities. These are then composed to give an approximation to the exact probabilities of the original CSP. In computing the probabilistic approximation for C we make the general assumption that the subproblems C_1 through C_N are independent. This assumption is based on the observation that they do not share constraints and thus can be regarded as a set of disjoint subproblems of C. It is important to note however, that the subproblems are disjoint in terms of their constraints only. It terms of their respective solutions sets, they are obviously not independent since a global solution to C must also be a solution in each C_i. For each of the individual subproblems C_i, $P_{C_i}(X = v)$ computes the the probability that $X = v$ is part of a solution to C_i. For a given variable X and value v in P, we thus approximate the probability $P(X = v)$ as the probability that $X = v$ is part of a global solution to P where:

$$P(X = v) = P_{C_1}(X = v) \cdot .... \cdot P_{C_N}(X = v) \tag{3}$$

We now formalize our independence assumption and give a derivation of the preceding formula 3. We define S as the set of solutions to the CSP C and $P(S)$ as the probability that a solution is achieved given a complete instantiation of values to variables. $P(S)$ can also be interpreted as the probability that a complete random instantiation is in the global solution set S. $P(S)$ is thus the total number of solutions ($|S|$) over the configuration space for C:

$$P(S) = \frac{|S|}{|D^n|} \tag{4}$$

Given a solution set $\{S_1, .., S_N\}$ corresponding to the decomposed subproblems $\{C_1, ..., C_N\}$:

$$S = S_1 \cap S_2 \cap ... \cap S_N \tag{5}$$

Essentially, if a configuration to the CSP C is in each S_i, it must satisfy all the constraints to C (by equations 4 and 5) and is thus an element of the global solution set S for C.

The second assumption we make in our model is that a global solution to the CSP does exists and thus $S \neq \phi$. This assumption is an artifact of our implementation. We use Bayesian networks to compute the exact beliefs for the subproblems and our representation assumes that each constraint in the CSP is not violated. Bayesian networks must maintain a consistent set of prior probabilities and thus a violated constraint violates the Bayesian network. It follows from equation 5 that $S_1, ..., S_N \neq \phi$. That is, each decomposed subproblem C_i is also assumed to contain a solution. Our approximation $P(X = v)$ is thus conditioned on S giving:

$$P(X = v|S) \tag{6}$$

By the inverse of the product rule we get:

$$\frac{P(X = v \cap S)}{P(S)} \tag{7}$$

We then apply the product rule to the numerator:

$$\frac{P(S|X = v) \cdot P(X = v)}{P(S)} \tag{8}$$

and by equation 5:

$$\frac{P(S_1 \cap ... \cap S_N|X = v) \cdot P(X = v)}{P(S_1 \cap ... \cap S_N)} \tag{9}$$

By our independence assumption we get:

$$\frac{P(S_1|X = v)}{P(S_1)} \cdots \frac{P(S_N|X = v)}{P(S_N)} \cdot P(X = v) \tag{10}$$

Rearranging this equation using Bayes' law we get:

$$\frac{P(X = v|S_1) \cdots P(X = v|S_N)}{P(X = v)^{N-1}} \tag{11}$$

Our approximation algorithm normalizes the approximations over a domain to sum to 1 since we assume that a solution S exists. Thus the term $P(X = v)^{N-1}$ is essentially eliminated from equation 11 leaving:

$$P(X = v|S_1) \cdots P(X = v|S_N) \tag{12}$$

The MST method thus computes probabilistic approximations for each subproblem and composes these through an independence assumption to approximate the probability for the complete CSP.

The MST method can be used to compute solution probabilities prior to search and thus give a static ordering to values (static MST). The SST and Uniform Propagation methods are also static ordering methods, but can only be implemented as such. We can however, use our approximation method as a dynamic value ordering heuristic. Previous work has shown that dynamic value-odering can improve performance on certain types of CSPs [15], [3].

Our dynamic heuristic (dynamic MST) uses the decomposition and approximation of static MST but dynamically maintains the current search state as evidence in the networks of the subproblems. Each instantiated variable in the CSP is part of the evidence set e and we use Bayesian networks to derive inferences based on evidence about the current state of the network for each subproblem C_i. Computing exact beliefs in *singly-connected* Bayesian networks, where there exists only 1 path between nodes, is linear in the number of nodes in the network [11], [8]. Since each C_i is a tree, belief updating on the subproblems is a tractable computation. Our algorithm is thus dynamic in the sense that the approximations are based on a set of evidence (e) about the current partial assignment. For a given variable X and value v, we evaluate $P(X = v|e)$.

Our approximation heuristic is incorporated into a backtracking algorithm to advise on the next most likely move to lead to a solution. At an instantiation point, we consider the next value to assign to a variable based on the corresponding beliefs associated with each value in the variable's domain. We first select that value which has the highest probability or support. Upon choosing a value for a variable, we enter that instantiation as evidence in each of the subproblems and update their beliefs.

Our heuristic is inserted into a backtracking algorithm with very little effort. We define a procedure Advise(X,e) shown in Figure 1. The Advise(X,e) procedure is called when considering a new variable to give advice on the search order over the domain. It takes as an argument the current variable X as well as the current instantiation or evidence e and returns a vector of values representing the search order for the domain of X. This procedure first calls the Bayesian belief algorithm on each subproblem C_i to get the exact probabilities over the variables given the evidence. Beliefs for the original CSP are then approximated through the independence equation of 3 in section 3.2. The next step of the Advise procedure creates the domain vector by adding as elements all values having non-zero probabilities and filtering out those known to be non-solutions. This step reflects the forward checking and arc-consistency algorithms described in the following section. We then call a sorting procedure (Sort(domain,P(X))) which arranges the values in the domain vector according to their corresponding probabilities and returns the ordered vector of values.

```
vector Advise(X,e) {
    vector domain = null;
    for each Cᵢ do
        Update_Beliefs(Cᵢ,e);
    for each value v do
        P(X = v) = 1;
    for each Cᵢ do
        P(X = v)* = P_Cᵢ(X = v);
    for each value v do
        if (P(X = v) > 0) then
            domain.add(v);
    if (domain!=null) then
        domain=Sort(domain,P(X));
    return domain;
}
```

Fig. 1. Advising algorithm for value-ordering

We use a commercial software package called *Netica* [9] to maintain the probabilities and compute beliefs for the Bayesian networks. It provides functionality through an API for entering and removing evidence for a variable instantiation and backtrack respectively. For an instantiation $X = v$, we enter the finding for each C_i and for a backtrack, we undo the finding by reverting back to the state of each C_i before $X = v$ was admitted. An instantiation occurs in the backtracking algorithm when choosing a value in the domain vector returned from the Advise(X,e) routing. The 2 conditions for backtracking are when Advise(X,e) returns an empty vector or there are no values left in the domain vector to instantiate.

4   Experiment and Results

Previous analysis comparing the SST and uniform propagation methods was on relatively small experimental problem sizes and did not grade problems based on their difficulty [7]. This resulted in limited insight into the performance of each method in varying regions of problem hardness. For the experimental analysis of each approximation method we use as test cases three categories of problems with increasing levels of difficulty.

The experimental problem set consists of randomly-generated CSPs characterized by four parameters: n, the number of variables; m, the domain size; p_1, the probability of a constraint between a given pair of variables; p_2 the probability that a pair of values for two variables is inconsistent given that a constraint exists. We restrict the size of our problems to CSPs with $n = 20$ and $m = 10$ and divide the problems into 3 sets varying in degrees of constrainedness where $p_1 = \{0.2, 0.5, 1.0\}$. The p_2 value for each set ranges from .01 to 1.0 in steps of .01 representing varying degrees of problem constrainedness. We generate 20 problems for each p_2 giving 2000 CSPs in each of the 3 sets. We are most interested in examining performance on hard CSPs. These types of problems can be found in the *phase transition* region where the solution probabilities have been found to decrease rapidly from 1 to 0 [1], [14]. The problems in our experiments consist of both soluble and insoluble problems instances so that we may generate a cover of this region.

For our search algorithm we use backtracking with forward checking and conflict-directed backjumping (Prosser 1993). To evaluate the heuristics, we consider the number of backtracks needed to find a solution or prove that no solution exists. A backtrack occurs when no values in the current variable's domain is consistent with the past instantiations and the assignment for the previous variable must be undone.

Figures 2, 3 and 4 show the results of our experiments on the three problems sets. We plot the number of backtracks on a logarithmic scale against the constraint tightness (p_2) for each problem set.

In the easy region where the CSPs are dense with solutions, all the value ordering heuristics do have a degree of utility. In the easy regions of Figures 2, 3 and 4 (the areas left of the peaks), a random value order results in the most number of consistency checks on average. In general, the MST and uniform propagation methods seem to be the most useful in the easy region while the SST method is closest to random.

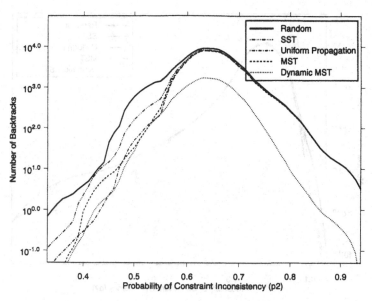

Fig. 2. Average Number of Backtracks for Sparsely Constrained CSPs (p1=0.2)

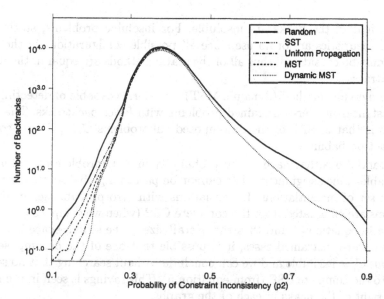

Fig. 3. Average Number of Backtracks for CSPs of Medium Constrainedness (p1=0.5)

There is very little difference between each of the static value-ordering heuristics especially in the hard regions (identified as the peaks in each of the graphs). It is important to note that almost all of the problems represented in the regions

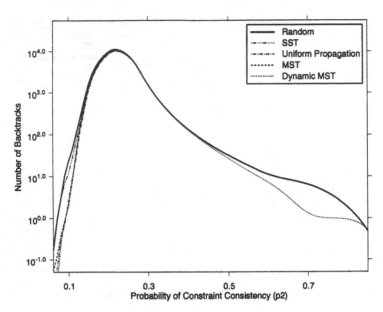

Fig. 4. Average Number of Backtracks for Densely Constrained CSPs (p1=1.0)

to the right of the peaks are insoluble. For insoluble problems, static value-ordering heuristics are of no use since all possible configurations in the search space must be considered, thus all of the static methods are equal in the number of backtracks.

The dynamic method (dynamic MST) however, is capable of detecting insoluble instances in over-constrained problems with fewer backtracks. The reason for this is that in each of the decomposed subproblems $C_1, .., C_N$ we compute the exact probabilities.

Instantiations that have a zero probability in a subproblem are interpreted as variable-value assignments that cannot be part of a global solution given the current set of instantiations. Instantiations with zero probabilities in the subproblems are eliminated from the complete CSP (when we compute the approximation in equation 5) and thus the overall size of the search space is reduced. In some over-constrained cases, it is possible that one of the decomposed subproblems C_i is insoluble and we can conclude without searching that no solution exists to the complete CSP (from equation 5). This savings is seen in the regions to the right of the peaks in each of the graphs.

However, dynamic MST seems to lose its advantage as the constraint density of the problems increases. In Figure 2, dynamic MST is noticeably better than any of the static methods in the hard region and as problems become over-constrained. However, in Figures 3 and 4, the dynamic method becomes increasingly closer to a random ordering. We conjecture that the independence assumption for our MST methods is stronger for CSPs that are sparsely constrained and begins to break down as CSPs become more dense and less tree-like. Indeed our independence assumption holds for trees since our decomposition results in one subproblem (the original CSP). In this case, our probabilistic approximations are exact and searching for solutions and non-solutions is backtrack-free. However, as the problems become more dense and less tree-like, our assumptions begin to break down and the number of backtracks increases to the point where the approximations are no longer useful in guiding the search (as seen in Figure 4).

5 Conclusions

We have given an empirical study of value-ordering in search and our results suggest that such heuristics do not improve performance on hard sets of problems. We've shown that as problem hardness increases, the utility of each approximation method as value-ordering advice decreases to the point where they perform as poorly as a random ordering in guiding the search.

We also introduced a dynamic value-ordering heuristic using Bayesian networks and evidence about to the current search configuration to approximate solution probabilities for CSPs. This method detects insoluble problem instances for over-constrained CSPs with fewer backtracks on average than static methods. Also, the dynamic method was shown to perform close to an order of magnitude better than static heuristics in the hard region of sparsely constrained CSPs. However, as the density of CSPs increases, the performance of our dynamic heuristic in the hard region becomes close to that of a random ordering.

References

1. Cheeseman, P.; Kanefsky, B.; and Taylor, W.M. 1991. Where the really hard problems are. *Proceedings of IJCAI-91*, 331-337.
2. Dechter R., and Pearl J., 1988. Network-based heuristics for constraint-satisfaction problems. *Artificial Intelligence*, 34:1-38.
3. Frost D., and Dechter R. 1995. Look-ahead value ordering for constraint satisfaction problems. *International Joint Conference on Artificial Intelligence*, Montreal, Canada.
4. Gent I.; MacIntyre E.; Prosser, P.; and Walsh, T. 1996. The constrainedness of search. *Proceedings of AAAI-96*, 246-252.
5. Golomb, S.W. and Baumert, L.D. 1965. Backtrack Programming. *Journal ACM*, 516-524.
6. Haralick, R. M., and Elliott, .L. 1980. Increasing tree search efficiency for constraint satisfaction problems. *Artificial Intelligence* 14:263-313.
7. Meisels A.; Shimony S.; and Solotorevsky G. 1997. Bayes networks for estimating the number of solutions to a csp, *AAAI Proceedings*.
8. Neopolitan E. 1990. *Probabilistic Reasoning in Expert Systems: Theory and Algorithms*. Wiley, New York.
9. Version 1.12, Netica from Norsys 1998. Norsys Software Corp. http://www.norsys.com.
10. Nudel, B. 1983. Consistent labeling problems and their algorithms: expected complexities and theory-based heuristics, *Artificial Intelligence* 21.

11. Pearl, J. 1988. *Probabilistic Reasoning in Intelligent Systems: Networks of Plausible Inference.* San Mateo, CA: Morgan Kaufmann.
12. Prosser, P. 1993. Hybrid algorithms for the constraint satisfaction problem. 1993. *Computational Intelligence.*
13. Sadeh, N. 1991. Look-Ahead Techniques for Micro-Opportunistic Job Shop Scheduling. Dissertation CMU-CS-91-102, Computer Science Department, Carnegie Mellon.
14. Smith, B. M. 1994. Phase transition and the mushy region in csp. In *UAI, Proceedings of the 12th Conference,* 477-484. Morgan Kaufmann.
15. Smith, B. M. and Grant, S. 1997. Trying harder to fail first. *ECAI-98.*
16. Tsang, E. 1993. *Foundations of Constraint Satisfaction.* Academic Press.

Heuristics and Experiments on BDD Representation of Boolean Functions for Expert Systems in Software Verification Domains*

Masahito Kurihara[1] and Hisashi Kondo[2]

[1] Hokkaido Institute of Technology
7–15 Maeda, Teine ward, Sapporo 060–8585, Japan
kurihara@hit.ac.jp
[2] Ibaraki University
4-12-1 Naka-Narusawa, Hitachi 316–8511, Japan
H.Kondo@dse.ibaraki.ac.jp

Abstract. Binary decision diagrams (BDDs) are graph-theoretical, compact representation of Boolean functions, successfully applied in the domain of expert systems for practical VLSI design. The authors have been developing the methods of using BDDs for expert systems that mechanically try to prove the termination of rule-based computer programs. To make BDD representation really practical, however, we need good heuristics for ordering Boolean variables and operations. In this paper, we will present some heuristic methods that could affect the performance and evaluate them through the comprehensive experiments on sample rule-based programs taken from practical domains such as hardware diagnosis, software specification, and mathematics. The results show the big difference among the heuristics and provide us useful information for optimizing the overall systems.

1 Introduction

Binary decision diagrams (BDDs) [1,2] are graph-theoretical, compact representation of Boolean functions, successfully applied in various fields of AI. In particular, its application in the field of practical VLSI design expert systems [10] has demonstrated the power of AI to many researchers and engineers outside the AI community. Many other works have been done for applying BDD technology to AI and other engineering fields. For example, in [9], BDD is used as a key technology for a truth maintenance system, and in [4], BDD is applied to the reliability analysis of huge and complex plant systems. This technology also interests the community of automated theorem proving [11].

---

* This work is partially supported by the Grants-in-Aid for Scientific Research of Education Ministry of Japan: No. 09650444 for the first author and No. 09780231 and No. 11780184 for the second. The first author is also supported by the Special Grants from Hokkaido Institute of Technology.

N. Foo (Ed.): AI'99, LNAI 1747, pp. 353–364, 1999.

However, it should be stressed that although this technology is quite general and may seem to be easily applied in various fields, it is known that it essentially contains some computationally hard problems to be solved, depending on the application domains. One of such problems is to determine an appropriate *variable ordering* for constructing BDDs. Without good variable orderings, the size of the BDDs could exponentially grow too large. Unfortunately, there are no efficient algorithms to compute a good variable ordering that minimizes the BDD size, because, as is often the case in typical AI problems, this problem is proved to be one of the NP-complete problems. Thus, all we can do is find a good heuristics for solving such a problem. Indeed, such a heuristic approach to hard problems is what AI is all about.

Recently, the authors have developed the framework of applying BDD technology in the field of computer software development. More exactly, we have developed the Boolean functions for verifying the correctness (termination, in particular) of rule-based programs and encoded them as BDDs. However, it does not necessarily imply a success in that field. As we mentioned, we need heuristics. In this paper, we present some heuristics suggested in the literature and evaluate them through comprehensive experiments on sample rule-based programs taken from practical domains such as hardware diagnosis, software specification, and mathematics. The results show the big difference among the heuristics and provide us useful information for optimizing the overall systems. Such information has been integrated into TERMINATOR/R, the expert system for verifying the termination of rule-based programs developed by the authors.

2 Preliminaries

2.1 Binary Decision Diagrams

A binary decision diagram (BDD), notation $BDD(F)$, is a directed acyclic graph representation of a Boolean function F. Given an assignment of Boolean values (0 or 1) to each variable of F, we can determine the value of the function by following the path from the root to a terminal (0 or 1), branching at each x_i node to either 0- or 1-labelled edge depending on the assigned value for the variable x_i. Usually, we fix a linear order (called a *variable ordering*) on the set of Boolean variables, and for every path from the root to a terminal, we let these variables appear in this ascending order. Figure 1 illustrates $BDD(x_1 + \overline{x_2}x_3)$ with the variable ordering $x_1 < x_2 < x_3$.

One of the most important aspects of BDDs is its uniqueness: with the variable ordering fixed, the BDD of the given function is uniquely determined. As a result, every Boolean function is unsatisfiable if and only if its BDD representation is $BDD(0)$. Another ramarkable aspect of BDDs is its compactness in size, compared with truth tables and other canonical representations. Actually, many practically important Boolean functions, particularly in the field of VLSI design, have been found to be represented in a moderate size of BDD.

The practically most important point in using BDDs is the choice of the variable ordering and the operation ordering. The variable ordering affects the

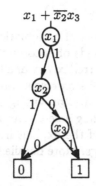

Fig. 1. $BDD(x_1 + \overline{x_2}x_3)$

size of the resultant BDDs, but the problem of determining the optimal variable ordering that yields the smallest BDD is known to be NP-complete. The operation ordering defines the order in which primitive and intermediate BDDs are combined by AND and OR operations to make the whole structure of the final BDD. It affects not on the size of the resultant BDDs, but on the size of the intermediate BDDs. Even if the final BDD is small, the intermediate BDDs created in the course of the process can be too large to be applied in practice. To be practical, therefore, we need good heuristics for ordering Boolean variables and operations, depending on problem domains.

2.2 Termination of Rule-Based Programs

Verification of correctness (including *termination*) is one of the most challenging and important applications of AI, because this kind of problems are often undecidable in general, meaning that there are no general algorithms for solving them. Thus, the heuristic, knowledge-based approach is essential. In this paper, we consider the application of BDD technologies to verification of the termination property of programs written in a language that has simple syntax and semantics, suitable for the foundational studies of verification.

The language is a rule-based language called *rewrite rules* [3,12]. In this language, a program is defined as a set of rules. Each rule is a pair (written in the form of $l \to r$) of terms. The terms may contain constants, function symbols, and variables as usual. Given an input term, the program rewrites it repeatedly by using pattern matching until you reach an irreducible answer term.

A program is *terminating* if there are no infinite rewrite sequences for any input terms. Termination is an undecidable property in general, but some sufficient conditions for its verification have been studied. In this paper, we focus on a popular class of such conditions based on *precedence*. A precedence, denoted by $\succ$, is a partial ordering on the set of function symbols. It is extended to a partial ordering $\succ_{lpo}$ (called the lexicographic path ordering, or LPO) on the set of terms. If all rules $l \to r$ satisfy $l \succ_{lpo} r$, we may conclude that the program is terminating [7].

2.3   Encoding Termination in BDD

We encode the sufficient condition of termination based on LPO as a Boolean function. We present three methods of encoding. The first method is based on natural encoding of LPO plus the irreflexivity and transitivity of partial orderings. The second encoding improves this representation by introducing the notion of explicit transitivity and irreflexivity, providing an encoding with less Boolean variables. Finally, the last encoding safely removes the transitivity part at the small cost of losing minimality of the explicit irreflexivity. In the following, we will briefly review these encodings. More detailed account is given in [8].

Basic encoding Let $\mathcal{F}(\mathcal{R})$ be the set of function symbols occurring in the program $\mathcal{R}$, and $X = \{x_{fg} | f, g \in \mathcal{F}(\mathcal{R})\}$ be the set of Boolean variables. By an assignment of a Boolean value to x_{fg}, we represent the truth of the proposition $f \succ g$. Thus a precedence $\succ$ is represented by an assignment of truth values to all the variables in X. Since the precedence is a strict partial ordering, it must satisfy the transitivity $(T(X))$ and irreflexivity $(I(X))$ represented by the following Boolean functions, respectively.

$$T(X) = \prod_{f,g,h \in \mathcal{F}(\mathcal{R})} [\overline{x}_{fg} + \overline{x}_{gh} + x_{fh}], \quad I(X) = \prod_{f \in \mathcal{F}(\mathcal{R})} \overline{x}_{ff}. \qquad (1)$$

The transitivity specifies that if $x_{fg} = 1$ and $x_{gh} = 1$ then $x_{fh} = 1$ (for all f, g, and h); and the irreflexivity simply means that $x_{ff} = 0$ for all f. In [8], the condition $l \succ_{lpo} r$ is encoded in a recursive way as a Boolean function denoted by $LPO_{l,r}(X)$, and the conjunction of such conditions for all rules in a program $\mathcal{R} = \{l_i \rightarrow r_i \mid i = 1 \ldots m\}$ is represented by the following function:

$$LPO_{\mathcal{R}}(X) = \prod_{i=1}^{m} LPO_{l_i,r_i}(X). \qquad (2)$$

For example, if $\mathcal{R}$ consists of a single rule $f(h(x)) \rightarrow g(x)$, then $LPO_{\mathcal{R}}(X) = x_{hg} + x_{fg}$. This means that if $h \succ g$ or $f \succ g$, then $f(h(x)) \succ_{lpo} g(x)$.

Now we can combine the three functions to yield the following encoding.

$$H_{\mathcal{R}}(X) = LPO_{\mathcal{R}}(X) \cdot T(X) \cdot I(X). \qquad (3)$$

It is proved that if $H_{\mathcal{R}}(X)$ is satisfiable, then $\mathcal{R}$ is terminating [6]. Note that the satisfiability of a Boolean function can be determined simply by checking if its BDD representation is not BDD(0), because every BDD distinct from BDD(0) contains a path from its root to the terminal vertex with truth value 1.

Encoding with explicit variables If the program $\mathcal{R}$ contains n different function symbols, then the set X consists of n^2 Boolean variables. The transitivity condition $T(X)$ consists of n^3 conjunctive clauses and tends to be the biggest part in $H_{\mathcal{R}}(X)$. In most cases, however, the set $X(R)$ of Boolean variables occurring in $LPO_{\mathcal{R}}(X)$ tends to be only a small part of X. We call them *explicit*

Boolean variables. This motivates the definitions of the explicit transitivity condition $T'(X(\mathcal{R}))$ and the explicit irreflexive condition $I'(X(\mathcal{R}))$ defined in [8]. These conditions are based on graph-theoretic enumeration of some sort of minimal paths and cycles of the graph $G = (V, E)$ with $V = \mathcal{F}(\mathcal{R})$ and $E = X(\mathcal{R})$. We can use them in place of basic transitivity and irreflexivity for encoding the termination as follows:

$$H'_\mathcal{R}(X(\mathcal{R})) = LPO_\mathcal{R}(X(\mathcal{R})) \cdot T'(X(\mathcal{R})) \cdot I'(X(\mathcal{R})) \tag{4}$$

where we have written $LPO_\mathcal{R}(X(\mathcal{R}))$ for $LPO_\mathcal{R}(X)$ to emphasize that all the Boolean variables occurring in this function are members of $X(\mathcal{R})$. It is proved that $H_\mathcal{R}(X)$ is satisfiable if and only if $H'_\mathcal{R}(X(\mathcal{R}))$ is satisfiable [6].

Encoding without transitivity Since the computation of transitivity part often requires a fairly amount of time even for explicit conditions, it can cause an efficiency problem. This motivates the encoding without transitivity defined in [8]. Let $I''(X(\mathcal{R}))$ be the explicit irreflexivity condition for $X(\mathcal{R})$ obtained by considering all minimal cycles plus all non-minimal simple cycles. Then we get the following encoding of termination:

$$H''_\mathcal{R}(X(\mathcal{R})) = LPO_\mathcal{R}(X(\mathcal{R})) \cdot I''(X(\mathcal{R})). \tag{5}$$

Note that this encoding has no transitivity part. Nevertheless, it is known that $H_\mathcal{R}(X)$ is satisfiable if and only if $H''_\mathcal{R}(X(\mathcal{R}))$ is satisfiable [6].

Example Figure 2 illustrates the BDDs for the two encodings $H'_\mathcal{R}(X(\mathcal{R}))$ and $H''_\mathcal{R}(X(\mathcal{R}))$, respectively, where

$$LPO_\mathcal{R}(X(\mathcal{R})) = (x_{hg} + x_{fg}) \cdot (x_{hf} + x_{gf})$$

$$T'(X(\mathcal{R})) = (\overline{x}_{hf} + \overline{x}_{fg} + x_{hg}) \cdot (\overline{x}_{hg} + \overline{x}_{gf} + x_{hf})$$

$$I'(X(\mathcal{R})) = I''(X(\mathcal{R})) = \overline{x}_{fg} + \overline{x}_{gf}$$

and $\mathcal{R}$ consists of two rules $f(h(x)) \rightarrow g(x)$ and $g(h(x)) \rightarrow f(x)$. Note that the size of the BDD for $H''_\mathcal{R}(X(\mathcal{R}))$ can be larger than that for $H'_\mathcal{R}(X(\mathcal{R}))$ as is the case of this example. However, without the transitivity part, $H''_\mathcal{R}(X(\mathcal{R}))$ can often be computed much faster, as will be shown later.

3 Heuristics

3.1 Basic Procedure and Policy for Heuristics

In this section we present the basic procedure for proving the satisfiability of $H'_\mathcal{R}(X(\mathcal{R}))$, using its BDD representation. Similar procedures for $H_\mathcal{R}(X)$ and $H''_\mathcal{R}(X(\mathcal{R}))$ should be clear from this construction. We suppose that the procedure is given a program $\mathcal{R}$, rule by rule, as an input and returns a truth value according to the satisfiability of $H'_\mathcal{R}(X(\mathcal{R}))$. After initializing $R = X(R) = \emptyset$ and $H(R) = BDD(0)$, the procedure executes the following steps repeatedly:

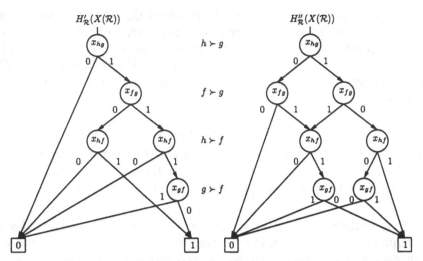

Fig. 2. Example BDDs for two encodings

1. If all rules have been input, then return true. $H'_R(X(R))$ is satisfiable.
2. Input a new rule $l \to r$, and add it to R, resulting $R' = R \cup \{l \to r\}$. Let ΔX be the set of Boolean variables occurring in $LPO_{l,r}(X)$ but not in $X(R)$. Introduce a variable ordering to make $X(R') = X(R) \cup \Delta X$ a linearly ordered set.
3. Let $\Delta LPO = BDD(LPO_{l,r}(X))$. Let $\Delta T'$ and $\Delta I'$ be the BDDs of the Boolean product of the minimal explicit transitivity and irreflexivity conditions, respectively, containing at least one Boolean variable from ΔX.
4. Let $H(R') = BDD(H(R) \cdot \Delta LPO \cdot \Delta T' \cdot \Delta I')$. If $H(R') = BDD(0)$, then return false. $H'_{R'}(X(R'))$ is unsatisfiable.
5. Set R', $X(R')$ and $H(R')$ to R, $X(R)$ and $H(R)$, respectively.

Note that the procedure is nondeterministic in the following three points.

(1) The order in which a new rule is input in step 2 is arbitrary.
(2) The linear ordering to be determined in step 2 is arbitrary.
(3) The order in which the product of four BDDs is taken in step 4 is arbitrary.

Implementation of this arbitrariness can affect the efficiency of the procedure. In general BDD terminology, this problem can be described as the problem of determining the variable ordering for (2) and the operation ordering for (1) and (3). We need good heuristic choices to implement the procedure effectively. However, we cannot devise and examine unlimited number of heuristics. In the following, we discuss the basic policy for the framework of the heuristics considered in this paper. The policy consists of the following three items.

1. We fix the order of rule input to the order of the rules specified by the users. This is because we assume the system verifies the termination incrementally (each time a rule is input) and on interactive systems we cannot control the order of input by the users.

2. We only consider classes of variable orderings that can be extended *incrementally*. This means that when a new Boolean variable has been created in the procedure, we add it to the current set of Boolean variables and extend the associated ordering consistently (without violating the current ordering). More restriction will be discussed later.

3. There are 18 possibilities for computing the product of four BDDs — 12 cases for liniar product of the form $((a \cdot b) \cdot c) \cdot d$, and 6 cases for the form $(a \cdot b) \cdot (c \cdot d)$, taking into account that multiplication is commutative. In our experiments, we consider all of them.

3.2 Variable Ordering

As we have already discussed, we only consider classes of orderings that can be extended incrementally. We further restrict ourselves to orderings depending only on the orderings in which Boolean variables and function symbols have been created or encountered by the procedure. This is because such orderings strongly depend on the orders of the user's input, which heuristically reflect the user's mental model associating symbols and rules with their meanings and structure in the real world. In other words, the orders of the user's input in interactive systems are not random but likely to be consistent with some implicit structure of meanings. In the following we introduce some classes of variable orderings satisfying these restrictions.

- **Random ordering (RAND)**: This ordering just orders the variables randomly, according to the uniform distribution. We do not think this ordering is effective but use it as the basis for evaluating other orderings.
- **Generation ordering (GO)**: This ordering orders variables as generated. More precisely, it is the ordering in which we encounter the Boolean variables while expanding the formula $LPO_{l,r}(X)$ for each input rule $l \rightarrow r$ in a depth-first, left-to-right manner according to the definition given in [8]. This scheme is quite natural in terms of implementation.
- **Left ordering (LO)**: We define two total orderings $<_L$ and $<_R$ on the set of function symbols:

    $f <_L g \Leftrightarrow f$ occurs before g in the left-hand sides of rules,
    $f <_R g \Leftrightarrow f$ occurs before g in the right-hand sides of rules.

    The left ordering is defined by $x_{fg} < x_{ij}$ if and only if $f <_L i$ or ($f = i$ and $g <_R j$).
- **Right ordering (RO)**: This ordering is the same as LO except that the ordering $<_R$ dominates over $<_L$.

We also consider the orderings obtained by reversing each one of the above orderings except RAND and call them the reversed generation ordering (RGO), the reversed left ordering (RLO), and the reversed right ordering (RRO), respectively.

3.3   Operation Ordering

The problem of operation orderings in our basic procedure includes the choice of order in which the Boolean multiplication of four BDDs are taken. From a more global viewpoint, however, it should be stressed that a kind of operation orderings is already built in the framework of the procedure itself, because it integrates the entire BDD as a product of interleaved increments of three kinds of constraints. More precisely, let $(\Delta LPO)_j$, $(\Delta T')_j$, and $(\Delta I')_j$ be the incremental constraints obtained from the j-th rule input with $1 \leq j \leq m$, and let $(\Delta H')_j$ be their product. Clearly, the basic procedure computes the product

$$H'_{\mathcal{R}}(X(\mathcal{R})) = (\Delta H')_1 \cdot (\Delta H')_2 \cdots (\Delta H')_m$$

from left to right. This order of integration of constraints is definitely different from the one that computes the product simply according to the original definition (4). We refer to the former and the latter as the *incremental* and the *batch* mode operation orderings, respectively, and will present a brief report on the experimental results in the next section.

4   Experiments and Comparison

We have performed comprehensive experiments on typical sample programs taken from several application domains, including hardware diagnosis, software specification, and mathematics. In this section, we present some results to show how the efficiency of our basic procedure is affected by the choice of variable orderings and operation orderings. In particular, we will see that in most cases the use of RGO for the variable ordering leads to good results. Then we will briefly report other experimental results which show that the proposed procedures implementing $H'_{\mathcal{R}}(X(\mathcal{R}))$ and $H''_{\mathcal{R}}(X(\mathcal{R}))$ are significantly more efficient than the implementation of the naive encoding $H_{\mathcal{R}}(X)$.

4.1   Effects by Variable Orderings

We have selected two particular problems for presenting the results in detail. One is taken from the field of the model-based hardware diagnosis. We refer to this problem as CIRCUIT [7]. The rules have been introduced by directing, from left to right, the equations that specify the behavior of the full adder. The number of explicit Boolean variables for this problem is 36.

The other problem referred to as SOLITAIRE consists of 28 rules taken from the field of the algebraic specification of software systems [13]. The number of explicit Boolean variables for this problem is 46.

The two problems are input to our basic procedure written in Lisp and run on a PC. The results are summarized in Tables 1 and 2. Each entry should be interpreted as follows. The *var order* shows the names of heuristic variable orderings. The *BDD size* is the number of nonterminal vertices of the resultant BDD, uniquely determined by the variable ordering employed. The *tree size*

Table 1. Experimental results for CIRCUIT

var order	RAND	GO	LO	RO	RGO	RLO	RRO
BDD size	39	33	32	33	33	32	33
tree size	41	41	39	40	54	55	55
max size	5804	751	1232	2625	594	965	2527
generation	19725	8776	13175	9965	2059	3307	4253
comparison	30713	11871	17387	12801	3668	6265	7679
CPU time	9533	797	1921	1067	70	225	357

Table 2. Experimental results for SOLITAIRE

var order	RAND	GO	LO	RO	RGO	RLO	RRO
BDD size	1459	398	451	494	400	515	482
tree size	8231	17574	18495	10951	12894	15365	17527
max size	2062	1601	1407	604	675	898	577
generation	11551	6192	6764	3994	1627	2243	3659
comparison	17787	8546	9828	6140	3945	5424	6240
CPU time	2479	452	666	220	74	169	242

is the number of vertices of the tree obtained by transforming the BDD into the equivalent tree form. Comparison of the BDD size with this tree size can show us how many duplicate vertices are shared in the BDD. The *max size* indicates the size of the biggest BDD temporarily generated in the course of the procedure. Even if the variable orders are the same, this value depends on the operation ordering employed. The values shown here are the results of employing the ordering that will be recommended in the next section. The *generation* shows the total number of vertices created in the procedure. The *comparison* counts the number of comparison (with respect to the variable ordering) of two Boolean variables in the generation of BDDs. The *CPU time* is the time (in seconds) required for getting a solution. The entries for the random ordering (RAND) are the average of the results of ten trials.

The results show that all the six heuristic variable orderings are more efficient than the random ordering (RAND) in both time and space. We notice that the difference of the BDD size and tree size for RAND is only two, meaning that only two vertices are shared in the BDD. In contrast, for the other orderings, at least seven vertices (17.5 %) are saved in adopting the BDD representation. In particular, the cases of RGO, RLO, and RRO are remarkable, because the tree sizes are greater but the BDD sizes are smaller than the case of RAND, thanks to the saving of more than twenty vertices (38.8 %).

The most efficient variable ordering depends on the problems and the definition of the "efficiency." However, we recommend the use of RGO, because in most cases it shows the best (or at least relatively good) perfomance in time and space. This is also true for other problems mentioned in the following subsections.

It has been found that the BDD structure provides compact representations for many practically important Boolean functions in VLSI design, etc. In general, however, not all Boolean functions are suitable for the BDD representation. Now let us see that our Boolean function $H'_\mathcal{R}(X(\mathcal{R}))$ is suitable for BDD representation. Surprisingly, for most cases (including our two sample problems) this is true even if we use RAND. Let us check it out for our sample problems. In most implementations, a BDD vertex is stored in three words of memory, with each word used for each pointer for the two outgoing edges and the identification of the Boolean variable. Supposing each word is 32 bits, we can store a single vertex in 96 bits. Then we can see that the 39 and 1459 vertices of the BDDs created in the sample problems with RAND can be stored in about 2^{12} and 2^{18} bits, respectively. On the other hand, the truth tables for representing the corresponding two Boolean functions with 36 and 46 Boolean variables would require 2^{36} and 2^{46} bits, respectively.

4.2   Effects by Operation Orderings

We have seen that our basic procedure implicitly incorporates a kind of operation ordering called the incremental mode, which is different from the mathematically natural way of the batch mode. By several experiments, we have clearly found the incremental mode superior to the batch mode. Actually, the BDD size and the CPU time for the batch mode were more than 10 and 18 times greater, respectively, than the incremental mode in all the experiments.

The order of taking the multiplication of the four BDDs did not affect the performance so dramatically, but the types of $((H(R) \cdot a) \cdot b) \cdot c$, imposing the constraints sequentially on top of the current BDD, performed better than the others. In particular, we can recommend the use of $((H(R) \cdot \Delta LPO) \cdot \Delta I') \cdot \Delta T'$, because in most cases it behaved the best.

Table 3 shows the results for five other problems taken from the domain of mathematics. Those are all the problems given in [14] that contain at least five function symbols and are terminating. The variable ordering is fixed to RGO, and the operation ordering is fixed to our recommendation above. The table includes two new entries for the number of rules and the number of explicit Boolean variables. We can say that all the problems have been solved efficiently.

4.3   Effects by Explicit Conditions

We briefly describe how the explicit transitivity and irreflexivity conditions on $X(\mathcal{R})$ result in more efficiency than the ordinary transitivity and irreflexivity conditions on X. Indeed, the use of $H'_\mathcal{R}(X(\mathcal{R}))$ is far better than $H_\mathcal{R}(X)$. This is justified by our experiments in which the use of $H_\mathcal{R}(X)$ did not yield a solution of the CIRCUIT problem within 48 hours. Actually, we found that this run required a temporary BDD whose maximum size is 35 times greater than the BDD required in the run for $H'_\mathcal{R}(X(\mathcal{R}))$.

Table 3. Experimental results for mathematical systems

No.	12	26	27	29	31
rules	9	10	11	7	7
explicit vars	14	18	17	18	11
BDD size	16	15	37	34	15
tree size	20	15	56	102	31
max size	85	81	116	43	16
generation	311	291	356	175	60
comparison	343	327	391	174	53
CPU time	1.16	0.94	1.33	0.35	0.10

Table 4. Experimental results for transitivity removal

No.	CIRCUIT		SOLITAIRE	
var order	GO	RGO	GO	RGO
BDD size	33	35	93	93
tree size	48	100	4500	4043
max BDD size	126	157	107	99
generation	1063	358	918	286
comparison	1199	846	1002	390
CPU time	8.95	6.95	7.56	2.62

4.4   Effects by Transitivity Removal

Table 4 shows the results of the experiments in which the previous two sample problems were solved by using $H''_{\mathcal{R}}(X(\mathcal{R}))$ in place of $H'_{\mathcal{R}}(X(\mathcal{R}))$. We only show the entries for the GO and RGO orders. Comparing this table with Tables 1 and 2, we can see that the use of $H''_{\mathcal{R}}(X(\mathcal{R}))$ is more efficient than $H'_{\mathcal{R}}(X(\mathcal{R}))$. Theoretically speaking, we could try to construct problems in which $H'_{\mathcal{R}}(X(\mathcal{R}))$ is more efficient, but we have not encountered such problems in practice, yet.

5   Conclusion

In conclusion, let us compare our method with two other works. One is a most simple way based on backtracking [5]. It is well-known that the simple backtracking suffers from inefficiency caused by futile backtracking, rediscovering contradictions, and rediscovering inferences. Actually, the CPU time for computing all solutions for the CIRCUIT and SOLITAIRE problems by the backtracking method was 108 and 2700 seconds, respectively, compared with 70 and 74 seconds by our method. The other work [7] uses a reason maintenance system to avoid the drawbacks caused by the simple backtracking. It is reported that this method was successful in getting a single solution efficiently. In contrast, our method is effective only if all solutions are sought (or if you want to check that there are no solutions).

References

1. Akers, S. B.: Binary decision diagrams, *IEEE Trans. Comput.*, Vol. C-27, No. 6, pp.509–516 (1978)
2. Bryant, R. E.: Graph-based algorithm for boolean function manipulation, *IEEE Trans. Comput.*, Vol. C-35, No. 5, pp.677–691 (1986)
3. Bundy, A.: Rewrite rules, *The Computer Modelling of Mathematical Reasoning*, Academic Press, pp.115–149 (1983)
4. Coudert, O. and Madre, J. C.: Towards an interactive fault tree analyser, *Proc. IASTED Int. Conf. on Reliability, Quality Control and Risk Assessment* (1992)
5. Detlefs, D. and Forgaad, R.: A procedure for automatically proving the termination of a set of rewrite rules, *Proc. of 1st Conf. on Rewriting Techniques and Applications*, Springer, LNCS 202, pp.255–270 (1985)
6. Kondo, H. and Kurihara, M.: Termination verification system for term rewriting systems using binary decision diagram, *Intern. Journal of Japanese Society for Artificial Intelligence*, Vol.13, No.5, pp.822–834 (1998) (in Japanese)
7. Kurihara, M., Kondo, H., et al.: Using ATMS to efficiently verify the termination of rewrite rule programs, *Intern. Journal of Software Engineering and Knowledge Engineering*, Vol.2, No.4, pp.547–565 (1992)
8. Kurihara, M. and Kondo, H.: Binary decision diagrams for mechanical verification of precedence-based termination of rewrite rules, *Poster Proc. of 5th Pacific Rim Int. Conf. on Artificial Intelligence*, pp.7–12 (1998)
9. Madre, J. C. and Coudert, O.: A logically complete reasoning maintenance system based on a logical constraint solver, *Proc. IJCAI*, pp.294–299 (1991)
10. Malik, S., et al.: Logic verification using binary decision diagrams in a logic synthesis environment, *Proc. IEEE Int. Conf. on Computer-Aided Design*, pp.6–9 (1988)
11. Moore, J. S.: Introduction to the OBDD algorithm for the ATP community, *Journal of Automated Reasoning*, Vol.12, pp.33–45 (1994)
12. Plaisted, D. A.: Equational reasoning and term rewriting systems, in Gabbay, D. M. (ed.), *Handbook of Logic in Artificial Intelligence and Logic Programming*, pp.274–364 (1993)
13. Steinbach, J.: Termination of rewriting , Ph.D thesis, Univ. Kaiserslautern, Germany (1994)
14. Steinbach, J. and Kühler, U.: Check your ordering — termination proofs and open problems, SEKI report SR-90-25(SFB), Univ. Kaiserslautern, Germany (1990)

Abduction without Minimality

Abhaya C. Nayak[1] and Norman Y. Foo[2]

[1] Computational Reasoning Group, Department of Computing,
Macquarie University, NSW 2109 Australia
abhaya@ics.mq.edu.au
[2] Knowledge Systems Group, School of Computer Science and Engineering,
The University of New South Wales, NSW 2052 Australia
norman@cse.unsw.edu.au

Abstract. In most accounts of common-sense reasoning, only the most preferred among models supplied by the evidence are retained (and the rest eliminated) in order to enhance the inferential prowess. One problem with this strategy is that the agent's working set of models shrinks quickly in the process. We argue that instead of rejecting all the non-best models, the reasoner should reject only the worst models and then examine the consequences of adopting this principle in the context of abductive reasoning. Apart from providing the relevant representation results, we indicate why an iterated account of abduction is feasible in this framework.

Keywords: belief revision, common-sense reasoning, philosophical foundations

1 Introduction

In many approaches to common-sense reasoning [6], belief change [3] and abductive reasoning [10] appeal is made to the *principle of minimal change*. This principle can be viewed as the commonsensical principle of selecting the best from the available set of alternatives [12]. In a recent work [9], Nayak *et al.* have advocated the adoption of the principle of rejecting the worst in lieu of the principle of selecting the best in the context of AGM style belief revision [1,3]. The aim of this work is to extend this idea to abductive reasoning – in particular, to explore the consequences of discarding the *choose the best* principle in favour of *reject the worst* principle in the context of abductive belief change [10].

This paper is organised as follows. In the next section we argue that the principle of selecting the best is inappropriate in contexts of a certain character, and should be discarded in favour of the principle of rejecting the worst. In section §3 we quickly present the account of abductive belief change due to Pagnucco [10] and argue that it is one of those contexts where adopting the principle of selecting the best has perilous consequences. Section §4 explores the consequences of adopting the principle of rejecting the worst in the context of abductive belief change. Section §5 is devoted to soundness and completeness results for this approach. We end with a brief discussion regarding the feasibility of an iterative account of abductive belief change in the proposed framework.

N. Foo (Ed.): AI'99, LNAI 1747, pp. 365–377, 1999.

2   The Perils of Choosing the Best

The principle of choosing the best essentially says that if there are multiple available ways of attaining a certain (desired) goal, one should choose those that one considers *best* (according to some contextually defined preference criteria). This principle is very appealing indeed. A moment's reflection shows that the appeal of this principle lies in a simple linguistic fact, namely, that the expression "best item" more or less *means* an item that should be chosen if offered as an alternative. The principle "select the best" is hence a glaringly obvious but entirely content-less principle. This principle means that one should select what should be selected, and hence is only as good as the underlying implementation of the concepts "best". More to the point, there is the underlying assumption that one already knows what is *best* in the given context. In particular, if one does not exactly know what the best item in the choice set is, and one considers x to be only a first approximation to what might be the best, the principle "select the best" has no prescriptive force as to whether or not one should select x.

Let us now consider a concrete situation. Suppose you are planning to fly from Australia to Europe and you are considering which airline to choose. Your choice set, of course, is the set of airlines that provide service from Australia to Europe. The simple suggestion, "Choose the best airline", is not of much help since it does not tell you which airline to choose. A bit of soul searching might explicate your criteria of choice – (low) price, (good) service, (less) number of stopovers, (less) hours of waiting at airports, (convenient) departure and arrival times, (good) safety record. [1]

Now, if you knew how to quantify these properties of an airline, and the relative importance of these properties (as weights) so far as your choice is concerned, then you could presumably take the weighted sum of the first figures as the desirability of an airline and easily determine what the best airline is. In other words, given that we have an exhaustive list of the preference criteria, their relative importance as weights and the relevant properties of individual airlines as quantities, the criteria in question can be combined in order to provide a single (read *ultimate*) preference criterion. Now, applying the principle of selecting the best we can find the desired airline to be contacted. (If there are more than one of them, we can devise some tie-breaking mechanism.)

In practice, however, the required quantifications may not be available. If so, we are not dealing with a single (read *ultimate*) preference criteria, but a bunch of them and we have to sequentially use these criteria to determine the item to be selected.

The question then is whether the principle of selecting the best can be applied in this situation. In our favourite example, suppose that the criteria in question

---

[1] This is not necessarily the only criteria you are going to consider – you might come up with more criteria, e.g. the type of frequent flyer program offered by the airline and want to add them to the list later without recomputing the best airline from scratch again. But without loss of generality, let us pretend that the list in question is complete.

were arrived at (and applied) in the given sequence. TABLE 2 encodes information as to the preference among airlines with respect to different criteria.[2] For

Price	Service	Stopovers	Waiting	Timing	Safety
AF, QA	JAL	BA	SW, KLM	LU, SA	LU
BA	SW, SA	SW, LU	LU	SW	SW, KLM
LU	QA, KLM	KLM, JAL	SA, JAL	JAL	JAL, BA
KLM, SA	BA, LU	AF, QA	QA, AF	AF, KLM	SA
JAL, SW	AF	SA	BA	QA, BA	QA, AF

Table 1. Preference over airlines based on different criteria.

instance, according to this table, Air France and Quantas offer the best price followed by British Airways which is in turn followed by Lufthansa. On the other hand, JAL and Swiss Air offer the worst price, whereas KLM and Singapore Airline offer next to worst. Suppose you consider low price as the primary factor. By applying the principle of selecting the best, the choice set is shrunk to just Air France and Quantas. Next you come up with the criterion "good service". Since your choice set is now {Air France, Quantas} and Quantas fares better than Air France on service count, your choice set is now reduced to the singleton set {Quantas}. After that you are stuck with Quantas, no matter how terrible its safety record is, no matter how inconvenient its timing is, etc. – unless you are prepared to go back to the original choice set and apply the criteria in a different sequence.[3] In fact, according to our table, Quantas has the worst safety record, the worst timing and only next to worst in both waiting and number of stopovers. You are still committed to choose this airline due to the principle of choosing the best!

If instead of price, you had started with the quality of service, you would have been stuck with JAL right at the outset although it is most expensive among the air lines and is only mediocre as far as stopovers, waiting time and timing are concerned and next to worst in safety record.

The perils of the "select the best" approach is obvious. By selecting the best, we are severely restricting the available choices for future selection, and end up choosing an option which is possibly not at all preferable on some other count. The way out of this peril is also equally obvious – we should follow some approach which is less restrictive. One way to achieve this goal is, instead of rejecting every option which is non-best, we should rather reject every option that is *worst*. Applying this alternative principle to our pet example, when we consider the criterion of price, we reject JAL and Swiss Air, and are still left with six other airlines. Next, on service count we eliminate Air France, on Stopover

---

[2] This table is completely fictitious, and has nothing to do with what really is or is not the case.

[3] But that does not solve the problem, only postpones it!

count we reject Singapore Airlines, on waiting count British Airways, on count of timing Quantas (BA is already eliminated at this point), and on safety count KLM (at this point SW, JAL, BA, SA, QA and AF are no longer available for elimination). Thus we end up selecting Lufthansa which is ranked mediocre on count of price, second best on count of stopovers and waiting, best on counts of timing and safety, and next to worst only on count of service. Many would agree that this is a lot more sensible choice than Quantas, given TABLE 2.

We have thus noticed that there are contexts when the "reject the worst" principle seems to be more sensible than the "select the best" principle. We will conclude this section with a sketchy outline of the features which, when present, make a context more appropriate for the "reject the worst" principle as opposed to the "select the best" principle.

- First of all, these principles apply to a choice context. If no choice is at issue, then these principles are irrelevant in that context.
- Given that a choice is to be made, the set of alternatives (or the choice set) is clearly specified – and that the choice must be made from members of that set. For instance, in our example, since Cathay Pacific is not an available option, the agent is not allowed to choose Cathay Pacific.
- It is understood that the choice being made is not necessarily the final choice. It is possible that the agent might be required to narrow down the choices further in light of hitherto unavailable criteria.

We will maintain that the above three are the salient features of a choice context in which the "choose the best" principle should be given up in favour of the "reject the worst" principle. In the next section we will show how abductive reasoning is a context with these features, and hence is appropriate for the "reject the worst" principle.

3   Abductive by Choosing the Best

Recently a very interesting account of abduction has been offered by Pagnucco [10] as an extension of the classic AGM system of belief change [1]. We will briefly recount the AGM system of belief change followed by Pagnucco's account of abductive belief change.

3.1   Belief Change

In the AGM system, a belief state is represented as a theory (i.e., a set of sentences closed under your favourite consequence operation), new information (epistemic input) is represented as a single sentence, and a state transition function, called revision, returns a new belief state given an old belief state and an epistemic input. If the input in question is not belief contravening, i.e., does not conflict with the given belief state (theory), then the new belief state is simply the consequence closure of the old state together with the epistemic input. In the other case, i.e., when the input is belief contravening, the model utilises a selection mechanism (e.g. an epistemic entrenchment relation over beliefs, a nearness relation over worlds or a preference relation over theories) in order to determine what portion of the old belief state has to be discarded before the input is incorporated into it.

From here onwards we will assume a finitary propositional object language $\mathcal{L}$.[4] Let its logic be represented by a classical logical consequence operation Cn. The yielding relation $\vdash$ is defined via Cn as: $\Gamma \vdash \alpha$ iff $\alpha \in Cn(\Gamma)$.

The AGM revision operation is required to satisfy the following rationality postulates: Let K be a belief set (a set of sentences closed under Cn), the sentence $x \in \mathcal{L}$ be the evidence, $*$ the revision operator, and K_x^* the result of revising K by x.

(1^*) K_x^* is a theory

(2^*) $x \in K_x^*$

(3^*) $K_x^* \subseteq Cn(K \cup \{x\})$

(4^*) If $K \nvdash \neg x$ then $Cn(K \cup \{x\}) \subseteq K_x^*$

(5^*) $K_x^* = K_\perp$ iff $\vdash \neg x$

(6^*) If $\vdash x \leftrightarrow y$, then $K_x^* = K_y^*$

(7^*) $K_{(x \wedge y)}^* \subseteq Cn(K_x^* \cup \{y\})$

(8^*) If $\neg y \notin K_x^*$ then $Cn(K_x^* \cup \{y\}) \subseteq K_{(x \wedge y)}^*$

Motivation for these postulates can be found in [3]. We call any revision operation that satisfies the above eight constraints "AGM rational". These postulates can actually be translated into constraints on a non-monotonic inference relation $\vdash$ [5].

3.2   Semantics of Belief Change

There are various constructions of an AGM rational revision operation. The one we will present is equivalent to the construction via "Systems of Spheres" (SOS) propounded by Adam Grove [7]. Let $\mathcal{M}$ be the class of maximally consistent sets w of sentences in the language in question. The reader is encouraged to think of these maximal sets as worlds, models or scenarios. We will use the following expressions interchangeably: "$w \models \alpha$", "α allows w" and $w \in [\alpha]$", where w is an element in $\mathcal{M}$ and α is either a sentence or a set of sentences.) Given the belief set K, denote by $[K]$ the worlds allowed by it, i.e., $[K] = \{w \in \mathcal{M} \mid K \subseteq w\}$. (Similarly, for any sentence x, let $[x]$ be the set of "worlds" in which x holds.)

A system of spheres is simply represented by a connected, transitive and reflexive relation (total preorder) $\sqsubseteq$ over the set $\mathcal{M}$ such that $[K]$ is exactly the set of $\sqsubseteq$-minimal worlds of $\mathcal{M}$. Intuitively, $w \sqsubseteq w'$ may be read as: w is at least as good/preferable as w' (or, w' is not strictly preferred to w). We define the Grove-revision function $G*$ as: $[K_x^{G*}] = \{w \in [x] \mid$ for all $w' \in [x]$,

---

[4] A finitary language is a language generated from a finite number of atomic sentences. So the number of sentences in this language is not finite.

$w \sqsubseteq w'$}, whereby $K_x^{G*} = \bigcap[K_x^{G*}]$. It turns out that the AGM revision postulates characterise the Grove revision operation $G*$.[5]

A visual representation of the crucial case in the Grove Construction is given in Figure 1.

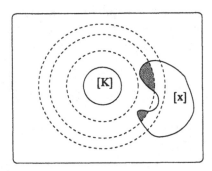

Fig. 1. Minimality Based revision – the principal case

In this, the area marked $[x]$ represents the models allowed by the evidence x. The area $[K]$ represents the model currently entertained by the agent, and the broken circles demarcate models according to their perceived plausibility. The farther a model is from the centre, the more implausible it is. The shaded part of $[x]$ represents the least implausible of the models allowed by the evidence x – hence identified with $[K_x^*]$.

Viewed from this semantic angle, belief change is about preferential choice: $[K_x^{G*}]$ essentially identifies the subset to be chosen from $[x]$ as the set of worlds that are $\sqsubseteq$-best in $[x]$.

We introduce the following notation for later use.

Definition 1 *A subset T of $\mathcal{M}$ is said to be $\sqsubseteq$-flat just in case $w \sqsubseteq w'$ for all members w, w' of T. In this case, the members of T are called $\sqsubseteq$-equivalent. $w \sqsubset w'$, on the other hand, is used as an abbreviation for $(w \sqsubseteq w') \wedge (w' \not\sqsubseteq w)$*

---

[5] Readers acquainted with Grove's work will easily notice that given a system of spheres Σ, the relation $\sqsubseteq_\Sigma$ can be generated as: $w \sqsubseteq_\Sigma w'$ iff for every sphere S' that has w' as a member, there exists sphere $S \subseteq S'$ with w as a member. On the other hand, given a total preorder $\sqsubseteq$ on $\mathcal{M}$, a system of spheres $\Sigma_\sqsubseteq$ can be generated as follows: A set $S \subseteq \mathcal{M}$ is a sphere in $\Sigma_\sqsubseteq$ iff given any member w of S, if $w' \sqsubseteq w$ then w' is also a member of S. It is easily noticed that the $\sqsubseteq$-minimal worlds of $\mathcal{M}$ constitute the central sphere, and for any sentence x, the $\sqsubseteq$-minimal members of $[x]$ constitute $[K_x^{G*}]$ in the corresponding SOS.

3.3 Minimality Based Abduction

In section §3.2 we offered a constructive approach to belief change via a similarity relation ⊑ among worlds. There is a well known alternative to this construction based on a binary relation over sentential beliefs, known as "epistemic entrenchment" [4]. This relation may be viewed as ranking the *beliefs* based on their comparative strengths of acceptance. Alternatively, a constructive approach to belief change can also be based on the pair-wise comparison of the *disbeliefs* with respect to their strength of denouncement [2]. None of these approaches allow any nontrivial comparison among plausible hypotheses that have neither been accepted nor rejected by the agent (henceforth *plausibilities*). A case can be made, however, that these plausibilities, namely the hypotheses that the agent has suspended judgement about, can be meaningfully compared with respect to their *plausibility*. After all, the whole Bayesian tradition is based the probabilistic comparison of such plausibilities!

If we grant that plausibilities can be meaningfully compared with each other, it has an interesting spin-off with respect to the Grovian Systems of Spheres. Let us say, for a start, that of two plausibilities x and y, the former is more plausible iff some x-validating scenario is preferable (closer to the reality) to every y-validating scenario. However, since x and y are plausibilities, the most preferred x-validating and y-validating worlds are members of $[K]$ and $[K]$ is ⊑-flat! So in order to allow meaningful comparison of plausibilities, we have to supplement the Grovian measure (primarily over $\mathcal{M} \setminus [K]$) with a measure over $[K]$. That is precisely what Pagnucco does in [10] in order to offer us an account of abduction.

Pagnucco effectively ignores (with good reason) the extra-$[K]$ systems of sphere and introduces an intra-$[K]$ systems of spheres and examines the consequences of adopting a minimality-based belief change operation with respect to the later. The result is not belief revision proper since the pieces of evidence that are of interest here are not disbeliefs but plausibilities, and hence are consistent with the current knowledge. Since the result is in general stronger than classical expansion, it is closest to what has been called *abduction* or *inference to the best explanation* in the literature [11]. The following figure provides a visual representation of the abductive process suggested in [10].

Pagnucco has examined the properties of this abduction operation. Let K be the current belief set, x the evidence and $+$ the abductive expansion operation. The following list fully characterises this operation.

(1^+) K_x^+ is a theory

(2^+) If $\neg x \notin K$ then $x \in K_x^+$

(3^+) $K \subseteq K_x^+$

(4^+) If $K \nvdash \neg x$ then $K_x^+ = K$

(5^+) If $K \nvdash \neg x$ then $\neg x \notin K_x^+$

(6^+) If $K \vdash x \leftrightarrow y$, then $K_x^+ = K_y^+$

(7^+) $K_x^+ \subseteq Cn(K_{(x \vee y)}^+ \cup \{x\})$

(8^+) If $\neg x \notin K_{x \vee y}^+$ then $K_{(x \vee y)}^+ \subseteq K_x^+$

The motivation behind these properties can be found in [10].

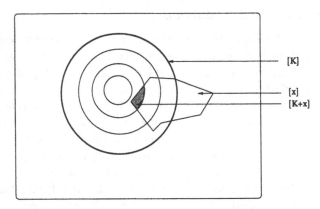

Fig. 2. Minimality based Abduction

3.4   Failure of Minimality Based Abduction

Despite its innovative approach, Pagnucco's suggestion soccumbs to a serious problem. It has been early recognised that any belief change operation should satisfy the properties of category matching: the object that undergoes change must result in an object of the same category. Without this property, there is no guarantee that the resultant object can face up to another change. This was a major problem with the classical AGM approach to belief change; extensions of this approach avoid this myopic problem [8]. However, Pagnucco's approach has not addressed this issue. In this, a structured object ($[K]$) undergoes an epistemic change and results in an unstructured object ($[K_x^+]$) which, in turn, cannot handle further abductive change.

In section §2 we outlined some features in presence of which the "reject the worst" principle is more appropriate than the "select the best" principle. It is easily verified that the context of abductive belief change has all these features. Hence we suggest that we give up "choose the best" principle in the context of abduction and adopt the reject worst principle instead.

4   Abduction by Rejecting the Worst

In the case of abduction, the crucial test is what happens when the evidence x is consistent with the current knowledge K. Accordingly, we will pretend that $\mathcal{M} \setminus [K]$ is $\sqsubseteq$-flat, although $[K]$ itself is, in general, not $\sqsubseteq$-flat. This assumption is granted in Pagnucco's account as well, and is similar in spirit to the assumption in [9] that K is $\sqsubseteq$-flat. For convenience, we will assume that K is consistent.

When the evidence is inconsistent with K, it is a boundary case, and it does not really matter how we deal with the boundery case. In this case, Pagnucco disallows any change in the current knowledge. On the other hand, we will stick to the classical AGM approach and assume that in this case the resultant state is inconsistent. (This accords well with the Reject worst principle – assuming that the worlds outside $[K]$ are all equally preferred, they are all rejected; so the resultant set is empty.)

Suppose now that the evidence x is consistent with the current knowledge K, namely, $[K] \cap [x] \neq \emptyset$. Then the choice set in question is the set of worlds $[K] \cap [x]$. If not all members of this set are equally preferred (or dispreferred), then according to the Reject Worst Principle, at least one member of this set will be rejected, and the rest will be returned as $[K_x^+]$.[6]

Accordingly, given an appropriate total preorder $\sqsubseteq$ on $\mathcal{M}$ for a belief set K we define the non-minimal abduction operation $\boxplus_{\sqsubseteq}$ (the subscript is henceforth dropped for readability except when the context is confusing) as follows:

Definition 2 (from $\sqsubseteq$ to $\boxplus$) *Where $\sqsubseteq$ is a total preorder on $\mathcal{M}$ and K a belief set such that $[K] = \{w \mid w \sqsubseteq w'$ for some $w' \in \mathcal{M}\}$,*

$$[K_x^{\boxplus}] = \begin{cases} \emptyset & \text{if } [K] \cap [x] = \emptyset \\ [K] \cap [x] & \text{else if } [K] \cap [x] \text{ is } \sqsubseteq\text{-flat} \\ \{w \in [K] \cap [x] \mid w \sqsubseteq w' & \\ \text{for some } w' \in [K] \cap [x]\} & \text{other wise.} \end{cases}$$

This definition separates three distinct ways of processing the evidence, as pictured in Figure 3. The first case is represented by $[z]$. In this case all the models in $[z]$ are eliminated. The area $[y]$ represents the second case. Here, since the models in $[K] \cap [y]$ cannot be discriminated on the basis of $\sqsubseteq$ alone, none of them is eliminated. The principal case, namely the third case, is represented by $[x]$. Here, among the models provided by $[K] \cap [x]$, the most implausible ones are eliminated and the rest are retained, perhaps, for future scrutiny.

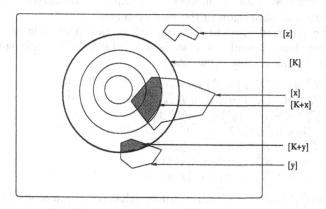

Fig. 3. Abduction Without Minimality

---

[6] We should not use the symbol $+$ here, since we have already used it to denote Pagnucco's abductive abduction. Later on we use a more appropriate symbol $\boxplus$.

How good is $\boxplus$, as defined above, as an abduction operation? We suggest that any abduction operation must have the following *basic* properties:

(1$\boxplus$) $K_x^\boxplus$ is a theory
(2$\boxplus$) $x \in K_x^\boxplus$
(3$\boxplus$) $K \subseteq K_x^\boxplus$
(4$\boxplus$) If $K \not\vdash \neg x$ then $K_x^\boxplus \not\vdash \neg x$
(5$\boxplus$) If $K \not\vdash \bot$ then $K_x^\boxplus = K_\bot$ iff $K \vdash \neg x$
(6$\boxplus$) If $K \vdash x \leftrightarrow y$, then $K_x^\boxplus = K_y^\boxplus$

The first three of these properties are obvious requirements for any expansion operation, abductive or otherwise. Given (2$\boxplus$), the fourth condition says that evidence consistent with the current knowledge cannot introduce inconsistency into one's body of knowledge. The fifth property says that an abductive process results in an inconsistent body of knowledge exactly when the evidence in question conflicts with the current knowledge. The sixth property says that the syntactic representation of evidence is irrelevant to the result of an abductive expansion, modulo the consequences of the current knowledge.

It is interesting to compare these basic properties with the first six postulates proposed by Pagnucco [10]. The basic difference is based on the difference between the corresponding second properties. Unlike (2$\boxplus$), Pagnucco's Success postulate is conditional upon the evidence being consistent with the current knowledge. When the evidence is inconsistent with the current knowledge, expansion is a boundary case, and how it is handled should not be given much importance. Accordingly, while we retain the AGM property of Success at the cost of allowing possible expansion into inconsistency, Pagnucco avoids such silly expansion at the cost of losing Success. This explains the difference between the fourth properties of abduction in the two systems.

As will be reported in section §5, our abduction operation $\boxplus$, apart from satisfying these basic postulates, also satisfies the following five *supplementary* postulates for the abductive expansion.

(7.1$\boxplus$) If $K_x^\boxplus \not\subseteq Cn(K \cup \{x, y\})$ then $K_{x \wedge y}^\boxplus \subseteq Cn(K_x^\boxplus \cup \{y\})$
(7.2$\boxplus$) If $K_y^\boxplus = Cn(K \cup \{y\})$ then $K_{x \wedge y}^\boxplus \subseteq Cn(K_x^\boxplus \cup \{y\})$
(7.3$\boxplus$) If $K_x^\boxplus \cap Cn(K \cup \{y\}) \subseteq Cn(K \cup \{x\})$
            then $K_{x \wedge y}^\boxplus \subseteq Cn(K_x^\boxplus \cup \{y\})$
(8$\boxplus$)   If $K_x^\boxplus \not\vdash \neg y$ then $Cn(K_x^\boxplus \cup \{y\}) \subseteq K_{x \wedge y}^\boxplus$
(9$\boxplus$)   If $K \not\vdash \neg x$, $K_x^\boxplus \vdash \neg y$ but $K \cup \{x\} \not\vdash \neg y$
            then $K_{x \wedge y}^\boxplus = Cn(K \cup \{x, y\})$.

Postulates (7.1$\boxplus$)–(7.3$\boxplus$) tell us under what condition a piece of evidence y loses its inferential power in presence of another piece of evidence x. For instance, (7.1$\boxplus$) may be paraphrased as follows: *Given some background knowledge K, if x is able to explain something that cannot be classically inferred from x and y together, then there is nothing that does not classically follow from y in presence of what x alone explains, and yet is jointly explainable by x and y together.* Postulate (8$\boxplus$) on the other hand says that x and y jointly fail to explain something that follows from y in presence of what is explainable by x only if y conflicts *with something that is explained by* x. Finally, postulate (9⊡) essentially says that *even though evidence* y *does not conflict with* x *(and the background knowledge* K), *if* y *conflicts with something explainable in terms of* x, *then* x *and* y *jointly have no abductive force.*

One striking difference between our supplementary postulates and those in [10] is that while in the latter constraints are sought for handling disjunctive evidence (i.e., on $K_{x \vee y}^{+}$), in the current approach constraints are sought on the result of processing conjunctive evidence (i.e., on $K_{x \wedge y}^{⊡}$). The primary reason for this is that we wanted the connection between the properties of ⊞ in [9] and ⊡ to be made obvious. We however believe that the same effect can be achieved by putting constraints on $K_{x \vee y}^{+}$ as are achieved by constraining $K_{x \vee y}^{+}$ in the postulates (7.1⊡)–(9⊡).

5   Technical Results

In section §4 we proposed and discussed a list of abduction postulates. It remains to be seen whether the proposed postulates in fact capture the semantic intuition behind Definition 2. The following results show that the postulates (1⊡)–(9⊡) indeed characterise the operation in question. The proofs have been omitted due to space constraints. Our first result, the soundness result, shows that the expansion operation ⊡ defined from the total preorder ⊑ operation via Definition 2 in fact satisfies properties (1⊡)–(9⊡).

Theorem 1 *Let* ⊑ *be a total preorder. Let the operation* ⊡ $=$ ⊡ ⊑ *be defined from* ⊑ *in accordance with Definition 2. The operation* ⊡ *satisfies the properties* (1⊡ – 9⊡).

Next we show the completeness result to the effect that given an abductive expansion operation ⊡ that satisfies (1⊡ – 9⊡) and a fixed belief set K we can construct a binary relation ⊑$_{⊡,K}$ with the desired properties. (We will trade off rigour against readability, and normally drop the subscripts.) In particular, we will show that, where ⊑ is the relation so constructed: (1) ⊑ is a total preorder over $\mathcal{M}$, (2) the SOS (System of Spheres) corresponding to ⊑ is a SOS whose maximal elements are exactly the members of $\mathcal{M} \setminus [K]$ and (3) $K_{x}^{⊡} = K_{x}^{⊡ ⊑}$ for any sentence x.

Definition 3 (from ⊡ **to** ⊑**)** *Given a revision operation* ⊡ *and a belief set* K, $w \sqsubseteq_{⊡,K} w'$ *iff either* $w' \notin [K]$ *or both* $\{w, w'\} \subseteq [K]$ *and* $w \in [K_{x}^{⊡}]$ *whenever* $w' \in [K_{x}^{⊡}]$, *for every sentence* x *such that* $\{w, w'\} \subseteq [K] \cap [x]$.

Theorem 2 *Let* ⊡ *be a revision operation satisfying* (1⊡) – (9⊡) *and* K *a belief set. Let* ⊑ *be generated from* ⊡ *and* K *as prescribed by Definition 3. Then* ⊑ *is a total preorder on* $\mathcal{M}$ *such that* $[K]$ *is the set of* ⊑*-non maximal elements of* $\mathcal{M}$.

Theorems 1 and 2 jointly show that the postulates (1⊞)-(9⊞) exactly characterise the abductive expansion operation constructed from the ⊑ relation.

Furthermore, the total preorder $\sqsubseteq_{⊞,K}$ constructed from a given non-minimal revision operation ⊞ and belief set K is the desired ⊑ in the sense that the non-minimal revision operation constructed from it, in turn, behaves like the original operation ⊞ with respect to the belief set K.

Theorem 3 *Let ⊞ be a non-minimal belief revision operator satisfying postulates (1⊞ − 9⊞) and K be an arbitrary belief set. Let ⊑ be defined from ⊞ and K in accordance with Definition 3. Let ⊞′ = ⊞$_⊑$ be defined from ⊑, in turn, via Definition 2. Then for any sentences x (and the originally fixed belief set K) it holds that $K_x^⊞ = K_x^{⊞'}$.*

Conversely, one can start with a total preorder ⊑, construct a revision operation ⊞ from it via Definition 2 and then construct a a total preorder ⊑ from that ⊞ in turn via Definition 3, then one gets back the original relation ⊑.

Theorem 4 *Let ⊑ be a total preorder on $\mathcal{M}$ and $[K]$ the set of ⊑-non maximal members of $\mathcal{M}$. Let ⊞ be defined (for K) from ⊑ via Definition 2. Let ⊑′=⊑$_{⊞'}$ be defined from ⊞, in turn, via Definition 3. Then $w ⊑ w'$ iff $w ⊑' w'$ for any two worlds $w, w' \in \mathcal{M}$*

6   Discussion: Iterated Abduction

In this paper, we examined the consequences of adopting the reject worst principle in the context of abductive belief change. This was done with the intent of extending a recently proposed account of abduction in [10] so that iterative abduction can be accommodated in the resulting framework. In the account of abduction provided in [10], there is no room for abduction. This is because Pagnucco's minimality based abduction relies on the degree of plausibility (of sentences that are at the time neither believed nor disbelieved) but provides no such measure in the resultant belief state. Graphically speaking, (see Figure 2) $[K_x^+]$, the candidate for $[K]$ in the next generation, is devoid of any structure, making it impossible to generate a measure of plausibility.[7] So, after one round of abduction, this account will reduce to classical AGM expansion.

The account of abduction provided in this paper addresses this shortcoming. In general, there is enough structure left in $[K_x^⊞]$ making further rounds of abduction possible. Of course, after each round of abduction, less structure is left in the new $[K]$, and eventually it will flatten out. Thus, it would appear as if our account merely postpones the problem of iterated abduction. Such a conclusion, however, is rather premature. Often, the evidence we handle is not consistent with our current knowledge. In such a case, it is understood that the agent should use a revision operation (instead of an expansion operation). And if the agent uses ⊞, although currently the plausibility measure is flat, the revision

---

[7] Strictly speaking, it will generate a flat plausibility measure.

is likely to inject structure into one's plausibility measure. A rigorous presentation of this material is beyond the scope of this paper, and is the subject of a different work.

References

1. Carlos E. Alchourrón, Peter Gärdenfors, and David Makinson. On the logic of theory change: Partial meet contraction and revision functions. *Journal of Symbolic Logic*, 50:510–530, 1985.
2. Didier Dubois and Henri Prade. Belief change and possibility theory. In Peter Gärdenfors, editor, *Belief Revision*, pages 142–182. Cambridge University Press, 1992.
3. Peter Gärdenfors. *Knowledge in Flux: Modeling the Dynamics of Epistemic States.* Bradford Books, MIT Press, Cambridge Massachusetts, 1988.
4. Peter Gärdenfors and David Makinson. Revisions of knowledge systems using epistemic entrenchment. In *Proceedings of the Second Conference on Theoretical Aspect of Reasoning About Knowledge*, pages 83–96, 1988.
5. Peter Gärdenfors and David Makinson. Nonmonotonic inference based on expectations. *Artificial Intelligence*, 65:197–245, 1994.
6. Michael R. Genesereth and Nils J. Nilsson. *Logical Foundations of Artificial Intelligence.* Morgan Kaufmann, 1987.
7. Adam Grove. Two modellings for theory change. *Journal of Philosophical Logic*, 17:157–170, 1988.
8. Abhaya C. Nayak. Iterated belief change based on epistemic entrenchment. *Erkenntnis*, 41:353–390, 1994.
9. Abhaya C. Nayak and Norman Y. Foo. Reasoning without minimality. In Hing-Yan Lee and Hiroshi Motoda, editors, *Proceedings of the Fifth Pacific Rim International Conference on Artificial Intelligence (PRICAI-98)*, pages 122–133. Springer Verlag, 1998.
10. Maurice Pagnucco. *The Role of Abductive Reasoning within the Process of Belief revision.* PhD thesis, University of Sydney, 1996.
11. Gabrielle Paul. Approaches to abductive reasoning: An overview. *Artificial Intelligence Review*, 7:109–152, 1993.
12. Yoav Shoham. *Reasoning About Change.* MIT Press, Cambridge, Massachusetts, 1988.

Causal Propagation Semantics — A Study

Mikhail Prokopenko, Maurice Pagnucco, Pavlos Peppas, and Abhaya Nayak

Computational Reasoning Group, Department of Computing, Division of ICS,
Macquarie University, NSW 2109, Australia
mikhail.prokopenko@cmis.csiro.au
{morri,pavlos,abhaya}@ics.mq.edu.au

Abstract. A unifying semantic framework for different reasoning approaches provides an ideal tool to compare these competing alternatives. A historic example is Kripke's *possible world* semantics that provided a unifying framework for different systems of modal logic. More recently, Shoham's work on *preferential* semantics similarly provided a much needed framework to uniformly represent and compare a variety of nonmonotonic logics (including some logics of action). The present work develops a novel type of semantics for a particular causal approach to reasoning about action. The basic idea is to abandon the standard state-space of possible worlds and consider instead a larger set of possibilities — a hyper-space — tracing the effects of actions (including indirect effects) with the states in the hyper-space. Intuitively, the purpose of these hyper-states is to supply extra context to record the process of causality.

Keywords: common-sense reasoning, nonmonotonic reasoning, temporal reasoning.

In recent artificial intelligence research into reasoning about action much attention has been focussed on the role of causality [8,13]. While there is significant consensus that a causal component to reasoning systems is not explicitly necessary to solve the frame and ramification problems, it is generally considered necessary for concise solutions to these problems.

Causal theories of action have become prominent in a proliferation of reasoning about action frameworks. Each of these frameworks is couched in its own syntax and calculus for providing solutions to the frame and ramifications problems. But a cursory glance at this situation is sufficient to clearly indicate that this is grossly inadequate. What is required is an independent semantic motivation for these various proposed frameworks.

A unifying semantics would provide a basis upon which to compare the myriad approaches to reasoning about action. Moreover, it would give a clearer insight into the nature of causality underlying these various frameworks. While the prospect of a unifying semantics is a bit too ambitious for the present work we hope that some of the morals drawn may be able to serve as a first step in this direction.

One landmark proposal in the early literature on reasoning about action was Shoham's [12] *preferential semantics*. This semantics provided insight into

N. Foo (Ed.): AI'99, LNAI 1747, pp. 378–392, 1999.

several areas of reasoning in artificial intelligence including belief change [1] and nonmonotonic reasoning [5]. Recently Peppas *et al.* [9] have shown that it is not possible to furnish a traditional preferential style semantics for a recent causal approach to reasoning about action — McCain and Turner's causal theory of action [8]. They provided an augmented preferential semantics capable of characterising this framework. Subsequent to McCain and Turner's framework Thielscher [13] has proposed a causal approach to reasoning about action which, under certain specific conditions, subsumes McCain and Turner's approach.[1] However, this framework is devoid of a suitable semantics. As a result, it is difficult to place this framework in perspective with competing proposals.

Put briefly, the main aim of this paper is to *furnish a semantics characterising Thieslscher's casual theory of action* . We do so by proffering a novel type of semantics. The basic idea is to abandon the standard state-space of possible worlds and consider instead a larger set of possibilities — a hyper-space — tracing the effects of actions (including indirect effects) with the states in the hyper-space. Intuitively, the purpose of these hyper-states is to supply extra context to record the process of causality.

In the following section we outline the necessary technical preliminaries for an understanding of this paper. In section 2 we briefly sketch Thielscher's causal theory of action. In Section 3 we introduce the hyper-space semantics that we shall use to characterise Thielscher's [13] approach. Section 4 will establish the necessary representation theorems. Section 5 discusses the importance of these results.

1 Technical Preliminaries

Let $\mathcal{F}$ be a finite set of symbols from a fixed language $\mathcal{B}$, called fluent names. A fluent literal is either a fluent name $f \in \mathcal{F}$ or its negation, denoted by $\neg f$. Let $L_{\mathcal{F}}$ be a set of all fluent literals defined over the set of fluent names $\mathcal{F}$. We will adopt from Thielscher [13] the following notation. If $\epsilon \in L_{\mathcal{F}}$, then $|\epsilon|$ denotes its affirmative component, that is, $|f| = |\neg f| = f$, where $f \in \mathcal{F}$. This notation can be extended to sets of fluent literals as follows: $|S| = \{|f| : f \in S\}$. By state we intend a maximal consistent set of fluent literals. We will denote the set of all states as W, and call the number m of fluent names in $\mathcal{F}$ the dimension of W. By $[\phi]$ we denote all states consistent with the sentence $\phi \in \mathcal{B}$ (i.e., $[\phi] = \{w \in W : w \vdash \phi\}$).

2 Background

The idea of minimising change in order to deduce the set of possible next states (successor states) is used quite broadly in action theories. Sometimes the notion of minimal change is defined by set inclusion (eg., PMA) [14,4,7,8], and often

---

[1] There is insufficient space for us to elaborate upon McCain and Turner's approach here and to furnish a comparison with Thielscher's alternate proposal.

incorporates the frame concept or the policy of categorisation [4,7], assigning different degrees of inertia to language elements (fluents, literals, formulas, etc.). Shortcomings of particular implementations of the principle of minimal change and the policy of categorisation are well-known: imprecise or capricious definitions of minimality metrics (eg., PWA [2] vs PMA [14]), difficulties in properly categorising fluents as inertial and non-inertial, leading to increasingly complex selection mechanisms of action languages [7,10,13]), etc. These problems have generated attempts to use some notion of causality instead of or in addition to the principle of minimal change. For instance, some action theories try to embody background information in the form of domain "causal laws", pointing to the fact that, in general, propositions embracing causal dependencies are more expressive than traditional state constraints [6,8].

However, despite numerous attempts to combine a notion of causality with the principle of minimal change and/or policy of categorisation, multiple counter-examples keep reappearing, highlighting the intractability of the ramification problem. The framework suggested by Thielscher [13] criticised the categorisation policy and the principle of minimal change, arguing for the necessity of an approach based on causality. Thielscher's approach was intended to provide a method to avoid unintuitive indirect effects (ramifications), while accounting for causal relationships of a domain in hand. One of the perceived strengths of the Thielscher approach was an ability to capture not only all intuitively expected resulting states with minimal distance to the initial state, but also non-minimal solutions - "perfectly acceptable provided all changes are reasonable from the standpoint of causality" [13]. In other words, the non-minimal solutions are those states which are reachable via causal propagation from an intermediate state. This intermediate state is determined as the nearest state to the initial state, where the direct action effects hold, while some domain constraints may be violated.

Thielscher [13] criticised minimal change on the grounds that, in his view, it rejects a potential resultant state if it is obtained by changing the values of more fluents than strictly necessary. Arguably, this skewed view of the principle is too restrictive to warrant complete abandonment of the general notion of minimal change. In this paper we question Thielscher's criticism of minimal change and contend that there is an element of minimal change at work in his framework. To demonstrate our claim we exhibit a semantics for Thielscher's causal theory of actions. This semantics can be clearly seen to employ a component of minimal change coupled with causality.

Thielscher employs two crucial notions: *action laws* and *causal relationships*. Action laws essentially describe the immediate (or direct) effects of performing an action in a given state. Causal relationships are responsible for producing the indirect effects of actions.

Thielscher employs the following notion of action specification. Each action law consists of:

– a condition C, which is a set of fluent literals, all of which must be contained in an initial state where the action is intended to be applied;

– a (direct) effect E, which is also a set of fluent literals, all of which must hold in the resulting state after having applied the action.

For simplicity, it is assumed that condition and effect are constructed from the very same set of fluent names.Therefore, the state resulting from a direct effect is obtained by simply removing set C from the initial state at hand and adding set E to it. However, execution of an action may cause further state transitions.

Definition 1. *Let $\mathcal{F}$ be the set of fluent names and let $\mathcal{A}$ be a finite set of symbols called action names, such that $\mathcal{F} \cap \mathcal{A} = \emptyset$. An action law is a triple $\langle C, a, E \rangle$ where C, called condition, and E, called effect, are individually consistent sets of fluent literals, composed of the very same set of fluent names (i.e., $|C| = |E|$) and $a \in \mathcal{A}$. If w is a state then an action law $\alpha = \langle C, a, E \rangle$ is applicable in w iff $C \subseteq w$. The application of α to w yields the state $(w \setminus C) \cup E$, where $\setminus$ denotes set subtraction.*

Thielscher's approach formally incorporates causal information through *causal relationships* of the form

$$\epsilon \ causes \ \rho \ if \ \Phi$$

where ϵ and ρ are fluent literals and Φ is a fluent formula based on $\mathcal{F}$, the set of fluent names.

Definition 2. *Let (s, E) be a pair consisting of a state s and a set of fluent literals E. Then a causal relationship ϵ causes ρ if Φ is applicable to (s, E) iff $\Phi \wedge \neg \rho$ is true in s, and $\epsilon \in E$. Its application yields the pair (s', E'), denoted as $(s, E) \rightsquigarrow (s', E')$, where $s' = (s \setminus \{\neg \rho\}) \cup \{\rho\}$ and $E' = (E \setminus \{\neg \rho\}) \cup \{\rho\}$.*

Intuitively, a causal relationship is applicable if the associated condition Φ holds, the particular indirect effect ρ is currently false, and its cause ϵ is among the current effects — in other words, the cause has been effected, i.e., it has *changed during causal propagation* from false in the past to being true at the moment. Importantly, if the literal ϵ is not among current effects, then it is not possible to apply the causal relationship - even if ϵ is an element of a current state.

States incorporating direct action effects may violate the underlying domain constraints.[2] So, "in order to obtain a satisfactory resulting state, we compute additional, indirect effects by (nondeterministically) selecting and (serially) applying causal relationships. If this procedure eventually results in a state satisfying the domain constraints, then this is called a *successor state*" ([13]). More precisely, the set of possible successor states $Res_T(a, w)$, given an initial state w and an action a, is determined as follows.

---

[2] The details of an algorithm translating domain constraints and the influence relation into causal relationships are described in [13].

Definition 3. *Let $\mathcal{F}$ be the set of fluent names, A a set of action names, $\mathcal{L}$ a set of action laws, $\mathcal{D}$ a set of domain constraints, and R a set of causal relationships. Furthermore, let w be a state satisfying $\mathcal{D}$ and let $a \in A$ be an action name. A state r is a successor state of w and a, $r \in Res_T(a, w)$, iff there exists an applicable (with respect to w) action law $\alpha = \langle C, a, E \rangle \in \mathcal{L}$ such that*

1. $((w \setminus C) \cup E, E) \overset{*}{\rightsquigarrow} (r, E')$ for some E', and
2. r satisfies $\mathcal{D}$,

where $\overset{*}{\rightsquigarrow}$ denotes the transitive closure of $\rightsquigarrow$.

As mentioned before, an occurrence of a literal ϵ in a state s does not guarantee that a causal relationship ϵ *causes* ρ if Φ is applicable to a pair (s, E) — to ensure applicability, the literal ϵ has to belong to the current effects E. It is interesting to note, however, that given a *transition* pair (s, E), if the literal ϵ is among current effects E, then it must be an element of the current state s. This observation can be formalised as follows.

Lemma 1. *If $(s', E') \overset{*}{\rightsquigarrow} (s'', E'')$, then $E'' \subseteq s''$.*

It is easy to observe that the set E' contains the *most recent* consistent effects that have taken place during the causal propagation $((w \setminus C) \cup E, E) \overset{*}{\rightsquigarrow} (r, E')$. In other words, although some of the effects may have been retracted from the effects set during propagation, their negations should have taken the respective places. The effects set is intended to account for both direct and indirect changes. However, it is not guaranteed that direct effects E are always preserved by the propagation. On the contrary, they can be lost (the indirect effects can be lost as well — but this obviously is less counter-intuitive).

Consider, for example, the simple action system with $\mathcal{F} = \{p, q\}$, $\mathcal{D} = \{\neg q \rightarrow \neg p\}$, $R = \{\neg q$ *causes* $\neg p$ if $\top\}$, and $\mathcal{L} = \{\langle \{p, q\}, a, \{p, \neg q\} \rangle\}$. The action a performed at the initial state $\{p, q\}$, results in a state $\{p, \neg q\}$. Clearly, this resultant state does not satisfy the domain constraint. The causal relationship is then applicable, whereby $(\{p, \neg q\}, \{p, \neg q\}) \rightsquigarrow (\{\neg p, \neg q\}, \{\neg p, \neg q\})$ and produces $Res_T(a, \{p, q\}) = \{\neg p, \neg q\}$, where the successor state satisfies $\mathcal{D}$, while leaving one of the direct effects (p) out.

We can strengthen the concept of successor states to *conservative* successor states (denoted $Res_T^*(a, S)$) as follows.

Definition 4. *Let $\mathcal{F}$, A, $\mathcal{L}$, $\mathcal{D}$, R, w, $\alpha = \langle C, a, E \rangle$ be the same as in Definition 3. A state r is a conservative successor state of w and a, $r \in Res_T^*(a, w)$, iff*

1. $r \in Res_T(a, w)$, and
2. $E \subseteq r$.

This definition allows the causal propagation to "travel" outside the $E-$states, but mandates that it finish in a state consistent with the direct effects E.

3 Hyper-space Semantics

It has been previously argued [9] that a preferential structure with a binary relation on states demonstrates that minimal change and causality — the former captured by preferential semantics and the latter by a binary relation — together are essential in furnishing a concise solution to the frame problem. Our approach here is intended to illustrate this idea once more, now with respect to Thielscher's causal theory of action. More importantly, it is our contention that a pure preferential semantics, in the spirit of [12], cannot be obtained for causal action systems without extending the underlying language. Thus, in addition, the proposed approach may serve as another step towards a uniform preferential semantics for (extended) causal action systems.

Our intention at this stage is to consider a formalisation of action systems which faithfully captures all successor states, as defined by $Res_T(a, w)$ (or $Res_T^*(a, w)$), using a simpler selection mechanism. More precisely, instead of keeping an explicit (and changing) account of context-dependent action effects, we would like to use a binary (causal) relation on states. The advantage of this proposal is that a causal relation would be action-independent, unlike a history of effects. Obviously, this objective is hardly achievable without extending the action system components in some way.

Let us begin by informally describing the semantics we develop, before proceeding to establish the formal results. An expansion of the standard state-space to a hyper-space of a larger dimension generates numerous hyper-states. Any state in the standard state-space can then be associated with a number of hyper-states, creating a hyper-neighbourhood. For instance, an intermediate state (defined, for a given action and an initial state, according to Thielscher's approach) can be represented by a set of hyper-states in the expanded space. This hyper-neighbourhood will be a starting point of a propagation. An appropriately constructed binary relation on hyper-states would allow us to propagate in the hyper-space in a very simple way — without the necessity to track the causal history, and resulting in a clearly defined "final" set of hyper-states. A projection from the resulting hyper-neighbourhood back to the normal state-space would pinpoint the desired successor state of the action at hand. Intuitively, the purpose of the hyper-states is to serve as possible causal extensions of normal states, providing necessary context to the process of causal propagation. In the remainder of this section we give a formal description of this semantics.

We suggest to extend the set of fluent names $\mathcal{F}$ and incorporate more causal information in states themselves rather than rely on context-dependent causal propagation. We begin with definitions of an extended (hyper-) state. First of all, we consider a set, denoted as $\overset{\circ}{\mathcal{F}}$, of the same cardinality as the set $\mathcal{F}$, such that $L_{\mathcal{F}} \cap \overset{\circ}{\mathcal{F}} = \emptyset$. Then we define a function $j : \mathcal{F} \to \overset{\circ}{\mathcal{F}}$. Intuitively, the element $j(f)$ of the set $\overset{\circ}{\mathcal{F}}$ is an extra space-dimension, corresponding to the fluent $f \in \mathcal{F}$. Now let us consider the set $L_{\overset{\circ}{\mathcal{F}}} = \overset{\circ}{\mathcal{F}} \cup \{\neg q : q \in \overset{\circ}{\mathcal{F}}\}$. Clearly, the cardinality of the set $L_{\overset{\circ}{\mathcal{F}}}$ is equal to the cardinality of the set of fluent literals $L_{\mathcal{F}}$, and $L_{\mathcal{F}} \cap \overset{\circ}{L}_{\mathcal{F}} = \emptyset$. Another function is needed to map from $L_{\mathcal{F}}$ to $\overset{\circ}{L}_{\mathcal{F}}$, and we introduce the function $l : L_{\mathcal{F}} \to \overset{\circ}{L}_{\mathcal{F}}$, such that $l(f) = j(f)$ if $f \in \mathcal{F}$ (f is a positive literal — a fluent name), and $l(f) = \neg j(|f|)$ if $f \in L_{\mathcal{F}} \setminus \mathcal{F}$ (f is a negative literal).

The following property of the function $l(f)$ can be easily obtained.

Lemma 2. *If $f \in \mathcal{F}$, then $l(\neg f) = \neg l(f)$.*

The function $l(f)$ is intended to produce extra literals, corresponding to fluent literals in $L_{\mathcal{F}}$. We will call a literal $l(f)$ a justifier literal, and will use the abbreviation $\overset{\circ}{f}$ instead of $l(f)$ for simplicity. In addition, the set $\overset{\circ}{\mathcal{F}}$ will be referred to as the set of all justifier fluents, and the $\overset{\circ}{L}_{\mathcal{F}}$ will be referred to as the set of all justifier literals.

Having defined the function l, we can define a justifier set $\overset{\circ}{J}$ for a set of fluent literals J as $\overset{\circ}{J} = \cup_{f \in J}\{l(f)\} = \cup_{f \in J}\{\overset{\circ}{f}\}$.

Definition 5. *Given a set of fluents $\mathcal{F}$, a hyper-state is a maximal consistent set of literals from $L_{\mathcal{F}} \cup \overset{\circ}{L}_{\mathcal{F}}$.*

We will denote the set of all hyper-states as Ω, where the dimension of Ω is $2m$, m being the dimension of W. The following two functions map hyper-space Ω to normal space W and vice versa.

Definition 6. *A projection from Ω to W, $p : \Omega \to W$, is the function mapping a hyper-state $s = \{f_1, ..., f_n, \overset{\circ}{f_1}, ..., \overset{\circ}{f_n}\} \in \Omega$ to a state $r = \{f_1, ..., f_n\} \in W$.*

We denote the hyper-part of a hyper-state $s \in \Omega$ as $h(s) = s \setminus p(s)$. Clearly, for any $s \in \Omega$, $h(s) \cap \mathcal{F} = \emptyset$.

Definition 7. *A hyper-neighbourhood of a state $r \in W$, $N : W \to 2^{\Omega}$, is the function mapping a state r to a set of hyper-states: $N(r) = \{s \in \Omega : r = p(s)\}$.*

Clearly, there are 2^m states in any hyper-neighbourhood, as there are m justifier fluent names in any hyper-state allowed to vary across the neighbourhood. Intuitively, justifier literals represent explicit causes for a set $r \in W$. In other words, the set $N(r)$ is the set of states where all possible causes vary, while the (proper) literals defined on $\mathcal{F}$ are fixed. For example, given the state $r = \{a, b\}$ in the normal space W, one can consider its hyper-neighbourhood $N(r)$ containing hyper-states $\{a, b, \overset{\circ}{a}, \overset{\circ}{b}\}$, $\{a, b, \overset{\circ}{a}, \neg\overset{\circ}{b}\}$, $\{a, b, \neg\overset{\circ}{a}, \overset{\circ}{b}\}$ and $\{a, b, \neg\overset{\circ}{a}, \neg\overset{\circ}{b}\}$, where the justifier fluents $\overset{\circ}{a}$ and $\overset{\circ}{b}$ vary. Hence any subset of $N(r)$ may represent a particular causal context — the set $\{\{a, b, \overset{\circ}{a}, \overset{\circ}{b}\}, \{a, b, \overset{\circ}{a}, \neg\overset{\circ}{b}\}\}$, for instance, may correspond to a partial state $\{a, b, \overset{\circ}{a}\}$, justifying the literal $a \in r$, and leaving the literal $b \in r$ somewhat unsupported (more precisely, any *change* in a truth value of a literal will be expected to have a justification).

It is worth noting that the history component E in any causally propagated pair (s, E) cannot have more elements than m — due to the consistency of the update defined in Definition 2, as shown by Lemma 1. In a simple case, when the history component E in a pair (s, E) has exactly m elements (or, in other words, $E = s$ by the Lemma 1), the pair can be easily represented by a single hyper-state $s \cup \overset{\circ}{s}$. For instance, the hyper-state $\{a, b, \overset{\circ}{a}, \overset{\circ}{b}\}$ can account for a causal transition pair $(\{a, b\}, \{a, b\})$. In the case when the component E has strictly less elements, $E \subset s$, the incompleteness may be represented by a partial hyper-state. A union of complete hyper-states, $\{\{a, b, \overset{\circ}{a}, \overset{\circ}{b}\}, \{a, b, \overset{\circ}{a}, \neg\overset{\circ}{b}\}\}$ can represent the pair $(\{a, b\}, \{a\})$ in a causal propagation chain where the second component carries the history of change $\{a\}$.

It is precisely the combinatorial variability of possible causes in a hyper-neighbourhood that allows us to account for different action-dependent histories in a causally propagated chain, leading to a successor state in $Res_T(a, \ w)$. Before we formally introduce the required notion of a binary causal relation on hyper-states, let us illustrate the intention with an example.

Consider an action system with $\mathcal{F} = \{a, b, c\}$, $\mathcal{D} = \{\neg b \rightarrow \neg a\}$, $R = \{\neg b$ causes $\neg a$ if $\top\}$, and $\mathcal{L} = \{\langle\{b\}, x, \{\neg b\}\rangle\}$. Let us perform the action x at the initial state $w = \{a, b, c\}$. The action direct effect, stored in an (initial) history component, is $\{\neg b\}$, and the intermediate state is, obviously, $\{a, \neg b, c\} = (w \setminus \{b\}) \cup \{\neg b\}$. This state violates the domain constraint, but the only causal law of the system is applicable: $(\{a, \neg b, c\}, \{\neg b\}) \rightsquigarrow (\{\neg a, \neg b, c\}, \{\neg a, \neg b\})$. The state component of the yielded pair satisfies the domain constraint and therefore belongs to $Res_T(x, \ w)$. It is easy to verify that $Res_T(x, \ w)$ is a singleton.

Now, let us sketch how this simple propagation could be traced in the hyper-space. The hyper-neighbourhood $N(r)$ of the intermediate state $r = \{a, \neg b, c\}$ contains eight hyper-states, some of which represent the initial history component $\{\neg b\}$ — these hyper-states are precisely the states in $N(r) \cap [\neg\overset{\circ}{b}]$. The hyper-neighbourhood of the successor state $r' = \{\neg a, \neg b, c\}$ contains some hyper-states accountable for the final history component $\{\neg a, \neg b\}$. These states are precisely the states in $N(r') \cap [\neg\overset{\circ}{a} \wedge \neg\overset{\circ}{b}]$ or $N(r') \cap [\neg\overset{\circ}{a}] \cap [\neg\overset{\circ}{b}]$. Our intention, therefore, is to construct, for an action system, such a binary relation on hyper-states that a transition in hyper-space faithfully corresponds to causal propagation driven by an action-dependent history.

Formally, we define a binary relation on states in Ω as follows.

Definition 8. *A binary relation $\mathcal{C}$ is defined on $\Omega \times \Omega$. We say that $\mathcal{C}(s, s')$ if and only if there exists a causal relationship ϵ causes ρ if Φ such that*

1. $p(s) \vdash \epsilon \wedge \Phi \wedge \neg\rho$
2. $h(s) \vdash \overset{\circ}{\epsilon}$
3. $p(s') = (p(s) \setminus \{\neg\rho\}) \cup \{\rho\}$
4. $h(s') = (h(s) \setminus \{\neg\overset{\circ}{\rho}\}) \cup \{\overset{\circ}{\rho}\}$

Figure 1 illustrates the generation of links by a causal relationship between hyper-states which belong to distinct hyper-neighbourhoods (the causal relationship is the same as in the example above).

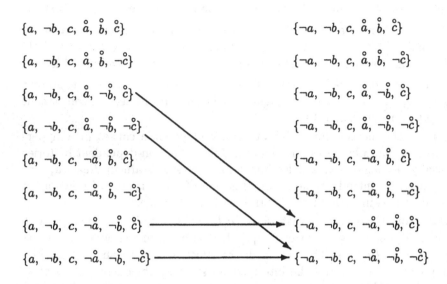

Fig. 1. The C-links between hyper-neighbourhoods of the states $\{a, \neg b, c\}$ and $\{\neg a, \neg b, c\}$, generated by a causal relationship $\neg b$ *causes* $\neg a$ *if* $\top$.

The fact that all the states in $N(r) \cap [\neg\overset{\circ}{b}]$ have links to the states in $N(r') \cap [\neg\overset{\circ}{a} \wedge \neg\overset{\circ}{b}]$ is not a coincidence, and will be formally captured in a definition of a successor state.

It is worth pointing out that the first condition in Definition 8 requires that the literal ϵ is a part of the $p(s)$ state — unlike Definition 2. However, Lemma 1 illustrated that this requirement is implicit in Definition 2 as well ensuring that, in this respect, the new definition is not going to be more restrictive than the former one (formally, it will be shown later).

A causal relationship ϵ *causes* ρ *if* Φ may, upon translation, generate quite a few links between hyper-states. But causal propagation expressed in terms of these links is much clearer and simpler than that of Thielscher's approach.

4   Representation Theorems

The following set will help in our analysis of causal links $C(s, s')$. Given two states $x \in W$ and $y \in W$, the set $L(x, y) = \{s \in N(x) : C(s, s'), \text{ for some } s' \in N(y)\}$

will be referred to as the *connection set* for the states x and y. In general, $L(x,y) \neq L(y,x)$.

An important property of the relation C is that there are at least 2^{m-1} links generated by one causal relationship (the minimum is attained when a causal relationship ϵ *causes* ρ if Φ is qualified by a complete state: $\Phi \leftrightarrow \bigwedge_{k=1}^{k=m} f_k$). This property leads to the following lemma.

Lemma 3. *For any two states $x \in W$ and $y \in W$, if the connection set $L(x,y) \neq \emptyset$ then there exists a justifier literal $\overset{\circ}{f}$ such that $[\overset{\circ}{f}] \cap N(x) \subseteq L(x,y)$.*

This lemma basically says that, if there is at least one C-link between two hyper-states, then there are at least $2^{m-1}-1$ more C-links between hyper-states in the respective neighbourhoods, and all these links are generated by the same causal relationship.

Figure 2 illustrates the existence of a justifier literal $\neg\overset{\circ}{b}$ such that $[\neg\overset{\circ}{b}] \cap N(\{a, \neg b, c\}) \subseteq L(\{a, \neg b, c\}, \{\neg a, \neg b, c\})$.

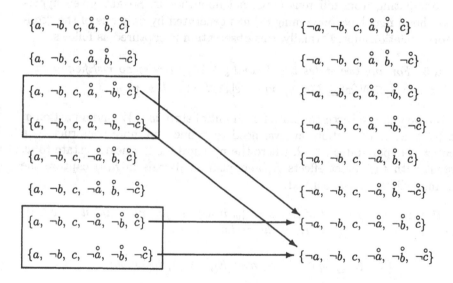

Fig. 2. All $[\neg\overset{\circ}{b}]$-states belong to the connection set $L(\{a, \neg b, c\}, \{\neg a, \neg b, c\})$.

It is possible to show that a qualified reverse observation holds as well.

Lemma 4. *For any two states $x \in W$ and $y \in W$, if there exists a justifier literal $\overset{\circ}{f}$ such that $[\overset{\circ}{f}] \cap N(x) \subseteq L(x,y)$, then there exists a causal relationship f causes ρ if Φ, for some Φ and where $\{\rho\} = y \setminus x$.*

The proof of this lemma progressively eliminates all literals except f, which might have been alternative causes. It capitalises on the fact that varying $m-1$ justifier literals (having fixed $\overset{\circ}{f}$) accounts for at most $2^{m-1}-1$ states in an hyper-neighbourhood, while there are 2^{m-1} states in the set $[\overset{\circ}{f}] \cap N(x)$.

Together, the last two lemmas show that the presence of a causal relationship underlying a C-link is equivalent to the existence of a justifier literal $\overset{\circ}{f}$ such that $[\overset{\circ}{f}] \cap N(x) \subseteq L(x,y)$.

Corollary 1. *For any two states $x \in W$ and $y \in W$, there exists a justifier literal $\overset{\circ}{f}$ such that $[\overset{\circ}{f}] \cap N(x) \subseteq L(x,y)$, if and only if there exists a causal relationship f causes ρ if Φ, where $\{\rho\} = y \setminus x$, for some Φ.*

It is not surprising to observe that any connection set may not contain all $[\overset{\circ}{\epsilon}]$-states and all $[\neg\overset{\circ}{\epsilon}]$-states in any hyper-neighbourhood. Although the set R of causal relationships is allowed to include causal relationships like f causes ρ if Φ and $\neg f$ causes ρ if Φ, such ("contradictory") relationships would generate C-links originating from different hyper-neighbourhoods. So any given hyper-neighbourhood may have outcoming C-links generated by only one of the "contradictory" relationships. Formally, this observation is captured as follows.

Lemma 5. *For any two states $x \in W$ and $y \in W$, there is no justifier literal $\overset{\circ}{\epsilon}$ such that both $[\overset{\circ}{\epsilon}] \cap N(x) \subseteq L(x,y)$ and $[\neg\overset{\circ}{\epsilon}] \cap N(x) \subseteq L(x,y)$ hold.*

Before we define a successor state for an initial state $w \in W$ and an action a, where $\langle C, a, E \rangle$ is the action law, we need to define one more construct — a *trigger set* of hyper-states $s \in \Omega$, where the $p(s)$ state is the nearest state to w, consistent with the direct effects E, and justifier literals in $h(s)$ capture the initial (immediate) causal context.

Definition 9. *A trigger set of states $\|E\|_w$ is defined for an initial state $w \in W$ and an action a, where $\langle C, a, E \rangle$ is the action law, as*

$$\{s \in N(q) : q \in W, q \in min([E], \ll_w), h(s) \vdash \overset{\circ}{E}\}$$

where $x \ll_w y$ if and only if $\mathit{Diff}(x, w) \subset \mathit{Diff}(y, w)$.

Here $\mathit{Diff}(p, q)$ represents the symmetric difference of p and q (i.e., $(p \setminus q) \cup (q \setminus p)$) as in PMA [14].

In other words, $\|E\|_w$ is the set contained in the hyper-neighbourhood $N(q)$ of the state q nearest to the initial state w (in terms of the PMA ordering), and the states $s \in \|E\|_w$ jointly represent the initial causally justified changes triggered by effects E. For example, consider an action law $\{\langle\{b\}, x, \{\neg b\}\rangle\}$, applied at the initial state $\{a, b, c\}$. Then the trigger set $\|\{\neg b\}\|_{\{a,b,c\}}$ contains exactly the states placed in boxes in Figure 2. The following observation can be obtained from the definition immediately.

Lemma 6. *For any initial state $w \in W$ and an action a, where $\langle C, a, E \rangle$ is the action law, $\cap_{s \in \|E\|_w} h(s) = \overset{\circ}{E}$.*

Intuitively, what the states $s \in \|E\|_w$ have in common in terms of justifier literals, is precisely literals in $\overset{\circ}{E}$.

Having defined a trigger set $\|E\|_w$, we can formally trace a causal propagation in the hyper-space Ω. Let C^* be the transitive closure of C.

Definition 10. *We say that a hyper-neighbourhood $N(q)$, where $q \in W$, is causally triggered by the set $\|E\|_w$, denoted as $\|E\|_w \succ N(q)$ if and only if $\forall s \in \|E\|_w$, $\exists s' \in N(q)$, such that $C^*(s, s')$ holds.*

A case shown previously in Figure 2 was an instance (assuming a direct action effect $\neg b$) when the trigger set $\|\{\neg b\}\|_{\{a,b,c\}}$ does trigger the hyper-neighbourhood on the right-hand side. Figure 3 gives an example when the same trigger set fails to trigger the same hyper-neighbourhood — because not all the states in the set $\|\{\neg b\}\|_{\{a,b,c\}}$ belong to the given connection set.

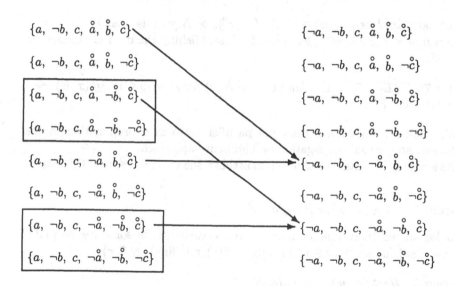

Fig. 3. The C-links between hyper-neighbourhoods of the states $\{a, \neg b, c\}$ and $\{\neg a, \neg b, c\}$, generated by a causal relationship c *causes* $\neg a$ *if* $\neg b$. Some $[\neg\overset{\circ}{b}]$-states do not belong to the connection set $L(\{a, \neg b, c\}, \{\neg a, \neg b, c\})$.

It is easy to check that the causal relationship which generated the connection set would not be applicable according to Thielscher's approach as well — because the cause (c) is not a part of a history component (equal to the direct effect at this stage).

Intuitively, changes triggered by the set $\|E\|_w$ propagate in hyper-space towards a hyper-neighbourhood of a possible successor state, tracing through some (causally triggered) hyper-neighbourhoods.

Definition 11. *A state $s \in \Omega$ is final if and only if $\{s' : C(s, s')\} = \emptyset$. A state $r \in W$ is final if and only if $\forall s \in N(r), s$ is final.*

Now we are ready to formally define a set of possible successor states $Res_\Omega(a, w)$ intended to faithfully capture Thielscher's resultant state set $Res_T(a, w)$.

Definition 12. *Let $\mathcal{F}$ be a set of fluent names, A a set of action names, $\mathcal{L}$ a set of action laws, C a causal binary relation defined by Definition 8. Furthermore, let $w \in W$ be an initial state and let $a \in A$ be an action name. A state $r \in W$ is a successor state of w and a, $r \in Res_\Omega(a, w)$, if and only if there exists an applicable (with respect to w) action law $\alpha = \langle C, a, E \rangle \in \mathcal{L}$ such that $\|E\|_w \succ N(r)$ and r is final.*

Alternatively, $Res_\Omega(a, w) \equiv \{r \in W : \|E\|_w \succ N(r), r \text{ is final }\}$.

We will need the following lemma before establishing the desired representation result.

Lemma 7. *If $\|E\|_w \subseteq N(x)$, then $\|E\|_w \succ N(y)$ for some $y \in W$ iff $(x, E) \overset{*}{\leadsto} (y, E')$ for some E'.*

This lemma establishes a principal parallel between a propagation in the hyper-space and causal propagation of Thielscher approach.

The foregoing results now allow us to estblish the central result of this paper.

Theorem 1. $Res_T(a, w) = Res_\Omega(a, w)$.

Analogous results can be obtained for conservative successor states as well if we define $Res_\Omega^*(a, w) \equiv \{r \in W : \|E\|_w \succ N(r), r \text{ is final}, E \subseteq r\}$.

Theorem 2. $Res_T^*(a, w) = Res_\Omega^*(a, w)$.

5   Discussion

The semantics proposed here extends the standard state-space to a hyper-space, and works by tracing the effects of actions (including indirect effects) in the hyper-space. The hyper-states are used to supply extra context to the process of causal propagation.

These additional states are reminiscent of a semantics provided by Kraus *et al.* [5] for nonmonotonic consequence relations. It would be interesting to extract a nonmonotonic consequence relation from the result function(s) investigated here. This would facilitate a wider comparison with a wider class of logics for nonmonotonic reasoning.

While we do not prove that the strategy proposed here is capable of furnishing a semantics for approaches to reasoning about action in general, we suggest that it is a fruitful strategy to pursue in supplying a unifying semantics for a large class of such frameworks. This is, at present, the subject of ongoing investigation.

There are several questions that one is tempted to ask. Are hyper-states necessary? What is the minimum number of hyper-states required to characterise a given result function? These, too, will be left for future investigation.

References

1. Peter Gärdenfors. *Knowledge in Flux: Modeling the Dynamics of Epistemic States*, Bradford Books, MIT Press, Cambridge Massachusetts, 1988.
2. Matthew L. Ginsberg and David E. Smith. Reasoning about action I: A possible worlds approach. Artificial Intelligence **35**:165–195, 1988.
3. Joakim Gustafsson and Patrick Doherty. Embracing occlusion in specifying the indirect effects of actions. In L. Aiello, J. Doyle, and S. Shapiro, editors, *Proceedings of the Fifth International Conference on Knowledge Representation and Reasoning*, pp. 87-98. Morgan-Kaufmann, 1996.
4. G. Neelakantan Kartha and Vladimir Lifschitz. Actions with indirect effects (Preliminary report). In *Proceedings of the Fourth International Conference on Principles of Knowledge Representation and Reasoning*, pages 341–350. Bonn, 1994.
5. Sarit Kraus, Daniel Lehmann and Menachem Magidor. Nonmonotonic reasoning, preferential models and cumulative logics, Artificial intelligence, **44**: 167–207, 1991.
6. Fangzhen Lin. Embracing causality in specifying the indirect effects of actions. In *Proceedings of International Joint Conference on Artificial Intelligence, Montreal* 1985 – 1991, 1995.
7. Vladimir Lifschitz. Two components of an action language. In *Proceedings of the Third Symposium on Logical Formalizations of Commonsense Reasoning*, Stanford, 1996.
8. Norman McCain and Hudson Turner. A causal theory of ramifications and qualifications. In *Proceedings of the Fourteenth International Joint Conference on Artificial Intelligence*, pages 1978–1984. Montreal, 1995.
9. Pavlos Peppas, Maurice Pagnucco, Mikhail Prokopenko, Abhaya Nayak and Norman Foo. Preferential semantics for causal systems. In *Proceedings of the Sixteenth International Joint Conference on Artificial Intelligence*, pp. 118–123. Stockholm, 1999.
10. Mikhail Prokopenko and Pavlos Peppas. Modelling inertia in action languages (Extended Report). In G. Antoniou, A. K. Ghose and M.Truszczynski (eds.) *Inducing and Reasoning with Complex Representations*, Springer Verlag Lecture Notes in AI, Volume 1359, pages 236-249, 1998.
11. Erik Sandewall. Assessments of ramification methods that use static domain constraints. In L. Aiello, J. Doyle, and S. Shapiro, editors, *Proceedings of the Fifth International Conference on Knowledge Representation and Reasoning*. Morgan-Kaufmann, 1996.
12. Yoav Shoham. *Reasoning About Change*. MIT Press, Cambridge, Massachusetts, 1988.

13. Michael Thielscher. Ramification and causality. Artificial Intelligence **89**: 317–364, 1997.
14. Marianne Winslett. Reasoning about actions using a possible models approach. In *Proceedings of the Seventh National Artificial Intelligence Conference*, pp. 89–93, San Mateo, CA., 1988. Morgan Kaufmann Publishers.

Arc Weights for Approximate Evaluation of Dynamic Belief Networks

Nathalie Jitnah and Ann E. Nicholson

School of Computer Science and Software Engineering
Monash University, Clayton, VIC 3168 Australia
tel: +613 9905 5211, fax: +613 9905 5146
{njitnah,annn}@csse.monash.edu.au

Abstract. Dynamic Belief Networks (DBNs) have become a popular method for monitoring dynamical processes in real-time. However DBN evaluation has the same problems of computational intractability as ordinary belief networks, with additional exponential complexity as the number of time-slices increases. Several approximate methods for fast DBN evaluation have been devised [1,3,11]. We present a new method which simplifies evaluation by selectively "forgetting" past events and their relationships to the present. This is done by pruning, from past time-slices, arcs and nodes which are deemed less relevant to the current time-slice, as determined by the arc weight measure introduced in [15]. This approach is more flexible than a fixed-size window and can be combined with other approximate evaluation techniques.

1 Introduction

Dynamic Belief Networks (DBNs) [5,14,12] extend the basic framework of belief networks [16] (BNs) by introducing a temporal aspect into the graphical representation. The building block is a traditional BN, where variable states change in accordance to the dependencies encoded in the structure. This basic unit is repeated in a series, each instance corresponding to a specific *time-slice*. Arcs connecting nodes across time-slices represent the dynamic behaviour of the domain and indicate the probabilistic dependence of a variable upon past states.

Exact and approximate methods developed for ordinary BN evaluation can also be used for DBN evaluation, with the same problem that undirected loops and large state-spaces lead to computational intractability. The temporal aspect of DBNs is an additional complicating factor, because as time-slices are added to the model, the total network size grows and evaluation complexity increases exponentially. DBNs have become a popular method for real-time applications such as traffic monitoring [8], medical monitoring [3] and process control [9], where it is crucial for the model to provide an acceptable response in real-time. Several approximate methods for fast evaluation of DBNs have been devised [1,3,11] (see Section 2). In this paper, we present a new approximate method which simplifies evaluation by selectively "forgetting" past events and their relationships to the present. This is done by pruning regions of past time-slices which are deemed to

N. Foo (Ed.): AI'99, LNAI 1747, pp. 393–404, 1999.

have less potential impact onto variables of the current time-slice, as determined by the arc weight measure. The pruning procedure creates a "tail" behind the current time-slice; the shape and size of the tail can be adjusted using a threshold parameter. This method offers more flexibility than a fixed-size window and can be combined with other evaluation techniques.

To select arcs for removal, we use the arc weight measure based on mutual information introduced in [15] (Section 3). Our algorithm is described in Section 4, together with an example of its application. Empirical results showing the performance of the algorithm for two example networks are given in Section 5. In particular we look at the trade-off between the error and the computational complexity compared to fixed-window evaluation, and for different threshold values. We conclude by indicating other approximate evaluation methods to which the arc weight measure may be applied.

2   Related Work

Algorithms developed for approximate evaluation of ordinary BNs such as [7,4] can also be applied to DBN evaluation and can be used in conjunction with methods which limit the size of the DBN by deleting arcs and/or nodes. The most common method of reducing DBN size is to maintain a "window" of a fixed number of time-slices [6], with a time-slice pruned off the past as each new time-slice is added. Using a larger window than 2 time-slices provides more accuracy at the expense of computation complexity. The disadvantage of any fixed window is that past slices are pruned completely, so that some dependencies, which may be important in the current context, are ignored. In this paper we provide a more selective pruning method.

The basic idea behind our approach is similar to that of Kjærulff's [13], that is, reducing computation complexity by the removal of weak dependencies. While our method deals directly with the network itself, Kjærulff's method involves the removal of arcs from the moralised independence graph. Also, his method does not directly exploit the structure of a DBN, although results are shown for the same WATER DBN that we investigate in Section 5.2. After simplifying the DBN structure using our algorithm, beliefs can be updated by any standard exact or approximate evaluation technique; however, the modified structure obtained by Kjærulff's procedure can only be used in conjunction with the Junction-tree evaluation algorithm. Hence, our method is more flexible.

Dagum and Galper's forecasting algorithm [3] also uses selective arc deletion to simplify computation while providing approximate beliefs. It performs k-step ahead forecast by removing arcs to render every uninstantiated node a root node in earlier time-slices, with priors equal to the posterior forecast distribution of the node. Instead of doing this over one large DBN, they use a series of smaller sections. While this method is efficient if many nodes are instantiated, given a complex DBN where only a few nodes have evidence in each time-slice, then few arcs will be deleted and the reduction in computational complexity is not significant. In contrast to both Kjærulff's, and Dagum and Galper's methods, our method uses a threshold parameter which can be adjusted to control arc removal to provide the required computation performance.

Boyen and Koller [1] use a 2 time-slice window for their evaluation method, which is based on the assumption that the current belief state summarises all historical information about the system. For each new slice, the window is "rolled" by copying values from the later slice to the earlier, and recomputing. They show that if a compact and approximate belief state is maintained over the current time, the error does not increase into the future, but remains bounded and even contracts. When testing our algorithm our experimental results also show the error is bounded over time. Their compact state is built by assuming the process can be decomposed into a number of weakly interacting subprocesses. They do not provide a method for automatically identifying good subprocesses; in [10] we show that our arc weight measure could be used for this purpose.

3   Arc Weight Based on Mutual Information

In this section we review the definition of an arc weight based on Mutual Information presented in [15]. Mutual Information (MI) [18,16] is a measure of the dependence between two random variables. It is the reduction in uncertainty of X due to knowing Y, and vice-versa. Since $p(X,Y) = p(X)p(Y|X)$, the MI between two variables X and Y can be written as:

$$I(X,Y) = \sum_x p(X) \sum_y p(Y|X) \ \log \frac{p(Y|X)}{p(Y)} \tag{1}$$

MI is symmetric, i.e. $I(X,Y) = I(Y,X)$. It is a non-negative quantity and is zero if and only if X and Y are mutually independent.

Given a node Y with single parent X in a BN, the MI between X and Y describes the influence of X on Y and vice-versa. The arc weight of $X \rightarrow Y$ is computed as the MI between X and Y:

$$w(X,Y) = \sum_{i \in \Omega(X)} p_{pr}(X = i) \sum_{j \in \Omega(Y)} p(Y = j | X = i) \ \log \frac{p(Y = j | X = i)}{p_{pr}(Y = j)} \tag{2}$$

where $\Omega(X)$ denotes the state space of X and $p_{pr}(X = i)$ denotes the prior probability of X being in state i. If X is a root node, its priors are stored in the BN. Otherwise $p_{pr}(X = i)$ is approximated by averaging the conditional probabilities of X, over all parent state combinations. Similarly, because $p_{pr}(Y = j)$ is not directly available in the BN, it is approximated by averaging the conditional probabilities of Y over all states of X.

Given a node Y with parent X and a set of other parents $\mathbf{Z} = \{Z_0, \ldots, Z_n\}$, we defined the weight of arc $X \rightarrow Y$ as:

$$w(X,Y) = \sum_{k \in \Omega(\mathbf{Z})} p_{pr}(\mathbf{Z} = k) \sum_{i \in \Omega(X)} p_{pr}(X = i)$$

$$\sum_{j \in \Omega(Y)} p(Y = j | X = i, \mathbf{Z} = k) \log \frac{p(Y = j | X = i, \mathbf{Z} = k)}{p_{pr}(Y = j | \mathbf{Z} = k)} \tag{3}$$

$p_{pr}(X = i)$ is obtained as for Eq 2. For each state of Y, $p_{pr}(Y = j \,|Z = \mathbf{k})$ is approximated by averaging the conditional probabilities of Y over all state combinations of parents in $\mathbf{Z}$. To estimate $p_{pr}(\mathbf{Z} = \mathbf{k})$, we first calculate $p_{pr}(Z)$ for every $Z \in \mathbf{Z}$, then multiply out the joint probabilities for each combination of states, i.e. $p_{pr}(Z_0 = l_0, \ldots, Z_n = l_n) = \prod_{m=0\ldots n} p_{pr}(Z_m = l_m)$. This is equivalent to assuming all $Z \in \mathbf{Z}$ are independent.

We also defined a combined arc weight of multiple converging arcs on a node, estimating the combined effect of all parent nodes. Consider a node Y with parents X and Z: $X \rightarrow Y \leftarrow Z$. In this configuration, the combined weight of the converging arcs to child node Y from its parents X and Z is:

$$
W(Y, \{X, Z\}) = \sum_{i \in \Omega(X)} p_{pr}(X = i) \sum_{k \in \Omega(Z)} p_{pr}(Z = k)
$$
$$
\sum_{j \in \Omega(Y)} p(Y = j \,|\, X = i, Z = k) \, \log \frac{p(Y = j \,|\, X = i, Z = k)}{p_{pr}(Y = j)} \qquad (4)
$$

$p_{pr}(X)$, $p_{pr}(Z)$ and $p_{pr}(Y)$ are obtained using the same averaging procedure used for the single parent situation. In general, given node Y with a set of parents $\mathbf{Z}$, the formula is:

$$
W(Y, \mathbf{Z}) = \sum_{k \in \Omega(\mathbf{Z})} p_{pr}(\mathbf{Z} = \mathbf{k}) \sum_{j \in \Omega(Y)} p(Y = j \,|\mathbf{Z} = \mathbf{k}) \log \frac{p(Y = j \,|\mathbf{Z} = \mathbf{k})}{p_{pr}(Y = j)} \qquad (5)
$$

4   The Algorithm

Our algorithm for simplifying DBN evaluation using arc weights, called DBN-AW, is shown in Figure 1. Initially, the DBN contains two slices, TS_0 and TS_1, and a parameter *threshold* is supplied as input to the algorithm. Evidence is entered into the current time-slice, the DBN is extended a time step and beliefs are updated.[1] Since the beliefs for nodes in the current time-slice summarise the historical information about the system, we store them for later use (Step 5(b)(ii)) as the node's priors if its incoming arcs are deleted.

Step 5 goes back through earlier time-slices, removing selected sets of converging arcs. For each node N, the weight $W(N, parents(N))$ of incoming arcs into N (see Section 3) is divided by the variable *stepBack*, which represents the distance in terms of time-slices from node N to the current slice. Since influence is generally decreased by distance [17], dividing in this way provides a heuristic estimate of the influence of deleted arcs onto the current queries. Note that when the CPDs are invariant in time (a common assumption for many applications) the arc weights need not be computed for each new time-slice, but can be pre-computed off-line.

The *threshold* parameter indirectly determines a tail size and shape. As time advances, arcs and nodes are removed from past slices, and eventually, an entire time-slice is deleted. When arcs are deleted, some past dependencies are

---

[1] As mentioned in Section 2, any standard evaluation algorithm may be used.

1. $t = 0$.
2. Enter evidence into TS_t.
3. For $N \in TS_t$
   (a) update and return $bel(N)$
   (b) store a copy of $bel(N)$ for use in step 5(b)ii
4. If $t < 2$, go to step 7.
5. For $i = t$ to 1 do
   (a) $stepBack = t - i + 1$
   (b) For each node $N \in TS_{stepBack}$, if N is not a
       root node and $(W(N, parents(N))/stepBack) <$
       $threshold$
       i. remove all incoming arcs into N
       ii. assign priors of the new root node N from
           the stored beliefs (Step 5)
   (c) $stepBack = stepBack - 1$
6. Delete all disconnected nodes.
7. Add a time-slice TS_{t+2} to the DBN.
8. $t = t + 1$
9. Go to step 2.

Fig. 1. Algorithm DBN-AW.

being "forgotten". Deleting temporal arcs corresponds to forgetting the influence of past events onto more recent events. On the other hand, deleting static arcs corresponds to forgetting dependencies between events which occurred simultaneously in the past. Both cases rely on the assumption that past events and influences can be ignored, at an acceptable cost in accuracy, to simplify the computation of current beliefs. The forgetting process happens gradually and preferentially preserves relationships which impact more on the current time-slice. Note that variants of algorithm DBN-AW are possible; for example, instead of using $W(N, parents(N))$ as the measure and removing all incoming arcs into node N, each arc could be considered individually for removal based on the value of $w(N, parent(N))$ for that arc. Results for such a variant are given in [10].

To illustrate the working of the algorithm we use a small example DBN, called **dbn6**, with 6 nodes per time-slice, obtained by taking a section of the water [9] network and preserving some of the original CPDs. Figure 2 shows the DBN generated by five steps of algorithm DBN-AW with a *threshold* value of .4 for **dbn6**. At the fifth step, all the nodes from the TS_0 time-slice are deleted; the shape of the tail remains the same in further steps.

Figure 3 shows **dbn6** with different *threshold* values, which clearly determine the shape and size of the tail. For the higher *threshold* value of .6, more arcs are removed earlier and the nodes in time-slice TS_0 are deleted at the fourth step; this threshold gives a network that is very close to a fixed 4-time-slice window. The lower *threshold* value of .2 takes until the eighth step to delete the nodes of TS_0 and the DBN has a longer tail; it is further from a fixed window DBN.

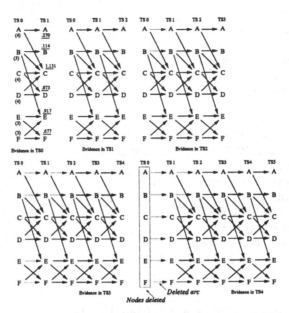

Fig. 2. Sequence of networks constructed for example DBN dbn6 using the DBN-AW algorithm with *threshold*=.4. The nodes of the DBN at the first step are labelled with the state spaces (in brackets) and the combined weight W of incoming arcs (underlined). Arcs deleted by algorithm DBN-AW are shown dotted in the third, fourth and fifth steps.

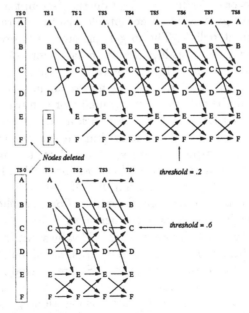

Fig. 3. Example DBN dbn6 produced by algorithm DBN-AW with *threshold*=.2 (above) and .6 (below).

5   Results

Our results were obtained using the Netica software [2] on a Pentium 2 at 300 MHz and 64Mb memory. Belief updating (Step 3(a)) is done using standard exact Junction-tree evaluation. For the purposes of evaluation, we assume that the main purpose is monitoring, i.e. maintaining a belief distribution over the current world state, hence the beliefs for the current time-slice TS_t are used for error estimation. The error is measured in terms of the Kullback-Leibler (KL) distance [16] between exact and approximate beliefs. When the algorithm is tested with evidence, results are plotted as a graph of the average error over 50 runs against the time-slice.

5.1   dbn6 DBN: Approximation Error

Figure 4 (LEFT) shows results from DBN-AW with *threshold* values of .3, .6 and .9, a 2 time-slice (2-TS) and a 6 time-slice (6-TS) fixed-window evaluation of dbn6 over 50 slices with no evidence. These errors are calculated by comparing to the beliefs from a complete 50-TS DBN. The best results are obtained with a 6-TS window, indicating that for this example network the state of the world at the current time-slice is largely independent of the world state more than 6 time steps ago. The order of the curves for DBN-AW show that a larger *threshold* results in larger errors, due to more arcs being deleted. The errors are highest for *threshold* value .9, smaller with .6 and least with .3.

Figure 4 (RIGHT) shows the results with evidence in each time-slice comparing evaluation using 2-TS, 6-TS and DBN-AW with *threshold* = .5. The order of the curves show that 2-TS gives the worst error, DBN-AW with *threshold* = .5 is better and the best performance is obtained using a 6-TS window. Z-tests on the averaged errors verified this hypothesis at the 5% significance level (see [10] for details of z-test results). Notice that the variance of the curves with evidence added at each step is more drastic than for no evidence; this effect is also mentioned by Boyen and Koller [1].

In Figure 5 (LEFT), the error curves are shown for evidence in each time-slice, with the *threshold* parameter for DBN-AW taking values .2, .4, .6 and .8. The error increases with increasing values of the *threshold* parameter, except for value .6 curve, which has a lower error than .4. The reason for this is that at *threshold*=.6, good approximate priors are obtained for nodes whose incoming arcs are deleted. Although this is not expected, it can happen "by chance". On the whole, the general trend of the curves indicate an error increase as *threshold* increases, which z-tests confirmed was the case for most points at the 5% significance level.

Randomised CPDs. Since arc weights are calculated based on the values in the CPDs, for a given DBN structure, the CPDs will determine which arcs are deleted from past time-slices. Hence, the errors in current beliefs also indirectly depend on the network's CPDs. To show the general applicability of the algorithm, we created five different versions of dbn6, with the same topology but

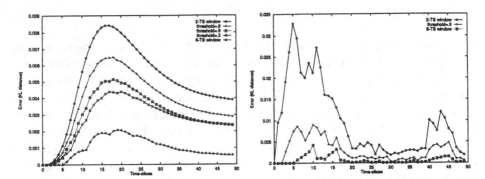

Fig. 4. LEFT: results from DBN-AW with *threshold* values .3, .6 and .9, a 2 time-slice, and a 6 time-slice window on example DBN dbn6 over 50 time-slices with no evidence. RIGHT: results from DBN-AW with *threshold* value .5, a 2-TS and a 6-TS window on example DBN dbn6 over 50 time-slices with evidence entered in each time-slice.

with the CPDs changed randomly. DBN-AW was then tested with the same values of *threshold* on the 5 networks, and the KL errors averaged over each *threshold*. Figure 5 (RIGHT) shows the results over 50 time-slices. The order of the curves show clearly that, as expected, errors grow larger with increasing *threshold* values. Although some of the curves are very close, z-tests confirmed the ordering between the .09, .05 and .01 threshold curves at the 5% significance level, while *threshold*=.07 produced a significantly larger errors than both .06 and .05, but the difference between the .06 and .05 curves was not significant.

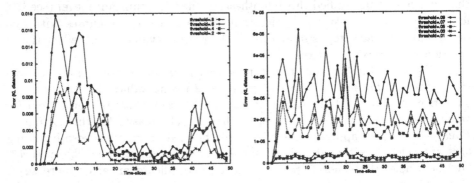

Fig. 5. LEFT: results from DBN-AW with *threshold* values .2, .4, .6, and .8. on example DBN dbn6 over 50 time-slices with evidence entered in each time-slice. RIGHT: average error over 5 versions of dbn6, for the indicated *threshold* parameter.

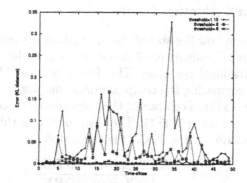

Fig. 6. Errors obtained DBN-AW with *threshold*=1.15, .8, .6, compared to a 4-TS window on **water** DBN.

5.2 water DBN: Approximation Error

Unlike the reduced **dbn6** example network, in our experimental environment the full **water** [9] network can only be evaluated exactly by Junction-tree for up to four time-slices. So, for the experiments shown here, we use the beliefs from a 4-TS window of the network as "exact" beliefs against which to compare the DBN-AW algorithm, with *threshold* values of 1.15, .8 and .6.

Figure 6 shows the performance of DBN-AW with *threshold* values of 1.15, .8 and .6, by comparing these beliefs with those obtained using a 4-TS window. As expected for DBN-AW, the errors decrease with decreasing *threshold*, while the errors are seen to remain bounded over time. Note that we also obtained results for a 2-TS window; z-tests showed no significant difference between the 2-TS window and DBN-AW with *threshold*=1.15. However, z-tests confirmed that *threshold* values of .8 and .6 produced lower errors than 2-TS at the 5% significance level. The effect of the threshold on the error can also be seen by the average errors over the 50 time-slices, listed in Table 1.

Algorithm	Average KL error
2TS-window	.112
DBN-AW, *threshold*=1.15	.060
DBN-AW, *threshold*=.8	.024
DBN-AW, *threshold*=.6	.003

Table 1. Average error over 50 time-slices for 2TS-window and DBN-AW with *threshold*=1.15, .8, .6 compared to a 4-TS window on **water** DBN.

5.3   Reduction in Evaluation Computation

Now that we have seen how the size of the approximation error depends on the pruning threshold used by algorithm DBN-AW, let us consider the corresponding reduction in computational resources. The Join-Tree Cost (JTC) [6] is an accepted measure for comparing the computational complexity of BN evaluation. Table 2 contains the results of comparing the Join-Tree Costs of the example networks with and without using DBN-AW. The final column in this table, "Savings" is the fractional reduction in the JTC. It is calculated as:

$$SF = 1 - \frac{JTC(approximateDBN)}{JTC(originalDBN)}$$

For comparison, the reductions for a fixed 2-TS window are also included in the table. These results show that the reduction in computation cost using DBN-AW decreases as the threshold is increased, and that the 2-TS window produces the largest reduction. Clearly this reduction for the 2-TS window is at the expense of a greater error in the approximate beliefs as seen in the results of the previous section.

Network	Original DBN	JTC	threshold for DBN-AW	JTC	SF
dbn6	6-TS	336629	.9	17825	.947
			.6	20495	.939
			.3	53144	.842
			2-TS	2663	.992
	50-TS	9364712	.9	17825	.998
			.6	20495	.998
			.3	53144	.994
			2-TS	2663	.999
water	4-TS	17392941	1.15	2571699	.852
			.8	5313675	.694
			.6	5313837	.694
			2-TS	12519	.999

Table 2. Computational savings in terms of the Junction-tree cost for DBN-AW using various *threshold* values and for 2-TS on dbn6 and water.

In [13], Kjærulff reports the computational saving achieved by applying his method of links removal on the water network. A reduction of 97% is achieved after removing 126 links from the moral graph; this is at a cost of .001 in total divergence, which represents the total error introduced in the network when links are deleted. Using the DBN-AW algorithm with *threshold*=1.15, the computational saving is about 85%, less than with Kjærulff's method. However, Kjærulff's global error measure does not provide control over which nodes of the network bear most of the cost, in terms of error in $bel'(Q)$, of simplifying the network structure. The issue of which nodes bear most of the error is important in DBN evaluation; for example, in the monitoring task, we would like to minimise error in nodes of the current time-slice and other nodes are less important. This is assured in the DBN-AW algorithm because arcs are deleted in past time-slices, in a way that least affects the beliefs of nodes of the current time-slice. Because Kjærulff does not specify the actual error in specific query nodes, it is difficult to make a comparative assessment of his .001 figure to the error produced by our algorithm for water. The results reported by Kjærulff for water are with a fixed-sized window of four time-slices. For the purposes of assessing his algorithm, this is treated as an ordinary network and the dynamic features of the structure are not exploited. There are no indications of how his algorithm performs when the DBN is extended by adding more time-slices and of how the error is affected over time. Using DBN-AW, we can guarantee that evaluation is feasible as more time-slices are added and our results showed that the error is bounded over time.

6   Conclusions and Future Work

We have presented a new method for approximate evaluation of dynamic belief networks. The algorithm DBN-AW is based on arc weights: at each time-slice, arcs are deleted from past slices if their weight is less than a pre-specified *threshold* parameter. Nodes which become disconnected are also deleted. This corresponds to a process of gradually forgetting past events, the relationships between them and their possible impact on present events. Since arcs of smaller weight are deleted first, information most relevant to the current belief state is retained. By adjusting the *threshold* value, one can vary the amount of information that is discarded at each step. The question of how to set the *threshold* value in practice is an issue for future work. In general, the best *threshold* will depend on the level of accuracy desired and the range of possible values will vary according to the DBN being used.

Our empirical testing of the algorithm on two example networks showed that the error introduced by the approximation stabilises over time and can be controlled by the *threshold* parameter. We also showed that our algorithm produces a corresponding reduction in computational complexity, as measured by the Join-Tree Cost. These results indicate that DBN-AW provides an efficient and more flexible alternative to using a fixed window for controlling the complexity of DBN evaluation. Our method can also be used in conjunction with other approximation algorithms; we intend to investigate the performance of such combinations of algorithms in the future.

The arc weight measure used to select arcs for deletion is based on mutual information. We are applying it in a range of other approximate evaluation methods, such as selecting nodes for state-space abstraction and partial join-tree evaluation [10].

References

1. X. Boyen and D. Koller. Tractable inference for complex stochastic processes. In *UAI'98*, pp 33–42, 1998.
2. Norsys Software Corp. Netica. http://www.norsys.com/.
3. P. Dagum and A. Galper. Forecasting sleep apnea with dynamic network models. In *UAI'93*, pp 65–71, 1993.
4. B. D'Ambrosio. Incremental probabilistic inference. In *UAI'93*, pp 301–308, 1993.
5. Thomas Dean and Keiji Kanazawa. A model for reasoning about persistence and causation. *Computational Intelligence*, 5:142–150, 1989.
6. Thomas Dean and Michael P. Wellman. *Planning and control*. Morgan Kaufman Publishers, San Mateo, Ca., 1991.
7. Denise L. Draper and Steve Hanks. Localized partial evaluation of a belief network. In *UAI'94*, pp 170–177, 1994.
8. Jeff Forbes, Tim Huang, Keiji Kanazawa, and Stuart Russell. The BATmobile: Towards a Bayesian automated taxi. In *IJCAI'95*, pp 1878–1885, 1995.
9. Finn V. Jensen, Uffe Kjærulff, Kristian G. Olesen, and Jan Pedersen. Et forprojekt til et ekspertsystem for drift af spildevandsrensning (an expert system for control of waste water treatment — a pilot project). Technical report, Judex Datasystemer A/S, Aalborg, Denmark, 1989. In Danish.
10. N. Jitnah. *Arc Weights for Approximate Evaluation of Bayesian Networks*. PhD thesis, Monash University, School of Computer Science and Software Engineering, 1999.
11. K. Kanazawa, D. Koller, and S. Russell. Stochastic simulation algorithms for Dynamic Probabilistic Networks. In *UAI'95*, pp 346–351, 1995.
12. U. Kjærulff. A computational scheme for reasoning in Dynamic Probabilistic Networks. In *UAI'92*, pp 121–129, 1992.
13. Uffe Kjaerulff. Reduction of computation complexity in bayesian networks through removal of weak dependencies. In *UAI'94*, pp 374–382, 1994.
14. A. E. Nicholson and J. M. Brady. Dynamic belief networks for discrete monitoring. *IEEE Systems, Man and Cybernetics*, 24(11):1593–1610, 1994.
15. Ann E. Nicholson and Nathalie Jitnah. Using Mutual Information to determine relevance in Bayesian Networks. In Hing-Yan Lee and Hiroshi Motoda, editors, *PRICAI'98: Topics in Artificial Intelligence*, volume 1531 of *LNCS/LNAI Series*, pp 399–410, Singapore, 1998. Springer.
16. J. Pearl. *Probabilistic Reasoning In Intelligent Systems: Networks of Plausible Inference*. Morgan Kaufmann, 1988.
17. K. L. Poh and E Horvitz. Topological proximity and relevance in graphical decision models. In *UAI'96*, pp 427–435, 1996.
18. C. E. Shannon and W. Weaver. *The mathematical theory of communication*. University of Illinois Press, 1949.

Finding Cutpoints in Noisy Binary Sequences – A Revised Empirical Evaluation

Murlikrishna Viswanathan, Chris S. Wallace, David L. Dowe, and
Kevin B. Korb

School of Computer Science and Software Engineering
Monash University VIC 3168
{krishna,csw,dld,korb}@cs.monash.edu.au

Abstract. Kearns et al. (1997) in an earlier paper presented an empirical evaluation of model selection methods on a specialized version of the segmentation problem. The inference task was the estimation of a predefined Boolean function on the real interval $[0, 1]$ from a noisy random sample. Three model selection methods based on the Guaranteed Risk Minimization, Minimum Description Length (MDL) Principle and Cross Validation were evaluated on samples with varying noise levels. The authors concluded that, in general, none of the methods was superior to the others in terms of predictive accuracy. In this paper we identify an inefficiency in the MDL approach as implemented by Kearns et al. and present an extended empirical evaluation by including a revised version of the MDL method and another approach based on the Minimum Message Length (MML) principle.

1 Introduction

The segmentation problem occurs when there is a need to partition some data into distinct homogeneous regions. The specialized binary sequence problem framework considered in this paper was introduced by Kearns et al. [1]. An unknown Boolean function $f(x)$ is defined on the real interval $0 < x < 1$. The interval is partitioned into $(k + 1)$ sub-intervals by k "cut points" $\{c_j : j = 1..k\}$ which are uniformly and randomly distributed in $[0,1]$ and indexed so that $c_j < c_{j+1}$, $(j = 1..k - 1)$. The function $f(x)$ is defined to be 0 in even-numbered sub-intervals, and 1 in odd-numbered sub-intervals, the sub-intervals being numbered from 0 to k so that cut-point c_j separates sub-intervals $j - 1$ and j. Data is generated from this model at N sample points $\{x_i : i = 1..N\}$. The Boolean datum y_i generated at x_i differs from $f(x_i)$ with probability $p < (1/2)$. Thus the probability that $y_i = 1$ alternates between p and $(1 - p)$, depending on whether x_i lies in an even or odd sub-interval.

The inference task, termed the "intervals model selection" problem by Kearns et al. [1], is to infer an approximation to the function $f(x)$ from the data $\{x_i, y_i : i = 1..N\}$. That is, we wish to infer the number and position of the cutpoints (and, incidentally, the unknown "noise" rate, p).

N. Foo (Ed.): AI'99, LNAI 1747, pp. 405–416, 1999.
© Springer-Verlag Berlin Heidelberg 1999

The intervals model selection problem was originally employed by Kearns et al. [1] in their evaluation of different model selection methods. These selection methods included the two penalty-based methods, Vapnik's Guaranteed Risk Minimization (GRM) [5] and a version (KMDL) [1] of Rissanen's Minimum Description Length (MDL) Principle [4], and cross validation (hold out) [8]. The motivation for this choice of problem was that, while being non-trivial, it appeared to Kearns et al. to permit exact solution of the optimizations required by the different methods and hence seemingly offered a comparison of the methods untainted by questionable mathematical approximations. Kearns et al. [1] reported that MDL performed no better than cross validation in this task.

Unfortunately, their application (KMDL) of the MDL method was flawed, and hence the comparisons presented in [1] are misleading. This paper replicates the experiments of [1], omitting their implementation of Vapnik's method (which appears correct). Minimum Message Length (MML) model selection [6] has been shown to perform significantly better than approaches based on GRM in the context of polynomial model selection [6]. We correct an approximation in KMDL, obtaining a slightly improved method which we term "CMDL", although it is still an improper application (see section 6) of the MDL principle. Consistent with [1], we find both KMDL and CMDL to perform relatively poorly unless the sample is large (with CMDL slightly superior). Finally, we develop a more correct MDL method, using the theoretical framework of the Minimum Message Length principle [2,3], with which we are more familiar. For this problem, there seems little significant difference between MDL (properly applied) and MML. The poor behaviour of KMDL is again observed, but the MML method works well, and compares well with the cross-validation (CV) method which we implement in the same form as in [1].

2   Definitions

This section presents standard definitions for all the terms used in this paper.

1. S : training set, $\langle x_i, y_i \rangle$.
2. N : sample size.
3. p : true probability (noise rate).
4. $\hat{p}$: estimated probability.
5. k : number of cuts.
6. d : number of alternations of label in S $(d = k + 1)$.
7. $f(x)$: true Boolean function from which S is generated.
8. $h(x)$: learning algorithm's estimate of $f(x)$ from S.
9. $H(x)$: binary entropy function given by $-(x \log x + (1 - x) \log(1 - x))$

We also define some standard error measures employed in the paper following notation used by Kearns et al. [1]:

- $\epsilon(h)$ represents the generalization error of a hypothesis $h(x)$ with respect to the target function $f(x)$. $\epsilon(h) = KL\left(f(x) \parallel h(x)\right)$, which is the Kullback-Leibler distance from $f(x)$ to $h(x)$.

- $\hat{\epsilon}(h)$ denotes the training error of h on sample S.
  $\hat{\epsilon}(h) = |\langle x_i, y_i \rangle \in S : h(x_i) \neq f(x_i)| /n$.

3   Kearns's Intervals Model Selection Problem

To test the various methods, Kearns et al. [1] chose a function $f(x)$ with 100 intervals each of length 0.01 (99 equally-spaced cutpoints). This function is the easiest to learn among all functions with 99 cuts. A randomly spaced set of cuts would increase the chance that some subintervals would contain few (or no) sample points, making them much harder to detect. In this study we employ generating functions with randomly-placed cuts. Note that none of the learning methods assume approximate or exact equality of subinterval lengths: they all assume the locations of the cuts to be random.

A single test problem is generated from $f(x)$ by fixing a sample size N and a noise probability, p. Then, N x-values are selected from the uniform distribution in (0,1), and for each x_i, a Boolean datum y_i is generated as $f(x_i)$ XOR $ran(p)$, where $ran(p)$ is a random noise bit with probability p of being 1. Many replications of a problem with given N and p are generated by making different random selections of the sample points and noise bits.

For a given sample S, Kearns et al. [1] see the essence of the learning problem as being the selection of a *model class*, where a class F_k is the set of all alternating functions with k cuts. That is, the essence is the estimation or selection of k. Within a class F_k, a simple dynamic programming algorithm suffices to find the model function $h'_k(x)$ with maximum likelihood, i.e. with minimum training error $\hat{\epsilon}(h'_k)$. Of course, the locations of the cutpoints of $h'_k(x)$ are determined only to within the interval between two adjacent sample points. In this work, we take the cutpoint of $h'_k(x)$ which lies between x_i and x_{i+1} to be midway between the sample points.

The learning task thus reduces to selecting a model from the set of model functions $\{h'_k(x); \ k = 1..k_{max}\}$, where k_{max} is the largest number of cuts resulting in any reduction in training error. This set of models was then given to the two model selection methods based on GRM [5] and a version (KMDL [1]) of the MDL [4] principle. For the cross-validation method, the protocol was slightly different. The sample S was divided randomly into a 90% fitting set and a 10% validation set. A set of maximum-likelihood models $\{h_k(x); \ k = 1..k^c_{max}\}$ was developed from the fitting sample, and the cross-validation method selected from that set the model with the lowest error on the validation sample. It is not claimed that this represents an optimal cross-validation, but it was chosen as a simple and representative application of the method. The generalization error for the model selected by each method was computed with respect to the problem target function $f(x)$.

4   The "KMDL" Method

We replicated the MDL encoding scheme employed by Kearns et al. in their paper. To distinguish from a modified method we consider later, we term it KMDL. According to them, MDL [4] is a broad class of algorithms with a common information theoretic motivation and each MDL algorithm is determined by a specific encoding scheme for both functions and their training errors. They present one such encoding scheme for the binary sequence problem.

Let h be a function with exactly k cut points. Description of $h(\cdot)$ first requires specification of its number k of cutpoints. The length of this description is neglected in KMDL. Given k, we can sufficiently describe $h(\cdot)$ by specifying the k sample points immediately before which $h(\cdot)$ changes value. Note that it makes sense for $h(\cdot)$ to have a cutpoint before the first sample point x_1, but not after the last, x_N. Thus, there are N places where $h(\cdot)$ may have cuts. Assuming, as in [1], that the cuts are equally likely to occur in any of these places, specifying their locations takes $\log_2 \binom{N}{k}$ bits. Given $h(\cdot)$, the training samples can simply be encoded by correcting the mistakes implied by $h(\cdot)$. Suppose $h(x)$ differs from $y(x)$ at m sample points, where $m = N \times \hat{\epsilon}(h)$. (KMDL neglects the cost of describing m.) Given m, the identity of the m sample points where y_i differs from $h(x_i)$ can be specified with $\log_2 \binom{N}{m}$ bits. Thus, KMDL arrives at a total description length of

$$\log_2 \left\{ \binom{N}{k} \times \binom{N}{m} \right\} \text{ bits}$$

In [1], expressions such as $\log_2 \binom{N}{m}$ are approximated by $N \times H(m/N)$ where $H()$ is the binary entropy function. Dividing by N leads to the KMDL choice of k:

$$k = argmin_k \{ H(k/N) + H(\hat{\epsilon}(h'_k)) \} \tag{1}$$

5   The "CMDL" Method

We attempt a modest correction to the KMDL method, which we term CMDL. An important point that we note in developing our MDL approach is that as we are only considering the maximum-likelihood model in each class there cannot be any misses adjacent to a cutpoint. Therefore, we can safely assume that the number of cuts $k \leq N - 2m$. The encoding scheme includes the lengths needed for the description of k and m. The training error count m can certainly not exceed $N/2$, so the cost of encoding m is $N/2$ bits. The cost of specifying a cutpoint from $N - 2m$ potential cuts is $\log(N - 2m)$ bits. We also replace the binary entropy approximation in KMDL by the accurate log-combinations expression. Thus, CMDL selects

$$k = argmin_k \left\{ \log(N - 2m) + \log(N/2) + \log \binom{N - 2m}{k} + \log \binom{N}{m} \right\} \tag{2}$$

6   The Flaw in KMDL

While the minor correction of KMDL to CMDL has some beneficial effect, there remains a serious flaw in the coding scheme used in both methods. The use of a *Minimum* Description Length principle to select among competing model-based encodings of the data can make sense only if the coding scheme used with each competing model indeed *minimizes* the length of the description employing that model. The scheme used in KMDL and CMDL does not come close.

These methods specify the location of the cutpoints of a model to within the interval between adjacent sample points. On average, this is a precision of about $(1/N)$. Except for very low noise rates, such precise specification is unwarranted, leads to an over-long description, and vitiates the comparison of competing models.

It is an essential feature of efficient model-based coding (whether MDL or MML) that *no estimated parameter be specified more accurately than it can be estimated*. Suppose, in this problem, that we decide to encode the cutpoints so that they are always required to precede an odd-numbered sample point. That is we encode them to an average precision of $(2/N)$. What effect will this have on the description length? First, we save approximately k bits, because for each of the k cutpoints there are now only $N/2$ possible locations to be selected among. Second, for each cut point, there is a probability $(1/2)$ that it is where we wanted it to be. If it is not, then one y-value will be encoded using probability $\hat{p}$ instead of $(1 - \hat{p})$ or vice-versa. The final result is that the description length is increased on average by $(k/2)(\log_2((1 - \hat{p})/\hat{p}) - 1)$ bits. This quantity is negative for $p > 0.2$, so by lowering the precision of cutpoint specification we actually *shorten* the description unless the noise rate is less than 0.2. The MML method now described generalizes this approach. (For a detailed recent comparison between MML and MDL, see Wallace and Dowe [7].)

7   MML Based Model Selection

In essence, MML [2,3,7] seeks to miminize a message length defined by the joint encoding of the model and data given the model. It will be more convenient now to measure lengths in nits rather than bits (1 nit $= \log_2 e$ bits) so now we switch to natural logs.

We start the message by stating the estimated k, with length $\log(N/2)$. (Henceforth, we use k and p to denote the estimated model quantities.) Next, the message states p, the estimated noise rate. This value determines that y-values agreeing with $h(x)$ will be encoded with length $- \log(1 - p)$ each, and those disagreeing, with length $- \log p$.

The MML principle [3,7] offers the following general expression for computing the MML message length for parameter vector $\boldsymbol{\theta}$ and data $\boldsymbol{x}$:

$$MessLen = - \log g(\boldsymbol{\theta}) - \log f(\boldsymbol{x}|\boldsymbol{\theta}) + 0.5 \log F(\boldsymbol{\theta}) - \frac{D}{2} \log 12 + \frac{D}{2} \quad (3)$$

where $g(\theta)$ is the prior density on θ, $f(x|\theta)$ is the likelihood of data x given θ, D is the number of parameters and $F(\theta)$ is the "Fisher Information". In this application of the MML principle, θ is the parameter p of a binomial sequence with n trials and m successes, so the relevant likelihood function is

$$f(m|p) = p^m (1-p)^{N-m} \tag{4}$$

Since we assume $0 \le p \le 0.5$ but have no other prior information, we assume a uniform prior $g(p)$.

The Fisher Information $F(p)$ is easily shown [3] to be

$$F(p) = \frac{N}{p(1-p)} \tag{5}$$

The value of p that minimizes the message length can be derived [3,2] by differentiating the expression for $MessLen$ to obtain,

$$p = (m + 0.5)/(N + 1.0) \tag{6}$$

7.1   Encoding a Cut-Point

As the cut-points are real-valued, it would require an infinite number of bits to specify them precisely. Thus, we need to find an optimal precision for our parameter specification. Let δ be the precision (range) with which we want to specify our cut-point. We assume that the true cut-point lies within this range. Let ϵ be the difference between the true cutpoint and the estimated one. Since we assume that our cut-point is uniformly distributed in δ, the difference ϵ is uniform in $[-\frac{\delta}{2}, +\frac{\delta}{2}]$.

The expected number of data points in a region of width δ is given by $n\delta$. Since our training values are uniformly distributed, the expected number of data points coded with the wrong probability (put in the "wrong" side of the cutpoint) is given by $n|\epsilon|$. The expected value of $|\epsilon|$ can be derived as,

$$E(|\epsilon|) = \frac{2}{\delta} \int_0^{\delta/2} x \, dx = \frac{2}{\delta} \times \frac{\delta^2}{8}$$

$$= \frac{\delta}{4} \tag{7}$$

The expected excess cost (in message length) of encoding a single data item with the wrong probability can be calculated by computing the difference between the expected cost of encoding the data item with the correct and incorrect probabilities. Thus, the expected loss per wrong item can be derived as,

$$\begin{aligned} ExpLoss &= -p\log(1-p) - (1-p)\log p - (-p\log p - (1-p)\log(1-p)) \\ &= p(\log(p) - \log(1-p)) + (1-p)(\log(1-p) - \log(p)) \\ &= p\log\frac{p}{1-p} + (1-p)\log\frac{1-p}{p} \end{aligned}$$

$$= (2p - 1) \log \frac{p}{1 - p}$$

$$= (2(1 - p) - 1) \log \frac{1 - p}{p} \tag{8}$$

which is symmetrical between p and (1 - p).

The expected increase in the cost of encoding the $N\delta/4$ y-values expected to be encoded with the "wrong" probability is

$$ExcessCost = \frac{N\delta}{4}(2p - 1) \log \frac{p}{1 - p} \tag{9}$$

The cutpoints of $h(\cdot)$ are parameters of the model and so must be encoded. To encode the position of a cut to precision δ within the range (0,1) requires length $- \log \delta$. Hence, for each cut point, the total cost incurred by encoding its position to precision δ is

$$TotalExcessPerCutpoint = - \log \delta + \frac{N\delta}{4}(2p - 1) \log \frac{p}{1 - p} \tag{10}$$

Differentiating $TotalLossPerCutpoint$ in (11), we find the value of δ that yields the minimum message length to be,

$$\delta = \frac{4}{N(2p - 1)\log \frac{p}{1-p}} \tag{11}$$

With this choice of δ, from (9) and (11), the expected $ExcessCost$ is just one nit per cutpoint. The total cost of encoding all k cutpoints to precision δ is

$$\log(N - 2m) - k \log(\delta/N) - \log(k!)$$

since the order in which they are specified is immaterial and $k \leq (N - 2m)$. As mentioned earlier, the use of an overly precise specification for δ is only justified when the noise rate p is very low. Substituting $1/N$ (as used in Kearns et al. [1]) for δ in expression (11) above we find that $p \approx 0.018$. In other words, the precision specified by Kearns et al. is only justified for quite extreme values, namely if $p \leq 1 - 0.982 = 0.018$.

7.2   The Total Message

The length of the entire MML message can now be computed. The components are the statement of k, the statement of p to precision $\sqrt{12/F(p)}$ within the range (0,1/2), the positions of the cutpoints to precision δ, and finally the expected $DataLoss$ of one nit per cutpoint resulting from imprecise specification of cutpoints. Given m, the identity of the m sample points where y_i differs from $h(x_i)$ can be specified with code length $\log \binom{N}{m}$, which is included in the data part of our message.

In estimating the noise parameter p, the number of mistakes m made by the maximum-likelihood model $h'_k(x)$ is increased by the expected additional number of disagreements resulting from the imprecision of cutpoints. The resulting estimated error count is used in place of m in estimating p, which affects the choice of δ, and hence the estimated error count. A few iterations of these calculations converge quickly.

As a result, our estimate of the noise rate exceeds m/N. The effect seems to correct for the overfitting of the maximum-likelihood model which, in KMDL and CMDL, leads to an underestimate of p.

8   Results

All four methods — MML, KMDL, CMDL and CV — were compared on noise rates of 0, 0.1, 0.2, 0.3 and 0.4 with sample sizes ranging from 100 to 3000 in steps of 100. For each choice of p and N, 100 replications were performed. The true cutpoint model consisted of 100 either evenly-spaced or randomly generated cutpoints, but here, due to space restrictions, we only include results from evaluation of all our methods on random cutpoint models. All methods were compared on the basis of the number of estimated cuts and the Kullback-Leibler (KL) distance between the true and estimated model. The Kullback-Leibler distance (also known as the "relative entropy") measures the expected excess cost of using an encoding based on the estimated model rather than the true model. Formally, the Kullback-Leibler distance between the true distribution $p(y)$ and the estimated distribution $q(y)$ is:

$$KL\ (p \parallel q) = \sum_y p(y) \log \frac{p(y)}{q(y)} \qquad (12)$$

Finally, although as above, all methods were evaluated with both fixed and randomly spaced cutpoints, it is important to remember that the original statement of the problem [1] and all the models implicitly assume that the cutpoints are randomly distributed. Figures 1-3 include comparisons of the KL distance and the number of estimated cuts for noise rates of 0.1, 0.2 and 0.3 respectively.

Each figure plots the generalization error as measured by the KL distance and the estimated number of cuts collated. All plots represent averages over 100 replications. With *no* noise (i.e., $p = 0$), all methods understandably performed well. But more important is how these methods perform given noise and random cut points. The robust performance of MML for small sample sizes in the presence of increasing noise values can be clearly observed from Figures 1-3. It is also important to observe that although MML tends to be conservative in estimating large numbers of cuts in comparison with CV, it does much better at minimizing the KL distance. Thus, in general, the MML approach performs significantly better than all the other methods evaluated when the models (cuts) are randomly distributed (as assumed in the problem framework).

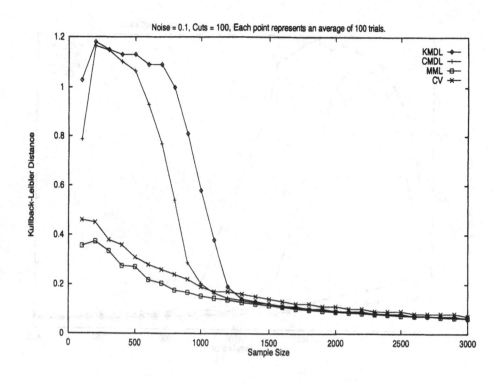

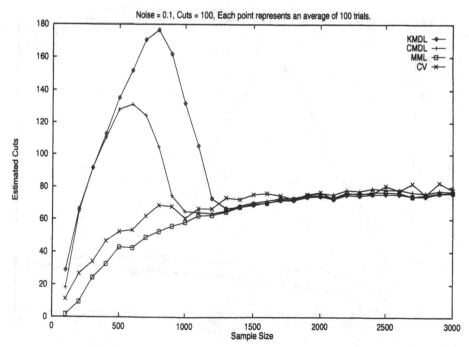

Fig. 1. Evaluation of Different Methods with Random Cutpoints

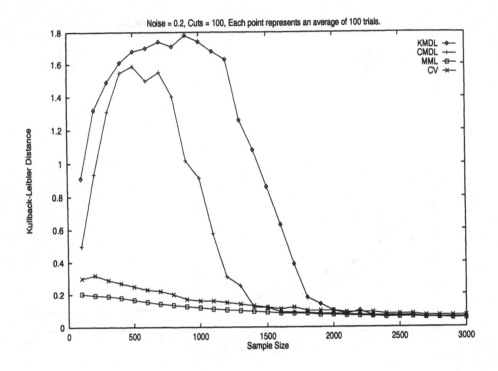

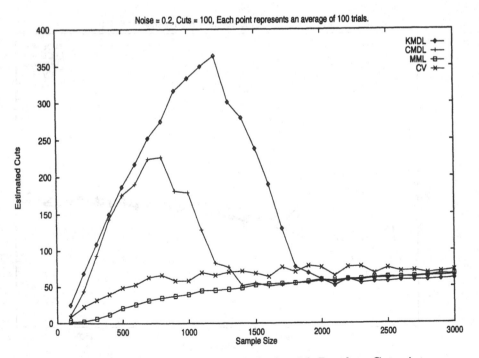

Fig. 2. Evaluation of Different Methods with Random Cutpoints

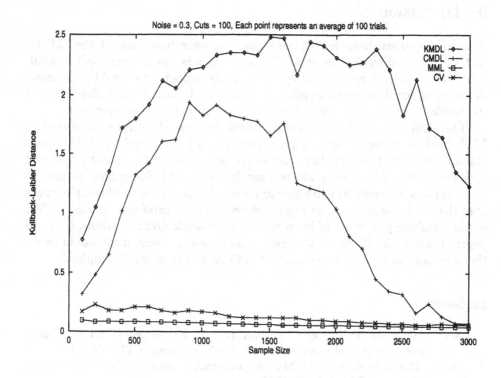

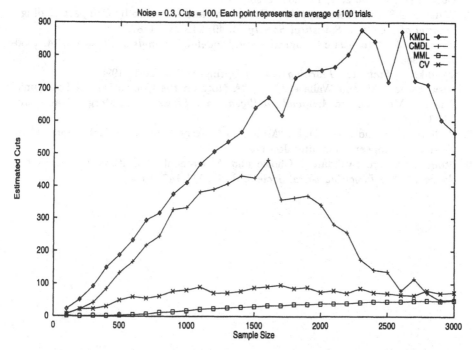

Fig. 3. Evaluation of Different Methods with Random Cutpoints

9   Discussion

The results shown here demonstrate that the poor behaviour of the "MDL" method reported by Kearns et al. (KMDL) [1] was not inherent in the MDL principle. Rather, it was caused by their failure properly to consider the minimization of the description lengths for each model, and in particular the need to encode estimates (here the cut positions) to an appropriate precision.

The MML method developed here (which may equally well be considered an MDL method) is itself only a rough application of the principle, and still uses a sub-optimal coding scheme. In particular, it uses a constant cutpoint precision δ for all cutpoints of the model, whereas our derivation of δ clearly implies that the precision used for each cutpoint should reflect the local density of sample points near the cut. In future work, we hope to develop a more carefully optimized MML method making proper use of knowledge of the sample point locations. Previous experience with MML leads us to expect that such a development would lessen the over caution of the present method in finding cuts in small samples.

References

1. Kearns, M., Mansour, Y., Ng, A. Y., Ron, D., "An Experimental and Theoretical Comparison of Model Selection Methods", *Machine Learning*, 27, 7-50, 1997.
2. Wallace, C.S. and Boulton, D. M., "An information measure for classification", *Computer Journal*, 2:11, 195-209, 1968.
3. Wallace, C.S. and Freeman, P.R., "Estimation and Inference by Compact Coding", *Journal of the Royal Statistical Society*, B, 49: 240-252, 1987.
4. Rissanen, J., "Stochastic Complexity and Modeling", *Annals of Statistics*, 14, 1080-1100, 1986.
5. Vapnik, V., *Statistical Learning Theory*, Springer, New York, 1995.
6. Viswanathan, M. and Wallace, C. S., "A Note on the Comparison of Polynomial Selection Methods", in *Artificial Intelligence and Statistics 99*, Morgan Kaufmann, 169-177, 1999.
7. Wallace, C. S. and Dowe, D. L., "Minimum Message Length and Kolmogorov Complexity", to appear, Computer Journal.
8. Stone, M., "Cross-validatory Choice and Assessment of Statistical Predictions", *Journal of the Royal Statistical Society*, B, 36, 111-147, 1974.

Q-Learning in Continuous State and Action Spaces

Chris Gaskett, David Wettergreen, and Alexander Zelinsky

Robotic Systems Laboratory, Department of Systems Engineering
Research School of Information Sciences and Engineering
The Australian National University,Canberra, ACT 0200 Australia
{cg,dsw,alex}@syseng.anu.edu.au

Abstract. Q-learning can be used to learn a control policy that maximises a scalar reward through interaction with the environment. Q-learning is commonly applied to problems with discrete states and actions. We describe a method suitable for control tasks which require continuous actions, in response to continuous states. The system consists of a neural network coupled with a novel interpolator. Simulation results are presented for a non-holonomic control task. Advantage Learning, a variation of Q-learning, is shown enhance learning speed and reliability for this task.

1 Introduction

Reinforcement learning systems learn by trial-and-error which actions are most valuable in which situations (states) [14]. Feedback is provided in the form of a scalar *reward* signal which may be delayed. The reward signal is defined in relation to the task to be achieved; reward is given when the system is successfully achieving the task. The *value* is updated incrementally with experience and is defined as a discounted sum of expected future reward. The learning systems choice of actions in response to states is called its *policy*. Reinforcement learning lies between the extremes of supervised learning, where the policy is taught by an expert, and unsupervised learning, where no feedback is given and the task is to find structure in data.

There are two prevalent approaches to reinforcement learning: Q-learning and actor-critic learning. In Q-learning [16] the expected value of each action in each state is stored. In Q-learning the policy is formed by executing the action with the highest expected value. In actor-critic learning [4] a critic learns the value of each state. The value is the expected reward over time from the environment under the current policy. The actor tries to maximise a local reward signal from the critic by choosing actions close to its current policy then changing its policy depending upon feedback from the critic. In turn, the critic adjusts the value of states in response to rewards received following the actor's policy.

The main advantage of Q-learning over actor-critic learning is exploration insensitivity—the ability to learn without necessarily following the current policy. However, actor-critic learning has a major advantage over current implementations of Q-learning; the ability to respond to smoothly varying states with

N. Foo (Ed.): AI'99, LNAI 1747, pp. 417–428, 1999.

smoothly varying actions. Actor-critic systems can form a continuous mapping from state to action and update this policy based on the local reward signal from the critic. Q-learning is generally considered in the case that states and actions are both discrete. In some real world situations, and especially in control, it is advantageous to treat both states and actions as continuous variables.

This paper describes a continuous state and action Q-learning method and applies it to a simulated control task. Essential characteristics of a continuous state and action Q-learning system are also described. Advantage Learning [7] is found to be an important variation of Q-learning for these tasks.

2 Q-Learning

Q-learning works by incrementally updating the expected values of actions in states. For every possible state, every possible action is assigned a value which is a function of both the immediate reward for taking that action and the expected reward in the future based on the new state that is the result of taking that action. This is expressed by the one-step Q-update equation,

$$Q(x, u) := (1 - \alpha) Q(x, u) + \alpha (R + \gamma \max Q(x_{t+1}, u_{t+1})) , \qquad (1)$$

where Q is the expected value of performing action u in state x; x is the state vector; u is the action vector; R is the reward; α is a learning rate which controls convergence and γ is the discount factor. The discount factor makes rewards earned earlier more valuable than those received later.

This method learns the values of all actions, rather than just finding the optimal policy. This knowledge is expensive in terms of the amount of information which has to be stored, but it does bring benefits. Q-learning is exploration insensitive, any action can be carried out at any time and information is gained from this experience. Actor-critic learning does not have this ability, actions must follow or nearly follow the current policy. This exploration insensitivity allows Q-learning to learn from other controllers, even if they are directed toward achieving a different task they can provide valuable data. Knowledge from several Q-learners can be combined, as the values of non-optimal actions are known, a compromise action can be found.

In the standard Q-learning implementation Q-values are stored in a table. One cell is required per combination of state and action. This implementation is not amenable to continuous state and action problems.

3   Continuous States and Actions

Many real world control problems require actions of a continuous nature, in response to continuous state measurements. *It should be possible that actions vary smoothly in response to smooth changes in state.*

But most learning systems, indeed most classical AI techniques, are designed to operate in discrete domains, manipulating symbols rather than real numbered variables. Some problems that we may wish to address, such as high-performance control of mobile robots, cannot be adequately carried out with coarsely coded inputs and outputs. Motor commands need to vary smoothly and accurately in response to continuous changes in state.

Q-learning with discretised states and actions scale poorly. As the number of state and action variables increase, the size of the table used to store Q-values grows exponentially. Accurate control requires that variables be quantised finely, but as these systems fail to generalise between similar states and actions, they require large quantities of training data. If the learning task described in Sect. 7 was attempted with a discrete Q-learning algorithm the number of Q-values to be stored in the table would be extremely large. For example, discretised roughly to seven levels, the eight state variables and two action variables would require almost 300 million elements. Without generalisation, producing this number of experiences is impractical. Using a coarser representation of states leads to aliasing, functionally different situations map to the same state and are thus indistinguishable.

It is possible to avoid these discretisation problems entirely by using learning methods which can deal directly with continuous states and actions.

4   Continuous State and Action Q-Learning

There have been several recent attempts at extending the Q-learning framework to continuous state and action spaces [17, 12, 11, 15, 6].

We believe that there are eight criteria that are necessary and sufficient for a system to be capable of this type of learning. Listed in in Fig. 1, these requirements are a combination of those required for basic Q-learning as described in Sect. 2 combined with the type of continuous behaviour described in Sect. 3. None of the Q-learning systems discussed below appear to fulfil all of these criteria completely. In particular, many systems cannot learn a policy where actions vary smoothly with smooth changes in state (criteria *Continuity*). In these not-quite continuous systems a small change in state cannot cause a small change in action. In effect the function which maps state to action is a staircase—a piecewise constant function.

Sections 4.1–4.6 describe various real valued state and action Q-learning methods and techniques and rate them (in an unfair and biased manner) against the criteria in Fig. 1.

4.1   Adaptive Critic Methods

Werbos's adaptive critic family of methods [17] use several feedforward artificial neural networks to implement reinforcement learning. The adaptive critic family includes methods closely related to actor-critic and Q-learning. A learnt dynamic model assists in assigning reward to components of the action vector (not meeting the *Model-Free* criteria). If the dynamic model is already known, or learning one is easier than learning the controller itself, model based adaptive critic methods

Action Selection:	Finds *action* with the highest expected value quickly.
State Evaluation:	Finds *value* of a *state* quickly as required for the Q-update equation (1). A state's value is the value of highest valued action in that state.
Q Evaluation:	Stores or approximates the entire Q-function as required for the Q-update equation (1).
Model-Free:	Requires no model of system dynamics to be known or learnt.
Flexible Policy:	Allows representation of a broad range of policies to allow freedom in developing a novel controller.
Continuity:	Actions can vary smoothly with smooth changes in state.
State Generalisation:	Generalises between similar states, reducing the amount of exploration required in state space.
Action Generalisation:	Generalises between similar actions, reducing the amount of exploration required in action space.

Fig. 1. Essential capabilities for a continuous state and action Q-learning system

are an efficient approach to continuous state, continuous action reinforcement learning.

4.2   CMAC Based Q-Learning

Santamaria, Ashwin and Sutton [12] have presented results for Q-learning systems using Albus's CMAC (Cerebellar Model Articulation Controller) [1]. The CMAC is a function approximation system which features spatial locality, avoiding the unlearning problem described in Sect. 6. It is a compromise between a look up table and a weight-based approximator. It can generalise between similar states, but it involves discretisation, making it impossible to completely fulfil the *Continuity* criteria. In [12] the inputs to the CMAC are the state and action, the output is the expected value. To find Q_{max} this implementation requires a search across all possible actions, calculating the Q-value for each to find the highest. This does not fulfil the *Action Selection* criteria.

Another concern is that approximation resources are used evenly across the state and action spaces. Santamaria et. al. address this by pre-distorting the state information using a priori knowledge so that more important parts of the state space receive more approximation resources.

4.3 Q-AHC

Rummery presents a method which combines Q-learning with actor-critic learning [11]. Q-learning is used to chose between a set of actor-critic learners. Its performance overall was unsatisfactory. In general it either set the actions to constant settings, making it equivalent to Lin's system for generalising between states [10], or only used one of the actor-critic modules, making it equivalent to a standard actor-critic system. These problems may stem from not fulfilling *Q Evaluation*, *Action Generalisation* and *State Generalisation* criteria when different actor-critic learners are used. This system is one of the few which can represent non-piecewise constant policies (*Continuity* criteria).

4.4   Q-Kohonen

Touzet describes a Q-learning system based on Kohonen's self organising map [15, 8]. The state, action and expected value are the elements of the feature vector. Actions are chosen by choosing the node which most closely matches the state and a the maximum possible value (one). Unfortunately the actions are always piecewise constant, not fulfilling the *Continuity* criteria.

4.5   Q-Radial Basis

Santos describes a system based on radial basis functions [13]. It is very similar to the Q-Kohonen system in that each radial basis neuron's holds a center vector like the Kohonen feature vector. The number of possible actions is equal to the number of radial basis neurons, so actions are piecewise constant (not fulfilling the *Continuity* criteria). It does not meet the *Q Evaluation* criteria as only those actions described by the radial basis neurons have an associated value.

4.6   Neural Field Q-Learning

Gross, Stephan and Krabbes have implemented a Q-learning system based on dynamic neural fields [6]. A neural vector quantiser (Neural Gas) clusters similar states. A neural field encodes the values of actions so that selecting the action with the highest Q requires iterative evaluation of the neural field dynamics. This limits the speed with which actions can be selected (the *Action Selection* criteria) and values of states found (the *State Evaluation* criteria). The system fulfils the *State Generalisation* and *Action Generalisation* criteria.

4.7   Our Approach

We seek a method of learning the control for a continuously acting agent functioning in the real world, for example a mobile robot travelling to goal location. For this application of reinforcement learning, the existing approaches have shortcomings that make them inappropriate for controlling this type of system. Many can't adequately generalise between states and/or actions. Others can't produce smoothly varying control actions or can't generate actions quickly enough for operation in real time. For these reasons we propose a scheme for reinforcement learning that uses a neural network and an interpolator to approximate the Q-function.

5   Wire-Fitted Neural Network Q-Learning

Wire-fitted Neural Network Q-Learning is a continuous state, continuous action Q-learning method. It couples a single feedforward artificial neural network with an interpolator ("wire-fitter") to fulfil all the criteria in Fig. 1.

Feedforward Artificial Neural networks have been used successfully to generalise between similar states in Q-learning systems where actions are discrete [10, 11]. If the output from the neural network describes (non-fixed) actions and their expected values, an interpolator can be used to generalise between them. This would fulfil the *State Generalisation* and *Action Generalisation* criteria.

Baird and Klopf [2] describe a suitable interpolation scheme called "wire-fitting". The wire-fitting function is a moving least squares interpolator, closely related to Shepard's function [9]. Each "wire" is a combination of an action vector, u, and its expected value, q, which is a sample of the Q-function. Baird and Klopf used the wire-fitting function in a memory based reinforcement learning scheme. In our system these parameters describing wire positions are the output of a neural network, whose input is the state vector, x.

Figure 2 is an example of wire-fitting. The action is this case is one dimensional, but the system supports many dimensional actions. The example shows the graph of action versus value (Q) *for a particular state*. The number of wires is fixed, the position of the wires changes to fit new data. Required changes are calculated using the partial derivatives of the wire-fitting function. Once new wire positions have been calculated the neural network is trained to output these new positions.

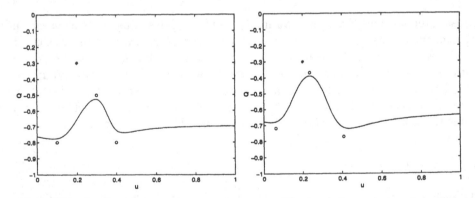

Fig. 2. The wire-fitting process. The action (u) is one dimensional in this case. Three wires (shown as o), this is the output from the neural network for a particular state. The wire-fitting function interpolates between the wires to calculate Q for every u. The new data (*) does not fit the curve well (*left*), so the wires are moved according to partial derivatives (*right*). In other states the wires would be in different positions.

The wire-fitting function has several properties which make it a useful interpolator for implementing Q-learning.

Updates to the Q-value (1) require $Q_{max}(x, u)$, which can be calculated quickly with the wire-fitting function (the *State Evaluation* criteria).

The action u for $Q_{max}(x, u)$ can also be calculated quickly (the *Action Selection* criteria). This is needed when choosing an action to carry out. A property of this interpolator is that the highest interpolated value always coincides with the highest valued interpolation point, so the action with the highest value is always one of the the input actions. When choosing an action it is sufficient to propagate the state through the neural network, then compare the output q to find the best action. The wire-fitter is not required at this stage, the only calculation is the forward pass through the neural network.

Wire-fitting also works with many dimensional scattered data while remaining computationally tractable; no inversion of matrices is required. Interpolation is local, only points nearby influence the value of Q. Areas far from all wires have a value which is the average of q, wild extrapolations do not occur (see Fig. 2). It does not suffer from oscillations, unlike most polynomial schemes.

Importantly, partial derivatives in terms of each q and u of each point can be calculated quickly. These partial derivatives allow error in the output of the Q-function to be propagated to the neural network according to the chain rule.

This combination of neural network and interpolator stores the entire Q function (the *Q Evaluation* criteria). It represents policies in a very flexible way; it allows sudden changes in action in response to a change in state by changing wires, while also allowing actions to change smoothly in response to changes in state (the *Continuity* and *Flexible Policy* criteria).

The training algorithm is shown in figure 3.

Training of the single hidden layer, feedforward neural network is by incremental backpropagation. The learning rate is kept constant throughout. Tansigmoidal neurons are used, restricting the magnitude of actions and values to between 1 and -1.

The wire-fitting function is

$$Q(x, u) = \lim_{\epsilon \to 0^+} \frac{\sum_{i=0}^{n} \frac{q_i(x)}{\|u - \hat{u}_i(x)\|^2 + c(q_{max}(x) - q_i(x)) + \epsilon}}{\sum_{i=0}^{n} \frac{1}{\|u - \hat{u}_i(x)\|^2 + c(q_{max}(x) - q_i(x)) + \epsilon}}$$
$$= \lim_{\epsilon \to 0^+} \frac{\sum_{i=0}^{n} \frac{q_i(x)}{distance(x, u)}}{\sum_{i=0}^{n} \frac{1}{distance(x, u)}} \qquad (2)$$
$$= \lim_{\epsilon \to 0^+} \frac{wsum(x, u)}{norm(x, u)},$$

where i is the wire number; n is the total number of wires; x is the state vector; $u_i(x)$ is the ith action vector; $q_i(x)$ is the value of the ith action vector; u is the action vector to be evaluated, c is a small smoothing factor and ϵ avoids division by zero. The dimensionality of the action vectors u and u_i is the number of continuous variables in the action. The two simplified forms shown simplify description of the partial derivatives. The partial derivative of Q from (2) in

1. In real time, feed the state into the neural network. Carry out the action with the highest q. Store the resulting change in state.

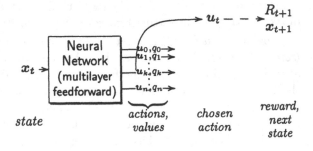

2. Calculate a new estimate of Q from the current value, the reward and the value of the next state. This can be done when convenient.

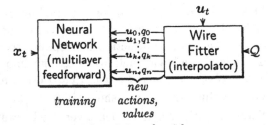

3. From the new value of Q calculate new values for u and q using the wire-fitter partial derivatives. Train the neural network to output the new u and q. This can be done when convenient.

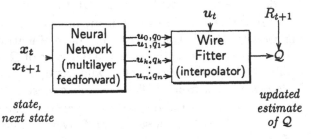

Fig. 3. Wire-fitted neural network training algorithm.

terms of $q(x)_k$ is

$$\frac{\partial Q}{\partial q_k} = \lim_{\epsilon \to 0^+} \frac{norm(x,u) \cdot (distance(x,u) + q_k \cdot c) - wsum(x,u) \cdot c}{[norm(x,u) \cdot distance(x,u)]^2} . \quad (3)$$

Equation (3) is inexact when $q_k = q_{max}$. The partial derivative of Q in terms of $u(x)_{k,j}$ is

$$\frac{\partial Q}{\partial u_{k,j}} = \lim_{\epsilon \to 0^+} \frac{[wsum(x,u) - norm(x,u) \cdot q_k] \cdot 2 \cdot (u_{k,j} - u_j)}{[norm(x,u) \cdot distance(x,u)]^2} , \quad (4)$$

where j selects a term of the action vector (u_j is a term of the chosen action). The summation terms in (3) and (4) have already been found in the calculation of Q with (2).

With partial derivatives known it is possible to calculate new positions for all the wires $u_{0...n}$ and $q_{0...n}$ by gradient descent. As a result of this change the Q output from the wire-fitter should move closer to the new target Q.

6   Practical Issues

When the input to a neural network changes slowly a problem known as un-learning or interference can cause the network to unlearn the correct output for other inputs because recent experience dominates the training data [3]. We cope with this problem by storing examples of state, action and next state transitions and replaying them as if they are being re-experienced. This creates a constantly changing input to the neural network, known as a persistent excitation. We do not store target outputs for the network as these would become incorrect through the learning process described in Sect. 5. Instead the wire-fitter is used to calculate new neural network output targets. This method makes efficient use of data gathered from the world without relying on extrapolation. A disadvantage is that if conditions change the stored data could become misleading.

One problem with applying Q-learning to continuous problems is that a single suboptimal action will not prevent a high value action from being carried out at the next time step. Thus the value of actions in a particular state can be very similar, as the value of the action in the next time step will be carried back. As the Q-value is only approximated for continuous states and actions it is likely that most of the approximation power will be used representing the values of the states rather than actions in states. The relative values of actions will be poorly represented, resulting in an unsatisfactory policy. The problem is compounded as the time intervals between control actions get smaller.

Advantage Learning [7] addresses this problem by emphasising the differences in value between the actions. In Advantage Learning the value of the optimal action is the same as for Q-learning, but the lesser value of non-optimal actions is emphasised by a scaling factor ($k \propto \Delta t$). This makes a more efficient use of the approximation resources available. The Advantage Learning update is

$$\mathcal{A}(x, u) := (1 - \alpha)\,\mathcal{A}(x, u)$$
$$+ \alpha \left[\tfrac{1}{k}\left(R + \gamma^k \max \mathcal{A}(x_{t+1}, u_{t+1})\right) + \left(1 - \tfrac{1}{k}\right) \max \mathcal{A}(x_t, u_t) \right] , \quad (5)$$

where $\mathcal{A}$ is analogous to Q in (1). The results in Sect. 7 show that Advantage Learning does make a difference in our learning task.

7   Simulation Results

We apply our learning algorithm to a simulation task. The task involves guiding a submersible vehicle to a target position by firing thrusters located on either side. The thrusters produce continuously variable thrust ranging from full forward to full backward. As there are only two thrusters (left, right) but three degrees on freedom (x, y, rotation) the submersible is non-holonomic in its planar world. The simulation includes momentum and friction effects in both angular and linear displacement. The controller must learn to slow the submersible and hold position as it reaches the target. Reward is the negative of the distance to the target (this is not a *pure* delayed reward problem).

Fig. 4. Appearance of the simulator for one run. The submersible gradually learns to control its motion to reach targets

Figure 4 shows a simulation run with hand placed targets. At the point marked zero the learning system does not have any knowledge of the effects of its actuators, the meaning of its sensors, or even the task to be achieved. After some initial wandering the controller gradually learns to guide the submersible directly toward the target and come to a near stop.

In earlier results using Q-learning alone [5], the controller learned to direct the submersible to the first randomly placed target about 70% of the time. Less than half of the controllers could reach all in series of 10 targets. Observation of Q-values showed that the value varied only slightly between actions, making it difficult to learn a stable policy. In our current implementation we use Advantage Learning (see Sect. 6) to emphasise the differences between actions. We now report that 100% of the controllers converge to acceptable performance.

To test this, we placed random targets at a distance of 1 unit, in a random direction, from a simulated submersible robot and allowed a period of 200 time steps for it to approach and hold station on the target. For a series of targets, the average distance over the time period, was recorded. A random motion achieves an average distance of 1 unit (no progress) while a hand coded controller can achieve 0.25. The learning algorithm reduces the average distance with time, eventually approaching hand coded controller performance. Recording distance rather than just ability to reach the target ensures that controllers which fail to hold station don't receive a high rating.

Graphs comparing 140 controllers trained with Q-learning and 140 trained with Advantage Learning are shown in the box-and-whisker plots in Fig. 5. The median distance to the target is the horizontal line in the middle of the box. The upper and lower bounds of the box show where 25% of the data above and below

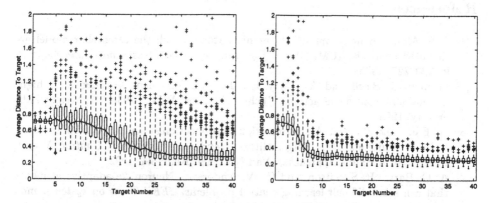

Fig. 5. Performance of 140 learning controllers using Q-learning (*left*) and Advantage Learning (*right*) which attempt to reach 40 targets each placed one distance unit away

the median lie, so the box contains the middle 50% of the data. Outliers, which are outside 1.5 times the range between the upper and lower ends of the box from the median, are shown by a "+" sign. The whiskers show the range of the data, excluding outliers. Advantage Learning converges to good performance more quickly and reliably than Q-learning and with many fewer and smaller magnitude spurious actions. Gradual improvement is still taking place at the 40th target. The quantity of outliers on the graph for Q-learning show that the policy continues to produce erratic behaviour in about 10% of cases.

When reward is based only on distance to the target (as in the experiment above) the actions are somewhat step like. To promote smooth control it is necessary to punish for both energy use and sudden changes in commanded action. Such penalties encouraged smoothness and confirmed that the system is capable of responding to continuous changes in state with continuous changes in action. A side effect of punishing for consuming energy is an improved ability to maintain position.

8   Conclusion

A practical continuous state, continuous action Q-learning system has been described and tested. It was found to converge quickly and reliably on a simulated control task. Advantage Learning was found to be an important tool in overcoming the problem of similarity in value between actions.

Acknowledgements

We thank WindRiver Systems and BEI Systron Donner for their support of the Kambara AUV project. We also thank the Underwater Robotics project team: Samer Abdallah, Terence Betlehem, Wayne Dunston, Ian Fitzgerald, Chris McPherson, Chanop Silpa-Anan and Harley Truong for their contributions.

References

[1] J. S. Albus. A new approach to manipulator control: the cerebrellar model articulated controller (CMAC). *J. Dynamic Systems, Measurement and Control*, 97:220–227, 1975.

[2] Leemon C. Baird and A. Harry Klopf. Reinforcement learning with high-dimensional, continuous actions. Technical Report WL-TR-93-1147, Wright Laboratory, 1993.

[3] W. Baker and J. Farrel. An introduction to connectionist learning control systems. In D. A. White and D. A. Sofge, editors, *Handbook of Intelligent Control: Neural, Fuzzy, and Adaptive Approaches*. Van Nostrand Reinhold, 1992.

[4] A. G. Barto, R. S. Sutton, and C. W. Anderson. Neuronlike adaptive elements that can solve difficult learning control problems. *IEEE Trans on systems, man and cybernetics*, SMC-13:834–846, 1983.

[5] Chris Gaskett, David Wettergreen, and Alexander Zelinsky. Reinforcement learning applied to the control of an autonomous underwater vehicle. In *Proceedings of the Australian Conference on Robotics and Automation (AuCRA99)*, 1999.

[6] H.-M. Gross, V. Stephan, and M. Krabbes. A neural field approach to topological reinforcement learning in continuous action spaces. In *Proc. 1998 IEEE World Congress on Computational Intelligence, WCCI'98 and International Joint Conference on Neural Networks, IJCNN'98*, Anchorage, Alaska, 1998.

[7] Mance E. Harmon and Leemon C. Baird. Residual advantage learning applied to a differential game. In *Proceedings of the International Conference on Neural Networks*, Washington D.C, 1995.

[8] T. Kohonen. *Self-Organization and Associative Memory*. Springer, Berlin, third edition, 1989.

[9] Peter Lancaster and Kęstutis Šalkauskas. *Curve and Surface Fitting, an Introduction*. Academic Press, 1986.

[10] Long-Ji Lin. Self-improving reactive agents based on reinforcement learning, planning and teaching. *Machine Learning Journal*, 8(3/4), 1992.

[11] Gavin Adrian Rummery. *Problem solving with reinforcement learning*. PhD thesis, Cambridge University, 1995.

[12] Juan C. Santamaria, Richard S. Sutton, and Ashwin Ram. Experiments with reinforcement learning in problems with continuous state and action spaces. *Adaptive Behaviour*, 6(2):163–218, 1998.

[13] Juan Miguel Santos. *Contribution to the study and design of reinforcement functions*. PhD thesis, Universidad de Buenos Aires, Universite d'Aix-Marseille III, 1999.

[14] Richard S. Sutton and Andrew G. Barto. *Reinforcement Learning: An Introduction*. Bradford Books, MIT, 1998.

[15] Claude F. Touzet. Neural reinforcement learning for behaviour synthesis. *Robotics and Autonomous Systems*, 22(3-4):251–81, 1997.

[16] Christopher J. C. H. Watkins. *Learning from Delayed Rewards*. PhD thesis, University of Cambridge, 1989.

[17] Paul J. Werbos. Approximate dynamic programming for real-time control and neural modeling. In D. A. White and D. A. Sofge, editors, *Handbook of Intelligent Control: Neural, Fuzzy, and Adaptive Approaches*. Van Nostrand Reinhold, 1992.

On Understanding Global Behavior of Teams in Robot Soccer Simulators

Victor Korotkich[1] and Noel Patson[2]

[1] Central Queensland University, Mackay Qld. Australia 4740
v.korotkich@cqu.edu.au
[2] Central Queensland University, Rockhampton Qld. Australia 4702
n.patson@cqu.edu.au

Abstract. An approach is investigated to identify an invariant in the team's behavior in order to characterize the global behavior of a robot soccer team. The existence of such an invariant confirmed by computational evidence is reported in this paper. The invariant is being studied with the view of using it as a possible means for developing intelligent strategies in robot soccer. ...

Keywords: robotics, multiagent systems, simulation, distributed AI, mathematical foundations, artificial life.

1 Introduction

The study of Robotics and Intelligent machines is becoming an important discipline in Artificial Intelligence [1]. Robot Soccer is used as a test bed for many branches of research that have arisen in this discipline. This paper gives attention to understanding the global behavior of teams in a Robot Soccer simulator. The aim is to identify any invariants in the team's behavior that can be used as its global signature. We report that the approach used in the paper is confirmed by computational evidence and indicates the existence of such an invariant. The invariant is being studied with the view of using it as a possible means for developing intelligent strategies in robot soccer.

Usually in the game of soccer between teams of human players, enthusiasts of the game have an intuitive understanding of the style of play exhibited by a particular team. The global behavior may be designated by terms like: an offensive team, a defensive team, the Italian style, the Brazilian approach etc. Because the style of robot soccer teams has been encoded algorithmically it should be able to be described and understood formally. It is hoped that the invariant will be useful as an identifier of the robot team's style.

2 Robot Soccer

The organizing of several world robot soccer competitions by the Federation of International Robot-soccer Association (FIRA) [2] and the RoboCup Federation [3] has stimulated much research in the field of robot soccer. In 1996 the

N. Foo (Ed.): AI'99, LNAI 1747, pp. 429–439, 1999.

Micro-Robot World Cup was held in Korea [4]. During the 1997 World Cup tournament FIRA was organized [5] and the categories NaroSot, MiroSot, RoboSot, and KheperaSot were established. These categories differ from each other in the number or size of robots on the playing field.

The RoboCup was initiated by a group of researchers into Artificial Intelligence in Japan. This competition is split into leagues, the Small Size League, Middle Size League, and the Simulator League. The Simulator League is a test bed for robot team strategies played in simulation on the official RoboCup Simulator [6]. In 1998 the World Cup for both competitions was held in Paris and in the year 2000 to coincide with the Olympic games in Sydney, the World Cup for both competitions will be held in Australia. The FIRA competion will be hosted by Central Queensland University in Rockhampton [7] and RoboCup will be hosted by RMIT University in Melbourne [8].

2.1   The Game of Robot Soccer

In both Robot Soccer competitions the game is played on a soccer field that is scaled down to about the size of a ping-pong table [2,3] (9 tables for RoboCup middle sized league MSL [3]). Depending on the category, there are between one and five robots on each team. The robots attempt to move a golf ball (200mm ball for MSL) into the opponent's goal. In general the RoboCup competition has larger robots that move slower than in the FIRA competition. FIRA is seeking to have micro and nano technology built into its robots.

Usually a central computer is used to transmit instructions to each robot based on information given by a global vision system except in MSL where all systems are on board the robot. The goal of both competitions is to have fully autonomous robots with on-board vision and control systems.

2.2   Robot Soccer Simulators

Autonomous robots must perform many complex computations such as cooperation with team members [1,9,10] coordination of movements [11], interpretation of visual signals [12], collision avoidance [13], machine learning [14] and calculation of trajectories [15]. These computational requirements are currently far too great to physically fit inside a robot. For this reason simulators are being used to test algorithms that improve the strategies and global behavior of robot soccer teams. Consequently understanding global behavior becomes a very important problem.

Some of these simulators can be found on the web and freely downloaded (see Table 1).

2.3   ASCII Soccer Simulator

The ASCII Soccer simulator is based on a text screen with a field 78 characters long and 21 lines wide. A team consists of 4 ">" characters playing against 4

Table 1. Robot Soccer Simulators and the internet address where they can be downloaded.

Simulator	Internet address
ASCII Soccer	http://www.cc.gatech.edu/grads/b/Tucker.Balch/soccer/
Java Soccer	http://www.cc.gatech.edu/grads/b/Tucker.Balch /JavaBots/EDU/gatech/cc/is/docs/index.html
RoboCup Soccer Server	http://ci.etl.go.jp/ noda/soccer/server/DownLoad.html

"<" characters with an "o" as the ball. The goals are the left hand and right hand sides of the field. The ASCII Soccer simulator was used in this research due to its simplicity and the ease of extracting the data of the successive positions of play throughout the game.

Thirteen different teams can be downloaded with the ASCII Soccer simulator. The strategies that are encoded in the teams vary from random players who move in any direction, to position-based strategies and continuous feedback learning and control.

3   An Approach to Understand Team Behavior

An approach used in this paper is based on the theory of Random Matrices [16] and Structural Complexity [17,18]. It may been seen as analogous to the spectral analysis procedure that physicists use to identify substances by how the substance absorbs and emits photons [19]. This approach is employed to identify an invariant in the team's behavior that can be used as a global signature. The invariant is being studied with the view of using this characterization of global behavior as a possible approach to developing intelligent strategies in robot soccer.

The core of this approach is based on eigenvalue statistics of matrices related to the dynamics of robots. The movements of the team of robots throughout the game are captured by a sequence of matrices. The approach is confirmed by computational evidence given in the paper that indicates the existence of an invariant. Computational results show that the statistics derived from the eigenvalues of these matrices are consistent over a number of games against the same opponent and also against different opponents. This encourages us to consider them as a signature of the team's global behavior in the same way as a spectrum identifies the behavior of atoms in a molecule.

3.1   Constructing Matrices that Describe Team Movements

In ASCII soccer the playing field is naturally divided into a grid 78 by 21. In order to speed up computations by decreasing the size of the matrix the resolution was changed to a grid 39 by 11. Starting from the bottom left-hand corner of the grid and moving from left to right and then to the next line, each cell was numbered from 1 to 429.

At each instant of time the robot players will be in a cell, denoted s_i. A "frame of action" represents the cell positions for the whole team at a given instant of time. Corresponding to the change in resolution, only every second frame of action was considered.

The movement from one frame of action to the next is captured by a 429 by 429 symmetric matrix $A = (a_{ij})$, $i, j = 1, \ldots, 429$ where $a_{ij} = a_{ji}$ equals 1 if a robot moves from cell s_i to s_j. The construction of matrix A is illustrated by the following example. The data in Table 2 shows the cell positions of the team players for frame 1 and frame 2. In the matrix A of zeros the following elements are changed to ones (15, 54), (54, 15), (132, 172), (172, 132), (249, 289), (289, 249), (366, 367), (367, 366).

Table 2. Table 2 Data for illustration of matrix construction

Players	1	2	3	4
Frame 1	15	132	249	366
Frame 2	54	172	289	367

This method of encoding has been used in order to preserve symmetry in the matrix and as a result the following situations arise. When a robot remains in the same cell it will contribute only one element which is on the diagonal of the matrix. In the case where two robots swap positions from one frame to the next, the matrix A would appear to "lose" a robot, i.e. only two ones would appear in A whereas normally four ones would encode the movements of the two robots. It can be shown that generality is not affected by these simplifications and we plan to take this into account in our future research.

3.2   Distribution of Eigenvalues

Statistics of spacings between eigenvalues has been found to be very useful in categorizing global behavior in the field of quantum chaology [20]. In particular it has been found that the probability distribution of these spacings reveal an invariant that is useful in classifying phenomena on the boundary between the classical and quantum realms.

The matrices $A_1, \ldots, A_t$ which encode the movements of the team of robots from one frame of action to the next over $t + 1$ frames are considered individually. The eigenvalues calculated for each matrix are arranged in ascending order $\lambda_1, \ldots, \lambda_n$. All but one of the zero eigenvalues are ignored by the process of considering the differences (spacing) d, between sequential eigenvalues given by: $d = \lambda_i - \lambda_{i+1}$ if λ_i and λ_{i+1} are both not zero. These spacings are stored for all $A_1, \ldots, A_t$. This data is then displayed as a probability histogram.

3.3 Results

Figure 1 shows the graphs of these statistics for 3 games played by the Soccer Spaniels team against the Dynamic Rollers. Each bar represents the probability of having a spacing between eigenvalues at its position on the x axis. Figure 2 shows the statistics for the Dynamic Rollers team for the 3 games. In both these figures the interval width for the sample is 0.0033... , which gives a very high resolution. Figure 3 and Figure 4 display the data collected over 5 games between the same two teams using a much lower resolution. Here the interval width is 0.2.

It is to be noted that the algorithms for the two teams use different approaches and are programmed by different authors. Quite surprisingly it is observed that the statistics for each team are very similar for each of the five games and appear as our results show, to be a signature of the global behavior for each team. That the games were completely different can be seen by the different game results as shown in Table 3.

Table 3. Scores for 5 games between Soccer Spaniels and Dynamic Rollers simulated robot soccer teams.

Team/Game	1	2	3	4	5
Soccer Spaniels	7	2	10	8	10
Dynamic Rollers	10	10	7	10	9

The Soccer Spaniels and the Dynamic Rollers teams also were pitted against other teams that had been downloaded with the ASCII Soccer simulator and remarkably the same signatures were consistently found for each team. The other teams also were seen to have their own individual signatures. It appears that the signature is an invariant of the team's global behavior and may be a formal way of describing the team's style of play. These similarities are established by the usual statistical methods.

4 Discussion

An approach for identifying a global invariant of a robot soccer team is confirmed by computational results that indicate the existence of such an invariant as presented in this paper. This encourages us to anticipate that this invariant could be viewed as a global signature of the team's style. This is a first step in the search to identify team style of play in a quantitative rather than qualitative way. It is a mathematical approach that formally describes a team's global behavior. Future research will focus on finding the link between a team's signature and its behavior.

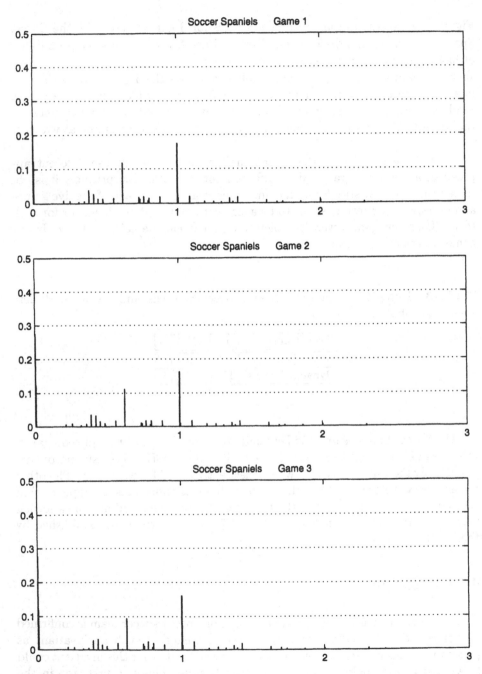

Fig. 1. Probability histograms with an interval width of 0.0033... of spacings between eigenvalues for matrices encoding the movement of the Soccer Spaniels Simulated Robot Soccer Team for 3 games.

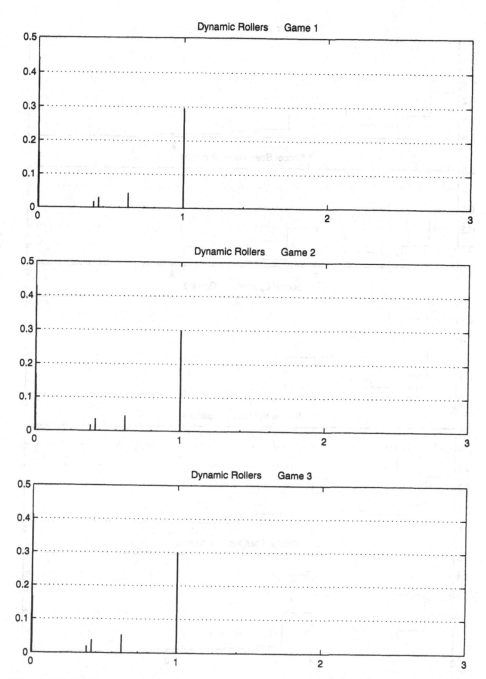

Fig. 2. Probability histograms with an interval width of 0.0033... of spacings between eigenvalues for matrices encoding the movement of the Dynamic Rollers Simulated Robot Soccer Team for 3 games.

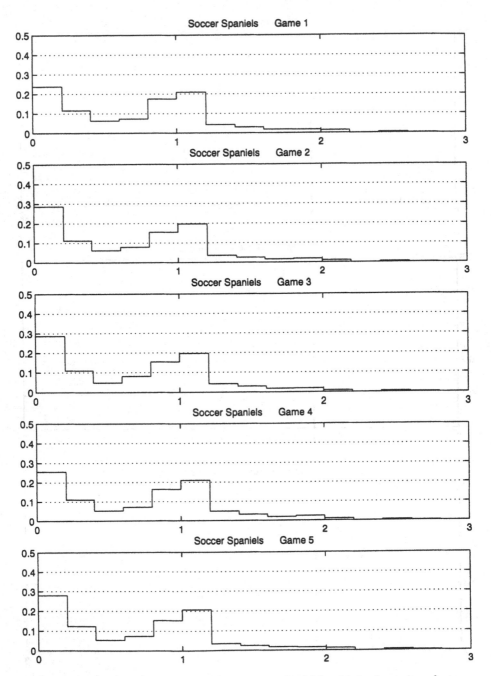

Fig. 3. Probability histograms with an interval width of 0.2 of spacings between eigenvalues for matrices encoding the movement of the Soccer Spaniels Simulated Robot Soccer Team for 5 games.

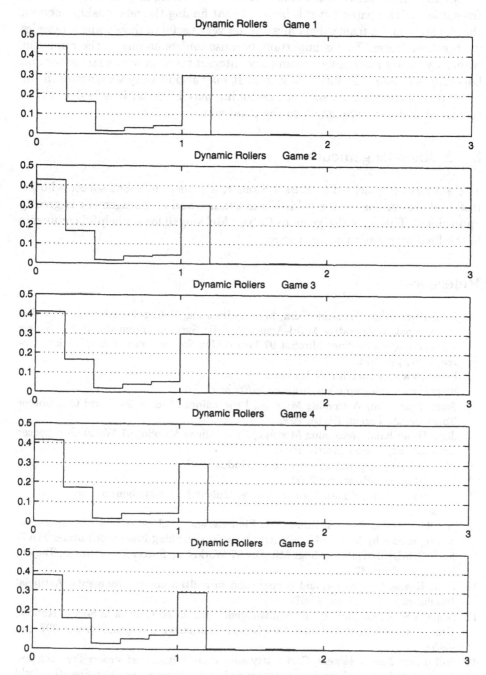

Fig. 4. Probability histograms with an interval width of 0.2 of spacings between eigenvalues for matrices encoding the movement of the Dynamic Rollers Simulated Robot Soccer Team for 5 games.

All the consequences and ramifications of this intriguing discovery are not the subject of this paper but it is believed that finding the relationship between the signature and a team's dynamics will be very useful in developing strategies for the home team. This is important because understanding of the opponent team's dynamics will enable a team to counteract the opponent's strategies and hopefully estimate their future positions. It may also identify weaknesses in the home team's coordination so that fine-tuning may be done. It is believed that the use of this signature may help the team win.

5 Acknowledgements

The authors are indebted to Russel Stonier, a pioneer in robot soccer who introduced the authors to the field. His assistance and encouragement is greatly appreciated. Thanks is also given to Robert McDougall for his helpful comments in the final preparation of this paper.

References

1. Jong-Hwan Kim, Hyun-Sik Shim, Myung-Jin Jung, Heung-Soo Kim, and Prahlad Vadakkepat, Cooperative Multi-Agent Robotic Systems: From the Robot-Soccer Perspective, Proceedings MiroSot 97 World Cup Soccer Tournament, Taejon, Korea, 1997, pp. 3-14.
2. http://www.fira.net/fira/index.html.
3. http://www.robocup.v.kinotrope.co.jp/02.html.
4. Jong-Hwan Kim, Welcoming Message, Proceedings MiroSot 96 World Cup Soccer Tournament, Taejon, Korea, 1996.
5. Jong-Hwan Kim, Welcoming Message, Proceedings MiroSot 97 World Cup Soccer Tournament, Taejon, Korea, 1997.
6. http://ci.etl.go.jp/ noda/soccer/server/index.html.
7. http://fira.cqu.edu.au/rwc2000.
8. http://www.rmit.edu.au/About/press-rel/July98.html#Melbourne wins RoboCup.
9. A. Oller, R. Garcia, J. A. Ramon, A. Figueras and J. LI. de la Rosa, Co-operation among robots by Means of Multi-Agent Decision making Framework under MATLAB/SIMULINK, Proceedings MiroSot 97 World Cup Soccer Tournament, Taejon, Korea, 1997 pp. 37-45.
10. Sarit Kraus, Negotiation and cooperation in multi-agent environments, Artificial Intelligence 94, 1997 pp. 79-97.
11. Sripada Subramanyam, et. al., Multi-Agent Centralized Control in Soccer Robots, Proceedings MiroSot 97 World Cup Soccer Tournament, Taejon, Korea, 1997, pp. 49-52.
12. Bill Bailey, Randy Sargent, Carl Witty and Anne Wright, Fast Vision Tracking and Coordinated Control for Soccer-Playing Robots, Proceedings MiroSot 97 World Cup Soccer Tournament, Taejon, Korea, 1997, pp.59-65.
13. P. Hannah, G. Springer, S. Smith, R. J. Stonier and P. Wolfs, Simple Strategies for Collision-Avoidance in Robot Soccer, Proceedings MiroSot 96 World Cup Soccer Tournament, Taejon, Korea, 1996 pp. 64-68.

14. Sorin Achim, Peter Stone and Manuela Veloso, Collaboration and Learning in Robotic Soccer, Proceedings MiroSot 96 World Cup Soccer Tournament, Taejon, Korea, 1996, pp. 26-37.

15. K. Kozlowski, Trajectory Control Algorithms for Robots in Terms of Quasi-Velocities, Proceedings MiroSot 97 World Cup Soccer Tournament, Taejon, Korea, 1997, pp.125-135.

16. M. L. Mehta, Random Matrices in Nuclear Physics and Number Theory, Contemporary Mathematics, Volume 50, American Mathematical Society, 1986, pp. 295-309.

17. V. Korotkich, Symmetry in Structural Complexity and a Model of Formation, in From Local Interactions to Global Phenomena, IOS Press, Amsterdam, 1996 pp. 84-95.

18. V. Korotkich, A Mathematical Structure for Emergent Computation, Kluwer Academic Publishers, Boston/Dordrecht/London, 1999 (forthcoming).

19. Raymond A. Serway, et. al., Modern Physics, Saunders College Publishing, Philadelphia, 1989, p. 294.

20. M.V. Berry, Quantum chaology, The Bakerian Lecture 1987, Proc. R. Soc. Lond. A413. 1987, pp 183-198.

Visual Human-Machine Interaction

Alexander Zelinsky

Research School of Information Sciences and Engineering
Australian National University, Canberra, ACT 0200, Australia
Alex.Zelinsky@anu.edu.au
http://syseng.anu.edu.au/rsl/

Abstract. It is envisaged that computers of the future will have smart interfaces such as speech and vision, which will facilitate natural and easy human-machine interaction. Gestures of the face and hands could become a natural way to control the operations of a computer or a machine, such as a robot. In this paper, we present a vision-based interface that in real-time tracks a person's facial features and the gaze point of the eyes. The system can robustly track facial features, can detect tracking failures and has an automatic mechanism for error recovery. The system is insensitive to lighting changes and occulsions or distortion of the facial features. The system is user independent and can automatically calibrate for each different user. An application using this technology for driver fatigue detection and the evaluation of ergonomic design of motor vehicles has been developed. Our human-machine interface has an enormous potential in other applications that allow the control of machines and processes, and measure human performance. For example, product possibilities exist for assisting the disabled and in video game entertainment.

1 Introduction

Throughout the era of computer vision research, much effort has been undertaken to improve the interface between humans and machines. [1] [2]. An important area of this research has been the recognition of gestures of the head and body, as well as expressions of the face. Gestures are regarded as the most natural forms of human expression. Particularly for disabled and totally inexperienced computer users, a gesture interface would open the door to many applications ranging from control of machines to "helping hands" for the elderly and disabled. A smart visual human-machine interface should recognise facial gestures such as "yes" or "no", as well as being able to determine the users gaze point i.e. the direction in which the person is looking and the focus attention. The ability to estimate a person's gaze point is very important. For example a robot assisting the disabled may need to pick up items that attract the user's gaze. The crucial aspect of such systems is the capability to process data in real-time, However, at present many computer vision systems still suffer from a lack of computational speed. In our research we describe a vision system that is capable of real-time feature tracking.

N. Foo (Ed.): AI'99, LNAI 1747, pp. 440–452, 1999.

The goal of our research is to build a visual human-machine interface based on a real-time stereo camera system, that works in natural scenes to track the human face as well as estimate the user's gaze direction. It is our belief that in the near future, vision-based interfaces will revolutionise the way people work with machines, and will open up a tremendous range of new applications.

Innovative applications of the technology for the automotive industry have been the a primary focus of our research. Driver Behaviour Analysis and Driver Safety Systems are the prime targets. Car manufacturers also need to analyse the ergonomic efficiencies of their motor vehicle designs. Where drivers look and how they behave in vehicles equipped with various configurations of instrumentation is of great importance. Our system completely automates the data capture and replay phase of driver behaviour analysis. We determine the instrument being observed using an internal computer model of the vehicle and the driver's gaze point as a reference. The duration and timing of the driver's gaze are automatically measured and logged. The impact on Driver-Safety of our system is apparent. It can detect whether the driver is not looking at the road or has fallen asleep. We have built, tested and successfully demonstrated a in-car prototype.

2 Visual Interfaces

2.1 Face and Gaze Detection

There are several types of commercial products in existence to detect head position and orientation, using magnetic sensors and link mechanisms. There are also several companies supporting products that perform eye gaze tracking. These products are generally highly accurate and reliable. However, all these products require either expensive hardware and/or artificial environments (helmets, infrared lighting, marking on the face etc). The restricted motion and discomfort to user caused by such equipment makes it difficult to measure natural and unihibited behavior of people.

To solve this problem, there have been many research results reported that are related to the visual detection of head pose [3,4,5,6]. Recent advances in computer hardware have allowed researchers to develop real-time face tracking systems. However all of the previously reported systems are based on monocular vision. Recovering the 3D pose from a monocular image stream is regarded as a difficult problem in general. High accuracy as well as robustness are particularly hard to achieve. Most reported systems do not compute the full 3D 6DOF posture of heads. Researchers have developed monocular systems to detect both the head pose and gaze point simultaneously [7,8], However, these systems do not accurately determine the 3D vector of the gaze direction.

In order to construct a system which observes a person without causing any discomfort, the system should satisfy the following requirements: non-contact, passive, real-time, robust to occlusions and lighting change, compact, accurate, and capable to detect head posture and gaze direction simultaneously.

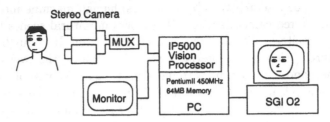

Fig. 1. System configuration of the human-machine interface.

Our system simultaneously satisfies all the listed requirements by utilizing the following techniques: stereo vision using field multiplexing, image processing using normalized correlation and 3D model fitting using virtual springs.

3   Real-Time Vision Hardware

Figure 1 illustrates the hardware setup of our real-time stereo face tracking system. It has a NTSC camera pair (SONY EVI-370DG × 2) to capture the person's face. The output video signals from the cameras are multiplexed into one video signal using the "field multiplexing technique"[9]. The multiplexed video stream is then fed into a vision processing board (Hitach IP5000), where the position and the orientation of the face are determined. The face tracking results are visualized on a SGI O2 graphics workstation.

3.1   Hitachi IP5000 Image Processor

The Hitachi IP5000 PCI half-sized image processing board is used in this research. The card is equipped with 40 frame memories of 512 × 512 pixels. It provides in hardware a wide variety of fast image processing functions such as binarization, convolution, filtering, labeling, histogram calculation, color extraction and normalized correlation. The frequency of these operations is 73.5MHz, which means the card can apply a single basic function (such as binarization) to a single image in 3.6ms.

3.2   Field Multiplexing Device

The field multiplexing is a method for generating an analog multiplexed video steam from two video streams. A diagram of the device is shown in Figure 2. The device takes two video steams which are synchronized into a video switching IC. The video switcher selects one signal and uses it as the odd field of the video output; the other signal becomes the even field of the video output. Since the frequency of the switching is only 60Hz, the multiplexer can be easily and cheaply implemented using only consumer electronic parts. A photo of the device is also shown in Figure 2; the size of the device is less than 5cm square.

The advantage of multiplexing video signals in the analog phase is that such an approach can be applied to any vision system. Single video stream processing is transformed into stereo vision processing. Since the multiplexed image is stored in a single video frame memory, stereo image processing can be performed within the memory. This means there is no overhead cost for transferring images, which is inevitable in stereo vision system with two image processing boards. Thus a system with a field multiplexing device can have a higher performance than a system with two boards.

A minor weak point of the field multiplexing is that the image looks strange to human eyes if you display the signal directly on a TV monitor, because two images are superimposed every two lines. However this doesn't make image processing any harder, since a normal image can be easily obtained by subsampling the multiplexed image in the vertical direction.

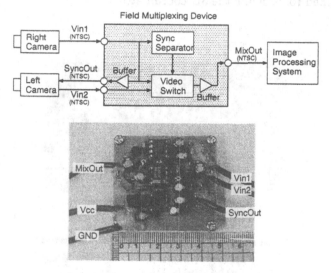

Fig. 2. Field Multiplexing Device.

4   Stereo Face Tracking

4.1   3D Facial Model

The 3D facial model used in our stereo face tracking is composed of three components:

– template images of the facial features,
– 3D coordinates of the facial features,
– an image of the entire face.

The facial features are defined as both of the corners of the eyes and the mouth. Thus there are six feature images and coordinates in a facial model, an example of which is shown in Figure 3. The facial model also has an image of the whole face stored in low resolution. This image is used to search for a face at the system initialisation stage and in cases when the system feature tracking fails.

The facial model can be acquired either "automatically" or "manually". In automatic acquisition mode, the eyes and mouth are detected by first finding skin colored regions in the image and then binarizing the intensity information contained in the skin colored facial region. Small image patches at both ends of the extracted eyes and mouth are memorized as feature templates, and the 3D coordinates of the features are calculated based on stereo matching. In the manual acquisition mode, the image patches of the features are selected by simply clicking with a mouse over positions of interest in the image. Stereo matching is then performed to calculate the 3D coordinates.

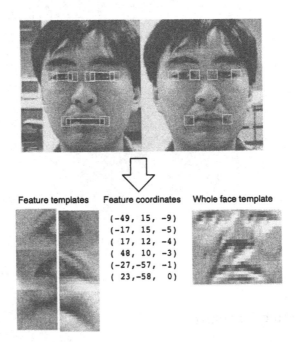

Feature templates   Feature coordinates   Whole face template

$$(-49, 15, -9)$$
$$(-17, 15, -5)$$
$$(17, 12, -4)$$
$$(48, 10, -3)$$
$$(-27, -57, -1)$$
$$(23, -58, 0)$$

Fig. 3. Upper: Extracted tracking features from stereo images, Lower: 3D facial model.

4.2   Stereo Tracking Algorithm

Before face tracking begins, the error recovery procedure is executed to determine the approximate position of the face in the live video stream using the whole face image.

Feature tracking and stereo matching for each feature are carried out to determine the 3D positions of each feature. A 3D facial model is fitted to the 3D measurements, and the 3D position and orientation of the face is estimated in terms of six parameters. Then the 3D coordinates for each feature are adjusted to maintain the consistency of the rigid body facial model. Finally, the 3D feature coordinates are projected back onto the 2D image plane in order to update the search area for feature tracking by the vision processor in the next frame.

At the end of each tracking process cycle, the overall reliability of the face tracking is determined using the correlation values of feature tracking and stereo matching. If the reliability is higher than a preset threshold, the system returns to the beginning of the tracking process again. Otherwise the system decides it has lost the face and jumps back to the error recovery phase.

3D Feature Tracking In the 3D feature tracking stage, it is assumed that each feature has only a small displacement between the current frame and the previous one. The 2D positions of features in the previous frame are used to determine the search area in the current frame. The feature images stored with the 3D facial model are used as templates. Images from the right camera are searched for features. The 2D features that have been found in the right image are used as templates for searching for matching images from the left camera. By stereo matching the 3D coordinates of each feature are acquired. The processing time of the whole tracking process (i.e. feature tracking + stereo matching for six features) is about 10ms by the IP5000.

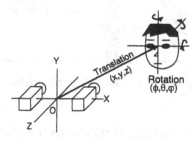

Fig. 4. Coordinate system for face tracking.

3D Model Fitting Figure 4 illustrates the coordinate system used to represent the position and the orientation of the face. The parameters (ϕ, θ, φ) represents

446   Alexander Zelinsky

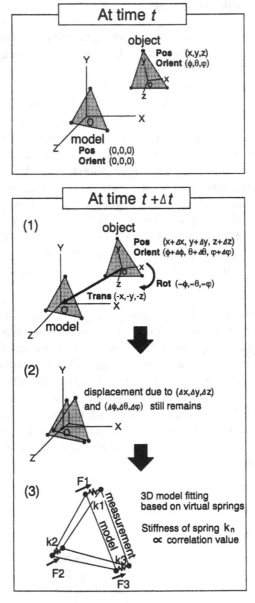

Fig. 5. 3D model fitting algorithm.

the orientation of the face, and (x,y,z) represents the position of the face center relative to the origin of the camera axis.

The diagrams in Figure 5 describe the model fitting scheme used in our system. In the actual implementation six features are used for tracking, however only three points are illustrated in the diagrams for simplicity. The basic idea of the model fitting is to iteratively move the model closer to the system measurements while considering the reliability results of feature tracking. As mentioned before, the face is assumed to have a small motion between the frames. This means there can be only small displacements in terms of the position and the orientation, which is described as $(\Delta x, \Delta y, \Delta z, \Delta \phi, \Delta \theta, \Delta \varphi)$ in Figure 5(1).

The position and the orientation determined in the previous frame (at time t) are used to rotate and translate the data set of measurements from the vision system to the same coordinate space as the model, as shown in Figure 5(2). After the rotation and translation, the data set of measurements have a small disparity from the model due to the motion which has occurred during the interval Δt. Fine fitting of the model is performed next. To realize a robust fitting of the model, it is essential to take the reliability values of the individual measurements into account. The least squares method is usually adopted for such purposes. In our system, a similar fitting approach based on virtual springs is used. The result of 3D tracking yields two correlation values (for the left and right images) which are between 0 and 1 for each feature. If a template and another matching region have exactly the same pattern, then the resulting image correlation value is 1. A value of 0 represents correlation where all pixels in the two correlation images are completely different. The product of the two correlation values for each feature can be regarded as a reliability value. The reliability values are used as the parameters of stiffness of springs that link each feature in the model. The spring based model fiiting is shown in Figure 5(3). The model is iteratively rotated and translated in order to reduce the elastic energy of the springs. Using the tracking reliability as a spring constant makes the results of model fitting insensitive to the partial matching failures, and ensures robust face tracking. The processing time of the iterative model fitting takes less than 2ms using a PentiumII 450MHz processor.

4.3   Error Recovery

The tracking method described above has only a small search area in the image, which enables the real-time processing and continuous stable result of tracking. However once the system fails to track the face, it is hard for the system to make a recovery by using only the local template matching, and a complementary method for finding the face in the image is necessary as an error recovery function. This process is also used at the beginning of the tracking when the position of the face is unknown.

The whole face image shown in Figure 3 is used in this process. In order to reduce the processing time, the template is memorized in low resolution. The live video stream is also reduced in resolution. The template is first searched in the right image, and then the matched image is searched in the left image. As a result, the rough 3D position of the face is determined and is then used as the initial state of the face for the face tracking. This searching process takes about 100ms.

5   Implementation Results

5.1   Face Tracking

Some snapshots of the results of the real-time face tracking system are shown in Figure 6. Images (1) and (2) in Figure 6a show results when the face rotates, while (3) and (4) show results when the face moves closer to and further from the camera. The whole tracking process takes about 30ms which is within a NTSC video frame rate. The accuracy of the tracking is approximately ±1mm in translation and ±1° in rotation.

The snapshots in Figure 6b show the results of tracking when there is some deformation of the facial features and partial occlusions of the face by a hand. The results indicate our tracking system works quite robustly in such situations owing to our model fitting method. By utilizing the normalized correlation function on the IP5000, the tracking system is tolerant of the fluctuation in lighting.

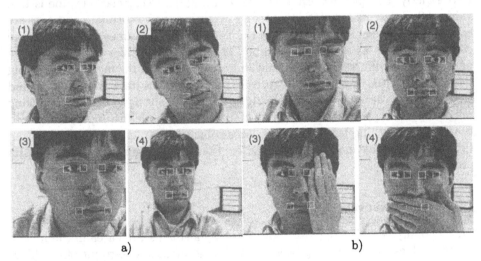

a)   b)

Fig. 6. Face tracking results.

5.2   Visualization

The results of the tracking are visualized using a SGI O2 graphics workstation. Figure 7a illustrates examples of the tracking results and the corresponding visualization. The 3D model used in the visualization consists of the rigid surface of the face and two eyeballs. The face has six DOF for position and orientation, and the eyeballs have two DOF respectively. The external border of the irises of the eyes is detected using the Circular Hough Transform, and then are used to position the eyes of the mannequin head. The visualization process is performed online during the tracking, and therefore the mannequin head can mimic the person's head and eye motions in real-time.

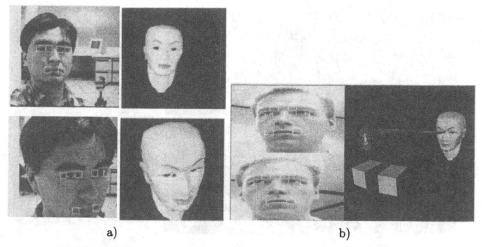

a)   b)

Fig. 7. Visualization of Face Tracking and Gaze Estimation.

5.3 Gaze Detection

Our system outputs the position and posture of the face, as well as the position
of the pupils. Pupil detection is done using the Circular Hough Transform. Gaze
point estimation is done by fusing the 3D face position and posture with the
2D positions of the pupils. The eyeball is modelled as a sphere, and using the
corners of the eye the center of the eyeball can be determined. The eyeball center
is connected to the detected pupil's center to form a gaze line for each eye. The
gaze lines are then projected into 3D space, and the intersection point becomes
the estimated gaze point. Figure 7b shows a stereo image pair of a face, and
the corresponding mannequin model shows the estimated face pose and gaze
direction. Pupil detection takes about 2ms. The combined face tracking and
gaze detection system runs at 20Hz.

6 Applications

Our system has been developed for use as a general vision-based human-machine
interface. We believe our interface can be applied to an enormous range of real
world applications. For example our system could be used as a measurement tool
in psychological experiments to determine where a human subject is looking. A
commercial application of gaze measurement lies in advertising. Marketing firms
could evaluate the effectiveness of television commercials by monitoring gaze direction while subjects are watching the TV. Another possible area of application
lies in the entertainment industry. Video games could be controlled simply by
a user's gaze direction. Likewise disabled people could steer wheelchairs using
gaze, or command robots to pick up items merely by looking at the object.

An important application area lies in evaluating the ergonomic design effectiveness of products and machines that people use. For example the operator

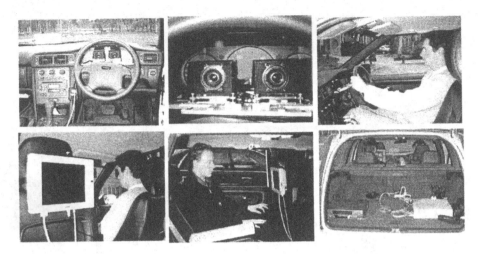

Fig. 8. Driver Performance Measurement System.

control panel in a nuclear plant should be designed and laid out in a manner that does not induce any confusion that causes the operator to press the wrong button. A non-intrusive means of observing the operator working is needed. In the case of a poor ergonomic design the operator's gaze will wander unnecessarily. In this application domain we have developed a system that measures the ergonomic design efficiency of its motor vehicles in driving tasks. We have built an in-car version of our system. Figure 8 shows the in-car installation. The figure shows the stereo cameras mounted in the dash, a close up of the cameras, the driver, the display monitor mounted in the rear seat, and the computer equipment in the rear compartment. We can measure the gaze direction and duration while a person is driving. For example the system can log how often the driver glances at the speedometer and side mirrors.

The system has been extensively tested with a variety of drivers in a wide range of driving conditions. It is able to work reliably over 85% of the time; on the occasions when feature tracking does fails our system recovers automatically. The onboard computer logs the user's gaze detection data. This feature allows design engineers to analyse the data off-line. The off-line analysis also allows users to visualise the gaze detection data using a CAD model of the motor vehicle. Figure 9 shows an example of gaze point visualisation inside a 3D CAD model of a motor vehicle.

An obvious extension of our work is to apply the system to Driver-Safety in motor vehicles, so that an alarm sounds if a driver falls asleep. Currently, our system can detect if a person has fallen asleep (by measuring eye closure) and can also determine if a driver has entered a hypnotic state (by measuring the blink rate of the eyes). Also, a person may be awake and not looking at the road ahead, and should be warned.

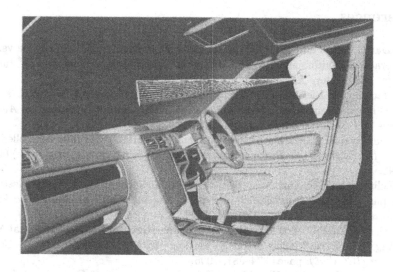

Fig. 9. Driver Performance Visualisation.

7   Conclusions

In this paper, we presented a vision-based human-machine interface. The interface is able in real-time reliably, accurately and robustly measure the 3D position and orientation of the face, as well as the user's gaze direction. The system is non-intrusive and passive, thereby making it a natural interface. Presently, this interface is the most advanced of its kind. In the course of this research project, we solved the longstanding problems of processing video images sufficiently fast enough to achieve reliable results, coping with different users and varying lighting conditions, as well as developing automatic error recovery mechanisms.

We believe that in the near future, vision-based interfaces will revolutionise the way people work with machines, and will open up a huge range of new applications. We have demonstrated the usefulness of the interface in two applications for motor vehicles. The interface could also be applied to measuring human performance in psychological experiments, ergonomic design, as well as products for the disabled and in video games for the entertainment industry.

Acknowledgements

Special thanks are extended to the students and research colleagues at the Robotic Systems Lab who contributed to the system described in this paper, particularly Tim Edwards, Jochen Heinzmann, Yoshio Matsumoto, Sebastien Rougeaux and Rhys Newman. Thanks are also extended to the anonymous referees.

References

1. T. Darrel, A.P. Pentland, "Attention-driven Expression and Gesture Analysis in an Interactive Environment", *Proceedings of the International Workshop on Automatic Face- and Gesture-Recognition*, pp. 135-140, 1995.
2. A. Jacquin, A. Eleftheriadis, "Automatic location tracking of faces and facial features in video sequences", *Proceedings of the International Workshop on Automatic Face- and Gesture-Recognition*, pp. 142-147, 1995.
3. A.Azarbayejani, T.Starner, B.Horowitz, and A.Pentland. Visually controlled graphics. *IEEE Trans. on Pattern Analysis and Machine Intelligence*, 15(6):602–605, 1993.
4. A.Zelinsky and J.Heinzmann. Real-time Visual Recognition of Facial Gestures for Human Computer Interaction. In *Proc. of the Int. Conf. on Automatic Face and Gesture Recognition*, pages 351–356, 1996.
5. Black and Yaccob. Tracking and Recognizing Rigid and Non-rigid Facial Motions Using Parametric Models of Image Motion. In *Proc. of Int. Conf. on Computer Vision (ICCV'95)*, pages 374–381, 1995.
6. A.Gee and R.Cipolla. Fast Visual Tracking by Temporal Consensus. *Image and Vision Computing*, 14(2):105–114, 1996.
7. J.Heinzmann and A.Zelinsky. 3-D Facial Pose and Gaze Point Estimation using a Robust Real-Time Tracking Paradigm. In *Proc. of the Int. Conf. on Automatic Face and Gesture Recognition*, 1998.
8. R.Stiefelhagen, J.Yang, and A.Waibel. Tracking Eyes and Monitoring Eye Gaze. In *Proc. of Workshop on Perceptual User Interface (PUI'97)*, 1997.
9. Y. Matsutmoto, T. Shibata, K. Sakai, M. Inaba, and H. Inoue. Real-time Color Stereo Vision System for a Mobile Robot based on Field Multiplexing. In *Proc. of IEEE Int. Conf. on Robotics and Automation*, pages 1934–1939, 1997.

Applying Ant Algorithms and the No Fit Polygon to the Nesting Problem

Edmund Burke and Graham Kendall

The School of Computer Science and Information Technology
The University of Nottingham
Nottingham NG7 2RD UK
{ekb,gxk}@cs.nott.ac.uk

Abstract. In previous work solutions for the nesting problem are produced using the no fit polygon (NFP), a new evaluation method and three evolutionary algorithms (simulated annealing (SA), tabu search (TS) and genetic algorithms (GA)). Tabu search has been shown to produce the best quality solutions for two problems. In this paper this work is developed. A relatively new type of search algorithm (ant algorithm) is developed and the results from this algorithm are compared against SA, TS and GA. We discuss the ideas behind ant algorithms and describe how they have been implemented with regards to the nesting problem. The evaluation method used is described, as is the NFP. Computational results are given.

Keywords. Genetic Algorithm, Search, Ant Algorithms, No Fit Polygon, Simulated Annealing

1 Introduction

In the nesting problem it is necessary to place a number of shapes onto a larger shape. In doing so the shapes must not overlap and they must stay within the confines of the larger shape. The usual objective is to minimise the waste of the larger shape. Only two dimensions, height and width, of the shapes are considered and the larger piece is sometimes considered to be of infinite height so that only the width of the placements need be checked. This is a realistic assumption for the real world as the larger shapes are sometimes rolls of material which can be considered as being of infinite length for the purposes of the placement procedure. In this paper a number of assumptions are made. The height of the bin (the larger piece) is considered infinite, although it remains the aim of the evaluation function to minimise this height. Only convex polygons are considered. Only one bin is used (that is, there is no concept of filling a bin and having to start another). Only guillotine cuts are allowed (that is, a cut must be made from one edge to the other). In future research, once we have shown the method to be effective, we will relax these constraints.

Ant Algorithms (described in section 4) are a relatively new search mechanism, having been introduced by Marco Dorigo in his PhD thesis [16] and in [9, 10]. Initially the algorithm was applied to the Travelling Salesman Problem (TSP) [19].

N. Foo (Ed.): AI'99, LNAI 1747, pp. 453–464, 1999.

In [25], when ant algorithms are compared against an iterated local search (ILS) algorithm, which is known to be among the best algorithms for the TSP, the ant algorithm finds a better average solution quality than ILS. In recent years, ant algorithms have also been applied to other problems. A recent paper [23] compares the results of an ant algorithm using test problems from QALIB. The ant algorithm was able to beat GRASP (greedy randomized adaptive search procedure) in all cases. The algorithm was also applied to a real world case and found a solution that was 22.5% better then the current one (although it is noted that this figure must be read with caution as other factors have been included in the real world planning). Ant Algorithms have also been applied to Vehicle Routing Problems (VRP) [4]. In [4] the algorithm could not improve on published results but it is seen as a viable alternative when tackling VRP's. Scheduling [11, 21], Graph Colouring [12], Partitioning Problems [22] and Telecommunication Networks [15] have also been addressed by ant algorithms. An overview of ant algorithms can be found in [17, 18].

We are not aware of any published work that applies ant algorithms to the nesting problem. The only work we have seen is a presentation at Optimization 98, University of Coimbra, Portugal (10-22 July 1998), which used an ant algorithm to place shapes. Unfortunately the conference did not publish proceedings.

In [3] the no fit polygon (NFP) is introduced (described in section 2). The NFP is also used in [1] to calculate the minimum enclosing rectangle for two irregular shapes. Albano [2] used a heuristic search method to place irregular pieces onto stock sheets. The search is based on the A* algorithm but some restrictions are introduced due to the size of the search space. For example the heuristic function is not admissible. Their evaluation function, f(n), is given by g(n) + h(n) where g(n) is the cost of the solution so far, which is a measure of the waste that cannot be used in later placements. h(n) is a heuristic measure that estimates the amount of waste in the optimal solution should the current piece be included in the placement. If it were possible to find suitable values for h(n) then an optimal solution could be found. However, this is not possible so only "good" solutions can be found. The Albano and Sapuppo approach makes use of the no fit polygon when deciding where pieces should be placed. More recently [24] also used the no fit polygon. Pieces are placed onto the stock sheet one at a time. The location of the next piece is calculated using the no fit polygon. Once the best placement has been found the piece is added to the partial solution and the next piece is placed. Oliveira experimented with three evaluation functions when considering the placement of the next piece.

This paper presents a method to produce solutions to the nesting problem. We employ an ant algorithm and compare our results with other evolutionary and meta-heuristic algorithms that have been applied to the same problem [5, 6].

2   No Fit Polygon

The no fit polygon (NFP) determines all arrangements that two arbitrary polygons may take such that the polygons touch but do not overlap. If we can find the NFP for two given polygons then we know we cannot move the polygons closer together in order to obtain a tighter packing. In order to find the placements we proceed as follows (see fig. 1). One of the polygons (P_1) remains stationary. The other polygon,

P_2, orbits around P_1, staying in contact with it but never intersecting it. Both polygons retain their original orientation. That is, they never rotate. As P_2 moves around P_1 one of its vertices (the reference point – shown as a filled circle) traces a line (this becomes the NFP).

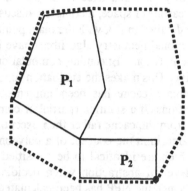

Fig. 1. No Fit Polygon

Fig. 1 shows the starting (and finishing) positions of P_1 and P_2. The NFP is shown as a dashed line. It is slightly enlarged so that it is visible. In fact, some of the edges will be identical to some of the edges of P_1 and P_2. Once we have calculated the NFP for a given pair of polygons we can place the reference point of P_2 anywhere on an edge or vertex of the NFP in the knowledge that P_2 will touch but not intersect P_1. In order to implement a NFP algorithm it is not necessary to emulate one polygon orbiting another. [13] and [14] present an algorithm that works on the assumption that (for convex polygons only) the NFP has its number of edges equal to the number of edges of P_1 and P_2. In addition, the edges of the NFP are simply copies of the edges of P_1 and P_2, suitably ordered. To build the NFP it is a matter of taking the edges of P_1 and P_2, sorting them and building the NFP using the ordered edges.

3   Evaluation

3.1   Placing the Polygons

In order to fill the bin we proceed as follows. The first polygon to be placed is chosen and becomes the stationary polygon (P_1 in the example above). The next polygon (P_2 from the above example) becomes the orbiting polygon. Using these two polygons the NFP is constructed. The reference point of P_2 is placed on each vertex of the NFP and for each position the convex hull for the two polygons is calculated. Once all placements have been considered the convex hull that has the minimum area is returned as the best packing of the two polygons. This larger polygon now becomes the stationary polygon and the next polygon is used as the orbiting polygon. This process is repeated until all polygons have been processed. As each large polygon (i.e. output from the convex hull operation) is created, its width is checked. If this exceeds the width of the bin, then a new row within the bin is started. In this case the polygon which forced the width of the bin to be exceeded becomes the stationary polygon. That is, the large polygon built thus far forms one row and the next row is constructed using a single polygon as a starting point.

There are a number of points that need to be considered when using the above evaluation method. For reasons of space, a complete discussion of these points cannot be provided but they are detailed in [7], with the main points summarised below

A number of computational geometry algorithms have been implemented in order to effectively manipulate polygons. Executing computational geometry algorithms is computationally expensive. This makes the evaluation function the slowest part of the algorithm. In view of this a cache has been implemented which retains n (user defined) previous evaluations. If a solution (partial or complete) is in the cache then the results are retrieved from the cache rather than executing the evaluation function. To further improve the algorithm the concept of a polygon type has been introduced. This allows polygons which are identical to be classified together so that the cache can work at a higher level of abstraction when deciding if a partial or complete solution is in the cache. Once the NFP has been calculated there may be a number of optimal placements for the two polygons being evaluated (that is, the convex hulls have equal area). In this case, the convex hull to use is selected at random. However, all the optimal solutions are stored in the cache so that if the solution (partial or complete) is seen again, one of the other convex hulls could be selected.

If n polygons have been evaluated the solutions in the cache for the nth polygon will be influenced by earlier evaluations. However, even though the convex hulls with the lowest area has been chosen earlier in the evaluation, this may not be the best choice once other polygons are added to the solution. Therefore, it may be beneficial to reevaluate a complete solution even if it is stored in the cache. In order to accommodate this a reevaluation parameter was introduced which, with some probability, forces a solution to be re-evaluated even if it is in the cache.

3.2. Evaluating the Placement

Our cost function is based on that used in [20]. It can be stated as follows

$$(\sum_{1}^{n}((1-(UsedRowArea/TotalRowArea))^2)*k)/n \qquad (1)$$

Where   *UsedRowArea* is the total area of the polygons placed in that row
         TotalRowArea is the total area of the bin occupied by that row
         k if a factor simply to scale the result. We used 100 but 1 could be used
         n is the number of rows in the bin

In words, we are trying to minimise the area used by each row.

This evaluation function is preferable to the more obvious method of simply measuring the bin height as, using the bin height, many solutions will map to the same evaluation function. This makes it much more difficult to effectively explore the search space. In previous work, we have compared these two different types of evaluation and we find that the above function (1) produces better quality solutions; which is the same experience as reported in [20].

4   Ant Algorithms

4.1   Ant Algorithms and the TSP

Ant algorithms are based on the real world phenomena that ants, despite being almost blind, are able to find their way to a food source and back to their nest, using the shortest route. In [19] this phenomena is discussed by considering what happens when an ant comes across an obstacle and it has to decide the best route to take around the obstacle. Initially, there is equal probability as to which way the ant will turn in order to negotiate the obstacle. If we assume that one route around the obstacle is shorter than the alternative route then the ants taking the shorter route will arrive at a point on the other side of the obstacle before the ants which take the longer route. If we now consider other ants coming in the opposite direction, when they come across the same obstacle they are also faced with the same decision as to which way to turn. However, as ants walk they deposit a pheromone trail. The ants that have already taken the shorter route will have laid a trail on this route so ants arriving at the obstacle from the other direction are more likely to follow that route as it has a deposit of pheromone. Over a period of time, the shortest route will have high levels of pheromone so that all ants are more likely to follow this route. This form of behaviour is known autocatalytic behaviour. There is positive feedback which reinforces that behaviour so that the more ants that follow a particular route, the more desirable it becomes.

To convert this idea to a search mechanism for the Travelling Salesman Problem (TSP) there are a number of factors to consider. Below is a summary of [19].

At the start of the algorithm one ant is placed in each city. Time, t, is discrete. t(0) marks the start of the algorithm. At t+1 every ant will have moved to a new city and the parameters controlling the algorithm will have been updated. Assuming that the TSP is being represented as a fully connected graph, each edge has an *intensity of trail* on it. This represents the pheromone trail laid by the ants. Let $T_{i,j}(t)$ represent the intensity of trail edge (i,j) at time t. When an ant decides which town to move to next, it does so with a probability that is based on the distance to that city and the amount of trail intensity on the connecting edge. The distance to the next town, known as the *visibility*, n_{ij}, is defined as $1/d_{ij}$, where, d_{ij}, is the distance between cities i and j.

At each time unit *evaporation* takes place. This is to stop the intensity trails building up unbounded. The amount of evaporation, p, is a value between 0 and 1.

In order to stop ants visiting the same city in the same tour a data structure, Tabu, is maintained. This prevents ants visiting cities they have previously visited. $Tabu_k$ is defined as the list for the kth ant which holds the cities that have already been visited.

After each ant tour the trail intensity on each edge is updated using the following formula

$$T_{ij}(t + n) = p \cdot T_{ij}(t) + \Delta T_{ij} \qquad (2)$$

where

$$\Delta T_{ij}^{k} = \begin{cases} \dfrac{Q}{L_k} & \text{if the kth ant uses edge(i, j) in its tour} \\ & \text{(between time } t \text{ and } t+n) \\ 0 & \text{otherwise} \end{cases} \qquad (3)$$

This represents the trail substance laid on edge (i, j) by the kth ant between time t and t+n. Q is a constant and L_k is the tour length of the kth ant. Finally, we define the transition probability that the kth ant will move from city i to city j.

$$p_{ij}^{k}(t) = \begin{cases} \dfrac{[T_{ij}(t)]^{\alpha} \cdot [n_{ij}]^{\beta}}{\sum k \in allowed_k \;\; [T_{ik}(t)]^{\alpha} \cdot [n_{ik}]^{\beta}} & \text{if } j \in allowed_k \\ \\ 0 & \text{otherwise} \end{cases} \qquad (4)$$

where α and β are control parameters that control the relative importance of trail versus visibility.

4.2   Ant Algorithms and the Nesting Problem

Using the TSP ant system as a model, an ant system has been developed for the nesting problem using the no fit polygon and the evaluation method described in section 3. Each polygon can be viewed as a city in the TSP and these are fully connected so that there is an edge between each polygon and every other. An ant is placed at each city (polygon) and using the trail and visibility values (formula 4) the ant decides which polygon should be visited (placed) next. Once an ant has placed all the polygons the edge trail values are updated. The edge trail values are calculated using the value returned from evaluating the nesting. This is equivalent to using the tour length in the TSP (L_k in formula 3).

Using the method described above we can use very similar formulae to those described in [19] (and shown above (2, 3, 4)), with some minor amendments. Visibility is now defined as how the polygon, just placed, fits with the piece about to be placed. For example, two rectangles of the same dimensions would fit together with no waste so the visibility would be high. Two irregular shapes, when placed together, may result in high wastage. This would result in a low visibility value. In order to calculate the visibility, the combined area of the two pieces is divided by the best placement of the two shapes (using the NFP). That is

$$n_{ij} = TotalArea_{ij} / BestPlacement_{ij} \qquad (5)$$

Where i is the polygon just placed and j is the polygon about to be placed. This returns a value between 0 and 1. In order to improve the speed of the algorithm all the visibility values are calculated at the start of the algorithm and held in a cache. The transition probability is defined as the probability of a polygon being placed next taking into account the polygons placed so far and the visibility of the next polygon. The same formula as 4, above, can be used to calculate the transition probability.

5   Testing and Results

5.1   Test Data

Two problems were used in our testing. The packing shown in fig. 2 is from [8]. The reason that this data was chosen is because it consists of convex polygons and the optimum is known. The only change made is to multiply the measurements in the original paper by a factor of two. This assists us when displaying results.

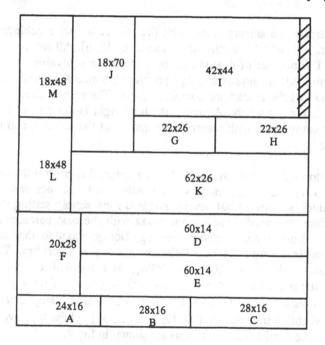
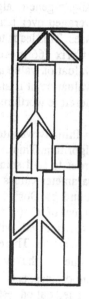

Fig. 2. Test Data 1   Fig. 3. Test Data 2

Our algorithms will not be able to find the optimum. The first two rows (A, B, C and D, E, F) can be constructed without problems. However, to find the optimum for the third row the polygons, would need to be presented in the order of G, H, I, J, K, L and M. The optimal solution could be built until the last polygon (M) came to be placed. At this time, due to the convex nature of the large polygon that had been built, the final polygon will not be placed in the position shown. In fact, the final polygon would be placed on a new row. Under these circumstances the total bin height would be 188 (as opposed to the optimal height of 140). Therefore, the permutation

ABCDEFGHIJKLM produces a bin height of 188. We accept that we will never achieve a value of 140 but would like to get as close as possible to this figure.

The second problem (fig. 3) is taken from the real world. A company has to cut polycarbonate shapes from larger stock sheets. The solution shown (fig. 3) is one stock sheet on a given day. Like the first problem, this is constrained by the convex properties of the algorithm. For example, the bottom four shapes cannot be packed in the way they have been as once three of the shapes have been packed, the fourth shape cannot be placed in the position shown. The same is true for the four shapes above (excluding the rectangle). The height of the stock sheet is 23940 units. Its width is 6240 units. Due to the convex properties of the algorithm it is not possible to achieve the solution shown but our main aim is to see if ant algorithms can match or beat the solutions we have already obtained.

5.2   Results

In this section we compare the ant algorithm with the results we have achieved using a genetic algorithm, tabu search and simulated annealing [5, 6]. All results are averaged over ten runs. The number of evaluations performed are equivalent in all cases. This leads to runtimes that are approximately equivalent (about 300 seconds on a Cyrix 166 processor) so that the results are compared fairly. The results show the evaluation value as well as the bin height. Although the bin height is not part of the evaluation, it is an important measure with regard to the quality of the solution and is therefore worth recording.

Initially we attempted to find suitable values for the parameters that control the ant algorithm. This aspect of advanced search remains an art, rather than a science and, in order to find suitable values we carried out several hundred runs simply setting the parameter values at random. We used these results, along with the best parameters found by Dorigo [19], to conduct more selective testing. Dorigo reported that the value of Q (the constant in formula 3) had little effect on the algorithm. We experimented with various values, {1, 10, 100, 1000}, and reached a similar conclusion. Therefore in the remainder of our tests Q = 100. In order to find a good value for the evaporation parameter, $p \in \{0.1, 0.5, 0.9\}$ was tested, using a trail importance, $\alpha = 1$ and a visibility importance, $\beta \in \{0, 1, 2, ..., 30\}$. These tests were carried out on test data 1. The results from these tests are shown in fig. 4.

All tests in fig. 4 show the highest evaluation when $\beta = 0$. This is expected as when $\beta = 0$ the search is effectively transformed into randomised greedy search with multiple starting points. All three runs also show, in the early stages, a downward trend as the visibility parameter increases. With $p = 0.1$ the evaluation values are generally higher than when p is 0.5 or 0.9. $p = 0.5$ performs better than when $p = 0.9$, at least in the early stages of the algorithm (until $\beta = 19$). In the latter stages, when the visibility is high, the graph has either flattened or is showing an upward trend for all values of p. Again, this would be expected as having too high a visibility starts returning the algorithm to a greedy search. This is due to the effect of the intensity trail becoming diminished. $p = 0.5$ as a good value agrees with the results in [19] in

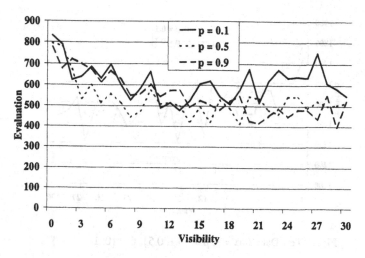

Fig. 4. Test Data 1, $\alpha = 1$, $p = \{0.1, 0.5, 0.9\}$, $\beta = \{0, 1, ..., 30\}$

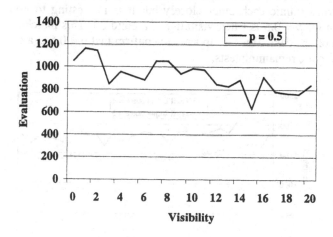

Fig. 5. Test Data 1, $\alpha = 5$, $p = 0.5$, $\beta = \{0, 1, ..., 20\}$

which it was reported that this was the best value found for p. In [19] the best value for α was found to be 1 (which is the value used above). In order to see if our algorithm agrees with this a test was carried that that set $p = 0.5$, $\alpha = 5$ and $\beta = \{0,1,..., 20\}$. Fig. 5 shows that this set of parameters produces worse results than when $\alpha = 1$. None of the tests produce an evaluation below 600, which was consistently done when $\alpha = 1$ (fig. 4)

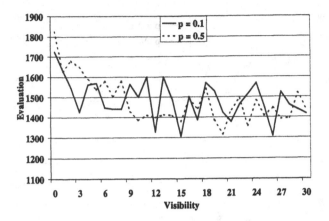

Fig. 6. Test Data 2, $\alpha = 1$, $p = \{0.1, 0.5\}$, $\beta = \{0, 1, ..., 30\}$

Having established a good parameter set we used test data 2 to confirm these values. Fig. 6 shows two runs that compare the effect of p (evaporation) on test data 2. In fact the two runs mimic each other closely but it is interesting to note that the lowest evaluation for $p = 0.5$ is when visibility is around 20. This matches the result from the first set of test data. This test appears to confirm that p = 0.5 is a good choice and we used this in the remaining tests.

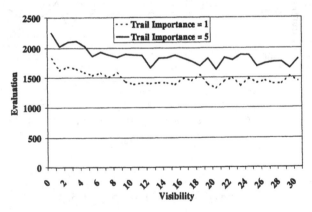

Fig. 7. Test Data 2, $\alpha = \{1, 5\}$, $p = 0.5$, $\beta = \{0, 1, ..., 30\}$

Fig. 7 shows the effect of trail importance, $\alpha = \{1, 5\}$ using test data 2. It shows that a higher value of α leads to inferior solutions. Again, this confirms the results from the first set of test data. In summary, the best results were achieved on both sets of test data when $\alpha = 1$, $p = 0.5$, $\beta = 20$. The best results we have achieved using other search algorithms [5, 6] and the modified Falkenauer function are shown in table 1. We also show the best results from the ant algorithm using the parameters just described.

Table 1. Results using the same test data with different search algorithms

Search Method	Test Data 1		Test Data 2	
	Evaluation	Bin Height	Evaluation	Bin Height
Genetic Algorithm	516.41	179.00	1377.99	30478.50
Tabu Search	323.77	165.80	1006.75	27566.40
Simulated Annealing	397.01	170.80	1661.77	33052.20
Ant Algorithm	412.97	173.20	1316.85	29316.60

Tabu search finds the best quality solutions of the algorithms implemented but the ant algorithm compares favourably with simulated annealing, performing significantly better with test data 2. The ant algorithm also out performs the other population based search method (genetic algorithm).

6   Summary

This is the first time that ant algorithms have been applied to the nesting problem and the results are encouraging. Ant algorithms out perform genetic algorithms and provide a viable alternative to simulated annealing, although more work is required for it to compete with tabu search. We will continue using ant algorithms in our future research when we will tackle more complex problems as well as relaxing some of the constraints we outlined above. The parameters to the ant algorithm are critical and we plan to carry out more work in this area. In addition we plan to look at hybridsation to combine ant algorithms with other search techniques in order to produce even better solutions.

References

1. Adamowicz, M., Albano, A. 1976. Nesting Two-Dimensional Shapes in Rectangular Modules. Computer Aided Design, 8, 27-33
2. Albano, A., Sappupo, G. 1980. Optimal Allocation of Two-Dimensional Irregular Shapes Using Heuristic Search Methods. IEEE Trans. Syst., Man and Cybernetics, SMC-10, pp 242-248
3. Art, R.C., 1966. An Approach to the Two-Dimensional Irregular Cutting Stock Problem. Technical Report 36.008, IBM Cambridge Centre.
4. Bullnheimer B., R.F. Hartl and C. Strauss (1999). An Improved Ant system Algorithm for the Vehicle Routing Problem. The Sixth Viennese workshop on Optimal Control, Dynamic Games, Nonlinear Dynamics and Adaptive Systems, Vienna (Austria), May 21-23, 1997, to appear in: Annals of Operations Research (Dawid, Feichtinger and Hartl (eds.): Nonlinear Economic Dynamics and Control, 1999
5. Burke, E., K., Kendall, G. 1999. Applying Evolutionary Algorithms the No Fit Polygon to the Nesting Problem. Accepted for The 1999 International Conference on Artificial Intelligence (IC-AI '99), Monte Carlo Resort, Las Vegas, Nevada, USA, 28 June - 1 July 1999

6. Burke, E., K., Kendall, G. 1999. Applying Simulated Annealing and the No Fit Polygon to the Nesting Problem. Accepted for WMC (World Manufacturing Congress), September 1999, Durham, UK
7. Burke, E., K., Kendall, G. 1999. Evaluation of Two Dimensional Bin Packing using the No Fit Polygon. Submitted to CIE26 (Computers and Industrial Engineering), December, 1999, Melbourne, Australia
8. Christofides, N., Whitlock, C. 1976. An Algorithm for Two_Dimensional Cutting Problems. Operations Research, 25, 30-44
9. Colorni A., M. Dorigo & V. Maniezzo (1992). An Investigation of Some Properties of an Ant Algorithm. Proceedings of the Parallel Problem Solving from Nature Conference (PPSN 92), Brussels, Belgium, R.Männer and B.Manderick (Eds.), Elsevier Publishing, 509-520
10. Colorni A., M. Dorigo & V. Maniezzo (1992). Distributed Optimization by Ant Colonies. Proceedings of the First European Conference on Artificial Life, Paris, France, F.Varela and P.Bourgine (Eds.), Elsevier Publishing, 134-142
11. Colorni A., M. Dorigo, V. Maniezzo and M. Trubian (1994). Ant system for Job-shop Scheduling. JORBEL - Belgian Journal of Operations Research, Statistics and Computer Science, 34(1):39-53. [116]
12. Costa D. and A. Hertz (1997). Ants Can Colour Graphs. Journal of the Operational Research Society, 48, 295-305
13. Cunninghame-Green, R. 1989. Geometry, Shoemaking and the Milk Tray Problem. New Scientist, 12, August 1989, 1677, pp 50-53
14. Cunninghame-Green, R., Davis, L.S. 1992. Cut Out Waste! O.R. Insight, Vol 5, iss 3, pp 4-7
15. Di Caro G. & Dorigo M. (1998). AntNet: Distributed Stigmergetic Control for Communications Networks. Journal of Artificial Intelligence Research (JAIR), 9:317-365
16. Dorigo M. (1992). Optimization, Learning and Natural Algorithms. Ph.D.Thesis (in italian), Politecnico di Milano, Italy, in Italian
17. Dorigo M. and G. Di Caro (1999). The Ant Colony Optimization Meta-Heuristic. In D. Corne, M. Dorigo and F. Glover, editors, New Ideas in Optimization, McGraw-Hill, in press
18. Dorigo M., G. Di Caro & L. M. Gambardella (1999). Ant Algorithms for Discrete Optimization. Artificial Life, 5(2), in press
19. Dorigo M., V. Maniezzo & A. Colorni (1996). The Ant System: Optimization by a Colony of Cooperating Agents. IEEE Transactions on Systems, Man, and Cybernetics-Part B, 26(1):29-41
20. Falkenauer, E. 1998. Genetic Algorithms and Grouping Problems. John Wiley and Sons
21. Forsyth P. and A. Wren (1997). An Ant System for Bus Driver Scheduling. Presented at the 7th International Workshop on Computer-Aided Scheduling of Public Transport, Boston, August 1997
22. Kuntz P., P. Layzell and D. Snyers (1997). A Colony of Ant-like Agents for Partitioning in VLSI Technology. Proceedings of the Fourth European Conference on Artificial Life, P. Husbands and I. Harvey, (Eds.), 417-424, MIT Press
23. Maniezzo V. and A. Colorni (1999). The Ant System Applied to the Quadratic Assignment Problem. IEEE Transactions on Knowledge and Data Engineering, to appear
24. Oliveira, J.F., Gomes, A.M., Ferreira, S. 1998. TOPOS A new constructive algorithm for nesting problems. Accepted for ORSpektrum
25. Stützle T. and M. Dorigo (1999). ACO Algorithms for the Traveling Salesman Problem. In K. Miettinen, M. Makela, P. Neittaanmaki, J. Periaux, editors, Evolutionary Algorithms in Engineering and Computer Science, Wiley, 1999

Fisheye Matching: Viewpoint–Sensitive Feature Generation Based on Concept Structure
Extended Summary

Yasufumi Takama[1] and Mitsuru Ishizuka[2]

[1] Interdisciplinary Graduate School of Science and Engineering,
Tokyo Institute of Technology, 4259 Nagatsuta, Midori-ku,
Yokohama, 226-8502, Japan
[2] Dept. of Information & Communication Engineering, School of Engineering,
University of Tokyo, 7-3-1 Hongo, Bunkyo-ku, Tokyo, 113-8656, Japan

Abstract. In this paper, we propose an extended Vector Space Model (VSM) called Fisheye Matching method, which generates features related to the users' viewpoints based on an electronic dictionary. We have also developed a GUI system employing Fisheye Matching method, which can help users order the vast collection of documents in several ways employing the users' viewpoint information extracted by the Fisheye Matching method.

When a user gets some ideas from papers or articles, he may organize his thoughts by relating incoming information with knowledge which already exists in his mind. This process is getting harder for him in proportion to the volume of information which he considers, and it is useful to illustrate a concept structure on a paper or on a display, which leads to reducing his confusion. We assert that ordering documents while reading is an effective way of dealing with the vast collection of documents, and the systems which assist such processes should be able to find relations among documents based on users' viewpoints/interests. From this point of view, we have proposed an extended VSM called *Fisheye Matching* method [1] to perform vector matching on the vector space sensitive to users' viewpoints. Each feature in the Fisheye Matching method is generated as a set of words which belong to the same concept (meaning) in a dictionary[1]. Choosing concepts (features) appropriate for the users' viewpoints from a dictionary, a vector space is constructed so that the matching results can be expected to be more preferable for them. We have also proposed the algorithm to find concepts appropriate for the users' viewpoints from training sets of documents. Furthermore, each concept in a dictionary has a heading information, which can be presented explicitly to the users as a kind of their viewpoint information. Some experiments on document retrieval tasks have been performed, and Table 1 shows parts of concepts found and used as features during the experiments. From both this table and its precision property, it was confirmed that the

---

[1] We have used the EDR electronic dictionary developed by Japan Electronic Dictionary Research Institute, Ltd. : http://www.iijnet.or.jp/edr/

N. Foo (Ed.): AI'99, LNAI 1747, pp. 465–466, 1999.

Table 1. Examples of concepts extracted as features in the case of retrieving documents about medical topics

ID	Heading Term	Group Words (stemmed)
3f98b3	value of health	diseas sickne health ...
444506	component of living body	protei immuno choles dna
30f6da	internal organs	eye heart lung knee ...
3f969e	disease	syndro aids cancer cold ...
44479c	medical supplies	drug medici laxati acid ...
30f6f7	medical instruments	bandag cathet glasse ...

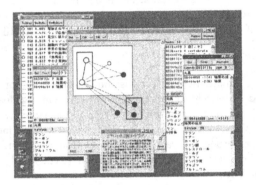

Fig. 1. Fview: GUI system for document ordering support

Fisheye Matching method can not only retrieve documents in which the users take interest, but also supply them with useful information on their viewpoints.

We have also developed the GUI system which assists users to order documents with the Fisheye Matching method (Fig. 1). By using the Fisheye Matching method, the system can extract the users' viewpoint information from the diagrams produced by them, which information cannot be used by the system only to retrieve documents suited for the users' current interests, but also to indicate the similarity among documents of which they may not be aware. Furthermore, the users' viewpoint information are also presented to them as a list of heading information of extracted concepts. Several students actually used this system, and it has been confirmed that an effective assist for users can be achieved.

References

1. Takama, Y., Ishizuka, M.: Fish–eye matching: A document organizing function based on the extraction of user's viewpoint using concept structure. Journal of the Japanese Society for Artificial Intelligence, Vol. 14 (1). (1999) 93–101(in Japanese)

A Procedural Approach for Rule Based Update
Extended Summary

Sai Kiran Lakkaraju and Yan Zhang

School of Computing and Information Technology
University of Western Sydney
Nepean Kingswood, NSW 2747, Australia
{slakkara,yan}@cit.nepean.uws.edu.au

Abstract. We consider the knowledge base update in which a knowledge base is realised by a normal logic program and can be updated with an inserting or deleting update rule. In this paper we propose a SLDNF resolution based procedure to implement this kind of rule based update. We prove a correctness theorem for our approach under the stable model semantics and show that a minimal change criterion is also satisfied in the underlying update formalization.

1 Introduction

The knowledge base is realised as a normal logic program. Basically, rule based update addresses the following problem: Given an initial knowledge base and an update rule, how to update the initial knowledge base such that whenever the body of the update rule is achieved in the initial knowledge base, the head and the body of the update rule are achieved in the resulting knowledge base.

2 Definitions and Concepts

A *rule* is of form:

$$A_0 \leftarrow A_1, \cdots, A_m, not B_{m+1}, \cdots, not B_n, \tag{1}$$

where $A_0, \cdots, A_m, B_{m+1}, \cdots, B_n$ are atoms of language $\mathcal{L}$. Now we specify a *Knowledge Base* is a normal logic program. An *update rule* is a rule with one of the following two forms:

$$Q \leftarrow P_1, \cdots, P_m, not P_{m+1}, \cdots, not P_n, \tag{2}$$

$$not Q \leftarrow P_1, \cdots, P_m, not P_{m+1}, \cdots, not P_n. \tag{3}$$

Rule (2) is called the *inserting update rule*, while rule (3) is called the *deleting update rule*. In our formalism, an update is a transformation on knowledge bases.

N. Foo (Ed.): AI'99, LNAI 1747, pp. 467–468, 1999.
© Springer-Verlag Berlin Heidelberg 1999

3   Formal Descriptions

It is well known that it is possible that a SLDNF tree may include infinite branch. In this case, no result is able to be proved from the SLDNF resolution proof. To avoid this problem, in our update context, we assume that during the update, each SLDNF tree is *finite*. We present the main procedures named checking, Insert/Delete update.

Algorithm 1. Checking($\mathcal{P}, r$)
Function: Checking the body of an update rule r in logic program $\mathcal{P}$.
Input: A logic program (knowledge base) $\mathcal{P}$ and an update rule r of form (2) or (3), where the body of r consists of $P_1, \cdots, P_m, notP_{m+1}, \cdots, notP_n$.
Output: A Boolean value True or False.
The function of algorithm **Checking($\mathcal{P}, r$)** is to check if the body of the update rule r is achieved by $\mathcal{P}$.

Algorithm 2. Insert/ DeleteUpdate($\mathcal{P}, r$)[1]
Function: Update $\mathcal{P}$ with a inserting/deleting update r.
Input: A logic program $\mathcal{P}$ and a update rule r of form (2) or(3).
Output: An updated logic program $\mathcal{P}'$.

Example 1. Consider a knowledge base $\mathcal{P} : \{A \leftarrow B, A \leftarrow notB, B \leftarrow C,\}$ and an inserting update rule r_1: $C \leftarrow A$. Suppose we update $\mathcal{P}$ with r_1. Firstly, by using algorithm **Checking($\mathcal{P}, r$)**, it is clear that A is derivable from $\mathcal{P}$. So **Checking($\mathcal{P}, r$)** =True. Then by algorithm **InsertUpdate($\mathcal{P}, r_1$)**, we simply obtain a unique resulting knowledge base $\mathcal{P}' = \mathcal{P} \cup \{C \leftarrow\}$. Note that the body A in r_1 can still be proved from $\mathcal{P}'$.

Now we consider to update $\mathcal{P}'$ with a deleting update rule r_2: $notA \leftarrow$. Consider the SLDNF tree for $\mathcal{P}' \cup \{\leftarrow A\}$ To make the successful branch fail, there are several options according to our algorithm. Firstly, if we choose node "$\leftarrow C$" as n_i and "$\Diamond$" as n_{i+1}, then to make this branch fail, we may remove fact $C \leftarrow$ from $\mathcal{P}'$ according to the case (1) in Algorithm 2. However, this does not achieve our purpose that $\mathcal{P}'' \not\vdash A$, where $\mathcal{P}'' = \mathcal{P}' - \{C \leftarrow\}$. This is clear that even if rule $A \leftarrow B$ cannot used to derive A in $\mathcal{P}''$, A still can be proved fror $\mathcal{P}''$ through rule $A \leftarrow notB$. According to Algorithm 2, we have to consider other options then. The only way available for us is to choose node "$\leftarrow A$" as node n_i and node "$\leftarrow B$" as node n_{i+1}. Then from the case (3) in the algorithm, we need to remove rule $A \leftarrow B$ from $\mathcal{P}'$. Therefore, after updating $\mathcal{P}'$ with the deleting update rule r_2, we obtain the resulting knowledge base $\mathcal{P}''$:
$\{ A \leftarrow notB, B \leftarrow C, C \leftarrow. \}$.
This example also shows that it is *not* always the situation of adding or removing simple facts from the initial knowledge base in order to achieve the update. □

---

[1] The detailed explanation for this algorithm is referred to our full paper.

Learning Logic Programs with Local Variables from Positive Examples

M.R.K. Krishna Rao and Abdul Sattar

[1] Computer Science Department, James Cook University,
Townsville 4811, Australia,
krishna@score.is.tsukuba.ac.jp
[2] School of Computing and Information Technology,
Griffith University, Nathan, Brisbane, Australia, 4111,
sattar@cit.gu.edu.au

Abstract. We present a **polynomial time** algorithm to learn a rich class of logic programs (called one-recursive programs) from positive examples alone. This class of programs uses the divide-and-conquer methodology and contains a wide range of programs such as **append, reverse, merge, split, delete, insertion-sort, preorder and inorder traversal of binary trees, polynomial recognition, derivatives, sum of a list of numbers** and allows local variables.

Main Results

Starting from the influential work of Gold [2], a lot of effort has gone into the development of a rich theory about inductive inference and the classes of concepts which can be learned from both positive (examples) and negative data (counterexamples), and the classes of concepts which can be learned from positive data alone. The study of inferability from positive data alone is important because negative examples are hard to obtain in practice. See [3] for further discussion and references.

The existing literature mainly concerns with either nonrecursive programs or recursive programs without local variables (variables occurring in the body of a clause but not occurring in the head of that clause), usually with a further restriction that programs contain a unit clause and at most one recursive clause with just one atom in the body. In other words, standard programs for various sorting and tree traversal algorithms, which use local variables, are beyond the scope of these results.

As established by many authors in the literature, learning recursive logic programs, even with the above restrictions, is a very difficult problem. We approach this problem from a programming methodology angle and propose an algorithm to learn a class of logic programs, that use divide-and-conquer methodology. Our endeavor is to develop an inference algorithm that learns a very natural class of programs so that it will be quite useful in practice. We measure the naturality of a class of programs in terms of the range of programs it covers from a standard Prolog book such as [5]. To summarize, major contributions of the paper

N. Foo (Ed.): AI'99, LNAI 1747, pp. 469–471, 1999.

include: (1) polynomial time learning algorithm that does not need negative examples and does not ask any queries, (2) ability to handle programs with local variables enlarging the class of learnable programs (and thereby enlarging the scope of applications) and (3) the novel approach to the learning problem from the programming methodology point of view.

One-Recursive Programs

The divide-and-conquer approach and recursive subterms are the two central themes of our class of programs. The predicates defined by these programs are recursive on the leftmost argument. The leftmost argument of each recursive call invoked by a caller is a recursive subterm of the arguments of the caller.

Notation: In atom $p(\mathbf{s}; \mathbf{t})$, $\mathbf{s}$ is the sequence of input terms and $\mathbf{t}$ is the sequence of output terms. The *size* of $\mathbf{t}$, denoted by $|\mathbf{t}|$, is the total number of variables, constants and functions occurring in it. In the following, *builtins* is a (possibly empty) sequence of atoms with built-in predicates having no output positions.

Definition 1 A linearly-moded well-typed logic program [3] without mutual recursion is *one-recursive* if each clause in it is of the form

$$p(\mathbf{s_0}; \mathbf{t_0}) \leftarrow builtins, \ p(\mathbf{s_1}; \mathbf{t_1}), \cdots, p(\mathbf{s_k}; \mathbf{t_k}) \qquad \text{OR}$$
$$p(\mathbf{s_0}; \mathbf{t_0}) \leftarrow builtins, \ p(\mathbf{s_1}; \mathbf{t_1}), \cdots, p(\mathbf{s_k}; \mathbf{t_k}), q(\mathbf{s}; \mathbf{t})$$

such that (a) $\mathbf{s_i}$ is same as $\mathbf{s_0}$ except that the leftmost term in $\mathbf{s_i}$ is a recursive subterm of the leftmost term in $\mathbf{s_0}$ for each $1 \leq i \leq k$, (b) the terms in $\mathbf{t_i}$, $i \geq 1$ are distinct variables not occurring in $\mathbf{s_0}$, the terms in $\mathbf{s_0}$ are variables or one of the first two generic-expressions[1] of the asserted types and $|\mathbf{s_0}| \geq |\mathbf{t_0}|$.

Due to space limitations, the learning algorithm is not presented. See [4] for it.

Comparison with Related Works

The works of Arimura et. al. [1] and Krishna Rao [3] are closely related to ours.

1. Our results are generalizations of the results in Arimura et. al. [1] and the class of context-free transformations (no local variables) considered in [1] is a proper subclass of our class of one-recursive programs.
2. In contrast to the results of Krishna Rao [3], we investigate **polynomial time learnability** from positive data alone (no negative examples).

---

[1]   The terms void and tree(T_1, X, T_2) are the first two generic-expressions of the type Binary $-$ tree. Similarly, [ ] and [H|L] are the first two generic-expressions of the type List. The first two generic-expressions of any given recursive type are unique upto variable renaming. The *recursive subterms of* tree(T_1, X, T_2) are T_1 and T_2. Similarly, L is the recursive subterm of [H|L].

References

1. H. Arimura, H. Ishizaka and T. Shinohara (1992), *Polynomial time inference of a subclass of context-free transformations*, Proc. of COLT'92, pp. 136-143.
2. E.M. Gold (1967), *Language identification in the limit*, Information and Control **10**, pp. 447-474.
3. M.R.K. Krishna Rao (1996), *A class of Prolog programs inferable from positive data*, Proc. of ALT'96, Lecture Notes in Computer Science **1160**, pp. 272-84.
4. M.R.K. Krishna Rao and A. Sattar (1999), *Learning logic programs with local variables from positive examples*, Technical Report, Griffith University.
5. L. Sterling and E. Shapiro (1994), *The Art of Prolog*, MIT Press.

Estimating Problem Value in an Intelligent Tutoring System Using Bayesian Networks

Michael Mayo and Antonija Mitrovic

Department of Computer Science, University of Canterbury
Private Bag 4800, Christchurch, New Zealand
mjm185@student.canterbury.ac.nz, tanja@cosc.canterbury.ac.nz

SQL-TUTOR [1,2] is an ITS for teaching the database language SQL to upper-level undergraduate students taking database courses. Students using SQL-TUTOR work through a series of problems where the solution is an SQL statement. Although SQL-TUTOR does not solve problems, it does have an ideal solution (IS) for each one. A correct student solution (SS) to a problem may be the same as the IS although there can be more than one correct solution. Figure 1 is an example of a problem in SQL-TUTOR, its IS, and an incorrect SS.

Problem	Ideal Solution	Student Solution
List the titles of all movies that have a critics rating.	`SELECT title FROM movie WHERE NOT(critics='NR');`	`SELECT title FROM movie WHERE critics NOT 'NR';`

Fig. 1. An SQL problem, its ideal solution, and a student's incorrect solution.

SQL-TUTOR models students using Ohlsson's Constraint-Based Modeling (CBM) [3]. CBM proposes the modeling of domains as a set of constraints of the form *(Cr, Cs)*. *Cr* specifies the set of student solutions to which the constraint is relevant, and *Cs* specifies the subset of the relevant student solutions where the constraint is satisfied. Each constraint has an associated feedback message that can be displayed if the constraint is violated. In figure 1, the student has violated constraint 168 and the feedback message is: *Make sure NOT is in the right place in the WHERE clause.*

Until recently, problem selection in SQL-TUTOR was based on one simple rule: the first problem relevant to the single constraint that the student has most frequently violated in the past was selected. In a real classroom, this is an overly simple strategy because it was often the case that selected problems were either too complex or too simple. Our research has been aimed at improving this situation.

We propose a new problem selection module based on Bayesian belief networks (BBNs) [4]. Our approach involves applying the following two steps to each potential next problem p. Firstly, the system predicts, for each constraint c, the potential teaching effects of p. The main calculation is of the posterior probability $P(Performance_{c,p} = VIOLATED)$, the probability that c will be violated by the student should he/she attempt problem p. Constraint violations lead to feedback messages, and constraint-specific feedback is the main way that students learn constraints in SQL-TUTOR. A BBN for this is depicted in figure 2. $RelevantIS_{c,p}$ is the probability of c being relevant to p's IS. The value for this node is always known with certainty. $RelevantSS_{c,p}$ is the probability of c being relevant to p's SS. $Mastered_c$ is the

N. Foo (Ed.): AI'99, LNAI 1747, pp. 472–473, 1999.

probability of the student having mastered the constraint c. Finally, $Performance_{c,p}$ predicts the behaviour of the student on constraint c. All the nodes except $Performance_{c,p}$ are binary variables. $Performance_{c,p}$ is a three-valued node taking values {SATISFIED, VIOLATED, NOT-RELEVANT}.

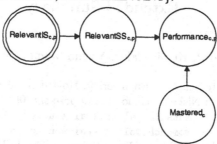

Fig. 2. A Bayesian network for predicting student performance on a single constraint.

The second step is to summarise the predictions for p over all the constraints c. Currently this is done by counting the number of constraints for which $P(Performance_{c,p} = \text{VIOLATED}) > 0.45$. This number, *Feedbacks*, is then compared to the student's *OptimalFeedback*. The value of p is (- | *Feedbacks* − *OptimalFeedback* |). That is, p has a high value if *Feedbacks* is close to or the same as *OptimalFeedback*. The rationale behind this rule is that if the predicted number of feedback messages exceeds *OptimalFeedback* then the student will be overwhelmed with information and the teaching effects of each message will be discounted. On the other hand, if the number of feedback messages is less than optimal, then student learning will be inefficient and the problems may be too easy. Presently *OptimalFeedbacks* starts at 2 and increases linearly with the competence level of the student.

After the student has submitted his solution, the prior probabilities of mastery for each constraint, $P(Mastered_1)$, $P(Mastered_2)$...etc, are updated if the constraint was relevant to the SS.

We have performed several off-line experiments using student history logs from previous user studies of SQL-TUTOR, comparing problems that were selected by the original system against problems that would have been selected by the proposed system. In the majority of cases, the new system outperforms the old system.

Future research will investigate the acquisition of probabilities for the BBNs both subjectively (by an expert) and from data. We also plan an on-line evaluation of the new system in a user study.

1. Mitrovic A., 1998. Learning SQL with a Computerized Tutor, Proc. 29th SIGCSE Tech. Symposium, 307-311.
2. Mitrovic A., Ohlsson, S., 1999. Evaluation of a constraint-based tutor for a database language, Int. J. Artificial Intelligence in education, 10, 3-4, to appear.
3. Ohlsson S., 1994. Constraint-based Student Modeling. In: Greer, J.E., McCalla, G.I. (eds.): Student Modeling: the Key to Individualized Knowledge-based Instruction. NATO ASI Series, Vol. 125. Springer-Verlag, Berlin, 167-189.
4. Pearl J. 1988. Probabilistic reasoning in intelligent systems: networks of plausible inference (revised 2nd edition). Morgan Kauffman, USA.

Evaluation of Number-Kanji Translation Method of Non-Segmented Japanese Sentences Using Inductive Learning with Degenerated Input

Extended Summary

Masafumi Matsuhara[1], Kenji Araki[2], Yoshio Momouchi[1], and Koji Tochinai[2]

[1] Graduate School of Engineering, Hokkai-Gakuen University,
Minami 26 Nishi 11, Chuo-ku, Sapporo-shi, 064-0926 Japan.
matsu@ai.eli.hokkai-s-u.ac.jp
momouchi@eli.hokkai-s-u.ac.jp
[2] Graduate School of Engineering, Hokkaido University,
Kita 13 Nishi 8, Kita-ku, Sapporo-shi, 060-8628 Japan.
{araki,tochinai}@media.eng.hokudai.ac.jp

Abstract. Our proposed method enables us to promptly and easily input Japanese sentences into a small device. All the keys for input are only 12 keys, which are 0, 1,..., 9, * and #. Therefore, we are able to input one *Kana* character per one keystroke. Furthermore, the system based on our method automatically generates the dictionary adapted to the target field because the system automatically acquires words by using inductive learning. The system is improved by its own learning ability.

1 Outline

The procedure for our proposed method consists of translation process, proofread process, learning process and feedback process in this order.

A user inputs the string of numbers corresponding to the pronunciation of the intended Japanese sentence by only 12 keys[1][2]. In translation process, the input sentence is translated into *Kanji-Kana* mixed sentence by using the words dictionary. The words in the words dictionary are applied in order of the higher certainty degree[3][4]. The certainty degree is based on the situation of the acquisition of the word, the rate of the correct translation and the appearance degree of neighboring characters[5]. If the translation result has errors, proofread process is performed. The user judges whether it is correct or not and proofreads it. In learning process, words are extracted by comparing the input sentence with its proofread translation result[3][4]. They are compared using their common segments. The extracted words are registered into the words dictionary. In feedback process, the certainty degree for the word in the words dictionary is updated. Thus, this system repeats these processes and improves.

N. Foo (Ed.): AI'99, LNAI 1747, pp. 474–475, 1999.

2 Evaluation Experiment

The system based on our proposed method has been developed for the experiment. The input data for the experiment are some sections of UNIX MANUAL. The number of characters is 122,000 in the input data. The initial dictionaries are empty for evaluation of adaptability of this method. The system translates each input sentence systematically. The results are evaluated by the translation rates to the number of input characters. The correct rate, erroneous rate and unfixed rate are calculated by each proportion to the number of input characters.

3 Results and Considerations

The rate of the correct translation increases as the input data increase. It shows that the system has acquired the words and improved. When the section of input data changes, the rate of correct translation decreases. The reason is that the number of the unregistered words in the words dictionary increases because the field of input data changes. However, the correct rate increases again because this system acquires words for the new fields. Thus, this system adapted to the new field immediately. The final rate of the correct translation is about 85[%].

Acknowledgements

This work is also partially supported by the Grants from the Government subsidy for aiding scientific researches (No. 09878070, No. 10680367) of Japan Society for the Promotion of Science and the High-Tech Research Center of Hokkai-Gakuen University.

References

1. Kushler, C.: AAC USING A REDUCED KEYBOARD. *Proc. CSUN98*, Los Angeles, America, Mar. 1998.
2. Higashida, M.: A Fully Automated Directory Assistance Service that Accommodates Degenerated Keyword Input Via Telephone. *Proc. PTC'97*, pp. 167–174, Honolulu, Hawaii, Jan. 1997.
3. Araki, K., Momouchi, Y. and Tochinai, K.: Evaluation for adaptability of Kana-Kanji translation of non-segmented Japanese Kana sentences using inductive learning. *Conference Working Papers of PACLING-II*, pp. 1–7, Brisbane, Australia, Aug. 1995.
4. Araki, K., Takahashi, Y., Momouchi, Y. and Tochinai, K.: Non-Segmented Kana-Kanji Translation Using Inductive Learning. *The Transactions of The Institute of Electronics, Information and Communication Engineers*, Vol. J79-D-II, No. 3, pp. 391–402, Mar. 1996.
5. Nagao, M., Mori, S.: A New Method of N-gram Statistics for Large Number of n and Automatic Extraction of Words and Phrases from Large Text Data of Japanese. *proc. COLING94*, pp. 2093–2100, Kyoto, Japan, Aug. 1994.

A Serving Agent for Integrating Soft Computing and Software Agents

Extended Summary

Zili Zhang and Chengqi Zhang

School of Computing and Mathematics
Deakin University, Geelong Victoria 3217, Australia
{zili,chengqi}@deakin.edu.au

Abstract. This paper discusses the design and implementation of a serving agent for integrating soft computing and software agents.

1 Introduction

When we build agent-based application systems, we need to integrate the symbolic and computational intelligence concepts and technologies for the design of truly robust, flexible and adaptive intelligent systems. One of the important computational intelligence technologies is known as soft computing (SC). The principal members of SC are fuzzy logic (FL), neural network (NN), genetic algorithm (GA) etc. The SC technologies such as FL, NN, and GA are complementary rather than competitive. Thus, it is necessary to equip a multi-agent system with different kinds of SC techniques, the more, the better. The problem left is how to integrate these SC techniques into multi-agent systems.

In recent years an increasing number of researchers have been working in the field of hybrid systems in an attempt to find new ways to integrate two or more technologies to tackle complex real world problems[1]. Some of the research work such as the IMAHDA architecture[2], and the PREDICTOR system (see [1] Ch.9) etc. involved in multi-agent systems. The way for integrating SC technologies and software agents (SA) in these systems is to embed the SC technologies in each individual SA. There are some limitations of such approaches: (1) It is impossible to embed many SC technologies within a single SA. Otherwise, the SAs will be overloaded; (2) It is not flexible to add more SC technologies to or delete some unwanted one from the software agent.

Our idea for integration is to move the SC abilities from the front-end agents in a multi-agent system to the back-end as independent SC agents. We equip these SC modules with the communication ability using KQML (Knowledge Query and Manipulation Language), and under the support of JATLite (http://java.stanford.edu/java_agent). According to Genesereth's statement: *An entity is a software agent if and only if it communicates correctly in an agent communication language such as ACL*[3], we call these SC modules agents. The emphasis of our work is trying to provide a universal approach to incorporate different SC technologies into multi-agent systems. There are two notable features

N. Foo (Ed.): AI'99, LNAI 1747, pp. 476–477, 1999.

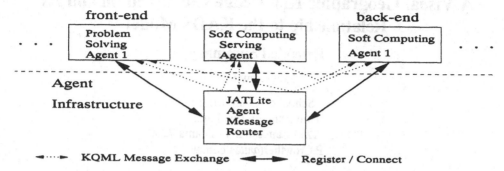

Fig. 1. Architecture of the Soft Computing Agent Society

in such a system: (1) Our approach shown here makes every problem solving agent easily access all the SC technologies available in the system; (2) The ability to add and delete SC agents dynamically as needed.

2 Modeling and Implementation of SC Serving Agent

The architecture of such a system is shown in Figure 1. The internal structure of SC serving agent consists of KQML message interpreter (KMI), *SC_Agent* maintenance, and *SC_Agent_List* (database). The KMI represents the interface between KQML router and the SC serving agent. The SC agent list maintenance module has three functions: Add a node which contains the SC agent's name, ability, and ontology to the list (database); Delete a node from the list; and retrieve the list to find out SC agents with specific ability. Actually, we combined its implementation with KQML message interpreter.

3 Concluding Remarks

A prototype has been implemented according to the architecture. There are two principal features that we mentioned Section 1.

Our goal is to provide a platform independent soft computing support environment. By using this support environment, the multi-agent system developers need only to build the problem solving agents for a specific application. Then the problem solving agents can use all the SC technologies in the system when necessary.

References

1. S. Goonatilake and S. Khebbal (Eds.), Intelligent Hybrid Systems, Wiley, Chichester, 1995.
2. R. Khosla and T. Dillon, Engineering Intelligent Hybrid Multi-Agent Systems, Kluwer Academic Publishers, Boston, 1997.
3. M. R. Genesereth and S. P. Ketchpel, Software Agents, Commun. ACM, Vol.37, No.7, 1994, 48-53.

A Visual Geographic Knowledge Classification and Its Relationship to the KADS Model

Extended Summary

Paul Crowther

School of Computing
University of Tasmania
PO Box 1214 Launceston Tasmania 7250
P.Crowther@utas.edu.au

Abstract. Visual geographic knowledge which can be extracted from satellite remote sensing images has characteristics which are not commonly found in non-visual domains. Traditionally geographic expert systems have worked either at the pixel level of raster images or the object level of vector images. This has shortfalls when knowledge acquisition from a human image interpreter has to be incorporated into an expert system to aid interpretation.

A framework for the classification of visual geographic knowledge will be presented that expands beyond the traditional per-pixel model and has been used as the theoretical basis of a knowledge acquisition toolkit, KAGES (Knowledge Acquisition for Geographic Expert Systems) [2]. This model will be compared with the KADS knowledge model to show the relationship with modeling in a non-visual environment.

Keywords: Expert systems, geometric or spatial reasoning, knowledge acquisition.

1 A Proposed Classification of Geographic Knowledge

Visual (including spatial) knowledge presents special problems for knowledge acquisition. Recognising visual features is easy for a human although the cognitive processing is complex. Describing those features without the use of diagrams is difficult. It is easy for a human expert to show what something looks like, but far more difficult to describe it in words, and more difficult again to describe it in terms of rules [3]. Given that geographic knowledge is visual and that domain experts work with images, a graphical system is required. The following classification is derived from and expands on those of McKeown et al [4] and Armstrong [1]. It is more rigorous and incorporates non-visual knowledge. It consists of six levels of knowledge which are:

- **Primitive Knowledge** about the identification of scene primitives, a readily identifiable object which cannot be subdivided into smaller named entities.
- **Relationship Knowledge** of the spatial relationships between scene primitives in terms of their proximity, orientation and degree of overlap.
- **Assembly Knowledge,** used to define collections of objects which form identifiable spatial decompositions.

N. Foo (Ed.): AI'99, LNAI 1747, pp. 478-479, 1999.

- **Non-Visual Knowledge** which helps refine classifications developed using visual knowledge including labelling of scene primitives and spatial relationships consisting of temporal knowledge of how a scene changes over time, algorithmic knowledge, including how to combine bands and heuristic knowledge of a non-visual nature.
- **Consolidation Knowledge** used to resolve and evaluate conflicting information.
- **Interpretation Knowledge** of how to combine the other five types of knowledge to produce a classified image.

2   Visual Knowledge and KADS

KADS (Knowledge Acquisition and Development System) consists of a four-layer model of expertise [5]. In terms of the suggested geographic knowledge classification, Primitive, Relationship and Assembly Knowledge are forms of knowledge at the Domain Level under the KADS methodology as is Heuristic knowledge in the Non-Visual category. This knowledge could be used in a variety of different ways to produce products showing different aspects of an area covered by an image.

Consolidation Knowledge on the other hand requires knowledge of how the rules are to be applied and is knowledge at the Inference level. Algorithmic Knowledge which contains knowledge of image band combinations and when they should be applied is also at the Inference level.

The Task Level in the KADS system is represented by Interpretation Knowledge and shows how to apply the problem solving strategy to the whole image set.

There is no equivalent of the Strategy Layer. In future extensions this would be knowledge of alternate ways of classifying images

References

1. Armstrong, M. P, 1991, Knowledge Classification and Organization, in Buttenfield B.P. and McMaster, R.B., Map Generalization: Making Rules for Knowledge Representation, Longman, Ch. 5, pp.86 - 102.
2. Crowther, P., Hartnett, J., 1996, Knowledge Acquisition for Expert Systems used with a Geographic Expert Systems, Proceedings of *AURISA '96*, Hobart.
3. Kweon, I. S. and Kanade, T., 1994, Extracting Topographic Terrain Features From Elevation Maps, *CVGIP: Image Understanding*, Vol. 59, No. 2, pp.171 - 182.
4. McKeown, D. M., Harvey, W.A. and Wixson, L.E., 1989, Automating Knowledge Acquisition for Aerial Image Interpretation, *Computer Vision and Graphics*, Vol. 46, pp. 37 - 81.
5. Wielinga, B. J., Schreiber, A. T. and Breuker, J. A., 1992, KADS: A Modelling Approach to Knowledge Engineering, *Knowledge Acquisition*, Vol. 4, No. 1.

A Constraint Optimization Framework
for
MultiAgent Anytime Scheduling

Extended Summary

Bill Havens[1], Randy Goebel[2], Jean Berger[3] and René Proulx

[1] Computing Science, Simon Fraser University, Burnaby, B.C., Canada V5A 1S6
email: havens@cs.sfu.ca

[2] Computing Science, University of Alberta, Edmonton, Alberta, Canada T6G 2H1
email: goebel@cs.ualberta.ca

[3] Department of National Defense, Defense Research Establishment Val Cartier,
Val Cartier, Québec, email: jean.berger@drev.dnd.ca

1. Introduction

Dynamic real-time scheduling applications are characterized by rapidly changing requirements and the need for timely response. We employ an approach combining *Constraint Programming* and *Anytime Algorithms* within a *Multiagent* framework. Agents implement various heuristic optimization algorithms which work concurrently on the same scheduling problem. A best solution is always available from some agent and agents collaborate to improve each others intermediate results. A multiagent resource allocation scheme for agents based on economic portfolio management is described. A report presenting the multiagent architecture and our early experiments using the prototype system is available [Havens *et.al* 99].

Our challenge has been to develop a viable planning system for *Tactical Air Mission Planning/Scheduling* (TAMP/S) which can effectively schedule helicopter missions under rapidly changing conditions in real-time. A mission is naturally viewed as a *vehicle routing problem* (VRP) [Christofides *et al.*, 76] with *time windows* (VRPTW) [Solomon, 87] and capacity constraints. VRPTW problems are NP-hard in general. Given an incoming stream of aircraft mission requests, the problem is to assign both helicopters and flight crews to satisfy these missions. The task is also a multiple criteria optimization problem to minimize delay, maximize utilization, *et cetera*.

We require initially feasible solutions but desire much better suboptimal solutions as time and computing resources allow. Hence the application is an anytime planning problem. We describe here our multiagent approach to this application. Given the strict time constraints, we do not use complete exhaustive scheduling methods. Neither do we rely on traditional batch-oriented constraint solvers and optimization methods. Instead, we exploit two compatible approaches: 1) heuristic constraint optimization; and 2) multiagent systems.

Heuristic constraint optimization methods can often find suboptimal solutions rapidly for even very large real-world scheduling problems (Minton *et al.*, 1990; Glover *et al.*, 1993) but such performance cannot be guaranteed. As well, pure heuristic ("greedy") methods often can find very good solutions in sublinear time.

N. Foo (Ed.): AI'99, LNAI 1747, pp. 480–481, 1999.
© Springer-Verlag Heidelberg Berlin 1999

Given heuristic search methods producing suboptimal solutions but without any performance guarantees, how can we improve the expected performance of the heuristic methods in an anytime framework? There exists a class of heuristic constraint optimization algorithms, called *iterative repair techniques* (IRT), which can incrementally improve a seed solution (perhaps from a greedy algorithm). Given good greedy algorithms to produce good seed solutions and a stable of good IRT methods, we have the opportunity to apply multiple methods (agents) in concert to the same scheduling problem. Agents both cooperate and compete. Greedy agents assigned the same scheduling problem compete to produce better seed solutions. IRT agents assigned the same seed solution compete to produce better and better anytime solutions over time. IRT agents cooperate by using seed solutions produced previously by other IRT agents.

2. Overview of the TAMP/S Architecture

Our multiagent architecture is illustrated in the figure below which includes:

1. a *Representation Manager* for creating new mission problems and assigning an initial greedy planning agent.

2. an *Environment Manager* for dynamically modifying the constraints under which the planning agents operate.

3. a *Solution Manager* for controlling the working set of anytime planning agents.

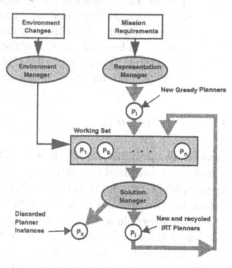

Initially, the Solution Manager gives each greedy planner sufficient resources to compute a heuristic answer and each IRT planning agent a seed and a fixed allocation of resources. All IRT planners report back their best solution found so far. The Solution Manager then adjusts its resource allocations to the planning agents based on a market economy metaphor which measures the both the quality (price) of their present solutions and their rate of improvement (return). If an agent is performing badly relative to the other agents in the working set (portfolio) then it is discarded and another agent created in its place.

3. Conclusion

A prototype version of the TAMP/S has been implemented and tested using two greedy seed algorithms and a TABU search [Glover93] IRT method. Initial experiments suggest that the architecture is indeed appropriate for anytime scheduling applications where good (but suboptimal) solutions are acceptable and the environment (problem specifications and external situation) changes unpredictably over time.

Evolving Modular Neural Networks Using Rule-Based Genetic Programming

Extended Summary

Bret Talko*, Linda Stern, and Les Kitchen

Department of Computer Science and Software Engineering
The University of Melbourne, Melbourne, Australia.
{talko,linda,ljk}@cs.mu.oz.au

Abstract. This paper describes a new approach for evolving recurrent neural networks using Genetic Programming. A system has been developed to train weightless neural networks using construction rules. The network construction rules are evolved by the Genetic Programming system which build the solution neural networks. The use of rules allows networks to be constructed modularly. Experimentation with decomposable Boolean functions has revealed that the performance of the system is superior to a non-modular version of the system.

1 Introduction

Genetic programming (GP) is a modification of the genetic algorithm which evolves variable-sized tree structures rather than fixed-length bitstrings. GP has been applied to neural network (NN) learning ([1,3]) and can automatically determine the necessary number of network neurons and the connection weights to solve the problem, as well as being able to produce recurrent networks. The GP-based Cellular Encoding system of Gruau [2] has shown the ability to exploit the decomposability of problems.

This paper summarizes a novel GP-based system for evolving neural networks (the GPNN system) that implement functions and can take advantage of decomposable problems. The system evolves weightless neural networks and evolves the activation functions of each neuron. Experimentation has demonstrated the ability of the system to find solution networks to test problems and shows that decomposable problems are efficiently learned.

2 System Description and Results

The GPNN system uses GP to evolve a collection or population of tree-structured rules. The rules, when read and executed in a left-to-right order, construct a

---

* Bret Talko is now with the Defence Science and Technology Organisation in Australia. The authors would like to gratefully acknowledge the support of the Agent Laboratory in the department.

N. Foo (Ed.): AI'99, LNAI 1747, pp. 482–483, 1999.

neural network. The GP system must find a set of rules which when executed constructs a neural network that solves the specified problem. Rules exist to add a neuron, add a connection, and to change the activation function of neurons. Full details of this method can be found in [4].

The GPNN system uses weightless networks. The operation of the network is determined solely by the activation functions of the neurons and the connections between the neurons. The activation functions are represented and evolved as arithmetical expression trees.

Networks are situated on two-dimensional grids, with neurons being located at grid vertices. Initially only the input and output neurons are on the grid, along with an initial neuron that is used to grow the full network. Each neuron is assigned a *class* number. Multiple neurons may share the same class. Rules specify which classes of neurons will apply the rules to themselves. By having multiple neurons share the same class, a rule can be simultaneously executed by multiple neurons. This ability is particularly useful for forming modular networks that have multiple copies of subnetwork modules.

Experiments using the system for learning 16 decomposable Boolean functions have been carried out. The functions have 4 input variables and two output variables, are decomposable in the sense that they are formed as an amalgamation of two identical smaller functions having two input variables and one output variable.

A non-modular system was used whereby rules can only affect at most one neuron instead of multiple neurons.

The performance of the modular system was found to be better than or equal to the performance for the non-modular system.

3 Conclusion

This paper presented a new approach to evolving neural networks. Experimental results indicate it is suited to solving decomposable problems efficiently.

References

1. Sung-Bae Cho and Katsunori Shimohara. Modular neural networks evolved by genetic programming. In *Proceedings of the IEEE International Conference on Evolutionary Computation*, volume 1. IEEE, 1996.
2. Frédéric Gruau. Cellular encoding of genetic neural networks. Technical Report RR92-21, Laboratoire de l'Informatique du Parallélisme, Ecole Normale Supérieure de Lyon, France, May 1992.
3. John R. Koza and James P. Rice. Genetic generation of both the weights and architecture for a neural network. In *IJCNN-91-Seattle: International Joint Conference on Neural Networks*, volume 2, pages 397–404, Seattle, Washington, USA, 8–14 July 1991. IEEE Press.
4. Bret Talko. A rule-based approach for constructing neural networks using genetic programming. Master's thesis, Department of Computer Science and Software Engineering, The University of Melbourne, Australia, March 1999.

A Trajectory Approach to Causality

(Extended Summary)

Victor Jauregui[1], Maurice Pagnucco[2], and Norman Foo[1]

[1] Knowledge Systems Group, School of Computer Science and Engineering,
University of New South Wales, NSW 2052, Australia.
{vicj,norman}@cse.unsw.edu.au.
[2] Computational Reasoning Lab, Department of Computing, Division of ICS,
Macquarie University, NSW 2109, Australia.
morri@ics.mq.edu.au.

Generally, having specified the *direct effects* of an action, approaches for handling the *ramification problem* in *reasoning about action and change* favour the the use of domain constraints to infer any additional *indirect effects*. This usually also requires the augmentation of the domain description with a dynamical specification, both syntactically and semantically, in order to accurately model the direction of the causal forces that govern the dependencies between various parts of the system.

In this paper we deviate from the convention that causal rules act to restore the integrity of the *static constraints* describing the system and argue, in a spirit similar to Denecker *et al.* [1], for the de-coupling of the causal rules describing the dynamical aspects of a system from a static domain description. Moreover, we argue for the dynamical nature of causation and extend propositional logic into a simple, abstract language for modelling the causal dependencies of dynamical systems, furnishing an underlying state transition semantics in the spirit of Thielscher [6] and Sandewall [5].

For example, consider the simple act of holding a pebble. If we release the pebble it will fall; coming to a rest on the floor. This intuition can be readily captured if we denote that 'the pebble is being held' by h, and that it is 'elevated' by e, and supply the constraint: $e \rightarrow h$.

If we modify our scenario by replacing the pebble with an egg we would, nonetheless, wish to model this system in terms of e and h, based on the symmetries in the domains and the desire to preserve the *modularity* of the description.

The difficulty arises in augmenting the system description to establish a *static* constraint that would lead to the egg breaking in terms of the properties e and h. We argue that neither $e \wedge \overline{h} \rightarrow b$, reflecting that an egg released while elevated will break, nor $\overline{e} \wedge \overline{h} \rightarrow b$, with the intuition that on reaching the ground the egg will break, offer accurate and faithful descriptions of the system. In particular, the second alternative, *while reflecting our intuition dynamically, does not do so correctly in a static context*, as provided above.

To model such systems we propose a *trajectory-based approach* in which the history of states through which a system evolves, in terms of a chain of indirect effects, is used to model the dynamics of a domain. We proceed to argue for the many-fold advantages of such an approach.

N. Foo (Ed.): AI'99, LNAI 1747, pp. 484–485, 1999.

Firstly, we need not augment the scenario above (e.g., by adding a fluent 'f' to indicate 'falling') to specify the dynamical behaviour of the system. Instead, we claim that the statement:

$$(e \rightsquigarrow \bar{e}) \wedge \bar{h} \Rightarrow b,$$

with the intended interpretation: 'If the system undergoes a transition from e to $\bar{e}$ (i.e., $e \rightsquigarrow \bar{e}$) while the egg was not held ($\bar{h}$), then the egg should break (b) in the ensuing state'; can *concisely* and accurately model the intended dynamical behaviour of the system where, otherwise, we encounter difficulties in obtaining a faithful static description. Moreover, by not introducing a 'falling' fluent f, as mentioned above, we avoid the possible introduction of indeterminacy and *cyclic* fluent dependencies that can appear when attempting to model *transient* properties (such as the *event* of 'falling').

Secondly, we inherit all the modelling features of a state-transition based approach, such as the possible dependence of an action on the intermediate effects that a system has assumed on course to its current state. This provides us with the *versatility* to model systems that include both sequential (time evolving) and simultaneous/concurrent effects within a common framework.

Thirdly, by augmenting a typical propositional language with the connective ($\rightsquigarrow$), having the interpretation indicated above, we can, at an abstract level, provide an ontological basis for events (e.g., 'falling') by associating them with multiple states within a trajectory. This allows us to generalise state-transition based approaches to modelling dynamical systems by using the trajectory as the fundamental descriptive and operational entity through which to obtain the dynamical properties of a system. Moreover, it permits us to retain a minimal state description (in terms of the number of basic properties—or *fluents*—of the system) and use this to extrapolate the dynamical state of the system.

Comparisons with respect to McCain & Turner [4] are also made while attempts to reconcile, translate or reformulate the approach outlined above with other formalisms in the literature (e.g., Denecker *et al.* [1], Gustafsson & Doherty [2], Lin [3], etc.) are left for further investigation.

References

1. Denecker, M., Dupré D., Belleghem, K. An Inductive Definition Approach to Ramifications. In *Linköping Electronic Articles in Computer & Information Science*. Linköping University Electronic Press, 3, 1998.
2. Gustafsson, J., Doherty, P. Embracing Occlusion in Specifying the Indirect Effects of Actions. In *Proc. of the 5th International Conference on Knowledge Representation & Reasoning*. 1996.
3. Lin, F. Embracing Causality in Specifying the Indirect Effects of Actions. In *Proc. of the 14th International Joint Conference on Artificial Intelligence*, 1995.
4. McCain, N., and Turner, M. A Causal Theory of Ramifications and Qualifications. In *Proc. of the 14th International Joint Conference on Artificial Intelligence*, 1995.
5. Sandewall, E. Transition Cascade Semantics and First Assessment Results for Ramification. Preliminary report. IDA Technical Report, 1996.
6. Thielscher, M. Ramification and Causality. *Artificial Intelligence*, 89:317-364, 1997.

Bayesian Reasoning for Diagnosing Student Misconceptions about Decimals
(Extended Summary)

Elise Dettmann[1], Ann Nicholson[2], Liz Sonenberg[1], Kaye Stacey[3], and Vicki Steinle[3]

[1] Department of Computer Science and Software Engineering
The University of Melbourne, Parkville, Victoria, 3052
[2] School of Computer Science and Software Engineering
Monash University, Clayton, Victoria, 3168
[3] Department of Science and Mathematics Education
The University of Melbourne, Parkville, Victoria, 3052
eas@cs.mu.oz.au

Abstract. Work in Bayesian student modelling is described, which draws on extensive analyses of the way that students think about the decimal numeration system. The model will form the basis of an adaptive tutoring system. We present an initial model and discuss issues arising.

This paper describes initial work towards the diagnostic component of a tutoring system, based on Bayesian modelling, that will monitor students engaged in various tasks, including standard tests [2], teaching activities, and interactive games involving the use of decimal notation [1], and adjust its choice of a next activity for the student according to its current classification of the student.

We briefly describe the extensive background data available that provide key parameters for the student model.

The student model used in this work derives from a very detailed analysis of student thinking based on data from over 2500 Victorian school students [3]. Understanding decimals is a complex task, which requires bringing together a web of related ideas. There are many sources of confusion and many opportunities for partial knowledge to lead children to make errors systematically. In this domain, the ideas that children hold can be grouped into three major categories: A, L and S, and several subcategories. The category of apparent experts (A) comprises students who generally can decide correctly which of two decimals is larger. Some of these students are indeed experts (subcategory ATE), others follow correct rules with little understanding. Others have misconceptions, for example believing that only the first two decimal places have meaning so that 2.4513 and 2.45 are precisely equal. This can be due to analogy with money (subcategory AMO). Students in the longer-is-larger (L) category generally think that longer decimals are larger numbers than shorter decimals and so believe 2.14 is greater than 2.8. The various reasons for this, the subcategories of L, can be diagnosed by careful examination of student responses to various item types.

N. Foo (Ed.): AI'99, LNAI 1747, pp. 486–487, 1999.
© Springer-Verlag Berlin Heidelberg 1999

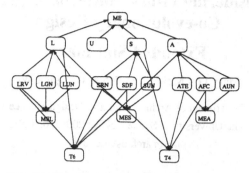

Fig. 1. Bayesian network used in testing

Figure 1 represents a partial model of the decimal domain. The longitudinal data and expert assessment provide the necessary (conditional) probabilities for the model. This model uses only two evidence nodes, corresponding to two types of test items (called Types 4 and 6), four category nodes (A, L, S, U), nodes for 9 of the (eventual 15) subcategories (LRV, LGN, LUN, SDF, SRN, SUN, ATE, AUN, AFC) and 4 dummy nodes included for technical reasons. The priors used in our initial tests are based on data from 294 Grade 5 students.

We conducted 16 tests with different patterns of static evidence using items of types T4 and T6. wich demonstrated that at the category and subcategory levels, the qualitative behaviour of the network was as intended.

As we scale-up, we need to: (i) instrument the games to extract key subsequences to use as additional evidence; (ii) explore the technology of dynamic belief networks to deal with learning over time; (iii) experiment with the effect of students accidentally not performing true-to-type; (iv) observe whether rare thinking patterns (with low priors) will ever be diagnosed and develop methods to give more weight to evidence which has particular significance in certain circumstances. Our model building shows considerable promise and we are optimistic about the next phase.

Acknowledgements The project is partially supported by a grant from the Australian Research Council. The teaching resource web site [1] was developed with the assistance of a grant from the Teaching and Learning (Multimedia and Educational Technologies) Committee at The University of Melbourne. We especially wish to thank the teachers and students who have participated in the project.

References

1. K Stacey, D Chambers, and V Steinle. Decimals project web site. Current address is at http://online.edfac.unimelb.edu.au/485129/DecProj/index.htm.
2. K Stacey and V Steinle. Refining the classification of students' interpretations of decimal notation. *Hiroshima Journal of Mathematics Education*, 6:49–69, 1998.
3. K Stacey and V Steinle. A longitudinal study of children's thinking about decimals: A preliminary analysis. In *Proceedings of the Psychology and Mathematics Education Conference*. Israel, August, 1999.

Reconsidering Fitness and Convergence in Co-evolutionary Design

Extended Summary

Mary Lou Maher and Peter Xianghua Wu

Department of Architectural and Design Science
The University of Sydney, NSW 2006, Australia
mary@arch.usyd.edu.au

Co-evolution is the term used to identify the process in nature in which two or more species interact so intimately that their evolutionary fitness depends on each other. Biological co-evolution has been the inspiration for a class of computational algorithms called co-evolutionary computing. Co-evolutionary design is an approach to design problem solving in which the requirements and solutions of design evolve separately and affect each other. A reconsideration of the purpose of the fitness function and its affect on convergence is necessary since the fitness function changes through the co-evolutionary cycles. The interactions between requirements and solutions of design may possibly add some new variables to both aspects of design, which redefines the search space for requirements and solutions as well as the fitness function. Based on the idea of mutualism, which is one of three types of co-evolution in nature, the interacting populations raise the level of fitness in both, rather than the two populations competing with each other or one population living off the other.

Co-evolutionary design is characterised by having a search space of problem requirements and a search space of problem solutions. The algorithm has two phases, each one corresponding to a simple genetic algorithm. In the first phase, the problem space provides the basis for a fitness function used to evaluate alternatives in the design space. In the second phase, the solution space provides the basis for a fitness function used to evaluate the problem space. Each of the two phases of co-evolutionary design is a search process using a simple GA and unchanging fitness function. Therefore, each phase corresponds to one design focus and a change in phase indicates a change in focus. In co-evolutionary design we need to reconsider concepts of evolution, their counterpart in GAs and their meaning in the co-evolutionary design process.

Fitness: Survival of the fittest in evolution has been translated as a fitness function in simple GAs. This fitness function is the basis for the comparison of alternative solutions. In design, when we let the definition of the fitness function change, the value of the fitness function can no longer serve as the basis for comparison for all alternative designs. The performance of individuals in the solution space can only be compared when they are evaluated using the same fitness function. This makes it difficult to compare the performance of solutions across

N. Foo (Ed.): AI'99, LNAI 1747, pp. 488-489, 1999.

different phases of the co-evolutionary design process. The performance of individuals is used to determine which members of the population "survive", or are selected to participate in the next generation of search. When searching a space, either the problem space P or the solutions space S, the performance is measured by how well the alternatives satisfy the focus. A focus for the search for a design solution is a function of the set of possible design requirements, and a focus for the design requirements is based on the current set of design solution alternatives.

Convergence: Convergence in evolutionary algorithms means that the search process has led to the "best" design in terms of the specified fitness function. Convergence is typically the criteria for termination of the evolutionary search process. Since the fitness function in co-evolutionary design changes from one phase to another, the idea of convergence needs to be reconsidered. This requires a consideration of the purpose of co-evolutionary design as compared to evolutionary search. The purpose of evolutionary search is to find the best solution for a given environment, where the environment is effectively represented by the fitness function. The purpose of co-evolutionary design is to explore both the problem and solution spaces, allowing both to change in reaction to each other, until a satisfactory combination of a problem statement and solution state is found. The exploratory nature of the co-evolutionary process implies that the process should search until the potential for new ideas is reduced. We propose then, that convergence is not related to fitness, but to the similarity of the members of the population. A population in which there is little change in the genotypes of the members when compared to the previous population indicates that the search process has converged.

Termination: The link between convergence and termination in evolutionary algorithms occurs because the convergence to the "best" solution indicates that the search should be terminated. In co-evolutionary design, convergence is determined for each phase of the search, that is, for a given focus, and following the convergence for one focus, another focus is determined and search commences in the other space. This indicates a separation of termination and convergence. We use termination to indicate when the co-evolutionary process should stop, and convergence to indicate when the search in a given space for a given focus should stop. One criterion for termination is the number of cycles of the co-evolution process. This criterion is equivalent to setting a time limit for the design process. Often, the time limit is a major criterion for signalling when exploration of changes in problem and solution should stop. Another criterion for termination is similar to the convergence criterion above − there are no new fitness functions being found. The significance of this criterion is that the algorithm is not able to identify a different focus for the design and therefore, new ideas have been exhausted.

Acknowledgments

This work is supported by a grant from the Australian Research Council.

A Proposal of Generating Artistic Japanese Calligraphic Fonts

Tsuyoshi Nakamura[1], Lifeng He[2], and Hidenori Itoh[1]

[1] Department of ICS, Nagoya Institute of Technology
Gokiso-cho, Showa-ku, Nagoya 466-8555, JAPAN
[2] Faculty of Information Science and Technology, Aichi Prefectural University
Nagakute-cho, Aichi-gun, Aichi 486-0069, JAPAN
tnaka@ics.nitech.ac.jp

1 Introduction

The purpose of this paper is to show a proposal of generating artistic calligraphic fonts. Japanese calligraphic art is to write brush characters by using a writing brush and black ink. Also, it is very popular art in Japan, China and so on. Needless to say, the brush characters are hand writing characters. The artists' pen (brush) pressure, pen speed, and ink quantity are very important factors for the artistic effect. A calligraphic character consists of several brush strokes. In Japanese calligraphic art, the artistic effect appears in the compositions, which are the position of each brush stroke and the stroke shape itself, but here we limit the discussion to scratched and blurred look of calligraphic characters.

Each of scratched and blurred look plays a very important role on brush strokes as essential artistic effect. Scratched look appears on brush strokes, when black ink sometimes does not reach paper from a writing brush. Scratched look is a white part on brush strokes. Similarly, blurred look appears on brush strokes, when black ink runs spread to paper from a writing brush. Blurred look is blurred black part with ink.

2 System Overview

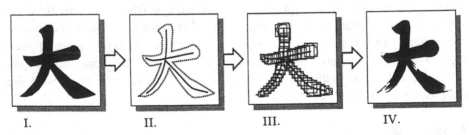

I.   II.   III.   IV.

Fig. 1. a process of generating artistic fonts by the system

N. Foo (Ed.): AI'99, LNAI 1747, pp. 490–491, 1999.

We will show the system which adopts our proposal method to generate artistic fonts. Here is a figure which shows the system overview. See Figure 1. Our proposal method is divided into the following four stages.

I. An original calligraphic font is inputted, and it is translated into a bitmap image format. We call it an original bitmap font.
II. The skeleton of the original bitmap font is detected. We employ the line-thinning algorithm by [Hil69][NESI98] for this task. It goes without saying that the skeleton is bitmap image and represented by a set of black pixels.
III. Brush-touch cursors are placed on each black pixel of the skeleton, and the artistic font with scratched or blurred look is completed.
IV. The artistic font is displayed and outputted.

The brush-touch cursors are represented as bitmap patterns (black and white). The black part of the brush-touch cursor expresses ink-colored part of calligraphic fonts, and while the white part expresses colorless part of calligraphic fonts, or rather, it expresses scratched look.

3   Experimental Results and Future Work

Below is a series of examples showing the variety of scratched or blurred look except the extreme left one. In case artistic fonts were need, it had needed to prepare data of artistic fonts until now, but it would have cause huger font database. The system solves the problem, and moreover it generates various type of artistic fonts. This system needs a lot of processing. The processing depends on the size of an input font, and at present we are fixing the problem.

Fig. 2. output examples except the extreme left input font

References

Hil69.   C.J. Hilditch. Linear skeleton from square cupboards. *Machine Intelligence* 6, pages 403–420, 1969.
NESI98.   T. Nakamura, H. Enowaki, H. Seki, and H. Itoh. Skeleton revision algorithm using maximal circles. In *14th International Conference on Pattern Recognition (ICPR'98)*, pages 330–335, 1998.

Using Competitive Learning in Neural Networks for Cluster-Detection-and-Labeling*

Extended Summary

Wen-Gong Chen, Chen-Sen Ouyang, and Shie-Jue Lee

Department of Electrical Engineering
National Sun Yat-Sen University
Kaohsiung 804, Taiwan, ROC

Abstract. The CDL network [1] produces too many prototypes. In this paper, we reduce the number of prototypes by using a competitive learning algorithm and adding a re-labeling procedure to obtain a correct labeling of clusters.

1 Our Model

In the training phase, If $s(z^j, x^i)$ [1]$> \xi$ for only one prototype z^j and any input pattern x^i, then z^j is updated with the following competitive learning formula:

$$z^j = z^j + \alpha(x^i - z^j) \tag{1}$$

where α is a learning parameter with a value between 0 and 1. Figure 1(a) shows the prototypes obtained by the CDL network and our network, respectively. Black rectangulars represnt prototypes obtained by the CDL network and ellipses reprsent prototypes obtained by our network.

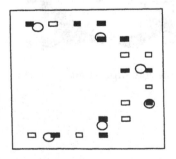

(a) Prototypes.

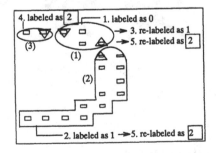

(b) Re-labeling.

Fig. 1. Description of prototypes generated and re-labeling process.

* Partially supported by National Science Council under grant NSC-88-2213-E-110-010.

We add re-labeling in our model to let two clusters that are similar enough be labeled with the same label. To illustrate how re-labeling works, we show an example of 19 patterns they belong to the same cluster in Figure 1(b) as follows:

Step 1. Four patterns are clustered together and labeled as 0. These patterns are placed in X_{cl}.

Step 2. Thirteen patterns are clustered and labeled as 1, and then placed in X_{cl}.

Step 3. Now we check whether there exist a pair of re-labeling patterns between cluster 1 and cluster 0. A pair of re-labeling patterns are two patterns which are sufficiently similar to each other. In this case, relabeling patterns, marked as upright triangles, are found between cluster 1 and cluster 0. So we re-label cluster 0 to be 1.

Step 4. Two patterns are clustered and labeled as 2, and are placed in X_{cl}.

Step 5. Now we check if there exist a pair of re-labeling patterns between cluster 2 and any cluster in X_{cl}. Re-labeling patterns, marked as downright triangles, are found between cluster 2 and cluster 1. Therefore, we re-label cluster 1 to be 2.

2   Experiment

To demonstrate the effectiveness of our method, we show the result of a data set of 400 patterns shown in Figure 2, where ξ_0=49, α=0.9, and γ=0.9. Figure 2(a) shows the data set and Figure 2(b) shows the results

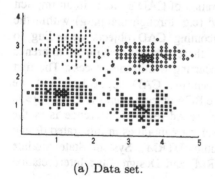

	Our Method		CDL network	
n_{min}	0.05	0.01	0.05	0.01
n_{limit}	0.80	0.90	0.80	0.90
no. of clusters	4	4	4	4
no.of prototypes	124	124	274	289
cluster 1	98	98	98	98
cluster 2	97	97	98	98
cluster 3	99	99	99	99
cluster 4	98	98	99	99

(a) Data set.   (b) Results.

Fig. 2. Description of experiment 1.

References

1. T. Eltoft and R. J. deFigueiredo, "A new neural network for cluster-detection-and-labeling," *IEEE Trans. on Neural Networks*, vol. 9, pp. 1021–1035, September 1998.

Knowledge-Based Communication Processes in Building Design
Extended Summary

Wei Dai and Robin Drogemuller

Commonwealth Scientific and Industrial Research Organisation (CSIRO)
Building, Construction and Engineering
PO Box 56, Highett, Victoria 3190, Australia
{Wei.Dai,Robin.Drogemuller}@dbce.csiro.au

The development of standardised product and process models for the building and construction industry has now reached a stage where collaborative design is feasible. The challenge comes from the appropriate adoption of emerging technologies to support advanced data interoperability at different levels of granularity. Interoperability is the enabling mechanism that allows information to be exchanged between collaborative systems. We focus on advanced coordination between the design system (e.g. CAD system) and the building code checking system based on the Building Code Australia (BCA). It will enable design tasks (e.g. drawings) produced within a CAD system to be automatically processed by an external system, e.g. building code checking system. One technical difficulty concerned is CAD and BCA objects recognition. The process covers the information flow from a CAD system to the code checking system. It contains the events and activities taking place within each separate CAD and compliance checking system, and through the communication channels between the two systems. The code checking system needs the recognition of CAD objects such as doors, walls and passageways and their relationships. This information is already available in the new generation of CAD systems in an implicit form. BCA objects may further be substantiated (e.g. through mapping) within the compliance checking system based on the incoming CAD objects according to building code requirements. Recognition of these objects requires inference techniques. There are two levels of inference occurring within the process. The first level is across the communication link between the CAD application and the compliance checking application. This derives the BCA objects from the CAD objects and maintains the mapping between them. The second level of inference is in the application of the BCA rules. There are several software modules in integrated design systems, e.g. Design Task Representation Module (DTRM), System State Module (SSM), Knowledge Representation Module (KRM) and Design Task Interpretation Module (DTIM).

In DTRM, design tasks are described in terms of data objects. A data object has an arbitrary number of properties. The features of these properties are their simplicity in structure, generality for different tasks and flexibility for linking with global representation standards, such as the international STEP standard, and existing research activities in the domain of artificial intelligence for design, e.g. the FBS model [1]. For this application, it satisfies various requirements from a building design perspective. The code checking system has been implemented to work cooperatively with external

N. Foo (Ed.): AI'99, LNAI 1747, pp. 494-495, 1999.

systems such as CAD systems to provide integrated solutions. The design task interpretation module is thus designed to be capable of converting external design task information into a processable form within the code checking system. In SSM, the system state information is the system's internal understanding of its problem-solving status, e.g. what has been achieved and what is to be done at a particular point in time, and how information can be derived from design tasks and users (through human/computer interaction). The SSM offers a set of operation routines to provide communication services with external systems for information exchange, e.g. CAD systems on building design-related applications. There are two types of BCA rules in the knowledge base: auxiliary rules and core rules managed by KRM. Auxiliary rules are used for verifying the presence of all the conditional elements of a BCA clause, and are optional. Core rules deal with the complying information of that clause, i.e. the core semantics of the clause, and are compulsory. The DTIM responds to any external events initiated from CAD systems by constructing a unique task model in the memory driven by the knowledge base. DTIM is based on event-driven inference strategy. Upon receiving a design task (an event), the task information is decomposed into subtasks until regional design areas are identified. Regional designs are the minimum design areas where the BCA can become effective, and are classified according to BCA rules from the knowledge base. The major advantage of dynamic design task modelling is its flexibility and cost effectiveness in delivering solutions, e.g. overcoming the bottleneck of total building modelling.

Concerning application impact, BCAider [2] is a commercial product developed at CSIRO for building compliance checking. It is a world-leading product but suffers from the fundamental drawback that a human must answer questions. The power of the new compliance checking system comes from its design knowledge base. One important feature of this knowledge base is that it is capable of describing regulation constraints at the design level, thus making it feasible for the building code checking system to be integrated with a design system such as CAD systems. The system components were written in Visual C++. The computing platforms are PC 486 onwards with Windows 95 or Windows NT.

Acknowledgments

The authors wish to thank CSIRO colleagues who have contributed to this work at various stages, particularly Kevin Gu, Mike Rahilly, Michael Ambrose and John Mashford.

References

1. Gero, J.: Design Prototypes: A Knowledge Representation Schema for Design. AI Mag. **11**(4) (1990) 26–36.
2. Sharpe, R., Oakes, S.: Advanced IT Processing of Australian Standards and Regulations. Int. J. Constr. Inform. Tech. 3(1) (1995) 73–89.

Information-Based Cooperation in Multiple Agent Systems

Extended Summary

Yuefeng Li and Chengqi Zhang

School of Computing and Mathematics
Deakin University, Geelong VIC 3217, Australia
{yuefeng,chengqi}@deakin.edu.au

Abstract. In this paper, we divide the cooperation in multiple agent systems into task-based cooperation and information-based cooperation. We describe information-based cooperation as information synthesizing and decision making. To implement information synthesizing, agents' beliefs are decomposed into two levels. The higher level represents the possible information, and the lower level subsequently estimates a number function for the belief by synthesizing the possible information.

1 Information-Based Cooperation

There are two distinct research fields in distributed artificial intelligence (DAI), distributed problem solving (DPS) and multiple agent systems (MAS). In DAI, the central goal is problem solving, and there are several scenarios, such as task decomposition, task unique-allocation and task multi-allocation. Based on these scenarios, we can divided the cooperation into task-based cooperation and information-based cooperation.

The sender agent knows which agents have the problem solving abilities (PSA) to do its subtasks in task-based cooperation (often within the area of DPS). As soon as it receives the answers about its tasks, the agent will treat these answers as gotten by itself. The situation is quite different from information-based cooperation (often within the area of MAS). The sender agent cannot be sure which agents have the PSA to do its tasks. Because it always assumes that other agents will help one another only when it is in their own best interests to do so, and in most cases the solutions sent by different agents for a same task are always different and even contain uncertainty information.

For task-based cooperation, one common approach is to use a central co-ordinator (agent) which has a centralized planning. In task-based cooperation, agents lose the autonomy, because the society of agents is just like a industry workshop or a management organization. Autonomy is an important characteristic in MAS. There are several notable efforts for describing autonomy, e.g., artificial social systems, social laws, establish cooperation through the formalization of agents' intentions, reaching consensus by negotiation or by economic

N. Foo (Ed.): AI'99, LNAI 1747, pp. 496–498, 1999.

decision process, and building ideal rational agents. For this kind of cooperation, the information-based cooperation is important, because the information an agent receives or sends is not only based on its belief, but also its interests. At this stage, agents could not expect to obtain certain information from other agents, and they have to synthesize (including conflict resolution) some uncertainty information before making decisions.

2 Information Synthesizing in MAS

The information mainly comes from two streams, one from agents' local sensors, and another from other agents. In order to capture these information properly, we represent an agent's belief as two levels. The higher level represents the possible information about the possible worlds, and the lower level subsequently estimates a number function for the belief.

A pair $B = (PW_\mathcal{A}(l), \Gamma_\mathcal{A})$ is used to describe the higher level when agent $\mathcal{A}$'s local state is l, where, $PW_\mathcal{A}$ is a mapping: $PW_\mathcal{A} : \mathcal{L}_\mathcal{A} \to 2^\mathcal{W}$, which describes the knowledge of how the agent explains its local states. If the local state is $l \in \mathcal{L}_\mathcal{A}$ (the set of agent $\mathcal{A}$'s local states), the agent believes that $PW_\mathcal{A}(l) \subseteq \mathcal{W}$ (the set of possible worlds) is the plausible world (i.e., the true world state is in $PW_\mathcal{A}(l)$). $\Gamma_\mathcal{A}$ is another mapping: $\Gamma_\mathcal{A} : \varXi \to 2^\mathcal{W} - \{\emptyset\}$, which represents the information (opinion) provided to agent $\mathcal{A}$ by other agents ($\varXi$, the set of other agents).

In the lower level, firstly the information provided by other agents can be captured reasonable by using a Dempster-Shafer mass function, which satisfies

$$m_\mathcal{A} : 2^\mathcal{W} \to [0,1], \text{ such that}$$

$$m_\mathcal{A}(S) = \begin{cases} Pr_\mathcal{A}(\{\xi \in \varXi \mid \Gamma_\mathcal{A}(\xi) = S\}) & \text{if } S \neq \emptyset \\ 0 & otherwise \end{cases}$$

for all $S \subseteq \mathcal{W}$. Where, we use a probability distribution $Pr_\mathcal{A}$ on $\varXi$ to describe the degrees of agent $\mathcal{A}$ believing other agents' PSAs.

Based on the local state l, then the agent will generates its belief by combining $m_\mathcal{A}$ and its observation, $PW_\mathcal{A}(l)$, $l \in \mathcal{L}_\mathcal{A}$. In this paper, we use Dempster rule of conditioning to synthesize the two kinds of information:

$$B_\mathcal{A}^l : 2^\mathcal{W} \to [0,1], \text{ such that}$$

$$B_\mathcal{A}^l(S) = \begin{cases} \dfrac{\sum_{T \cap PW_\mathcal{A}(l)=S} m_\mathcal{A}(T)}{1 - \sum_{T \cap PW_\mathcal{A}(l)=\emptyset} m_\mathcal{A}(T)} & \text{if } S \neq \emptyset \\ 0 & otherwise \end{cases}$$

Function $B_\mathcal{A}^l$ is still a Dempster-Shafer mass function.

We can prove that $\sum_{T \cap PW_\mathcal{A}(l)=S} m_\mathcal{A}(T) = Pr_\mathcal{A}(\{\xi \in \varXi \mid \Gamma_\mathcal{A}(\xi) \cap PW_\mathcal{A}(l) = S\})$, and, and $1 - \sum_{T \cap PW_\mathcal{A}(l)=\emptyset} m_\mathcal{A}(T) = 1 - Pr_\mathcal{A}(\{\xi \in \varXi \mid \Gamma_\mathcal{A}(\xi) \cap PW_\mathcal{A}(l) = \emptyset\})$, where set $\{\xi \in \varXi \mid \Gamma_\mathcal{A}(\xi) \cap PW_\mathcal{A}(l) = S\}$ contains all agents whose opinions do not completely conflict with agent $\mathcal{A}$'s observation, and set $\{\xi \in \varXi \mid$

$\Gamma_{\mathcal{A}}(\xi) \cap PW_{\mathcal{A}}(l) = \emptyset\}$ contains all agents whose opinions completely conflict with agent $\mathcal{A}$'s observation. So function $B_{\mathcal{A}}^l$ synthesizes all opinions of these agents whose opinions do not completely conflict with agent $\mathcal{A}$'s observation $PW_{\mathcal{A}}(l)$.

3   Conclusion

We have formalized a method for information-based cooperation in multiple agent systems. The new method can synthesize (including conflict resolution) the information which comes from agents' local sensors and other agents by using Dempster-Shafer theory.

Author Index

Lecture Notes in Artificial Intelligence (LNAI)

Lecture Notes in Computer Science